NATIVE HAWAIIAN RIGHTS HANDBOOK

CONTRIBUTORS

Edward Halealoha Ayau
John Castle
Catherine Kau
Cynthia Lee
Paul Nahoa Lucas
Alan Murakami
Marie Riley
Livia Wang

ADDITIONAL CONTRIBUTORS

Charles E. N. Dickson
Jackie Mahi Erickson
Monica Lee Loy
Louis Turbeville

ARTISTS

Cover: ʻImaikalani Kalāhele
Section Dividers: Douglas Poʻoloa Tolentino

NATIVE HAWAIIAN RIGHTS HANDBOOK

Edited by

Melody Kapilialoha MacKenzie

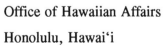

Published By

Native Hawaiian Legal Corporation
Honolulu, Hawai'i

Office of Hawaiian Affairs
Honolulu, Hawai'i

ISBN 0-8248-1374-X

Production coordination and assistance
for this volume was provided by
Professional Communications, Honolulu.

Design and manufacture of this book was
through the production services of the
University of Hawaii Press.

This book is printed on acid-free paper and meets
the guidelines for permanence and durability
of the Council on Library Resources.

Distributed by
University of Hawaii Press
Order Department
2840 Kolowalu Street
Honolulu, Hawai'i 96822

CONTENTS

ACKNOWLEDGMENTS

There are many people who contributed to the research, writing, and editing of this book. Cynthia Lee, Gina Green, and Elizabeth Fujiwara, who at the time were law students at the University of Hawai'i's William S. Richardson School of Law, initially approached the Native Hawaiian Legal Corporation with the idea of the *Handbook*. Without their initial vision and groundwork, this *Handbook* would not be a reality. Cynthia Lee also deserves much of the credit for seeking and obtaining funds to initiate the project and keep the vision alive.

Marie Riley and Louis Turbeville both worked extensively on researching and drafting portions of the *Handbook*. While their work has been substantially revised, it was an invaluable contribution to the writers and editors. Numerous other law students at the William S. Richardson School of Law, under the direction of Professor Jon Van Dyke, worked on various sections of the *Handbook*. We have built on their research and case summaries.

Denise Balanay and Catherine Remegio checked the citations and text for accuracy and consistency. Stacy Rosehill-Baker read the text to check the accuracy and spelling of Hawaiian words, names, and places.

A substantial portion of the original word processing for the *Handbook* was done by Carleen Ornellas. Karen Gates, typist and proofreader extraordinaire, however, slogged through countless revisions and is largely responsible for the final product. The editor thanks her for her skills, patience, and good humor. Ruth Academia and Mark Zeug also should be acknowledged for their many long hours of production work.

Financial support for this work has been provided by the Office of Hawaiian Affairs, the Department of Hawaiian Home Lands, the Wallace Alexander Gerbode Foundation, the American Bar Association -- Law Student Division, the Legal Aid Society of Hawai'i, Princess Po'omaikelani Kawānanakoa, and Marchesa Kapi'olani K. Marignoli.

The Trustees of the Office of Hawaiian Affairs -- Chairman Thomas K. Kaulukukui, Sr., Rodney Burgess, III, Moanikeala Akaka, Clarence F.T. Ching, A. Frenchy DeSoto, Louis Hao, Manu Kahaiali'i, Moses K. Keale, Sr., and Kevin M.K. Mahoe -- deserve special thanks for their continuing support and confidence.

On a more personal note, I would like to acknowledge Mahealani Kamauu, Alan Murakami, and Jon Van Dyke for their encouragement, guidance, and counsel during the many years it took to complete the *Handbook*. My deepest *mahalo* to Linda Kawai'ono Delaney who never swayed in her belief in this work. Finally, while I have been the chief editor of the *Handbook*, the Board of Directors and staff of the Native Hawaiian Legal Corporation have nurtured and sustained this project throughout the years. They deserve full recognition for their professional commitment and personal dedication to protecting and advancing the rights of Native Hawaiians.

The Editor

INTRODUCTION

This book discusses and analyzes the rights of Native Hawaiians. Until recently, American society did not acknowledge that Native Hawaiians have rights that are unique and distinct from those of other citizens. With the exception of the Hawaiian Homes Commission Act, little recognition existed that Native Hawaiians are a separate native people. The spiritual and political disintegration of Hawaiians after the illegal destruction of the Hawaiian nation, the pervasive belief that Hawaiians were a "dying race," and the prolonged territorial period which culminated in the statehood declaration that "we're all haoles now" -- would not and could not acknowledge Native Hawaiian rights. Thus, little more than a decade ago this *Handbook* would have been unimaginable. Even today, Native Hawaiians must constantly assert and defend their rights in a foreign, and often hostile, legal system if they are to remain a separate and distinct native people.

Why do Native Hawaiians have rights that are different from others who live in Hawai'i? The answer to that question combines complex historical and political factors. Many rights emanate from the unique status of Native Hawaiians as an aboriginal people, and from the political status of the Hawaiian Kingdom prior to the destruction of the Hawaiian Monarchy in 1893. Thus, the Hawaiian Homes Commission Act and the section 5(f) trust of the Admission Act implicitly acklowledge a special relationship between Native Hawaiians and their traditional lands. These same measures also recognize a trust relationship between the federal and state governments and the Hawaiian people. The 1978 amendments to the Hawai'i State Constitution establishing the Office of Hawaiian Affairs clearly arose out of the state's efforts to address earlier wrongs as well as a recognition of Native Hawaiian aboriginal status. The Native Hawaiian self-governance and sovereignty movement is a direct reflection not only of the earlier political relationship between the Hawaiian Kingdom and the United States, but also the Kingdom's standing in the international community as a sovereign nation.

Other rights discussed in this *Handbook* are rights which the general population exercises. For instance, any person may bring a quiet title action, or claim land under the adverse possession doctrine, or be entitled to a certain amount of water for growing taro. And everyone has a right of access to the beach and along the shoreline. These areas of law are discussed in the *Handbook* because they have a great impact on Native Hawaiians as original inhabitants of the *'aina* of Hawai'i and because they are necessary in maintaining a traditional lifestyle. Moreover, some rights exercised by the general public are based on or find their roots in ancient Hawaiian customs and practices.

The term "rights" can be misleading since it implies static and unchanging conditions. The rights that a society recognizes and validates are a deep expression of its innermost beliefs and values. Rights develop and change over time. They can arise out of customary practice and receive recognition by the courts, thus becoming part of the common law. They can be created by constitution or statute and then be interpreted or altered by the courts. Equally true, however, is that rights can be abrogated or limited by judicial decisions, legislative changes or constitutional amendments. It is important then, to remember that the rights discussed in this *Handbook* are in a constant state of change -- expanding and contracting with the passage of new laws and current rulings by the courts.

The concept of a handbook on Native Hawaiian rights came from law students enrolled in the Native Hawaiian Rights class at the University of Hawai'i's William S. Richardson School of Law. Frustrated with the lack of a textbook, they approached the Native Hawaiian Legal Corporation with the idea of compiling all of the pertinent cases and statutes in one manual. It soon became apparent, however, that a mere compilation of the materials was insufficient and that an analysis of the applicable statutory and case law would be of greater value to the legal community. At the same time, members of the Hawaiian community also expressed the need for a work that would help explain, in simple language, the law most relevant to Native Hawaiians.

The Native Hawaiian Legal Corporation undertook this project as a long-term commitment to the development of Native Hawaiian rights law. Initially, other members of the legal community who had litigated Native Hawaiian rights cases were asked to participate by writing various chapters. Unfortunately, for many of them the time commitment proved too great a burden. Consequently, the writing and editing of the *Handbook* has been done primarily by the staff attorneys of the Native Hawaiian Legal Corporation or attorneys and law students working under their direction. Thus, work on the *Handbook* has necessarily taken a secondary position to the active litigation and case commitments of the staff attorneys. This *Handbook* is long overdue. For those who have been waiting, thank you for your patience and understanding.

Every chapter of the *Handbook* was written by an attorney and reviewed and edited numerous times. Each chapter has a unique history. Some chapters are the discrete work of an individual author -- this is particularly true for the chapter on the Hawaiian Homes Commission Act written by Alan Murakami and the Native Hawaiian Burials chapter by Edward Halealoha Ayau. These chapters were written by the named authors and the editor's role has been merely to clarify and streamline the text. Most chapters, however, are the accumulated work and knowledge of many people. For instance, the chapter on adverse possession was drafted by Cynthia Lee, reviewed and edited by Alan Murakami, edited by myself, reviewed by Charles Dickson, and rewritten and edited by myself several additional times. For the most part, then, this volume is the product of many minds.

As overall editor, my function has been to make the *Handbook* as consistent and integrated a work as possible. This has been a great challenge, given the number of people involved in the writing, and the complexity of the issues addressed in the *Handbook*. I have read and reread every chapter numerous times, sometimes making massive revisions and sometimes minor modifications. Each chapter in the *Handbook* can be read independently of the others for information on a specific subject area. This means, however, that some of the historical or background information is discussed more than once. Thus, several chapters may briefly review the ancient land tenure system, or the Organic Act, or the Admission Act, in order to set the context for discussion of a particular topic.

The changes that have occurred in the law since the Native Hawaiian Legal Corporation began the *Handbook* project, have been another challenging aspect of this undertaking. Each year, additional sections and chapters have been added due to the tremendous activity in this area of law. As this *Handbook* was in its final stages, the state and the Office of Hawaiian Affairs reached a settlement of the ceded lands revenue dispute, landmark state legislation on Native Hawaiian burials was passed, and the state legislature approved a statement of purpose clause for the Hawaiian Homes Commission Act. Case law also has not remained static. The developments in water rights litigation, recent suits filed on violations of the Hawaiian Homes trust, and challenges to the state's disposition of ceded lands are only a few of the areas that have been in active litigation during this period.

A word about Hawaiian usage. In the Hawaiian language, nouns are not pluralized by adding an "s." Thus, we have not used words such as "konohikis" or "kuleanas." We have attempted, wherever possible, to italicize Hawaiian words and use the correct diacritical marks as set out in M.K. Pukui and S.H. Elbert, *Hawaiian Dictionary* (1986 edition). However, places and proper names, with the exception of the *akua* and *'aumākua,* have not been italicized. Diacritical marks in proper names and place names have been used only when a source could be found for such usage. If no source was found, no diacritical marks were used. In case names and quotations, the Hawaiian words appear as they did in the original text.

Except where specifically indicated in the text, the term Native Hawaiian as used in this *Handbook* means any person of Hawaiian ancestry without regard to blood quantum. The text calls special attention to those statutes or trust provisions in which a specific blood quantum is required.

The authors and editors of this work are attorneys. To the extent possible, we have tried to minimize "legalese" and present the material in a direct and straightforward manner. We hope that the *Handbook* is an accessible tool for members of the Hawaiian community. At the same time, we envision the *Handbook* as a point of departure for further research and analysis of the critical legal issues facing Native Hawaiians today. In the American tradition, people are supposed to stand up for their rights. This book is intended to help Native Hawaiians do just that. It is also intended to be a legal primer for individuals and legal professionals, to enable them to better understand Native Hawaiian rights, and to provide a basis for their pursuit.

We live in a society which increasingly impels its members toward conformity and unanimity. A true measure of a society's vitality and spirit, however, is its ability to protect, and even honor, diversity. Native Hawaiians, like other native people, are pressured to assimilate and conform to the goals and values of the larger society. Given that pressure, the ability to exercise native rights, to preserve a traditional lifestyle and, most importantly, to exert meaningful control over their resources and destiny, allows individual Native Hawaiians a choice -- to assimilate, or to maintain their integrity and values as an independent native people. It also provides the larger society with an increased and broadened range of world views and perspectives.

The Editor

PART ONE

NATIVE HAWAIIAN LANDS
AND SOVEREIGNTY

CHAPTER 1

HISTORICAL BACKGROUND

> The Polynesians who settled Hawaii, perhaps as early as 300 A.D., brought with them a long Pacific island history and a distinctive Polynesian culture: their language, religion, their art, navigational knowledge, agriculture and fishing technologies, their legends and history, and the plants and animals which they cultivated and domesticated.
>
> It was their belief that their gods had created the land and the sea and everything on the land and in the sea. These resources were there for everyone's use--land, water, sea. Because these were created by the gods, they must be cared for. No one must take more than they need, and everything must be shared.
>
> Marion Kelly (1984)[1]

1. INTRODUCTION

Traditional Hawaiian life and culture was intimately tied to the land. It is no wonder then that the development of law relative to Native Hawaiians reflects this relationship. Land, and the vast changes in the Hawaiian land tenure system upon contact with the West, provide a foundation for understanding the current problems and issues facing Native Hawaiians. This chapter will give an overview of ancient Hawaiian land tenure and the impact of Western contact on Native Hawaiian lands and society.

2. TRADITIONAL LAND TENURE SYSTEM

Prior to Western contact, Hawaiians had developed a complex culture and stable land tenure system that supported a population conservatively estimated to be 300,000 people.[2] The success of this system can be explained not only by the cooperative arrangements which bound Hawaiian society, but also the physical shape of Hawaiian land divisions.

The eight main islands were divided into several separate kingdoms, with an *ali'i 'ai moku* or *mō'ī*, or high chief, controlling one island or section of an island.[3] The *ali'i 'ai moku*, meaning the one who receives the provender of the *moku* or district, usually reserved certain lands for personal use and distributed the remaining lands to the most loyal chiefs, relatives, or allies. In turn, the chiefs retained lands for themselves and distributed the rest to their followers. All lands were given subject to revocation at will, and when conquest or death brought a new *ali'i 'ai moku*, lands would be redistributed according to the preference of the new high chief.[4]

While other land divisions existed, the *ahupua'a*[5] was the land unit most closely related to the everyday life of the people. An *ahupua'a* could range in size from 100 to 100,000 acres. Ideally, it was an economically self-sufficient, pie-shaped unit which ran from the mountain tops down ridges, spreading out at the base along the shore.[6] An *ali'i 'ai ahupua'a* or *ahupua'a* chief, or sometimes a *konohiki* or land agent, administered the *ahupua'a*. An early Hawai'i case explained that the *ahupua'a* afforded to the chief and people "a fishery residence at the warm seaside, together with the products of the high lands, such as fuel, canoe timber, mountain birds, and the right-of-way to the same, and all the varied products of the intermediate land as might be suitable to the soil and climate of the different altitudes from sea soil to mountainside or top."[7]

Many *ahupua'a* were further divided into smaller units termed *'ili* and *'ili kūpono*. *'Ili* were merely subdivisions of the larger *ahupua'a* unit created for the convenience of the *ahupua'a* chief, while *'ili kūpono* were independent political units administered by separate chiefs or *konohiki*.[8]

Hawaiian society paralleled this land division pattern. At the top were the *ali'i 'ai moku* and *kahuna nui* (priest), then the *ali'i 'ai ahupua'a*, the *ahupua'a konohiki* and finally, the *maka'āinana*, literally, people of the land.[9] The *maka'āinana* worked together under the direction of chiefs and priests in clearing the land, constructing irrigation systems, cultivating taro, building fishponds for breeding fish, and many other communal endeavors. Each strata of society owed allegiance to those above and the *maka'āinana* supported the chiefs and priests by their labor and its products. Common areas within the *ahupua'a* were worked to support the chiefs and priests. Within the boundaries of the *ahupua'a*, the *maka'āinana* also had liberal rights to use the *ahupua'a* resources. These included the right to hunt, gather wild plants and herbs, fish off-shore, and use parcels of land for taro cultivation together with sufficient water for irrigation.[10] *Maka'āinana* could freely trade and move within the *ahupua'a*. All of these activities were regulated by an intricate system of rules designed to conserve natural resources and provide for all *ahupua'a* residents.

The concept of private ownership of land had no place in early Hawaiian thought. Although some scholars have described Hawaiian land tenure as if the high chief owned the land in the Western sense, these descriptions tend to oversimplify and distort the ancient Hawaiian system.[11] Within the Hawaiian hierarchical structure, the high chief had ultimate power, but it was not without limits. As the Hawaiian scholar David Malo wrote, "the king was over all the people; he was the supreme executive, so long, however, as he did right."[12] From a religious viewpoint, the *mō'ī* was a person of divine power. Yet his authority was not a personal authority. It was, instead, a power channeled through him by the gods. In relation to land and natural resources, he was analogous to a trustee.[13] He administered the land and other resources on behalf of the gods.

This trust concept continued throughout the political hierarchy and was reinforced by reciprocal rights and obligations of each strata of society. Even though the *maka'āinana* owed a work obligation to those above them in the societal structure, they were not serfs bound to the land. They could freely move to other areas if treated unfairly. Since the responsibility of an *ahupua'a* chief was to make the *ahupua'a* productive, and a stable workforce was necessary to achieve that end, abuses by *ahupua'a* chiefs were minimized. Hence the chiefs' powers were checked and balanced by their reliance on the mutual cooperation of the *maka'āinana*. If the people of an *ahupua'a* were ill-treated and moved to another district, it was likely that the high chief would replace the *ahupua'a* chief for failing to make the land productive.[14] Finally, unlike European serfs, the *maka'āinana* were not required to provide military service to the chiefs.[15]

A 1979 report on Hawai'i's land and water resources drew the following conclusion about the traditional land tenure system:

> This ancient land system was thus sharply different from Western ideas of private land ownership. The ali'i nui (or mo'i) himself enjoyed no absolute ownership of all the land. The ali'i nui was a trustee of all the people within an island (moku) or some other larger district. The konohiki also maintained a similar tentative position because the maka'ainana were free

to leave the ahupua'a if they were unhappy with a particular chieftain (ali'i) or konohiki. In short, the members throughout the political hierarchy shared a mutual dependence in sustaining their subsistence way of life.[16]

3.   TRANSITION

Contact with the West brought startling changes in both the Hawaiian land tenure system and Hawaiian social structure. In 1795, the traditional rivalries between island chiefs ended when Kamehameha I, using Western arms and allies, brought all of the islands, with the exception of Kaua'i, under his control. In 1810, Kamehameha gained the allegiance of Kaua'i's chief. While Kamehameha divided the lands among his subchiefs in the customary way, he also created another administrative level by appointing loyal chiefs to be governors on each of the islands. In this manner, he sought to prevent chiefs on other islands from gathering sufficient power to challenge his control. Kamehameha did not make substantial alterations in land tenure, but his rule provided a measure of security previously unknown in island life.

After Kamehameha's death in 1819, his son Liholiho (Kamehameha II) took the throne and, with the Dowager Queen Ka'ahumanu, ruled until 1825. Kamehameha II did not redistribute land to *his* supporters, but allowed the majority of his father's subchiefs to retain their land.[17] Understandably, foreigners approved of this action, since they feared that changes in land tenure might lead to civil wars and disrupt trade. Further, many foreigners had been given land by the king and other chiefs in return for services. These grants were made with the understanding that the lands would eventually return to the king, but foreigners and chiefs alike began to feel that the right to pass land on to their heirs was only reasonable. Thus, when Kamehameha III took the throne at the age of 12, the Council of Chiefs convinced him to adopt a formal policy, later called the Law of 1825, allowing chiefs to retain their lands upon the death of the king and permitting hereditary succession.[18]

Early commerce and trade in this period centered around the active fur and sandalwood trade and the whaling industry. But when overharvesting collapsed the sandalwood trade and whaling stocks diminished, some Westerners with substantial capital in the islands sought new ways to make money. Large-scale agricultural products for the growing market in California provided the obvious answer. Since investment of capital required a more secure land tenure system, pressure to change the traditional system mounted. In 1839, Kamehameha III proclaimed a Declaration of Rights securing protection to "all the people, together with their lands, their building lots, and all their property . . . nothing whatever shall be taken from any individual, except by express provision of the laws."[19]

The following year, the Constitution of 1840 formally declared that the land belonged to the chiefs and people, with the king as trustee for all:

> Kamehameha I, was the founder of the kingdom, and to him belonged all the land from one end of the Islands to the other, *although it was not his own private property. It belonged to the chiefs and people in common, of whom Kamehameha I was the head, and had the management of the landed property.* Wherefore, there was not formerly, and is not now any person who could or can convey away the smallest portion of land without the consent of the one who had, or has the direction of the kingdom.[20] (Emphasis added.)

5

This provision formalized trust concepts with which Hawaiians were already familiar, but for the first time the interests of the people, the chiefs, and the king in the land were specifically acknowledged.

The 1840 Constitution also established a governmental structure for the kingdom. It created a two-body legislative council, with a house of nobles and house of representatives chosen by the people.[21] Also created was a judicial system including a supreme court, consisting of the king, *kuhina nui* (prime minister) and four others appointed by the house of representatives.[22]

The 1840 Constitution and the laws enacted immediately thereafter attempted to deal with the increasing conflicts between Hawaiians and foreigners over land.[23] While preserving the traditional land system and stating that land could not be conveyed without the consent of the king, these laws were also designed to appease foreign interests. For example, one provision of the constitution was interpreted to mean that land already held by foreigners would not be reclaimed by the crown.[24] In 1841, another concession was made by the adoption of a plan allowing the various island governors to enter into 50-year leases with foreigners.[25]

As their economic interests progressively increased, foreigners exerted even greater pressure in order to secure their land holdings. In some instances, foreigners were aided by diplomatic agents of the government to which they owed allegiance and the frequent visits of foreign gunboats.[26] In one such incident, Lord George Paulet, captain of the British warship *Carysfort*, took control of the Hawaiian government for five months, partially in response to a lease dispute involving the British counsel.[27]

Even with an uncertain land tenure system, foreigners managed to gain enormous economic power in the islands. A naval officer visiting the islands in 1839 commented upon the extent of American holdings in Hawai'i:

> The Americans alone have at least $572,000 worth of property at stake upon Hawaiian grounds. They have two or three sugar mills already in successful operation, and two extensive silk plantations on Kauai Island alone . . . . They will soon have a mill for extracting paint oil from the abundant candle nuts . . . . At least thirty merchant vessels are annually reported to our American Counsel, and not less than fifty whale ships stop annually at Honolulu, for refreshment and repairs.[28]

4. THE *MAHELE* PERIOD

The demand for change in the land tenure system intensified and in 1845 a law was passed establishing a Board of Land Commissioners.[29] The commission was to investigate and ascertain or reject all claims of private individuals, whether natives or foreigners, to land acquired prior to the creation of the commission. Its decisions were to be based on the existing land laws of the kingdom, including "native usages in regard to landed tenures"[30] and could be appealed only to the Hawai'i Supreme Court. The commission had five members: two Hawaiians, one half-Hawaiian, and two Americans.[31]

The act creating the Land Commission required that a notice be published declaring that all persons must present their claims to interest in land within two years after publication.[32] However, since the interests of king, chiefs, and commoners were intertwined and undivided, the commission at first could not act on the bulk of Hawaiian lands. Consequently, it handled a small number of claims during the first two or three years of its existence and, even though fee simple ownership was not yet part of the Hawaiian system, fee patents were issued on these awards.[33]

In 1846, the commission adopted seven principles, subsequently ratified by the legislative council, to guide them in their work.[34] The first five principles dealt with the kind and degree of proof necessary to bring a claim. The sixth principle set the commutation due to the government at one-third and recognized the rights of tenants. The seventh principle barred claims not brought by February 14, 1848, with any unclaimed lands forfeited to the government.[35] The preface to the principles stated that "there are but three classes of persons having vested rights in the land -- 1st, the government (the King), 2nd, the landlord, and 3rd, the tenant."[36] The commission's goal was to totally partition these undivided interests.

However, a specific plan to fulfill the principles was debated for almost two years until Justice William Lee's formulation for division of the lands was accepted by the king and chiefs.[37] Under Lee's plan,[38] the king would retain his private lands "subject only to the rights of the tenants." The remaining land of the kingdom would be divided into thirds: one-third to the Hawaiian government, one-third to the chiefs and *konohiki*, and the final third to the tenant farmers, "the actual possessors and cultivators of the soil."

The *Mahele* -- meaning division -- followed enactment of these rules. Beginning on January 27, 1848, all the lands of Hawai'i were divided between the king and chiefs and recorded in the *Mahele* Book. The king quit-claimed his interest in specific *ahupua'a* and *'ili* to 245 chiefs and the chiefs quit-claimed their interest in the balance of the lands to the king. These quit-claims did not confer title on the chiefs or *konohiki*, but merely acknowledged that the king had no claims to these specific lands and the chiefs had no claim to the king's personal lands.

a. Government and King's Lands

After the last division between Kamehameha III and the chiefs on March 7, 1848, the king held almost 2.5 million acres or 60.3 percent of the total land, while the chiefs had received a total approximating 1.5 million acres. The king then divided his lands into two parts. The larger portion, 1.5 million acres, he "set apart forever to the chiefs and people" of the kingdom. Later in the year, the legislative council ratified and accepted the lands conveyed to the chiefs and people, declaring them to be "set apart as the lands of the Hawaiian government, subject always to the rights of tenants."[39] These lands were designated as Government Lands.

Kamehameha III retained for himself, his heirs and successors, the remaining lands, approximately one million acres.[40] These private lands became known as the King's Lands. When this action was ratified by the legislature, the King's Lands were also made subject to the rights of native tenants.

b. Konohiki Lands

After the *Mahele*, the *konohiki* were still required to go before the Land Commission and make claim to their lands. In addition, they had to pay a commutation tax of one-third the value of the unimproved land or cede one-third of the land to the government.[41] The *konohiki* were entitled to receive full allodial title to their lands in the form of royal patents. These awards specifically reserved the rights of the native tenants. Consequently, all lands of the king, government, and chiefs were given *subject to the rights of native tenants*. The *konohiki* received awards to their lands by name only, with the ancient boundaries controlling until a survey could be made. Subsequently, in 1862, a Boundary Commission was established to settle questions of the boundaries of the *ahupua'a* and *'ili kūpono* awarded by name only.[42]

c.   **Kuleana *Lands***

The final step in the *Mahele* process was determining the interests of the *maka'āinana*. The *Kuleana* Act of August 6, 1850 authorized the Land Commission to award fee simple title to native tenants for their plots of land.[43] Each tenant farmer could apply for his own plot of land or *kuleana*.[44] A *kuleana* parcel could come from lands of the king, government or chiefs. Moreover, native tenants were not required to pay a commutation tax since the chief or *konohiki* of the *ahupua'a* or *'ili kūpono* in which the *kuleana* was located was responsible for the commutation. Consequently, upon the death of a *kuleana* owner without an heir, the *kuleana* escheated to the owner of the *ahupua'a* or *'ili kūpono* who had a reversionary interest as a result of paying the commutation.[45]

While *kuleana* lands were generally among the richest and most fertile in the islands, there were a number of restrictions placed on *kuleana* claims. First, *kuleana* could only include the land which a tenant had actually cultivated plus a houselot of not more than a quarter acre. Second, the native tenant was required to pay for a survey of the lands as well as bring two witnesses to testify to the tenant's right to the land.

It is estimated that of the 8,205 awards given by the Land Commission, 7,500 awards involved *kuleana* lands. This resulted, however, in only 26 percent of the adult male native population receiving such lands.[46] The plan adopted by the king and chiefs for division of the land had stated that the *maka'āinana* were to receive, after the king partitioned out his personal lands, one-third of the land of Hawai'i. However, only 28,600 acres, much less than one percent of the total land, went to the *maka'āinana*.

Numerous reasons explain why the *maka'āinana* did not secure more *kuleana* land. Many Hawaiians did not know of or understand the law; some lacked the money to pay for a survey; others felt that to claim land was an act of betrayal to the chiefs; or they feared reprisal from the chiefs. Additionally, increasing numbers of Hawaiians, unable to support themselves in a cash economy system, had left the land to find jobs in the cities. One commentator has suggested that the major reason the *maka'āinana* received so little land was that *kuleana* grants were severely limited by the "really cultivated" clause of the act.[47] The area actually cultivated by an individual farmer was relatively small since Hawaiians had always cultivated large portions of the *ahupua'a* in common. Others have suggested that the rapid decrease in the Hawaiian population because of devastating epidemics in 1848 and 1849 resulted in fewer claims.[48] Finally, the *maka'āinana* had a relatively short period of time in which to make their claims. All *kuleana* claims were barred if not proved by 1854, giving the *maka'āinana* only four years in which to prove their claims.[49]

The 1850 *Kuleana* Act also protected the rights of tenants to gain access to the mountains and the sea and to gather certain materials.[50] However, an early Hawai'i case, *Oni v. Meek* (1858),[51] held that the rights enumerated in the *Kuleana* Act were the full extent of native tenant rights within the *ahupua'a*. The *Kuleana* Act did not allow the *maka'āinana* to exercise other traditional rights, such as the right to grow crops and pasture animals on unoccupied portions of the *ahupua'a*. The court's interpretation of the act prevented tenants from making traditional use of commonly cultivated land, so essential to the continued residency on *kuleana*.

When the Land Commission dissolved in 1855, 1.5 million acres of land had been distributed to the chiefs or *konohiki*, another 1.5 million acres had been set aside as Government Lands, approximately one million acres had been retained by the king, and only 28,600 acres had been claimed by the people.

As the rights of the native people in land diminished, the rights of Westerners simultaneously increased. An 1846 act authorized sales of Government Lands and within four years over 27,000 acres of land had been sold, establishing a precedent for alienating Hawaiian lands.[52] In 1850, a second major piece of legislation permitted any resident of Hawai'i to own and convey land *regardless* of citizenship.[53] These changes set the stage for a swift and massive transfer of land title from Hawaiian to Western hands.

5. AFTER THE *MAHELE*

The 50-year period after the *Mahele* brought the growth of large-scale plantation agriculture, especially sugar, and the steady loss of lands from Hawaiian control. One commentator aptly described the situation:

> With a permanent population of fewer than two thousand, Westerners took over most of Hawaii's land in the next half-century and manipulated the economy for their own profit. They had already stripped the land of its only readily exploitable resource, sandalwood. After the Reciprocity Treaty of 1876, which allowed Hawaiian sugar to enter the United States duty-free, Western-owned sugar plantations dominated the Hawaiian economy. That the local population did not participate in this economy proved no obstacle; laborers were imported from the Orient and Europe. By the turn of the century Hawaiians were a minority in their own homeland.[54]

The ancient land divisions seemed well-suited to the needs of the sugar industry. Control of several contiguous *ahupua'a* often provided the basis for plantation operations since *ahupua'a* included extensive level areas of rich soil, water supplies, and forested areas for lumber for plantation mills. Land not suited for agriculture was used for ranching, augmenting the plantation operations.

Numerous *kuleana* grants were lost as a result of changes in the economy and the failure by Hawaiians to understand the foreign legal and judicial systems.[55] *Kuleana* lands became isolated islands in the midst of large agricultural or ranching operations. Lacking access to previously shared grazing and cultivation areas, native farmers were unable to earn a subsistence living on their small plots of land. Without the shared labor to maintain irrigation systems, it became more difficult, if not impossible, to gain sufficient water for taro cultivation. Moreover, *kuleana* owners often had to contend with grazing cattle from surrounding ranches. Faced with all of these obstacles, native farmers were forced to leave their lands. Some *kuleana* lands that had been leased to Westerners were never returned and others were lost to surrounding landholders through adverse possession.

The chiefs, as well as the commoners, were unable to maintain control of their lands. The great majority of chiefs were already heavily in debt, primarily to Westerners, for past liabilities linked to a growing demand for material goods. Sandalwood was gone and the only thing left of value was land. Many of the chiefs paid their debts to Westerners in land. Those chiefs who attempted large-scale agriculture were unable to manage plantations and the cash demands for supplies and equipment. Consequently, large estates were lost through foreclosure.[56]

Government Land also fell under Western control. By 1864, 213 Westerners had purchased over 320,000 acres of Government Land.[57] By 1893, 613,233 acres of land had been sold by the kingdom at an average price of 92 cents per acre. While Native Hawaiians made the largest *number* of purchases, the bulk of the land acreage went to Westerners.[58]

Additionally, in the years after the *Mahele*, Hawai'i's monarchs freely sold and used the King's Lands as their personal property. Such sales did not always reflect the real value of the land. For instance, in 1855 Kamehameha IV conveyed the entire *ahupua'a* of Waihe'e on O'ahu for $48.00.[59]

The legal status of the King's Lands was clarified in 1864. When Kamehameha IV died without a will, his widow, Queen Emma, claimed her intestate share of one-half of the King's Lands and rights of dower in the remaining half. In *Estate of Kamehameha IV* (1864),[60] the Hawai'i Supreme Court held that it was not intended that the King's Lands descend to the heirs of the king, rather the lands should descend to the successors of the throne. Each successive possessor, however, had the right to dispose of the lands as private property. Finally, by the Act of January 3, 1865, the legislature designated the King's Lands as Crown Lands and declared them inalienable, to descend to the heirs and successors of the Hawaiian crown forever.[61]

As plantation agriculture flourished, concentration of land ownership and control increased. Plantations had purchased considerable quantities of Government Land and had secured long-term leases on other portions of Government and Crown Lands. Long-term leases at low prices enabled sugar companies to mortgage the land to secure working capital with little risk. By 1890, 76 lessees controlled 752,431 acres of Crown and Government Land through leases at an annual rate equalling pennies per acre.[62] The 1890 census, the last taken before the overthrow of Hawai'i's monarchy, revealed the extent to which land had been concentrated in American and European hands. Of a total population near 90,000, fewer than 5,000 actually owned land. Hawaiians, if they had any lands, owned small acreages. Consequently, for every four acres belonging to private owners, three were held by Westerners.[63] The relatively small number of Westerners owned over a million acres.[64]

The 1890 census also reflects the severe decimation of the Hawaiian population, which had dropped by two-thirds since the time of Western contact. In addition to the loss of their lands, Hawaiians were clearly losing the battle to survive as a race.

6.   OVERTHROW OF THE HAWAIIAN MONARCHY

The struggle to control land was reflected in Hawai'i's political institutions and particularly in its constitution. While the 1840 Constitution had set forth some basic principles, it provided only the rough outlines of government structure. In 1852, Kamehameha III proclaimed a new constitution, drafted in the main by Justice William Lee, reflecting his American and democratic point of view. That document gave the vote to male taxpayers over the age of 20 who had resided in Hawai'i for more than a year, provided that the legislature should meet every year, and made most of the acts of the king subject to approval of the privy council and *kuhina nui*.

When Kamehameha IV took the throne in 1855, he felt the Constitution of 1852 placed unacceptable limitations on his royal prerogatives.[65] Throughout his reign he fought to have the constitution amended to reflect his views.

Kamehameha V, who came to the throne in 1863, refused to take an oath to maintain the constitution. Instead, a constitutional convention was convened. When the convention became deadlocked over the question of universal suffrage, which the king opposed, the convention was dissolved and the constitution abolished.[66] For a week, Hawai'i was without a constitution, until Kamehameha V signed the Constitution of 1864, which reasserted the monarch's powers.[67]

William Lunalilo, Hawai'i's first elected king, made no changes in the Constitution of 1864 although he did advocate eliminating property qualifications for voters. Lunalilo died and David Kalākaua was elected to the throne in 1874. Kalākaua also supported an amendment abolishing voter property qualifications, which subsequently was adopted.[68]

In 1887, however, Kalākaua yielded to demands by Western interests to appoint a new cabinet whose foremost task was to write a new constitution.[69] After vociferous protest, Kalākaua reluctantly signed the Constitution of 1887 which reduced him to the status of a ceremonial figure, made his military powers subject to legislative control, placed executive powers in the hands of a cabinet appointed by him but responsible to the legislature, and made the house of nobles an elective office.[70] Under this so-called "Bayonet Constitution," the privilege of voting was extended to American and European males regardless of citizenship, and two classes of voters were created: (1) those who could vote only for representatives and (2) those who could vote for both representatives and nobles.[71] Property qualifications for voting were so high that many Native Hawaiians were disenfranchised.[72]

In 1892, Lili'uokalani succeeded to the throne upon Kalākaua's death. She, like her brother, felt the 1887 Constitution not only limited the monarch's prerogatives but resulted in too much power being placed in the hands of Westerners. On January 14, 1893, Lili'uokalani was on the verge of declaring a new constitution limiting the vote to Hawaiian-born or naturalized citizens and making cabinet ministers subject to removal by the legislature.[73] Knowing the opposition such changes would face, Lili'uokalani was persuaded by her advisors to postpone that action.

As rumors of the new constitution spread, members of the annexation club met. These men, who controlled the economy and much of the private property of Hawai'i, advocated annexation to the United States.[74] A year earlier, they had sent one of their members, Lorrin Thurston, to Washington, D.C. to assess the U.S. government's view of the matter.[75] There, the Secretary of the Navy, after meeting with President Harrison, told Thurston:

> [T]he President . . . authorizes me to say to you that, if conditions in Hawaii compel you to act
> as you have indicated, and you come to Washington with an annexation proposition, you will
> find an exceedingly sympathetic administration here.[76]

While the struggle over Hawai'i's constitution was the apparent catalyst for the overthrow of the monarchy, economic forces also played a major role in the annexation movement. In 1891, a tariff had been placed on Hawaiian sugar imports into the United States, with disastrous effects on the local sugar industry. While sympathetic to annexation, the Harrison administration was not sympathetic to lifting the tariff. It appeared to some

11

that the only way Hawaiian sugar could be guaranteed a portion of the American market was for Hawai'i to become part of the United States.[77]

Using the queen's proposed constitution as an excuse, these annexationists plotted to overthrow the monarchy.[78] In their efforts, they sought and received the help of the U.S. Minister to Hawai'i, John L. Stevens, an advocate of annexation.[79] On January 16, 1893 Stevens ordered United States Marines to land in Honolulu. The asserted reason for landing troops was to protect American lives and property.[80] With American troops for support, the insurrectionists took control of the government building, declared the monarchy abolished, and proclaimed the existence of a provisional government until annexation with the United States could be negotiated. Minister Stevens immediately recognized the provisional government, even before the queen's line of defense had surrendered.[81]

Lili'uokalani, realizing the futility of resisting American forces, and in order to prevent bloodshed, relinquished her authority to the superior forces of the United States.[82]

It took only a few days to accomplish the overthrow, but whether the provisional government could maintain control was highly questionable. On February 1, 1893, Minister Stevens placed the provisional government under the protection of the United States, pending annexation negotiations, and hoisted the American flag over Hawai'i.[83]

Immediately after the fall of the monarchy, a delegation was sent to Washington, D.C. to seek a treaty of annexation. Such a treaty was negotiated and sent to the U.S. Senate by President Harrison on February 15th. Harrison asked for prompt and favorable action and denied that the United States was in any way involved in overthrowing the monarchy. But the American national elections in November 1892 had already replaced Harrison's pro-annexation administration with Grover Cleveland. Cleveland was sworn into office in March 1893, and before the annexation treaty passed the senate he withdrew it "for the purpose of re-examination."[84]

After receiving the report of a commissioner specially appointed to examine the situation, President Cleveland determined that the United States had been responsible for the overthrow of the monarchy. In a forceful and moving speech to congress, Cleveland recommended restoration of the monarchy and declared:

> [I]f a feeble but friendly state is in danger of being robbed of its independence and its sovereignty by a misuse of the name and power of the United States, the United States can not fail to vindicate its honor and its sense of justice by an earnest effort to make all possible reparation.[85]

In the months following Cleveland's message, the Hawaiian issue was debated and argued in congress.

In February of 1894, the U.S. Senate Foreign Relations Committee, controlled by pro-annexationists,[86] held hearings on the Hawaiian question and issued a report condoning Stevens' actions and recognizing the provisional government. The report classified U.S. relations with Hawai'i as unique and not to be judged by the normal precepts of conduct between nations since "Hawaii has been all the time under a virtual suzerainty of the United States."[87] As a consequence, congress failed to act by either restoring the queen to power or annexing Hawai'i to the United States.[88]

7. THE REPUBLIC OF HAWAI'I

In Hawai'i, members of the provisional government had not given up on the idea of annexation. While annexation did not appear immediately possible, they felt it was only a matter of time until the political tide in the United States turned. However, the title of the provisional government projected an undesirable image of impermanence. Plans were made for establishing the Republic of Hawai'i. The name of the republic, however, belied its true nature:

> When the provisional government on March 15, 1894, called a convention to draft a constitution for the proposed 'Republic of Hawaii,' they made certain that the revolutionary leaders would retain control. There would be thirty-seven members in the convention. Automatically named to the convention were the president and members of the executive and advisory councils of the provisional government. They numbered nineteen -- a clear majority of one. The voters were then privileged to choose the minority of eighteen. But the oligarchy did not stop there. Even to allow the franchise to those who had voted before the revolution, under the limitations imposed by the Constitution of 1887, was considered dangerous. Therefore, those who were allowed to vote for a minority of the convention, besides possessing a certain amount of wealth, had to take an oath of allegiance to the provisional government and to oppose any attempt to re-establish the monarchy. In the finished constitution the qualifications for voting and holding office were so stringent that comparatively few natives, and no Orientals, could vote. Fewer still were eligible to serve in either house of the legislature.[89]

Another commentator wrote on the Native Hawaiian attitude toward the new regime:

> Native Hawaiians were, perhaps, not extremely sophisticated in governmental matters, but it took no great amount of political insight to perceive that this constitutional system was a beautifully devised oligarchy devoted to the purpose of keeping the American minority in control of the Republic. Hence, even those Kanakas (Hawaiians) who could fulfill the requirements generally refused to register, to vote, and to take part in the Government when it was established.[90]

A new constitution was proclaimed and Sanford Dole was declared president on July 4, 1894.[91] Although Lili'uokalani protested to the United States and Great Britain, all the foreign powers with whom Hawai'i had diplomatic relations soon recognized the republic.

The republic had claimed title to all those lands designated as Government Lands at the time of the overthrow. Under the republic's constitution, the republic also expropriated the Crown Lands, without compensation to the monarch.[92]

In January of 1895, those loyal to Lili'uokalani attempted to regain control of the government. In a skirmish between government and royalist groups, a prominent government supporter was mortally wounded. Martial law was proclaimed and during the next few days several skirmishes occurred. Some of the royalists were killed and others wounded. Within two weeks, the royalist movement was completely suppressed and over 200 persons were arrested. Among them were Lili'uokalani and the young princes, David Kawānanakoa and Jonah Kūhiō Kalaniana'ole. While confined under house arrest, Lili'uokalani signed a document in which she formally abdicated and renounced all claims to the throne. She also signed an oath of allegiance to the republic. Later she wrote that she did so because of fears that her supporters would be condemned to death.[93] The republic gained strength by defeat of the royalists.

It was never intended that the republic last for a long period of time:

> It was a kind of interim government. Its purposes, all of which were successfully carried out, were to give a greater appearance of regularity and permanence than did the Provisional Government, to keep the way clear for annexation whenever the United States government became ready to take up that question again, and in the mean time to maintain in authority the group that had carried through the Revolution of 1893.[94]

By 1896, it seemed apparent that the mission of the republic would soon be fulfilled. In the United States, Cleveland had been replaced by McKinley, whose campaign platform had advocated a Hawai'i "controlled" by the United States. On June 16, 1897, a new treaty of annexation was signed by the Hawaiian annexation commissioners and Assistant Secretary of State William R. Day. In Hawai'i, island annexationists were delighted by news of the treaty. President Dole was advised to call a special session of the senate to ratify the document.

On September 7th, the U.S. Minister to Hawai'i, H.M. Sewall, as well as Dole and his cabinet, were given a set of resolutions in Hawaiian which had been adopted at a mass meeting of natives the day before. The resolutions represented the views of Native Hawaiians and made two points: first, that the natives were largely against annexation and second, that they wanted independence under a monarchy.[95] Ironically, at the same time the resolutions were being presented, the republic's senate was ratifying the annexation treaty.

The treaty was not so readily welcomed in the United States Senate. Mainland sugar interests, fearful of importation of Hawaiian sugar, organized labor opposing the contract labor system in the islands, and anti-expansionist forces mounted a vigorous campaign against annexation.[96] The arguments of the anti-expansionists were constitutional, historical, moral, and racial. Perhaps the strongest argument raised against the annexation treaty was that the United States should adhere to her republican tradition and forgo a policy of imperialism.[97]

The opponents of annexation exhibited a wide range of attitudes concerning the racial make-up of the islands' population. In spite of the spectrum of opinion on the suitability of Hawai'i's indigenous people for American citizenship "the critics of empire were nearly unanimous in their belief that no transfer of sovereignty should take place without the consent of the natives of Hawaii."[98]

The U.S. Senate rejected the McKinley annexation treaty. However, during the spring of 1898, the Spanish-American war, the prospect for increased trade in the Far East, and developments in China where the European powers were scrambling for spheres of influence, combined to revive the annexation move in congress. After Dewey's victory in Manila on May 1st, many annexationists insisted that the United States had to annex Hawai'i in order to send supplies and reinforcements to American forces in the Philippines. Pearl Harbor, whose military importance had long been recognized, became a primary objective of annexation. Although America had rights to a base at Pearl Harbor, those rights derived from a treaty that could be abrogated. Annexationists argued that it was necessary for the United States to have permanent rights to Pearl Harbor, which only annexation could provide.[99]

8.   ANNEXATION

On May 4, 1898, Representative Francis G. Newlands of Nevada introduced a joint resolution of annexation in the U.S. House of Representatives. The constitutionality of annexing a territory by way of resolution rather than by treaty was hotly debated.[100] Nevertheless, by July, the "Newlands resolution" had moved through both houses of congress. President McKinley signed it into law on July 7th.

On August 12, 1898, the Republic of Hawaiʻi ceded sovereignty of the islands to the United States under the terms of the Joint Resolution of Annexation.[101] With cession of sovereignty, the republic also conveyed absolute title of Hawaiʻi's public lands to the United States. These lands, which included both the Government and Crown Lands under the monarchy, amounted to almost 1.75 million acres valued at $5.5 million.[102] The Joint Resolution, while ceding absolute title to the public lands, declared that:

> The existing land laws of the United States relative to public lands shall not apply to such land in the Hawaiian Islands; but the Congress of the United States shall enact special laws for their management and disposition: *Provided, That all revenue from or proceeds of the same*, except as regards such part thereof as may be used or occupied for the civil, military, or naval purposes of the United States, or may be assigned for the use of the local government, *shall be used solely for the benefit of the inhabitants of the Hawaiian Islands for educational and other public purposes.*[103] (Emphasis added.)

The Joint Resolution set up an interim government for the islands, and provided that municipal legislation of the republic not inconsistent with federal laws, treaties, or the federal constitution should remain in effect until congress could provide for a territorial government.[104]

9.   TERRITORIAL PERIOD

In 1900, congress passed an Organic Act establishing Hawaiʻi's territorial government. The Organic Act confirmed the cession of public lands to the United States, and provided specific laws to administer those lands.[105] Section 91 of the Organic Act, one of two sections dealing directly with lands, stated in relevant part:

> [E]xcept as otherwise provided, the public property ceded and transferred to the United States by the Republic of Hawaii under the joint resolution of annexation . . . shall be and remain in the possession, use, and control of the government of the Territory of Hawaii, and shall be maintained, managed, and cared for by it, at its own expense, until otherwise provided for by Congress, or taken for the uses and purposes of the United States by direction of the President or of the Governor of Hawaii.[106]

Section 73 of the Organic Act stated that the proceeds from the territory's sale, lease, or other disposition of these ceded lands should be deposited in the territory's treasury for "such uses and purposes for the benefit of the inhabitants of the Territory of Hawaii as are consistent with the joint resolution of annexation."[107]

Although the republic had ceded title of Hawaiʻi's public lands to the United States, both the Joint Resolution of Annexation and Hawaiʻi's Organic Act recognized that these lands were impressed with a special trust under the federal government's proprietorship.

15

In fact, it has been suggested that Hawai'i's ceded lands never became an integral part of the federal public domain. Rather, due to their unique status, the United States received legal title to the land, while the beneficial title rested with the inhabitants of Hawai'i:

> The territorial government had in effect become a conduit of Congress. For all practical purposes the ceded lands had not changed hands. Building on Hawaii's existing land administration scheme, Congress prescribed several significant changes in the Organic Act to insure widespread use of public lands for settlement and homesteading. Otherwise, the territory was given direct control over the public lands and was authorized to dispose of them as a governmental entity .... The federal government continued to hold absolute title to the public domain, but did so only 'in trust' for the islands' people.[108]

Nevertheless, the federal government also reserved the right to withdraw lands for its own use.

The Organic Act established a territorial government structurally similar to that of most states in the Union. The differences arose from the ultimate authority possessed by the federal government. Congress, having erected the territorial government, could abolish it and substitute some other government form. The principal officers of the territory, the governor and secretary, were appointed by the U.S. president with the consent of the senate.[109] The secretary became acting governor in event of the disability of the governor. Heads of the various territorial departments were appointed by the governor.[110] Territorial supreme court, circuit court, and federal district court judges were appointed by the president, while district magistrates were appointed by the chief justice of the territorial supreme court.[111] A bi-cameral legislature was established with universal suffrage for anyone who had held citizen status under the republic. Although the legislature could pass laws on substantially the same range of subjects as do state legislatures, congress had the right to amend or invalidate any territorial law.[112] The act also assigned Hawai'i a non-voting delegate to congress.[113]

a. The Crown Lands

In 1910, Queen Lili'uokalani brought suit against the United States in the U.S. Court of Claims to recover the value of the Crown Lands. In *Liliuokalani v. United States* (1910),[114] the court, relying upon the earlier Hawai'i Supreme Court decision in *Estate of Kamehameha IV* (1864), and the Act of January 3, 1865, determined that the Crown Lands belonged to the office of the crown and not to the individual monarch. The court stated:

> [T]he crown lands were treated not as the King's private property in the strict sense of the term. While possessing certain attributes pertaining to fee-simple estates, such as unrestricted power of alienation and incumbrance, there were likewise enough conditions surrounding the tenure to clearly characterize it as one pertaining to the support and maintenance of the Crown, as distinct from the person of the Sovereign. They belonged to the office and not to the individual.[115]

In essence, the court upheld the confiscation of the Crown Lands and their eventual transfer to the United States, by concluding that:

> It seems to the court that the crown lands acquired their unusual status through a desire of the King to firmly establish his Government by commendable concessions to his chiefs and people out of the public domain. The reservations made were to the Crown and not the

16

King as an individual. The crown lands were the resourceful methods of income to sustain, in part at least, the dignity of the office to which they were inseparably attached. When the office ceased to exist they became as other lands of the Sovereignty and passed to the defendants as part and parcel of the public domain.[116] (Citations omitted.)

b. *Hawaiian Homes Commission Act*

Prior to annexation, some public lands had been opened up in homesteading programs.[117] A 1910 amendment to the Organic Act directed the territory to open land for homesteading in a given area when 25 or more qualified homesteaders applied for the land.[118] Since many sugar leases were due to expire during the 1920s and 1930s, growers were afraid that when their leases expired, choice sugar lands might be put into homesteading under the 1910 amendment. "The managers of Hawaii's large plantations feared that the net result of this homesteading experiment would be to destroy a thriving plantation enterprise . . . ."[119]

During the same period, Hawaiian leaders began to encourage racial consciousness among the Hawaiian people, whose social and economic condition was rapidly deteriorating. A 1964 report describes the situation:

> Available social statistics indicate that as of 1920 the position of the Hawaiian community had deteriorated seriously. The general crime rate for people of Hawaiian ancestry was significantly higher than that of other groups. The rate of juvenile delinquency was also higher, an ominous omen for the future. Economically depressed, internally disorganized and politically threatened, it was evident that the remnant of Hawaiians required assistance to stem their precipitous decline.[120]

All of these forces converged in 1921 to promote congressional passage of the Hawaiian Homes Commission Act. Under the act, about 188,000 acres of public lands were designated as "available lands" and put under the jurisdiction of the Hawaiian Homes Commission to be leased out to Native Hawaiians, those with 50 percent or more native blood, at a nominal fee for 99 years.[121] The homesteading approach to rehabilitation

> was consistent with long-established American and Hawaiian traditions. It was further reinforced . . . by the suggestion that dispossessed Hawaiians would be returning to the soil, going back to the cultivation of at least a portion of their ancestral lands . . . . Finally, the threat which extension of general homesteading programs had posed to Hawaii's sugar industry was eliminated by exclusion of all sugar producing lands from the acreage set aside as 'available' for the Hawaiian Homes homesteading program.[122]

The act was supported by the sugar interests because it carefully defined the lands which Native Hawaiians might receive. Forest reserves were excluded and so were cultivated sugar cane lands and lands under homestead lease, right of purchase lease, or certificate of occupation.[123] Most lands made available were arid and of marginal value.[124] Many were actually lava rock. Moreover, while Hawaiian leaders had originally proposed a bill which would have allowed Hawaiians with even small amounts of aboriginal blood to be eligible for homesteading, the local sugar growers, fearful that large numbers of Hawaiians would demand lands, maneuvered to have the blood quantum set at 50 percent.[125]

Homesteading was originally conceived of as an agricultural experiment, but since the lands were arid and of marginal agricultural quality, virtually none of the homestead areas designated for diversified agriculture were successful. Consequently, the homestead program turned its attention to providing houselots and some pasture lands to Native Hawaiians.[126] When Hawai'i became a state in 1959, only 1,673 Native Hawaiians had been provided with homesteads, although there were more than four *houselots* to every *farmlot*.[127] An additional 2,200 Native Hawaiians were on the waiting list for homestead lands.[128] Thirty years later, 5,778 Native Hawaiians lease 32,713 acres of Hawaiian homestead land while almost 19,000 Native Hawaiians remain on the waiting list for homestead lands.[129]

Primary responsibility for administration and management of the Hawaiian Homes program was transferred to the state as a condition of statehood. The program is now administered by a state agency, the Department of Hawaiian Home Lands. However, the federal government retains responsibility for certain aspects of implementing the original act.[130]

c. *Federal Use of Hawai'i's Lands*

Undoubtedly, one of the major justifications for annexing Hawai'i was national defense. Many annexationists had argued that Hawai'i was needed to protect the West Coast of the United States and to maintain U.S. military strength in the Pacific.[131] No site in the Pacific area was better suited for refueling ships, storing munitions, and quartering troops than Pearl Harbor. Since Hawai'i's public lands were now controlled by the United States, congress and the president had the power to use them and large tracts of land were set aside for military use.

This policy of using Hawai'i's lands for military purposes continued, accelerating during the Second World War. By statehood in 1959, 287,078.44 acres of Hawai'i's public lands had been set aside for federal government use.[132] Of this acreage, 227,972.62 acres were located in national parks, with the remainder being utilized by the Department of Defense.[133] In addition, the federal government had permits and licenses for an additional 117,412.74 acres of land.[134] Finally, the United States had acquired the fee interest, through purchase or condemnation, of 28,234.73 acres.[135]

10. STATEHOOD AND THE ADMISSION ACT

In 1959, Hawai'i was admitted to the Union as a state.[136] Hawai'i's Admission Act recognized the special status of Hawai'i's public lands and reflected the intent to return those lands to the new state. This approach differed significantly from the legal treatment of lands in other states admitted to the Union, where only a small portion of land was allocated to the new states. Hawai'i's public lands, formerly the Crown and Government Lands, had been ceded to the United States at annexation. In an unprecedented action, the federal government relinquished title to the new state for most of the ceded lands held at the time of statehood.[137] However, certain lands -- those that had been set aside pursuant to an act of congress, executive order, presidential proclamation, or gubernatorial proclamation -- remained the property of the United States.[138] The Admission Act provided a mechanism for return of these "retained" lands within five years of Hawai'i's admission if the United States no longer needed them.[139] Subsequently, congress passed an act allowing the return of these lands to the state at any time they are declared unnecessary to federal needs.[140]

Section 5(f) of the Admission Act requires the state to hold all ceded lands, with limited exceptions:

> [A]s a public trust for the support of the public schools and other public educational institutions, for the betterment of the conditions of native Hawaiians, as defined in the Hawaiian Homes Commission Act, 1920, as amended, for the development of farm and home ownership on as widespread a basis as possible[,] for the making of public improvements, and for the provision of lands for public use. Such lands, proceeds, and income shall be managed and disposed of for one or more of the foregoing purposes in such manner as the constitution and laws of said State may provide, and their use for any other object shall constitute a breach of trust for which suit may be brought by the United States.[141]

a. *1978 Constitutional Amendments*

Prior to 1978, little attention was focused on section 5(f) of the Admission Act and its trust language. The state had interpreted the provision to require only that the proceeds and income be used for the fulfillment of any *one* of the five trust purposes and the state chose to make that one purpose public education. At the 1978 Constitutional Convention, however, the Hawaiian Affairs Committee sought to clarify and implement the Admission Act's trust language as it relates to Native Hawaiians.[142] As a result, three new sections were added to the constitution fundamentally altering the state's role in implementing the section 5(f) trust language.

The first section added to the state constitution specified that the lands granted to the state by section 5(b) of the Admission Act (with the exception of the Hawaiian Home Lands) were to be held by the state as a public trust for two beneficiaries -- Native Hawaiians and the general public.[143] The second section established an Office of Hawaiian Affairs (OHA), to be governed by a nine-member board of trustees, which would hold title to all real or personal property, set aside or conveyed to it, as a trust for Native Hawaiians and Hawaiians.[144] A final section set forth the powers of the OHA board of trustees and made it clear that included within the property that OHA was to hold in trust would be a *pro rata* portion of the income and proceeds from sale or other disposition of the lands granted to the state by section 5(b) of the Admission Act.[145]

b. *The Office of Hawaiian Affairs*

OHA was established to serve all Hawaiians. However, it is clear from the amendments' language and the relevant committee reports[146] that the Constitutional Convention structured OHA as the entity to receive and administer the share of the public land trust funds designated for the betterment of the conditions of Native Hawaiians under the Admission Act. The definition of Native Hawaiian in section 5(f) of the Admission Act is tied to the definition of Native Hawaiian under the Hawaiian Homes Commission Act. Benefits under the Hawaiian Homes Commission Act are limited to those with 50 percent or more aboriginal blood.[147] Thus, although the OHA amendment names two beneficiaries of the OHA trust -- Native Hawaiians (those with 50 percent or more Hawaiian blood) and Hawaiians (those with any quantum of Hawaiian blood) -- OHA is restricted to utilizing its public land trust funds solely for the benefit of its Native Hawaiian beneficiaries.

The Admission Act left to state law the allocation of the public land trust proceeds and income among the five trust purposes.[148] In 1980, in response to the new constitutional provision establishing OHA, the state legislature set the amount to be received by OHA from those proceeds and income at 20 percent.[149] However, many unresolved issues relative to the public land trust and its proceeds and income remained. Disputes over the classification of specific parcels of land as ceded or non-ceded, questions as to whether section 5(f) contemplates gross or net income, and problems in defining "proceeds," have plagued the state and hampered OHA in effectively carrying out its responsibilities to Native Hawaiians.

Securing a *pro rata* portion of the public land trust fund for Native Hawaiians was a primary motive for establishing the Office of Hawaiian Affairs. Of equal importance, however, were the objectives of providing all Hawaiians with the right to choose their leaders through the elective process and providing a vehicle for self-government and self-determination.

OHA is a unique entity combining features of both a public trust and government agency. Under Hawai'i law, OHA is a separate state agency, independent of the executive branch.[150] Its independence is assured by its primary funding mechanism (the public land trust fund), its control over internal affairs, its ability to acquire and manage property, its power to enter into contracts and leases, and the elective process by which the board of trustees is chosen.[151] At the same time, OHA is mandated to act as a trustee in administering its funds for the benefit of Native Hawaiians and Hawaiians. OHA's statutory purposes[152] include promoting the betterment of conditions of Native Hawaiians and Hawaiians; serving as the principal state agency for the performance, development, and coordination of programs and activities relating to Hawaiians; assessing the policies and practices of other agencies impacting on Hawaiians; conducting advocacy efforts; receiving and disbursing grants and donations from all sources for Hawaiians; and, serving as a receptacle for reparations from the federal government.

11.   CONCLUSION

The state has begun to address, at least partially, its trust duties to Hawaiians. However, the federal government has been reluctant to clearly recognize and respond to its trust responsibilities. The federal government has never actively involved itself in enforcing the trust provisions of section 5(f) of the Admission Act. Arguments for restitution and reparations based upon the loss of Hawaiian sovereignty and land at the time of the overthrow of the Hawaiian kingdom in 1893 have been advanced by Hawaiians for almost 100 years but congress has yet to give recognition to these longstanding claims. While recent federal legislation for Native Americans has included Hawaiians as beneficiaries, such legislation falls far short of addressing and clarifying the relationship between Native Hawaiians and the federal government. In the next decade, increasing demands from the Hawaiian community for rights of self-governance and sovereignty must be resolved by both the federal and state governments.

NOTES

1. *Hearings on the Report of the Native Hawaiians Study Commission Before the Senate Comm. on Energy and Natural Resources*, 98th Cong., 2nd Sess. 104 (1984) (statement of Marion Kelly).

2. Native Hawaiians Study Commission, *Report on the Culture, Needs and Concerns of Native Hawaiians (Majority)* 102-104 (1983). *But see generally* D.E. Stannard, *Before the Horror* (1989) (arguing that the pre-*haole* population was between 800,000 to one million).

3. E.S. Handy and E.G. Handy, *Native Planters in Old Hawaii* 53 (1972).

4. J.J. Chinen, *The Great Mahele* 5 (1958).

5. Handy and Handy, *supra* note 3, at 48.

6. *In re Boundaries of Pulehunui*, 4 Haw. 239-241, 242 (1879).

7. *Id.* at 241.

8. Chinen, *supra* note 4, at 3-4.

9. Handy and Handy, *supra* note 3, at 41-53.

10. M. Kelly, *Changes in Land Tenure in Hawaii, 1778-1850*, 20-26 (1956) (unpublished thesis available in University of Hawai'i Library).

11. *Compare, for instance*, Chinen, *supra* note 4, at 5 and R. Kuykendall, *The Hawaiian Kingdom 1778-1854*, at 269 (1938) with Kelly, *supra* note 10, at 20-26 and Handy and Handy, *supra* note 3, at 57-59.

12. D. Malo, *Hawaiian Antiquities* 53 (1951 ed.).

13. Handy and Handy, *supra* note 3, at 63.

14. J. Wise, "The History of Land Ownership in Hawaii," in *Ancient Hawaiian Civilization* 85 (1965); Kelly, *supra* note 10, at 42.

15. Chinen, *supra* note 4, at 6.

16. Hawai'i State Dept. of Budget and Finance (Hawai'i Institute for Management and Analysis in Government), *Land and Water Resource Management in Hawaii* 148 (1979) [hereinafter *Land and Water Resource Management*].

17. Levy, *Native Hawaiian Land Rights*, 63 Calif. L. Rev. 848, 850 (1975).

18. *See* R. Kuykendall, *The Hawaiian Kingdom 1778-1854*, 119-122 (1938) [hereinafter 1 *Hawaiian Kingdom*] (account of the adoption of the Law of 1825 and early law-making in Hawai'i).

19. *Id.* at 160.

20. L. Thurston, *The Fundamental Law of Hawaii* 3 (1904).

21. *Id.* at 5-6.

22. *Id.* at 8-9.

23. *See* 1 *Hawaiian Kingdom*, *supra* note 18, at 273-298 (thorough discussion of the factors involved in the enactment of these laws).

24. Thurston, *supra* note 20, at 1 and Haw. Const. preamble (1840). The preamble was virtually identical to the 1839 Declaration of Rights.

25. Royal Proclamation of May 31, 1841, in 1 *Hawaiian Kingdom*, *supra* note 18, at 275-276.

26. Other instances of foreign interference in Hawaiian affairs involved the visits of French warships during the years 1836-1839, the action of Captain LaPlace in compelling the Hawaiian government to accept a treaty in 1839, and the virtual seizure of Honolulu's fort and government offices by the French Admiral de Tromelin in 1849.

27. 1 *Hawaiian Kingdom*, *supra* note 18, at 206-226.

28. Quoted in J. Hobbs, *Hawaii: A Pageant of the Soil* 31 (1953).

29. 1 *Laws of Kamehameha III* 107 (1840); Thurston, *supra* note 20, at 137; 2 *Revised Laws of Hawaii, 1925*, 2120, *et seq.* [hereinafter *Revised Laws 1925*].

30. *Revised Laws 1925*, *supra* note 29, § 7, at 2123.

31. 1 *Hawaiian Kingdom*, *supra* note 18, at 280.

32. *Revised Laws 1925*, *supra* note 29, §§ 5-6, at 2121-2122.

33. *Id.*, § 10, at 2123.

34. Principles Adopted by the Board of Commissioners to Quiet Land Titles in Their Adjudication of Claims Presented to Them, in *Revised Laws 1925*, *supra* note 29, at 2124. Approved by the Legislative Council October 26, 1846.

35. *Id.* at 2136.

36. *Id.* at 2126.

37. 4 Privy Council Records 205-308 (1847).

38. *Id.* at 296-306.

39. *See Revised Laws 1925*, *supra* note 29, at 2152-2176 (listing of lands and act ratifying division of lands).

40. *See Estate of Kamehameha IV*, 2 Haw. 715, 722-723 (1864).

41. It should be noted that the *Mahele* did not give the *konohiki* title to their lands. They were required to present their claims to the Land Commission, pay the commutation, and receive awards for their land. The *konohiki* were given several extensions of time in which to file and prove their claims. *See*, Act of August 10, 1854, *Revised Laws 1925, supra* note 29, at 2147; Act of August 24, 1860 *Revised Laws 1925, supra* note 29, at 2148; and Act of December 16, 1892 *Revised Laws 1925, supra* note 29, at 2151. The latter act allowed claims until January 1, 1895 after which all lands not claimed reverted to the government.

42. *Laws of Hawaii, 1862*, 27.

43. *Revised Laws 1925, supra* note 29, at 2141-2142.

44. *Id.*

45. Chinen, *supra* note 4, at 30.

46. Marion Kelly, Associate Anthropologist, Bishop Museum, in a lecture on April 22, 1982 noted that of the 8,205 awardees, 200 were foreigners, 560 were chiefs of various ranks and 7,500 were *maka'āinana*.

47. Levy, *supra* note 17, at 856.

48. *Land and Water Resource Management, supra* note 16, at 156.

49. All *kuleana* claims must have been filed by February 14, 1848, the date on which the Land Commission was to have terminated. Although the commission's powers were extended, the deadline for filing native tenants' claims was not. The Act of May 26, 1853 barred claims not proved by May 1, 1854, *Revised Laws 1925, supra* note 29, at 2145. *Compare* to the provisions extending the time period in which the *konohiki* had to file claims, discussed *supra* note 41.

50. *Revised Laws 1925, supra* note 29, § 7, at 2142.

51. *Oni v. Meek*, 2 Haw. 87 (1858), interpreted the *Kuleana* Act as declaring all rights of native tenants (with the exception of fishing rights) and abrogating all customary and statutory rights not specifically stated.

52. Hobbs, *supra* note 28, at 54.

53. *Revised Laws 1925, supra* note 29, at 2233.

54. Levy, *supra* note 17, at 858.

55. *Land and Water Resource Management, supra* note 16, at 163.

56. Levy, *supra* note 17, at 860.

57. *Id.* at 859.

58. R. Horowitz, *Public Land Policy in Hawaii: An Historical Analysis* 186 (Legislative Reference Bureau Report No. 5, 1969) [hereinafter *Historical Analysis*].

59. P. Thompson, Kahalu'u and the Development of Windward Oahu 3 (Hawaii Observer Report No. 1).

60. *Estate of Kamehameha IV*, 2 Haw. 715 (1864).

61. *Revised Laws 1925, supra* note 29, at 2177-2179.

62. *Historical Analysis, supra* note 58, at 137.

63. L.H. Fuchs, *Hawaii Pono: A Social History* 251 (1961).

64. R. Horowitz, *Public Land Policy in Hawaii: Major Landowners* 4-5 (Legislative Reference Bureau Report No. 3, 1967).

65. R. Kuykendall, *Constitutions of the Hawaiian Kingdom* 21 (papers of the Hawaiian Historical Society, No. 21, 1940) [hereinafter *Constitutions*].

66. *Id.* at 27-36.

67. *Id.* at 36-40.

68. *Id.* at 43.

69. *Id.* at 45.

70. *Id.* at 46-49.

71. Qualification of voters for nobles were set forth in art. 59 of the Constitution of 1887:

> Every male resident of the Hawaiian Islands, of Hawaiian, American or European birth or descent, who shall have attained the age of twenty years, and shall have paid his taxes, and shall have caused his name to be entered on the list of voters for Nobles for his District, shall be an elector of Nobles, and shall be entitled to vote at any election of Nobles, provided:
> *First*: That he shall have resided in the country not less than three years, and in the district in which he offers to vote, not less than three months immediately preceding the election at which he offers to vote:
> *Second*: That he shall own and be possessed, in his own right, of taxable property in this country of the value of not less than three thousand dollars over and above all encumbrances, or shall have actually received an income of not less than six hundred dollars during the year next preceding his registration for such election:
> *Third*: That he shall be able to read and comprehend an ordinary newspaper printed in either the Hawaiian, English or some European language:

> *Fourth*: That he shall have taken an oath to support the Constitution and laws, . . .
>
> Provided however, that the requirements of a three years' residence and of ability to read and comprehend an ordinary newspaper, printed either in the Hawaiian, English or some European language, shall not apply to persons residing in the Kingdom at the time of the promulgation of this Constitution, if they shall register and vote at the first election which shall be held under this Constitution.

Compare with qualifications of voters for representatives set forth in art. 62:

> Every male resident of the Kingdom, of Hawaiian, American, or European birth or descent, who shall have taken an oath to support the Constitution and laws in the manner provided for electors of Nobles; who shall have paid his taxes; who shall have attained the age of twenty years; and shall have been domiciled in the Kingdom for one year immediately preceding the election; and shall know how to read and write either the Hawaiian, English or some European language, (if born since the year 1840,) and shall have caused his name to be entered on the list of voters of his district as may be provided by law, shall be entitled to one vote for the Representative or Representatives of that district, provided however, that the requirements of being domiciled in the Kingdom for one year immediately preceding the election, and of knowing how to read and write, either the Hawaiian, English, or some European language, shall not apply to persons residing in this Kingdom at the time of the promulgation of this Constitution, if they shall register and vote at the first election which shall be held under this Constitution.

72. *Constitutions, supra* note 65, at 50.

73. R. Kuykendall, *The Hawaiian Kingdom 1874-1893*, 585-586 (1967) [hereinafter 3 *Hawaiian Kingdom*] summarizes the most important changes the queen planned to make in the constitution:

> (1) Cabinet ministers were to serve "during the queen's pleasure," but also subject to impeachment and to removal by legislative vote of want of confidence; (2) nobles were to be appointed for life by the queen instead of being elected for a term of years; (3) only male subjects (i.e., Hawaiian born or naturalized) were to be allowed to vote; (4) justices of the supreme court were to be appointed for a term of six years instead of life; (5) article 78 of the Constitution of 1887 was dropped out; this was the article that required all official acts of the sovereign to be performed "with the advice and consent of the Cabinet."

74. L.A. Thurston, *Memoirs of the Hawaiian Revolution* 249-250 (1936) [hereinafter *Memoirs*].

75. *Id*. at 230-232.

76. *Id*.

77. *But see* R.D. Weigle, *Sugar and the Hawaiian Revolution*, 16 *Pacific Historical Review* 41-58 (Feb. 1947), in which it is argued that many sugar planters were opposed to annexation because they feared that annexation to the United States would interfere with the immigration laws and contract labor system in Hawai'i.

78. *Memoirs, supra* note 74, at 250.

79. Stevens had written in 1892:

> Destiny and the vast future interest of the United States in the Pacific clearly indicate who at no distant day must be responsible for the government of these islands. Under a Territorial government they could be as easily governed as any of the existing territories of the United States . . . I can not now refrain from expressing the opinion with emphasis that the golden hour is near at hand.

J. Blount, *Report of Commissioner to the Hawaiian Islands*, Exec. Doc. No. 47, 53rd Cong., 2d Sess. 356-357 (1893) [hereinafter *Blount's Report*].

80. *Id*. at 497.

81. 3 *Hawaiian Kingdom, supra* note 73, at 601.

82. Liliuokalani, *Hawaii's Story by Hawaii's Queen* 387 (12th ed. 1976).

83. 3 *Hawaiian Kingdom, supra* note 73, at 608.

84. *See* T. Osborne, *"Empire Can Wait"* 10-16 (1981), for a discussion of Cleveland's purposes in withdrawing the treaty.

85. 3 *Hawaiian Kingdom, supra* note 73, at 364.

86. Osborne, *supra* note 84, at 74-80.

87. S. Rep. No. 277, 53rd Cong., 2d Sess. 21 (1894).

88. On February 7, 1894, the House of Representatives resolved that there should be neither restoration of the queen nor annexation to the United States. The senate passed a similar resolution on May 31, 1894.

89. 3 *Hawaiian Kingdom, supra* note 73, at 649.

90. W.A. Russ, Jr., *The Hawaiian Republic (1894-1898)*, 33-34 (1961).

91. *Id*. at 36.

92.   The constitution provided:

> That portion of the public domain heretofore known as crown land is hereby declared to have been heretofore, and now to be, the property of the Hawaiian Government, and to be now free and clear from any trust of or concerning the same, and from all claim of any nation whatsoever upon the rents, issues, and profits thereof.

Thurston, *supra* note 20, at 237.

93.   Liliuokalani, *supra* note 82, at 273-277.

94.   R. Kuykendall and A.G. Day, *Hawaii: A History* 183 (1948).

95.   Russ, *supra* note 90, at 198. *See also id.* at 209 (description of another petition against annexation by native Hawaiians).

96.   *See* Osborne, *supra* note 84, at 85-95 (discussion of the arguments against annexation propounded by sugar and labor interests).

97.   *Id.* at 95.

98.   *Id.* at 100.

99.   *See, e.g., Congressional Record*, 55 Cong., 2nd Sess. 5982 (June 15, 1898); Appendix at 669-70 (June 13, 1898).

100.   The primary argument against the resolution was that only under the constitutional treaty-making power could the United States gain territory. To acquire Hawai'i by a legislative act, a joint resolution, would usurp the power of the senate and executive to act in matters relating to acquisition of new territories and set a dangerous precedent. Although annexationists pointed to the acquisition of Texas in 1845 by joint resolution as precedent, most anti-annexationists believed that Texas had been brought into the Union legally under congress' power to admit new states. Since statehood was not proposed for Hawai'i, the Texas acquisition had no precedential value. Further, the joint resolution utilized in the Texas case was approved by a plebiscite held in Texas. No plebiscite was proposed for Hawai'i. One senator offered an amendment to the Newlands measure providing for such a vote by all adult males, but it was defeated. Finally, on June 15, 1898, by a vote of 209 to 91, the U.S. House approved the Newlands resolution. On July 6, 1898 the Newlands measure passed the senate by 42 to 21, with 26 abstentions. *Id.* at 6149 (June 20, 1898); *id.* at 6310 (June 30, 1898); *id.* at 6709-10 (July 6, 1898); *id.* at 6018 (June 5, 1898); *id.* at 6712 (July 6, 1898).

101.   Joint Resolution of Annexation of July 7, 1898, 30 Stat. 750 [hereinafter *Joint Resolution*].

102.   J. Hobbs, *supra* note 28, at 118. *But see* L. Thurston, *A Handbook of the Annexation of Hawaii* 24 (n.d.), in which the amount of land involved is set at 1,740,000 acres valued at $4,389,550 in 1894.

103.   *Joint Resolution, supra* note 101.

104.   *Id.*

105.   *Id.*

106.   Act of April 30, 1900, ch. 339, § 91, 31 Stat. 141, 159 [hereinafter *Organic Act*].

107.   *Id.* at § 73(4)(c).

108.   Note, *Hawaii's Ceded Lands*, 3 U. Haw. L. Rev. 101, 121 (1981) [hereinafter *Ceded Lands*]. *See also* S. Rep. No. 675, 88th Cong., 1st Sess. (special status implicitly recognized).

109.   *Organic Act, supra* note 106, at §§ 66, 69.

110.   *Id.* at § 80.

111.   *Id.*

112.   *Id.* at § 55. *See Inter-Island Steam Nav. Co. v. Territory*, 305 U. S. 306 (1938) (noting that congress may abrogate territorial laws or legislate directly for territories).

113.   *Id.* at § 85.

114.   45 Ct. Cls. 418 (1910).

115.   *Id.* at 427.

116.   *Id.* at 428.

117.   The Land Act of 1895, *Civil Laws of 1897*, § 169 *et seq. See Historical Analysis, supra* note 58, at 5-15 (detailed analysis of the Act).

118.   *Organic Act, supra* note 106, at 5.

119.   *The Hawaiian Homes Program: 1920-1963*, 6 (Legislative Reference Bureau Report No. 1, 1969) [hereinafter *Homes Program*]. *See* Chapter 3, *infra,* for an exhaustive analysis of the Hawaiian Homes Commission Act.

120.   *Id.* at 2-3.

121.   Act of July 9, 1921, Pub. L. No. 34, ch. 42, §§ 203, 207, 208, 42 Stat. 108 [hereinafter *HHCA*].

122.   *Homes Program, supra* note 119, at 7.

123.   *HHCA, supra* note 121, at § 203.

124.   *See Land Aspects of the Hawaiian Homes Program* 19-26 (Legislative Reference Bureau Report No. 1b, 1964) [hereinafter *Land Aspects*].

125. H.R. Rep. No. 839, 66th Cong., 2nd Sess. (1920). *See generally,* M.M. Vause, *The Hawaiian Homes Commission Act, History and Analysis* (June 1962) (unpublished master's thesis).

126. *Land Aspects, supra* note 124, at 19-26.

127. *Id.* table at 17.

128. 1980-81 Dept. of Hawaiian Home Lands Ann. Rep., *'Aina Ho'opulapula,* graph at 8.

129. 1990 Dept. of Hawaiian Home Lands Ann. Rep., *'Aina Ho'opulapula* 12, 16.

130. *Admission Act of March 18, 1959,* Pub. L. No. 86-3, §§ 4, 5(f), 73 Stat. 4, 5-6 [hereinafter *Admission Act*].

131. Osborne, *supra* note 84, at 107.

132. *Historical Analysis, supra* note 58, at 68.

133. *Id.* at 74.

134. *Id.* at 68.

135. *Id.*

136. *Admission Act, supra* note 130.

137. *Ceded Lands, supra* note 108, at 102.

138. *Admission Act, supra* note 130, § 5(c).

139. *Id.* § 5(e).

140. Act of Dec. 23, 1963, Pub. L. No. 88-233, 77 Stat. 472.

141. *Admission Act, supra* note 130, § 5(f).

142. The state had channeled the majority of the public land trust funds toward public education.

143. Haw. Const., art. XII, § 4:

> PUBLIC TRUST. The lands granted to the State of Hawaii by Section 5(b) of the Admission Act and pursuant to Article XVI, Section 7, of the State Constitution, excluding therefrom lands defined as "available lands" by Section 203 of the Hawaiian Homes Commission Act, 1920, as amended, shall be held by the State as a public trust for native Hawaiians and the general public. [Add Const Con 1978 and election Nov. 7, 1978]

144. *Id.* § 5:

> OFFICE OF HAWAIIAN AFFAIRS; ESTABLISHMENT OF BOARD OF TRUSTEES. There is hereby established an Office of Hawaiian Affairs. The Office of Hawaiian Affairs shall hold title to all the real and personal property now or hereafter set aside or conveyed to it which shall be held in trust for native Hawaiians and Hawaiians. There shall be a board of trustees for the Office of Hawaiian Affairs elected by qualified voters who are Hawaiians, as provided by law. The board members shall be Hawaiians. There shall be not less than nine members of the board of trustees; provided that each of the following Islands have one representative: Oahu, Kauai, Maui, Molokai and Hawaii. The board shall select a chairperson from its members. [Add Const Con 1978 and election Nov. 7, 1978]

145. *Id.* § 6:

> POWERS OF BOARD OF TRUSTEES. The board of trustees of the Office of Hawaiian Affairs shall exercise power as provided by law: to manage and administer the proceeds from the sale or other disposition of the lands, natural resources, minerals and income derived from whatever sources for native Hawaiians and Hawaiians, including all income and proceeds from that pro rata portion of the trust referred to in section 4 of this article for native Hawaiians; to formulate policy relating to affairs of native Hawaiians and Hawaiians; and to exercise control over real and personal property set aside by state, federal or private sources and transferred to the board for native Hawaiians and Hawaiians. The board shall have the power to exercise control over the Office of Hawaiian Affairs through its executive officer, the administrator of the Office of Hawaiian Affairs, who shall be appointed by the board. [Add Const Con 1978 and election Nov. 7, 1978]

146. *See generally* Hawaiian Affairs Comm. Rep. No. 59 and Comm. of the Whole Report No. 13, in 1 *Proceedings of the Constitutional Convention of Hawaii of 1978,* 643, 1017.

147. *See supra* text accompanying notes 121-125.

148. *Admission Act, supra* note 130, § 5(f).

149. Act 273 of 1980, codified at Haw. Rev. Stat. § 10-13.5 (1985).

150. Haw. Rev. Stat. § 10-4 (1985).

151. *Id.* at § 10-5 sets forth the powers of the OHA trustees.

152. *Id.* at § 10-3.

CHAPTER 2

THE CEDED LANDS TRUST

1. INTRODUCTION

When Hawai'i was annexed in 1898, the Republic of Hawai'i ceded approximately 1.75 million acres[1] of Government and Crown Lands to the United States. The Government Lands had been set aside by Kamehameha III in 1848 for the benefit of the chiefs and people. The Crown Lands, reserved to the sovereign, provided a source of income and support for the crown and, pursuant to an 1865 act, were made inalienable. While the fee simple ownership system instituted by the *Mahele* and the laws that followed drastically changed Hawaiian land tenure, the Government and Crown Lands were held for the benefit of all the Hawaiian people. They marked a continuation of the trust concept that lands were held by the sovereign on behalf of the gods and for the benefit of all.

At the time of annexation, the United States implicitly recognized the trust nature of the Government and Crown Lands. Nevertheless, large tracts of these lands were set aside by the federal government for military purposes during the territorial period and continue under federal control even to this day. The trust nature of the Government and Crown Lands was clearly articulated in the 1959 Hawai'i Admission Act transferring the lands from U.S. control to the State of Hawai'i. The following chapter examines the Government and Crown Lands, now commonly termed "ceded lands," because they were ceded to the United States and back to the State of Hawai'i, and explores the trust as interpreted under current law.

2. THE TRUST UNDER FEDERAL CONTROL

The Joint Resolution annexing Hawai'i to the United States, "cede[d] and transfer[red] to the United States the absolute fee and ownership of all public, Government, or Crown lands . . . belonging to the Government of the Hawaiian Islands, together with every right and appurtenance thereunto appertaining."[2] Existing federal laws dealing with public lands were not made applicable to lands in Hawai'i. The Joint Resolution stated that congress would enact "special laws for [the] management and disposition" of Hawai'i's public lands.[3]

Another section of the Joint Resolution provided that

> [A]ll revenues from or proceeds of the [public lands], except as regards such part thereof as may be used or occupied for the civil, military, or naval purposes of the United States, or may be assigned for the use of the local government, *shall be used solely for the benefit of the inhabitants of the Hawaiian Islands for educational and other public purposes.*[4] (Emphasis added.)

In an 1899 opinion, the United States Attorney General interpreted this language as subjecting the public lands in Hawai'i to "a special trust, limiting the revenue from or proceeds of the same to the uses of the inhabitants of the Hawaiian Islands for educational and other purposes."[5]

The Joint Resolution was followed by Hawai'i's Organic Act, approved April 30, 1900.[6] The Organic Act established Hawai'i's territorial government, confirmed the cession of lands to the United States, and provided specific laws for the administration of public lands. Section 91 of the Organic Act stated:

> [T]he public property ceded and transferred to the United States by the Republic of Hawaii under the joint resolution of annexation . . . shall be and remain in the possession, use, and control of the government of the Territory of Hawaii, and shall be maintained, managed, and cared for by it, at its own expense, until otherwise provided for by Congress, or taken for the uses and purposes of the United States by direction of the President or of the governor of Hawaii.[7]

Another section of the Organic Act provided that the proceeds from the territory's sale, lease, or other disposition of these ceded lands should be deposited in the territory's treasury for "such uses and purposes for the benefit of the inhabitants of the Territory of Hawaii as are consistent with the Joint Resolution of Annexation."[8]

Consequently, in the period between annexation and statehood, although the legal title to the Government and Crown Lands was vested in the United States, the Territory of Hawai'i had administrative control and use of the lands. Moreover, funds received from disposition of the lands were used for the benefit of Hawai'i's people. While the republic had ceded absolute title of the Crown and Government Lands to the United States, both the Joint Resolution of Annexation and the Organic Act recognized that these lands were impressed with a special trust under the federal government's proprietorship. In fact, it could be argued that Hawai'i's ceded lands never became part of the federal public domain, but because of their unique status, the United States received legal title to the lands, while beneficial title rested with the inhabitants of Hawai'i.

Undoubtedly, one of the major reasons for annexing Hawai'i was to strengthen U.S. military defenses. Annexationists had argued that Hawai'i was needed to protect the West Coast of the United States and to maintain U.S. military presence in the Pacific. Pearl Harbor was best suited, of all Pacific sites, for refueling ships, storing munitions, and quartering troops. Since Hawai'i's public lands were now controlled by the United States, congress and the president had the power to use them. Under the provisions of the Organic Act, lands could be formally "set aside" by presidential executive orders for use by the United States. Large tracts of land were set aside.[9] Other lands, while not formally "set aside," were used by the United States under permits, licenses, or by permission from the territorial government.[10] At statehood in 1959, 287,078.44 acres of Hawai'i's public lands had been set aside for federal government use. Of this acreage, 227,972.62 acres were located in national parks with the remainder being utilized for military purposes.[11] Moreover, the federal government had permits and licenses for an additional 117,412.74 acres of land.[12] The United States had also acquired the fee interest, through purchase or condemnation, of 28,234.73 acres.[13]

One recognition of the unique status of the Government and Crown Lands, as well as the special relationship between the federal government and Native Hawaiians, came in 1921 with the passage of the Hawaiian Homes Commission Act.[14] The act effectively withdrew approximately 188,000 acres of ceded lands and brought them under the jurisdiction of the Hawaiian Homes Commission to be leased to Native Hawaiians at a nominal fee for 99 years.[15] A Native Hawaiian was defined in the act as "any descendant of not less than one-half part of the blood of the races inhabiting the Hawaiian Islands previous to 1778."[16]

In 1959, Hawai'i became a state.[17] Upon admission, the Government and Crown Lands were transferred to the State of Hawai'i and the state assumed the role of trustee. Section 5 of the Admission Act provides the key to understanding Hawai'i's ceded lands and the state's responsibilities in relation to those lands.[18] Section 5(a) names the state as successor in title to the lands and properties held by the territory. Section 5(b) of the act states:

> Except as provided in subsection (c) and (d) of this section, the United States grants to the State of Hawaii, effective upon its admission into the Union, the United States' title to all the public lands and other property, and to all lands defined as "available lands" by section 203 of the Hawaiian Homes Commission Act, 1920, as amended, within the boundaries of the State of Hawaii, title to which is held by the United States immediately prior to its admission into the Union.

Section 5(g) defines public lands and other public property as the "lands and properties that were ceded to the United States by the Republic of Hawaii under the joint resolution of annexation . . . or that have been acquired in exchange for lands or properties so ceded."

Section 5(c) of the Admission Act specifically omitted from the lands to be returned to the state any lands that had been set aside for federal use pursuant to an act of congress, executive order, presidential proclamation, or gubernatorial proclamation. According to section 5(c), such lands should remain the property of the federal government.

Furthermore, section 5(d) gave the federal government five years to set aside any ceded lands it was using under permit, license, or permission of the territory immediately prior to statehood. Once set aside, those lands also would become the property of the United States.

However, section 5(e) provided some relief from the federal government's ability to keep ceded lands. Under section 5(e,) land and property unnecessary for federal needs could be conveyed "freely to the State of Hawaii." This provision required federal agencies to assess their needs for ceded lands and report to the president. It set a five-year deadline for reporting and conveying lands to the state. After August 21, 1964, five years from the date on which Hawai'i formally entered the union, title to ceded lands retained by federal agencies vested permanently in the United States.

State officials had high hopes that substantial portions of federally held lands would be returned. At the end of the five-year period, however, of the 287,078.44 acres set aside for the federal government, only 595.41 were returned.[19]

Furthermore, the federal government chose to retain control of virtually all of the 117,412 acres it had held under lease, permit, or license prior to statehood. Of this number, under the provisions of section 5(d), 87,236 acres were subsequently added to the lands set aside for federal use. While the remaining 30,176 acres became the property of the state, under pressure from federal officials these lands were leased to the federal government for 65 years at a nominal cost.[20] Consequently, as the five-year deadline approached, the federal government retained title to 373,719.58 acres and leased an additional 30,176.18 acres.

TABLE I

Lands Retained by the U.S. Under
§ 5(c) and § 5(d) of the Admission Act

Category		Acres
Lands set aside for U.S. during territorial period and retained by U.S. under § 5(c)		287,078.44
Lands returned under § 5(e)	-	595.41
TOTAL		286,483.03
Lands set aside by U.S. under § 5(d)	+	87,236.55
TOTAL lands retained by U.S.		373,719.58
Lands leased to U.S.		30,176.18

Hawai'i's political leaders objected to the five-year deadline set on the return of the land under federal use.[21] They contended that Hawai'i had a unique claim to these lands and property since they were originally given to the United States by the republic and were held as a trust for the people of Hawai'i. On December 23, 1963, congress passed Public Law 88-233 (P.L. 88-233), which abolished the five-year deadline in subsection 5(e). This meant that the federal government could relinquish section 5(c) and 5(d) ceded lands to the state at any time.[22] However, all lands that had been set aside for national parks (227,972.62 acres) became the fee simple property of the federal government. Thus, under the provisions of P.L. 88-233, approximately 145,746.96 acres (58,510.41 acres of section 5(c) lands and 87,236.55 acres of section 5(d) lands) became eligible for return to the state. Since 1964, one source estimates that only 1,906 acres have been returned under the act's provisions.[23]

TABLE II

Lands Eligible for Return After Passage of P.L. 88-233

Category		Acres
Lands set aside for U.S. during territorial period and retained by U.S. under § 5(c)		287,078.44
Lands returned under § 5(e)	-	595.41
TOTAL		286,483.03
National parks -- fee simple title in U.S.	-	227,972.62
TOTAL		58,510.41
Lands set aside by U.S. under § 5(d)	+	87,236.55
TOTAL lands eligible for return to state after passage of P.L. 88-233		145,746.96
Lands returned since 1964		1,906.00

The exact number of acres of ceded lands currently under federal control is unknown. Various federal government documents give conflicting figures.[24]

An egregious example of federal abuse of trust lands is the island of Kaho'olawe, originally part of the Government Lands. Kaho'olawe is one of the eight major islands in the Hawaiian archipelago. The island had been leased to private ranching operations until 1941, when it was seized under martial law during World War II. In 1953, the island was set aside for naval operations by a presidential order until no longer needed.[25] The Navy has used the island primarily as a bombing target and has consistently maintained that it is indispensable to national security.

In 1976, individual Native Hawaiians sought to gain access to Kaho'olawe and were arrested and convicted for criminal trespass on a U.S. military installation. However, the resulting awareness of the island's beauty and cultural significance led to the filing of a civil suit[26] by the Protect Kaho'olawe 'Ohana and others to stop the bombing and return the island to Native Hawaiian control. The suit alleged violations of environmental and historic preservation laws. In 1980, a consent decree was filed in the suit. Under the consent decree, the Navy is required to survey and protect historic sites on the island, begin soil conservation and revegetation programs, and allow regular religious, cultural, scientific, and environmental access to the island. The consent decree also granted the 'Ohana stewardship to part of the island, and set guidelines for the Navy's bombing practices. A complete archaeological survey of the island has revealed thousands of archaeological features such as petroglyphs, fishing shrines, temples, and house sites. In 1981, the entire island was placed on the National Register of Historic Places as a National Historic District.

While the island of Kaho'olawe may be the most extreme example of federal abuse of trust lands, there are others. On O'ahu, Mākua Valley on the Wai'anae coast is also used for target practice. Over 3,000 acres of Mākua are lands set aside by the federal government and retained under section 5(d) of the Admission Act, while an additional 1,500 acres are leased by the federal government from the state for a nominal fee.[27] Other lands, such as portions of Bellows Air Force Base on the windward side of O'ahu, do not appear to be put to any significant use by the federal government and could readily be returned to Native Hawaiian use.

3. THE TRUST UNDER THE STATE'S ADMINISTRATION

The state's primary responsibilities with regard to the Government and Crown Lands are established in section 5 of the Admission Act. Section 5(f) of the act provides that these lands and the income and proceeds derived from them are to be held by the state as a public trust:

(1) for the support of the public schools and other public educational institutions;
(2) for the betterment of the conditions of Native Hawaiians, as defined in the Hawaiian Homes Commission Act of 1920;
(3) for the development of farm and home ownership on as widespread a basis as possible;
(4) for the making of public improvements; and
(5) for the provision of lands for public use.

Section 5(f) also provides that these lands, proceeds, and income shall be managed and disposed of for one or more of the trust purposes "in such manner as the constitution and laws of said state may provide and their use for any other object shall constitute a breach of trust for which suit may be brought by the United States."[28]

Unfortunately, the legislative history of the Admission Act provides little insight into the trust language of section 5(f). This language originated in deliberations on a 1947 bill for Hawai'i's statehood. The Department of the Interior suggested amendments to the bill, including the trust language contained in section 5(f). The House Committee on Public Lands adopted the amendments and the trust language was carried forward into every subsequent statehood bill. While the legislative history of section 5(f) fails to provide detailed guidance as to the trust language, it is clear that the welfare of Native Hawaiians was of specific concern to congress. Looking to the considerations which earlier had guided congress in enacting the Hawaiian Homes Commission Act, several factors stand out. First, there was a fear that Hawaiians were dying out as a race; their economic, social and physical conditions were dismal and their continued existence was at risk. Second, it was recognized that with the drastic economic and political changes brought by Western contact, Native Hawaiians had been displaced from native lands and their rights in such lands had not been adequately protected.[29] It is fair to assume that these same concerns prompted the inclusion of the section 5(f) language on the betterment of conditions of Native Hawaiians. Thus section 5(f), in part, can be viewed as a further safeguard to the continued existence of Native Hawaiians and additional protection of their rights in native lands.

Since statehood, the Department of Land and Natural Resources (DLNR) has been charged with the administration of the public land trust.[30] However, a 1979 audit of the DLNR showed that the DLNR had failed to properly dispose of the revenue and income from the trust.[31]

Hawai'i Revised Statutes (Haw. Rev. Stat.), section 171-18, the implementing legislation for section 5(f) of the Admission Act, established a public land trust fund for the receipt of funds derived from the sale, lease, or other disposition of *ceded lands*.[32] Haw. Rev. Stat. section 171-19, created a special land and development fund, to receive all proceeds from the disposition of *non-ceded* lands (lands which the state may have acquired by condemnation, purchase or other means).[33] This second fund was established for the maintenance and development of all public lands. These two funds were intended to serve different purposes: Monies deposited in the public land trust fund were to come from the disposition of ceded lands and were to be used as directed in section 5(f) of the Admission Act. Monies deposited in the special land and development fund were to come from the disposition of non-ceded lands (lands not subject to the section 5(f) trust) and were to be used to maintain and develop all public lands.

The 1979 audit revealed, however, that the DLNR had failed to make this distinction between the two funds and instead deposited monies from the *leases* of all public lands into the public land trust fund and monies from the *sale* of all public lands into the special land and development fund.[34] Thus, in depositing money in the two funds, DLNR ignored the distinction between ceded lands and non-ceded lands; instead, it deposited monies on the basis of a lease/sale dichotomy. The reason given for the failure to conform to the mandate of section 5(f) of the Admission Act was even more disturbing: No inventory of public lands existed, and the DLNR was unable to distinguish between ceded and non-ceded public lands.[35]

a. Inventory of Ceded Lands

The absence of an inventory and the confusion of funds impeded the administration of the section 5(f) public trust in several ways.[36] First, because the DLNR did not use the ceded/non-ceded distinction in recording receipts, there is no way of knowing the accuracy of its figures for each fund or of determining which monies belong to which fund. Since most of the income from public lands is derived from ceded lands, this failure to distinguish ceded and non-ceded lands has probably worked to the disadvantage of the public land trust fund. Second, the wrongful deposits may have resulted in expenditures of public trust monies for the purposes of the special land and development fund and vice versa. Finally, because section 5(f) requires the state to hold ceded lands separately in trust, the state's failure to identify ceded lands, like a private trustee's failure to identify and segregate trust assets, constitutes an independent breach of its 5(f) obligations.

As a result of the disclosures in the 1979 audit and the 1978 amendments to the state constitution, discussed below, the DLNR began to compile an inventory of all the state-owned public lands for which it is accountable. By September, 1981, the DLNR had completed its initial inventory, listing approximately 1,271,652 acres. The department itself conceded, however, that its inventory was not complete.

In 1982, the legislature appropriated funds for the Office of the Legislative Auditor to complete the inventory of ceded lands and to study the legal issues relating to revenues from the ceded lands.[37] The Legislative Auditor issued a progress report[38] in 1983, requesting additional time to complete its task. In December 1986, the Legislative Auditor's Final Report on the public land trust was issued. With regard to the inventory, the report stated:

> The inventory put together by the DLNR is as precise and complete as can be expected given the circumstances under which it was prepared. The DLNR is the first to admit, however, that the inventory contains inaccuracies. The inaccuracies are in the classification of land as ceded or non-ceded and as trust land or non-trust land and in the acreages of parcels.[39]

The report went on to detail the numerous problems, including survey and title search expenses, which would be involved in compiling a completely accurate and comprehensive inventory. The report recommended that such work be done only for those lands which generate considerable revenues or whose land title history is complex or obscure.[40] Finally, the report recommended that the ceded versus non-ceded lands distinction be abolished and that *all* public lands, including all lands which vested in the state as a result of section 5(a) of the Admission Act, should be held in the public trust.[41]

b. The 1978 Constitutional Amendments

Until 1978, little attention had been given to the trust language of section 5(f) of the Admission Act. At the 1978 Constitutional Convention, however, members of the Hawaiian Affairs Committee examined the Admission Act's trust language as it relates to Native Hawaiians.[42] As a result of these deliberations, new sections were added to the state constitution to implement the trust provisions.

The first new section stated that the lands granted to the state by section 5(b) of the Admission Act (with the exception of the Hawaiian Homes Commission Act's "available lands") were to be held by the state as a public trust for Native Hawaiians and the general public.[43] The second section established an Office of Hawaiian Affairs (OHA), to be governed by a nine-member elected board of trustees, which would hold title to all real or personal property set aside or conveyed to it as a trust for Native Hawaiians and Hawaiians.[44] The final provision gave the powers of the board of trustees and made clear that OHA was to hold in trust the income and proceeds derived from a *pro rata* portion of the trust established for lands granted to the state by section 5(b) of the Admission Act.[45] An additional section defined the terms "Hawaiian" and "Native Hawaiian," but the Hawai'i Supreme Court subsequently determined that this section had not been validly ratified in the 1978 general election.[46]

A careful reading of the relevant committee reports,[47] as well as the OHA amendments, reveals that the Constitutional Convention structured OHA as the body which would receive and administer the share of the public land trust funds designated for the betterment of the conditions of Native Hawaiians under the Admission Act. Section 5(f) of the Admission Act tied the definition of Native Hawaiian to the Hawaiian Homes Commission Act. Benefits under the Hawaiian Homes Commission Act are limited to those with 50 percent or more Hawaiian blood. Thus, although the OHA amendment names two beneficiaries of the OHA trust -- Native Hawaiians (those with 50 percent or more Hawaiian blood) and Hawaiians (those with any quantum of Hawaiian blood) -- OHA is restricted to using its public land trust funds solely for the benefit of its Native Hawaiian beneficiaries. The constitution does not establish a source of funding for OHA's Hawaiian beneficiaries.

The Admission Act did not set a specific formula for allocation of the public land trust proceeds and income among the five trust purposes.[48] While the OHA constitutional provision stated that the proceeds and income from a *pro rata* share of the trust should be directed to OHA, the amendment did not define that *pro rata* share. That determination was left to the state legislature, who set OHA's *pro rata* share at 20 percent.[49]

c. *Defining the Trust* Res *and Income*

The 1978 constitutional amendments were meant to insure that the Admission Act's section 5(f) trust provision on Native Hawaiians would be implemented. Numerous questions immediately arose regarding what constitutes the trust *res,* or body of the trust, and what constitutes income. The answers to these questions have greatly impacted on the amount of income OHA is entitled to receive.[50] From June 16, 1980 to June 30, 1989, OHA received a total of $12,466,383.00 from the ceded lands trust, representing 20 percent of the revenue collected for those section 5(b) and 5(e) lands under the control of the DLNR.[51] There were, however, other lands that could have been included in the trust *res* and whose inclusion would have substantially increased revenues to OHA.[52]

(1) *The Trust* Res   Article XII, section 4, of the state constitution provides that the lands granted to the state by section 5(b) of the Admission Act shall be held by the state as a public trust for Native Hawaiians and the general public. Article XII, section 6, empowers OHA to manage and administer "all income and proceeds from that pro rata portion of the trust referred to in section 4 of this article." While this language is subject to interpretation,[53] OHA has received a *pro rata* share of the income and proceeds derived from lands held by the DLNR under section 5(b) of the Admission Act.

The Admission Act's section 5(f) trust covers not only the lands granted to the State of Hawai'i by section 5(b), but also lands conveyed to the state under section 5(e), together with the proceeds from the sale or other disposition of those lands and the income therefrom. Additionally, P.L. 88-233 provides that any lands, property, improvements, and proceeds conveyed to the state under its terms also shall be considered a part of the section 5(f) trust.[54] Consequently, while the state constitution makes no specific provision with regard to section 5(e) lands or P.L. 88-233 lands or the income and proceeds derived from them, since those lands are part of the ceded lands trust, the constitutional provisions could be interpreted to include them. Indeed, the legislature seems to have reached the same conclusion with regard to section 5(e) lands. Haw. Rev. Stat. chapter 10, the legislation implementing the constitutional amendments, includes section 5(e) lands along with section 5(b) lands as part of the public trust lands from which OHA derives its income.[55]

Until recently, however, the state's position was that OHA was entitled to 20 percent of the revenues from section 5(b) and 5(e) lands, but none of the revenues from P.L. 88-233 lands. The Legislative Auditor's Final Report supported OHA's entitlement, reasoning that P.L. 88-233 lands are subject to the section 5(f) trust and that P.L. 88-233 in effect amends section 5(e) of the Admission Act.[56] Since section 5(e) lands had been included in the trust *res*, it seemed reasonable that P.L. 88-233 lands should also be included.

While OHA had received modest revenues from the trust lands under the jurisdiction of the DLNR, it had not received any funds from other governmental agencies who use or administer trust lands. Many of the state's lands with the highest potential for development -- those adjoining harbors and airports, for example -- have been set aside to other agencies, principally the Department of Transportation (DOT), for nominal fees or for no money at all. The DOT in turn develops the land. Substantial revenues have been earned from concessions and other private uses of the lands. These revenues were not paid into the trust fund.

A 1983 attorney general's opinion[57] upheld this practice. It reasoned that Haw. Rev. Stat. section 10-3 defines the public land trust as "all proceeds and income from the sale, lease, or other disposition of lands" conveyed to the state under sections 5(b) and 5(e) of the Admission Act. The opinion concluded that transfers of public lands to governmental agencies for public use are neither sales, leases, nor dispositions of public lands. Consequently, OHA would not be entitled to a share of the revenues generated by such trust lands.

However, the definition contained in Haw. Rev. Stat. section 10-3 was narrower than that contained in section 5(f) of the Admission Act. Section 5(f) specifies not only the proceeds from the sale, lease or other disposition of the lands, but also the lands and *income* from the lands as part of the public land trust. As the Legislative Auditor's Final Report points out, it is doubtful that the legislature intended to limit OHA's entitlement to funds generated by sales, leases or other dispositions since the constitutional amendments provide for OHA sharing in the trust, including the *income* generated by trust lands, established in the Admission Act.[58]

The Legislative Auditor also has suggested that lands acquired by the state under section 5(a) of the Admission Act be included in the trust *res*. For the most part, these lands were ceded lands which were turned over to the territory prior to statehood. While not specifically mentioned in the trust established by section 5(f) of the Admission Act, adding section 5(a) lands would be consistent with the notion that all public lands have been held in trust from annexation to the present time. Moreover, as the Legislative Auditor's Final Report notes, the inclusion of section 5(a) lands would also ease the administration of the trust and mitigate the need for an accurate inventory to distinguish between trust lands and non-trust lands.[59]

These issues surrounding the trust *res* have been one aspect of a larger problem. Additional and more complex questions have been raised as to what should be considered "income" subject to OHA's 20 percent entitlement.

(2)   *Trust Income*   Trust lands are used in a variety of ways. Some are sold, some are leased, some trust lands house governmental offices from which little or no income is derived. On other trust lands, however, government and private businesses may generate substantial revenues. It has been clear that OHA is entitled to share in the proceeds from the sale or lease of trust lands. It is equally obvious that where trust lands house government offices, no income is derived.

However, difficult problems have arisen when trust lands are used to operate government enterprises, such as harbors and airports, which do generate income; or when private businesses operate public facilities on trust lands; or when government allows privately operated concessions within government office buildings or public facilities. Until recently, the state's position had been that the revenues derived from these activities do not constitute "income" subject to OHA's *pro rata* share.

Moreover, neither the Admission Act nor the relevant statutes state whether "income" means gross or net income. The Legislative Auditor's Final Report points out some of the difficulties in defining "income" as gross income and advocates a net income approach:

> The usual meaning given to the word "income" is net income, not gross income, in the absence of something showing a contrary intent. Defining "income" as gross income could adversely affect important governmental programs.
>
> Except where expressly established for the purpose of raising revenues for the State or county, a public enterprise is generally intended to be no more than self supporting. The revenues of the enterprise are expected to do no more than defray the cost of its operation and maintenance and the cost of making improvements to the facilities of the enterprise. Government strives to set fees at a level sufficient to enable the enterprise to break even. However, the fees set are often insufficient to cover costs, and many public enterprises are subsidized from the general fund of the State or the county. If the 20 per cent provision of chapter 10 is applied to the gross income of these enterprises, the fees will need to be raised or additional subsidies will need to be made.[60]

Consequently defining "income" as net income could be appropriate. It would result in shielding income derived from those government programs or operations which are not intended to raise revenue, but are more in the nature of government services. However, if a public enterprise or program is established in order to raise revenues, the net income should be subject to OHA's 20 percent share.

The gross versus net income issue has been of particular importance in the case of the state's harbors and airports. As noted earlier, an attorney general's opinion determined that transfers to the DOT are not "dispositions" and consequently not subject to OHA's 20 percent entitlement. However, another rationale for the opinion rests on the fact that the airports and harbors are constructed by floating revenue bonds and the revenues from airports and harbors are used to secure these bonds.[61] The bonds themselves prescribe the order in which payments are to be made out of airport and harbor revenues. Usually principal and interest are paid first, with cost for operations, maintenance and repair of the airport properties second. Under this system, all revenues go into the operation and maintenance of the airport and harbor system so, it has been argued, no net income is realized. The Legislative Auditor's Report points out another problem in that the bonds require some excess of revenues over costs. The report states:

> The application of the gross income approach to airport and harbor revenues raises a constitutional issue concerning the impairment of obligation of contracts. Indeed, even the net income approach, as that term is traditionally defined, raises the same constitutional issue. The airport and harbor systems can and do raise revenues in excess of the cost of construction, operation, maintenance and repair; but none of that excess can be reached by chapter 10 without raising the impairment of contract issue, unless and until all of the requirements of the bond covenants are met. It is possible, under the certificates, for the State to raise revenues in excess of the requirements specified in the certificates. To the extent that there is such an excess, and the excess is attributable to lands subject to chapter 10, OHA probably may legitimately claim a share of it. However, the stated policy of the State is to operate the airport and harbor systems on a self-sustaining basis by producing only that amount of revenues which are required to pay all expenses of the systems, including bond requirements.[62]

Finally, another difficult issue arises when a public facility is located on both trust and non-trust lands. How are revenues generated from a facility located on trust and non-trust land to be categorized? Honolulu International Airport illustrates the problem. Most revenues at the airport are generated from concessions located on non-trust lands.[63] Yet, were it not for the use of trust lands as landing strips, no concessions could exist and no revenues would be generated. Several solutions have been suggested, including attributing to the trust only the revenues that are actually generated on trust lands or taking the total acreage of the facility and attributing revenues in the same proportion that trust lands bear to the total acreage.[64]

d. *Litigation to Define the Trust* Res *and Income*

All of these problems dealing with the identification of the trust *res* and income, have prevented OHA from realizing its full potential income in the past ten years. Initial efforts by the trustees to resolve these issues through the courts were frustrated.

The Hawai'i Supreme Court, in *Trustees of the Office of Hawaiian Affairs v. Yamasaki* (1987),[65] refused to determine two important questions on OHA's entitlements, basing its ruling on the doctrine of "political question." The court declined to rule on the issues stating that, after examining the facts, they found the issues "to be of a peculiarly political nature and therefore not meet for judicial determination."[66]

This case involved two separate suits filed by the trustees which were consolidated for appeal. The first suit sought a declaration that OHA was entitled to 20 percent of the damages received by the state in settlement of a lawsuit for the illegal mining of sand from Pāpōhaku Beach, ceded lands on Moloka'i. The second suit sought a declaration that OHA was entitled to 20 percent of the income and proceeds from sales, leases, or other disposition of lands surrounding harbors on all the major islands, of land on Sand Island, of land on which Honolulu International Airport is located, and of land on which the Aloha Tower complex stands. The court appeared to be influenced by the fact that the state had already made commitments for the revenues from the harbors and airports. The court stated:

> [The OHA Trustees] would have the circuit court apply HRS Sec. 10-13.5 literally and declare that OHA should receive twenty per cent of the revenues generated through the use of the

foregoing lands, which concededly are part of the trust res. A ruling to that effect, however, would be at odds with legislative commitments relative to such revenues.

The construction of the State's harbors and airports is primarily financed through the sale of bonds which carry the State's pledge that revenues obtained from their operation shall be employed to repay bondholders. These pledges are supported by legislation establishing special funds to meet the State's obligations . . . .

Were the circuit court to enjoin the Director of Transportation as prayed by the Trustees, he would be compelled to renege on the State's pledge. It would be unrealistic, to say the least, for us to conclude this could have been the intent of the legislature when the language of HRS Sec. 10-13.5 was adopted.[67]

Moreover, the court appeared to believe that even when OHA's share of the public lands trust fund was fixed at 20 percent by the state legislature, the trust *res* was undetermined. The court found evidence of this in the act authorizing the legislative auditor to complete the inventory of ceded lands and study the use and distribution of revenues from ceded lands. The court noted that all four committees to which the measure was referred found there were uncertainties with respect to ceded lands comprising the trust and the funds derived therefrom. The court also noted that the Legislative Auditor's Final Report of December 1986 stated that the uncertainties surrounding the trust and funds derived therefrom could not be resolved without further legislative action. Consequently, the court, following the lead of the Legislative Auditor's Report, concluded that the issues were ones better left for resolution by the legislature than the judiciary. In October 1987, the U.S. Supreme Court declined to review the decision of the Hawai'i Supreme Court.[68]

e. *Resolution of the OHA Entitlements Dispute*

Governor Waihe'e, in his State of the State Address in January 1988, made it clear that the state was committed to resolving the ceded lands revenue issues once and for all.[69] Since that time, OHA and members of the governor's staff have been meeting to attempt to resolve these issues without further resort to the courts. On February 8, 1990, the OHA Trustees and Governor Waihe'e announced a settlement of the ceded lands dispute.[70] Under the terms of the settlement, both the trust *res* and trust revenues have been defined.

The agreement provides that all section 5(b), 5(e), and P.L. 88-233 lands, with the exception of Hawaiian Home Lands, are subject to the trust, regardless of departmental jurisdiction.[71] This means that all lands in these categories, whether administered by the DLNR, DOT, or any other state department, are subject to the 20 percent income entitlement.

Under the agreement, revenues from the section 5(b), 5(e), and P.L. 88-233 lands are segregated into two categories -- sovereign and proprietary revenue.[72]

Sovereign revenue is the revenue which the state generates as an exercise of governmental or sovereign power. This revenue is not subject to the OHA trust provision. Among the revenues included in the sovereign category are personal and corporate income taxes, general excise taxes, fines collected for violations of state law, and federal grants or subsidies.[73]

Proprietary revenue is generated from the use or disposition of the public trust lands. Included in this category are rents, leases, and licenses for the use of trust lands, minerals, and runway landing fees. Proprietary revenue is subject to the OHA trust provision.

The settlement also sets forth the following guidelines with regard to determining the amounts due for previous years:

(1)   Section 5(b), 5(e), and P.L. 88-233 lands will be determined based on the current DLNR inventory of public lands and the final report of the Legislative Auditor;

(2)   The sovereign and proprietary revenue categories will be used to segregate income generated on trust lands and will be calculated from the effective date of the 20 percent formula -- June 16, 1980;[74]

(3)   The State Department of Budget and Finance will calculate and present actual year-by-year income figures to determine the full amount due;[75]

(4)   The state has agreed to pay the allowed statutory interest -- six percent through June 30, 1982 and ten percent for the years thereafter -- compounded annually, on the actual amounts due.[76]

After all the calculations have been made and the total amounts due for previous years are determined, the trustees and governor have agreed that OHA may take amounts due for previous years in the form of money, land, or a combination of money and land.[77] While the exact amounts are still being calculated, it is estimated that OHA will be entitled to an additional $7 to $8 million a year as a result of the settlement. Thus, the past due amount, with statutory interest, could be in the neighborhood of $100,000 million. In recognition of the immediate impact resulting from the settlement, the governor submitted a measure to the 1990 legislature containing a $7.2 million payment to OHA to meet the expected increase over current OHA trust income for the 1990-91 fiscal year.[78]

As the 1990 Hawai'i legislative session ended, the legislature and governor approved the negotiated settlement as Act 304. The trustees and administration have announced their intent to continue negotiations on the form of payment -- either as money or money and land. Moreover, the parties apparently have agreed that while many issues regarding entitlements for those of 50 percent or more Hawaiian blood have been resolved, the question of entitlements for all Hawaiians, regardless of blood quantum, will be negotiated in the coming year.[79]

f.   *State Trust Duties Under the Admission Act*

The OHA entitlement under the 1978 constitutional amendments and Haw. Rev. Stat. chapter 10 is only one aspect of the state's trust responsibilities in relation to the Government and Crown Lands. Indeed under the constitution and chapter 10, the Native Hawaiian entitlement is to a portion of the *revenues* and *proceeds* generated by the trust lands. The state, however, also has a duty in administering the trust lands to follow the requirements of section 5(f) of the Admission Act.

In the 30 years since statehood, the state's trust responsibilities under section 5(f) have never been closely scrutinized by the courts. Indeed, only recently have Native Hawaiians and others challenged the state's use and disposition of the trust lands. In *Ulaleo v. Paty*,[80] a case filed in 1988, an individual Native Hawaiian beneficiary and the Pele Defense Fund challenged an exchange of trust lands between state officials and a private party, Campbell Estate. The lands involved are located on the Big Island of Hawai'i in the Puna area. The state officials exchanged 27,785.891 acres of trust lands for about 25,807.055 acres of private lands to allow for geothermal development on the trust lands. The plaintiffs argued that the lands had been exchanged without any attempt to assess the impact on the trust purposes and that at least two of the trust purposes -- the betterment of the conditions of Native Hawaiians and public use of the lands -- were violated by the exchange. Moreover, the complaint contained allegations that the private lands received in the exchange were improperly valued because the state's appraiser had failed to consider recent lava flows covering the private lands. The plaintiffs further argued that because section 5(f) states that the trust lands shall be used consistent with the constitution and laws of the state, state laws protecting the lands must be read as part of the section 5(f) trust. In this particular instance, state law had set aside the trust lands in a natural area reserve to be preserved in perpetuity and the trust lands were used by *ahupua'a* tenants for traditional access, gathering, and religious practices.

The *Ulaleo* case was dismissed by the federal district court on the grounds that it was barred by the state's immunity under the Eleventh Amendment.[81] The suit, however, had been filed against *state officials* pursuant to 42 U.S.C. section 1983, which allows suits against state officials who, acting under color of state law, deprive an individual of rights guaranteed by federal law. The state had not been named as a party in the suit, but the district court believed that the only remedy available to plaintiffs would be to require the *state* to pay damages or repurchase the land. Since this would involve the use of state funds, the court characterized the suit as one against the state, and thus barred by the Eleventh Amendment.

In a startling opinion filed on May 4, 1990, the Ninth Circuit Court of Appeals affirmed.[82] The court held that the relief sought was retrospective in nature.

> [S]ometime in the past, the BLNR undertook an action, the land exchange, which allegedly injured the plaintiffs by violating the trust of which the plaintiffs are beneficiaries . . . . The immediate relief plaintiffs seek would require the state to purchase the land from its present holder by way of cash or other land. We hold that to grant the requested relief would be a retrospective remedy, as opposed to stopping an ongoing violation of federal law. If the trust duty was violated, it happened when the BLNR executed the exchange.[83]

Given this reasoning, however, it would have been impossible for the plaintiffs ever to have challenged the land exchange. Prior to the exchange, filing an action would have been premature since no trust breach had yet taken place. According to the court, after the exchange, no lawsuit could be filed since it would challenge a past action of the board, not an ongoing breach of trust. Since no action could be filed before the exchange and no action could be filed after the exchange, the court, in essence, has rendered the section 5(f) trust unenforceable in federal court in relation to land exchanges. This decision casts doubt on whether the federal courts will be willing, even given the best factual situation, to enforce the section 5(f) trust.

4.   CONCLUSION

The state has taken a major step in resolving the issue of entitlements owed to OHA under Hawai'i Revised Statutes chapter 10. Further negotiations promise even greater financial benefits to the Hawaiian community. Yet, it is clear that additional and much more difficult issues need to be addressed by the state, particularly relating to use and management of ceded lands. Many Native Hawaiian advocates maintain that the Admission Act requires that the ceded lands, the former Crown and Government lands, be managed consistent with the trust purposes set forth in the act. The state has only grudgingly acknowledged this aspect of its trust responsibilities. Moreover, the state has taken the position, at least in the *Ulaleo* case, that it need not dispose of lands consistent with the trust purposes as long as the funds generated by the disposition or the lands received in exchange are used for a trust purpose.

While the federal government retains title to proportionately less of the Government and Crown lands than does the state, many of the lands held, such as the island of Kahoʻolawe, have deep spiritual and cultural significance for Native Hawaiians. To date, the federal government has given very little recognition to Native Hawaiian claims to these lands.

Ultimately, Native Hawaiians seek return of Government and Crown Lands from both the state and federal governments. How such lands would be cared for and managed, who would have jurisdiction over them, and what rights Native Hawaiians could exercise upon them are crucial aspects of Native Hawaiian self-governance and sovereignty.

NOTES

1. J. Hobbs, *Hawaii: A Pageant of the Soil* 118 (1935). *But see* L. Thurston, *A Handbook of the Annexation of Hawaii* 24 (n.d.), in which the amount of land involved is set at 1,740,000 acres valued at $4,389,550 in 1894 and R. Horowitz, *Public Land Policy in Hawaii: An Historical Analysis* 15, 59-107 (*Legislative Reference Report* No. 5, 1969) [hereinafter *Historical Analysis*], in which the amount of land involved is estimated to be 1.8 million acres.

2. Joint Resolution of Annexation of July 7, 1898, 30 Stat. 750.

3. *Id.*

4. *Id.*

5. 22 Op. Att'y Gen. 574 (1899).

6. Act of April 30, 1900, ch. 339, 31 Stat. 141.

7. *Id.* at § 91.

8. *Id.* at § 73(4)(c).

9. For a list of executive orders setting aside public lands between annexation and 1955, see Chronological Notes of Federal Acts Affecting Hawaii, *Revised Laws of Hawaii, 1955,* 9-12.

10. *Historical Analysis, supra* note 1, at 68.

11. *Id.* at 74.

12. *Id.* at 68.

13. *Id.*

14. Act of July 9, 1921, Pub. L. No. 34, ch. 42, 42 Stat. 108.

15. *Id.* at §§ 203, 207, 208. *See also* Chap. 3, *infra*, for a discussion of the lands made available for Hawaiian homesteading.

16. *Id.* at § 201(a)(7).

17. *Admission Act of March 18, 1959,* Pub. L. No. 86-3, 73 Stat. 4 [hereinafter *Admission Act*].

18. *Id.* at § 5.

19. *Historical Analysis, supra* note 1, at 70-71.

20. *Id.* at 75.

21. *See id.* at 72.

22. Act of Dec. 23, 1963, Pub. L. No. 88-233, 77 Stat. 472 [hereinafter Pub. L. No. 88-233].

23. Public Land Inventory, DLNR (1988).

24. In September 1989, the Office of Hawaiian Affairs released a draft report entitled "Federal Land Holdings in Hawaiʻi" which attempts to list all federal land holdings by tax map key number, with the status of each parcel, how it was acquired, and current assessed valuation.

25. Presidential Executive Order No. 10346.

26. *Aluli v. Brown*, Civ. No. 76-0380 (D.Haw. 1976).

27. Presidential Executive Order No. 11166 and General Lease No. 3848.

28. *Admission Act, supra* note 17, at § 5(f).

29. *See Congressional Record*, May 21, 1920, at 7448, 7451-7453.

30. The DLNR is charged with managing all of Hawai'i's public lands. *See generally* Haw. Rev. Stat. § 171 (1985) and Haw. Rev. Stat. § 26-15 (1985).

31. Legislative Auditor, Audit Report No. 79-1 (January 1979) [hereinafter *Audit*].

32. Haw. Rev. Stat. § 171-18 (1985) provides:

    Public Land Trust. All funds derived from the sale or lease or other disposition of public lands shall be appropriated by the laws of the State; provided that all proceeds and income from the sale, lease, or other disposition of lands ceded to the United States by the Republic of Hawaii under the joint resolution of annexation, approved July 7, 1898 (30 Stat. 750), or acquired in exchange for lands so ceded, and returned to the State of Hawaii by virtue of section 5(b) of the Act of March 18, 1959 (73 Stat. 6), and all proceeds and income from the sale, lease or other disposition of lands retained by the United States under sections 5(c) and 5(d) of the Act and later conveyed to the State under section 5(e) shall be held as a public trust for the support of the public schools and other public educational institutions, for the betterment of the conditions of native Hawaiians as defined in the Hawaiian Homes Commission Act, 1920, as amended, for the development of farm and home ownership on as widespread a basis as possible, for the making of public improvements, and for the provision of lands for public use.

33. The current version of Haw. Rev. Stat. § 171-19(a) lists the purposes for which the land board may use the special land and development fund. These purposes have not changed substantially in the last 10 years.

34. *Audit, supra* note 31, at 32-33.

35. *Id.* at 35.

36. Note, *Hawaii's Ceded Lands*, 3 U. Haw. L. Rev. 101, 121, 141-142 (1981).

37. 1982 Haw. Sess. Laws 121.

38. Legislative Auditor, *Progress Report on the Public Land Trust*, Audit Report No. 83-13 (May 1983).

39. Legislative Auditor, *Final Report on the Public Land Trust*, Audit Report No. 86-17, 33 (December 1986) [hereinafter *Final Report*].

40. *Id.* at 34.

41. *Id.* at 131-132.

42. *See, e.g.*, Hawaiian Affairs Comm. Rep. No. 59, 1 *Proceedings of the Constitutional Convention of Hawai'i of 1978*, 643, and Comm. of the Whole Rep. No. 13, *id.* at 1017.

43. Haw. Const., art. XII, § 4:

    PUBLIC TRUST. The lands granted to the State of Hawaii by Section 5(b) of the Admission Act and pursuant to Article XVI, Section 7, of the State Constitution, excluding therefrom lands defined as "available lands" by Section 203 of the Hawaiian Homes Commission Act, 1920, as amended, shall be held by the State as a public trust for native Hawaiians and the general public. [Add Const Con 1978 and election Nov. 7, 1978]

44. *Id.* § 5:

    OFFICE OF HAWAIIAN AFFAIRS; ESTABLISHMENT OF BOARD OF TRUSTEES. There is hereby established an Office of Hawaiian Affairs. The Office of Hawaiian Affairs shall hold title to all the real and personal property now or hereafter set aside or conveyed to it which shall be held in trust for native Hawaiians and Hawaiians. There shall be a board of trustees for the Office of Hawaiian Affairs elected by qualified voters who are Hawaiians, as provided by law. The board members shall be Hawaiians. There shall be not less than nine members of the board of trustees; provided that each of the following Islands have one representative: Oahu, Kauai, Maui, Molokai and Hawaii. The board shall select a chairperson from its members. [Add Const Con 1978 and election Nov. 7, 1978]

45. *Id.* § 6:

    POWERS OF BOARD OF TRUSTEES. The board of trustees of the Office of Hawaiian Affairs shall exercise power as provided by law: to manage and administer the proceeds from the sale or other disposition of the lands, natural resources, minerals and income derived from whatever sources for native Hawaiians and Hawaiians, including all income and proceeds from that pro rata portion of the trust referred to in section 4 of this article for native Hawaiians; to formulate policy relating to affairs of native Hawaiians and Hawaiians; and to exercise control over real and personal property set aside by state, federal or private sources and transferred to the board for native Hawaiians and Hawaiians. The board shall have the power to exercise control over the Office of Hawaiian Affairs through its executive officer, the Administrator of the Office of Hawaiian Affairs, who shall be appointed by the board. [Add Const Con 1978 and election Nov. 7, 1978]

46. The definitional section in the proposed amendment defined Hawaiian as "any descendant of the races inhabiting the Hawaiian Islands, previous to 1778" and Native Hawaiian as "any descendant of not less than one-half of the blood of races inhabiting the Hawaiian Islands previous to 1778 as defined by the Hawaiian Homes Commission Act, 1920, as amended or may be amended." 1978 Constitutional Convention Proposal No. 13, R.D.2, S.1. *Kahalekai v. Doi*, 60 Haw. 324, 590 P.2d 543 (1979), held that this section was not validly ratified.

47. Hawaiian Affairs Comm. Rep. No. 59 and Comm. of the Whole Rep. No. 13, *supra*, note 42.

48. *Admission Act, supra* note 17, at § 5(f).

49. Act 273 of 1980, codified at Haw. Rev. Stat. § 10-13.5 (1985).

50. From June 16, 1980 through June 30, 1986, OHA had received a total of $8.3 million from the public land trust, representing 20 percent of the rentals collected by DLNR for those lands held by the state under §§ 5(b) and 5(e) of the Admission Act. *Final Report, supra* note 39, at 103.

51. Testimony of William Paty, Chairman, Board of Land & Natural Resources, August 8, 1989 in joint hearings before the U.S. Senate Select Committee on Indian Affairs and House Committee on Interior and Insular Affairs.

52. For instance, if § 5(a) lands and Pub. L. No. 88-233 lands at Sand Island had been included in the trust, revenues to OHA would have increased by over a million dollars a year. *Final Report, supra* note 39, at 109.

53. *See Audit, supra* note 31, at 130-131. The constitutional provision can be read to mean that OHA is entitled to all of the income of a *pro rata* portion of the trust *res* rather than a *pro rata* portion of all of the income from the trust *res*.

54. Pub. L. No. 88-233, *supra* note 22, at § 2.

55. Haw. Rev. Stat. § 10-3 (1985).

56. *Final Report, supra* note 39, at 106-109.

57. Opinion letter to the Director of the State Department of Transportation (Sept. 23, 1983) [hereinafter *Opinion Letter*].

58. *Final Report, supra* note 39, at 112-113.

59. *Id.* at 111.

60. *Id.* at 116.

61. *Opinion Letter, supra* note 57.

62. *Final Report, supra* note 39, at 123.

63. *Id.* at 124.

64. *Id.* at 126-127.

65. 69 Haw. 154, 737 P.2d 446 (1987).

66. *Id.* at 175, 737 P.2d 458 (1987) (quoting *Colegrove v. Green*, 328 U.S. 549, 552 (1946)).

67. *Id.*

68. 484 U.S. 898 (1987).

69. Governor John Waiheʻe, State of the State Address to the 1988 Hawaiʻi State Legislature (Jan. 25, 1988).

70. D.L. Ward and A.L. Moore, *OHA to get 20% Ceded Land Share*, 7 Ka Wai Ola O Oha, No. 3, at 1 (March 1990).

71. 1990 Haw. Sess. Laws, Act 304, § 3 defining public land trust.

72. *Id.*, defining revenue.

73. *Id.*

74. *Id.* at § 8.

75. *Id.*

76. *Id.*

77. *Id.* at § 9.

78. *Id.* at § 11.

79. H.R. Conf. Rep. No. 9, 15th Leg., 2nd Sess., at 3 (Haw. 1990).

80. *Ulaleo v. Paty*, No. 88-00320 (D. Haw. 1988).

81. *Id.*, Order Granting Motion to Dismiss, July 26, 1989.

82. *Ulaleo v. Paty*, No. 89-16130 (9th Cir., May 4, 1990).

83. *Id.* at 4378.

CHAPTER 3

THE HAWAIIAN HOMES COMMISSION ACT

1.   INTRODUCTION

On July 9, 1921, the Hawaiian Homes Commission Act of 1920 (HHCA) was signed into law.[1] The HHCA set aside between 188,000 and 203,000[2] of the 1.75 million acres of Government and Crown Lands, "ceded" by the Republic of Hawai'i upon annexation to the United States, for homesteading by Native Hawaiians. Under the act, Native Hawaiians could obtain 99-year leases at a dollar a year, for residential, pastoral, and agricultural lots. The HHCA also provided for services to assist the beneficiaries with the establishment of these homesteads. Congress, however, restricted eligibility for the program to Native Hawaiians of 50 percent or more Hawaiian blood.[3]

Pursuant to the HHCA, the United States assumed a trust obligation to benefit and rehabilitate Native Hawaiians.[4] Conspicuously, the HHCA did not contain a statement of purpose. However, congress apparently intended to provide homesteads and financial assistance in order to promote the rehabilitation of Native Hawaiians, whose numbers were seriously declining due to a combination of complex sociological, economic, medical, and political factors. Nevertheless, other interested parties, primarily the powerful sugar growers, successfully incorporated provisions in the HHCA to neutralize any potential impacts of the act on the valuable public lands then being leased to them by the territory. These provisions, cloaked under the guise of "rehabilitation" of Hawaiians, largely favored the continuation of public land leasing to sugar and ranching interests, at the expense of the Native Hawaiian.

These features of the program, and associated administrative problems and political obstacles, have plagued the act's implementation. Accordingly, the track record of HHCA administrators has been dismal. Only recently have administrators seriously examined the fundamental problems preventing Native Hawaiians from occupying the lands set aside for their benefit. In 1990, fewer than 3,800 families actually reside, farm, or ranch on only 17.5 percent of the lands originally set aside. In contrast, at least 62 percent of the land is used for non-homestead purposes, almost exclusively by non-beneficiaries, for an average annual yield of $26 per acre per year.[5] Over 19,000 Native Hawaiians are on the waiting list for homestead awards. Currently, there is renewed interest in restructuring the HHCA to increase federal involvement in developing resources for the program, monitoring or reducing state control, and enhancing direct accountability to beneficiaries.

2.   BACKGROUND

a.   *Prelude to the Passage of the HHCA*

By adopting the HHCA, congress appeared to be reacting, although indirectly, to the serious political repercussions of the westernization of Hawai'i and the loss of a communal land base by Hawaiians. Much of the political and economic fate of Hawaiians was sealed in the aftermath of the *Mahele* of 1848, which transformed Hawai'i's communal land tenure system into a *private* property system. In a few short years, this change resulted in a phenomenal concentration of land ownership in the large plantations, estates, and ranches that came to dominate Hawai'i's economic development.[6]

Government and Crown Lands also fell within the grasp of these powerful economic forces. For example, during the reign of King Kalākaua the government executed 39 long-term leases to sugar interests covering 26,653 acres of the best agricultural land on the four major islands. All of the leases were due to expire between 1917 and 1921.[7] Nearly half of the leased lands were Crown Lands, the lands once specifically reserved for the Hawaiian monarchy.[8]

A small group of economically and politically powerful Westerners formed a Committee of Safety to block the attempts of Queen Lili'uokalani to reassert greater political power by the monarchy. In 1893, the Committee of Safety, assisted by the landing of U.S. Marines, successfully overthrew the Hawaiian monarchy and imposed their own provisional government. The overthrow eventually cleared the way for the 1898 annexation of Hawai'i to the United States. These events consolidated and formalized Western control over the Government and Crown Lands.

b.   Condition of the Hawaiian People

Conversely, in this process, many Hawaiians found they no longer could farm or gain access to the traditional gathering areas in the mountains and the ocean that once supported them. Other Hawaiians were left landless. As a result, many were forced to move to urban areas to seek employment. They abandoned traditional subsistence living, which had supported the Hawaiian culture for centuries.[9] Many Hawaiians became members of the "floating population crowding into the congested tenement districts of the larger towns and cities of the Territory" under conditions which many believed would "inevitably result in the extermination of the race."[10]

Stripped of their resource base, Hawaiians faced a cultural crisis and the decimation of their population. In the century following Western contact, hundreds of thousands of Hawaiians died from a variety of infectious diseases introduced by the white man. Ailments seldom fatal to foreigners were deadly for Hawaiians who had acquired no immunity to these diseases.[11] Under conservative estimates, from 1778 to 1893, the Hawaiian population dropped by at least 87 percent, from approximately 300,000 to less than 40,000.[12] More recent theorists believe that this population decline has been grossly understated.[13]

The pure Hawaiian population had plummeted from an estimated 142,650 people in 1826 to about 22,500 people in 1919.[14] On the other hand, some evidence suggests that the *part*-Hawaiian population grew from 2,487 in 1872 to about 16,660 in 1919, due to the large number of mixed marriages at the time.[15] Nevertheless, the higher infant mortality and disease rates for Hawaiian families resulted in the disparate decline of the pure Hawaiian population, especially for those living in congested urban areas.[16] By 1921, devastated by poverty, disease, and political powerlessness, Hawaiians were clearly in danger of losing the battle to survive as a race.[17]

c.   The Dichotomy of Political Influences

Alarmed by the decimation of the Hawaiian population and the social conditions under which they lived, political leaders became interested in providing Hawaiians with greater opportunities for homesteading.[18] Several earlier attempts to provide Hawaiians with more land had failed.[19] For example, in 1895, the Republic of Hawai'i enacted a

44

general homesteading law, allowing 999-year homestead leases to those who could meet various occupancy, alienation, and descent restrictions. While Hawaiians obtained over half of these leases, many lost their leases because they could not meet the lease restrictions and others sold their interests to more wealthy non-Hawaiians for nominal sums.[20]

In the 1900 Hawai'i Organic Act, congress provided that the land laws of Hawai'i would continue to govern the use of the public lands ceded to the United States in 1898.[21] However, the Organic Act imposed two restrictions: (1) the term of any agricultural lease was limited to no longer than five years; and (2) no corporation, including a sugar plantation, could acquire and hold more than 1,000 acres of land, subject to vested rights.[22] These restrictions reflected the prevailing view that the plantation economy should give way to an economy more diversified among small farms.[23] In 1908, congress loosened the first restriction by extending the lease term to 15 years, but also provided that agricultural leases would be subject to withdrawal if needed for homesteading or public purposes.[24]

In 1910, congress amended the Hawai'i Organic Act to provide that any 25 persons, upon petition to the Commissioner of Public Lands, could obtain title to agricultural homesteads.[25] This provision, in combination with the withdrawal provision, opened the door for breaking the sugar planter's grip on the best agricultural lands leased from the territory. Critics had long cited this concentration of leases as the primary reason for the failure of earlier homesteading attempts. Without the availability of these prime lands, homesteaders had been denied the best chance of succeeding.[26]

General homesteading had its detractors as well. Some were critical of this "unbusinesslike" use of the best public lands.[27] Others decried the speculation that homesteading had attracted.[28] Finally, others were opposed to homesteading simply because it threatened use of the land for sugar cultivation and ranching.[29]

Proponents of Hawaiian rehabilitation through homesteading believed that a return to a land base and a traditional agrarian and fishing lifestyle was the only means of rehabilitating and arresting the death rate of Hawaiians.[30] However, some of the act's supporters had ulterior motives.[31] Since the reign of King Kalākaua, large sugar interests in Hawai'i enjoyed the use of 26,000 acres of prime agricultural lands, largely Crown Lands, then under lease from the territory.[32] None of these leases contained a withdrawal clause, which would allow for cancellation if the lands were needed for other public purpose.[33] Even without the withdrawal clauses, these lands would become available for general homesteading once the leases expired. In all, government leases to some 200,000 acres of public land were due to expire between 1917 and 1921. Most of the leases apparently allowed for rents favorable to lessees and covered large acreages of pasture land.[34] The 1910 Organic Act amendments threatened to end leasing to sugar and ranching interests and put these public lands into homesteading.

The HHCA was used as a vehicle to continue the sugar and ranching leases. In 1920, the 10th Territorial Legislature sent a legislative commission to Washington, D.C. to lobby for approval of various resolutions. One of these resolutions, House Concurrent Resolution No. 28 (HCR 28), requested that congress amend the Hawai'i Organic Act to empower the governor to exempt one-fifth of the highly cultivated lands under general lease from any homesteading laws and to continue those leases.[35] This resolution was conditioned on making "adequate provision . . . to accomplish the purpose set forth in Senate Concurrent Resolution No. 2."[36] Senate Concurrent Resolution No. 2 (SCR 2) requested congress to amend the Hawai'i Organic Act to provide:

> [F]rom time to time there may be set aside suitable portions of the public lands of the Territory of Hawaii by allotments to or for associations, settlements or individuals of Hawaiian blood in whole or in part, the fee simple title of such lands to remain in the government, but the use thereof to be available under such restrictions as to improvement, size of lots, occupation and otherwise as may be provided for said purposes by a Commission duly authorized or otherwise giving preference rights in such homestead leases for the purposes hereof as may be deemed just and suitable by the Congress assembled . . . .[37]

The legislative commission was composed of Senator John H. Wise, a proponent of Hawaiian rehabilitation and homesteading, and three other commissioners who favored amendments to the Hawaiʻi Organic Act that would allow the leasing of public lands to sugar interests.[38] This division in opinion was reflected in the commission's presentation to the House Committee on Territories.[39]

Senator Wise made an impassioned plea for a rehabilitation program for Hawaiians as outlined in the territory's SCR 2. Other members, including then-Governor Charles McCarthy,[40] attempted to steer the discussion to Organic Act amendments proposed in the territory's HCR 28, which called for allowing one-fifth of the highly cultivated lands to be re-leased to the highest bidder.

Concerned about the demise of the Hawaiian race, the committee reacted more favorably to Senator Wise's proposal. However, it was also fueled by the "rabidly anti-Japanese" sentiment of its chairman, Representative Charles F. Curry of California.[41] He feared that the Japanese in Hawaiʻi would out-compete Hawaiians for the limited amount of land available for homesteading and outvote them at the ballot box.[42]

Ultimately, Representative Curry urged the commission to submit one bill harmonizing the two pieces of legislation. The result was House Resolution 12683 (HR 12683), a measure drafted for Prince Jonah Kūhio Kalanianaʻole, Hawaiʻi's delegate to congress, by Territorial Attorney General Harry Irwin.[43] Unlike the limited amendments suggested in the territory's HCR 28, this draft exceeded even the hopes of the sugar planters and general homestead opponents by making major changes to the 1910 Organic Act amendments.[44]

Specifically, the Kūhio bill allowed public auction leasing of *all*, rather than one-fifth, of the "highly cultivated public lands." The measure repealed the provision requiring homesteading upon demand by 25 persons. Furthermore, the bill allowed such leases to be executed without any withdrawal clause.[45] Finally, the nature of the public auction process assured that the sugar planters would win any bid for these lands.[46]

When word of Prince Kūhio's proposed draft reached Hawaiʻi, it touched off a firestorm of protest.[47] It was alleged that the legislative commission had violated the will of the territorial legislature and had succumbed to a sugar planter "conspiracy . . . to prevent homesteading" of the cultivated sugar lands.[48] Even Secretary of Interior Franklin Lane predicted:

> If the [Kūhio] bill is passed in its present form, it will virtually kill homesteading in Hawaii, for the land which will be left for homesteading is second class.[49]

Several editorial writers agreed. Most scoffed at the efforts to disguise the efforts to "kill homesteading" under the cloak of Hawaiian rehabilitation.[50]

Despite these protests, another resolution emerged, giving strength to the sugar interests' position. House Resolution 13500 (HR 13500) exempted "all cultivated sugar-cane lands" and any lands under an existing form of homestead contract from the "available lands" to be set aside for Hawaiian homesteading.[51] This provision insulated those prime sugar-cane lands previously covered by the Kalākaua leases from Hawaiian homesteading. Simultaneously, HR 13500 designated those lands with poor soils, remote locations, and low rainfall or little nearby irrigation water, for homesteading by Native Hawaiians.[52] HR 13500 also deleted a provision found in HR 12683 that would have allowed additional public lands to be added to the HHCA inventory when needed for homesteading.[53] Other provisions allowed homesteading to those with 1/32 or more Hawaiian blood and shortened the lease term from 999 years to 99 years.[54]

In 1920, congress deferred action on HR 13500. In the ensuing period territorial leaders heatedly debated the bill's merits.[55] During this debate, Representative William Jarrett, accurately diagnosing the thrust of the bill, pointedly challenged Governor McCarthy, the bill's advocate:

> They want to give the Hawaiians lands that a goat couldn't live on. This whole thing is a joke. The real purpose of this bill is to cut out homesteading. If you want to cut out homesteading, then pass the bill.[56]

In spite of these prophesies, Senator Wise, seeking to assure passage of a Hawaiian rehabilitation bill, negotiated a compromise with the sugar and ranching interests.[57] As a result, the 1921 territorial legislature passed Senate Concurrent Resolution No. 8 which recommended, among other things: (1) a change in the definition of "Native Hawaiian" from 1/32 to 1/2 Hawaiian blood; (2) a requirement that the program initially be experimental for five years on 37,900 acres on the islands of Hawai'i and Moloka'i;[58] and (3) the repeal of the requirement that no corporation could hold a real interest to more than 1,000 acres.[59]

In the next congress, the Hawaiian rehabilitation section of the HHCA was relegated to a minor role in an omnibus bill that ultimately gained congressional approval and restructured Hawai'i's land laws.[60] On July 9, 1921, the president signed the HHCA into law. The final bill was the product of compromises with ranching interests who had sought similar concessions a year earlier:[61]

> [W]hile HR 13500 favored the sugar interests, [this bill] favored both the sugar and ranching interests. Thus both large interests had been pacified. The bill had become law.[62]

The large corporations who controlled Hawai'i's economy were now free to control bidding at the public auction of leases to the 26,000 acres of highly cultivated public land, without the threat of withdrawal for homesteads and without the 1,000-acre limitation imposed in 1900. What these interests acting alone could not accomplish for ten years -- amending the Organic Act -- was now realized with the help of proponents of Hawaiian rehabilitation.

This dichotomy in the motivation for passing the act may explain why congress never specified the purpose of the HHCA.[63] Accordingly, courts have had to turn to the legislative history of the HHCA to identify its purpose. The congressional record appears to establish that the act's goal was "the rehabilitation of Native Hawaiians."[64] In passing the HHCA, congress sought to lay the foundation for a comprehensive program to resettle

Hawaiians on land that could be farmed and ranched, with adequate water and financial assistance to get them started.[65]

In reality, those fearing the loss of their leases successfully exploited Delegate Kūhio and Senator Wise by masking their agenda under the guise of rehabilitating the Hawaiian people. The major thrust of the HHCA was to amend the Hawai'i Organic Act land laws by repealing homesteading for the general public. This history largely explains why the Hawaiian Homes program was destined to disappoint both its proponents and Native Hawaiian beneficiaries.

3. TRUST RESPONSIBILITIES

Under the HHCA, the United States and, subsequently, the State of Hawai'i, assumed the duties of a trustee for the aboriginal people of Hawai'i.[66] The Hawai'i Supreme Court has analogized the trust duties the state acquired upon statehood with those owed by the federal government to other Native Americans.[67]

a. *Nature of the Trust Duty*

The power of the United States over Indian affairs derives from congress' special authority under the Indian Commerce Clause, which allows congress to "regulate commerce with . . . the Indian Tribes."[68] While this power is broad, it is something short of plenary since it is subject to certain procedural and constitutional limits. Accordingly, the acts of congress and executive officials are subject to judicial review under constitutional and administrative law principles.[69] Furthermore, in order for the exercise of the trust responsibility of the U.S. to be valid, the federal government must show that it acted in a way that "can be tied rationally to the fulfillment of Congress' unique obligations toward the Indians."[70]

The United States Supreme Court first analyzed the federal trust relationship with Native Americans in its historic decisions found in the "Marshall trilogy."[71] In sum, these decisions established that the United States dealt with Indian tribes as separate, distinct sovereign entities which did not surrender their independence and right to self-government by associating with a stronger government and "taking its protection."[72] Rather, the federal government, as a result of treaties and other agreements negotiated with the tribes, and as a trustee for the Indians, had a special role to oversee and protect many of the possessions of Indians from non-Indians.[73] Indian tribes are not foreign nations, but are distinct political entities akin to "domestic dependent nations" whose relation to the United States is like that "of a ward to his guardian."[74] Thus, as a trustee, the United States holds legal title to many Indian lands for the benefit of the tribes. Accordingly, Indian tribes cannot convey land without the federal government's consent, since the tribes only hold equitable title to the land.[75]

The Hawai'i Supreme Court also has evaluated the trust duties of the Hawaiian Homes Commission (HHC), the body charged with implementing the HHCA, using "the most exacting fiduciary standards."[76] This trust responsibility is of the highest order and is judged according to the same strict standards set for any trustee of a private trust.[77] In *Ahuna v. Department of Hawaiian Home Lands* (1982),[78] a homesteader challenged the HHC's refusal to award him the total acreage of an additional lot located next to the agricultural homestead which he farmed. Previously, a court had ordered the HHC to award him an additional lot located as close to his agricultural homestead as possible. The HHC, however, awarded him only 6.5 acres of the 10-acre lot located next to his agricultural homestead. The HHC believed that it was necessary to reserve the remainder of the land for a future street extension planned by the county for general public use.

The Hawai'i Supreme Court held that the HHC impermissibly withheld trust land from the beneficiary because of its concern for the interests of the general public. This concern was a breach of its trust duty to act solely in the interest of the beneficiary.[79] Furthermore, the court found that setting aside 3.5 acres of trust land in unproductive use under these circumstances was also a breach of trust duty.[80] Consequently, the court condemned the HHC's breach of trust duty, and found that the trust duty included: (1) the obligation to administer the trust solely in the interest of the beneficiary, and (2) the use of reasonable skill and care to make trust property productive.

In another decision, *Keaukaha-Panaewa Community Association v. Hawaiian Homes Commission* (1976),[81] the U.S. District Court determined that the HHC's prior policy of failing to consummate land exchanges was a breach of trust. The commission had failed to assure timely receipt of full value for trust lands it had previously transferred to the County of Hawai'i for a flood control project. During the delay, the HHC deprived beneficiaries of any income or return from the property conveyed. The court held that a reasonable trustee would not act in the same way in dealing with the trustee's own property.

b. *Partial Transfer of Trust to State*

For 38 years, the United States government served as the sole trustee of Hawaiian Home Lands for the benefit of Native Hawaiians. At the time of Hawai'i's admission into the Union in 1959, the U.S. transferred this primary obligation to the State of Hawai'i as a condition of statehood,[82] under a compact that the state accepted and incorporated into its constitution.[83]

During this same period, the United States sought to terminate its trust relationship with Indian tribes in an effort to assimilate Indian people into mainstream America, even at the cost of denying them their sovereign rights.[84] For example, in 1953 congress enacted Public Law No. 280, which extended state jurisdiction over Indian country for the first time in several areas.[85] The Hawai'i Admission Act was consistent with this policy, transferring administration of the HHCA to the state.

Under the provisions of sections 4 and 5 of the Admission Act, however, the federal government retained oversight responsibility for certain aspects of the administration of the HHCA. This oversight responsibility requires, for example, that the U.S. Secretary of Interior approve any land exchanges involving Hawaiian Home Lands.[86] Congress also retains the power to alter, amend, or repeal the provisions of the HHCA.[87] Similarly, the United States must approve any amendments to the act, enacted by the state legislature, which may alter the qualifications or diminish the benefits of the program to its beneficiaries.[88]

4. PROGRAM FEATURES

a. *Administrative Framework*

The state has delegated primary administrative responsibility for the program to the Department of Hawaiian Home Lands (DHHL), headed by the Hawaiian Homes

Commission.[89] Eight members, representing each island upon which trust lands are located, sit on the Hawaiian Homes Commission.[90] The governor appoints the eight commission members and a ninth member to serve as chair. The chair is also the director of the department and a member of the governor's cabinet. The commission "is the specific state entity obliged to implement the fiduciary duty under the HHCA on behalf of eligible Native Hawaiians."[91] However, the law does not provide for any direct accountability to beneficiaries. None of the commissioners are elected. The governor need not even consult with beneficiaries in selecting commission members. Thus, there is no mechanism for self-determination in the implementation of the HHCA.

The DHHL performs the day-to-day functions of the program. Currently, it has 98 positions authorized by the legislature. Most of these positions are located in Honolulu. The DHHL also maintains district managers with limited staffing on each island with homestead land.

b. *Homesteading Program*

The HHC may award homestead leases for residential, agricultural, pastoral, and aquacultural lots to individual beneficiaries for 99 years for $1.00 per year.[92] Under section 209, lessees may designate one of the specified relatives listed in the section as a successor to the leasehold upon the lessee's death. The lessee may change the designation at any time. If the lessee fails to designate a successor, the DHHL may offer the leasehold to a qualified spouse or one of the children. To be a qualified successor, a spouse or child of the decedent must be at least one-quarter Hawaiian. Otherwise, the eligible relative must be at least one-half Hawaiian.[93]

To preserve trust assets, the HHCA does not allow homesteaders to alienate their land.[94] It also prohibits a lessee from subletting the interest in the leasehold.[95] Accordingly, title to the land may not be encumbered absent commission consent.[96] Nevertheless, after an initial seven-year grace period, the lessee is liable for all taxes assessed on the parcel.[97]

The DHHL is authorized to assist lessees in all phases of farming, ranching, and aquacultural operations, including marketing and other kinds of economic development. Section 219 of the HHCA permits the DHHL to employ agricultural and aquacultural experts to instruct and advise the lessees on the best methods of diversified farming, stock raising, and aquacultural operations. Section 219.1 authorizes the DHHL to assist lessees in fully utilizing their lease awards, and under sections 214 and 215, the DHHL may make loans to lessees to support these activities. Finally, the HHCA authorizes the DHHL to develop water projects and, to a limited degree, tap "government-owned water" to support activities on Hawaiian Home Lands.[98]

c. *General Leases*

In addition, under section 204 of the HHCA, the DHHL may lease land not needed for homestead awards to the public, including Native Hawaiians, by issuing general leases.[99] These leases are subject to the same terms, conditions, restrictions, and uses applicable to the disposition of public lands.[100] Until 1988, the revenue generated from general leasing was the only source of income available to the department for administrative operations, even though every other state department received appropriations from the state's general revenues for administrative expenses.

5. **PRINCIPAL PROBLEM AREAS**

a. *Past Administrative Abuses*

Throughout most of the 69-year history of the program, the administration of the HHCA received little or no scrutiny. Questionable administrative practices, combined with an inadequate land base, poor financial support, and insufficient water resources made many of the apparent goals of the program impractical and unattainable. Many trust lands are located in mountainous areas where the slope, precipitation, and topography make homesteading untenable. In addition, even where topography is not a problem, soil conditions or lack of water and transmission lines are typically major obstacles to farm or ranch development. Finally, past commissioners have allowed the trust to be depleted by illegal transfers of land and use of trust land for little or no compensation by other public agencies.

With neither sufficient natural resources to sustain agricultural or pastoral activities on these lands, nor the financial or political commitment by the federal and state governments to aggressively place Native Hawaiians on homesteads, the program predictably languished. Consequently, relatively few Native Hawaiians have been placed on the land. Most of those awarded leases obtained residential leases only, despite congress' initial focus on farming and ranching when the program was created. As of June 30, 1988, the HHC had awarded a total of 5,803 homestead leases, 2,059 of which were completely unimproved "raw land" awards.[101] These 5,803 Native Hawaiians held leases to 32,713 acres, or 17.5 percent of the lands set aside for the program.[102] Curiously, a year later, Native Hawaiians continued to hold leases for the same amount of land, under only 5,778 homestead leases -- 25 leases *fewer* than the year before.[103] Of the 5,778 leases, 4,592, or 79 percent of the total, were residential leaseholds (2,366 or 41 percent on Oʻahu alone). In contrast, the HHC has awarded only 1,093 agricultural and 93 pastoral leases.[104] (*See* Table 1.)

The 2,059 beneficiaries who received unimproved "raw land" awards during an acceleration program between 1984-1987, must wait in frustration for funds to develop on- and off-site infrastructural improvements before they can farm, ranch, or reside upon homestead lands.[105] Thus, in the 69 years of the program, the HHC has awarded only about 3,800 leaseholds on which beneficiaries are actually settled.

The heavily residential character of the present homestead program is either a reflection of the current needs and economic situation of Hawaiians or an indictment of the utter failure to place Hawaiians back on the land so they may "make a good living"[106] or to provide "for their self-sufficiency and initiative."[107] Nevertheless, demand for homesteads remains high. As of June 30, 1989, there were 11,289 on the residential homestead waiting lists, 6,615 on the agricultural waiting list, and 862 on the pastoral waiting list, for a total of 18,766 applications.[108] (*See* Table 1.) Many on these waiting lists, especially for agricultural and pastoral lots, have waited up to 40 years or more. Some have died waiting.[109] After the 1984-87 award acceleration program, the DHHL began receiving homesteading applications at a rate of 300 per month, a rate which has dropped to about 200 per month.[110]

Currently, over 19,000 Native Hawaiians are on the waiting list for homestead leases throughout the state.[111] In the meantime, non-beneficiaries utilize trust land for a variety of commercial, industrial, and public uses, as shown in Table 2 below.

TABLE 1

Comparison of Lease Award Distribution with Waiting List Distribution
(As of June 30, 1989)

	Leases Awarded*		On Waiting List	
Residential	4,592	(79.5%)	11,289	(60.2%)
Agricultural	1,093	(18.9%)	6,615	(35.2%)
Pastoral	93	(1.6%)	862	(4.6%)
Total	5,778	(100.0%)	18,766	(100.0%)

*Includes raw land awards (lessees have yet to occupy 2,059 lots previously awarded).

TABLE 2

Dispositions of DHHL Land to Non-Beneficiaries as of June 30, 1989[112]

Conveyance	No.	Acres	Annual Revenues ($/Per Acre)	
General leases	114	73,465	$2,563,673	($34.90)
DLNR leases	4	16,365	78,446	(4.79)
Licenses	180	9,902	178,984	(18.07)
Revocable permits	46	8,697	122,798	(14.12)
Right of entry	10	6,348	43,106	(6.79)
Executive orders	4	1,410	0	(00.00)
		116,187	$2,987,007	($25.71)

The 116,187 acres of documented use primarily by non-beneficiaries is more than three and a half times the total acreage being used by beneficiaries and comprises 62 percent of the entire Hawaiian Home Lands inventory. Three ranchers, including Richard Smart, lease a total of 40,257 acres in Humuʻula and Piʻihonua, more land than all the beneficiaries combined.[113] The $3 million in revenue generated by general leases averages out to less than $26 per acre per year. Finally, another 38,513 acres of Hawaiian Home Lands appear to be vacant or lack formal conveyances.[114]

b. *Restoration of the Trust Corpus*

(1) *Illegal Conveyances of Trust Land* Section 206 of the HHCA explicitly states that the governor does not have the power to dispose of trust lands by executive order or proclamation. Nevertheless, over the 69-year history of the program, Hawaiʻi's governors illegally transferred over 30,000 acres of Hawaiian Home Lands to other agencies and departments under executive orders and proclamations.[115] Public agencies have used these lands for parks, airports, military reserves, schools, and forest reserves with no compensation to DHHL. None of these transfers were authorized by the HHCA.[116]

For example, under one executive order, the former Board of Agriculture and Forestry acquired the use of 11,124 acres in Humuʻula for a game reserve and hunting ground at no cost.[117] In 1930 and 1933, the governor issued two executive orders illegally transferring 1,356 acres of valuable land at Lualualei to the U.S. Navy for military use.[118] Finally, the Department of Health currently utilizes 1,247 acres at Kalaupapa on Molokaʻi for no compensation without *any* formal conveyance at all.[119] This last uncompensated and undocumented use apparently continues to this day. Recently, the HHC agreed to lease the area to the U.S. National Parks Service as part of a plan to convert the entire Kalaupapa peninsula into a national park.[120]

In 1978, the U.S. District Court for Hawai'i declared in *Aki v. Beamer*[121] that the use of a gubernatorial executive order to create a county park in Anahola, Kaua'i was illegal.[122] Similarly, in 1980, a state court declared void the executive order allowing the State Department of Transportation to use homestead lands for the Hilo airport.[123] The HHC subsequently resolved the litigation by issuing a general lease to the Department of Transportation for the lands. One paragraph in the lease waived the DHHL's claims for back rent for a one-time payment of $482,000. Similar leases were issued for lands used for the Waimea and Moloka'i airports with similar back rent claim waivers. On November 30, 1984, the HHC agreed to exchange 204 acres of trust land used for airport purposes for 13.8 acres of industrial land at Shafter Flats.[124] DHHL will apparently also collect payments for back rent totalling $3.7 million over six years.[125] However, the DHHL has not resolved what compensation it will seek for the past free use of other lands by public agencies.[126]

In December 1984, Governor Ariyoshi finally withdrew or cancelled 27 executive orders and proclamations, returning 27,835.6 acres of land to the control of the DHHL.[127] After the cancellation of the executive orders and proclamations, the DHHL issued two-year licenses to the same agencies who once managed and utilized the Hawaiian Home Lands for use by the general public. This two-year period was to give the DHHL time to plan for the management of these lands upon their ultimate return to department use and to resolve any compensation issue.[128] Subsequently, some of these lands have been exchanged, but the HHC has issued a variety of conveyances generally allowing other lands to continue being used as they had been under the rescinded orders and proclamations.

(2) *Land Exchanges* Section 204 of the HHCA allows the HHC to exchange Hawaiian Home Lands for public or private lands of equal value, if the purpose of the exchange is to consolidate the holdings of the DHHL or to better effectuate the purposes of the act. The U.S. Secretary of Interior must approve all land exchanges.

In the past, the HHC allowed trust lands to be altered or taken for public uses before the territory or state agreed on the amount and location of the exchange parcels. For instance, in *Keaukaha-Panaewa Community Association v. Hawaiian Homes Commission* (1978),[129] homesteaders challenged the decision of the HHC allowing the County of Hawai'i to acquire and use 24 acres of trust lands to complete a county flood control project pending a land exchange to be worked out later. When the action was challenged, the HHC then issued a license to the county for $1.00 a year. The U.S. District Court found that the HHC violated section 204(4) of the HHCA by: (1) failing to make the required factual findings to support its decision; (2) allowing the county to use and alter trust lands before obtaining legal title to lands of equal value in exchange; and (3) depriving Native Hawaiian beneficiaries of the protection inherent in the legal requirement to obtain approval for the exchange *before* allowing use and alteration of trust lands by the county.[130] The commission finally consummated the exchange in 1987.[131]

Another example stems from a 1972 agreement by the HHC allowing the Department of Land and Natural Resources (DLNR) the use of 17.188 acres of land in Waimea to construct the Waikoloa II reservoir, pending an exchange with DLNR for equally valued land.[132] The HHC never consummated the land exchange. It allowed free use of the trust land for 15 years, in spite of a 1983 request from DLNR to complete the transaction.[133] Then, in 1987, the HHC issued a 50-year license to the Hawai'i County Water Commission to allow use of the 17.188-acre site for nominal compensation.[134] In short, the HHC ratified its 1972 decision, without completing the contemplated land exchange, in spite of the *Keaukaha* decision eight years earlier.

(3) *Inadequate Compensation* Other trust lands remain in the hands of general lessees without obvious benefit to the trust and for nominal or inadequate compensation. Prior to 1965, the DHHL exercised no authority over general leases to non-beneficiaries. The DLNR managed trust lands deemed "not immediately needed" by DHHL for homesteading. In 1965, the legislature amended the HHCA to transfer general leasing authority from DLNR to DHHL.[135] While DHHL is now empowered to assume direct responsibility for managing its own properties, it has allowed DLNR to retain control over four general leases, for no obvious reason. Two of these properties are leased to the military for 65 years, at $1.00 for the term, ending in 2029.[136]

c. *Resource Limitations*

In 1978, in recognition of the severe lack of funds for programs and administration of the HHCA, the Hawai'i State Constitution was amended to include Article XII, section 1, which provides, in part:

> The legislature *shall* make sufficient sums available for the following purposes: (1) *development of home, agriculture, farm and ranch lots;* (2) home, agriculture, aquaculture, farm and ranch loans; (3) rehabilitation projects to include, but not limited to, educational, economic, political, social and cultural processes by which the general welfare and conditions of native Hawaiians are thereby improved; (4) *the administration and operating budget of the department of Hawaiian home lands;* in furtherance of (1), (2), (3) and (4) herein, by appropriating the same in the manner provided by law. (Emphasis added.)

The purpose of the amendment was to provide the DHHL with monies for administrative and program costs, thereby eliminating the need to general-lease lands for revenues for department operating costs, and allowing the DHHL to focus on leasing to beneficiaries.[137] The legislature and governor ignored the 1978 amendment for nine years.[138] During this period, the DHHL continued its reliance on the revenue generated from general leases and interest to fund its administrative and program costs. This reliance perpetuated the DHHL practice of allowing the majority of trust lands to be used by non-Native Hawaiians for private uses.[139] The funds received were necessarily diverted from programs to pay administrative costs, prolonging the harm that the 1978 constitutional amendment sought to remedy.[140]

In 1987, the state legislature finally appropriated state general revenues to fund one-half of the department's administrative staffing budget. That appropriation of $1.2 million covered funding for only 49 of 98 staff positions in the DHHL, and only for the second half of the fiscal biennium, *i.e.*, fiscal year 1988-89.[141] The 1989 legislature provided the DHHL with $3.8 million per year in general revenue funding for its administrative budget covering the 1989-91 biennium.[142] While this amount is a significant increase over the prior biennium, it still constitutes *less than 0.2 percent* of the total state general fund budget, which is about $3.2 billion each year for the 1989-91 biennium.[143]

Simultaneously, the state enjoyed a $480 million cash surplus as of June 30, 1989. The 1989 legislature committed much of the surplus to other state projects for the funding biennium 1989-91, allocating less than $4 million (0.83 percent of the surplus) in cash to the DHHL for its capital improvements projects (CIP). In addition, the 1989 legislature authorized another $46.8 million in *revenue* bond funds for other DHHL capital improvements projects for the 1989-91 biennium.[144] This authorization of approximately $50.7 million initially appears to be a major increase over the $22.7 million in *general obligation* bonds authorized for the prior biennium (1987-89).[145] Indeed, the CIP funds authorized for the period January 1, 1987 to June 30, 1992 represent more financing to the DHHL than it has expended over the previous 12 years of the program.[146] Also, for the first time, the U.S. Congress in 1989 appropriated $1.2 million to DHHL in additional funds for infrastructural improvements.[147]

Despite this increased attention to the program, the DHHL has estimated that it would require $1 billion to meet infrastructural costs needed to support homesteads for the 8,000 eligible beneficiaries on the waiting list in 1984.[148] In 1989, that list had mushroomed to over 19,000.[149] As of June 27, 1989, the DHHL's next *ten-year* CIP program called for expending only $200 million, a sum it did not anticipate coming from the legislature.[150] By June 30, 1990, the DHHL plans to encumber the 1987 CIP funds ($22.7 million) to improve 265 lots, construct on 369 lots, and design another 865 lots out of the 2,500 total lots already awarded during the 1984-87 raw land acceleration program.[151]

Furthermore, most of the 1989 legislature's authorization of an additional $50 million cash and bond funding to support the DHHL over the 1989-91 fiscal biennium will be devoted primarily to installing infrastructure for only 881 of the raw land lots already awarded under the 1984-87 acceleration program. The DHHL projects that some of the CIP money will go to making improvements to 306 new homestead lots so lessees can occupy them.[152] However, none of these CIP funds include the required mortgage assistance funds needed for the next ten years -- $140 million -- to finance home construction.[153]

An even more troubling development is the fact that the 1989 legislature simultaneously authorized DHHL to issue *revenue* bonds to raise 92 percent of its $50.7 million CIP budget for 1989-91.[154] Since the state had already reached its general obligation debt ceiling, the governor apparently could not issue additional general obligation bonds to cover this authorized CIP amount.[155] While authorizing DHHL to issue revenue bonds would appear to give DHHL additional flexibility to raise the sum authorized,[156] it will also make the department more dependent on its general leasing revenues.

The DHHL's current income stream will enable it to issue only $13-25.9 million in revenue bonds, depending on the term of the bond issue, credit rating and other security features.[157] This amount falls short of the DHHL's current projected short-term capital costs of $43 million.[158] Furthermore, without greater revenue sources, the DHHL cannot meet its recently revised $1 billion, ten-year capital improvements goal to settle beneficiaries on the waiting lists statewide in affordable housing. This inability to fund infrastructure projects will pressure the DHHL to use more of its lands to generate income in the absence of significantly enhanced fiscal support from the state and/or federal governments.[159] Thus, unless substantial government support is devoted to the DHHL's ambitious ten-year infrastructural improvement goal, the DHHL may be forced to resort to more general leasing of trust lands to non-beneficiaries.

This practice places the DHHL right back in the conflict of having to raise money through general leasing to non-beneficiaries to pay its debts, utilizing the same limited land base from which it must also lease homesteads to Native Hawaiians. It also diverts precious resources of the DHHL from directly serving beneficiaries to managing property for the benefit of non-beneficiaries. The DHHL is currently seeking to shift revenue bond appropriations to general funds or general obligation bonds.[160]

Furthermore, because of these limitations, the DHHL is attempting to restrict the size of future *pastoral* homestead lots to five to 20 acres each without any definite timetable for making larger pastoral lots available. These smaller lots were sized to support only two animal units (one unit equals one cow and one calf). In response to this policy, the Aged Hawaiians[161] sued to stop the DHHL from implementing this policy without assisting those applicants seeking to become economically self-sufficient as ranchers.[162] Members of the Aged Hawaiians have been on the pastoral lot waiting list for Waimea since 1952.

On October 4, 1989, Judge Shunichi Kimura of the Hawai'i Third Circuit Court preliminarily enjoined the DHHL from proceeding with its plan until it properly promulgated rules, pursuant to Haw. Rev. Stat. section 91-3.[163] This statute requires any state agency to give notice and hold a public hearing before adopting any rules affecting the rights of the public it serves. As a result, the DHHL is now offering 16, out of 204, pastoral lots ranging in size from 100 to 200 acres. However, even these larger lots will not be able to successfully support commercial ranching.

Judge Kimura must now decide whether the HHCA requires the DHHL to offer those, like the Aged Hawaiians, pastoral lots large enough to give pastoral homesteaders an opportunity to develop the land "for their highest and best use commensurate with the purposes for which the land is being leased" and thereby become economically self-sufficient.[164]

The DHHL is playing a catch-up game which it is soundly losing. In an apparent reaction to recent congressional hearings, Governor John Waihe'e is pressing DHHL to meet the housing demand of its beneficiaries -- 20,000 homes by the year 2000.[165] DHHL responded by setting housing objectives to build or develop 10,792 master-planned residential units plus 3,400 homestead lots. It will need $990 million in increments until the year 2002.[166] Apparently, DHHL will fall short of the identified needs of its beneficiaries even with this housing initiative. In addition, in spite of the commitments of new financial resources, DHHL has not even filled its personnel vacancies while it is undergoing a multi-year reorganization plan. This practice has left DHHL with a greater than 30 percent vacancy rate in its authorized personnel count.[167]

d. *Water Rights and the Lack of Water Resources*

One of the most critical failures of the homesteading program has been the inability to secure adequate water resources to support ranching, farming and, more recently, aquacultural activities. Because of the locations of homestead areas, and the lack of financial resources to overcome the obstacles, potential beneficiaries of the HHCA have often been frustrated by the lack of adequate irrigation water to support homesteading. Furthermore, lack of administrative coordination among state agencies has left homesteaders without water resources which otherwise could have been made available to them. Finally, legal uncertainties limit the ability of homesteaders to obtain water resources ostensibly reserved for them.

(1)   *Legal Rights to Water*   In *Winters v. U.S.* (1908),[168] the U.S. Supreme Court recognized an implied reservation of water to support farming on tribal lands set aside for an Indian reservation. The court held that these water rights were superior to the rights of other users who had settled on their lands *after* the reservation was created. The water rights of the Indians were not subordinate to those of the settlers, even if the white settlers began their uses *before* the Indians had established any use.

A similar analysis applies to the HHCA. In enacting the HHCA, congress intended to rehabilitate Native Hawaiians by placing them back on the land as farmers and ranchers.[169] When the federal government set aside lands in Hawai'i for farms and ranches, it also must have intended to assure that adequate water would be reserved for homesteaders to make the lands productive.[170]

Until recently, however, section 221(c) of the HHCA explicitly empowered the DHHL to use government-owned water, with certain exceptions, free of charge only "[i]n order adequately to supply livestock, aquaculture operations, or the domestic needs" of homesteaders.[171]

The DHHL is authorized, under section 221(d) to also use government-owned *surplus* water tributary to the Waimea river upon the island of Kaua'i, not covered by a water license or covered by a water license issued after July 9, 1921, for the additional purposes of providing irrigation to homesteads on Kaua'i.[172]

Thus, in contrast to other water needs, any demand for *irrigation* water, at least on Kaua'i, may be limited to "surplus water" tributary to the Waimea River.[173] The HHCA also authorizes DHHL to make use of any water transmission facilities needed to transport water to homestead lands.[174]

In recognition of the shortcomings of section 221 of the HHCA, the 1990 Hawai'i State Legislature passed, and the governor approved, Act 24, adding "agricultural operations" to the list of purposes for which "government-owned water" may be used by the DHHL. It is unclear how the DLNR, the state agency issuing water licenses, will implement this provision in issuing future water licenses. However, the State Attorney General has testified that this provision will give the DHHL "first call" on the government water being licensed.[175]

The DHHL has largely failed or been unable to exercise its rights under section 221 because of financial and physical limits to developing the infrastructure to transport the necessary water supplies the long distances to generally remote locations of trust lands. Secondly, DHHL's failure to successfully obtain water for its beneficiaries is partially due to its failure to aggressively assert its dominion over trust assets. Too often, the need for water to serve homesteaders has been subordinated to water use by more economically powerful forces.

(2)   *Moloka'i -- Physical and Financial Limits*   The most prominent example of the department's exercise of water rights involves the Moloka'i irrigation system (MIS) which supplies irrigation water to a homestead area on Moloka'i, and the Moloka'i water system, which provides domestic water. The MIS currently serves fewer than 50 homesteaders in Ho'olehua, Moloka'i. In the 1920s, the HHC also installed a parallel and separate *domestic* water system to serve Ho'olehua. Over the past eight years, the HHC has spent $9 million to replace, enhance, and restore that 40- to 50-year-old system.[176]

These systems are limited to homesteads that were established long ago. During the 1984-87 raw land award acceleration program,[177] the HHC awarded an additional 392 agricultural and residential lots in Hoʻolehua and Kamiloloa without any infrastructure. Without resources to pay for water meters or feeder water lines to connect homesteaders to trunk lines, no one has settled on these lease awards. The DHHL has no funds to improve these lots in the near future.[178] Nevertheless, additional irrigation water is available in the MIS for homestead development. In fact, under Hawaiʻi statutes, homesteaders are entitled to a two-thirds preference to water in the MIS.[179] Nevertheless, the system remains vastly under-utilized for homestead use because the homesteaders are unable to afford expensive agricultural water meters, and there are no feeder water lines to connect individual homesteaders to the main trunklines of the MIS.[180]

The MIS is also the source of irrigation water for other non-beneficiary farmers in Hoʻolehua and, because of an unauthorized "temporary" emergency diversion to the county domestic water system, residents in Kaunakakai. It also serves as the pipeline through which water is transmitted for a portion of the distance between a private Hoʻolehua well site and the west end resort at Kaluakoʻi, under a 1975 lease agreement between the DLNR and the resort developer. Under the lease, Kaluakoʻi is entitled to remove up to two million gallons per day (mgd) from the western end of the MIS, in exchange for pumping an equivalent amount plus ten percent, up to 2.2 mgd, into the system from its well located near the eastern end of the MIS.[181]

This latter arrangement has been the source of numerous conflicts between farmers and resort developers over the availability of water in the system. In *Ah Ho v. Cobb* (1980),[182] the Hawaiian homestead farmers in Hoʻolehua unsuccessfully raised numerous procedural objections to the issuance of the state water lease with Kaluakoʻi. In *Molokai Homesteaders Cooperative Association v. Morton* (1973),[183] the U.S. District Court and the Ninth Circuit Court of Appeals upheld the lease arrangement as an allowable lease for *space* within the MIS and not a prohibited *sale* of the irrigation water in that system.[184]

(3)   *Kekaha Water System -- Legal/Administrative Problems*   Over the course of several years, commencing in 1955, the HHC permitted beneficiaries to attempt ranching on five 90-acre ranch lots in an area known as Puʻuʻōpae, Kekaha, Kauaʻi.[185] These lands have been classified as Class C lands of marginal soil with low productivity unless irrigated. Without irrigation, the carrying capacity of the Puʻuʻōpae area is five to ten acres per animal unit year. With irrigation the land could be elevated to Class A and have a carrying capacity of less than 2.5 acres per animal unit year. To assist the homesteaders, the HHC built a 10,000-gallon water tank for the beneficiaries to store water from the Kōkeʻe ditch.[186] However, this source has proven inadequate and none of the lessees have ever received adequate water to support self-sufficient ranching operations in the area.

In fact, despite the perennial problem with water resources, in 1969, the DLNR granted Kekaha Sugar Company a general lease covering: (1) 14,558 acres of Hawaiian Home Lands and another 13,000 acres of public land, and (2) the right to store, take and use all surface water flowing from the Waimea river and its irrigation ditch systems and ground waters from existing wells and shafts. This general lease, which runs from January 1, 1969 to December 31, 1993, provided no explicit irrigation water reservation for Hawaiian homesteaders in the area.[187] Thus, Kekaha Sugar has utilized the trust lands and a state water license without regard for the irrigation water needs of the homesteaders in the Kekaha area.

Due to the repeated problems in obtaining water, four of the five homesteaders eventually abandoned their leases.[188] The remaining lessee and another beneficiary assumed the acreage surrendered by the other lessees and have attempted to continue their ranching operations with whatever water is available.

Unable to obtain sufficient irrigation water over the years, the Puʻuʻōpae homesteaders sought to obtain more water from the Kōkeʻe ditch by resorting to self-help.[189] In two instances, Kekaha Sugar successfully got court injunctions to stop the homesteaders' attempts to increase their water from the ditch.[190] After 35 years, the two Kekaha homesteaders still do not receive adequate water to support self-sufficient ranching operations, and cannot do so without greater administrative coordination between DLNR and DHHL and funds for infrastructure. Furthermore, the HHC has awarded no new homestead leases for the Kekaha area.

Kekaha Sugar refuses to supply any irrigation water to the beneficiaries, because it maintains that there is no "surplus water" available from the Waimea river under its water license. Kekaha claims it has superior rights to this water, particularly during the drier summer months. This interpretation is based on section 221(d) of the HHCA which authorizes the DHHL to utilize "surplus water tributary to the Waimea river" and section 221(a)(1), which defines "surplus water" as:

> so much of any government-owned water covered by a water license or so much of any privately owned water as is *in excess of the quantity required for the use of the licensee* or owner, respectively. (Emphasis added.)

Hence, the HHCA appears to allow priority water use by a water licensee of the state over any water needs of an HHC beneficiary. This interpretation would mean that the state is free to issue a water license without any regard for the irrigation water needs of its trust beneficiaries. However, the state agreed to "faithfully" carry out the *"spirit"* of the HHCA as an explicit condition of statehood.[191] As an agent of the state, DLNR should not turn a blind eye to the beneficiaries of this trust under the guise of enforcing a water license to a third party.

Furthermore, under section 212 of the HHCA, the DHHL has the statutory power to withdraw its trust lands from the lease arrangement with Kekaha Sugar, at any time upon notice "that the lands are required." The DHHL has refused to give notice to withdraw the lands from the general lease, even though almost 900 Native Hawaiians wait for pastoral homestead awards.[192] This lease, while generating revenues for the DHHL,[193] also creates the demand for the same irrigation water the homesteaders need. In other words, the DHHL's failure to assert its rights over its trust lands directly contributes to the water problems of its beneficiaries.[194]

(4) *Puʻukapu, Waimea -- Failure to Adequately Reserve Water* In Puʻukapu, on the island of Hawaiʻi, DHHL has allowed various state, county, and private entities to develop water storage and transmission facilities on Hawaiian Homes trust land for nominal consideration, even though most of the water consumption is for the general public. For example, the DHHL has issued nine licenses to the Hawaiʻi County Department of Water Supply, the DLNR, and Parker Ranch for the construction of water storage facilities and water transmission lines across Hawaiian Home Lands for generally nominal rent. In all, the nine DHHL licenses to these entities encumber over 72 acres of trust land. The DHHL has received no firm commitment from these entities insuring adequate irrigation water for current and future agricultural homesteaders on the Big Island.

In 1987, the DHHL issued a 50-year license allowing the Hawaiʻi County Department of Water Supply to continue operating the Puʻu Nani domestic water storage tank, the Waikoloa II reservoir, and the Puʻukapu booster pumping station on trust land to serve both Hawaiian homesteaders and the general public in the Waimea area.[195] In exchange for the license, the DHHL belatedly secured 108 "water commitments" to supply domestic water from the Waimea-Puʻukapu Domestic Water System to beneficiaries previously awarded unimproved farm and residential lots in 1984-86. These 108 "water commitments" would supposedly allow the DHHL to secure county approval for DHHL subdivision plans previously delayed by the lack of water supply to support the subdivisions.[196] While the DHHL has apparently gotten these commitments from the county, no formal binding agreement has been signed.

In this 1987 arrangement, the DHHL obtained partial commitments for water; commitments that it should have gotten *before* it allowed the land to be used for a reservoir in 1972. The public benefitted from the continued operation of the Waimea-Puʻukapu Domestic Water System. However, the DHHL allowed depletion of trust assets without compensation. It also apparently ignored back rent claims -- past compensation for the illegal uses of trust land. Furthermore, the 108 "commitments" fall short of the total number of planned homesteads for the Waimea area.

The State Department of Agriculture (DOA) currently manages the Waimea Irrigation System, which the DLNR administered until 1988, when the State Water Code required it to transfer this function to DOA.[197] This system currently utilizes Hawaiian Home Lands for a 60-million-gallon reservoir in upper Puʻukapu II and another overflow reservoir at Puʻu Pūlehu, for nominal compensation. The system supplies irrigation water to 28 private leasehold farmers in the Lālāmilo Farm Lots on public lands leased by the state,[198] and to 16 Hawaiian homesteaders with agricultural lots.[199] In the meantime, 75 Native Hawaiians who received agricultural lots in Waimea during the 1984-87 raw land award acceleration program continue to wait for irrigation water to make their lots usable.[200]

In addition, the 28 Lālāmilo farmers and 16 Hawaiian homesteaders currently on the Waimea Irrigation Water System pay ten cents per 1,000 gallons for irrigation water. Those Hawaiian homesteaders with agricultural leaseholds who cannot tie into the water system because of DOA restrictions and/or their inability to afford expensive water meters and feeder lines to their lots,[201] must pay $1.00 per 1,000 gallons for use of domestic water to irrigate their crops. Several homesteaders have abandoned farming because of the higher cost of water and the periodic droughts in Waimea. Those who have persisted have been forced to haul water to their homesteads by truck to irrigate their crops.[202]

Furthermore, fewer than 60 Native Hawaiians hold leases to *pastoral* Hawaiian homesteads in Waimea, while more than twice that number are on the waiting list for Waimea.[203] None of these homesteaders receive irrigation water. They also must rely on stockwater from the Waimea-Puʻukapu Domestic Water System operated by the Hawaiʻi County Department of Water Supply, which charges their customers $1.00 per 1,000 gallons. If irrigation water was made available to homesteaders, the DHHL could at least triple the number of pastoral homestead lots it might otherwise award unirrigated.[204]

Hawaiian homesteaders do not understand why their trust assets are being used for nominal compensation simply because they derive some benefit from these water systems. Any private landowner would demand fair compensation, priority use, or concessions in water charges for use of the system. The HHC appears to allow or condone the use of these lands by forgoing adequate compensation when Native Hawaiians obtain only *some* benefit from a water project.[205]

6.   PROSPECTS FOR IMPROVING THE PROGRAM

a.   *Judicial Relief*

In *Keaukaha-Panaewa Community Association v. Hawaiian Homes Commission* (1978),[206] the Ninth Circuit Court of Appeals held that Native Hawaiians did not have a right to bring a lawsuit directly under the Hawaiian Homes Commission Act to challenge decisions involving the HHCA's administration.

However, in a sequel to that case, *Keaukaha-Panaewa Community Association v. Hawaiian Homes Commission* (1984),[207] the same court ruled that an independent action could be brought under 42 U.S.C. section 1983, which allows suits against state officials who, acting under color of state law, deprive individuals of federal rights. The court inferred that sections 4 and 5(f) of the Hawai'i Admission Act conferred the requisite federal right that could be addressed and protected in a lawsuit filed in federal court.[208] This right of action is limited to seeking declaratory and injunctive relief (orders declaring that certain actions are illegal and enjoining improper actions by state and local officials). Such federal actions cannot include requests for damages or monetary relief (judgments that order payments directly from the state treasury) absent an explicit waiver of sovereign immunity.[209] Litigants can bring 42 U.S.C. section 1983 actions in either state or federal court.[210]

b.   *Waiver of Sovereign Immunity*

After several years of debate, the 1988 Hawai'i Legislature passed legislation authorizing a limited "right to sue."[211] The Native Hawaiian Trusts Judicial Relief Act provides a limited waiver of sovereign immunity, enabling Native Hawaiians to initiate litigation in state courts to rectify certain problems involving the Hawaiian Homes and ceded lands trusts accruing after July 1, 1988.

The act allows claimants to bring actions to challenge official decisions, to restore the trust lands and funds depleted by a breach of trust, and to seek only actual damages limited to out-of-pocket losses directly related to the claimed injury.[212] It specifically excludes relief for consequential "pain and suffering," or punitive damages.[213] It also imposes a two-year statute of limitations.[214]

On the other hand, it also grants an initial grace period of two years, until June 30, 1992, allowing claimants to seek relief for actions accruing after July 1, 1988.[215] It also provides for attorneys' fees if a claimant is successful.[216] The act explicitly preserves any legal rights afforded by other statutes.[217] Accordingly, actions under 42 USC section 1983 are not affected. Finally, it provides for a three-year period during which the governor may prepare and submit a plan to the legislature for addressing the claims which are not covered under the act's provisions.[218] If the governor fails to present the plan to the 1991 legislature or if one house of the legislature rejects his plan by a two-thirds vote, then claimants who suffered damages *prior* to July 1, 1988 may seek judicial relief in state court. However, the legislature also is free to withhold taking any action on the plan and to ignore any claims for damages arising prior to July 1, 1988.[219]

This legislation supplements the judicial remedies currently available through the *state* courts only and does not affect judicial relief available in federal courts -- particularly where federal agencies may have improperly used Hawaiian Home Lands. Congress would have to enact legislation to provide for a right of action in federal court directly under the HHCA and to waive the sovereign immunity of the U.S. from damage claims. However, congress has not given Native Hawaiians comparable or expanded rights in federal courts beyond that available under 42 U.S.C. section 1983.[220] Currently, only the United States has the *explicit* right to sue for breaches of trust under section 5(f) of the Hawai'i Admission Act. It has never done so.

c. *Federal-State Task Force on the HHCA*

Several fundamental problems plague the administration of the HHCA. First, DHHL does not have sufficient resources to operate its programs. Both the federal and state governments have failed to make an adequate financial commitment to funding the program, leaving many beneficiaries on waiting lists for 40 years.

Second, the location, topography, availability of irrigation water and quality of soils of the lands originally set aside for homesteading made homesteading very difficult and expensive. Little effort has been expended to upgrade these lands by acquisition or exchange.

Third, Native Hawaiians seeking homesteads have typically encountered an administrative bureaucracy with confusing policies, haphazard record-keeping, closed records, poor fiscal control, inadequate staffing, and a host of other management problems.[221] These problems have led to serious administrative and management problems that regularly frustrate beneficiaries.

Finally, various federal, state, and county agencies failed to fairly compensate DHHL for the illegal use of Hawaiian Home Lands. Through a variety of conveyances which were generally without legal authority, the county, state and federal governments made free use of trust lands intended for Native Hawaiians.[222] These exploitive practices deprived Native Hawaiians of income and proceeds for programs under the HHCA.

In recognition of these problems, on July 14, 1982, the Secretary of Interior and the Governor of the State of Hawai'i jointly convened a Federal-State Task Force on the Hawaiian Homes Commission Act to make recommendations for improving the program. In August 1983, that Task Force issued a comprehensive report describing the nature and scope of problems facing the HHC and making positive recommendations for actions to correct these problems.

The responsible entities have not implemented many of the Task Force recommendations. For example, the Task Force recommended the appointment of an advisory committee on funding sources. The governor never appointed such a committee and, without explanation, DHHL assumed that function internally.[223] In addition, the secretary has not studied all existing federal laws to determine how they may be used to fund an acceleration strategy. Furthermore, neither the federal nor state governments have provided the funding for the acceleration strategy that was to have been devised by the committee on funding sources.[224] The federal government appropriated only $1.2 million in 1989. During 1987-89 the state authorized $32.4 million in general obligation bonds[225] and another $46.7 million in *revenue* bonds.[226]

Most of the CIP funds appropriated by the 1987 and 1989 legislatures must be used to improve the 2,059 unimproved lots awarded between 1984-86. Very little will be left for infrastructural improvements for the 19,000 beneficiaries on the current waiting list.[227]

In light of these problems, in 1986 the DHHL terminated the acceleration program it had begun in 1984, still 1,500 lots short of its original goal of 4,000 awards.

d. *Recovery of Trust Land*

In 1986, the DHHL filed a federal quiet title lawsuit, *State of Hawaii v. United States*, seeking the return of, or compensation for, some 1,356 acres of land at Lualualei, Oʻahu from the U.S. Navy. Under the purported authority of two gubernatorial executive orders issued in 1930 and 1933, the Navy had been using the property as a radio transmitting facility and ammunition depot. On January 6, 1988, the U.S. District Court ruled that the DHHL had filed its suit too late, beyond the statute of limitations, and dismissed the action.[228] The Ninth Circuit Court of Appeals subsequently upheld that decision.[229] The Navy's use of the Lualualei acreage effectively deprives beneficiaries of the use of flat and arable land on the island where demand for residential homesteads is the greatest.[230] The Lualualei lands alone could satisfy much of the demand for homesteads on Oʻahu.[231]

The HHC also has continued its practice of leasing trust land to public agencies, without clear benefits to beneficiaries. In 1985, the HHC leased 4.3 acres to the Department of Transportation for a public boat ramp at Kaulana, Kamāʻoa-Pueo, Kaʻū for $10,575, or the construction of certain improvements designed to accelerate homesteading in the area. Several beneficiaries challenged the HHC's ability to lease the area to a public agency under section 204 of the HHCA. The Hawaiʻi Supreme Court in *Ahia v. Department of Transportation* (1988),[232] in a three-to-two opinion, approved this arrangement, agreeing with the HHC that the section allows such a disposition. The court did not address the issue of whether this use was a breach of DHHL's trust duties.

In addition, various older uses of trust lands by public agencies have continued substantially unabated. For example, the City and County of Honolulu had utilized Hawaiian Home Lands at Makapuʻu and Waimānalo Beach Parks with nominal compensation to the DHHL, under the authority of two gubernatorial executive orders issued in 1930 and 1950.[233] The city made improvements to the properties and opened the parks up for general public use. Although the executive orders were declared illegal and consequently rescinded, the DHHL does not have the resources to manage the park exclusively for Native Hawaiians. Citing benefits to Native Hawaiians who use these "desirable and accessible" parks, the HHC issued a five-year license at $1.00 for the term of the license to allow the city to continue managing these parks.[234] The rent also covered the previous two-year license term.[235] The DHHL, however, has never established criteria for situations in which it would be appropriate to charge nominal rents to public agencies allowed to use trust land.[236]

Similarly, contrary to a Task Force recommendation, the HHC has not revoked the 65-year general lease issued by DLNR for nominal consideration to the U.S. Army for the use of 295 acres at Pōhakuloa on the island of Hawaiʻi for a military training ground.[237] DHHL claims it does not have the resources to pursue a claim for the return of the lands at Pōhakuloa.[238] The HHC also allows DLNR to lease 25.7 acres of trust land at Kekaha, Kauaʻi to the U.S. Navy for a storage facility, charging $1.00 for the 65-year term.[239] In fact, contrary to a Task Force recommendation, the HHC has allowed the DLNR to continue management of that parcel with no benefit to the program.[240]

Finally, the Federal-State Task Force noted that the Territory of Hawaiʻi apparently illegally conveyed the fee title to 650 acres of trust land to private interests, despite HHCA restrictions against such alienation. Several of these owners subsequently obtained judgments quieting title to these properties.[241] DHHL staff is currently researching the title history of the lands to determine whether it can seek their return.

Many other general leases and uses of trust land by non-beneficiaries raise serious questions about the propriety of utilizing trust lands for income-generating purposes. The HHC clearly has authority to general-lease trust lands to non-beneficiaries, but *only where the lands are not needed for homesteading.*[242] The Federal-State Task Force report revealed that the lack of clear policies and guidelines for the issuance of general leases, licenses, revocable permits, and rights of entry to non-beneficiaries allowed non-beneficiaries the use of more land than that leased to beneficiaries.[243]

In the past, the DHHL may have justified some of these practices as necessary to generate revenues for administrative costs. However, since 1988-89, the legislature has fully funded the DHHL budget request. Nevertheless, the DHHL persists in general-leasing trust land now as it did previously. In fact, it is concentrating on *increasing* its general lease revenues on a smaller land base, apparently in an effort to enhance its income stream to support the issuance of revenue bonds.[244]

e.   *Federal Oversight*

For 26 years prior to 1986, the DHHL failed to get congressional approval for a host of legislative amendments the state legislature had made to the HHCA. In 1986, the DHHL, in response to a recommendation of the Federal-State Task Force, belatedly obtained congressional approval for these amendments.[245]

In the process of approving this consent measure, Public Law No. 99-557, then-President Reagan perhaps aptly reflected the traditional attitude of federal officials about the program by declaring:

> I am signing this joint resolution because I believe, as the Department of the Interior testified when the resolution was pending, that the matters with which the Hawaiian Homes Commission Act is concerned should be left entirely to the State of Hawaii. The administration of the public lands in question can be competently handled by the State government.[246]

Under section 5(f) of the Admission Act, the United States may bring suit if the state breaches its trust responsibilities to Native Hawaiians.[247] However, the United States has never exercised this duty, despite numerous opportunities to enforce the trust provisions on behalf of the beneficiaries. In fact, until recently, congress had never even conducted hearings on the implementation of the HHCA. President Reagan demonstrated his distaste for any further federal involvement in the administration of the program by questioning its legality on equal protection grounds, and urging congress to re-examine the HHCA because of its "troubling racial classification."[248]

Nevertheless, on August 7-11, 1989, Senator Daniel K. Inouye, Chairman of the Senate Select Committee on Indian Affairs, held extensive oversight hearings on the HHCA throughout Hawai'i. This effort was unprecedented. Throughout the hearings, Senator Inouye acknowledged the trust duty of the United States and explored ways to remedy the multitude of problems confronting the program.

As a result of these hearings, the 1990 State Legislature passed and the governor approved, a bill adding a statement of purpose to the HHCA. Act 369[249] establishes: (1) a policy of self-determination and greater self-sufficiency for beneficiaries; (2) the congressional intent to create a permanent homeland for Native Hawaiians under the

HHCA; and (3) the explicit trust duties of the federal and state governments for administering and supporting the program with funds for infrastructure and reservations for irrigation water. If passed by congress this statement of purpose will help guide future administration of the Hawaiian Home Lands.

When congress turned over the responsibility for the Hawaiian Home Lands trust in 1959, the federal government also was attempting to end its trust responsibilities with other Native Americans.[250] In the late 1960s, congress repudiated this "termination" policy, embarking on the present policy of native self-determination.[251] The current era has been characterized by expanded powers of tribal self-government and diminishment of state authority over Indian affairs. These policies have been accompanied by increased native initiatives over matters of self-determination, mineral resource management, education, and economic development.[252] The models of Indian tribal government and sovereignty, combined with federal programs for Indians, provide potential options for management of the Hawaiian Home Lands trust and greater self-determination by beneficiary groups.

Congress and the Native Hawaiian beneficiaries must explore a means to make the administration of the trust more accountable and responsive. This inquiry could and should include consideration of the establishment of a sovereign entity, controlled by Hawaiians and divorced from state government, to administer the trust.[253] Congress should determine what land better suited for homesteading, including the former Government and Crown Lands, as well as federal and other lands, could be added to the trust inventory. Finally, it must resolve what mix of federal and state funding support, as well as revenues from general-leasing trust land, would be appropriate to fully support the program.

7. CONCLUSION

By any measure, the performance of the United States and the State of Hawai'i in their roles as trustees for Native Hawaiians over the past 69 years has been dismal. The United States played a pivotal part in setting the tone for initial implementation of the Hawaiian Homes Commission Act, allowing, if not causing, the loss of thousands of acres of trust land. The federal government has done little in regard to the trust since 1959, sometimes claiming it has no continuing trust responsibility. When the State of Hawai'i assumed its duties, it continued many of the detrimental practices begun under the federal government's administration. Even today, the DHHL is understaffed, underfunded, and often unresponsive to beneficiary needs.

Consequently, 69 years after the passage of the HHCA, 3,800 Native Hawaiian families occupy only 17.5 percent of the trust lands on homesteads, while general lessees control 62 percent of the lands in the inventory. Over 19,000 Native Hawaiians are on the waiting list for homestead awards.

The Hawaiian Home Lands trust presents a clear opportunity for the federal government, the state, and Native Hawaiians to work toward increased self-determination and self-governance. The history of abuse and mismanagement of the trust leads to the conclusion that, consistent with the federal policy of native self-determination, trust lands should be administered and managed by Native Hawaiians themselves.

NOTES

1. 42 Stat. 108, *reprinted in* 1 Haw. Rev. Stat. 167-205 (1985, 1989 Supp.) [hereinafter "HHCA"].

2. The HHCA did not specify the boundaries of these lands, but identified them only by place names, with estimates of acreage. The lands were not accurately surveyed. The original HHCA purported to set aside 203,500 acres, more or less, as "available lands." Accounting for subsequent additions and withdrawals of lands by congress, and land exchanges, this figure should mathematically be 207,695 acres. However, modern inventories of Hawaiian Home Lands indicate that the true acreage is about 17,000 acres less.

    Various individuals have determined that the acreage should be 190,919 (1971 Study by Clegg and Bird), 189,878 (1972 Study by Akinaka), and 187,561.49 (1983 Study by Kaeo). Federal-State Task Force Report on the Hawaiian Homes Commission Act, Appendix 15 (August, 1983) [hereinafter *Federal-State Task Force Report*]. The Department of Hawaiian Home Lands (DHHL) is currently using a figure of 187,413 acres in its most recent annual report.

3. HHCA § 201(a)(7).

4. *Ahuna v. Department of Hawaiian Home Lands*, 64 Haw. 327, 336-338, 640 P.2d 1161, 1167-1168 (1982).

5. Department of Hawaiian Home Lands, 1989 Annual Report 16 (n.d.) [hereinafter *1989 DHHL Annual Report*]. This report indicates that about 20 percent of the land is either vacant, or has been conveyed without any written conveyance document (*i.e.*, leases, permits, licenses, rights-of-entry).

6. *See generally* Chapter 1.

7. M.M. Vause, *The Hawaiian Homes Commission Act, History and Analysis* 17, App. VII (June 1962) (unpublished master's thesis).

8. *Id.*

9. H.R. Rep. No. 839, 66th Cong., 2d Sess. 4 (1920).

10. S. Con. Res. 2, 10th Leg. of the Territory of Hawai'i, *1919 Senate Journal* 25-26.

11. H.R. Rep. No. 839, 66th Cong., 2d Sess. 5 (1920); *Hearings on Rehabilitation and Colonization of Hawaiians and Other Proposed Amendments to Organic Act of Hawaii and on Proposed Transfer of Buildings of Federal Leprosy Investigation Station of Kalawao on Island of Molokai to Hawaii, Before the House Comm. on Territories* [hereinafter *Hearings*], 66th Cong., 2d Sess. 121-122, 127-128 (1920) (Testimonies of Senator John Wise and Secretary of Interior Franklin Lane).

12. Native Hawaiians Study Commission, *Report on the Culture, Needs, and Concerns of Native Hawaiians (Majority)* 102-104 (1983). Senator Wise testified that Captain Cook estimated there were 400,000 Hawaiians in 1778. H.R. Rep. No. 839, 66th Cong., 2d Sess. 3 (1920).

13. *See generally* D. Stannard, *Before the Horror: The Population of Hawaii on the Eve of Western Contact* (1989).

14. H.R. Rep. No. 839, 66th Cong., 2d Sess. 2 (1920).

15. In a 1921 population study, Professor Alonzo Sullivan of the New York Museum of Natural History in fact concluded that while pure Hawaiians were declining in number, "the part Hawaiians were the most prolific group in the territory . . . ." *Id.* at 2-3.

16. Vause, *supra* note 7, at 3.

17. Vause, *supra* note 7, at 2 (citing *Hawaiian Almanac and Annual*, 1897 through 1922, inclusive (Honolulu, 1897-1921)).

18. It was evident that there was great demand for homesteads after annexation. For example, in anticipation of the 1920 opening of the planned 261 homesteads in Waiākea and Pāpa'aloa on Hawai'i island, over 2,905 people applied. S. Con. Res. 2, 10th Leg. of the Territory of Hawai'i, *1919 Senate Journal* 25-26. Ten months before the scheduled Waiākea drawing, nearly 2,500 applications had been received for only 243 lots. Vause, *supra* note 7, at 21-22.

19. R.S. Kuykendall and A.G. Day, *Hawaii: A History from Polynesian Kingdom to American Statehood* 203-209 (1948); H.R. Rep. No. 839, 66th Cong., 2d Sess. 5-6 (1920).

20. H.R. Rep. No. 839, 66th Cong., 2d Sess. 5-6 (1920).

21. An Act to Provide for a Government for the Territory of Hawaii, ch. 339, 31 Stat. 141 (1900) (amended in 1908, 1910 and 1921) [hereinafter *Organic Act*].

22. *Id.* §§ 55, 73.

23. Kuykendall and Day, *supra* note 19, at 206.

24. *Id.* at 206-207.

25. *Id.* at 207.

26. *Id.*

27. Vause, *supra* note 7, at 18 (citing *Hearings*, *supra* note 11, at 105).

28. *Id.* at 19.

29. *Id.* at 27.

30. A major proponent of the HHCA, Senator John H. Wise, testified:

The Hawaiian people are a farming people and fishermen, out of door people, and when they were frozen out of their lands and driven into the cities they had to live in the cheapest places, tenements. That is one of the reasons why the Hawaiian people are dying. Now, the only way to save them, I contend, is to take them back to the lands and give them the mode of living that their ancestors were accustomed to and in that way rehabilitate them.

H.R. Rep. No. 839, 66th Cong., 2d Sess. 4 (1920).

31. M.M. Vause, in introducing her study on the HHCA, stated:

This study questions a myth -- a myth that the Hawaiian Homes Commission Act of 1920 was made possible because of humanitarian motives. It suggests that this moral consideration was not the impelling motive for the enacting of the rehabilitation program, rather that the Hawaiian Homes Commission Act was thought important to the Hawai'i of the 1920s because it amended the basic land laws of the territory and assured stability of control over the public lands for at least 15 more years. The rehabilitation program was the political accident which enabled these laws to be amended.

Vause, *supra* note 7, at iii.

32. *Id.* at 115.

33. *Id.* at 17.

34. *Id.*

35. H. Con. Res. 28, 10th Leg. of the Territory of Hawai'i, *1920 Senate Journal* 1672-1673.

36. *Id.*

37. S. Con. Res. 10th Leg. of the Territory of Hawai'i, *1920 Senate Journal* 25-26.

38. Vause, *supra* note 7, at 33-36, 40. The other three members were Senator Robert Shingle, Representative William T. Rawlins, and Representative Norman Lyman. *Id.* at 35.

39. *Id.* at 40-41; *Hearings, supra* note 11, at 37.

40. Governor McCarthy at first sided with Senator Wise by opposing any amendments to the Organic Act. Later, he supported the re-leasing of the highly cultivated public lands. In 1920, it was announced that Governor McCarthy was going to assume the position as the Washington representative of the Chamber of Commerce, following his term as governor. The salary for this position was higher than that of Delegate Kūhio. Vause, *supra* note 7, at 69-70, 94.

41. *Id.* at 46-47.

42. *Id.* at 46-51. The legislative commission did little to dispel these racist notions. *Id.* at 49, n.38.

43. *Id.* at 54.

44. Section 5 of HR 12683 contained the critical language long sought by the sugar interests and other opponents to general homesteading, stating:

That for the purpose of raising the necessary revenues for the accomplishment of the purpose of this section the land commissioner with the approval of the governor and two-thirds of the land board, is hereby authorized and empowered to lease by sale at public auction the highly cultivated public lands of the Territory of Hawaii for a term not to exceed fifteen years, and any such lease sold under the provisions of this section shall not contain the withdrawal clause now provided for by law. *Id.* at 55.

The provision in effect nullified the power of 25 persons to compel homesteading, and restored administrative discretion to issue leases without withdrawal clauses at public auction. The most likely winners at such auctions would have to be the sugar growers, the only ones with enough capital to compete. Vause, *supra* note 7, at 55-56.

45. *Id.*

46. *Id.*

47. *Id.* at 56-64.

48. *Id.* at 57.

49. *Id.* at 59.

50. *Id.* at 63-64.

51. *See also* HHCA § 203.

52. *See* letter from A. Horner to U.S. Senator Miles Poindexter (November 18, 1920), *reprinted in* Vause, *supra* note 7, Appendix X.

53. Vause, *supra* note 7, at 72.

54. *Id.* Furthermore, following the Kūhio version, congress kept key amendments to the Hawai'i Organic Act in HR 13500. Those amendments included: (1) repeal of the clause requiring homesteading upon demand of 25 or more persons; (2) authorization to continue leasing the highly cultivated public lands at public auction for a term not in excess of 15 years; and (3) the elimination of any requirement to include a withdrawal clause in those leases. *Id.* at 74.

55. *Id.* at 87-89. Representative Lyman asked Governor McCarthy: "Why not put Hawaiians on the best lands and give them a fair trial?" The governor suggested that if that were done, Hawaiians would not

till the land but merely hire Japanese cultivators. *Id.* At one point, during the debate, Representative Lyman punched and injured Representative A.M. Christy. *Id.* at 90, n.56.

56. *Id.* at 89 (citing Honolulu Star Bulletin, April 23, 1921).

57. *Id.* at 86-87, 91.

58. *Id.* at 90 (*see also id.* at 172-173 (Appendix VI)), *1921 Senate Journal* 672-685.

59. *Id.* at 91. The Hawai'i Organic Act, § 55 had provided:

> No corporation, domestic or foreign, shall acquire and hold real estate in Hawaii in excess of one thousand acres; and all real estate acquired or held by such corporation or association contrary hereto shall be forfeited and escheat to the United States, but existing vested rights in real estate shall not be impaired. (Footnote omitted.)

In her thesis, M. Vause describes the background for the amendment:

> In order to avoid this law separate corporations had been formed under full knowledge of the territorial and federal officials in Hawaii. In 1921 it was reported that U.S. District Attorney Robert D. Breckons, aware of this circumvention of the law, was filing suit against the corporations. It was agreed in Washington between the attorney for the sugar planters and the interested federal agencies that the suit would be dropped if Congress would repeal the law. The amendment was consequently drafted "for the purpose of complying with the law." At the U.S. House hearings in 1921 interest was centered on this proposal. The sugar interests were able to argue a convincing case and the proposal passed. (Footnotes omitted.)

Vause, *supra* note 7, at 96.

60. *Id.* at 84. Ultimately, this section was relegated to only one part of an omnibus bill that fundamentally restructured Hawai'i's land laws. As Kūhio stated:

> After all, the rehabilitation provisions of the bill are not of such tremendous importance. It is, in a way, unfortunate that this feature has been allowed to overshadow other extremely important provisions of the bill. There is, for instance, the provision for prohibiting the employment of alien labor on federal construction work. That is most important in my mind, but has not received due consideration. . . . *Id.* at 84, n.36 (citing Honolulu Star Bulletin, April 5, 1921).
>
> . . .
>
> The rehabilitation portion is only one of many important features. The increase in salary of the judges and federal officials, the residence qualifications of office holders, and most of all, the employment of citizen labor only on all federal work in the Territory are just as important to the Territory and in fact more important than the rehabilitation feature. . . . *Id.* (citing letter from J. Kūhio Kalaniana'ole to Will Carden, February 21, 1921).

S. 1881, 67th Cong., 1st Sess. (1921).

61. In particular, the five-year experimental period allowed the ranchers time to renegotiate new general leases for public land not initially included in the Moloka'i experiment. Many of these leases of grazing land were issued at very favorable lease rents for tens of thousands of acres of public land. Thereafter, these ranchers could count on withdrawal clauses which first required approval by the Secretary of Interior before additional homestead lands could be made available to beneficiaries. Vause, *supra* note 7, at 91-92.

62. *Id.* at 92.

63. In light of this omission and at the urging of U.S. Senator Daniel K. Inouye, the 1990 Hawai'i Legislature passed and Governor John Waihe'e signed a bill to add a purpose section in the HHCA. Act 369, 15th Leg., 2d Sess. (1990).

64. Senator John H. Wise, an author of the HHCA and a member of the Legislative Commission of the Territory of Hawai'i declared:

> The idea in trying to get the lands back to some of the Hawaiians is to rehabilitate them. I believe that we should get them on lands and let them own their own homes. I believe it would be easy to rehabilitate them. The people of New Zealand are increasing today because they have the lands to live on and are working out their own salvation.

H.R. Rep. No. 839, 66th Cong., 2d Sess. 4 (1920); *Hearings, supra* note 11, at 38-39.

65. The Committee on the Territories described in part the general policy underlying the bill for the enactment of the HHCA in these words:

> Your committee is . . . of the opinion that (1) the Hawaiian must be placed upon the land in order to insure his rehabilitation; (2) alienation of such land must, not only in the immediate future but also for many years to come, be made [im]possible [sic]; (3) accessible water in adequate amounts must be provided for all tracts; (4) the Hawaiian must be financially aided until his farming operations are well underway. In framing such a program your committee is in a general way following the broad outlines of Senator Wise's plan.

H.R. Rep. No. 839, 66th Cong., 2d Sess. 7 (1920).

66.   Ex-Secretary of the Interior Franklin K. Lane testified before the House Committee on the Territories:

> One thing that impressed me . . . was the fact that the natives of the islands who are our wards, . . . and *for whom in a sense we are trustees,* are falling off rapidly in numbers and many of them are in poverty.

    H.R. Rep. No. 839, 66th Cong., 2d Sess. 4 (1920) (emphasis added). The term "ward" connotes a notion of trusteeship. *Ahuna v. Dept. of Hawaiian Home Lands,* 64 Haw. 327, 336, 640 P.2d 1160, 1167 (1982) (citing *Cherokee Nation v. Georgia,* 30 U.S. (5 Pet.) 1 (1831)).

67.   In *Ahuna v. Dept. of Hawaiian Home Lands,* 64 Haw. 327, 339, 640 P.2d 1160, 1168-1169, the Hawai'i Supreme Court stated:

> In our opinion, the extent or nature of the trust obligations of the appellant toward beneficiaries such as the appellee may be determined by examining well-settled principles enunciated by the federal courts regarding lands set aside by Congress in trust for the benefit of other native Americans, *i.e.,* American Indians, Eskimos, and Alaska natives. In *Pence v. Kleppe,* 529 F.2d 135 (9th Cir. 1976), the circuit court recognized that the word "Indian" is commonly used in the United States to mean "the aborigines of America." *Id.* at 138-39 n.5; *see also* 42 C.J.S. *Indians* § 1 (1944). Congress recently passed a religious freedom act which specifically included native Hawaiians among other American Indians. *See* American Indian Religious Freedom Act, Pub. L. No. 95-341, 92 Stat. 469 (1978) (codified at 42 U.S.C. § 1996 (Supp. III 1979)). Essentially, we are dealing with relationships between the government and aboriginal people. Reason thus dictates that we draw the analogy between native Hawaiian homesteaders and other native Americans.

68.   U.S. Const. art. 1, § 8.

69.   *Delaware Tribal Business Committee v. Weeks,* 430 U.S. 73 (1977); *U.S. v. Sioux Nation,* 448 U.S. 371 (1980).

70.   *Morton v. Mancari,* 417 U.S. 535, 555 (1974).

71.   *Johnson v. M'Intosh,* 21 U.S. (8 Wheat.) 543 (1823); *Cherokee Nation v. Georgia,* 30 U.S. (5 Pet.) 1 (1831); *Worcester v. Georgia,* 31 U.S. (6 Pet.) 515 (1832).

72.   *Worcester v. Georgia,* 31 U.S. (6 Pet.) 515, 560 (1832).

73.   F. Cohen, *Handbook of Federal Indian Law xxv* (1986 Reprint of 1942 Edition).

74.   *Cherokee Nation v. Georgia,* 30 U.S. (5 Pet.) 1-2 (1831).

75.   *Johnson v. M'Intosh,* 21 U.S. (8 Wheat.) 543, 603-604 (1823).

76.   *Ahuna v. Dept. of Hawaiian Home Lands,* 64 Haw. 327, 339, 640 P.2d 1161, 1169 (1982) (citing *Seminole Nation v. U.S.,* 316 U.S. 286, 296-297 (1942)).

77.   *Id.* at 339, 640 P.2d at 1169, citing *U.S. v. Mason,* 412 U.S. 391 (1973).

78.   64 Haw. 327, 640 P.2d 1161 (1982).

79.   *Id.* at 342, 640 P.2d at 1171.

80.   *Id.*

81.   Civ. No. 75-0260 (D.Haw. Sept. 1, 1976). The *Keaukaha* case was later reversed on jurisdictional grounds by the Ninth Circuit Court of Appeals, rather than on the merits of the legal conclusions. *Keaukaha-Panaewa Community Association v. Hawaiian Homes Commission,* 588 F.2d 1216 (9th Cir. 1978). The U.S. Supreme Court refused to review that decision, 444 U.S. 826 (1979). However, a refusal does not signify the supreme court's view of the legal merits of a decision.

82.   Admission Act of March 18, 1959, Pub. L. No. 86-3, § 4, 73 Stat. 4, § 4 (1959), provides, in part:

> As a compact with the United States relating to the management and disposition of Hawaiian home lands, the Hawaiian Homes Commission Act, . . . shall be adopted as a provision of the Constitution of said State . . . .

83.   Haw. Const. art. XII, §§ 1 and 2, provide that:

> Section 1. Anything in this constitution to the contrary notwithstanding, the Hawaiian Homes Commission Act, 1920, enacted by the Congress, as the same has been or may be amended prior to the admission of the State, is hereby adopted as a law of the State, subject to amendment or repeal by the legislature, provided that if and to the extent that the United States shall so require, such law shall be subject to amendment or repeal only with the consent of the United States and in no other manner; . . . .

> Section 2. The State and its people do hereby accept, as a compact with the United States, or as conditions or trust provisions imposed by the United States, relating to the management and disposition of the Hawaiian home lands, the requirement that section 1 hereof be included in this constitution, in whole or in part, it being intended that the Act or acts of the Congress pertaining thereto shall be definitive of the extent and nature of such compact, conditions or trust provisions, as the case may be. The State and its people do further agree and declare that the spirit of the Hawaiian Homes Commission Act looking to the continuance of the Hawaiian homes projects for the further rehabilitation of the Hawaiian race shall be faithfully carried out.

See In re Ainoa, 60 Haw. 487, 488, 591 P.2d 607, 608 (1979).

84. American Indian Lawyer Training Program, Inc., *Indian Tribes as Sovereign Governments* 11-14 (1988) [hereinafter AILTP].

85. Originally, Pub. L. No. 280 delegated state jurisdiction over most crimes and many civil matters to six states. In addition, the statute allowed any other state the option of asserting its jurisdiction over various matters except the regulation and taxation of trust property and the hunting and fishing rights of Indians. 25 USC § 1162 (1953). In 1968, congress amended Pub. L. No. 280 to require tribal consent to a state's exercise of this option. 25 USC §§ 1321, 1322 (1968). *See* AILTP, *supra* note 84, at 41-42.

86. HHCA § 204(3) provides, in part:

> The department, with the approval of the Secretary of the Interior, in order to consolidate its holdings or to better effectuate the purposes of this Act, may exchange the title to available lands for land, privately or publicly owned, of an equal value . . . .

87. HHCA § 223 provides:

> The Congress of the United States reserves the right to alter, amend, or repeal the provisions of this title.

88. Admission Act of March 18, 1959, Pub. L. No. 86-3, § 4, 73 Stat. 4, § 4; *see also* Haw. Const. art. XII, §§ 1 and 3; *Federal-State Task Force Report*, *supra* note 2, Appendix 8.

> [A]ny amendment to increase the benefits to lessees of Hawaiian home lands may be made in the constitution, or in the manner required for State legislation, but the qualifications of lessees shall not be changed except with the consent of the United States.

89. HHCA § 202.

90. HHCA § 202 currently provides that the commission be composed of three members from Oʻahu, one member from west Hawaiʻi, one member from east Hawaiʻi, one member from Molokaʻi, one member from Maui and one member from Kauaʻi. Under Act 265, the 1989 State Legislature authorized the additional commissioner from east Hawaiʻi.

91. *Ahuna v. Dept. of Hawaiian Home Lands*, 64 Haw. 327, 338, 640 P.2d 1161, 1168 (1982).

92. HHCA §§ 207(a) and 208(2). Initially, the HHCA provided that leases be awarded only for pastoral and agricultural purposes. In 1923, congress added residential lots to section 207. More recently, it added aquacultural lots to the same section.

93. The eligible relatives are a spouse, child, grandchild, brother, sister, widow or widower of a child, grandchild, or sibling, or niece, or nephew. HHCA § 209.

94. HHCA §§ 207(b) and 208(5).

95. HHCA § 208(5).

96. HHCA § 208(6).

97. HHCA §§ 208(7) and (8); *see In re Ainoa*, 60 Haw. 487, 591 P.2d 607 (1979).

98. HHCA § 221(d). The 1990 legislature passed, and the governor approved, Act 24 which expands the beneficiaries' rights to irrigation water by making all "government-owned water" subject to a water reservation for homesteaders, regardless of whether it is "surplus," *i.e.*, in excess of the needs of any holder of a water license issued by the Department of Land and Natural Resources pursuant to Haw. Rev. Stat. § 171-58.

99. HHCA § 204(2).

100. *Id.*

101. Department of Hawaiian Home Lands, 1988 Annual Report 8 (n.d.) [hereinafter *1988 DHHL Annual Report*].

102. *Id.* at 2.

103. *1989 DHHL Annual Report*, *supra* note 5, at 12.

104. *Id.* at 12.

105. Department of Hawaiian Home Lands, 1987 Annual Report 10 (n.d.) [hereinafter *1987 DHHL Annual Report*].

106. Letter from Deputy Attorney General F. Hustace to Hawaiian Homes Commission (March 20, 1964).

107. *Federal-State Task Force*, *supra* note 2, at 14.

108. *1989 DHHL Annual Report*, *supra* note 5, at 12.

109. No comprehensive statistics are available. However, by one informal survey of the 127 applicants on the 1952 Waimea Pastoral Waiting List, 36 (or 28.3 percent) had died by the time this material went to print.

110. *1987 DHHL Annual Report*, *supra* note 105, at 10; *Informational Hearing Before the Senate Select Committee on Indian Affairs and the House Committee on Interior and Insular Affairs*, 101 Cong., 1st Sess. (1989) (testimony of I. Piianaia, Chairperson, DHHL) [hereinafter *Testimony of I. Piianaia*].

111. The statewide Hawaiian Homestead waiting list grows each month. The DHHL has indicated in public meetings that the list is now over 19,000. *Id.*

112. *1989 DHHL Annual Report*, *supra* note 5, at 16, 28, 29, 38, 49, 51.

113. *Id.* at 16, 30, 32.

114.   If the DHHL considers the land inventory total to be 187,413 acres as indicated in its 1989 annual report, only 148,900 acres are under homestead leases, general leases, licenses, revocable permits, illegal executive orders and rights of entry. The remaining 38,513 acres are either vacant or used without any written documentation. *See 1989 DHHL Annual Report, supra* note 5, at 16.

115.   In total, Hawai'i's past governors illegally withdrew 13,580 acres of Hawaiian Home Lands under 34 illegal executive orders. However, since statehood, Hawai'i's governors withdrew only two acres of land of this total under five executive orders. Similarly, Hawai'i's territorial governors illegally utilized nine proclamations to withdraw 16,586 acres of Hawaiian Home Lands for forest reserves. *See, Federal-State Task Force Report, supra* note 2, at 265-301 App. 12.

116.   *Id.*

117.   *Id.* at 267-268, 284.

118.   *Id.* at 287.

119.   *Id.* at 281.

120.   As yet, no formal lease has been issued to either the Park Service or the Hawai'i State Department of Health, which operates a Hansen's Disease Settlement under its authority to govern Kalawao County. Haw. Rev. Stat. § 326-34 (Supp. 1989).

121.   No. 76-1044 (D.Haw. Feb. 21, 1978).

122.   *Id.*

123.   *Department of Hawaiian Home Lands v. Aloha Airlines, Inc.*, Civil No. 6122 (3rd Cir. Ct. of Hawai'i, Sep. 24, 1980).

124.   The Secretary of Interior approved this exchange during fiscal year 1986-87. *1987 DHHL Annual Report, supra* note 105, at 16.

125.   11 DHHL Newsletter, "Ka Nūhou," No. 1, at 1 (Feb. 1985).

126.   It is unclear what DHHL has done about the remaining 2,330 acres still purportedly encumbered under 15 executive orders and one proclamation. In its 1988 annual report, DHHL lists only four outstanding executive orders it has failed to cancel. In the only other exchange consummated since the Task Force report, DHHL acquired 20 acres of land in Wai'anae for 84.6 acres of trust land used illegally for schools in Waimānalo and Nānākuli, O'ahu and a health care center in Wai'anae, O'ahu. *Id.* These exchanges apparently did not involve a resolution of any back rent issue.

127.   *Id.* at 1. However, if past governors illegally withdrew a total of 30,166 acres of trust land by illegal executive orders and proclamations, there are still 2,331 acres in use by other agencies. The *1989 DHHL Annual Report, supra* note 5, at 28, lists only four of those orders, accounting for only 1,410 acres, leaving 921 acres still unresolved without mention in the report.

128.   Memorandum from D. Yagodich to HHC (October 31, 1986).

129.   Civ. No. 75-0260 (D. Haw. Sept. 1, 1976); *see supra* 81 and accompanying text.

130.   *Id.* at 10-11.

131.   Secretary of the Interior Donald Hodel approved an exchange of 20 acres of Hawaiian Home Lands in Waiakea, Hilo, being used for a flood control project for over a decade, for 54 acres of state public lands adjacent to the DHHL's Panaowa homestead area. 13 DHHL Newsletter "Ka Nūhou," No. 2, at 2 (April 1987) [hereinafter *13 DHHL Newsletter 4/87*].

132.   Letter from HHC Chairperson W.G. Among to DLNR Chairperson Sunao Kido (February 4, 1972).

133.   Letter from DLNR Chairperson Susumu Ono to HHC Chairperson Georgianna Padeken (July 25, 1983).

134.   *Id.*; HHC Minutes (Sep. 27, 1987).

135.   1965 Haw. Sess. Laws, Act 271.

136.   *1989 DHHL Annual Report, supra* note 5, at 28; *see also, Federal-State Task Force Report, supra* note 2, at 277-279.

137.   Stand. Comm. Rep. No. 56, *reprinted in* 1 *Proceedings of the Constitutional Convention of Hawaii 1978*, at 632 (1980) [hereinafter *1978 Proceedings*].

138.   The legislature apparently interpreted the language of art. XII, § 1 to be satisfied if funds came from the DHHL special funds, into which revenues from trust land leases and licenses, and interest income, are deposited. The history of the Constitutional Convention proceedings does not support this interpretation.

139.   *1978 Proceedings, supra* note 137, at 631.

140.   *Id.* at 632.

141.   13 DHHL Newsletter, "Ka Nūhou," No. 3, at 1 (May 1987).

142.   This level covers *all* 98 staff positions.

143.   1989 Haw. Sess. Laws, Act 316.

144.   Memorandum from DHHL Deputy Director John Rowe to HHC (June 27, 1989) [hereinafter *Memo from J. Rowe*].

145.   *13 DHHL Newsletter 4/87, supra* note 131, at 1.

146.   *Id.*

147. 15 DHHL Newsletter, "Ka Nūhou," No. 3, at 4 (November 1989) [hereinafter *15 DHHL Newsletter 11/89*].

148. 10 DHHL Newsletter, "Ka Nūhou," No. 1, at 6, 8 (January 1984).

149. *Testimony of I. Piianaia, supra* note 110.

150. *Memo from J. Rowe, supra* note 144, at 2-3.

151. *15 DHHL Newsletter 11/89, supra* note 147. The 1987 Legislature appropriated $22.7 million to DHHL in capital improvement cash and bond funding for infrastructural improvements and planning. At the time, DHHL estimated that this amount was only sufficient to fund the infrastructural improvements for 480 unimproved lots previously awarded and to finance the planning for improving another 620 lots. *Hearing on S. 2018 Before the House Committee on Finance*, 14th Leg., 2d Sess. (Haw. 1988) (testimony of I. Piianaia, DHHL Chairperson). These lots had been previously awarded as part of the 1984-87 award acceleration program. The legislature refused to increase this budget by another $9.8 million during its 1988 session.

152. These funds will also allow for the awarding of another 306 leases during 1987-90, in addition to infrastructure work for 881 more lots already awarded earlier, and engineering design work for another 774 lots already awarded earlier, which are slated for construction during FY 1991-92. *Memo from J. Rowe, supra* note 144, at 2.

153. *Id.* at 2-3.

154. 1989 Haw. Sess. Laws, Act 283. Art. VII, § 12 of the Hawai'i State Constitution provides:

> 2.   The term "general obligation bonds" means all bonds for the payment of the principal and interest of which the full faith and credit of the State or a political subdivision are pledged and, unless otherwise indicated, includes reimbursable general obligation bonds.
>
> . . . .
>
> 7.   The term "revenue bonds" means all bonds payable from the revenues, or user taxes, or any combination of both, of a public undertaking, improvement, system or loan program and any loan made thereunder and secured as may be provided by law.
>
> . . . .
>
> The legislature, by a majority vote of the members to which each house is entitled, shall authorize the issuance of all general obligation bonds, bonds issued under special improvement statutes and revenue bonds issued by or on behalf of the State and shall prescribe by general law the manner and procedure for such issuance. The legislature by general law shall authorize political subdivisions to issue general obligation bonds, bonds issued under special improvement statutes and revenue bonds and shall prescribe the manner and procedure for such issuance. All such bonds issued by or on behalf of a political subdivision shall be authorized by the governing body of such political subdivision.

155. Under Haw. Const. art. VII, § 13, the state may not issue general obligation bonds if such issuance will cause the total amount of principal and interest payable in the current or any future year on such bonds and any outstanding general obligation bonds to exceed 18.5 percent of the average of the general fund revenues of the state in the three years preceding the issuance. Revenue bonds are generally excluded from this calculation.

156. *Id.; see supra* notes 144, 154.

157. Public Financial Management, Inc., State of Hawaii Department of Hawaiian Home Lands Evaluation of Revenue Bonding Capacity for Infrastructure Improvement Projects 4, 23 (1990).

158. *Id.*

159. The DHHL's consultant has recommended deferring immediate financing for some "non-revenue projects in the short-term," believing that "the alternative of focusing existing capital resources entirely on non-revenue producing projects essentially *guarantees* that the Department will fall well short of its 10-year capital program goal." *Id.* at 24.

160. *Memo from J. Rowe, supra* note 144, at 2.

161. The story of those on the 1952 Pastoral Waiting List is a tragic one. In 1952, 427 applied for pastoral homesteads in Waimea. The HHC selected 187 as most likely to succeed as ranchers. Of these 48 were awarded pastoral leases and the remaining 139 placed on the 1952 list. Contrary to legal authority, the HHC purportedly cancelled that list without taking a formal vote or notifying those on the list so they could reapply. Subsequently, the HHC awarded pastoral homestead leases to beneficiaries without following the order of the 1952 list, as those on the list continued to wait in anticipation of getting their own awards. Since the HHC refused to disclose the identities or the order of those on its waiting lists until 1989, none of those on the waiting list could check how, and in what order, the HHC was awarding lots in Waimea. (The State Office of Information Practices (OIP) finally ruled in 1989 that such lists were public records that should be made available to the public. OIP Opinion No. 89-4 (Nov. 9, 1989).) Finally in 1983, the HHC restored the 1952 list under pressure from Sonny Kaniho and the Aged Hawaiians, an association of those on the 1952 list. *See generally* HHC Minutes (Nov. 17, 1983).

162. *Akiona v. DHHL*, No. 89-244 (3d Cir. Ct. of Hawai'i, filed July 17, 1989).

163. *Id.* (order granting preliminary injunction).

164. Under § 219.1 of the HCCA:
> The Department is authorized to carry on any activities it deems necessary to assist the lessees in obtaining maximum utilization of the leased lands, including *taking any steps necessary to develop these lands for their highest and best use commensurate with the purposes for which the land is being leased* as provided for in Section 207, and assisting the lessees in all phases of farming, ranching and aquaculture operations and the marketing of their agricultural or aquacultural produce and livestock. (Emphasis added.)

165. 16 DHHL Newsletter, "Ka Nūhou," No. 1, at 4 (January 1990).

166. *Id.*

167. *Hearing on H.R. Con. Res. 298 Before the House Committee on Economic Development and Hawaiian Affairs,* 15th Leg., 2d Sess. (1990) (statement of DHHL Deputy Director John Rowe).

168. 207 U.S. 564 (1908).

169. *Ahuna v. Dept. of Hawaiian Home Lands,* 64 Haw. 327, 338, 640 P.2d 1161, 1168 (1982).

170. This implied reservation is known as the "Winters doctrine." In *Winters v. United States,* 207 U.S. 564 (1908), the U.S. Supreme Court inferred that the United States had reserved water rights to support the settlement of certain Indian tribes on the Ft. Belknap reservation, which the U.S. created by agreement with those tribes in 1888. The agreement had not explicitly mentioned water rights. These rights were deemed to be superior to upstream diversions initiated after the creation of the reservation. Furthermore, the court held that the tribes had superior rights even if they had not actually established water usages before the upstream diverters of water. Federal law assured the preservation of tribal water rights, albeit unexercised, even if state law would dictate that those who established earlier water uses would have superior rights. In a later case, the court extended this doctrine to other federal enclaves and defined the scope of the rights to include enough water to develop all "practicably irrigable acreage." *Arizona v. California,* 373 U.S. 546, 600-601 (1963).

171. HHCA § 221(c).

172. All water licenses issued *after* July 9, 1921 are deemed subject to a condition, whether explicit or not, that the licensee must allow the DHHL the right to use, free of all charge, any of the surplus water tributary to the Waimea river, covered by the license in order for the DHHL to adequately irrigate any tract it deems necessary. HHCA § 221(d).

173. The 1990 Legislature considered measures to expand this water right to all water on public land. *See* H.R. 3094, H.R. 2487 and S. 2701, 15 Leg., 2d Sess. (Haw. 1990); *see also* H.R. Rep. No. 839, 66th Cong., 2d Sess. 10 (1920). Initially, congress reserved rights to water for the homestead program on Moloka'i as well. However, that reservation was scaled back in subsequent amendments to the HHCA.

174. Section 221(e) also specifies that the rights conferred on the DHHL by this section include "the right to use, contract for or acquire the use of any ditch or pipeline constructed for the distribution and control of such water and necessary to such use by the Department."

175. *Oversight Hearings on State and Federal Trust Responsibility for Hawaiian Homes and Other Related Matters Before Senate Select Committee on Indian Affairs,* 101 Cong., 2d Sess. (May 30, 1990) (testimony of State Attorney General Warren Price).

176. *See 13 DHHL Newsletter 4/87, supra* note 131, at 4.

177. Originally designed to award 4,000 Native Hawaiians homestead lots between July 1, 1984 and June 30, 1987, the DHHL ultimately awarded only 2,541 lots through June 30, 1986. *Compare* 11 DHHL Newsletter, "Ka Nūhou," No. 3 at 5 (August 1985), 12 DHHL Newsletter, "Ka Nūhou," No. 3 at 1, 4 (August 1986) with 13 DHHL Newsletter, "Ka Nūhou," No. 1, at 2 (January 1987) and *Memo from J. Rowe, supra* note 144.

178. *Memo from J. Rowe, supra* note 144; *15 DHHL Newsletter 11/89, supra* note 147 at 4.

179. Initially, the MIS was designed to support the Ho'olehua homesteaders exclusively. Section 221(d) of the HHCA provided for the use of any government-owned water on Moloka'i free of charge, even if a water license was issued to another party subsequent to the passage of the HHCA. In 1955, the legislature and congress amended Section 221 to allow for joint use of the MIS so that lessees would retain a prior right to two-thirds of the water from an irrigation project which was being planned to tap the waters of Waikolu Valley through a tunnel. (1955 Haw. Sess. Laws, Act 164 (as amended by Act 306, 1987 Haw. Sess. Laws), *reprinted in* Haw. Rev. Stat. § 168-4 (Supp. 1989).) That project ultimately resulted in funding by the federal government under the Small Projects Reclamation Act for the construction of the MIS. However, in order to meet project requirements, DHHL exchanged 1,050 acres of its land at Ho'olehua for 243 acres of equally valued land at Waimānalo in 1962. Letter from W.C. Kea to H. Fong (February 19, 1962).

180. Beneficiaries are entitled to receive two-thirds (currently up to 5.1 mgd) of the water transmitted through the MIS, which has a capacity of delivering 7.6 mgd. In reality, because homesteader water demand is currently low, less than two-thirds of the water delivered through the MIS reaches beneficiaries. Agricultural water meters can exceed $10,000 in cost. The lack of adequate water feeder lines from the MIS poses another obstacle to use.

181. *See Ah Ho v. Cobb,* 62 Haw. 546, 549, 617 P.2d 1208, 1210-1211 (1980).

182. 62 Haw. 546, 612 P.2d 1208 (1980).

183. 356 F. Supp. 148 (D. Haw. 1973), *aff'd,* 506 F.2d 572 (9th Cir. 1974).

184. 506 F.2d 572, 580 (9th Cir. 1974).

185. Originally, the HHC awarded five pastoral lots of 90 acres each on a "permissive use" or experimental basis, rather than under a homestead lease. HHC Minutes (July 28, 1983); letter from W.G. Among to H.S. Doi (February 5, 1971). The HHC refused to issue leases until the five could live on those lots. After four of the five "permittees" gave up attempts to ranch the land, the HHC issued two homestead lots to Alice Akita and Joe Manini in 1971. Later, the Hawai'i Supreme Court held that the HHC was not authorized to grant land to beneficiaries using this method. *Ahuna v. Dept. of Hawaiian Home Lands*, 64 Haw. 327, 330, 640 P.2d 1161, 1163-1164 (1982) n.4. *See also*, Memorandum from S. Matsunaga to HHC (August 30, 1988).

186. HHC Minutes, Item XI at 68 (July 28, 1983).

187. DLNR General Lease No. S-4222 issued to Kekaha Sugar Co. (Jan. 23, 1969).

188. Memorandum from S. Matsunaga to the HHC (August 30, 1988); HHC Minutes (July 28, 1983).

189. Memorandum from S. Matsunaga to the HHC (August 30, 1988); HHC Minutes (July 28, 1983); Memorandum from S. Matsunaga to M.S. Jones 2 (November 8, 1983); letter from DHHL Chairperson Padeken to DLNR Chairperson Ono (July 1, 1982); HHC Minutes Item XI, at 62-70 (July 28, 1983); HHC Minutes 89-90 (March 25, 1982); letter from V.P. Loomis to G. Padeken (December 22, 1983); letter from G. Padeken to A. Zenger (April 11, 1984); *Kekaha Sugar Ltd. v. Joseph Manini*, Civil No. 88-0156 (Order Granting Motion for Permanent Injunction, February 27, 1990).

190. *Kekaha Sugar Co. v. Manini*, Civil No. 2129 (5th Cir. Ct. of Hawai'i 1979) (complaint filed May 23, 1979) (Preliminary Injunction granted September 26, 1979). *Kekaha Sugar Ltd. v. Joseph Manini*, Civil No. 88-0156 (Order Granting Motion for Permanent Injunction, February 27, 1990).

191. *See* Haw. Const. art. XII, § 2.

192. DHHL maintains that it must compensate a general lessee for the value of improvements to the leased property if it seeks an early termination of the lease upon exercise of the withdrawal statute. That premise is debatable. The amount of compensation owed, if any, for improvements is reduced proportionately by the number of years remaining on the 25-year general lease. Since the Kekaha Sugar lease has only three years remaining, any liability for improvements must be reduced by 91 percent. *See* DLNR General Lease No. S-4222, *supra* note 187, at 8.

193. Kekaha Sugar's general lease No. S-4222, managed by DLNR, expires on December 31, 1993. Until then, the lease generates $55,000.00 per annum for DHHL. *Id.* at 16. In addition, the lease also calls for six percent of the gross proceeds from sugar sales to be paid to DLNR. It is not clear how much of this latter amount is paid to DHHL. However, under art. XII, § 1 of the Hawai'i State Constitution, the state has allocated 30 percent of all leases to sugar plantations and water licenses to the Native Hawaiian Rehabilitation Fund administered by DHHL. For fiscal year 1987-88, this income source was only $492,109, or 7.4 percent of all DHHL revenues. *See id.*

194. The continuation of the DLNR general lease to Kekaha Sugar of 14,558 acres of Hawaiian Home Lands is contrary to the recommendation of the Federal-State Task Force that such lease be turned over to DHHL unless some advantage is gained by the consolidation of these areas under DLNR. *Federal-State Task Force Report, supra* note 2, at 45. Even if financial or practical considerations might dictate the consolidation of the 27,000 acres being leased by Kekaha Sugar in Kekaha, the operation of the lease has clearly run contrary to the interest of the two beneficiaries in this area. Apparently, the DHHL is content to let the lease expire in 1993, claiming it neither has the resources nor a clear management plan to utilize its lands for homesteading at this time. Hearings on H.R. Con. Res. 295 Before House Committee on Economic Development and Hawaiian Affairs, 15th Leg., 2d Sess. (Haw. April 2, 1990) (statement of H. Drake, Chairperson, DHHL).

195. The DHHL issued license No. 156 to Parker Ranch for a waterline easement without obtaining rights to use this line. The DHHL also allowed a license to the DLNR to develop a reservoir on 54 acres of trust land at Pu'u Pulehu without adequate reservations for water to supply homesteaders. *1988 DHHL Annual Report, supra* note 101, at 39.

196. Memorandum from D. Yagodich to the HHC (Sep. 22, 1987).

197. Haw. Rev. Stat. §§ 167-5, 167-6, 168-1, 168-2 (Supp. 1989).

198. U.S. Dept. of Agriculture Soil Conservation Service, Watershed Plan and Environmental Assessment -- Waimea-Paauilo Watershed 24 (Sep. 1989).

199. *Id.* at 24.

200. Memo from D. Yagodich, *supra* note 196.

201. One DOA estimate for a two-inch water meter is $1,500-$2,000. Telephone conversation with Paul Matsuo (April 23, 1990). DHHL estimates the cost to be $12,000 per meter. Conversation with Hardy Spoehr (April 19, 1990).

202. Conversation with Waimea agricultural homesteader Pat Ah Sing (December, 1989).

203. The DHHL has now decided to limit most future pastoral homesteads to 20 acres, or enough to raise two head of cattle and two calves.

204. The maximum acreage for an unirrigated pastoral homestead lot is 1,000 acres; the maximum acreage for an irrigated pasture lot is 100 acres. HHCA § 207(a). Most pastoral homestead lots previously awarded in the Waimea area have been for 200 to 300 acres each.

205. Letter from Hawai'i County Department of Water Supply Manager Engineer W.Y. Thompson to HHC Chair A.K. Piianaia (Sep. 11, 1964).

206. 588 F.2d 1216 (9th Cir. 1978).

207. 739 F.2d 1467 (9th Cir. 1984).

208. The Ninth Circuit held that § 5(f) did not establish a comprehensive scheme to enforce its terms so as to preclude relief under 42 USC § 1983. *Id.* at 1471. It also held that (1) even if the State of Hawai'i manages the home lands pursuant to the incorporation of the HHCA in its constitution, "the trust obligation is rooted in federal law" and Hawai'i Admission Act §§ 4, 73 Stat. 4, and (2) "the power to enforce the HHCA is contained in federal law" *id.* at 1472; *see also Kila v. Hawaiian Homes Commission*, Civ. No. 74-12 (D.Haw. Sep. 17, 1974).

209. *Keaukaha-Panaewa Community Association v. Hawaiian Homes Commission*, 739 F.2d 1467, 1472; *Makanui v. Department of Education*, 6 Haw. App. 397, 406 (1986) (citing *Quern v. Jordan*, 440 U.S. 332, 341 (1979)).

210. *Martinez v. California*, 444 U.S. 277, 283-84, n.7 (1980).

211. 1988 Haw. Sess. Laws, Act 395, codified at Haw. Rev. Stat. ch. 673.

212. Haw. Rev. Stat. §§ 673-2(a), 673-4(a), (b).

213. *Id.*

214. *Id.*

215. *Id.*

216. *Id.*

217. *Id.*

218. 1988 Haw. Sess. Laws, Act 395, § 5; *see* note following Haw. Rev. Stat. ch. 673.

219. *Id.*

220. The 1990 legislature passed a resolution calling on the congress to enact appropriate federal legislation to allow for a private right of action in federal court to seek damage relief. H.R. Con. Res. 301, 15th Leg., 2d Sess. (Haw. 1990).

221. *Federal-State Task Force Report, supra* note 2, at 29, 42, 44-68.

222. *Id.* at 39, 41-51.

223. Recent Developments Relating to the Hawaiian Homes Commission Act, 1920, As Amended, Hearings Before the Hawai'i Advisory Committee to the United States Commission on Civil Rights, 100th Cong., 2d Sess. (Sep. 6, 1988) (testimony of I. Piianaia, Chairperson, DHHL).

224. *But see supra* notes 141-159 and accompanying text.

225. *Id.* Also in 1986 the state legislature appropriated only $6.7 million in CIP for the program. 11 DHHL Newsletter, "Ka Nūhou," No. 2, at 1 (May 1985). In 1985, it only authorized $3 million in CIP funding. 12 DHHL Newsletter, "Ka Nūhou," No. 2, at 2 (June 1986).

226. *See supra* notes 141-159 and accompanying text.

227. *Id.*

228. *State of Hawaii v. United States*, 676 F.Supp. 1024, 1039 (D. Haw. 1988).

229. *State of Hawaii v. United States*, 866 F.2d 313 (9th Cir. 1989).

230. Of the 10,798 applicants on the statewide waiting list for residential homesteads, as of June 30, 1988, 4,602 were seeking homesteads on O'ahu. *1988 DHHL Annual Report, supra* note 101, at 7.

231. Lualualei (1,356 acres) constitutes nearly 21 percent of all DHHL land on O'ahu (6,600 acres). *Id.* at 12. As of June 30, 1988, there were 5,031 applicants on the O'ahu waiting list, 4,602 of whom were seeking residential leaseholds. *Id.* at 7. Conceivably most on this list could be accommodated at Lualualei on 10,000-square-foot lots, if made available.

232. 69 Haw. 538, 751 P.2d 81 (1988). The specific issue in this case was whether a state agency is a member of the "general public" for purposes of § 204, which allows such general leases.

233. Executive Order Setting Aside Land for Public Purposes No. 437 issued on October 17, 1930 purportedly withdrew 67.07 acres. Executive Order Setting Aside Land for Public Purposes No. 1393 issued on September 11, 1950 purportedly withdrew 20.8 acres.

234. Letter from I. Piianaia to A. Murakami (May 10, 1988); DHHL License Agreement No. 213 (January 26, 1987).

235. DHHL License No. 213 to City and County of Honolulu (January 26, 1987).

236. *Federal-State Task Force Report, supra* note 2, at 268, 276.

237. *Id.* at 279, 299 (Appendix 12).

238. Letter from Chairperson H. Drake to A. Murakami (January 17, 1990).

239. *Federal-State Task Force Report, supra* note 2, at 299 (Attachment E to Appendix 12).

240. *Id.* at 45; *1988 DHHL Annual Report, supra* note 101, at 26.

241. *Federal-State Task Force Report, supra* note 2, at 301 (Attachment G to Appendix 12).

242. HHCA § 204(2).

243. *Federal-State Task Force Report, supra* note 2, at 265-301 (Appendix 12).

244. *Compare 1989 DHHL Annual Report, supra* note 5, at 16 ($3 million) and *1987 DHHL Annual Report, supra* note 105, at 17 ($1.7 million).

245. Approval of Amendments to HHCA, Pub. L. No. 99-557, 100 Stat. 3143 (1986).

246. Presidential Statement on signing H.R.J. Res. 17, Pub. L. No. 99-557, into law (Oct. 27, 1986) [hereinafter *Presidential Statement*].

247. Hawai'i Admission Act of March 18, 1959, Pub. L. No. 86-3, § 5(f), 73 Stat. 4, § 5(f) (1959) provides, in part:

> Such lands, proceeds, and income shall be managed and disposed of for one or more of the foregoing purposes in such manner as the constitution and laws of said State may provide, and their use for any other object shall constitute a breach of trust for which suit may be brought by the United States. The use of the trust assets for any purpose other than those specified in the Admission Act constitutes a breach of trust for which suit may be brought by the United States against the State of Hawaii.

248. *Presidential Statement, supra* note 246.

249. *See* H.R. Rep. No. 839, 66th Cong., 2d Sess. (1920).

250. AILTP, *supra* note 84, at 11-14, citing H.R. Con. Res. 108, 67 Stat. B132 (1953).

251. AILTP, *supra* note 84, at 12-13, 14-20, citing the Indian Civil Rights Act of 1968, 25 USC § 1301-1303; Indian Self-Determination and Education Assistance Act of 1975, 25 USC §§ 450a-450n.

252. *Id.* at 14-17.

253. In public meetings, Senator Inouye has declared his support for the establishment of a sovereign entity controlled by Hawaiians which would have dominion over a land base comprised in part of the land inventory of the DHHL.

CHAPTER 4

SELF-DETERMINATION AND SELF-GOVERNANCE

1.   INTRODUCTION

In 1893 when the Hawaiian government was overthrown, the inherent self-governing rights of Native Hawaiians were severely restricted. Native Hawaiians also lost control of their traditional lands. Chapters 2 and 3 have discussed the subsequent history of the Government and Crown Lands and the rights Native Hawaiians still retain in those lands. This chapter examines the basis of the claim for sovereignty, reviews the evolution of the Native Hawaiian movement from "reparations" to self-determination and self-governance, and discusses some of the recent Native Hawaiian initiatives for self-governance.

The claims of Native Hawaiians have often been analogized to those of other Native American groups.[1] While there may be similarities, there is one significant difference: Indian nations had some, but not all, of the aspects of sovereignty; the Kingdom of Hawai'i possessed all of the attributes of sovereignty and was so recognized by the world community of sovereign nations. Native Hawaiians were citizens of an organized, self-governing nation whose status as an independent sovereign was acknowledged by other nations, including the United States.

2.   THE SOVEREIGNTY OF THE HAWAIIAN KINGDOM[2]

The most basic right of a nation is its right to exist.[3] From this first right, a nation derives all of its other rights: the right to control internal affairs, the right to chose a form of government, make and amend laws, provide for its citizens, and administer its domain.[4] In international affairs, the right to exist gives rise to the right to enter into intercourse with other nations, to conclude special relationships and agreements with other nations, to acquire territory, and to admit and expel aliens.[5] Perhaps the primary right arising from the right to exist is the right of independence. A corollary *duty* arising from the right of independence is the principle of non-intervention, the duty not to intervene in the internal affairs or the external sovereignty of another nation.[6]

As early as 1826, the first formal agreement between the United States and the Hawaiian Kingdom was negotiated.[7] That treaty was never ratified by the United States Senate as required by the U.S. Constitution. The document, however, was

> clearly an international act, signed as such by the authorities of the then independent Hawaiian government, and by a representative of the United States, whose instructions, while vague, must be regarded as sufficient authority for his signature, in view of the then remoteness of the region from the seat of government and the general discretion which those instructions granted . . . .[8]

Further, "for more than a decade [after the treaty was signed], American officials and residents of the Hawaiian Islands were seeking to impress upon the perplexed chiefs the sanctity of this agreement which the government of the United States had refused to accept."[9] The first section of the unratified treaty acknowledged that "the peace and friendship" between the United States and the sovereign and people of Hawai'i "[are] hereby confirmed, and declared to be perpetual."[10]

In 1842, President John Tyler recognized the sovereignty of Hawai'i and declared it the official policy of the United States to support Hawaiian independence.[11] As a result, congress appropriated funds for the appointment of a minister from the United States to Hawai'i.

The first formal treaty between the United States and the Kingdom of Hawai'i was ratified by congress in 1849.[12] That treaty dealt with friendship, commerce, and navigation. Article I provided for the "perpetual peace and amity between the United States and the King of the Hawaiian Islands, his heirs and successors."[13] The initial life-span of this Friendship Treaty was ten years. After the initial ten years, each party had the right to terminate the treaty after a year's notice. This treaty was still in effect at the time the Hawaiian monarchy was overthrown. In 1875, another treaty between the United States and Hawai'i was signed, providing duty-free entry of certain American goods and products into Hawai'i and vice versa.[14] In 1884, the Reciprocity Treaty was amended to give the United States the exclusive right to enter and use Pearl Harbor as a coaling and repair station.[15] The Reciprocity Treaty was also still in effect in 1893. The treaties signed between the Kingdom of Hawai'i and the United States were never cancelled; nevertheless, the United States government violated the international standards of conduct between sovereigns bound by their treaties.[16]

As earlier chapters have demonstrated, the government formed by and for the benefit of Native Hawaiians was deprived of the most basic right of a nation, the right to exist. This deprivation was accomplished with the assistance of the United States Minister to Hawai'i and the aid of American troops upon a pretense that not even a special commissioner appointed by then-President Cleveland could accept.[17] Those actions represented a clear violation of the right to independence of the Hawaiian Kingdom and the principle of non-intervention. In 1893, those actions were condemned by the president's special envoy, by U.S. Secretary of State Walter O. Gresham, and ultimately, by President Cleveland.[18] While time may have changed the circumstances of the native people, it has not changed the initial wrong, made it any less ignominious, or alleviated the consequential damage that followed.

As a result of that initial wrong, Native Hawaiians lost both the internal and external rights and control that are paramount to a sovereign nation. Hawaiians lost the right to choose a form of government, to make laws, to oversee their domain, and to provide for their common good. They lost the right to stand as an equal in the international community, to make agreements and treaties with other nations, and to exhibit the external manifestations of sovereignty. While these losses may not be actionable in the American judicial system, they nevertheless require redress.[19]

These losses resulted not solely from the acts of the United States Minister to Hawai'i, but also from the entire process leading to annexation. As early as 1887, a significant number of Native Hawaiians had been disenfranchised due to restrictive voting qualifications contained in the 1887 Constitution.[20] This constitution had been forced upon King David Kalākaua by a small, but powerful, group of Western businessmen. It is clear that the moving force in overthrowing the monarchy was this same group of businessmen -- most of whom were American or European.[21] There was no pretense on their part that their cause was supported by the native population. Indeed they took the paternalistic attitude that the natives did not know what was best for them and that, ultimately, Hawaiians would benefit from annexation to the United States.[22]

When union with the United States did not immediately materialize, the annexationists formed the Republic of Hawai'i.[23] Again, there was no significant representation of native views in forming that government[24] and there was minimal participation by Native Hawaiians once that government was formed. On O'ahu, for instance, only 509 natives registered to vote in the legislative elections, as opposed to 466 Americans, 274 from England and its colonies, 175 Germans, 362 Portuguese, and 131 others.[25] Moreover, the republic's constitution set such strict voting qualifications, including property restrictions, that few Hawaiians could have participated even if they had wished.[26] As one historian has stated, the legislature of the republic was "predominately American, republican, and Annexationist."[27]

In 1895, when an attempt was made to restore the monarchy, Native Hawaiians constituted the overwhelming majority of those arrested for participation in the "rebellion."[28] In 1897, when an annexation treaty appeared imminent, Native Hawaiians presented petitions and resolutions to the republic's president and to the United States Minister to Hawai'i protesting annexation and requesting, at the very least, for a vote on the subject.[29]

The Senate of the Republic of Hawai'i ratified a treaty of annexation with the United States on September 8, 1897. It was not until the summer of the *following year*, however, that the Joint Resolution of Annexation passed both houses of congress and was signed.[30] The joint resolution made no provision for a vote by Native Hawaiians or other citizens of Hawai'i to accept annexation. It was merely assumed that the action of the republic's senate in ratifying an annexation treaty almost a year earlier was sufficient to show assent of the people.[31]

In congress, the annexation of Hawai'i by joint resolution rather than by treaty was hotly debated. Many argued that the United States could acquire territory only under the treaty-making power of the constitution, which would require a ratification vote by two-thirds of the senate.[32] Those favoring annexation pointed to the annexation of Texas in 1845 as precedent.

Several significant factors, however, differentiated the Texas situation.[33] The Texas joint resolution merely signified the willingness of the United States to admit Texas as a *state* if it fulfilled certain conditions, one of which was acceptance of annexation.[34] There was a time limit imposed on Texas in that it had to adopt a duly ratified state constitution on or before January 1, 1846. The Texas Congress accepted annexation and, subsequently, a special convention approved annexation and wrote a state constitution. Finally, the people of Texas ratified the constitution in a referendum, and also voted to accept annexation. Thus, Texas accepted annexation not just once, but three times. In a technical sense then, a joint resolution did not admit Texas to the Union -- it merely invited Texas to accept annexation and form a state. In contrast to Hawai'i, the Texas joint resolution required Texas to act *after* the United States had first acted. In the case of Hawai'i, the United States required neither a vote on annexation nor further acceptance of the joint resolution.

The entire process of annexation, from the 1887 Constitution to the 1898 Joint Resolution of Annexation, denied Native Hawaiians the most fundamental rights of self-determination. As expressed simply and most eloquently by Ka Pākaukau, a coalition of Hawaiian sovereignty groups:

[Sovereignty] is the right possessed by a culturally distinct people inhabiting and controlling a definable territory, to make all decisions regarding itself and its territory free from outside interference. It is what Hawaiians enjoyed under their own culture and constitution before armed U.S. intervention brought about the overthrow of the Hawaiian Kingdom in 1893. Sovereignty is not something that can be given to us -- we can only assert it or give it up . . . .

We Native Hawaiians have never voluntarily surrendered our sovereignty. We were never allowed to vote on the Republic or Annexation, and we had no chance to vote separately on statehood. We can achieve sovereignty when nations of the world accept the fact that a people make their own decisions and refuse to allow others to decide their fate for them.[35]

3. REPARATIONS

Reparations are commonly viewed as the settlement of a claim for monetary compensation.[36] In terms of Native Hawaiian claims, reparations have often been associated with settlement of the claim for the loss of Crown and Government Lands. However, reparations can encompass not only claims for loss of land, but also for loss of sovereignty and self-governing powers. Moreover, reparations can come not only in the form of money, but can also include restoration of self-governing powers. It does seem clear though that in the early stages of the Hawaiian reparations movement, financial compensation was seen as the most viable form of settlement.

a.   *Early Efforts*
Beginning in the early 1970s, several organizations were formed in Hawai'i for the purpose of examining and reassessing the historical and legal relationships between Native Hawaiians and the federal government. The ALOHA Association[37] was most active among the groups who called attention to the United States' involvement in the overthrow of the Hawaiian government. In a 1975 hearing, the president of the ALOHA Association noted the growth in the Hawaiian reparations movement:

[T]he ALOHA Association . . . was founded in 1972 by Louisa K. Rice . . . . First there were only a handful of members, who joined, because the Hawaiian natives felt that the United States of America is such a powerful Government and they would not listen to the native Hawaiians, who claimed their kingdom was lost over 80 years ago.

The native Hawaiians were made aware of the Alaskan Native Claims Bill and that the Alaskan natives were successful in their claims. The membership and interest in the ALOHA Association began to increase and the native Hawaiians started to investigate the basis of the claim, which they found to be true. Today, the ALOHA Association has a membership of 30,000 . . . . The mission of ALOHA is to get legislation to justly and fairly compensate the Hawaiian natives for what the United States of America took from them.[38]

As a result of these efforts, a series of "reparations" bills[39] was introduced in congress. These bills were modeled after the Alaska Native Claims Settlement Act[40] and called for the creation of a Hawaiian Native corporation which would receive monetary reparations in the amount of one billion dollars from the federal government.[41] A Hawaiian Native roll would be established, with eligible members electing the corporation's board of directors.[42] The Hawaiian Native corporation would have, among other powers, the ability to adopt and amend by-laws for its governance and structure;[43] to acquire, hold, manage, and invest property and funds;[44] to engage in business for profit and pay dividends and make distributions of money and property to Hawaiians;[45] and, to finance and conduct programs in order to provide housing and education and promote the economic and social health and welfare of Hawaiians.[46] The Hawaiian Native corporation would be exempt for a 20-year period from all local, state, and federal taxation laws and laws regulating corporations.[47] The bill also gave the Hawaiian Native corporation the first option to receive, without cost, all federal lands in Hawai'i declared surplus to federal needs.[48]

During the hearings which were held to consider these bills, the complexity of the issues and related social concerns emerged. When it became clear that congress was not ready to address the Native Hawaiian claim by direct legislation, those who advocated the claim suggested other forums[49] including a model loosely based on the Indian Claims Commission (ICC) Act.[50] That act, passed in 1946, established a "judicial" commission which was given a specific grant of jurisdiction by congress to hear and determine claims of American Indian groups.[51] Native Hawaiians were not eligible to file claims under the ICC Act since only identifiable groups of Indians could make claims.[52] The act establishing the ICC allowed native groups to bring some types of claims which had not been previously allowed. For instance, claims based on "fair and honorable dealings [between the United States and the native group] not recognized by any existing rule or law or equity" and "claims arising from the taking by the United States, whether as the result of a treaty or cession or otherwise, of lands owned or occupied by the claimant without . . . payment for such lands" were allowed.[53] It seems likely that if Native Hawaiians had been able to present claims to the ICC for less than fair and honorable dealings or for the taking of their lands, they would have been successful. The ICC, however, could only award monetary damages -- return of land was not within its power.

Rather than attempting to enact a special jurisdictional statute for Native Hawaiian claims, the Hawai'i congressional delegation sought to establish a Hawaiian Native claims settlement study commission.[54] Senate Joint Resolution No. 4[55] would have created a commission to "conduct a study of the culture, needs, and concerns of the Hawaiian Natives; the nature of the wrong committed against and the extent of injuries to Hawaiian Natives by reason of the actions set forth in the preamble of this resolution; and various means to remedy such wrong."[56] The preamble of the resolution basically acknowledged the involvement of Minister Stevens and U.S. troops in the events of 1893. While a settlement study commission measure passed the senate, it died in the house of representatives. Evidently, congress was unwilling to allow an impartial body to give full consideration to the Native Hawaiian claim.

These early attempts to obtain federal reparations were unsuccessful. In retrospect, it was perhaps to the benefit of Native Hawaiians that their claims were not resolved by congress at that time. Many Native Hawaiians now believe that mere monetary settlement is insufficient, especially in light of the strong sovereignty claims currently being advanced. One positive result of these early reparations efforts, however, was to bring attention to Native Hawaiian claims on a national and state level and to encourage a more searching inquiry into the events of 1893.

b. The Native Hawaiians Study Commission

In 1980, the initial efforts to establish a commission to study the Native Hawaiian claims appeared to come to fruition. Congress created the Native Hawaiians Study Commission (NHSC) to study the "culture, needs and concerns of Native Hawaiians."[57] The act appeared to be a weakened version of earlier proposals -- there was no specific mention of the events of 1893, of the "wrong" committed, or of a remedy for the wrong.

The NHSC act called for the president to appoint a nine-member commission, three of whom were to be Hawai'i residents.[58] Nine members were appointed by President Carter during the last week of his administration. These commissioners were dismissed when President Reagan took office. It was not until eight months later that new commissioners were appointed. The three commissioners from Hawai'i were distinguished members of the Hawaiian community, while five of the six non-Hawaiian members were mid-level U.S. government officials.[59]

Although the NHSC act did not specifically so state, it is clear from the legislative history of earlier proposals for a settlement commission, that the NHSC's primary mission was to make an inquiry into the extent of U.S. involvement in the 1893 overthrow of the Hawaiian monarchy and the validity of Native Hawaiian claims resulting from those actions. The commission held eight public hearings in Hawai'i, and heard testimony and received written statements from hundreds of individuals during dozens of hours of hearings.[60] The NHSC's draft report was issued in September of 1982, and a five-month comment period was allowed.[61] Almost 100 written comments on the draft report were received, many of them quite critical of the draft report's findings on the Native Hawaiian claim.[62] Finally, in March of 1983, the NHSC met in Washington, D.C. to finalize its report.[63]

At the conclusion of the commission's meeting, the nine members found themselves irreconcilably divided on fundamental issues involving the overthrow of the Hawaiian government. The three Hawaiian commissioners filed a separate report[64] disputing the majority's finding that the United States government was blameless in connection with the overthrow of the Hawaiian monarchy.[65] Moreover, the majority concluded that there was no basis for federal action to redress the claims of Native Hawaiians stemming from the events of 1893.[66]

Significantly, the majority report acknowledged the involvement of U.S. Minister Stevens and American troops in the events leading to the overthrow of the Hawaiian monarchy.[67] In spite of this finding, it determined that the actions of U.S. agents and military personnel were not based on "express authority from the United States Government."[68] Thus, the majority concluded, no reparations were owed to the Native Hawaiian people.

In subsequent hearings before the Senate Committee on Energy and Natural Resources, the findings of the majority were soundly repudiated. Numerous legal scholars and historians questioned the methodology and motives of the majority.[69] As one analysis pointed out, "[a]s a general rule of international law, a government is responsible for the illegal acts of its agents ... regardless of whether such acts were authorized by the government or not."[70] In a 1988 hearing on Hawaiian claims before the Senate Select Committee on Indian Affairs, Office of Hawaiian Affairs Chair Moses Keale, Sr., summarized the applicable law:

> The issue is not one of express authority to act, as the majority report attempts to frame it, but whether the apparent and inherent authority of the United States possessed by its agent (Stevens) was rightfully or wrongfully exercised. Under international and domestic law, the *United States is responsible for the actions of its agents when they act within areas where they appear to others to have authority even if the U.S. government did not specifically authorize those acts.*

The agent-principal relationship is essential to government. It is necessary that governmental authority be delegated to agents who will act on the government's behalf .... Such agency authority was particularly essential to the functioning of diplomacy in the 19th century. United States agents overseas were so physically isolated from their superiors that their ability to represent U.S. interests would have been hopelessly paralyzed by a requirement that each of their actions be subjected to prior review and express approval.

A nation bears general liability for the unauthorized actions of its administrative agents and military forces which "fall within the normal scope of their duties" or are "committed in the exercise of their official functions."

. . . .

If we apply this principle to the actions of Minister Stevens in 1893, it is clear that the United States is liable for the harm suffered by native Hawaiians. The United States had the capacity to select its agents carefully and the opportunity to train them about the proper use of U.S. authority. If a government sends agents to an island kingdom over 5,000 miles away from the government's capital, the government must expect the agents to exercise discretion when using their power. A government must therefore anticipate the types of actions that are appropriate and instruct the agent with some care. If the government fails to instruct its agents, and the agents use their power to harm the citizens of the Kingdom, the government that sent the agents with their military power must logically bear responsibility for the agents' action.[71] (Emphasis added.)

Unfortunately, the report of the majority commissioners now stands as an additional obstacle to congressional action on the Native Hawaiian claim. The NHSC, however, did serve a useful purpose. The resulting report provided needed statistical and background information on education, health, and social welfare needs of Native Hawaiians. More importantly, the process revealed that Native Hawaiians had turned their focus from a mere monetary settlement of their claims and instead were seeking restoration of their land and their self-governing powers.[72]

4. THE LIMITED SOVEREIGNTY AND FEDERAL RECOGNITION OF NATIVE AMERICAN GOVERNMENTS

Precedents set by other Native Americans have served as a model for restructuring the relationship of Native Hawaiians with the federal government. In recent years, Native American governments have made tremendous progress in reasserting their sovereignty within their territorial boundaries. As the following section discusses, however, Native American sovereignty is limited by federal power. Moreover, Native Hawaiians can probably only gain federal recognition for their self-governing rights through direct congressional legislation. Administrative or judicial recognition appear to be foreclosed to Native Hawaiians.

a.   *The Limited Sovereignty of Native American Governments*
In federal Indian law, the sovereignty of native groups is assumed to be inherent, subject only to the power of congress:

Perhaps the most basic principle of Indian law, supported by a host of decisions . . . is the principle that *those powers which are lawfully vested in an Indian tribe are not, in general, delegated powers granted by express acts of Congress but rather inherent powers of a limited sovereignty which has never been extinguished.* Each Indian tribe begins its relationship with the

> Federal Government as a sovereign power, recognized as such in treaty and legislation. The powers of sovereignty have been limited from time to time by special treaties and laws . . . . These statutes of Congress, then, must be examined to determine the limitations of tribal sovereignty rather than to determine its sources or its positive content. What is not expressly limited remains within the domain of tribal sovereignty.[73] (Emphasis added.)

Unfortunately, the sovereignty of Indian nations has been limited by congress at various times in American history. For instance, in the 1950s, congress adopted a termination policy in an attempt to end tribal sovereign status and absorb Indians into mainstream America.[74] While that policy has since been repudiated,[75] it stands as an example of the near "plenary power" congress exercises in its dealings with Native Americans.

In recent years the United States Supreme Court has stated that tribal governments are "unique aggregations possessing attributes of sovereignty over both their members and their territory."[76] Under certain circumstances this power may even extend over non-members or extend beyond territorial limits, the determinative issue being whether the matter falls within "the ambit of internal self-government."[77] Most external attributes of sovereignty -- such as the ability to enter into treaties with other nations -- have been implicitly lost because of the tribes' incorporation into the federal system.

The right of Indian nations to self-governance was first articulated by Chief Justice Marshall in *Worcester v. Georgia* (1832),[78] when the state of Georgia sought to impose state law within the territory of the Cherokee Nation. Marshall acknowledged that the "Indian nations [are] distinct political communities, having territorial boundaries, within which their authority is exclusive . . . ."[79] Marshall further elaborated on the status of the Indian nations:

> [They have] always been considered as distinct, independent, political communities, retaining their original natural rights, as possessors of the soil, from time immemorial, with the single exception of that imposed by irresistible power, which excluded them from intercourse with any other European potentate than the first discoverer of the coast of the particular region claimed . . . .[80]

Marshall then went on to hold that congress' authority to regulate commerce with the Indians, in conjunction with the treaty-making power, was the basis for federal regulation of Indian affairs.[81] The *Worcester* case established the principle that the sovereignty of Indian nations is limited only by federal authority. Marshall further found that because of the nature of the federal-Indian relationship, the United States had assumed a protectorate over Indian nations. This protectorate does not extinguish Indian sovereignty, but preserves it and insulates it from state interference.

Consequently, native governments today exercise certain fundamental and inherent powers of self-governance. These include the power to establish a form of government, determine membership, exercise police powers, administer justice, and maintain immunity from suit.[82]

Indian nations may adopt the form of government best suited to their own cultural, religious, or practical needs.[83] Moreover, Indian governments are not limited by the federal constitution and are not subject to the same constraints as the federal or state governments. Native governments need not have republican forms of government and are not bound by the one-person, one-vote principle. There is no requirement that the branches of government be separated or even that religious and government action be independent.[84] Thus, native governments can make decisions through religious leaders, traditional hereditary leaders, or by consensus.

Indian governments also have the power to determine their own membership. The ability to define membership is crucial to self-governance. As the United States Supreme Court noted in *Santa Clara Pueblo v. Martinez* (1978),[85] a "tribe's right to define its own membership for tribal purposes has long been recognized as central to its existence as an independent political community."[86] This case involved an Indian mother who challenged a tribal ordinance denying tribal membership to children of Santa Clara women who married outside the tribe. The same law permitted children of Santa Clara men who married outside the tribe to be members, thus giving males a benefit denied to women. Plaintiff Martinez claimed that she and her daughter had been denied equal protection and due process by the tribal ordinance, in violation of the 1968 Indian Civil Rights Act (ICRA).[87] The ICRA restricts tribal governments by extending many protections of the U.S. Bill of Rights to tribal members. In this instance, the United States Supreme Court found that it lacked jurisdiction to review tribal enrollment disputes, in spite of the argument that the tribe's ordinance amounted to sexual discrimination. The court held that tribal institutions must first address membership disputes, and that any federal court review could only come much later, if at all. In so doing, the court emphasized the "extraordinarily broad" powers of congress over Indian matters, and stated that in the absence of express laws allowing judicial intrusion, the court could not interfere in relations between a tribe and its members.[88]

Indian nations also have the authority to enact substantive civil and criminal laws on internal matters. Such power is considered inherent since it is necessary for the maintenance of an ordered and peaceful society. Legislative authority includes the power to regulate the conduct of individuals within the tribe's jurisdiction, to determine domestic rights and relations, to dispose of non-trust property and to establish rules for inheritance, to regulate commercial and business relations, to levy taxes, to zone trust lands, and to administer justice.[89] A tribe's ability to regulate trust lands and resources is essential in order to maintain any degree of sovereignty, especially where it is necessary to protect tribal interests.

The maintenance of law and order is also an inherent attribute of sovereignty. Included in this right is the power to establish criminal laws, form a police force, establish courts and jails, and to prosecute and punish tribal members who violate tribal law.[90] While congress has specifically legislated to take many offenses out of the jurisdiction of native governments,[91] and tribal criminal jurisdiction does not extend over non-Indians, the tribes do possess broad authority to administer justice within their territories and may fashion a system which best reflects their practical and cultural needs. Court systems vary, but many tribes appear to follow common state and federal court systems. Some tribes, however, such as the New Mexico Pueblos, rely heavily on customary procedure, and may operate quite informally, using traditional methods of dispute resolution.[92]

Establishing the limits of federal and state authority in areas involving native peoples and native governments is the most serious issue currently facing Native Americans. Congress' "plenary power" in Indian affairs is broad, but limited by procedural and constitutional restraints. Executive action is also constrained by the trust doctrine. Nevertheless, in recent years, there have been serious incursions into the internal sovereignty of the tribes.

A recent decision by the United States Supreme Court, *Brendale v. Confederated Tribes and Bands of the Yakima Indian Nation* (1989),[93] reflects the tension between state and tribal government authority. It also appears to limit the inherent sovereignty of native governments. The narrow issue presented in that case was whether the Yakima Nation could zone both the "open" and "closed" areas of the Yakima reservation in Washington state. The state and county asserted authority to zone by granting petitioners Brendale and Wilkinson the right to develop their properties, despite the fact that tribal zoning laws prohibited such development. Both petitioners' properties were located within the reservation boundaries. However, Wilkinson's property was located in an "open" area of the reservation, while Brendale's lot was located in a "closed" area. Ninety-seven percent of the "closed" area was Indian trust land while the remaining three percent was held by non-Indians and Indians in fee. Nearly 50 percent of the "open" area of the reservation was held in fee, either by Indians or non-Indians. The supreme court upheld the county's zoning authority for the fee lots in the "open" area of the reservation, but denied the state authority to zone fee lots in the "closed" area.

The *Brendale* decision has serious ramifications for tribal government powers within Indian reservations that go far beyond zoning authority. Even though the fee lands in the "open" area of the reservation had passed out of trust status, the tribe argued that, in order to maintain its internal self-governance, it should have the authority to zone lands within the confines of its territory. The court held that the tribe's inherent sovereignty did not include the power to zone fee lands within the reservation because tribal sovereignty beyond that necessary to protect tribal self-government or to control internal relations is inconsistent with the tribe's dependent status, and cannot survive without express congressional delegation.[94] The court utilized a test which appears extremely difficult for tribes to meet -- in order for a tribe to regulate the conduct of non-Indians, the tribe must show a "demonstrably serious impact" which "imperils tribal political integrity, economic security, or health and welfare."[95] Today, there are over 400 federally recognized native entities in the United States.[96] No two are exactly alike. However, the typical example of a federal-tribal relationship is one where the tribe is recognized by the federal government, and is thus eligible for protectorate status. The state in which the tribe resides is precluded from interfering in tribal affairs without express congressional consent. The thread common to all of these native entities is the right to internal self-governance. Thus, as one authority notes:

> Far and away the greatest achievement [for Native governments] . . . has been the attainment of political power. The overriding point of constitutional law and political science made by the United States Supreme Court in modern times is that there are three -- not two, as we all were taught from grade school on -- there are three sovereigns in our federal constitution system: the federal government, the states, and Native governments.[97]

b. *Seeking Federal Recognition*

Despite the drawbacks in the limited sovereignty of Native American governments, many native groups, including Native Hawaiians, have sought similar status. Federal recognition may be obtained administratively through the executive branch of the federal government or legislatively through congress. While federal courts give deference to congress and the executive in making determinations of tribal or native entity status, courts are sometimes called upon to interpret congressional and executive action regarding tribal recognition.

(1)   *The Administrative Process*   In October 1978, the Department of Interior put into effect federal recognition regulations.[98]   These regulations, found at 25 Code of Federal Regulations (CFR), part 83, set forth the criteria by which a Native American group can establish its existence as a tribe and the procedure to obtain federal acknowledgment. Once recognized as a tribe, the group is eligible for the full range of services available to federally recognized Native American groups.   As one authority has pointed out, "the regulations can be reduced to four essential requirements: (1) a common identification ancestrally and racially as a group of Native Americans; (2) the maintenance of a community distinct from other populations in the area; (3) the continued historical maintenance of tribal political influence or other governmental authority over members of the group; and (4) the status of not being part of a presently recognized tribe."[99]   Once a group meets this criteria and is determined to be a native entity, it is "entitled to the privileges and immunities available to other federally recognized tribes by virtue of their status as Indian tribes with a government-to-government relationship to the United States as well as having the responsibilities and obligations of such tribes."[100]   Acknowledgment subjects native groups to the same authority of congress and the United States to which other federally acknowledged native entities are subject.   Acknowledgment does not create immediate entitlement to existing Bureau of Indian Affairs' (BIA) programs.   Those programs become available upon appropriation of funds by congress.

The federal recognition regulations exclude aboriginal people outside the continental United States.   The regulations are intended to cover "only those American Indian groups indigenous to the continental United States which are ethnically and culturally identifiable, but which are not currently acknowledged as Indian tribes."[101]   On this basis alone, Native Hawaiians would be precluded from applying for federal recognition through the acknowledgment process.   Moreover, many Native Hawaiians strongly object to coming under the jurisdiction of the BIA.   Finally, the recognition process requires extensive resources, is cumbersome and lengthy, and has resulted in limited success for other native groups.   Since 1978, the Interior Department has received approximately 123 petitions for federal recognition; eight of those petitions have been approved, 12 have been denied, and 12 have been resolved outside of the acknowledgment process.[102]

(2)   *Judicial Attempts*   In *Price v. State of Hawaii* (1985),[103] the Hou Hawaiians, claiming to be a Native Hawaiian tribal body, brought suit alleging that the State of Hawai'i had breached its trust obligations by failing to expend funds received from the public lands trust for the betterment of the conditions of Native Hawaiians, as required by the Hawai'i Admission Act.   The Hou filed suit under 28 U.S.C. section 1362, an act giving federal district courts jurisdiction of suits arising under federal law brought by any "Indian tribe or band with a governing body duly recognized by the Secretary of the Interior."[104]   The Ninth Circuit Court of Appeals examined whether the Hou fell within the definition set forth in the statute and determined that neither the Hou nor its governing body were "duly recognized by the Secretary."   The court noted that "[n]o statute explicitly details the procedure by which a tribe may become 'duly recognized by the Secretary' for purposes of establishing § 1362 jurisdiction."[105]   The court stated that "[a]lthough native Hawaiians *in general* may be able to assert a longstanding aboriginal history, the issue before us is

whether the particular subgroup seeking recognition -- the Hou Hawaiians -- can establish that they are a longstanding aboriginal sovereign rather than a recently formed association."[106] The court determined that under both the BIA's current regulations and the BIA's pre-regulation standard for recognizing a tribe, the Hou failed to demonstrate eligibility for recognition. The court found that the Hou did not fulfill the requirements of 25 CFR 83 in that it lacked historical continuity, longstanding tribal political authority, and was not representative of a substantial portion of the Native Hawaiian community inhabiting a specific area or living in a distinct community.[107] Neither had the Hou met the non-statutory standards that the BIA used to establish tribal status prior to the 1978 regulations. The Hou had no treaty relations with the United States, had not been denominated as a tribe by congress or the executive, had not been treated as a tribe by other Indian nations, and had not demonstrated that it exercised political authority over its members.[108]

5.   THE OFFICE OF HAWAIIAN AFFAIRS

While self-governance and self-determination efforts have been focused primarily on the relationship with the federal government, Native Hawaiians have achieved a measure of self-governance and autonomy on the state level. In 1978, the Office of Hawaiian Affairs (OHA) was established by amendments to the Hawai'i State Constitution.[109]

Native Hawaiian participants in the 1978 Constitutional Convention saw the convention as an opportunity to further the goal of self-determination. Their vision was to establish a governing entity, as well as to reaffirm the state's obligation with regard to the ceded lands trust. The delegates contemplated that OHA would be an independent entity, as reflected in the committee report of the Hawaiian Affairs Committee:

> The committee intends that the Office of Hawaiian affairs will be independent from the executive branch and all other branches of government although it will assume the status of a state agency . . . . The status of the Office of Hawaiian Affairs is to be unique and special. The establishment by the Constitution of [OHA] with power to govern itself through a board of trustees . . . results in the creation of a separate entity independent of the executive branch of the government.[110]

The Constitutional Convention delegates also examined the rights of other Native Americans and found that they "traditionally enjoyed self-determination and self-government," retained power to make their own substantive laws on internal matters, and were a "separate people with the power of regulation over their internal and social problems[,]" although no longer possessed of all attributes of sovereignty.[111] By establishing OHA, the Constitutional Convention delegates intended to further the cause of Hawaiian self-government and grant similar rights to Native Hawaiians.

Another interesting aspect of the Hawaiian Affairs Committee report is its express statement that the OHA amendments were intended to be sufficiently broad enough to include the administration and management of the Hawaiian Home Lands. The Hawaiian Affairs Committee envisioned that one day, the ceded lands and Hawaiian Home Lands trusts would be combined and the elected OHA board of trustees would assume the trust responsibilities of the Hawaiian Homes Commission.[112]

After the 1978 amendments were adopted, the legislature was charged with implementing the amendments. The legislature, however, declined to follow the express language of the Constitutional Convention committee reports. For instance, the Senate Judiciary Committee stated:

> In dealing with all bills addressed to implementation of Constitutional amendments, we have considered only the text to have been ratified by the voters and therefore entitled to consideration as mandatory. Conversely, matters in the committee reports were considered entitled to serious consideration, but were nonetheless only advisory.[113]

Consequently, even though the Constitutional Convention delegates had stated in their committee reports the rationale for OHA's independent status, the legislature ignored those statements and determined that "the voters did not intend to give the board of trustees . . . exclusive jurisdiction over its internal organization and management."[114] The legislature also chose to ignore the Hawaiian Affairs Committee recommendation of eventual transfer of the administration of the Hawaiian Home Lands to OHA. Instead, the OHA legislation specifically *excludes* administration of the Hawaiian Homes Commission Act from OHA's jurisdiction.[115]

Nonetheless, the main elements of the OHA amendments were implemented by the legislature. Hawai'i Revised Statutes (Haw. Rev. Stat.) chapter 10 sets out the powers and duties of the office. Haw. Rev. Stat. section 10-4 establishes OHA as a body corporate "which shall be a separate entity independent of the executive branch." OHA has the power to acquire, hold, and manage property, enter into contracts and leases, sue and be sued, manage and invest funds, and formulate public policy relating to Hawaiian affairs.[116] In comparison to other state agencies, OHA is a unique entity. It is established in the state constitution and is independent from all other branches of state government.

The electoral process for choosing the board of trustees ensures OHA's independence. The trustees, who must be of Hawaiian ancestry, form a nine-member board with one member residing on each of the islands of Kaua'i, O'ahu, Moloka'i, Maui, and Hawai'i. The remaining four trustees may reside on any of the islands and are designated as "at-large" trustees. From their membership, the trustees elect a chair and vice-chair. Trustees are elected for four-year staggered terms. Some 63,432 people are currently registered as OHA voters, while more than 50,000 votes have actually been cast in each election.[117]

Under the state constitution, OHA was established to serve both Native Hawaiians (those with 50 percent or more Hawaiian blood) and Hawaiians (those with any amount of Hawaiian blood).[118] However, OHA presently receives ceded land trust revenues which are restricted to benefit only Native Hawaiians. The state constitution does not establish a source of funding for Hawaiians. Consequently, while OHA's independence from other branches of government is clear, its dealings with the legislature can be problematic since the state legislature has been the primary source of funding for Hawaiians. OHA has been burdened by a legislative process that mandates the submission of expenditures of general and public funds to the legislature, thereby limiting OHA's financial independence.[119]

Although imperfect, the creation of the Office of Hawaiian Affairs is a step toward self-governance. Indeed, in analyzing how Native Hawaiians could obtain a status similar to other Native Americans, a staff attorney with the U.S. Senate Select Committee on Indian Affairs commented that "it appears that the logical starting point for such a change might rest with the Hawaiian Homes Commission and the Office of Hawaiian Affairs (OHA). Both entities are institutions that are responsible for certain benefits and protections to native Hawaiians. Their origins are in Federal law."[120] The analysis went on to note that while the Hawaiian Homes Commission has administrative authority over a land base (the Hawaiian Home Lands), its powers are limited:

> On the other hand, the Office of Hawaiian Affairs (OHA), *would appear to be an appropriate vehicle for changing the status of native Hawaiians* to allow for participation in policies and programs that affect them. Again, it would appear that a statutory change in its structure is necessary to effectuate such a change. Under current law, native Hawaiians have limited powers in the administration of this office.
>
> In examining the role of native Hawaiians in the Hawaiian Homes Commission and the Office of Hawaiian Affairs, it is apparent that native Hawaiians do exercise a limited form of self-government. Furthermore, it is apparent that such limited power can be traced directly to their membership in the Hawaiian monarchy, which exerted political control and authority over its members. It can be argued that native Hawaiians are political "successors in interest" to what was their aboriginal sovereign powers.[121] (Emphasis added.)

6. RECENT INITIATIVES FROM THE NATIVE HAWAIIAN COMMUNITY

While Native Hawaiians have not had their self-governing status recognized by congress, the executive, or the courts, they retain their inherent right to self-determination and self-governance. The most fundamental element of sovereignty is the right to establish and choose a form of government. Native Hawaiians have already made significant steps in exercising that right.

a. *The Hawaiian Sovereignty Movement*

In the last two decades, numerous native groups have organized around self-governance issues. These organizations represent a broad spectrum of ideas, structures, and governing styles. Notable among these groups is Nā 'Ohana O Hawai'i, with its focus on the extended 'ohana as a basis for organization and leadership and its efforts to bring the Native Hawaiian claim to international judicial forums. The Hou Hawaiians have actively asserted status as a tribal government in litigation in the federal courts.[122] Self-governance on lands set aside under the Hawaiian Homes Commission Act has also served as a focal point for Hawaiian homesteaders.[123] The recent formation of the State Council of Hawaiian Homesteaders, representing 27,000 Native Hawaiians of 50 percent or more Hawaiian blood, has facilitated the discussion of self-governance. Another recent development is the formation of Ka Pākaukau, a coalition of groups and individuals supporting Native Hawaiian sovereignty. Ka Pākaukau provides a forum for different ideas and strategies for achieving self-determination and self-governance. The Pro-Hawaiian Sovereignty Working Group also plays an important function by publishing a bi-monthly newsletter, *Ka Mana O Ka 'Aina*, containing articles on sovereignty and its interaction with issues such as reparations, ceded lands, and the Hawaiian Home Lands. The increased activity and the multiplicity of views among native sovereignty groups is a healthy sign of greater interest in and awareness of the question.

While there is great diversity in the Hawaiian sovereignty movement, there are some points of agreement. A five-plank resolution regarding self-governance was adopted at an August 1988 Native Hawaiian Rights Conference attended by many supporting self-determination and self-governance. The resolution called for:

(1)   An apology by the United States government to Native Hawaiians and their government for the United States' role in the coup of 1893.

(2)   A substantial land and natural resource base comprised of a reformed Hawaiian Homes program, a fair share of the ceded lands trust, the return of Kaho'olawe and other appropriate lands.

(3)   Recognition of a Native Hawaiian government with sovereign authority over the territory within the land base.

(4)   Recognition and protection of the subsistence and commercial hunting, fishing, gathering (including beach access), cultural and religious rights of Native Hawaiians, and the legitimate exercise of sovereign powers over such rights.

(5)   An appropriate cash payment.[124]

Significantly, in subsequent oversight hearings before the Senate Select Committee on Indian Affairs, almost all speakers referred to the five-plank resolution with approval.[125]

A Native Hawaiian Sovereignty Conference held in December of 1988[126] produced an even stronger statement on sovereignty. The conferees agreed that sovereignty is a *birthright* for all ethnic Hawaiians, entitling them to self-government and control of their land and lifestyle. Morever, participants agreed that a Hawaiian nation could be independent from state and federal jurisdiction and gain the recognition of other nations. While no single form of government was endorsed by the conferees, they acknowledged that options could range from a democracy, to a federation, to limited sovereignty similar to that exercised by other Native Americans. The participants also concluded that the nation's territory should include all ceded lands, Hawaiian Home Lands, and the marine and mineral resources of the Hawaiian archipelago.

b.   *The OHA Draft Blueprint for Native Hawaiian Entitlements*

In September 1989, the Office of Hawaiian Affairs' committee on Status and Entitlements released a document entitled the Draft Blueprint for Native Hawaiian Entitlements,[127] which incorporates many of the principles articulated in the five-plank resolution.[128] The draft blueprint was intended to be a "discussion paper for Native Hawaiians" and presents a comprehensive plan for seeking return of native lands and acknowledgment of self-governing rights. The draft blueprint affirms that Native Hawaiians have a right to self-determination and self-governance pursuant to their culture, traditions, and current goals.[129] In the document, OHA suggests a process for developing a self-governing entity.[130] A gathering of Native Hawaiian representatives, elected by Native Hawaiians from single-member districts, would draft a governing document. The gathering would then recess for three months to hold hearings on the draft governing document. Upon reconvening, amendments would be made to the document. Once approved by the representatives, the governing document would be voted upon by Native Hawaiians. The document must be ratified by a majority of those Native Hawaiians voting at the ratification election. If the document fails to receive a majority vote, another gathering would be called to draft another governing document. This process would continue until a governing document receives a majority vote.

The draft blueprint suggests that the Native Hawaiian self-governing entity have the following powers:

the power to adopt ordinances for the health, safety, and welfare of Native Hawaiians; the power to levy taxes, zone trust lands, produce income from such lands, and regulate conduct on trust lands; the power to receive and manage any lands, resources or funds; the power to allot lands to individuals; and the power to regulate hunting, fishing, gathering, access and other traditional rights and practices of Native Hawaiians.[131]

In addition, the draft blueprint contemplates that OHA itself could be named as the self-governing entity or that a separate sovereign entity could be created in the governing document.[132] In any event, the sovereign entity would be given federal status by congress and would hold all funds and lands returned by the federal government.[133] Moreover, the self-governing entity would not come under the jurisdiction of the Bureau of Indian Affairs.[134]

The OHA draft blueprint also includes provisions that call for a land base composed of returned Government and Crown lands from the state and federal governments, including Hawaiian Home Lands;[135] provides for monetary compensation for the past use of ceded lands;[136] and guarantees the protection of native rights.[137] The blueprint gives a single definition of Native Hawaiian as one with any degree of Hawaiian blood,[138] but also guarantees that the rights of Native Hawaiian beneficiaries under the Hawaiian Homes Commission Act who are currently on homesteads or on the waiting list cannot be diminished.[139]

In September and October of 1989, hearings were held throughout the islands on the draft blueprint. While many Native Hawaiians supported OHA's efforts and the basic principles of the draft blueprint, the primary criticism had to do with OHA's involvement in the creation of a self-governing entity. The question continually posed was whether a state agency, such as OHA, was the appropriate entity to be guiding or leading the sovereignty discussion. Moreover, could OHA itself be the self-governing entity when it is a part of the state government?

While there is little precedent, there appears to be no reason why OHA could not *evolve* into such an entity. It was founded as a result of Native Hawaiian efforts, even though it is now a part of state government. As OHA has stated:

> In 1978, grass roots Hawaiians seized the opportunity to use the Constitutional Convention as a mechanism to develop a native governmental structure. Many Hawaiians then went into the community to convince other Hawaiians, as well as the general populace, to support OHA and the OHA amendments to the Constitution. They were successful. At its heart, OHA is the result of a native initiative for self-governance.[140]

OHA's position is that given the appropriate federal legislation, as well as amendments to the state constitution, it would be possible for OHA to evolve into the self-governing entity. OHA recognizes that "[l]egislation would have to be drafted to separate OHA from the state and give it federal recognition. In that way, it would be protected from the vagaries of state politics and would be able to deal with the state and federal governments at arms length."[141]

c.   *Ka Lāhui Hawaiʻi*

Ka Lāhui Hawaiʻi is a native self-governance initiative with an enrollment estimated to be over 4,000. In 1987, individual Hawaiians determined that it was time for the native people themselves to assert self-governance and self-determination. As a result, they called a constitutional convention and adopted a governing structure. The Constitution of Ka Lāhui Hawai'i[142] lays the groundwork for a democratically elected nation of Hawai'i within the American federal and state system. Ka Lāhui Hawai'i endorses a government-to-government relationship with the federal and state governments, free from external controls.[143]

Any Native Hawaiian or Hawaiian can enroll as a citizen of Ka Lāhui.[144] Native Hawaiians must be of 50 percent or more Hawaiian blood. While all Hawaiians, regardless of blood quantum, are extended the full rights of citizenship, only Native Hawaiians have the right to determine legislation and/or benefits relating to the Native Hawaiian land trusts.[145] The constitution also allows for honorary citizenship, with no voting rights or privileges for those of non-Hawaiian blood.[146]

The Ka Lāhui Constitution provides for an elective executive, legislature, and judiciary.[147] In addition, the office of ali'i nui is established to represent and advise the nation on matters of protocol.[148] The ali'i nui appoints two councils to give advice on cultural and social traditions and protocol. The first council, the ali'i council is comprised of representatives of the chiefly lines from each island.[149] The second council, the advisory council, is composed of kūpuna, maka'āinana, and professional people.[150]

The Ka Lāhui National Legislature is a unicameral body with each island, except Kaho'olawe, having eight voting representatives.[151] As an interim measure, until the issue of residency on the island of Kaho'olawe is resolved, the island has eight non-voting representatives. These representatives are elected from the Kaho'olawe caucus, composed of citizens who have demonstrated three years' involvement with the island, have been members of Ka Lāhui for not less than one year, and actively participate in the caucus.[152]

In electing legislators, each island is divided into districts, with voters in each district electing district chairs, officers, and chairs for standing committees on health, education, and land/natural resources. For some of the islands, the district chairs are the representatives in the national legislature. On other islands, depending on the number of districts, the district chairs and other district officers serve in the national legislature. Finally, some islands elect at-large representatives in addition to district chairs to serve in the national legislature.[153] While this elective system appears complex, it was designed to increase representation and responsiveness at the district, grass-roots level. Recent amendments to the Ka Lāhui Constitution also create district councils and island caucuses. Half of each island's delegation must be of 50 percent or more Hawaiian blood; the remaining representatives are elected without respect to blood quantum.[154] A representative must be at least 21 years old and have resided in his or her district for two years.[155] While legislative power is vested in the legislature, the constitution provides for initiative, referendum, and recall.[156]

The executive power of Ka Lāhui is vested in the office of the kia'āina, or governor.[157] The kia'āina serves for four years, must be a Native Hawaiian, a citizen, and at least 30 years of age.[158] The kia'āina has the power to veto legislation, subject to a two-thirds override vote by the legislature.[159]

The present kia'āina of Ka Lāhui Hawai'i, Mililani B. Trask, believes that the federal policy endorsing greater self-determination for Native Americans and offering direct grants to aid and improve tribal development and self-government should be extended to Native Hawaiians. "[T]here is no reason for native Hawaiians to be the only native American group excluded [from these benefits]."[160] She notes that the prior federal policies of guardianship and wardship have been abandoned. "The new policy encourages tribal self-government and provides a basis to become economically self-sufficient. It is almost a godsend for the Hawaiian people who have been thrashing around since 1893 for a solution."[161]

The Ka Lāhui Constitution contains a bill of rights, providing for separation of church and government, and protecting many of the rights recognized in the United States Constitution.[162] The Ka Lāhui Constitution also protects customary and traditional rights exercised throughout the Hawaiian archipelago. These rights include *kuleana*, water, access, gathering, fishing, and burial rights.[163]

In a presentation at a 1988 conference on Native Hawaiian sovereignty, *Kiaʻāina* Trask defined sovereignty as "the ability of a people who share a common culture, religion, language, value system and land base, to exercise control over their lands and lives, independent of other nations."[164] *Kiaʻāina* Trask listed the following elements of sovereignty: a people with a shared history, language, and culture; spiritual guidance; a national economy; a mechanism for self-governance; and, a land base.[165] The land base Ka Lāhui seeks includes the Hawaiian Home Lands and half the Government and Crown lands, to be reserved for Native Hawaiians, and additional ceded and federal lands to be reserved for those of less than 50 percent Hawaiian blood.[166]

d. *Institute for the Advancement of Hawaiian Affairs*

In the international arena today, greater attention is being focused on self-determination as a fundamental human right. Native Hawaiian attorney, Pōkā Laenui (Hayden F. Burgess), advocates the use of international human rights principles in pursuing self-determination for the nation of Hawaiʻi. He points out that the citizens of the Hawaiian nation never had an opportunity to choose from the full spectrum of political options. Hawaiians did not have a choice as to the events of 1893. Many Hawaiian citizens refused to participate in the formation of the Republic of Hawaiʻi or were "legislated" out of their citizenship by restrictive voting laws. Native Hawaiians also actively opposed annexation to the United States. Finally, in 1959, when statehood was voted upon, any American citizen having made Hawaiʻi their residence for at least one year was eligible to vote. There was no independent vote by citizens of the Hawaiian nation. Moreover, as Pōkā Laenui points out:

> in 1959, Hawaiʻi's political choices did not address the full range of political status but were limited to remaining a territory or becoming a "state" of the United States. The lesser of the two evils was selected, but that selection did not constitute an act of self-determination for there was not the full range of choices including independence and freedom from American occupation.[167]

Pōkā Laenui proposes that Hawaiʻi reassert its international integrity as an independent nation in regional and international forums. Moreover, with regard to citizenship, he makes the forceful argument that when Hawaiʻi was invaded by the United States, Hawaiian citizenship was politically defined, not racially or culturally defined. While the vast majority of Hawaiian citizens were Native Hawaiians, citizenship was based on allegiance and loyalty to the place one considered his or her "homeland." Consequently, he suggests that in asserting self-determination, the "self" -- or collective group -- should not be solely the indigenous people of Hawaiʻi, but must include those who consider Hawaiʻi their homeland.[168] He states:

> We cannot build a Hawaiian Nation on racism. The Nation of Hawai'i in 1893 was composed of citizens of the indigenous Hawaiian race as well as of people of many other races and cultures: The crucial determination for citizenship was not race but relationship to Hawai'i -- "ka po'e aloha 'aina."[169]

He does acknowledge though, that "the protection and increase of the Po'e Hawai'i (the indigenous people of Hawai'i) must take special priority. The Hawaiian language should be the official language of the Nation and as quickly as possible become the everyday language of Hawai'i. The traditional economic system and collective land relationship should be respected . . . . The traditions and customs of the Po'e Hawai'i should have the force and effect of law for those citizens opting to live under that system."[170]

7.   SELF-DETERMINATION AS A HUMAN RIGHT

While international recognition of Native Hawaiian sovereign status may appear improbable, one of the current focal points in international human rights law is the right of self-determination for indigenous peoples. In the United States, critics of the traditional Indian-federal government relationship have called for a restructuring of that relationship based upon international human rights doctrines:

> Existing and developing sources of international human rights principles secure the right to self-determination for indigenous peoples generally, and for American Indian nations specifically. The recognition and enforcement of Indian people's right to self-determination under international law will empower them to determine freely both their political relationship with the United States and their own economic, social and cultural development.[171]

Native Hawaiians, as well as Indians and Alaskan Natives, could apply international human rights principles to their situation.

There are various United Nations' human rights instruments that speak directly to the issue of self-determination and sovereignty for native people. The United States, as a signatory to the United Nations Charter and various accords, has acknowledged the right to self-determination of indigenous people.

The U.N. Charter is among the most comprehensive of the human rights instruments. Article 1 calls for the development of "friendly relations among nations based on respect for the principle of equal rights and self-determination of peoples."[172] Article 55 also demonstrates a commitment to self-determination by stating that the United Nations shall promote, among other values, "universal respect for, and observance of, human rights and fundamental freedoms for all without distinction as to race, sex, language, or religion."[173] Articles 1 and 55 have been cited by American Indian nations to support their claims that the United States must recognize their right to self-determination.[174]

Article 73 of the U.N. Charter, addressing the rights of peoples in the non-self-governing territories, also supports Native Hawaiian self-determination rights:

> Members of the United Nations which have or assume responsibilities for the administration of territories whose peoples have not yet attained a full measure of self-government recognize the principle that the interests of the inhabitants are paramount, and accept as a sacred trust the obligation . . . to develop self-government, to take due account of the political aspirations of the peoples, and to assist them in the progressive development of

their free political institutions, according to the particular circumstances of each territory and its people and their varying stages of advancement.[175]

Article 73 has limitations, as noted by some Native American advocates, because it "indirectly legitimizes the negative aspects of the present 'trust' relationship between the United States and [native] people by implying that the subjugated peoples may not have reached a level of advancement enabling them to be fully self-governing."[176]

The most severe limitation of Article 73 is the so-called "blue water thesis." The "blue water thesis" asserts that Article 73 should be applied only to territories geographically separated from the dominant society by a sea or ocean (blue water).[177] The thesis was developed because of the "conflict between freedom of subjugated peoples and concern for the territorial integrity of a nation . . . . The blue water interpretation of article 73 . . . excludes most indigenous people from the rights outlined in the article, because they generally have been colonized within the borders of existing nations."[178] While the reasoning and validity of the "blue water thesis" is highly questionable, it does not affect Native Hawaiian claims. Native Hawaiians would not be excluded from the rights articulated in Article 73 by application of the "blue water" thesis since Hawai'i is separated from the dominant society by over 2,500 miles.

The meaning and interpretation of these articles of the U.N. Charter have been established by three declarations adopted by the U.N. general assembly. While the declarations are not legally binding, they interpret and define the obligations of U.N. member nations. The 1960 Declaration on Granting of Independence to Colonial Countries and Peoples states:

> The subjection of peoples to alien subjugation, domination, and exploitation constitutes a denial of fundamental human rights, is contrary to the Charter of the United Nations and is an impediment to the promotion of world peace and co-operation.
> All peoples have the right to self-determination; by virtue of that right they freely determine their political status and freely pursue their economic, social and cultural development.[179]

The 1965 Declaration on the Inadmissibility of Intervention in Domestic Affairs of States and Protection of Their Independence and Sovereignty reaffirms that "[a]ll States shall respect the right of self-determination and independence of peoples and nations, to be freely exercised without any foreign pressure, and with absolute respect for human rights and fundamental freedoms. Consequently, all States shall contribute to the complete elimination of racial discrimination and colonialism in all its forms and manifestations."[180] The 1970 Declaration on Principles of International Law Concerning Friendly Relations and Cooperation Among States provides, in part:

> all peoples have the right freely to determine, without external interference their political status and to pursue their economic, social and cultural development . . . .[181]

These U.N. declarations extend the scope of the right to self-determination, affirming it as a right of all peoples regardless of current political status or geographical territory.

The Universal Declaration of Human Rights, passed unanimously by the U.N. General Assembly in 1948, is the source of most post-World War II human rights documents. It provides that everyone has the right to a nationality, and that no one shall be arbitrarily deprived of that right.[182] The declaration goes on to state that: "The will of the people shall be the basis of the authority of government; this will shall be expressed in periodic and genuine elections which shall be held by universal and equal suffrage . . . ." Obviously, if the Universal Declaration had been in effect in 1893, or in 1898 at the time of annexation, the United States would have been in violation of the declaration. Native Hawaiians were never consulted or given an opportunity to vote on whether incorporation into the United States was desirable.[183]

Other important sources of human rights law are The International Covenant on Civil and Political Rights and the International Covenant on Economic, Social and Cultural Rights.[184] These instruments were approved by the U.N. General Assembly in 1966, and became legally binding in 1977. They are international treaties, binding the nations that ratify them. President Carter signed the covenants in 1977 but the United States Senate has yet to ratify them. The first article in each covenant indicates the fundamental importance of the right of self-determination in international law:

> All peoples have the right of self-determination. By virtue of that right they freely determine their political status and freely pursue their economic, social and cultural development.[185]

All of these United Nations' declarations on human rights support the self-determination of "peoples." However, the definition of peoples has been a problematic one in international law. On the one hand, some existing states fear that a broad definition would encourage secessionist movements, threatening their territorial integrity. On the other hand, indigenous people support the broadest possible definition, since limiting the definition would exclude many native groups.

The term "peoples" has been analyzed by various organizations and individuals. The International Court of Justice has employed the following definition:

> a group of persons living in a given country or locality, having a race, religion, language and traditions of their own and united by this identity of race, religion, language and traditions, in a sentiment of solidarity, with a view to preserving their traditions, maintaining their form of worship, insuring the instruction and upbringing of their children in accordance with the spirit and traditions of their race and rendering mutual assistance to each other.[186]

The International Commission of Jurists, a non-governmental organization with consultative status at the U.N., identifies a group as a people if it shares a common history; racial or ethnic ties; cultural or linguistic ties; religious or ideological ties; a common territory or geographical location; a common economic base; and a sufficient number of individuals.[187] Native Hawaiians presently meet these criteria, with the possible exception of a common economic base. Of course, Native Hawaiians did share a common economic base until the disruption of their economy by Western capitalism. Under either of the definitions, Native Hawaiians appear to constitute a "people" and thus would be entitled to the self-determinative rights established in human rights documents.

Another major development in the protection of indigenous peoples' rights took place in 1982 with the establishment of the U.N. Working Group on Indigenous Populations. The U.N. Working Group was created to provide a permanent forum for the protection of indigenous rights and to establish standards concerning the rights of indigenous peoples.[188]

These standards should include principles regarding self-determination for indigenous peoples.[189]

Self-determination is a fundamental human right extended to all peoples. It is recognized and affirmed in existing declarations of international law. As a member of the United Nations, the United States is bound to protect and advance the human rights articulated in the United Nations Charter. The United States is also a signatory to the Declaration of Human Rights and the Human Rights Covenants and thus has committed itself to the right of self-determination for all peoples. Given the original sovereignty exercised by Native Hawaiians and the loss of that sovereignty through direct action of U.S. agents, the United States, in keeping with human rights declarations, must restructure its political relationship with Native Hawaiians. Native Hawaiians should fully embrace the international human rights doctrines supporting their claim and continue to assert their self-determination rights as an indigenous people.

8. CONCLUSION

Native Hawaiians, like many native peoples around the world, seek greater self-determination. In concrete terms, this means the ability to choose a form of government, to have control of Native Hawaiian lands, natural resources, and assets, and to be able to make decisions that have real and lasting effects on their lives and environment.

At the present time, Native Hawaiians have the ability to exercise a greater degree of self-determination and self-governance, through the Office of Hawaiian Affairs, than they did 15 years ago. However, all Native Hawaiians recognize OHA's limitations -- it does not have the autonomy and independence necessary to be able to deal on a government-to-government level with either the state or federal governments. Nevertheless, OHA is an important first step in that direction. Many individual Hawaiians and Native Hawaiian organizations, including OHA and Ka Lāhui Hawai'i, believe that it is possible for Native Hawaiians to remain within the structure of the existing federal-state system and maintain a separate native government. A Native Hawaiian government, like other Native American nations, would be recognized as an independent sovereign exercising jurisdiction over its lands and natural resources. The precedents for such a government are clearly established and recognized under federal law. Finally, Native Hawaiians are now being made aware, through international human rights forums, of other political status options available to them.

In all of these arenas, whether state, national or international, it is clear that Native Hawaiian efforts to assert self-governing status will be the critical determining factor. As one source aptly states:

> History suggests that those who maintain and assert their self-government, their freedom from outside domination, and their own economic, social and cultural development are most likely to eventually gain international recognition as people who have the right to self-determination, regardless of formal rules.[190]

NOTES

1.   *See, e.g.,* R.H. Houghton III, *An Argument for Indian Status for Native Hawaiians -- The Discovery of a Lost Tribe,* 14 Am. Ind. L. Rev. 1 (1989).

2.   Some of the material in this section is taken directly from M.K. MacKenzie, *Land and Sovereignty: Honoring the Hawaiian Native Claim* (1982).

3.   C.H. Rhyne, *International Law* 77 (1971).

4.   C.C. Hyde, *International Law,* vol. I, 209-212 (1945).

5.   *Id.* at 212-218.

6.   Rhyne, *supra* note 3, at 78. *See also* discussion in part 7 of this chapter on human rights principles.

7.   C. Bevans, 3 *Treaties and Other International Agreements of the United States of America, 1776-1949,* 861 (1971); R. Stauffer, *The Hawaii-United States Treaty of 1826,* 17 Hawaiian Journal of History 40, 55-558 (1983). *See* Houghton III, *supra* note 1, at 14-19, for a comparison of the treaties negotiated between the United States and the Kingdom of Hawai'i with the treaties between the United States and Indian tribes, arguing that the claims of Native Hawaiians are very similar to those of Indian tribes.

8.   U.S. State Department, *Treaties and Conventions Concluded Between the United States of America and Other Powers Since July 4, 1776,* 274 (1886).

9.   H. Bradley, *Thomas Ap Catesby Jones and the Hawaiian Islands, 1826-1829,* 39 Hawaiian Historical Society Rep. 23 (1931).

10.   Bevans, *supra* note 7, at 681.

11.   Sen. Ex. Docs., 52nd Cong., 2d. Sess., No. 77, at 35-37. *See also* Letter from John C. Calhoun, Secretary of State, to Timoteo Haalilio and William Richards, Comm'rs. of the Hawaiian Gov't. (July 6, 1844).

12.   *Bevans, supra* note 7, at 864, 9 Stat. 977.

13.   *Id.*

14.   *Id.* at 874, 19 Stat. 625.

15.   *Id.* at 878, 25 Stat. 1399.

16.   I. Brownlie, *Principles of Public International Law* 595 (2d ed. 1973).

17.   President Cleveland appointed a special commissioner, James Blount, former chair of the House Committee on Foreign Affairs, to examine the Hawai'i situation. When Blount reached Honolulu, he found the American flag flying and American troops still ashore. He ordered the flag lowered and the troops returned to their ship. Blount, after interviewing dozens of people from different factions, concluded that Minister Stevens had helped to overthrow the Hawaiian monarchy. He also reported that American troops were landed, not to protect American lives and property, but to aid in overthrowing the existing government. J. Blount, *Report to United States Congress: Hawaiian Islands,* Exec. Doc. No. 47, 53rd Cong., 2d Sess., 13-24, 35-37, 59-62 (1893) [hereinafter *Blount Report*].

18.   Based on Blount's report, Secretary of State Gresham laid the blame for the "revolution" directly on Minister Stevens, and recommended that action be taken to restore the government of Hawai'i. *See* Osborne, *infra* note 32, at 50-60. President Cleveland condemned Steven's actions in the most forceful language:

    > This military demonstration upon the soil of Honolulu was of itself an act of war, unless made either with the consent of the Government of Hawaii or for the *bona fide* purpose of protecting the imperiled lives and property of citizens of the United States. But there is no pretense of any such consent on the part of the Government of the Queen, which at that time was undisputed and was both the *de facto* and the *de jure* Government. In point of fact the existing Government, instead of requesting the presence of an armed force, protested . . . .
    > Thus it appears that Hawaii was taken possession of by the United States forces without the consent or wish of the Government of the islands, or of anybody else so far as shown except the United States minister. Therefore the military occupation of Honolulu by the United States on the day mentioned was wholly without justification . . . .

    9 *Messages and Papers of the President* 31-32, Special Message of President Cleveland to Congress (December 18, 1893).

19.   *See, e.g.,* D.H. Getches, *Alternate Approaches to Land Claims: Alaska and Hawaii,* in *Irredeemable America: The Indians' Estate and Land Claims* 331 (1985), stating:

    > The overthrow of the Hawaiian government itself could well be the subject of claims . . . . Other Native Americans have not been compensated for loss of sovereignty or the right of self-determination. The Hawaiians' situation may merit a different treatment, however, because their government was one fully recognized as a member of the international community. Indian tribes were seen as having some, but not all, aspects of a sovereign.

20.   *See* discussion of 1887 Constitution in Chapter 1, *supra,* notes 69-72 and accompanying text.

21.   R. Kuykendall, *Hawaiian Kingdom 1874-1893,* 367 (1967) lists those involved with helping to draft the 1887 Constitution. Many of these same men were members of the Committee of Safety. *Id.* at 587.

22. Commissioner Blount reported to Secretary of State Gresham that "while in Honolulu he did not meet a single annexationist who expressed willingness to submit the question to a vote of the people, nor did he talk with one . . . who did not insist that if the Islands were annexed suffrage should be so restricted as to give complete control to foreigners or whites." Blount Report, *supra* note 17, xv, xxvi.

23. *See* discussion of the formation of the Republic of Hawai'i in Chapter 1, *supra*, text accompanying notes 89-94.

24. W.A. Russ, *The Hawaiian Republic (1894-1898)*, 26-34 (1961).

25. *Id.* at 46.

26. *See id.* at 34.

27. *Id.*

28. *Id.* at 49-104, particularly 82-94.

29. *See, e.g., id.* at 189, 209.

30. For the legislative history of the joint resolution, *see* Chapter 1, *supra*, at note 100.

31. Russ, *supra* note 24, at 328.

32. T. Osborne, *"Empire Can Wait"* 111-112 (1981).

33. J.H. Smith, *The Annexation of Texas* 323-333 (1911); Russ, *supra* note 24, at 325-330 for a discussion of the Texas annexation.

34. Russ, *supra* note 24, at 328.

35. Letter to the Forum by Paul D. Lemke, member of Ka Pākaukau, Garden Isle, March 21, 1990. *See also Ka Mana O Ka 'Āina*, Vol. II, No. 1 (May 1990) for a more extensive discussion.

36. Historically, "reparations" is the term applied to the compensation a *defeated* country must make for damages or injury to the enemy during war. Thus, another term, such as restitution, would probably be more appropriate in this situation. Nevertheless, reparations has been the term most often used in regard to settlement of the Native Hawaiian claim.

37. The ALOHA Association, the Aboriginal Lands of Hawaiian Ancestry, Inc., is generally acknowledged in the Hawaiian community as being the organization that first focused congressional attention on the Hawaiian claim. In the reparations bills proposed by the Hawai'i congressional delegation, the ALOHA Association would have been reimbursed for fair and reasonable unpaid obligations incurred in preparing, presenting, and advancing the claim and obtaining a settlement. *See, e.g.,* H.R. 1944 § 6(f)(14), § 8. Other groups active in the reparations movement included the Council of Hawaiian Organizations, the Congress of the Hawaiian People, the Hawaiians, the Friends of Kamehameha, and the Hawaiian Civic Clubs.

38. *Hawaiian Native Claims Settlement Act: Hearings on H.R. 1944 Before the Subcomm. on Indian Affairs of the House Comm. on Interior & Insular Affairs*, 94th Cong., 1st Sess. 28 (1975) (statement of C. Maxwell, President of ALOHA Assn.).

39. *See, e.g.,* H.R. 15666, 93rd Cong., 2d Sess. (introduced June 27, 1974); H.R. 1944, 94th Cong., 1st Sess. (introduced January 23, 1975).

40. 43 U.S.C. §§ 1601-1628, Pub. L. No. 92-203 (1971). *See generally* Comment, *The Alaska Native Claims Settlement Act: An Illusion in the Quest for Native Self-Determination*, 66 Or. L. Rev. 195 (1987) and T. Berger, *Village Journey* (1985).

41. H.R. 1944, *supra* note 39, at § 5.

42. *Id.* at §§ 6(b),(d), and (h).

43. *Id.* at § 6(f)(1).

44. *Id.* at § 6(f)(5).

45. *Id.* at § 6(f)(4).

46. *Id.* at §§ 6(f)(7), (8).

47. *Id.* at §§ 6(f)(11), (13).

48. *Id.* at § 7.

49. *See, e.g.,* R. Jones, *A History of the Alaska Native Claims Settlement Act of 1971, Together with a History of the Determination and Disposition of the Property Rights of Native Hawaiians* 30-32 (1973).

50. 25 U.S.C. § 70-70v (1970).

51. Prior to 1946, Indian claims were handled by special jurisdictional acts passed by congress allowing particular Indian tribes to sue the United States. In the period between 1926 and 1945, over 140 claims were litigated, but others were stalled in congressional committees awaiting jurisdictional acts. The process was slow and expensive, generally taking many years. For example, it took the Turtle Mountain Band of Chippewa Indians from 1892 until 1964 to get final action on their claim. Realizing the piecemeal effect of these jurisdictional grants, congress enacted a broad statutory grant of jurisdiction to hear tribal claims cases to the Indian Claims Commission for claims accruing prior to August 13, 1946 and to the Court of Claims for claims accruing after that date.

52. 25 U.S.C. § 70(a) (1970).

53. *Id.*

54. *See* S.J. Res. 155, 94th Cong., 2d Sess. (introduced December 18, 1975), and S.J. Res. 4, 95th Cong., 1st Sess. (introduced January 10, 1977).

55. An identical resolution was introduced in the House of Representatives, H.J.Res. 526, 95th Cong., 1st Sess. (introduced June 21, 1977).

56. S.J. Res. 4, *supra* note 54, at § 3(a).

57. Pub. L. No. 96-565, Title III, § 303(a) (December 22, 1980).

58. *Id.* at § 302(b).

59. The six non-Hawaiian members were Stephen Shipley, Executive Assistant to the Secretary of the Department of Interior; Carl A. Anderson, Counselor to the Under Secretary, Department of Health and Human Services; Carol E. Dinkins, Assistant Attorney General, Land and Natural Resources Division, Department of Justice; James C. Handley, Special Assistant to the Secretary of Agriculture; Diane K. Morales, Member of the Civil Aeronautics Board; and Glenn R. Schleede, President, North East Energy, Inc. The Hawai'i members were Kina'u Boyd Kamali'i, House Minority Leader of the Hawai'i Legislature; Winona K.D. Beamer, teacher at Kamehameha Schools; and H. Rodger Betts, Corporation Counsel for the County of Maui. Kina'u Boyd Kamali'i served as chair of the commission, while Stephen Shipley held the vice-chair position.

60. Native Hawaiians Study Commission, *Report on the Culture, Needs and Concerns of Native Hawaiians (Majority Report)* 4 (1983) [hereinafter *1 NHSC (Majority)*].

61. *See id.* at 4-6 for a synopsis of the methodology employed by the NHSC.

62. *See, e.g.,* Comments by Sen. Daniel K. Inouye on the Draft Report of Findings of the Native Hawaiians Study Commission (Nov. 23, 1982); letter to NHSC from Pauline N. King (Nov. 5, 1982); letter to NHSC by Alexander H. Raymond (Nov. 23, 1982), *id.,* at Appendix.

63. For one account of the final meeting of the NHSC, *see* M.K. MacKenzie, J. Van Dyke, *The Native Hawaiians Study Commission: A Bizarre Charade,* Honolulu Star Bulletin, April 21, 1983, at A-23:

> As we sat in the background during these two days of meetings, we had the strange sensation of seeming to see the whole 19th century of Hawaiian history pass before our eyes, in which the fast-talking and goal-oriented Westerners were succeeding in manipulating the Hawaiian [commissioners] through their efforts at imposing Western values on the situation.
> Like Queen Liliuokalani in 1893, the Hawaiian commissioners were unwilling to play the Western game and thus chose instead to withdraw from the battlefield, with at least their personal integrity intact, in hopes of prevailing in a subsequent forum.

64. Native Hawaiians Study Commission, *Report on the Culture, Needs and Concerns of Native Hawaiians (Minority Report)* v (1983).

65. *1 NHSC (Majority)*, *supra* note 60, at 28.

66. *Id.* at 26-28.

67. *Id.* at 28.

68. *Id.* at 25.

69. *See Hearings on the Report of the Native Hawaiians Study Commission Before the Senate Comm. on Energy and Natural Resources,* 98th Cong., 2nd Sess. (April 16, 1984) (statement of Dr. Pauline Nawahineokalai'i King at 34, statement of Jon Van Dyke, Professor of Law, University of Hawai'i at 133, statement of David H. Getches at 48).

70. *Id.* at 116 (statement of Cecelia Y. Chang).

71. *Oversight Hearings on Native Hawaiian Reparations Before the Senate Select Comm. on Indian Affairs,* Testimony of Moses Keale, Sr., Chair of the Board of Trustees OHA, at 6-8 (August 16, 1988). Unpublished.

72. *See, e.g., Towards Reparations/Restitution,* Adopted by the Trustees of the Office of Hawaiian Affairs (May 13, 1982) and submitted to the NHSC, in which restoring self-governance and a land base are cited as two of the principles for reparations and restitution.

73. F. Cohen, *Handbook of Federal Indian Law* 122 (1986 reprint of 1942 original).

74. *See* American Indian Lawyer Training Program, Inc., *Indian Tribes as Sovereign Governments* 10-14 (1988) [hereinafter AILTP]. In 1953, congress adopted House Concurrent Resolution 108 which called for ending the federal trust relationship with Indian tribes. Over 50 tribes were "terminated" under this policy although many have since been restored to federal status. *Id.* at 12-13.

75. *Id.* at 13. Congress has not explicitly repudiated the termination policy, but more recent legislation calling for Native American self-determination implicitly reverses the policy.

76. *United States v. Wheeler,* 435 U.S. 313 (1978).

77. Cohen, *supra* note 73, at 246.

78. 31 U.S. (6 Pet.) 515 (1832).

79. *Id.* at 557.

80. *Id.* at 559.

81. U.S. Const. art. I, § 8, cl. 3 (Indian commerce clause), art. II, § 2, cl. 2 (Treaty power).

82. AILTP, *supra* note 74, at 36-39.

83. *But see* the Indian Reorganization Act (IRA), 25 U.S.C. §§ 467-79 (1982), adopted by congress in 1934 to aid tribes in government organization. The IRA supported the adoption of either tribal constitutions or federally chartered corporations, and provided funds to the tribes for that purpose. Tribes had a choice of whether or not to proceed under the IRA, but many federal funds were specifically earmarked for IRA tribes. The constitutions adopted by these IRA tribes were based upon sample governing documents developed by the BIA and were subject to approval by the Secretary of the Interior. Consequently, almost 80 tribes chose not to adopt IRA constitutions. The IRA process has raised controversy amongst some tribes. For instance, traditional Hopi leaders and people dispute the authority of the IRA-developed Hopi Tribal Council since many Hopi refused to participate in the vote to establish an IRA government.

84. AILTP, *supra* note 74, at 36.

85. 436 U.S. 49 (1978).

86. *Id.* at 71, n.32.

87. The Indian Civil Rights Act is found at 25 U.S.C. §§ 1301-03 (1982).

88. 436 U.S. at 60.

89. AILTP, *supra* note 74, at 35.

90. S. Pevar, *The Rights of Indians and Tribes* 74 (1983).

91. *See, e.g.,* the Major Crimes Act, 18 U.S.C. § 1153 (1982) extending federal jurisdiction over certain classes of crimes such as murder, manslaughter, and rape, and Pub. L. No. 280, 18 U.S.C. § 1162 (1982) extending state jurisdiction for many offenses even between Indians on reservation.

92. Pevar, *supra* note 90, at 26.

93. ___ U.S. ___, 109 S.Ct. 2994 (1989).

94. *Id.*, 109 S.Ct. at 3005-3006 (citing *Montana v. United States*, 450 U.S. 544, 564 (1981)).

95. *Id.*, 109 S.Ct. at 3008.

96. *See* 50 Federal Register 52829-52835 (December 29, 1988) for a listing of Indian and Alaskan Native entities recognized and entitled to receive federal services.

97. C.F. Wilkinson, *The Idea of Sovereignty: Native Peoples, Their Lands, and Their Dreams*, speech given at Native Hawaiian Rights Conference (August 5, 1988), *reprinted in* 13 NARF Legal Rev. No. 4, 1 (Fall 1988).

98. 25 CFR Part 83.

99. AILTP, *supra* note 74, at 26.

100. 25 CFR § 83.11(a).

101. 25 CFR § 83.3.

102. The 12 petitions resolved outside of the acknowledgment process include five groups that were recognized by congress and seven groups who were determined ineligible to apply under the regulations. *Status of Federal Acknowledgement Petitions*, BIA Div. Law Enf. Serv. 1-2 (Sept. 24, 1990), provided by Steve Heely, staff of Senate Select Comm. on Indian Affairs.

103. 764 F.2d 623 (9th Cir. 1985), *cert. denied sub nom. Hou Hawaiians v. Hawaii*, 404 U.S. 1055 (1986).

104. *Id.* at 626.

105. *Id.*

106. *Id.* at 627.

107. *Id.* at 627.

108. *Id.* at 628.

109. *See,* Haw. Const., art. XII, §§ 4, 5, 6.

110. Hawaiian Affairs Comm. Rep. No. 59, 1 *Proceedings of the Constitutional Convention of Hawaii of 1978*, 645.

111. Comm. of the Whole Rep. No. 13, in *id.* at 1019.

112. Hawaiian Affairs Comm. Rep. No. 59, *supra* note 110, at 645.

113. Senate Judiciary Comm. Rep. No. 784, *1979 Senate Journal* 1352.

114. *Id.*

115. *See* Haw. Rev. Stat. § 10-3(3) (1985).

116. *See* Haw. Rev. Stat. §§ 10-4, 10-5, 10-6 (1985) for the powers and duties of OHA and its board of trustees.

117. *See Special Report: OHA at a Crossroads*, Honolulu Star Bulletin, June 18, 1990, at A-6.

118. Haw. Const., art. XII, § 6; Haw. Rev. Stat. § 10-3 (1985).

119. *See* chapter 2, *supra*, for details of the OHA funding mechanism and the current settlement of funding disputes relating to the ceded lands trust.

120. Memorandum from Staff Attorney Michael Mahsetky to Sen. Daniel K. Inouye, Chair of Senate Select Comm. on Indian Affairs 9 (August 19, 1987).

121. *Id.*

122.   *See* discussion of the Hou Hawaiians' claim of tribal status in *Price v. State* in text accompanying note 103, *supra*.

123.   *See* S. Glauberman, *Third Hawaiian group enters self-determination fight*, Honolulu Advertiser, July 25, 1989, at A-3.

124.   Resolution adopted at Native Hawaiian Rights Conference, August 7-8, 1988.

125.   *See, e.g., Oversight Hearings on Native Hawaiian Reparations Before the Senate Select Comm. on Indian Affairs*, Testimony of Liko O Kalani Martin at 2-3, Testimony of Steven C. Moore of the Native American Rights Fund at 9, Testimony of Moses Keale, Sr., Chair of the Board of Trustees OHA, at 9-11 (August 26, 1988). Unpublished.

126.   The Native Hawaiian Sovereignty Conference was held on December 3-4, 1988. Participants included Ka Lāhui Hawai'i, the Institute for the Advancement of Hawaiian Affairs, Nā 'Oiwi O Hawai'i, the Protect Kaho'olawe 'Ohana, E Ola Mau, and the Council of Hawaiian Organizations.

127.   Office of Hawaiian Affairs, *Draft Blueprint for Native Hawaiian Entitlements* (September 2, 1989) [hereinafter *Blueprint*].

128.   Significantly, the OHA trustees had adopted a position statement in 1982 that is quite similar to the five-plank resolution. *See Towards Reparations/Restitution, supra* note 72.

129.   *Blueprint, supra* note 127, at § D.10.

130.   *Id.* at § D.10.a.

131.   *Id.*

132.   *Id.* at § D.10.b.

133.   *Id.* at §§ D.10.b and c.

134.   *Id.* at § D.10.d.

135.   *Id.* at §§ D.1.a-b, D.2, D.3.

136.   *Id.* at § D.5.

137.   *Id.* at §§ D.6, D.7.

138.   *Id.* at § D.11.

139.   *Id.* at § D.3.

140.   *Questions Answered from OHA Blueprint Meetings*, 6 Ka Wai Ola O Oha, No. 11, at 5 (November 1989).

141.   *Id. See also* discussion in text accompanying note 120, *supra*.

142.   Constitution of Ka Lāhui Hawai'i, with amendments through 1990.

143.   In answer to questions posed on the most desirable status for Hawaiians in a post-restitution period, Mililani B. Trask responded:

> The status which is most desirable is independent, native, sovereign, separate from the state and federal governments which can relate to the federal government and state government on a nation to nation/government to government status. This will require a continuing relationship to the U.S. and to the State of Hawaii.

Ms. Trask, however, was not responding in her capacity as the *kia'āina* of Ka Lāhui Hawai'i. Memo from Mililani Trask to Melody MacKenzie (n.d.). *See also* discussion of self-determination in Written Statement of Ka Lāhui Hawai'i, *infra* note 164.

144.   Ka Lāhui Constitution, *supra* note 142, at art. II, § 1.

145.   *Id.* at art. II, § 3.

146.   *Id.* at art. II, § 4.

147.   *Id.* at art. IV, § 6(B).

148.   *Id.* at art. III.

149.   *Id.* at art. III, § 5.

150.   *Id.* at art. III, § 6.

151.   *Id.* at art. IV, § 6 (B).

152.   *Id.* at art. IV, § 9.

153.   *Id.* at art. IV.

154.   *Id.*

155.   *Id.* at art. IV, § 9.

156.   *Id.* at art. IV, §§ 2, 3, 4, 5.

157.   *Id.* at art. VI, § 1.

158.   *Id.*

159.   *Id.*

160.   Statement of Mililani Trask, *kia'āina* of Ka Lāhui Hawai'i, in S. Glauberman, *Hawaiian group sets course for sovereignty*, The Sunday Star-Bulletin & Advertiser, July 23, 1989, at A-8.

161.   *Id.*

162.   *See* Ka Lāhui Constitution, *supra* note 142, at art. I, §§ 1, 2, 5, 6, 7, 8.

163. *Id.* at art. I, § 18.

164. Mililani B. Trask, *kia'āina* of Ka Lāhui Hawai'i, written statement of Ka Lāhui Hawai'i, Native Hawaiian Sovereignty Conference, 1 (December 3-4, 1988).

165. *Id.*

166. *Id.* at 3.

167. Pōkā Laenui (H.F. Burgess), written statement of the Institute for the Advancement of Hawaiian Affairs, Native Hawaiian Sovereignty Conference, 2 (December 3-4, 1988).

168. *Id.*

169. *Id.* at 5.

170. *Id.* at 3.

171. R.S. Kronowitz, J. Lichtman, S.P. McSloy, M.G. Olsen, *Toward Consent and Cooperation: Reconsidering the Political Status of Indian Nations*, 22 Harv.C.R.-C.L.L.Rev. 507, 587 (1987) [hereinafter *Political Status*].

172. United Nations Charter, art. 1, para. 2.

173. *Id.*, art. 55(c). In art. 56 of the U.N. Charter, member nations pledge themselves to take action for the achievement of the purposes set out in art. 55.

174. *Political Status, supra* note 171, at 604-612, discusses complaints lodged by the Hopi and Mohawk Nations against the United States before the U.N. Human Rights Commission.

175. U.N. Charter, art. 73.

176. *Political Status, supra* note 171, at 591.

177. Barsh, *Indigenous North America and Contemporary International Law*, 62 Or. L. Rev. 73, 84-90 (1983).

178. *Political Status, supra* note 171, at 591.

179. G.A. Res. 1514, 15 U.N. GAOR Supp. (No. 16) at 66-67, U.N. Doc. A/4684 (1960).

180. G.A. Res. 2131, 20 U.N. GAOR Supp. (No. 14) at 11-12, U.N. Doc. A/6014 (1966).

181. G.A. Res. 2625, 25 U.N. GAOR Supp. (No. 28) at 121, U.N. Doc. A/8082 (1970).

182. G.A. Res. 217A(III), U.N. Doc. A/810 (1948), art. 15.

183. The Universal Declaration was in effect at the time of the 1959 statehood vote. As suggested by Pōkā Laenui, *see* text accompanying notes 167-170, *supra*, the citizens of the nation of Hawai'i did not have an opportunity to vote on statehood. Statehood was voted on by all Americans who had resided in Hawai'i for a year. Moreover, the full range of choice on political status was not given to Hawaiians.

184. G.A. Res. 2200A, 21 U.N. GAOR Supp. (No. 16) at 52, U.N.Doc. A/6546 (1966). G.A. Res. 2200, 21 U.N. GAOR Supp. (No. 16) at 49, U.N. Doc. A/6316 (1966).

185. *Id.*

186. The Greco-Roman "Communities," Collection of Advisory Opinions (Greece v. Bulgaria), 1930 P.C.I.J. (ser. B) No. 17, at 21 (July 31).

187. International Commission of Jurists, *The Events in East Pakistan, 1971* (A Report by the Secretariat) 70 (1972).

188. 1983 Working Group Rept., E/CN.4/Sub.2/1983 at 3.

189. At the 1985 session of the Working Group, an ambitious set of standards was submitted by indigenous organizations. The first principle states:

> The right to self-determination is fundamental to the enjoyment of all human rights. From the right to self-determination flows the right to permanent sovereignty over the land, including aboriginal, ancestral-historical lands, and other natural resources, the right to maintain and develop governing institutions, the right to life, health and physical integrity, and the rights to culture, way of life and religion.

IWGIA Yearbook 1987: Indigenous Peoples and Development 92 (1988). At the time of this writing, the Working Group had not finalized its principles which, in draft form, were more conservative than those submitted by indigenous organizations. The 1989 meeting of the Working Group considered the first revised text of the draft Universal Declaration on the Rights of Indigenous Peoples. That draft did not contain a specific provision on self-determination, although it did call upon all nations to adhere to the fundamental rights and freedoms recognized in the U.N. Charter and existing human rights instruments. 1989 Working Group Rept., E/CN.4/Sub.2/1989/36 at 31.

190. Indian Law Resource Center, *Handbook for Indians on International Human Rights Complaint Procedures* 15 (1984).

PART TWO

SECURING INDIVIDUAL
HAWAIIAN LAND TITLES

CHAPTER 5

JUDICIAL METHODS OF SECURING LAND TITLE

1. INTRODUCTION

The limited availability of land in Hawai'i accounts for the importance of land ownership. For Native Hawaiians, who hold special reverence for the 'aina or land, land ownership assumes particular significance. Accordingly, establishing and protecting title to land are important aspects of preserving Native Hawaiian rights.

All methods of settling, determining or securing title to real property in Hawai'i, whether by a quiet title action, through the land court, or by a claim of adverse possession, can be considered judicial methods of securing title in that the courts are invariably involved in determining interests in real property. However, the quiet title and land court methods of securing title are statutorily based. As such, they differ from an adverse possession claim which, although subject to statutory requirements, has a deepseated common law history. Bringing a quiet title action and registering title in land court are judicial processes, which result in a confirmation of title; adverse possession is a claim to title which is asserted *in* a quiet title or land court action. The following chapter discusses the two judicial mechanisms for settling title to real property -- the quiet title action and land court registration -- while adverse possession is discussed in a separate chapter.

2. QUIET TITLE ACTIONS

Quieting title to property determines legal ownership and can include settling boundary disputes, removing clouds on title, resolving breaks in the chain of title caused by invalid or missing prior deeds or the absence of a probate for a deceased prior owner. As of 1985, a person can also use the quiet title procedure to secure ownership of lands created by accretion.[1]

a. *Commencement of a Quiet Title Action*

A quiet title action begins by filing a complaint in the circuit court where the property is located.[2] In the complaint the plaintiff identifies the defendants with adverse claims against whom the claim should be filed. All persons with a claim or interest in the land need not be made parties,[3] but the judgment of the court is only binding as to those persons who have been made parties to the action and as to those persons who have been appropriately notified and subsequently suffer entry of judgment against them for failure to pursue claims.

b. *Response to Complaint*

A defendant who is personally served with a complaint must file an answer within 20 days, unless a different time has been ordered by the court.[4] Two extra days are allowed if service is made by mail. A defendant who is given notice by publication must file an answer by the date stated in the publication, but the response date set in the notice must be at least 21 days following the last date of publication, unless a different time is ordered by the court.[5]

c.   *Parties to Action*

Although there has been a quiet title statute in existence in Hawai'i since 1890,[6] it applied only to known and named persons. A major change came about in 1959, when the state legislature added three sections to the quiet title statute.[7] The change permitted claimants by adverse possession to use publication as a means of serving unknown persons. As such, the statute offered claimants a complete determination of title against all the world.[8]

The quiet title statute today permits unknown persons to be named as defendants to a quiet title action when the complaint shows that there are or may be unknown persons claiming by, through, or under any named person, or if the complaint shows an actual controversy between plaintiff and persons unidentified or unknown.[9]

Defense of a quiet title action may also be maintained as a class action to prevent property interests of numerous unidentified persons from being transferred by default.[10]

Insofar as they are known, adjoining landowners and occupants must be joined as defendants in an action to quiet title to property claimed through adverse possession.[11] As a practical matter, adjoining landowners and occupants are named as defendants in almost all quiet title actions to insure against or resolve any potential boundary disputes.

d.   *State of Hawai'i as Defendant*

Prior to 1977, the interests of the state could not be determined in a quiet title action, since under the doctrine of sovereign immunity, the state could not be sued without its consent, usually in a specific statutory provision permitting such suits.[12] In 1977, the legislature enacted a law allowing the state to be joined as a defendant when it is an adjoining property owner or when the party making the claim can demonstrate, by a title search, that the state has an interest in the subject matter of the suit which is adverse to the plaintiff's claim.[13]

Consequently, many actions now name the state. The state's responses may include claims of specific interest in land held by the state under reservation, deed, court order, quitclaim, escheat and effect of law; claims of prehistoric or historical remains upon or under the land; claims of lands never clearly awarded by the government; and claims of mineral rights, rights of native tenants, and public access. The state's rights to minerals and mines usually derive from express reservations of rights in royal patents or land commission awards, or from statute.[14] No action against the state may be maintained based on adverse possession.[15]

e.   *Jurisdiction*

The settling of adverse claims relating to real property in state court can be accomplished only if the court has jurisdiction over the parties or the property; that is, only if the state can subject the property or the defendants to the decisions of its courts. Some actions require the courts to have jurisdiction over the defendants themselves (actions *in personam*), and others require the courts only to have jurisdiction over the property (actions *in rem*).

In personam jurisdiction gives the court power to order a defendant to act or refrain from acting with regard to the property. Additionally, *in personam* jurisdiction allows a state court's decision to be binding against that defendant in the courts of other states and against *all* property of that defendant, wherever located.

The basis of the court's *in rem* jurisdiction is the presence of the particular property within the state. *In rem* jurisdiction is binding against all the world but only with regard to the particular property that is the subject of the dispute. The court does not have power over the person of the defendant, to enable it to collect a deficiency judgment, for example, nor is the court able to satisfy its judgment by moving against other property of the defendant.

In Hawai'i, a quiet title action against known defendants who can be served after due diligence is an *in personam* action.[16] A quiet title action against unknown persons is an *in rem* proceeding.[17]

f. *Constitutional Requirements: Due Process of Law*

A court's exercise of its jurisdiction must satisfy the constitutional requirements of due process of law,[18] the cornerstone of which is reasonable notice and an opportunity to be heard. "Reasonable" notice is that method which, given the circumstances, the resources, and the nature of the suit, is reasonably calculated to reach the defendant.[19]

The type of notice "reasonably calculated" to notify defendants about an action has traditionally depended upon whether the action was *in personam* or *in rem*. For *in personam* actions, the defendant has to be personally served with process or has to consent (actually or constructively) to the jurisdiction of the court. Traditionally, the valid exercise of *in rem* jurisdiction required merely notice by publication in a newspaper of general circulation and posting of summons upon the land. However, today the "reasonably-calculated-to-notify-defendants" standard appears to govern actions *in rem* as well. Thus, all known persons whose interests will be affected by the suit, and whose addresses are known or knowable through diligent search, must at least be notified by ordinary mail.[20]

g. *Notice/Service of Process in Hawai'i*

(1) *Known Persons Who Can Be Personally Served Within the State* There are several constitutionally acceptable ways of giving personal service to an individual: personal delivery, delivery into the possession of a responsible person at the party's residence, or delivery to the party's authorized agent.[21] A plaintiff must use reasonable, due diligence to determine who are known defendants with adverse claims, and where their claims (or those of their predecessors) were recorded. Where the law requires personal service, notice by publication will not suffice.[22] Notice by publication will also not be effective against someone whom a plaintiff, by the exercise of reasonable diligence, should have known had an adverse claim.[23]

Failure to name and provide personal service to known defendants will not bind the court's determination of plaintiff's claims as to those defendants. In the case of *In re Vockrodt* (1968),[24] the Vockrodts claimed to have acquired ownership of Maui land by adverse possession. In their complaint to quiet title, the Vockrodts alleged that there were no other persons with an interest in the land, that there were other persons claiming an interest, but that these persons could not be found. The complaint contained a list of adjoining landowners and occupants and their addresses, where known. The Vockrodts published notice of the hearing to quiet title in a newspaper prescribed by the court, and they posted notice upon the land. Every person named in the complaint whose address was known received a copy by registered mail from the court clerk. Appellants, four adjoining landowners who had not been personally served, moved to dismiss the complaint for lack of personal jurisdiction and insufficient service of process. On appeal the issue was whether, in amending the notice provision, the legislature intended to convert the quiet title action from an *in personam* to an *in rem* proceeding by permitting service by publication upon known but unlocated defendants. The amended statute stated:

> Section 242-2.1 R.L.H.: Notice by publication. In any action brought under section 242-1(b), if there are persons who may claim interests in the property adverse to the plaintiff and cannot be found, notice in the form required by section 342-25 shall be published in a newspaper of general circulation and the provisions of section 342-26 shall also be made applicable therein.[25]

The court held that the statute permitting notice by publication applied *only* to persons who could not be found. As to the adjoining landowners, the action was *in personam*, and thus they should have been served personally.

(2) *Known Persons Who Are Absent From or Who Cannot Be Served Within the State* Known persons who are absent from the state or reside out-of-state, or persons who, after due diligence, cannot be served within the state, may be served: (1) by personal service wherever they can be found, (2) by registered or certified mail, return receipt requested, as ordered by the court,[26] or (3) by publication.[27] Service by publication is not valid unless the plaintiff convinces the court in an affidavit that the means, methods, and attempts made to locate defendant and to effect personal service showed due diligence.

It has been unclear just how far a plaintiff must go to determine the address of a known nonresident for service. In *Calasa v. Greenwell* (1981),[28] the Hawai'i Intermediate Appellate Court did not explain what constituted satisfactory proof that service could not have been made personally or by registered mail.

Calasa filed a complaint to quiet title to a piece of land in Kula, Maui, naming defendants Greenwell and Aruda and joining unnamed persons claiming an interest in the property. Aruda was personally served; Greenwell was not. A copy of the summons was posted on the property and published in the Maui Sun. When no defendants appeared, the court entered default and a decree in favor of Calasa. Two years later, Greenwell tried to vacate the decree, attesting that despite the little trouble it would have taken to ascertain his out-of-state address, he had not been served notice.

The issue before the court was whether service by publication of a known nonresident whose address was unknown was sufficient. The Hawai'i Intermediate Appellate Court found service of Greenwell by publication adequate. Plaintiff's failure to locate Greenwell's mailing address did not deny due process, since notice was reasonably calculated under the circumstances to give Greenwell notice: "[W]hen the proceedings involve title to land located in the jurisdiction and a non-resident defendant whose address is unknown, service by posting a copy of the summons on the land and by publication satisfies the requirements of due process."[29] (Citations omitted.)

In 1976, the statute interpreted by the *Greenwell* court was amended to require due diligence in locating unknown or nonresident defendants.[30]

In 1986, the Hawai'i Intermediate Appellate Court indicated the inquiry which, at a minimum, would constitute conscientious effort and due diligence in attempting to identify defendants in satisfaction of the statute. In *Hustace v. Kapuni* (1986),[31] the plaintiff's complaint to quiet title named four individual defendants, including Kapuni. It also listed 100 unknown John Doe defendants, for whom the court approved service by publication. Plaintiff amended the complaint to name 21 other defendants and their heirs, and the trial court authorized service by publication for these defendants as well. Only the four defendants personally served entered an answer, and default was entered against all the others.

Kapuni then obtained quitclaim deeds to the land at issue from two persons claiming to be heirs of two of the named defendants added in the amended complaint. Kapuni moved the court to set aside the default judgment against these heirs, claiming that plaintiff had failed to use due diligence in his attempt to identify and locate the heirs. The trial court denied the motion and ruled that Hustace had established title to the parcels through adverse possession.

One of the issues on appeal was whether Kapuni had standing to object to service of process, and whether plaintiff's affidavit of inquiry was sufficient to warrant substituted service.

The court ruled that Kapuni had acquired whatever interest the conveyors had in the property, including the right to move to set aside the default. The court also held that the test of diligent inquiry and conscientious effort under the notice statute was not satisfied by mere affidavits devoid of averments of fact. As a starting point, the court held that the plaintiff should have reviewed tax rolls, deed records, judicial records, telephone directories, and city directories in order to find defendants. The court took judicial notice of the following sources of genealogical information: the state library, Bishop Museum, churches, circuit and supreme courts, Mission House, Hawaii Sugar Planters' Association, Department of Health, Department of Immigration and Naturalization, and the state archives. Since the affidavit was insufficient, the order authorizing service by publication was void and the judgment against the heirs was void on its face.

(3) *Unknown Parties* Plaintiff may also elect to make unknown persons parties to the action.[32] Unknown defendants may be given notice by newspaper publication in accordance with Haw. Rev. Stat. sections 669-3, 634-23(2), and 634-23(3), and applicable court rules.[33]

An action against unknown persons is an *in rem* proceeding. Haw. Rev. Stat. sections 634-23(4) and 634-25 indicate that an action against a defendant served by publication, personal service out of state, or registered mail is an *in rem* proceeding, thus affecting only the property which is the subject of the action, unless the defendant (a) appears and defends the claim on the merits or (b) is a resident not found within the state but is nonetheless personally served.[34]

Service by publication is not unconstitutional.[35] While publication may be an indirect and possibly futile means of notification, it is not unconstitutional even when a final decree may foreclose a defendant's rights.[36]

h. *Default*

If a defendant fails to respond by answer or appearance to service or publication within the prescribed time, a default judgment may be entered, barring the defendant from pursuing a claim in the future.[37] Such default judgments can be entered against defendants who procrastinate, persons who have potential claims based on inheritance but who do not recognize an ancestor's name cited in the publication, and even persons who have good paper title but fail to defend their claims in court. However, no default judgment can be entered against the state or county unless plaintiff has established his claim to the court's satisfaction.[38]

i.   *Jury Trial*
Parties disputing legal title to real property have a right to try the issue by jury.[39]

j.   *Relief from Judgment*
For good cause shown, the court may set aside a default judgment.[40] In addition, pursuant to Hawai'i Rules of Civil Procedure Rule 60(b), relief from judgment may be granted by the court for various reasons, including voidness or "any other reason justifying relief from the operation of the judgment." A motion for relief must be made within a reasonable time.

The doctrines of collateral estoppel and *res judicata* bar relitigation of default judgments and final judgments entered in a quiet title case. However, even after a default judgment and final judgment are entered in a quiet title action, subsequent litigation may raise disputes relating to ownership and rights of adverse claimants. For example, when a landowner attempts to eject a party from property, that party may dispute the landowner's title and superior rights. Residents within an *ahupua'a* may dispute the landowner's right to prevent them from exercising rights as native tenants. A landowner may attempt to bar the public from using a previously available beach access. A person returning to Hawai'i after an extended absence may dispute the unexpected subdivision of *hui* lands.

The court may resolve such disputes by reviewing cases that have already been litigated and by determining the applicability of the prior judgment to the issues and facts in the current dispute. Since the judicial system favors and will enforce the conclusiveness of prior judgments, unless a party can prove the inapplicability of *res judicata* and collateral estoppel to the present claim, the court will most likely uphold the prior judgment.

3.   LAND COURT REGISTRATION

There is an alternate process to the quiet title action also designed to settle title and other real property claims: land court registration. The quiet title action and land court registration accomplish similar goals, but there are differences. For example, land court registration costs more: registration in land court requires a survey, abstract of title, examination of title, check by the state surveyor, and fee to an insurance fund, none of which is required by the quiet title procedure.[41] Land court registration also involves longer delays. On the other hand, land court registration offers greater benefits, including title insurance backed by the state, and express statutory protection against claims of adverse possession and prescription.[42]

a.   *Historical Background*
One method of confirming ownership to real property is the land court or Torrens system. Adapted by Sir Robert Torrens from the system of registering title to shipping vessels,[43] the purpose of the land court system is to clearly establish absolute title to land.[44] As a result, under the land court system of registration, title itself is registered.[45]

After registration, a property owner acquires complete title to the land and those dealing with the property need only concern themselves with the contents of the title registration.[46]

In Hawai'i, the territorial legislature adopted the land court system in 1903 in response to dissatisfaction with the existing recording system.[47] An 1898 report had specified the drawbacks of the existing system and urged its abandonment.[48] The 1898 legislature, however, refused to adopt the land court system, a position it maintained for five years.[49] When the territorial legislature finally established the new system, its purpose was to offer a "simple, rapid, inexpensive and secure" method of dealing with land ownership.[50] While the land court system today offers security to the titleholder, it is also a somewhat confusing, time-consuming, and expensive registration process.

b. *Land Court Procedures*

Chapter 501 of the Hawai'i Revised Statutes supplies the statutory guidelines for the land court system. Persons claiming fee simple ownership of property must submit a registration application in writing, signed and sworn to by the applicant, to the land court.[51] The application must include information on the applicant,[52] and a legal description, a map or plan, and a title abstract of the land.[53] The application may include several parcels, however, the applicant's interest in each parcel must be identical and each parcel must be located in the same district.[54] The land court may also require additional facts in the application.[55]

After an application is filed, the land court registrar refers it to a court-appointed title examiner.[56] The examiner investigates all facts asserted in the application and files a certificate of opinion about the title of the property.[57] At the same time, a state surveyor verifies the accuracy of the map of the land. Upon the examiner's favorable opinion, the application advances to the process of notice and hearing in the land court. In the event of an adverse opinion, the applicant may proceed or withdraw the application.[58]

Following an approving opinion, the registrar must publish the filing of the application in a newspaper of general circulation.[59] Notice is also provided by registered mail, posting or any other means deemed appropriate.[60] Other parties may dispute the applicant's claim of title via a court hearing.[61] If, after a court hearing, the court finds registration of title is appropriate, a decree of confirmation and registration is entered.[62] Thereafter, the decree of registration binds the land.[63] The land court registrar sends a certified copy of the decree to the bureau of conveyances, where the decree is transcribed in a registration book.[64]

Once a land court decree is entered, the property always maintains its land court status.[65] Moreover, once title to land is registered, it cannot be the subject of an adverse possession or prescription claim.[66] Other critical advantages of the land court system are the state guarantee of title and a compensation fund for losses sustained by errors in the registration book.[67] The fund also covers any deprivation of land created by the registration of any other persons as owners.[68] Applicant fees in the amount of one-tenth of one percent of the assessed value of the land and improvements generate the fund.[69] Despite the expensive and time-consuming nature of the land court system, its assurance of absolute title to land qualifies it as a worthwhile method of securing land ownership.

4. CONCLUSION

Persons seeking to determine ownership and other interests in land bring a quiet title action more frequently than they apply to register land in land court. Quieting title is less expensive and provides a fair degree of security to the interest protected. In Hawai'i, most significant litigation has arisen over questions concerning the adequacy of notice and service of process. Thus, anyone who contemplates bringing such an action to quiet title must exercise diligence in ascertaining all possible adverse parties and insure that the means of service can be reasonably expected to notify claimants of the pending action.

NOTES

1. Haw. Rev. Stat. § 669-1(e) (1985):

    Action may be brought by any person to quiet title to land by accretion. The person bringing the action shall prove by a preponderance of the evidence that the accretion is natural and permanent. "Permanent" means that the accretion has been in existence for at least twenty years. The accreted portion of land shall be considered within the conservation district unless designated otherwise by the land use commission under chapter 205. Prohibited uses are governed by section 183-45.

    Id. at § 183-45:

    Accreted land. No structure, retaining wall, dredging, grading, or other use which interferes or may interfere with the future natural course of the beach, including further accretion or erosion, shall be permitted on accreted land as judicially decreed under section 501-33 or 669-1(e). This provision shall not in any way be construed to affect state or county property.

    Any structure or action in violation of this provision shall be immediately removed or stopped and the property owner shall be fined in accordance with section 183-41(e). Any action taken to impose or collect the penalty provided for in this section shall be considered a civil action.

2. *Id.* at § 669-1(d):

    Action under subsection (a) or (b) shall be brought in the circuit court of the circuit in which the property is situated.

    Haw. R. Civ. P. 4(a):

    Summons: Issuance. Upon the filing of the complaint the clerk shall forthwith issue a summons and deliver it for service to a person authorized to serve process. Upon request of the plaintiff separate or additional summons shall issue against any defendants.

3. *Kahoiwai v. Limaeu*, 10 Haw. 507, 510 (1896).

4. Haw. R. Civ. P. 12.

5. Haw. Rev. Stat. § 669-3 (1985).

6. The 1890 statute provided:

    Section 1. Action may be brought in the Supreme Court or in any of the Circuit Courts by any person, against another person, who claims adversely to the plaintiff an estate or interest in real property, for the purpose of determining such adverse claim.

    Section 2. Any person may be made a defendant in such action who has, or claims an interest in the property adverse to the plaintiff, or who is a necessary party to a complete determination or settlement of the question involved therein.

    Section 3. If at the time of the commencement of such action the property in question is in the possession of a tenant, the landlord may be joined as a party defendant.

    Section 4. If in such action the defendant disclaim in his answer any interest or estate in the property or suffer judgment to be taken against him without answer, the plaintiff shall not recover costs.

    Section 5. This Act shall take effect from the date of its passage.

7. Haw. Rev. Stat. § 242 (1959):

    242-1. **Object of action.** Action for the purpose of establishing title to real property may be brought in any of the circuit courts by any person who has been in adverse possession of such real property for not less than ten years.

242-2.1. **Notice by publication.** In any action brought under section 242-1(b), if there are persons who may claim interests in the property adverse to the plaintiff and cannot be found, notice in the form required by section 342-25 shall be published in a newspaper of general circulation and the provisions of section 342-26 shall also be made applicable herein.

242-2.2. **Default; effect.** If no person appears and answers within the time allowed, the court may at once, upon motion of the plaintiff and no reason to the contrary appearing, order a general default to be recorded and the claim of plaintiff taken to be correct. By the description in the notice "to whom it may concern," all the world are made parties defendant and shall be concluded by the default and order. After such default and order the court may enter a decree confirming the title in the plaintiff.

8. Constitutional requirements differ significantly between service of process to known defendants and service to unidentified or unlocatable defendants. Great care must be taken that notice and service are adequate.

9. Haw. Rev. Stat. § 669-2(b) (1985):

> Unknown persons may be made parties as provided by the rules of court, if:
> (1) It shall be shown by the complaint that there are or may be persons unknown, claiming by, through, or under any named person; or
> (2) Other facts shall be shown by the complaint giving rise to an actual controversy between plaintiff and persons unidentified or whose names are unknown.

10. *See e.g. State v. Pioneer Mill*, Civ. No. 3673 (2nd Cir. Haw., Order entered June 15, 1982).

11. Haw. Rev. Stat. § 669-2(c)(1) (1985):

> (c) In any action brought under section 669-1(b):
> (1) There shall be joined as defendants, in addition to persons known to have an adverse interest, the adjoining owners and occupants so far as known.

12. *Waugh v. University of Hawaii*, 63 Haw. 117, 125, 621 P.2d 957, 964-965 (1980); *Big Island Small Ranchers Association v. State*, 60 Haw. 228, 236, 588 P.2d 430, 436 (1978); *Helela v. State*, 49 Haw. 365, 369, 418 P.2d 482, 485 (1966).

13. Haw. Rev. Stat. § 669-2(d)(2) (1989 Supp.) (the party attempting to join the state as a defendant must have a title search done by a licensed abstractor and provide a copy to the state).

14. *See, e.g., In re Robinson*, 49 Haw. 429, 430, 421 P.2d 570, 573-574 (1966) (upheld government's rights to "all mineral or metallic mines, of every description," reserved in royal patent).

15. *Kahoomana v. Minister of Interior*, 3 Haw. 635 (1875); *In re Kelley*, 50 Haw. 567, 581, 445 P.2d 538, 547 (1968); *In re Kamakana*, 58 Haw. 632, 641, 574 P.2d 1346, 1351 (1978).

16. *In re Vockrodt*, 50 Haw. 201, 204-205, 436 P.2d 752, 753-755 (1968). In general, ownership of real property within the state confers *in personam* jurisdiction when the cause of action arises from the property itself. *See also* Haw. Rev. Stat. § 634-35 (a)(3), (b), (c) (1985).

17. *In re Vockrodt*, 50 Haw. 201, 204-205, 436 P.2d 752, 753-755 (1968).

18. U.S. Const. amend. XIV states, in part, that no person shall be deprived of life, liberty, or property without due process of law.

19. *Mullane v. Central Hanover Bank & Trust Co.*, 339 U.S. 306, 318 (1950), in which Central Hanover Bank, trustee of a trust fund consisting of 113 separate trusts, petitioned the court for settlement of accounts, as required by state law. The court appointed Mullane as representative and special guardian of all persons known or unknown with an interest in the trust fund. Central Hanover published notice of the petition in a newspaper in an effort to notify beneficiaries, a method approved by New York law. Since the beneficiaries were quite numerous, personal service was deemed prohibitively expensive. Mullane objected to the notice on behalf of out-of-state parties whose names and addresses were known, arguing that notice by publication was not adequate to provide them due process. The court agreed that notice by publication of known beneficiaries was not adequate, but also held that such notice was sufficient for beneficiaries whose addresses the trustee did not know and could not reasonably discover through due diligence.

20. *Walker v. City of Hutchinson*, 352 U.S. 112, 116 (1956).

21. Haw. R. Civ. P. 4(d).

22. *Thayer v. McCandless*, 32 Haw. 745, 748-749 (1933).

23. *Id.* at 749.

24. 50 Haw. 201, 436 P.2d 752 (1968).

25. *Id.* at 203, n.2, 436 P.2d at 753, n.2.

26. Haw. Rev. Stat. § 634-24 (1985):

> **Service outside the State or by registered mail.** In any case in which, under section 634-23, provision is made for service of summons as provided by this section, personal service shall be made upon the defendant wherever found or the defendant shall be served by registered or certified mail with request for a return receipt and marked deliver to addressee only, as ordered by the court. A certified copy of the order, the summons and the complaint shall be served, and the service shall be

evidenced by an affidavit showing that the required papers were sent by registered or certified mail as aforesaid, and by the receipt signed by the defendant and filed with the affidavit, or in the case of personal service by the return of the serving officer or the affidavit of any other person authorized to serve process in the place where the defendant is found or appointed by the court to make the service.

The affidavit required by this section shall set forth facts based upon the personal knowledge of the affiant concerning the methods, means, and attempts made to satisfy the requirements of this section and any other pertinent facts.

See also Robinson v. McWayne, 35 Haw. 689, 712 (1940).

27. Haw. Rev. Stat. § 634-23(2) (1985):

> (2) If a defendant is unknown or does not reside within the State or if, after due diligence, the defendant cannot be served with process within the State, and the facts shall appear by affidavit to the satisfaction of the court, it may order that service be made as provided by section 634-24 or by publication, as may be appropriate; provided that service by publication shall not be valid unless, it is shown to the satisfaction of the court that service cannot be made as provided by section 634-24. The affidavit required by this paragraph shall set forth facts based upon the personal knowledge of the affiant concerning the methods, means, and attempts made to locate and effect personal service on the defendant and any other pertinent facts.

28. 2 Haw. App. 395, 633 P.2d 553 (1981).

29. *Id.* at 399, 633 P.2d at 556.

30. S. Rep. No. 754, 8th Leg., 2nd Sess. (1976):

> Your committee is in agreement that the existing law relating to service of process upon a defendant who is unknown or does not reside within the State is inadequate. This bill requires that the plaintiff shall use due diligence in locating the defendant. If, after due diligence, defendant cannot be served with process within the State and the facts shall appear by affidavit to the satisfaction of the court, the court may order that service be made as provided by Section 634-24, Hawaii Revised Statutes, or by publication, as may be appropriate. The affidavit shall set forth facts based upon the personal knowledge of the affiant concerning the methods, means and attempts made to locate and effect personal service on the defendant and any other pertinent facts.

31. 6 Haw. App. 241, 718 P.2d 1109 (1986).

32. Haw. Rev. Stat. § 669-2(b), 634-23(1) (1985). Haw. Rev. Stat § 634-23, 634-23(1) (1985) states:

> **Joinder of unknown persons; service when defendant unknown or absent.** Where an action or proceeding involves or concerns any property, tangible or intangible, within the jurisdiction of a circuit court, or any legal or equitable estate, right or interest, vested or contingent, in any such property, or any status or res within the jurisdiction of a circuit court:
> (1) Any person having a claim, interest or concern so as to be a necessary or proper party, who cannot be identified or whose name is unknown to the plaintiff, may be made party to the action or proceeding as provided by the rules of court.

33. *Id.* at § 669-3:

> **Notice by publication or registered mail.** In any action brought under section 669-1(a) or (b), unknown persons and any known persons who do not reside within the State or cannot after due diligence be served with process within the State may be served as provided by sections 634-23, 634-24, and 634-26; provided that 634-23(3) notwithstanding, service by publication in any action brought under section 669-1(a) or (b) shall be made in an English language newspaper published in and having a general circulation in the circuit in which the action or proceeding has been instituted, and if the action or proceeding has been instituted in any circuit other than the first circuit, service by publication shall also be made in an English language newspaper having a general circulation in the State. Publication shall be made in such manner and for such time as the court may order, but not less than once in each of four successive weeks, the last publication to be not less than twenty-one days prior to the return date stated herein unless a different time is prescribed by order of the court. A copy of the summons also shall be posted upon the real property concerned in the action or proceeding.

Id. at § 634-23(2); *see also In re Vockrodt*, 50 Haw. 201, 204-205, 436 P.2d 752, 753-755 (1968).

Id. at § 634-23, 634-23(3):

> **Joinder of unknown persons; service when defendant unknown or absent.** Where an action or proceeding involves or concerns any property, tangible or intangible, within the jurisdiction of a circuit court, or any legal or equitable estate, right or interest, vested or contingent, in any such property, or any status or res within the jurisdiction of a circuit court:
>
> . . . .

(3) Service by publication shall be made in at least one newspaper published in the State and having a general circulation in the circuit in which the action or proceeding has been instituted, in such manner and for such time as the court may order, but not less than once in twenty-one days prior to the return date stated therein unless a different time is prescribed by order of the court. If the action or proceeding concerns real property the court shall order additional notice by posting a copy of the summons upon the property.

See also Haw. R. Civ. P. 4(e).

Circuit Court Rule 11:

Proof of Publication.
Whenever the publication in a newspaper of any summons, process, notice or order is required, evidence of such publication shall be given by the affidavit of the editor, publisher, manager, foreman, clerk or printer of such newspaper, not interested in the suit, action, matter or proceeding to which such publication relates, to which affidavit shall be attached a copy of such summons, process, notice or order, and which affidavit shall also specify the dates and times when and the newspaper in which the publication was made. The publisher shall file said affidavit with the clerk before the time fixed for hearing.

34. Haw. Rev. Stat. § 634-23(4) (1985).
(4) Any adjudication shall, as regards a defendant served by publication pursuant to this section, or served as provided by section 634-24, affect only the property, status or res which is the subject of the action, unless (A) the defendant appears in the action and defends on the merits, in which case he shall be liable to a personal judgment with respect to the claim so defended, including in the case of a foreclosure action a deficiency judgment, or (B) the service is authorized by section 634-25 or other provision of law, in which case he shall be liable to any judgment authorized by such law.

Id. at § 634-25.

Personal service on resident outside the State. Whenever a defendant, being a resident of the State, cannot be served within the State personal service may be made upon the defendant outside the State by any person authorized to serve process in the place in which the defendant may be found or specially appointed by the court to make the service which service shall be evidenced by the return of the serving officer or by affidavit and shall be of the same legal force and validity as if made within the State.
The affidavit required by this section shall set forth facts based upon the personal knowledge of the affiant concerning the methods, means, and attempts made to satisfy the requirements of this section and any other pertinent facts.

35. *Manley v. Nelson*, 50 Haw. 484, 443 P.2d 155 (1968).

36. *Mullane v. Central Hanover Bank & Trust Co.*, 339 U.S. 306, 317-318 (1950).

37. Haw. R. Civ. P. 55(b)(2)
(b) **Judgment.** Judgment by default may be entered as follows:
. . . .
(2) *By the court.* In all other cases the party entitled to a judgment by default shall apply to the court therefor; but no judgment by default shall be entered against an infant or incompetent person unless represented in the action by a guardian, or other such representative who has appeared therein, and upon whom service may be made under Rule 17. If the party against whom judgment by default is sought has appeared in the action, he (or, if appearing by representative, his representative) shall be served with written notice of the application for judgment at least 3 days prior to the hearing on such application. If, in order to enable the court to enter judgment or to carry it into effect, it is necessary to take an account or to determine the amount of damages or to establish the truth of any averment by evidence or to make an investigation of any other matter, the court may conduct such hearings or order such references as it deems necessary and proper and shall accord a right of trial by jury to the parties when and as required by any statute.

38. Haw. R. Civ. P. 55(e):
Judgment Against the State, Etc. No judgment by default shall be entered against the State or a county, or an officer or agency of the State or a county, unless the claimant establishes his claim or right to relief by evidence satisfactory to the court.

39. Haw. Rev. Stat. § 669-3.5 (1985):
Trial when legal title in controversy. Whenever in an action brought under this chapter the legal title is in controversy, the issue shall be triable of right by a jury.

40. Haw. R. Civ. P. 55(c):

> **Setting Aside Default.** For good cause shown the court may set aside an entry of default and, if a judgment by default has been entered, may likewise set it aside in accordance with Rule 60(b).

41. *See* Steiner, *Adverse Possession Against Unknown Claimants Under Land Court and Quiet Title Procedures*, 2 Hawaii B. J. 4, 11 (Dec. 1964).

42. *Id.* at 12.

43. J. Reilly, *The Language of Real Estate* 485 (2d ed. 1982).

44. *Id.* at 484.

45. *Id.*

46. *Id.*

47. *Land Court Registration (Torrens Titles) and Conveyancing in Hawaii* 9 (2d ed. 1946).

48. *Id.* One major complaint of the existing system was the inability to determine who held title by an examination of the recording devices. Another problem occurred when persons known by several different names conveyed property.

49. *Id.*

50. *Id.*

51. Haw. Rev. Stat. § 501-23 (1985).

52. *Id.*

53. *Id.* at § 501-28.

54. *Id.* at § 501-25.

55. *Id.* at § 501-30.

56. *Id.* at § 501-32.

57. *Id.*

58. *Id.*

59. *Id.* at § 501-41.

60. *Id.* at § 501-42.

61. *Id.* at § 501-51.

62. *Id.* at § 501-71. If the applicant's title is encumbered, the court issues a decree subject to any encumbrances.

63. *Id.* Aggrieved parties may appeal to the supreme court. *Id.* at § 501-63.

64. Haw. Rev. Stat. § 501-75 (1989 Supp.).

65. Haw. Rev. Stat. § 501-86 (1985).

66. *Id.* at § 501-87.

67. *Id.* at § 501-212.

68. *Id.*

69. *Id.* at § 501-211.

CHAPTER 6

THE DOCTRINE OF ADVERSE POSSESSION

1. INTRODUCTION

Adverse possession is a legal means to acquire fee title to property. The adverse possessor may be either a stranger to the land and acquire fee title to land owned by someone else, or one who has a legitimate interest in the land but cannot prove ownership due to a break in the chain of paper title.

Whether the adverse possessor is a stranger to the land or someone with a legitimate interest in the land, the legal requirements for establishing adverse possession are the same. The adverse possessor must occupy the land for a statutory length of time in a visible, notorious, continuous, exclusive and hostile manner.[1] The statutory length of time can vary from jurisdiction to jurisdiction. In 1871, Hawai'i's adverse possession statute was adopted and the statutory length of time was set at 20 years. In 1898, the statutory length of time was changed to 10 years. It was changed back to 20 years in 1973.[2] Once the statutory period of time has been met, the doctrine of adverse possession denies the initial landowner the ability to use the courts to sue and remove the adverse possessor from the property.

Thus, under one view of adverse possession, when all the requirements have been met, title passes automatically from the initial owner to the adverse possessor.[3] The initial owner's title is extinguished, and a new title is created in the adverse possessor. The interest obtained by the adverse possessor is often referred to as an original title -- a new title obtained in opposition to the former record owner -- unlike a derivative title, which is obtained by descent, devise, or purchase. The adverse possessor's title is not a record title, because it is not based upon recorded documents. However, title acquired by adverse possession is as "perfect as if it had been conveyed by deed."[4] Moreover, the adverse possessor may go to court and get record title to the property in either a quiet title or land court action.

Another view holds that under Hawai'i's adverse possession statute, title does not pass automatically to the adverse possessor once the adverse possession requirements are met.[5] Rather, the adverse possession statute merely bars the true owner from going into court and making a claim; the statute does not give the adverse possessor any substantive rights in the property. Unfortunately, Hawai'i case law does not clearly support this interpretation.[6]

While adverse possession in Hawai'i often has been used as a tool to dispossess small landholders, it is not just a means for someone or some entity, like a corporation, ranch, or plantation, to take land from another. It is also the legal means by which an occupant of land or a *kuleana* owner, without clear "paper title," can obtain fee ownership to the land.

2. THE ORIGIN AND PURPOSE OF ADVERSE POSSESSION

a. *Purpose in Common Law*

The doctrine of adverse possession may appear to involve "robbery, burglary, piracy, and the like."[7] It also may seem to be contradictory to fundamental notions of fair play and the right to own and keep private property. However, to understand adverse possession, it must be viewed historically.

The law on adverse possession evolved out of the English common law. Under the old English feudal system, emphasis was placed on the possession of land rather than its ownership.[8] In early English law, rightful ownership was akin to "seisen" and adverse possession was akin to "disseisin." Seisin meant possession,[9] rather than outright ownership. The tenant seised of land was obligated to render feudal services to the lord.[10] The feudal lord's reliance upon the tenant's services caused great emphasis to be placed upon the person who was seised of land and who could produce the services required.[11] This system did not allow a tenant to suspend use or possession of the land. There always had to be some person responsible to the lord for the performance of these services.[12] Therefore, the person who provided these services, even a trespasser, would be rewarded with possession or seisen of the land and the former tenant, who had not performed feudal services, was punished by losing all right to and use of the land.

Besides punishing the former landholder, the doctrine of adverse possession was developed and formalized as law to function as a statute of limitations.[13] This limitation set a deadline by which a landowner could recover land, either by physically ousting the trespasser from the land (self-help), or by bringing suit in a court of law (real action). The deadline assured that there would be stability in land ownership or occupancy.[14] The modern purpose for having a statute of limitations is similar -- promoting stability in land ownership and giving a degree of certainty to one possessing land under a claim of ownership.[15]

Moreover, the purpose of a statute of limitations is to bar stale claims.[16] That is, as time passes, people's memories fade, witnesses become unavailable and physical evidence may be lost. Therefore it is only fair that a landowner act as promptly as possible in bringing a suit to court. The statutory deadline helps assure that promptness.

b. *Adverse Possession in America*

In America, every jurisdiction has statutory provisions fixing the period of time after which a landowner cannot bring an action, or undertake self-help, to recover land from a person in possession of that land.[17] In England, the primary function of the statute of limitations is to bar stale claims and to deter the lazy true owner who neglects rights to property.[18] But in America, the primary purpose of the statute is to confer ownership upon the adverse possessor, and not merely to bar stale claims.[19] Thus, under the American rule, the acts of the adverse possessor are examined before granting property ownership to the adverse possessor. Also, in America vast tracts of land available for settlement made the doctrine of adverse possession useful in achieving maximum land utilization.[20]

c. *Adverse Possession in Hawai'i*

(1) *Origin and Function* Hawai'i's first adverse possession statute was enacted in 1870, to take effect on July 31, 1871.[21] It was a logical time for passing a statute of limitations on actions to recover real property since the *Mahele* of 1848 had occurred barely 20 years previously.[22] Twenty years was the traditional statutory time period in the common law world and the 1870 enactment called for a 20-year statutory limit to recover possession of land.

The purpose of the 1870 adverse possession statute is not clear. However, it is clear who benefitted from the passage of such a statute. Of the five classes of persons who received land after the *Mahele* -- government, king, *konohiki*, *maka'ainana*, and foreigners -- the king and government can be eliminated as beneficiaries of the adverse possession statute since it was the king's purpose to relinquish his interest in the land granted to individuals -- after he and the government received their share.

The *maka'ainana* also did not benefit from passage of the adverse possession statute. If the *maka'ainana* remained on cultivated lands after 1850, but did not apply for *kuleana*, their continued possession was deemed permissive rather than adverse.[23] Thus, it became practically impossible for a commoner to adversely possess land owned by a *konohiki*.[24] Moreover, the very early case of *Kahoomana v. Minister of Interior* (1875)[25] held that adverse possession would not run against the government, so the *maka'ainana* could not avail themselves of an adverse possession claim against the government.

Thus, the landowners who would benefit most from the passage of the adverse possession statute were the *konohiki* and foreigners. The tiny *kuleana* parcels situated within large tracts of *konohiki* land rendered these parcels most attractive to unscrupulous *konohiki* or grantees of *konohiki*.[26] And from the perspective of the large-scale grower of sugar and pineapple, or perhaps of a rancher who sought to pasture cattle, a *kuleana* parcel within larger holdings presented an invitation for an adverse possession claim.[27] After the Reciprocity Treaty of 1875-76, which allowed Hawai'i sugar to enter the U.S. duty free, Western-owned sugar plantations dominated the Hawai'i economy and the need for land increased.[28] In short, many have asserted that adverse possession has been used primarily by large landholders to absorb the enclosed *kuleana* of Native Hawaiians.[29]

(2)　*Modern Purpose*　Accordingly, Native Hawaiian advocates have attempted to eliminate adverse possession at least twice in Hawai'i's history. Political leaders have made several arguments against retaining the adverse possession doctrine in Hawai'i:

- (a) Adverse possession is a concept foreign to the Hawaiian system of land use, which was based upon respect for the use rights of others.[30]
- (b) Adverse possession is an obsolete anachronism, used many years ago in countries that wanted to encourage the development of unused tracts of land.[31] On the mainland, adverse possession is used in states that have large open spaces that can be utilized. In Hawai'i, where land is very scarce and precious, lack of development is hardly the problem.[32]
- (c) Adverse possession has historically been used in Hawai'i by the rich as a weapon against the poor.[33] It has been used primarily by large landholders to absorb the *kuleana* of Native Hawaiians.[34]
- (d) It is unconstitutional for the government to authorize private individuals to take land without paying just compensation to the true owner.[35]

In 1973, the state legislature considered Senate Bill 660 for the purpose of abolishing "prescription and adverse possession as a means of acquiring title, right or interest in and to real property."[36] In 1978, the Constitutional Convention considered section 5 of the Hawaiian Affairs Committee Proposal No. 12: "No person shall be deprived of title to an estate or interest in real property by another person claiming actual, continuous, hostile, exclusive, open and notorious possession of such lands."[37] In both cases, the doctrine of adverse possession survived, but with substantial restrictions to help eliminate its abuses.

The 1973 Senate Judiciary Committee reported: "After much consideration, your Committee has determined that complete abolition of adverse possession is too drastic a measure and unwarranted at the present time. Your Committee agrees, however, that the present law relating to adverse possession needs to be tightened."[38] Accordingly, the time period necessary to establish adverse possession was extended from 10 years to 20 years.

Similarly, the 1978 Constitutional Convention restricted adverse possession claims to "real property of 5 acres or less," and provided that "such claim may be exercised in good faith by any person not more than once in 20 years."[39]

Two predominant lines of reasoning surfaced in 1973 and 1978 for retaining the adverse possession doctrine. The first is that adverse possession "is an *essential* method of expressing good title where record title is not good, and this applies to the title of poor Hawaiians . . . as much as it does to big corporations."[40] Delegate Burgess in 1978 argued that adverse possession was "a method for small landowners or real property owners to establish good title to their property . . . that the Hawaiian titles especially are not good paper title . . . [they are] titles that have come down by descent . . . without . . . formal conveyance."[41] The delegates believed it was necessary to retain adverse possession in order to allow Hawaiians to clear title to their land.[42] Following this line of reasoning, adverse possession serves three purposes: (1) to provide proof of meritorious titles; (2) to correct errors in conveyancing (breaks in the chain of title due to a mistake); and (3) to quiet all titles which are openly and consistently asserted.[43]

The second line of reasoning advanced for maintaining adverse possession is that "it protects the expectations of both the possessor and the community [and] that it acts in cutting off stale claims apt to be invested with fraud or perjury."[44] The public interest mandates that title to property should not remain uncertain and in dispute. The doctrine of adverse possession enhances the interest of society, and at the same time promotes private justice, putting an end to and fixing a limit to contention and strife.[45]

Thus, although the doctrine of adverse possession has been retained in Hawai'i, it has been severely limited to eliminate its worst abuses. Since 1973, an adverse possessor needs 20 years to perfect a claim. Since 1978, an adverse possessor can assert a claim not more than once every 20 years and to an area of no more than five acres. The small landowner who needs to establish a meritorious claim can still do so, but wholesale claims to large parcels of land appear to be barred unless the claims matured prior to 1978.

3. LIMITATIONS ON ADVERSE POSSESSION

a. *Adverse Possession Against the Government*

Title to land owned by the government, including property such as streets and parks dedicated to the public, cannot be obtained by adverse possession.[46] As early as 1875, the Hawai'i Supreme Court ruled in *Kahoomana v. Minister of Interior*[47] that adverse possession or prescription does not run against the government. The court reasoned that since the king was occupied with the cares of government, he ought not to suffer from the negligence of his officers and servants charged with administering public property. This principle was seen as "essential to a promotion of the interests and property of the public."[48]

b.　Disabilities

If at the time of entry by the adverse possessor, the owner is under a disability to sue, either as a minor, mental incompetent, or prisoner, the landowner or successor has five years *after* the removal of the disability within which to bring the suit, even if the statutory period has expired.[49]

Hawai'i's disability statute has not been the subject of much litigation.[50] Only two cases stand out and both are fairly early ones. Prior to 1898, marriage was considered a disability. The plaintiff in *George v. Holt* (1893),[51] argued that since the defendant was married during a period of time when she was establishing her adverse possession claim, she could not obtain a prescriptive title. The court ruled: "We are not aware that a married woman's coverture, which is considered in law as a disability, can be invoked against her. Such disability is considered as something she can invoke for her protection."[52] The policy then is that owners who are not able to exert their rights against an adverse possessor, due to a disability, should be allowed a grace period in which to do so.

However, once the statutory period begins to run against an owner, even if the owner becomes disabled, the statute will continue to run. In other words, the exemption only protects the owner who has a disability *when* the adverse possessor initially enters the property. Moreover, it does not protect successors of the owner who may have a disability. In *Waianae Co. v. Kaiwilei* (1917),[53] the court ruled that "[w]here the statute of limitations had commenced to run in favor of defendant the subsequent delivery of a deed of the property by the holder of the paper title thereto, to two minor children . . . would not destroy the continuity of defendant's possession."[54] The legal disability of the children who succeeded to title did not protect them from a pre-existing adverse possession claim against the property nor stop the running of the statute of limitations. In other words, once started, the statute continued to run, even if the minor children succeeded to paper title and are legally presumed to be unable to claim their right to the land.

c.　Future Interests

An adverse possessor cannot claim adverse possession against an owner who has no *present* right to possession at the time the adverse claimant enters the property. Accordingly, the statute of limitations is tolled, or does *not* run against holders of future interests in the property, such as a remainderman or the holders of a reversion.[55] There are two reasons for this rule of law. First, the holder of a future interest in land does not have a right to claim land from the adverse possessor until the future interest becomes a present possessory interest. Second, the adverse possessor can acquire only the interest that the present owner possesses, whatever that may be. For example, if A has a life estate and B will get the land after A dies, then the adverse possessor against A only gets A's life estate, not B's fee simple possession of the land. In *Atcherley v. Lewers & Cooke* (1908),[56] the court held: "Where land is devised to A for life, remainder to B for life, remainder to C in fee, and A conveys all his interest to B and then outlives B, the statute of limitations does not begin to run against a grantee of C until the death of A."[57]

d.　Liens and Encumbrances

If the true owner's property was subject to outstanding liens, restrictions, or covenants at the time of entry by the adverse possessor, the title acquired by the adverse possessor is also subject to such legal liens and encumbrances.[58] For instance, A owns a *kuleana*. In 1950, A deeds a right-of-way easement across A's *kuleana* to B. In 1951, C, A's judgment creditor, secures a lien against A's *kuleana*. In 1952, an adverse possessor enters A's *kuleana* and possesses it for the statutory period while fulfilling all requirements of adverse possession. The adverse possessor cannot interfere with B's easement over the land nor C's judgment lien.[59]

e. *Conclusion*

Even the strongest proponents of adverse possession would not dispute the four common law limitations placed on the doctrine. These restrictions are nearly as old as the doctrine itself and have a firm basis in public policy. The limitations imposed by the 1978 constitutional amendment are relatively new with no case law by which to assess their impact. However, they do reflect a less tolerant attitude toward wholesale application of the law of adverse possession, a trend that the courts also seem to have adopted.[60]

4. RIGHTS OF ADVERSE POSSESSOR BEFORE CLAIM HAS RIPENED

Until the statutory period has expired, an adverse possessor has no actual estate or interest in the property which can defeat the interest of the true owner. The true owner may legally reclaim the property at any time before the expiration of the statutory period.

However, an adverse possessor has rights that are based upon possession alone. For example, the adverse possessor owns the crops harvested during the period of possession.[61] Moreover, with the exception of the true owner, the adverse possessor can legally protect possession of the property against the world. Since trespass is a possessory action, an adverse possessor is entitled to a judgment in such an action against a person who invades the adverse possessor's legally protected interest.[62] For example, if a trespasser enters the property and starts uprooting taro plants, the adverse possessor may legally eject the trespasser and sue for damages.

The adverse possessor also has the right to transfer the interest, or number of years already spent on the property, to another person who can in turn use it to eventually satisfy the statutory requirement.[63] Thus, an adverse possessor can devise rights to another and that person, if all the other elements of adverse possession are satisfied, will then become the rightful owner of the property once the statutory period is met.

On the other hand, the true owner may try to convey the interest but if nothing is done to interrupt the statutory period, then that conveyance is nullified and the adverse possessor will take the property rather than the true owner's transferee. In short, the adverse possessor holds title not merely against the owner but also against transferees. Confirming this rule in *Waianae Co. v. Kaiwilei* (1917),[64] the Hawai'i Supreme Court held that the mere delivery of a deed to two minor children of defendant would not destroy the continuity of the adverse possessor's possession nor stop the running of the statute.[65]

5. ELEMENTS OF ADVERSE POSSESSION

The mere possession of land for 20 years alone is not enough to acquire title by adverse possession. The adverse possessor must show by clear and positive proof that the possession was (1) actual, (2) open and notorious, (3) exclusive, (4) continuous, and (5) hostile.[66] While each of these elements of adverse possession must be met, the facts and evidence proving one element will very often be used to prove another element.

a. *Actual Possession*

(1) *Actual Possession by Adverse Claimant*   In order for the statute of limitations to run, it is necessary not only that the true owner be out of actual possession, but also that there be an entry upon the land by another. The statute does not run against the true owner in favor of one who has never entered the land.[67] In 1880, the Hawai'i Supreme Court, in *Akowai v. Lupong*,[68] held that in order for a *konohiki* to adversely possess a *kuleana* located within land owned by the *konohiki*, the *konohiki* must show actual possession. In *Akowai*, the *kuleana* had been abandoned for over 20 years. On the other hand, the *konohiki* had never actually occupied the lot. The court noted that it was aware that "there are many kuleanas in the same position as this, totally deserted for over twenty years, hitherto deemed valueless by their owners, and only recently of any market value."[69] Thus, the court made it clear that for an adverse possession claim to succeed there must be "*actual, visible*, notorious, distinct and hostile"[70] possession. This rule applies not only to private parties but also to the government when it claims property by adverse possession.[71]

The policy considerations for requiring actual possession are two-fold: (1) if no one is in possession, there is nothing to suggest to the rightful owner the desirability or propriety of asserting rights in the land; and (2) if no one is in possession, there is no one against whom the rightful owner can enforce a right of action or entry.[72] In *Manumanu v. Rickard* (1879), the Hawai'i Supreme Court addressed the issue of notice, stating that "although the character of . . . possession may be varied . . . still it must be of such notoriety as that the owner may be presumed to have notice of it."[73]

(2) *Actual Possession Depends on Facts and Circumstances*   What is sufficient to constitute actual possession of the land depends on the nature, size, and location of the property, the uses to which it can be applied, and all the facts and circumstances of a particular case.[74] To be in actual possession, the claimant need not reside on the land.[75] All that is required to meet this element is that the land be used in a reasonable way, whether it be urban or rural land. However, occasional or infrequent visits, without residence or occupation, are insufficient to establish actual possession.[76] In one Hawai'i case, the supreme court noted that infrequent visits to the property to pick and gather fruits do not constitute continual possession or "even possession at all."[77]

An agent or tenant of the adverse possessor can occupy or use the land and satisfy the actual use requirements.[78] In *Kaae v. Richardson* (1907),[79] the court found the evidence slight but held that cutting wood and payment of taxes by a plaintiff who claimed title by purchase and prescription, combined with leasing the land to a tenant who made actual use of the land, justified an inference of adverse possession.

The evidence in each of the following three cases -- *Deponte v. Ulupalakua Ranch* (1964), *Gomes v. Upchurch* (1967), and *Thomas v. State* (1973) -- was considered substantial enough to constitute actual possession.[80] In *Deponte*, claimant Ulupalakua Ranch had used the land for 33 years continuously, cleared and planted grass, ran cattle in, paid taxes for over 20 years, paved the land, and cut down Deponte's fence two weeks after it was completed. Moreover, no one else used or was permitted to use the land.[81] In *Gomes*, claimant had a fattening pen on the land, continuously maintained a stone wall, constructed a water pipeline system, seeded the land, cut trees, and controlled growth.[82] In *Thomas*, uncontroverted evidence showed claimants had built a lumber shed, tool shed, and garage on the land and used it to store automobiles, firewood, and tools.[83]

b. *Open, Notorious, and Visible Possession*

Similar to the actual possession requirement and often used interchangeably, open, notorious, and visible possession means that the claimant's possession must be of such a character that the owner or owner's agent "on visiting the premises might readily see that the owner's rights are being invaded."[84] There must be evidence of use such that the neighbors or passers-by would reasonably assume that the adverse possessor is the true owner.

The Hawai'i courts have ruled that an adverse possession must be within the knowledge of the owner,[85] and an assertion of the adverse right must be brought home to the owner.[86] In *Manumanu v. Rickard* (1879),[87] the supreme court found that occasional visits to the land, without residence or occupation, and declarations that the land belonged to the claimant, which were not brought to the knowledge of the landowner, were not sufficient. One hundred years later in *In re Keamo* (1982),[88] the Intermediate Appellate Court found that attempts to rent out the property, payment of property taxes, and three visits to the property were not enough to meet the burden of proving "open and notorious" possession.

The purpose of both the actual and the open and notorious requirements is to give owners *notice* or put them on guard sufficiently to enable them to take preventive action.[89] Hence, title may never be acquired by mere possession, however long continued, which is surreptitious or secret or is not such as will give unmistakable notice of the nature of the occupant's claim.[90] It has been declared that the disseisor "must unfold his flag" on the land, and "keep it flying," so that owners may see, if they will, that an enemy has invaded their domain, and planted the standard of conquest.[91]

c. *Exclusive Possession*

Exclusivity of possession is an essential element of adverse possession.[92] "Exclusive" possession means that the claimant holds possession of the property for the claimant alone and not for another. Possession must exclude the true owner; possession that is concurrent with that of the true owner is never exclusive.[93]

In *Bishop v. Kala* (1889),[94] the court found that the adverse claimants' ancestor Keau, head fisherman of chiefess Ke'elikōlani, did not have exclusive possession of the property claimed. According to the claimants' own testimony, the chiefs, who were the true owners of the land, had placed their canoes and nets on the property and removed them as they pleased. Keau cared for their canoes and nets and used them in the adjacent fisheries.[95] Thus, the court found that the chiefs' continuing use of the parcel, without question from Keau, indicated that Keau's use of the premises was not exclusive and not hostile.[96]

On the other hand, two or more claimants can jointly obtain title by adverse possession, provided there is no element of hostility in the holding of one toward the other or others. In *Magoon v. Hong Yee Chuck* (1930),[97] three claimants, Kala, his wife Kaui, and his *hanai* sister Rose, were held to be joint disseisors for the full term of the statutory period. They acquired undivided interests to the property as tenants-in-common.[98]

Earlier, the Hawai'i Supreme Court had held that if all the elements of an adverse possession claim had been met, two tenants-in-common could claim undivided interests against a third co-tenant. In *Pebia v. Hamakua Mill Co.* (1927),[99] the court allowed an adverse claim against a third co-tenant where neither of the co-tenants claiming adverse possession knew, or reasonably could have known, of the interests of the third co-tenant during the period of possession.

Without exclusivity, there can be no possession, and consequently no adverse possession claim. If a person does not exclude others, it does not appear that that person is acting as an owner. If the true owner continues to exert control over the property, then a would-be adverse possessor will fail in a bid to claim the land. As noted earlier, there must be visibility in possession. Non-exclusive use does not indicate visible or open possession.

d. Continuous Possession

The element of continuous possession overlaps that of actual possession. "Continuous" does not mean constant. There is no requirement that the claimant possess every minute of the day. In determining what use is "continuous," the location and condition of the land must be considered as well as the claimant's acts of ownership. While the claimant must demonstrate a clear use or exercise of dominion over the property, minimal use may be considered continuous if the location and condition of the land so dictates. However, periodic or sporadic acts of ownership are not sufficient to constitute adverse possession.[100]

(1) *Statutory Period* Except for the number of years specified, the language of the Hawai'i statute of limitations on actions to recover real property has changed little over the years. In 1870, when the first statute was enacted, the law called for a 20-year limitations period.[101] In 1898, the limitations period was decreased to 10 years.[102] In 1973, the 20-year period was restored.[103]

The 1898 act decreasing the limitations period from 20 years to 10 years contained a savings clause stating that an action by the true owner could be brought within one year based on the old statutory period of 20 years. Thus, if the true owner was faced with an adverse possessor of 14 years, the true owner had to sue by New Year's Day of 1900 or be barred.[104] After January 1, 1900, the adverse possessor with 10 or more years of possession would have a vested right in the property.

The 1973 act also contained a savings clause stating: "This Act shall take effect upon its approval and should govern any case or controversy which shall arise after the effective date of the Act; provided, however, that this Act does not affect rights and duties that matured, penalties that were incurred, and proceedings that were begun, before its effective date."[105] The Hawai'i Supreme Court pointed out, in *Campbell v. Hipawai Corp.* (1982),[106] that this savings clause was prompted by the legislature's concern to protect vested rights and that the bill was specifically amended to insure that the act would be prospective in nature and would not affect the rights and duties existing under the law at the time.[107] Thus, anyone who had satisfied the requirements for adverse possession for the full 10-year period, had a vested adverse possession claim even if they had not filed a quiet title or land court action.

On the other hand, an adverse possessor whose claim had not matured before May 4, 1973, the effective date of the act, had to add 10 more years to the length of possession before rights could vest. Hawai'i's statute is explicit in acknowledging that no possible rights accrue to the adverse possessor before the full statutory period.[108] A guide to understanding the statute is to remember that it is fundamentally designed to limit a remedy.[109] Statutes of limitations, as commonly understood, are time limits within which judicial relief must be sought, otherwise, any action will be barred.[110]

It is not only what the adverse possessor does that confers title, but also what the true owner fails to do when an adverse claimant is in possession of the owner's land.[111] Therefore, the true owner has rights until the full statutory period has run, and the 1973 amendment increased that period from 10 to 20 years. Thus, a claimant with eight years of possession on May 4, 1973, would have to possess the property for an additional 12 years before title would vest.

The Hawai'i courts have also ruled that periods of adverse use prior to the grant of an award from the Land Commission cannot be included in an adverse possession claim. In the first case to consider the issue, *Kanaina v. Long* (1872),[112] claimant's adverse possession claim dated from the *Mahele* of 1848. However, the court held that the prescriptive period could run only from the date of the Land Commission Award in 1854. The court found that the Land Commission was a court of record and that there had thus been an adjudication of title of which all parties in interest were obliged to take note.[113] In *Kahoomana v. Minister of Interior* (1875),[114] the claimant's adverse possession claim dated from 1820 but the Land Commission had not granted an award on the parcel. The court stated that it did not regard the evidence of possession of the property previous to the organization of the Land Commission as evidence of title to land acquired anterior to that date, "for the Land Commission was authorized to take evidence of the previous possession, among other elements of title, upon which to base grants to land."[115] Since the land had never been awarded, it remained with the government and not the chief of the *ahupua'a*.[116] Finally, in *Dowsett v. Maukeala* (1895),[117] the court held that the possession of tenants living on an *ahupua'a* by permission of the chief or *konohiki*, previous to the establishment of the Land Commission, is presumed to continue to be permissive after the award of title to the owner of the *ahupua'a*, unless facts are known which would render the possession adverse.[118] In all three cases, whether a Land Commission Award was granted or not, all possessions prior to the award or the formation of the Land Commission were, in some sense, considered permissive. Thus, none of that time could be tacked on to later periods of adverse possession.

Whether a 10- or 20-year statutory period, Hawai'i's case law makes it clear that possession must be continuous. In numerous cases, the courts have failed to find adverse possession if the full statutory period was not satisfied.[119]

(2) *Tacking of Possession* An adverse claimant does not have to depend solely upon personal possession to establish title. By "tacking" together separate periods of possessions of different adverse possessors, the last adverse possessor may fulfill the statutory period. Tacking has been upheld in a number of Hawai'i cases. The first and foremost case is *Kainea v. Krueger* (1929),[120] which states the well-established general rule: "[W]here there is such a privity of estate or title so that the several possessions can be referred to the original entry they may be joined, and are regarded as a continuous possession, as in the case of landlord and tenant, ancestor and heirs, and vendor and vendee."[121] Cases involving tacking usually occur where the adverse claimant is trying to use a predecessor's years of possession to fulfill the 20-year requirement. However,

Hawai'i's statute on computing time allows for tacking insofar as the true owner is concerned: "If the right first accrued to any ancestor or predecessor of the person bringing the action or making the entry, or to any persons from, by, or under whom he claims, the twenty years shall be computed from the time when the right first accrued to the ancestor, predecessor, or other persons."[122]

In order to tack successive periods of possession, there must always be "privity" between the possessors. *Kainea v. Krueger* (1929)[123] furnishes a comprehensive definition of privity: "Privity denotes merely a succession of relationships created by deed or other act or by operation of law, a continuous possession by mutual consent, so that possession of the true owner shall not constructively intervene. It is not essential that there should be conveyances between successive occupants provided they claim under each other in some sufficient way."[124]

It is important, though, that there be an agreement or understanding which has for its object, a transfer of the rights of the original entry.[125] Since no such transfer occurred in *Wilder v. McFarlane* (1906),[126] the court found that there was no privity between father and daughter and the defendant's action in taking possession of the disputed land was a separate act of disseisin on her part. While the father did transfer some property to his daughter, there was no mention of the disputed piece of property and thus, his years of possession could not be tacked onto hers.

To establish privity, there must be a transfer of property. The transfer, however, need not be in writing. It may be proven by oral evidence.[127] The only essential element of the transfer is that the predecessor passes it to the successor by mutual consent, as distinguished from the case where a possessor abandons possession generally, and another, finding the premises unoccupied, enters without consent or relation to the former.[128]

As pointed out earlier, in order to tack possessions, all of the elements of adverse possession must be met by each successive possessor. Thus, if a parent acknowledges a true owner's interest and is in possession by permission of the true owner, the parent's possession cannot be tacked onto the child's possession, which is adverse to the owner, to meet the duration requirement.

In *In re Sing Chong Co.* (1945),[129] the court did not allow tacking because there had been no denial of the true owner's title, nor did the court find any evidence of disseisin of the true owner. Similarly, in *Suzuki v. Garvey* (1952),[130] the defendants could not tack on their predecessor's possession since their predecessor had recognized the true owner's ownership of an easement.[131]

Since the whole purpose of tacking is to satisfy the adverse possession requirement of continuity for a certain period of time, it is essential that there be no breaks between the successive periods -- that these periods be continuous. In *McCandless v. Honolulu Plantation Co.* (1908),[132] there was a break in possession, with the current adverse possessors obtaining the prior adverse possessor's claim after a four-year break. The court found that the ouster of the initial adverse possessor was a separate act of disseisen, and obtaining the initial adverse possessor's claim four years afterwards did not enable the current adverse claimants to tack their possession to the prior possession.[133]

Akin to tacking is the use of a tenant to help an adverse possessor establish actual, hostile, continuous, exclusive, and notorious possession of a piece of property. The possession of a tenant inures to the benefit of the landlord and constitutes the possession of the landlord both for purposes of showing adverse possession and benefitting from the statute of limitations bar.[134] It is important to remember that in order to utilize a tenant's possession, all of the elements of adverse possession must be met by that tenant. For instance, in *In re Kamakana* (1978),[135] the government argued that A.F. Cooke's possession of Kānoa fishpond under a lease from the government could be used to establish the government's adverse possession claim. However Cooke also held title to the fishpond under a quit-claim deed. The court determined that Cooke's possession of Kānoa fishpond could not be presumed to be hostile to, and impart a denial of, his *own* title to the pond.[136] Generally, however, an adverse possessor can use a tenant's possession as part of an adverse possession claim if the tenant is an agent for the adverse possessor.

(3)   *Break in Continuity of Possession*   A break in the continuity of possession by the adverse possessor interrupts the running of the 20-year period and places the land back into the constructive possession of the true owner. A "substantial continuous cultivation" of land is sufficient for continuity of possession.[137]   But if, for example, after eight years of adverse possession, the possessor decides to move from the property, he or she may be deemed to have "abandoned" the property with no intent of returning. If so, the continuity of possession is terminated. Therefore, if the adverse possessor subsequently returns, the previous eight years cannot be used to satisfy the 10- or 20-year requirement. The adverse possession period must begin anew.

In *Leialoha v. Wolter* (1913), defendants left the property due to a quarantine order and failed to return as soon as was reasonably practicable after the quarantine was lifted. The time away from the property due to the quarantine was exempted. However, defendants left the property vacant, unenclosed and unused for 2-1/2 years following the quarantine. The court concluded that they had failed to satisfy the required continuity of possession.[138]

On the other hand, "a mere absence is not an abandonment."[139]   In *Keawe v. Kana* (1927),[140] the adverse claimant left the property in order to earn money to meet his temporary needs. While he was gone, no one else took possession of the land. Since the absence was caused by "hard times," and not an intent to abandon the property, the court found that "under these circumstances plaintiff's absences did not constitute abandonment."[141]

Recognition of the true owner's title also interrupts the continuity necessary to acquire title by adverse possession.[142]   In Hawai'i, the courts have held that recognition of the true owner's title will not alone defeat an adverse possession title. However, "such recognition is evidence to be considered in determining whether in fact the prior possession of the adverse claimant was in fact adverse or a possession in subordination to the title of the true owner."[143]

Possession adversely commenced is presumed to continue as adverse so long as maintained.[144]   However, acts recognizing the owner's title will defeat an adverse possession claim, or because the running of the statute is interrupted, an adverse claim may become permissive. Simply put, "[i]nterruption of the continuity necessary to acquire title by prescription occurs when the adverse claimant recognizes the title of the disseizee."[145]

In *McCandless v. Mahelona* (1899),[146] the court found that acceptance of money for taxes on the land from the true owner, with other slight evidence, was sufficient to support a finding by the jury that the possession was not adverse. In contrast, in *Deponte v. Ulupalakua Ranch* (1964),[147] the acceptance of a quit-claim deed by the adverse possessor, after a possession of 31 years, was not deemed an acknowledgement of the superiority of the true owner's title.

A third way to interrupt the continuity of a possession is through the owner's entry on the land or action in bringing suit. Hawai'i Revised Statutes (Haw. Rev. Stat.) section 657-38, entitled "Possession, interrupting statute," requires that after entry, the owner continue in open and peaceable possession for one year or commence an action within one year after ouster. However, one expert contends that an adverse claimant must still meet the common law requirement of continuous possession, uninterrupted by the true owner or any third party.[148] Thus, possessory retaking, even if less than a year in duration, would succeed in defeating the adverse possession claim.

An overt act of dominion over or claim to the property in dispute is needed to interrupt the continuity of possession.[149] A mere transitory entry without the adverse possessor's knowledge is insufficient.[150] Moreover, brief visits by third parties not claiming title to the property do not interrupt the running of the statute.[151] Finally, the fact that an owner deeds to another person does not destroy the continuity of an adverse claimant's possession.[152]

e. *Hostile Possession*

(1) *Hostility Is Necessary* Without hostility there would be no "adversity" in an adverse possession claim. *Every* adverse possession claim must address the issue of hostility in one way or another and all four previously discussed elements of adverse possession may be viewed as different forms of hostility. Actual use means that the adverse possessor uses the land in opposition to the true owner's rights. Notorious visible possession means that the owner is put on notice of a claim of right. Continuous means that the use continues hostile for the statutory length of time. Exclusive use means excluding use by the true owner.

Throughout the history of adverse possession in Hawai'i, the courts have upheld the necessity of this very important element. As early as 1876, the court held in *Kahukuleionohi v. Kaikainahaole*,[153] that no right to bring suit for possession of land can accrue to a plaintiff unless the possession by defendant is "adverse." In 1904, the court found: "It is, of course of the essence of adverse possession that it should be hostile and that the circumstances of the holding be such as to give the true owner notice, at least if he paid attention to his rights, that the possession is under claim as owner . . . ."[154] Simply put, this means "possession . . . to be adverse must be hostile."[155]

(2) *Denial of the Owner's Right, Claim of Right, and Notice to the Owner* Mere possession is not enough to show hostility -- there must be a claim of right and a distinct disavowal of the owner's title to the land.[156] The rightful owner of land is deemed to have the possession until ousted from it or disseised. It is the denial of the owner's right and the owner's failure to do anything about it that starts the running of the statute of limitations.

"A possession, in order to be adverse within the meaning of the rule and in order to transfer title to the adverse holder . . . must be hostile to the true owner and must have been such as to inform the true owner that it was being held in hostility to him."[157] The logical justification for this requirement is that, without it, the true owner is lulled into a false sense of security and would refrain from asserting a right by entry or action.[158] The requirement of notoriety or notice has been discussed previously. Mere mental reservations,[159] or a claim made only in the privacy of the attorney-client relationship,[160] or a mere secret, mental process[161] are insufficient notice and do not amount to a claim of right.

Actions recognizing the true owner's title do not show hostility. One such recognition is payment of rent. In *Smith v. Hamakua Mill Co.* (1904),[162] the court found a possible construction of the facts to be that "Kia believed that Kapehe had a valid claim and feared that she might assert it . . . ." Therefore, he "gave her money so as to lead her to believe . . . that it was a portion of the rent . . . and in that way misled her into thinking that he was not holding adversely to her."[163]

In *Smith v. Laamea* (1927),[164] individuals were permitted to live upon portions of the 'ili in exchange for payment of $1.00 per year for fishing rights and a duty to perform labor. The court found that nothing less than clear and explicit notice to the owner by word or act could change the character of the possession from a permissive to an adverse one, and a permissive possession cannot ripen into an adverse title no matter how long it may continue.[165]

Similarly, in *In re Nelson* (1923),[166] trustees had paid the beneficiary, who was the true owner, all of the net rents, issues, and profits from the land, but then claimed to hold the property adversely to the beneficiary. The court asked: "How can there be any hostility when all the time the whole of the rents and profits of the land are being handed to the true owner?" The answer: "It cannot be."[167] The court found in *Waimea Falls Park v. Brown* (1985),[168] that the defendants' conduct in entering into numerous rental agreements with Waimea Falls Park was "a representation that they did not have title, and a recognition of the title of Waimea and its predecessors."[169]

Other instances in which title of the true owner has been recognized include accepting money from the owner for taxes on the land,[170] leasing the land from the owner,[171] not leasing out the portion of property being claimed,[172] recognizing an easement,[173] or requesting permission to use an easement.[174] The deciding factor hinges on whether these acts would lead the true owner to believe that possession was in subordination of his or her title. If so, the adverse claim would fail for lack of hostility and notice.[175]

On the other hand, in *Pebia v. Hamakua Mill Co.* (1927),[176] the court found a claim of right and notice based on the following factors: actual possession, payment of all taxes, repeated acts of leasing and mortgaging by the adverse claimants, conveyance of part of the land, statements of claiming in fee, lack of knowledge of the alleged true owners' deed, collection of all rents, and failure to pay alleged true owners any part of the income produced from the land. The court concluded, "[W]hen all of these things concur they are sufficient to give notice to the alleged true owners that the actual holders are holding adversely to them or would be sufficient if the true owners had paid proper attention to their rights."[177]

(3) *Permissive Possession Can Become Hostile Possession* Where a possessor is on the land by contract or by permission of the true owner, such as a tenant or licensee, hostility is not shown. Such relationships are interpreted as an acknowledgement or admission of the true owner's superior right to the property. A claim of right or disseisen with some kind of notice is pivotal to making a possession hostile. The rule is that "the rightful owner of land is deemed to have the possession until he is ousted from it or disseized, and . . . he is restored to possession when the hostile possession or disseizen ceases."[178]

Possession which begins as permissive is presumed, in the absence of any showing to the contrary, to continue to be permissive.[179] However, an entry which was initially permissive can become hostile. As pointed out in *Kaaihue v. Crabbe* (1877), permissive possession may become hostile by "[a] clear, positive and continued disclaimer and disavowal of the title" and "an assertion of an adverse right brought home to the owner."[180] Without this, the length of the occupancy is immaterial and does not affect the title.

Although the best evidence of a disclaimer or disavowal is actual notice in some form, in most cases disavowal is shown by the exercise of control over and use of the property inconsistent with the rights of the owner. Constructive notice of a disclaimer or disavowal may suffice to make a permissive possession hostile.[181] For example, in *Kalakaua v. Keaweamahi* (1883), the court determined that even if the adverse claimant was a trustee, his permissive possession could become hostile and that the award, which he accepted in his name, "constituted an open and constant repudiation of any trust" and operated as notice that "he claimed the possession as owner."[182]

In *John Ii Estate, Ltd. v. Mele* (1903),[183] the land in question originally had been awarded to the *konohiki* by the Land Commission. It adjoined the adverse claimant's property and he treated it as his own, enclosed it within a fence, and maintained it continuously. Moreover, the only dwelling on the premises stood on the portion in controversy, and later houses replaced that one on the same spot. Further, the claimant was not a servant of the *konohiki*, never paid any rent in money or in labor, and after a time began paying the taxes on the land.[184] The Hawai'i Supreme Court had previously held in *Dowsett v. Maukeala* (1895),[185] that the possession of land prior to a Land Commission Award was presumptively permissive. However, in this case, the court determined that under these circumstances, possession could become hostile *after* the Land Commission awarded the land to the *ahupua'a* owner.[186]

(4) *Color of Title* "Color of title" is defined as any writing which on its face appears to pass title but which fails to do so either because the person making the writing does not have title or because the conveyance mode used is defective.[187]

In the first Hawai'i case to deal with color of title, *Kalakaua v. Keaweamahi* (1883), the Hawai'i Supreme Court held: "We believe the law to be well settled, that the circumstance that the title claimed was void or commenced in fraud of law, does not detract from the force of adverse possession commenced under it."[188] Ten years later, the court in *George v. Holt* (1893)[189] stated a principle that the courts have continued to uphold. "While it is true that the possession must be under claim of title, it is not essential that there should be a rightful title. An invalid and defective title, *if believed to be good*, will be equally operative with a valid one in giving effect to a possession taken and held under it."[190] (Citations omitted; emphasis added.)

Furthermore, under common law, color of title is not necessary to show adverse possession, and is just one factor to consider in determining hostility. The Hawai'i Supreme Court stated in *Territory v. Pai-a* (1938):[191] "It is the rule in this jurisdiction that color of title is not indispensable to prove title by adverse possession if the other necessary elements, namely, actual, open, notorious, continuous and exclusive possession for the statutory period as the apparent owner, are shown to exist, and is not explained."[192] (Citations omitted.)

While not essential nor indispensable, "color of title reflects the character of the occupants' possession and, if shown to exist, is unquestionably an element tending to prove hostility of possession."[193] In other words, "color of title, even under a void and worthless deed, has always been received as evidence that the person in possession claims for himself, and of course adversely to all the world."[194] In a co-tenancy situation, "[t]he existence or non-existence of color of title is one factor for the jury to consider in evaluating whether a party in possession reasonably believed himself to be sole owner."[195]

Under the common law, the chief effect of color of title is to define the limits of the claim. It is used as evidence of *constructive* possession when only a portion of the entire property described in the instrument actually has been occupied by the adverse possessor.[196] Conversely, where a claimant has no color of title, the claimant must prove actual possession to all parts of the property being claimed.[197]

However, to be effective as color of title, the property must be described with a degree of certainty so that the boundaries may be ascertained.[198] Moreover, in *Malani v. Kaahumanu Society* (1935),[199] the Hawai'i Supreme Court held that adverse possession under color of title is limited to the area described in the deed or instrument conveying title.[200]

In 1983, the legislature passed Act 222,[201] which amended Haw. Rev. Stat. section 669-1 of the Quieting Title chapter by adding to section (b):

> For purposes of this section, any person claiming title by adverse possession shall show that such person acted in good faith. Good faith means that under all the facts and circumstances, a reasonable person would believe that the person has an interest in title to the lands in question and such belief is based on inheritance, a written instrument of conveyance, or the judgment of a court of competent jurisdiction.[202]

This statute appears to require color of title, unless the claim is based upon inheritance, in order to prevail in an adverse possession claim. However, the law has never been specifically interpreted by the Hawai'i courts.

In sum, color of title, under the common law, has not been necessary for adverse possession claims. Color of title, even though invalid or defective, has been accepted to show the character of an occupant's possession. The major effect of color of title is to help define the limits of a claim. However, since 1983, statutory law appears to require color of title for many claims as an element of good faith in adverse possession cases. It remains to be seen what effect this statute will have on case law relating to color of title.

(5) *Rebuttable Presumption* In *Albertina v. Kapiolani Estate* (1902),[203] the Hawai'i Supreme Court, in broadly defining the element of hostility, held that "where one is shown to have been for the statutory period in actual, open, notorious, continuous and exclusive possession, apparently as owner, and such possession is unexplained, either by showing that it was under a lease from, or other contract with or otherwise by permission of the true owner, the presumption is that such possession was hostile."[204] The court qualified this presumption in another case decided the same year, *Kapiolani Estate v. Cleghorn* (1902),[205] in which it held: "[w]here one is shown to have been in possession of land for the period of limitation, apparently as owner, and such possession is not explained or otherwise accounted for, it will be presumed to have been adverse, *although this presumption is open to rebuttal*."[206] (Emphasis added.)

Since these earlier cases, the court has more strictly construed hostility. In 1938, in *Territory v. Pai-a*,[207] the court reflected: "[W]e think [the defendant's counsel] have failed to recognize the well-known rule that the *presumption* of hostility may be rebutted by other facts and circumstances shown to exist."[208] Furthermore, the court added, "Adverse possession is to be taken strictly, and every presumption is in favor of a possession in subordination to the rightful owner. Title by adverse possession, therefore, must be established by clear and positive proof."[209] In fact, for the most part,[210] the court has used the stricter "clear and positive proof" standard set out by *Territory v. Pai-a* rather than the broader definition of hostility used in the earlier cases.[211]

(6) *Payment of Taxes* The rule on payment of taxes is fairly simple and straightforward. It is not necessary that an adverse claimant have paid taxes -- payment of taxes is only one of the factors to be considered in establishing adverse possession.[212] In fact, in several cases, the adverse possessors did not pay taxes and the court still found in their favor.[213] Moreover, there are several Hawai'i cases in which the claimants did pay taxes but failed to prevail in showing hostility.[214]

The court examines the totality of acts and circumstances, not just the payment of taxes, in determining hostility. For instance, in the first payment-of-taxes case, *Paulo v. Malo* (1883),[215] the defendants had cultivated or improved the land *and* paid taxes on the land for over 20 years. The court found "the character of their acts and possession may be taken as notice to the owners of a claim of title."[216] In three other cases, the adverse possession claimants did not pay taxes but they still prevailed, mainly because their acts taken altogether were sufficient to establish hostility and a claim of right.[217] There is no requirement that taxes be paid throughout the adverse period to establish adverse possession.

Just as the totality of facts is important in cases where no taxes were paid and adverse possession was found, so too is it important for cases where taxes were paid and no adverse possession was found. In *Territory v. Pai-a* (1938),[218] in addition to not paying taxes, the appellant and his predecessors lacked color of title, failed to communicate an intent of hostility to the owners of the property, and at all times seemed to have an amicable and friendly relationship with the owner. The court found that the failure to pay taxes "while not of itself controlling, detracts from the strength of the appellant's present claim of ownership."[219] Failure to pay taxes for a long period of time tends to weaken an adverse possession claim.[220]

In two other cases, the totality of facts, including the failure to pay taxes, added up to a finding of no adverse possession. In *In re Sing Chong Co.* (1945),[221] the adverse possession claimant consistently leased out less than the total area claimed, did not collect or pay territorial real property taxes on the whole parcel, and upon transferring the property, did not include covenants of warranty in the papers. Similarly, in *Okuna v. Nakahuna* (1979),[222] claimant's father made infrequent visits to the property, did not pay taxes, and did not have color of title; plaintiff himself continued to visit the property infrequently, did not pay taxes, and failed to list the property as part of his father's estate. In reviewing all of the factors in the above cases, the court found that the facts and circumstances did not amount to adverse possession.

Finally, payment of taxes must be supported by evidence. In *Oahu Railway & Land Co. v. Kaili* (1915),[223] no tax receipts were produced and it did not appear that the defendant who testified was cognizant of how long or how often taxes were paid. In *Kainea v. Krueger* (1929),[224] the respondent offered certain tax receipts but the receipts did not indicate on what property the taxes were paid. Therefore, the court concluded that they had "no proper tendency to prove the fact in support of which they were offered, to wit, payment of taxes on that particular piece of land."[225] Thus, although payment of taxes may be shown in support of a claim of adverse possession, the evidence must be sufficient and show a connection to the property in dispute.

(7) *Co-Tenancy* In disputes between co-tenants, the presumption is that a co-tenant in possession occupies the premises in common with other co-tenants.[226] Each co-tenant is entitled to enter and occupy the common property. The co-tenant in possession is deemed to hold the property permissively. Hence, the remaining co-tenants are justified in assuming that the co-tenant in possession is not asserting a claim of exclusive ownership.[227] On the other hand, if the parties are strangers in title, the true owner out of possession would and should naturally scrutinize any acts sufficient to notify him or her of the existence of adverse claims.[228]

Not only are co-tenants entitled to share the property, but "[t]he authorities are unanimous and clear that the possession of one co-heir enures to the benefit of the other co-heirs or tenants in common."[229] Stated another way, "[t]he entry and possession of one tenant in common, is ordinarily deemed the entry and possession of all the tenants."[230] In fact, if two or more persons adversely possess a piece of property, and one of these co-tenants should abandon the land, the other co-tenant(s), not the original owner, would acquire the share of the co-tenant out of possession.[231]

Although co-tenants are deemed to hold for one another, co-tenants can still adversely possess property against one another: "One co-tenant may, by an adverse holding of the common property, of which the other has notice, acquire title to the whole as against the ousted tenant."[232] The earlier courts speak of an ouster requirement: "Actual ouster is always said to be required before a co-tenant can bring ejectment . . . ."[233] An ouster is the wrongful dispossession or exclusion from real property of a party who is entitled to the possession.[234] It amounts to the adverse possession requirements of exclusion, notoriety, and hostility.

Over the years, the courts have clarified the requirements that must be met for an adverse claim between co-tenants. In 1877, the court in *Nakuaimanu v. Halstead & Gordon*[235] called for "an ouster, or what is equivalent, a demand for possession and a refusal."[236] In 1893, the court stated: "The proof of ouster between tenants in common ought to be of the most satisfactory nature. The law will deem the possession amicable until the tenant out of possession has in some method been notified that it has become hostile."[237]

In 1901, in *Smith v. Hamakua Mill Co.*,[238] the court appeared to make an exception to this rule for co-tenants who are ignorant of the existence of fellow co-tenants. On the one hand, the court acknowledged that in co-tenant cases, "more significant acts or conduct would generally be required, for the co-tenant in possession would in such case naturally be supposed to be acting merely in the exercise of his own rights and not in denial of his co-tenant's rights."[239] It also laid out the rule that "the circumstances must be such as to bring home to the ousted owner the adverse character of the possession, or be such as would bring it home to him if he paid proper attention to his rights."[240]

On the other hand, the court made it clear that it was not requiring "that there must be actual notice to or knowledge on the part of the one out of possession, or that the more stringent rule applicable to cases of co-tenancy applies where there is no recognition or knowledge of the existence of a co-tenancy."[241] It also felt that it would be absurd to require co-tenants, who were ignorant of the existence of a co-tenancy, "to hunt the world over for possible co-owners."[242]

Fifty-nine years later, the same language of *Smith v. Hamakua Mill Co.* was approved in *Poka v. Holi* (1960):[243] "[A]n heir and tenant in common of the property . . . would have a fiduciary relationship to the other heirs, his co-tenants, and this in itself would require that [the co-tenant in possession] *bring home* to the other heirs the knowledge or notice of the adverse claim."[244] (Citations omitted; emphasis added.)

In 1971, *Yin v. Midkiff*[245] examined the law and the necessary sufficiency of evidence in cases of co-tenants, and noted that traditionally courts have held that a co-tenant claiming adversely has the burden of showing the following essential requirements: "(1) a clear intent to claim adversely; (2) adverse possession in fact; and (3) knowledge or notice of the hostile holding brought home to the cotenant or cotenants out of possession."[246]

In addition to these requirements, in cases where the co-tenants are "closely related by ties of blood, the burden of the cotenant claiming adversely is intensified."[247] The additional element of "actual knowledge," rather than "mere circumstances putting the possessor's co-tenants on notice" is required.[248] Because the adverse claimants in *Redfearn v. Kuhia* (1972)[249] did not exclude their co-tenant from the property, they failed to meet all three *Yin* requirements: (1) there was no clear intent, (2) there was no adverse possession in fact ("possession was of an equivocal nature"), and (3) one co-tenant did not bring home to the other co-tenant notice of hostile holding.[250]

Subsequently, in *City and County of Honolulu v. Bennett* (1976),[251] the court expanded on these earlier holdings, stating:

> Following in the line of *Yin* and *Poka*, we lay down in this case the rule that, because of the general fiduciary relationship between cotenants, a tenant in common claiming by adverse possession must prove that he acted in *good faith* towards the cotenants during the statutory period. In most circumstances, this requirement of good faith will in turn mandate that the tenant claiming adversely must *actually notify* his cotenants that he is claiming against them. In the following exceptional circumstances, however, good faith is satisfied by less than actual notice: where the tenant in possession has *no reason to suspect* that a cotenancy exists; or where the tenant in possession makes a *good faith, reasonable effort to notify* the cotenants but is unable to locate them; or where the tenants out of possession already have *actual knowledge* that the tenant in possession is claiming adversely to their interests. In these limited circumstances, the notice requirement will be satisfied by constructive notice and "open and notorious possession."[252]

Although there are a number of cases interpreting *Bennett*'s good faith requirement,[253] *Bennett* itself provides the most cogent discussion of good faith. For instance, mere ignorance is not sufficient. Where a co-tenant claims adversely, the standard of good faith includes an objective requirement of *reasonableness*, in addition to a subjective requirement that the claimant actually believe that he or she is the sole owner.[254]

The existence or non-existence of color of title is one factor for the jury to consider in evaluating whether a party in possession reasonably could believe he or she was the sole owner. On the other hand, evidence that the co-tenant in possession knew or ought to have known that there existed a co-tenancy, together with evidence that the party in possession did not attempt to notify the co-tenants of the claim to sole ownership, can justify a finding of bad faith, assuming that the co-tenants did not already have actual knowledge of the adverse claim.[255]

In summary, since co-tenants are entitled to enter and occupy the property in common, a higher standard of hostility must be met before a co-tenant can adversely possess against another co-tenant. That standard has become clearer through the years, evolving from a vague "ouster or its equivalent," to the *Yin* three-prong test for non-related co-tenants plus the "actual knowledge" requirement for closely related co-tenants. Presently, the *Bennett* requirement of "good faith" amplifies the *Yin* holding.

6. CONCLUSION

Historically, the doctrine of adverse possession in Hawai'i stands in marked contrast to the communal system of Native Hawaiian land tenure in which land was held in trust by the *ali'i* for the benefit of all. Adverse possession as applied to land ownership subsequent to the *Mahele*, served to isolate and privatize land tenure.[256] Historically, and even in contemporary times, the beneficiaries of the adverse possession doctrine have been large plantations, ranches, and *konohiki* heirs or assigns. Indeed, these entities continue to apply the doctrine to settle title to large tracts of land.

Under the current constitutional, statutory, and procedural scheme, there appears to be a greater concern for the rights of heirs of original grantees. This is reflected in the relatively recent adoption of such requirements as statewide publication of notice to unknown heirs, the requirement of a "good faith" premise for a claim, the five-acre-or-less limitation as to property which can be claimed through adverse possession, and the limitation on the filing of each claim to once in each 20-year period. Since many adverse possession claims matured or accrued prior to changes in the adverse possession law, these statutory and procedural changes have had a prospective rather than retroactive effect.

However, it is questionable whether even these recent changes to the adverse possession laws are sufficient to redress historical dispossession of Native Hawaiians from their lands. To some extent, the adverse possession doctrine in its modern context does give small landowners a more accessible means to settle title to their parcels. This is particularly important when title has to be resolved amongst family members. However, proving an adverse possession claim in court is financially prohibitive for many. In truth, the proportionate cost burden on the small landowner is a practical bar to settling interests in family property.

Efforts by the Hawaiian community to abolish adverse possession have been unsuccessful, in part because adverse possession can be a useful tool for Native Hawaiians to clear title to family property. Moreover, without an appropriate mechanism to establish and settle title to property, the entire private property system would be in chaos. At least one solution has been offered by William S. Richardson, then-Chief Justice of the Hawai'i Supreme Court. He suggested the creation of a state agency that would determine and register title to ancestral lands and absorb the prohibitive financial cost to individual Native Hawaiians.[257] It may be time to seriously consider such an alternative if Native Hawaiians are to retain their *kuleana* and family lands.

NOTES

1. *See Manumanu v. Rickard*, 4 Haw. 207 (1879); *Bishop v. Kala*, 7 Haw. 590 (1889); *Deponte v. Ulupalakua Ranch, Ltd.*, 48 Haw. 17, 395 P.2d 273 (1964), rehearing denied 48 Haw. 149, 396 P.2d 826 (1964); *Gomes v. Upchurch*, 50 Haw. 125, 432 P.2d 890 (1967); and *Thomas v. State*, 55 Haw. 30, 514 P.2d 572 (1973), *appeal after remand*, 57 Haw. 639, 562 P.2d 425 (1977).

2. The original act establishing adverse possession in the Kingdom of Hawai'i is entitled "An Act Limiting the Time, Within Which Actions May be Brought to Recover Possession of Land." *Session Laws English*, ch. XXII, at 28-30 (1870-82), effective July 31, 1871. In 1898, the government amended the 1870 law so that the time to bring actions was reduced to 10 years, *Session Laws*, ch. 19, § 1, 22 (1898), effective January 1, 1899. Then, in 1973, the legislature lengthened the statutory period back to 20 years, *Session Laws*, Act 26, § 4 (1973), effective May 4, 1973.

3. Steadman, *The Statutory Elements of Hawaii's Adverse Possession Law*, 14 Hawaii B.J. 67, 70 (1978).

4. *Leialoha v. Wolter*, 21 Haw. 624, 630 (1913). This case goes on to state:

   > By adverse possession of land for the statutory period of limitation the adverse holder acquires a title in fee simple which is as perfect as a title by deed. Its legal effect is not only to bar the remedy of the owner of the paper title, but to divest his estate and vest it in the party holding adversely for the required period of time, so that he may maintain an action of ejectment for the recovery of the land even as against the holder of such paper title who has ousted him.

   Id. (quoting 1 Am. and Eng. Ency. Law 883, 886 (2d ed.)).

5. Hirayasu, *Adverse Possession and Quiet Title Actions in Hawaii -- Recent Constitutional Developments*, 19 Hawaii B.J. 59, 69-71 (1985).

6. *See Leialoha v. Wolter*, 21 Haw. 624 (1913).

7. Hirayasu, *supra* note 5, at 59-60 (quoting Bordwell, *Seisin and Disseisin*, 34 Harv. L. Rev. 592 (1920-21)).

8. W.E. Burby, *Handbook of the Law of Real Property* 267 (3d ed. 1965).

9. Hirayasu, *supra* note 5, at 60.

10. *Id.* (quoting Moynihan, *Introduction to the Law of Real Property* 90 (1962)).

11. A.J. Casner & W.B. Leach, *Cases: Text on Property* 245 (2d ed. 1969).

12. *Id.*

13. The statute of St. James, 21 Jac. 1, ch. 16, § 1, 2 (1623):

    > For quieting of men's estates and avoiding of suits [described types of action] shall be sued and taken within twenty years next after the title and cause of action first descended or fallen, and at no time after the said twenty years; . . . and that no person or persons shall at any time hereafter make any entry into any lands, tenements or hereditaments, but within twenty years next after his or their right of title which shall hereafter first descend or accrue to the same, and in default thereof, such persons, so not entering and their heirs, shall be utterly excluded and disabled from such entry after to be made . . . .

    R. Powell, 7 *The Law of Real Property*, Para. 1012 [1], at 91-3 n.7 (1982) [hereinafter *Powell on Property*].

14. Burby, *supra* note 8, at 267.

15. *Powell on Property*, *supra* note 13, Para. 1012 [3], at 91-9.

16. 3 *American Law of Property* 759, § 15.2 (1952).

17. *Powell on Property*, *supra* note 13, Para. 1012 [1], at 91-2.

18. Burby, *supra* note 8, at 268.

19. *Id.*

20. *Powell on Property*, *supra* note 13, Para. 1012 [3], at 91-9.

21. "An act limiting the time within which actions may be brought to cover possession of land," Hawaiian Statutes Session Law (English), ch. XXII, at 28-30 (1870-82).

22. For an in-depth discussion of this process, *see generally* J. Chinen, *The Great Mahele* (1952), and *Original Land Titles in Hawaii* (1961).

23. Levy, *Native Hawaiian Land Rights*, 63 Calif. L. Rev. 848 (1975).

24. *Id.*

25. 3 Haw. 635, 640 (1875). *See also Dowsett v. Maukeala*, 10 Haw. 166 (1895), and *In Kamakana*, 58 Haw. 632, 574 P.2d 1346 (1978).

26. Hirayasu, *supra* note 5, at 64.

27. *Id.*

28. Levy, *supra* note 23, at 858.

29. *Id.* at 869.

30. W.S. Richardson, *Chief Justice Challenges Conference*, 1 The Native Hawaiian 6 (July 1977).

31. Senator Kawasaki on the Hawai'i Senate Floor, March 30, 1973.

32. Delegate Okamura, 2 *Proceedings of the Constitutional Convention of Hawaii of 1978*, 448 (1978).

33. Town and Yuen, *Public Access to Beaches in Hawaii, A Social Necessity*, 10 Hawaii B.J. 21 (1973).

34. Levy, *supra* note 23, at 869.

35. Delegate Hoe, 2 *Proceedings of the Constitutional Convention of Hawaii of 1978*, 447.

36. S. Rep. No. 387 7th Leg., 1st Sess., *1973 Senate Journal* 811.

37. 2 *Proceedings of the Constitutional Convention of Hawaii of 1978*, 926.

38. S. Rep. No. 387, 7th Leg., 1st Sess., *1973 Senate Journal* 811.

39. "Quieting Title," art. XVI, § 12, Hawai'i State Constitution:

> Article XVI, Section 12. Quieting Title. No person shall be deprived of title to an estate or interest in real property by another person claiming actual, continuous, hostile, exclusive, open and notorious possession of such lands except to real property of 5 acres or less. Such claim may be asserted in good faith by any person not more than once in 20 years.

(As amended by the Hawai'i State Constitutional Convention, 1978 and adopted by voters on November 7, 1978.)

40. Acquiring Title by Adverse Possession, Hearing on S. 660 Before the Senate Committee on Judiciary, 7th Leg., 1st Sess., February 28, 1973 (written testimony of Page Anderson).

41. Delegate Burgess, 2 *Proceedings of the Constitutional Convention of Hawaii of 1978*, 446.

42. *Id.*

43. *Powell on Property, supra* note 13, Para. 1012[3], at 91-9. *See* S. Rep. No. 541, 7th Leg., 1st Sess., *1973 House Journal* 995.

44. *Id.*

45. *Waianae Co. v. Kaiwilei*, 24 Haw. 1, 7 (1917); *see also Kalakaua v. Keaweamahi*, 4 Haw. 577 (1883) (The policy of the law is to give quiet and repose to titles. After great lapse of time and long peaceable possession equity courts ought not to interfere.).

46. *See* Haw. Rev. Stat. § 501-87 (1980). Some cases enunciating this principle are: *In re Kamakana*, 58 Haw. 632, 574 P.2d 1346 (1978); *State v. Zimring*, 52 Haw. 477, 479 P.2d 205 (1970); *In re Kelley*, 50 Haw. 567, 445 P.2d 538 (1968).

47. 3 Haw. 635 (1875).

48. *Id.* at 641.

49. *See* Haw. Rev. Stat. §§ 657-34 and 657-36 (on Disabilities), and Steadman, *supra* note 3, at 75-76.

50. Steadman, *supra* note 3, at 75.

51. 9 Haw. 135 (1893).

52. *Id.* at 139.

53. *Id.* at 24 Haw. 1 (1917).

54. *Id.* at 2 (1917). For more rules of law, *see* Burby, *supra* note 8, at 272-278.

55. Haw. Rev. Stat. § 657-33 (1985).

56. 18 Haw. 625 (1908).

57. *Id.*

58. *See* Haw. Rev. Stat. § 501-82 (1985) re: types of encumbrances that may affect a transfer of property title. *See also Packaging Products Co. v. Teruya Bros., Ltd.*, 58 Haw. 580, 585, 574 P.2d 524, 528 (1978), stating that "one who takes a certificate of title to registered land for value and in good faith holds the land free from all encumbrances except those noted on the certificate and those enumerated in the statute." (Referring to Haw. Rev. Stat. § 501-82 (1985).)

59. *See generally* 1 K. Watson, *Report for Alu Like: Adverse Possession* (November 21, 1977) (unpublished paper).

60. In *City and County of Honolulu v. Bennett*, 57 Haw. 195, 208, 552, P.2d 1380, 1389 (1976), the Hawai'i Supreme Court noted:

> In general, we approach the issue of notice in a spirit opposed to the unduly facile acquisition of title by adverse possession. We take judicial notice that a critical attitude towards over-generous rules of adverse possession has manifested itself recently in law commentaries and legislative activity.

61. Burby, *supra* note 8, at 269-270.

62. *Id.* at 270.

63. *See infra* text accompanying notes 120-133.

64. 24 Haw. 1 (1917).

65. *Id.* at 6.

66. *Manumanu v. Rickard*, 4 Haw. 207, 208 (1879): "The law is clear that 'the nature of that adverse possession of land which is required to constitute a bar to the legal title, must be an *actual*, visible, notorious, distinct and hostile possession.'" (Quoting 2 Washburn on Real Property, p. 489.)

67. Tiffany, 4 *Real Property*, ch. 26, § 1137, at 704 (3d ed. 1975) [hereinafter *Tiffany*].

68. *Akowai v. Lupong*, 4 Haw. 259 (1880).

69. *Id.* at 261.

70. *Id.* at 262.

71. *In re Moiliili, Waikiki-Waena, City and County of Honolulu*, 49 Haw. 537, 553, 425 P.2d 83, 92-93 (1967).

72. *Tiffany, supra* note 67.

73. *Manumanu v. Rickard*, 4 Haw. 207, 208 (1879).

74. *Tiffany, supra* note 67, at 706. *See, also, Powell on Property, supra* note 13, Para. 1013[2][a], at 91-12.

75. *Thomas v. State*, 55 Haw. 30, 514 P.2d 572 (1973).

76. *Manumanu v. Rickard*, 4 Haw. 207, 208 (1879).

77. *Okuna v. Nakahuna*, 60 Haw. 650, 657, 594 P.2d 128, 132 (1979).

78. *Kainea v. Krueger*, 31 Haw. 108, 114 (1929).

79. *Kaae v. Richardson*, 18 Haw. 503 (1907).

80. *Deponte v. Ulupalakua Ranch*, 48 Haw. 17, 395 P.2d 273 (1964); *Gomes v. Upchurch*, 50 Haw. 125, 432 P.2d 890 (1967); *Thomas v. State*, 55 Haw. 30, 514 P.2d 572 (1973).

81. *Deponte v. Ulupalakua*, 48 Haw. 17, 18, 395 P.2d 273, 274 (1964).

82. *Gomes v. Upchurch*, 50 Haw. 125, 126, 432 P.2d 890, 891-892 (1967).

83. *Thomas v. State*, 55 Haw. 30, 31-32, 514 P.2d 572, 574 (1973).

84. *Marengo Cave Co. v. Ross*, 10 N.E.2d 917, 920 (Indiana 1937).

85. *Kanaina v. Long*, 3 Haw. 332, 335 (1872).

86. *Kaaihue v. Crabbe*, 3 Haw. 768, 774 (1877).

87. *Manumanu v. Rickard*, 4 Haw. 207 (1879).

88. *In re Keamo*, 3 Haw. App. 360, 650 P.2d 1365 (1982).

89. *Powell on Property, supra* note 13, Para. 1013[2][b], at 91-13, 14.

90. *Tiffany, supra* note 67, § 1140.

91. *Marengo Cave Co. v. Ross*, 10 N.E.2d 917, 920 (Indiana 1937). In *Kalakaua v. Keaweamahi*, 4 Haw. 577, 581 (1883), the claimant received an award from the Land Commission and occupied the land for more than 30 years. The Hawai'i court found that the award constituted an open and constant repudiation of any trust and served as notice to the plaintiff's grantor that he claimed the possession as owner.

92. *Nihoa v. Chow*, 57 Haw. 172, 552 P.2d 77 (1976).

93. *Powell on Property, supra* note 13, Para. 1013[2][d] at 91-9.

94. *Bishop v. Kala*, 7 Haw. 590 (1889).

95. *Id.* at 592-593.

96. *Id.* at 593.

97. *Magoon v. Hong Yee Chuck*, 31 Haw. 661 (1930).

98. *Id.* at 671.

99. *Pebia v. Hamakua Mill Co.*, 30 Haw. 100 (1927).

100. *Powell on Property, supra* note 13, Para. 1013[2][e], at 91-21.

101. "An Act Limiting the Time Within Which Actions May Be Brought to Recover Possession of Land," Hawaiian Statutes Session Law (English), ch. XXII, at 28-30 (1870-82). *See also* Haw. Rev. Stat. § 657-31 (1985) stating:

    > Twenty Years. No person shall commence an action to recover possession of any lands, or make any entry thereon, unless within twenty years after the right to bring the action first accrued.

102. "An Act Relating to the Limitation of Time Within Which Action May Be Brought to Recover Possession of Land," Hawaiian Statutes Session Law (English), ch. 19, § 1 (1898).

103. S. 660, 7th Leg., 1st Sess., 1973 Haw. Sess. Laws C. 26, § 2.

104. Steadman, *supra* note 3 at 69.

105. S. Rep. No. 838, 7th Leg., 1st Sess., *1973 House Journal* 1163-1164.

106. *Campbell v. Hipawai Corp.*, 3 Haw. App. 11, 639 P.2d 1119 (1982).

107. *Id.* at 14, 639 p. 29 at 1121.

108. Hirayasu, *supra* note 5.

109. Steadman, *supra* note 3, at 67.

110. *Id.* at 70.

111. It is not simply a matter of an owner abandoning a piece of property for 20 years but a matter of that owner's inaction *in relation* to an adverse possession claimant. As pointed out in *Akowai v. Lupong*, 4 Haw. 259 (1880), an adverse possession claim is required before the statutory period can begin to run and that claim must satisfy all of the elements of adverse possession in order to bar legal title to a piece of property. *Id.* at 262.

112. *Kanaina v. Long*, 3 Haw. 332 (1872).

113. *Id.* at 335.

114. *Kahoomana v. Minister of Interior*, 3 Haw. 635 (1875).

115. *Id.* at 637.

116. *Id.* at 639.

117. 10 Haw. 166 (1895).

118. *Id.*

119. *Fong Hing v. Yamaoka*, 31 Haw. 436 (1930) (adverse possession did not continue for statutory period of 10 years prior to commencement of the action); *Kailianu v. Lumai*, 8 Haw. 256 (1891) (plaintiffs had not possessed for period of 20 years prior to bringing of action of ejectment); *Smith v. Hamakua Mill Co.*, 13 Haw. 716 (1901) (alleged adverse possession was not hostile for a portion of the necessary statutory period).

120. 31 Haw. 108 (1929).

121. *Id.* at 115.

122. Haw. Rev. Stat. § 657-32 (1985).

123. 31 Haw. 108 (1929).

124. *Kainea v. Krueger,* 31 Haw. 108, 116 (1929).

125. *Id.* at 115.

126. 18 Haw. 121, 124-125 (1906).

127. *Kainea v. Krueger*, 31 Haw. 108, 115 (1929); *Territory v. Pai-a*, 34 Haw. 722, 725 (1938) (it is recognized in this jurisdiction that an oral transfer is sufficient to authorize tacking).

128. *Kainea v. Krueger*, 31 Haw. 108, 115 (1929).

129. *In re Sing Chong Co.*, 37 Haw. 49 (1945).

130. *Suzuki v. Garvey*, 39 Haw. 482 (1952). Also, as pointed out in *Territory v. Pai-a*, 34 Haw. 722, 725 (1938), there was no hostility found since a person could not adversely possess against himself.

131. *Suzuki v. Garvey,* 39 Haw. 482, 483-484 (1952).

132. 19 Haw. 239 (1908).

133. *Id.* at 241.

134. *In re Sing Chong Co.*, 37 Haw. 49, 52 (1945); *Kainea v. Krueger,* 31 Haw. 108, 115 (1929).

135. 58 Haw. 632, 574 P.2d 1346 (1978).

136. *Id.* at 642-643, 574 P.2d at 1352.

137. *Paulo v. Malo*, 6 Haw. 390 (1883).

138. *Leialoha v. Wolter*, 21 Haw. 624, 628-629 (1913).

139. *Kailianu v. Lumai*, 8 Haw. 256, 258 (1891).

140. 30 Haw. 204 (1927).

141. *Id.* at 207. *See also Kailianu v. Lumai*, 8 Haw. 256, 258 (1891) ("a mere absence is not an abandonment").

142. *Oahu Railway & Land Co. v. Kaili*, 22 Haw. 673, 674 (1915).

143. *Id.* at 679-680.

144. *Kalakaua v. Keaweamahi*, 4 Haw. 577, 581 (1883).

145. *Oahu Railway & Land Co. v. Kaili*, 22 Haw. 673, 680 (1915).

146. 12 Haw. 258 (1899).

147. 48 Haw. 17, 395 P.2d 273 (1964).

148. Steadman, *supra* note 3, at 78.

149. *Waianae Co. v. Kaiwilei*, 24 Haw 1, 8 (1917).

150. *Keawe v. Kana*, 30 Haw. 204, 208 (1927).

151. *U.S. v. Fullard-Leo*, 66 F.Supp. 782 (1944).

152. *Waianae Co. v. Kaiwilei*, 24 Haw. 1, 8 (1917).

153. 6 Haw. 183 (1876).

154. *Smith v. Hamakua Mill Co.*, 15 Haw. 648, 656 (1904). Similarly: "A possession, in order to be adverse within the meaning of the rule and in order to operate to transfer title to the adverse holder, must be not only continuous and exclusive, . . . but it must be hostile to the true owner . . . ." *In re Nelson*, 26 Haw. 809, 816 (1923).

155. *In re Sing Chong Co.*, 37 Haw. 49, 52 (1945) ("hostile" as that term is employed is the definition of adverse possession, *i.e.* possession for oneself under claim of right).

156. *Kaaihue vs. Crabbe*, 3 Haw. 768, 774 (1877). *See also Kalakaua v. Keaweamahi*, 4 Haw. 577, 580 (1883) (a possession to be adverse must be under a claim of title against all the world); *Territory v. Pai-a*, 34 Haw. 722, 726 (1938) ("[a] possession, however open and long continued it may be, will not operate as a disseisen and commencement of a new title unless it imports a denial of the owner's title"); *In re Kamakana*, 58 Haw. 632, 642, 574 P.2d 1346, 1351 (1978) ("[h]ostility imports denial of the owner's title, and possession, however open and long it may be, is not adverse without such a denial of the rightful owner's title") quoting from *Territory v. Pai-a*, 34 Haw. 722, 726 (1938).

157. *In re Nelson*, 26 Haw 809, 816 (1923).

158. *Tiffany, supra* note 67, § 1142, 743.

159. *In re Nelson*, 26 Haw. 809, 817 (1923).

160. *Poka v. Holi*, 44 Haw. 464, 481, 357 P.2d 100, 110, *rehearing denied*, 44 Haw. 582, 358 P.2d 53 (1960).

161. *Smith v. Laamea*, 29 Haw. 750, 759 (1927).

162. 15 Haw. 648 (1904).

163. *Id.* at 656.

164. 29 Haw 750 (1927).

165. *Id.* at 757-758.

166. 26 Haw. 809 (1923).

167. *Id.* at 816-817.

168. 6 Haw. App. 83, 712 P.2d 1136 (1985).

169. *Id.* at 99, 712 P.2d at 1146.

170. *McCandless v. Mahelona*, 12 Haw. 258, 261 (1899) ("acceptance of money as taxes on the land from the true owner by one in possession, knowing it to be paid by the true owner as taxes due by him, and not accepted as a gift or a loan, would constitute a recognition of the title of the true owner").

171. *Oahu Railway & Land Co. v. Kaili*, 22 Haw. 673 (1915) (new trial granted to consider whether a lease amounted to a recognition of title).

172. *In re Sing Chong Co.*, 37 Haw. 49 (1945) (adverse possessors leased out no more than their proportionate interest in the land, and also paid taxes on the property, but not for the lost *kuleana*).

173. *Suzuki v. Garvey*, 39 Haw. 482, 485 (1952) ("the rental paid by the Suzukis was a nominal one for the reason that Mrs. Kim recognized the Suzukis' rights, both in the property and the easement").

174. *Tagami v. Meyer*, 41 Haw. 484 (1956) (where a party requests permission to use an easement or pays a consideration for the use of such easement during a part of the prescriptive period, this constitutes an admission fatal to the claimant).

175. *See supra* text accompanying notes 84-91 (earlier discussions on open and notorious possession). *See also supra* text accompanying notes 156-177 (discussion on notice).

176. 30 Haw. 100 (1927).

177. *Id.* at 110.

178. *Rose v. Smith*, 5 Haw. 377, 378 (1885).

179. *Smith v. Hamakua Mill Co.*, 15 Haw. 648, 657 (1904).

180. 3 Haw. 768, 774 (1877). *Also in Kalaeokekoi v. Kahanu*, 4 Haw. 481, 482 (1882) (quoting *Kaaihue v. Crabbe*), *Smith v. Laamea*, 29 Haw 750, 758-759 (1927) (quoting 2.C.J. 134 § 230).

181. *Dowsett v. Maukeala*, 10 Haw. 166, 168 (1895) ("where the occupation has been with the permission of the owner of the land, in order that adverse possession may begin to run it is necessary that *some direct notice* be given to the owner that the occupier is holding hostile to himself") (quoting lower court's instructions) (emphasis added).

182. 4 Haw. 577, 581 (1883).

183. *John Ii Estate, Ltd. v. Mele*, 15 Haw. 124 (1903).

184. *Id.* at 126-127.

185. 10 Haw. 166 (1895).

186. 15 Haw. at 127.

187. Thompson on Property, § 2550, at 640.

188. 4 Haw. 577, 581 (1883).

189. 9 Haw. 135 (1893).

190. *Id.* at 139-140. *See also Waianae Co. v. Kaiwilei*, 24 Haw. 1, 7 (1917), and *Thomas v. State*, 55 Haw. 30, 32, 514 P.2d 572, 574-575 (1973).

    This qualification in *George* can be harmonized with *Kalakaua* by examining the underlying facts. In *Kalakaua*, the fraud involved the actions of a predecessor-in-interest to the adverse claimant, who was not an active participant in the fraud. In view of the doctrine's equitable underpinnings, it would be ironic for a court to sanction the willful wrong-doing of an adverse claimant. The court in *Kalakaua* was apparently willing to overlook the actions of the predecessor, so long as the current claimant was not a direct party to the fraud. No court has sanctioned any willful misconduct by quieting title in an adverse claimant who engaged in such activity. Rather, the court has consistently required the adverse claimant to show that he/she honestly believed that title was good, whether title is actually valid or not. More zealous adverse claimants would maintain that the absence of an honest belief in good title is immaterial, *i.e.,* no good faith is required. In other words, an adverse claimant is entitled to commence possession whether or not he/she has an honest belief in good title. However, the case law does not go quite so far.

191. 34 Haw. 722 (1938).

192. *Id.* at 725-726; *see also Albertina v. Kapiolani Estate*, 14 Haw. 321, 325 (1902), *Lai v. Kukahiko*, 58 Haw. 362, 368, 574 P.2d 1346, 1351 (1977), and *Minatoya v. Mousel*, 2 Haw. App. 1, 5, 625 P.2d 378, 381-382 (1981).

193. *Territory v. Pai-a*, 34 Haw. 722, 726 (1938).

194. *U.S. v. Carter*, 2 U.S. Dist. Ct. 326, 336 (1905).

195. *City and County of Honolulu v. Bennett*, 57 Haw. 195, 211, 552 P.2d 1380, 1391 (1976).

196. *Apo v. Dillingham Investment Corp.*, 50 Haw. 369, 370, 440 P.2d 965, 966 (1968), 57 Haw. 64, 69, 549 P.2d 740, 744 (1976).

197. *Powell on Property, supra* note 13, Para. 1013[2][g] at 91-42.

198. Thompson on Property § 2550, at 641.

199. 33 Haw. 387 (1935).

200. *Id.* at 393.

201. 1983 Haw. Sess. Laws Act 222, § 1.

202. Haw. Rev. Stat. § 669-1(b) (1985).

203. 14 Haw. 321 (1902).

204. *Id.* at 325 (1902), citing 1 Am. & Eng. Encycl. Law, 2nd ed., 888, 890; 1 Cycl. L. & P. 1146; *Morse v. Churchill*, 41 Vt. 649, 651; *Neel v. McElhenny*, 69 Pa. St. 305; *Wilkins v. Nicolai*, 99 Wis. 178, 182, 183; *Meyer v. Hope*, 101 Wis. 123, 125. *Also upheld* in *Oahu Railway & Land Co. v. Kaili*, 22 Haw. 673, 677-678 (1915). Somewhat related is the adverse use of an easement and the presumption of a lost grant, see *Lalakea v. Hawaiian Irrigation Co.*, 36 Haw. 692, 707 (1944), where the court stated: "The longer the period the stronger the presumption of a grant."

205. 14 Haw. 330 (1902).

206. *Id.* at 337-338.

207. 34 Haw 722 (1938).

208. *Id.* at 726.

209. *Id.,* citing 1 R.C.L. 695.

210. *See however Deponte v. Ulupalakua Ranch*, 48 Haw. 17, 19, 395 P.2d 273, 275 (1964) (upholding *Albertina v. Kapiolani Estate*, 14 Haw. 321, 325 (1902) and *Kapiolani Estate v. Cleghorn*, 14 Haw. 330 (1902)).

211. *Tagami v. Meyer*, 41 Haw. 484, 488 (1956) ("[a]dverse possession is to be taken strictly, and every presumption is in favor of a possession in subordination to the rightful owner") (quoting 1 R.C.L. 695); *Territory v. Pai-a*, 34 Haw. 722 (1938); *Redfearn v. Kuhia*, 53 Haw. 378, 381, 494 P.2d 562, 564 (1972) ("title by adverse possession must be established by clear and positive proof") (citation omitted); *Okuna v. Nakahuna*, 60 Haw. 650, 656, 594 P.2d 128, 132 (1979) ("the undisputed findings of the trial court demonstrate that this element [of hostility] was not established by clear and positive proof").

212. *In re Wong*, 47 Haw. 472, 477, 391 P.2d 403, 405 (1964). *See Territory v. Pai-a*, 34 Haw. 722 (1938); *Kainea v. Krueger*, 31 Haw 108 (1929); *Oahu Railway & Land Co. v. Kaili*, 22 Haw. 673 (1915); *Paulo v. Malo*, 6 Haw. 390 (1883); *Deponte v. Ulupalakua Ranch*, 48 Haw. 17, 395 P.2d 273 (1964); *Gomes v. Upchurch*, 50 Haw. 125, 432 P.2d 890 (1967); *Lai v. Kukahiko*, 58 Haw. 362, 569 P.2d 352 (1977).

213. *Paulo v. Malo*, 6 Haw. 390 (1883); *Deponte v. Ulupalakua Ranch*, 48 Haw. 17, 395 P.2d 273 (1964); *Gomes v. Upchurch*, 50 Haw. 125, 432 P.2d 890 (1967); *Lai v. Kukahiko*, 58 Haw. 362.

214. *In re Wong*, 47 Haw. 472, 391 P.2d 403 (1964); *In re Keamo*, 3 Haw. App. 360, 650 P.2d 1365 (1982).

215. *Paulo v. Malo*, 6 Haw. 390 (1883).

216. *Id.* at 390-91.

217. *Deponte v. Ulupalakua Ranch*, 48 Haw. 17, 20 (1964); *Gomes v. Upchurch*, 50 Haw. 125, 126-127, 432 P.2d 892 (1967); *Lai v. Kukahiko*, 58 Haw. 362, 367-368, 569 P.2d 352, 356 (1977).

218. 34 Haw. 722 (1938).

219. *Id.* at 728.

220. *Id.*

221. *In re Sing Chong Co.*, 37 Haw. 49 (1945).

222. *Okuna v. Nakahuna*, 60 Haw. 650, 594 P.2d 128 (1979).

223. 22 Haw. 673 (1915).

224. 31 Haw. 108 (1929).

225. *Id.* at 109.
226. *Redfearn v. Kuhia,* 53 Haw. 378, 381, 494 P.2d 562, 564 (1972) (citing *Yin v. Midkiff,* 52 Haw. 537, 541, 481 P.2d 109 (1971); *Aiona v. Ponahawai Coffee Co.,* 20 Haw. 724, 727 (1911); *Hawaiian Commercial & Sugar Co. v. Waikapu Sugar Co.,* 9 Haw. 75 (1893); *Nakuaimanu v. Halstead,* 4 Haw. 42 (1877)).
227. *Id. See also Hawaiian Commercial & Sugar Co. v. Waikapu Sugar Co.,* 9 Haw. 75, 80 (1893):

> As between tenants in common where all are entitled to the possession, the intent with which possession is taken is material, for a stranger having no title may enter land and exercise acts of ownership over it and leave little room to doubt that he thereby intends to oust the true owner. But a co-tenant may enter the whole or any part of the common estate as he has legal right to do, and the presumption of law is, when nothing more is done, that he intends to do nothing beyond the assertion of his right.

228. *Smith v. Hamakua Mill Co.,* 13 Haw. 716, 722 (1901).
229. *Nakuaimanu v. Halstead,* 4 Haw. 42, 43 (1877). *See McAulton v. Smart,* 54 Haw. 488, 491-492, 510 P.2d 93, 96 (1973) (citing the *Nakuaimanu* case for the proposition that: "an entry by one tenant in common is deemed in law to be an entry by all co-tenants").
230. *Peters v. Kupihea,* 39 Haw. 327, 331 (1952) (quoting *Clymer, et al. v. Dawkons, et al.,* U.S. 674).
231. *Kauhikoa v. Hobron,* 5 Haw. 491, 493 (1885) (citing *Allen v. Holton,* 20 Pick. 458).
232. *Aiona v. Ponahawai Coffee Co.,* 20 Haw. 724 (1911). *Also Yin v. Midkiff,* 52 Haw. 537, 540 (1971) ("[t]hat one co-tenant may hold adversely to another co-tenant is recognized in this jurisdiction").
233. *Nahinai v. Lai,* 3 Haw. 317, 318 (1871); *also Nakuaimanu v. Halstead,* 4 Haw. at 42, 43-44 (1877) ("[t]he Statute of Limitations does not run against a tenant in common unless there has been an actual ouster or its equivalent"); *Kaia v. Kamaile,* 4 Haw. 352, 358 (1880) (prescription not applicable if parties were co-tenants and there had been no ouster); *Kaahanui v. Kaohi,* 24 Haw. 361, 363 (1918) (one co-tenant in common may acquire the title of a co-tenant by adverse possession where the one ousts the other and claims the title which the other held, all of the necessary elements of adverse possession being present).
234. *Hawaiian Commercial & Sugar Co. v. Waikapu Sugar Co.,* 9 Haw. 75, 80 (1893).
235. 4 Haw. 42 (1877).
236. *Id.* at 44.
237. *Hawaiian Commercial & Sugar Co. v. Waikapu Sugar Co.,* 9 Haw. 75, 80 (1893). The case goes on to add:

> In Vermont it is said that the acts relied upon to prove ouster between tenants in common must be such as would constitute ouster between landlord and tenant.
> In New York it is held that to establish an adverse possession by one tenant in common such as will effect the ouster of his co-tenant, notice in fact of the adverse claim is required, or unequivocal acts, open and public, making the possession so visible, hostile, exclusive, and notorious that notice may be fairly presumed. (Citations omitted.)

238. 13 Haw. 716 (1901).
239. *Id.* at 722.
240. *Id.* at 721-722.
241. *Id.* at 722-723. *See also Pebia v. Hamakua Mill Co.,* 30 Haw. 100 (1927).
242. 13 Haw 716, 721 (1901).
243. 44 Haw. 464, 357 P.2d 100 (1960).
244. *Id.* at 481, 357 P.2d at 110.
245. 52 Haw. 537, 481 P.2d 109 (1971).
246. *Id.* at 540, 481 P.2d at 111.
247. *Id.* at 540, 481 P.2d at 111-112.
248. *Id.* In *Waimea Falls Park v. Brown,* 6 Haw. App. 83, 89-90, 712 P.2d 1136, 1141 (1985), the *Yin* requirement of knowledge or notice was not met since there was no indication that the co-tenant was named as party in case even though her interest was on record at Bureau of Conveyances, nor was she ever served or did she make an appearance.
249. 53 Haw. 378, 494 P.2d 562 (1972).
250. *Id.* at 382, 494 P.2d at 564-565.
251. 57 Haw. 195, 552 P.2d 1380 (1976).
252. *Id.* at 209-210, 554 P.2d at 1390.
253. Three cases illustrate the *Bennett* standard of "good faith": *Hana Ranch, Inc. v. Kanakaole,* 4 Haw. App. 573, 580, 623 P.2d 885, 889 (1981) (no actual notice given to any possible co-tenants and nothing to excuse such notice); *In re Keamo,* 3 Haw. App. 360, 368, 650 P.2d 1365, 1371 (1982) (case falling within "limited circumstances" category since appellees had "no reason to suspect" co-tenants existed); *Kipahulu Investment Co. v. Seltzer Partnership,* 4 Haw. App. 625, 628-629, 675 P.2d 778, 782 (1983) (the breaks in Kipahulu's chain of record title provided "reason to suspect" the existence of one or more co-tenants).
254. *City & County of Honolulu v. Bennett,* 57 Haw. 195, 210-211, 552 P.2d 1380, 1391 (1976).

255.   *Id.*

256.   While adverse possession did foster use of land, it also allowed for dispossession of land in favor of non-natives.

257.   Richardson, *supra* note 30.

PART THREE

NATURAL RESOURCE RIGHTS

CHAPTER 7

WATER RIGHTS

1. INTRODUCTION

The concept of water ownership did not exist in ancient Hawai'i. Water was a procreative force identified with the gods. The *ali'i 'ai moku* or district chief exercised dominion over the waters as an instrument of the gods. In other words, the *ali'i 'ai moku* was trustee of the waters for the people.[1] From the ancient Hawaiian perspective, water was not owned, but was subject to a right of use for productive purposes. The development of water rights in Hawai'i reveals the tension between this ancient concept of use rights and the Western-imposed private-ownership system. This conflict remains unresolved in Hawai'i case law, but the recent adoption of the State Water Code has provided a partial, if incomplete, solution to the difficult issues surrounding water management and use. The following chapter discusses and analyzes water rights in Hawai'i from ancient times to the present.

2. THE ANCIENT HAWAIIAN WATER SYSTEM

The ancient Hawaiians used surface waters primarily for the cultivation of taro, the staple crop of the islands. They constructed a complex system of *'auwai* or irrigation ditches for that purpose, and developed an administrative system to apportion the water among taro patches adjacent to a ditch or stream. A *luna wai* or watermaster, appointed by the *konohiki* or land agent, supervised the distribution of water.[2]

An *'auwai* typically ran from a stream through a series of taro patches adjacent to the *'auwai*. Sometimes the taro patches were terraced to permit drainage from upper to lower levels. At specified times, designated by the *luna wai*, the stream was dammed with loose stones and clods of dirt, causing it to rise sufficiently to flow into the *'auwai*.[3] Each taro grower then took water directly from the *'auwai*, or took the excess from the neighboring upstream grower.[4] To contain the water, taro farmers built dirt embankments along the boundaries of each taro patch. They planted secondary crops, like bananas, sugar cane, and yams, on these embankments.[5]

The usual method of water distribution was rotation according to time. For example, those farming a smaller plot of land might take the entire flow of the *'auwai* for a few hours, while those cultivating a larger one would take the flow for several days. Taro growers on large neighboring tracts of land might alternate day and night usage until all of the subdivisions in each tract had been irrigated. In times of abundant water supply, an upper taro grower might take all the water needed without regard to time, and then release the water to flow to lower planters for use in the same manner. In times of scarcity, each taro grower suffered proportionately from the diminished supply.[6]

In any event, the needs of downstream growers had to be respected. The *luna wai* did not permit any one *'auwai* to take more than half the flow of a stream. The quantity actually taken was usually less. Downstream users would enforce this rule by dismantling

149

a dam which diverted too much water.[7] In some instances, surplus water, meaning water beyond that needed for irrigation, was returned to the main stream for use by downstream planters.[8] Sometimes the *luna wai* allowed diversion of the surplus water to dry *kula* lands for a secondary crop of sweet potatoes. However, such surplus was never diverted if any of the taro patches needed water.[9] The transfer of water to upland areas far from the stream, or to lands beyond the watershed, was not an issue to the ancient Hawaiians, since they did not have the engineering tools to accomplish such large diversions.[10]

All of the taro growers were entitled to use the water, provided they helped to build and maintain the irrigation system and kept their lands productive. Each parcel of land shared the water in proportion to the number of laborers it provided to build a particular *'auwai* or dam.[11] Thus, a smaller land unit might be entitled to more water than a larger one, if it contributed more people to the project. When a single *'auwai* served two or more *ahupua'a*, the *konohiki* of the two lands joined in the construction of the *'auwai*. The *konohiki* who contributed the most hands to the effort supervised the work and often became the water master of the *'auwai*.[12] Distribution likewise was determined by the number of laborers contributed by each *ahupua'a*. The taro farmers worked to maintain the *'auwai* under the supervision of the *konohiki*. They could lose their water privileges if they failed to provide such maintenance labor or to keep their land productive.[13]

The powers of the *konohiki* were tempered by reliance on the people for labor. It was the responsibility of the *konohiki* to make the *ahupua'a* productive, and to pay tribute to superiors in the hierarchy. Therefore, the *konohiki* endeavored to treat all planters fairly and to avoid disputes among them. The *konohiki* was reluctant to impose unreasonable burdens on the tenants, since tenants were free to leave the land if they became dissatisfied. Under these circumstances, water disputes were rare, and a system of mutual support developed among the taro growers themselves and their chiefs.[14]

3.   WESTERN INFLUENCE

The traditional Hawaiian system of land tenure and water rights began to change with the arrival of foreigners, particularly Western merchants, to the islands.[15] Those merchants who had acquired land rights needed a more stable system of land ownership to advance their economic interests. In 1825, they prevailed upon King Kamehameha III to allow the chiefs to retain their lands upon the death of the previous king and to permit hereditary succession. Some Hawaiian lands were "given" to Westerners by the king or chiefs in return for services. Those Westerners who had received land rights from the king sometimes attempted to transfer these rights to other foreigners without the king's approval. Likewise, many chiefs attempted to transfer their land rights to Westerners without the approval of the crown.[16] As more and more Westerners acquired land interests, confusion and conflict increased.

The Declaration of Rights and the Constitution of 1839-1840 attempted to adjust the changing land rights of the chiefs, the people, and Westerners. The constitution declared that all lands had belonged to Kamehameha I, but not as his own private property. The land belonged to the chiefs and the people, subject to the king's management. The traditional Hawaiian notion of the king's trusteeship of land was therefore codified into law. The constitution also provided that all people were to be secure in their lands, and that nothing would be taken from any person, except by express provision of law. Thus, for the first time, the law recognized that the people had some form of ownership interest in land, as distinguished from a mere right of use.[17]

In contrast to the movement toward private ownership of land, the laws of 1839 treated water as a natural bounty reserved to all of the people. Specifically, the law "Respecting Water for Irrigation" provided that:

> In all places which are watered by irrigation, those farms which have not formally received a division of water, shall, when this new regulation respecting lands is circulated, be supplied in accordance with this law, the design of which is to correct in full all those abuses which men have introduced. All those farms which were formally denied a division of water, shall receive their equal proportion. Those bounties which God has provided for the several places should be equally distributed, in order that there may be an equal distribution of happiness among all those who labor in those places. The allowance of water shall be in proportion to the amount of taxes paid by the several lands. For it is not the design of this law to withhold unjustly from one, in order to unjustly enrich another according to the old system which has been in vogue down to the present time. That the land agents and the lazy class of persons who live about us should be enriched to the impoverishment of the lower classes who with patience toil under their burdens and in the heat of the sun is not in accordance with the designs of the law . . . such is considered to be the proper course by this law, regulating the property of the kingdom; not in accordance with the former customs of the country which was for the chiefs and land agents to monopolize to themselves every source of profit.[18]

This language revealed the king's intent to assert his sovereign power to regulate water for the common good. The right to use water was dependent upon taxes paid to the king, not upon servience to the *konohiki* of the *ahupua'a*. The implication is that the central government controlled the distribution of waters.

This law was apparently aimed at correcting certain abuses which arose during the transition from the traditional taro economy to a Western mercantile economy. In the process of change, the system of cooperation between the *konohiki* and tenants broke down along with the traditional restraints on the powers of the *konohiki*. With the introduction of the Western concept of material wealth, water came to be viewed as a commodity that could be separated from the land and consumed, rather than as a resource to be shared equally. The attainment of wealth would, therefore, depend more upon maximum use of the "commodity," and less upon the working of the land. The shift in thinking from equal rights to maximum use may have led the *konohiki* to neglect the irrigation rights of some tenants. These changes would assume great importance as the sugar industry rose to dominate the political and economic life of the islands. In any event, the law may have been the government's attempt to guard the rights of all the people against the intrusion of foreign practices.[19]

In 1845, the government created the Board of Land Commissioners to investigate and settle all land claims of private individuals, whether native or foreign. The Land Commission subsequently adopted seven principles to guide them in deciding all claims. The commission's work led to the *Mahele* of 1848, the division of lands between the king and the *konohiki*. Those lands retained by the king were subsequently divided into Government Lands and King's Lands.

All lands of the king, the government, and the *konohiki* were awarded subject to the rights of native tenants. In 1850, the enactment of further principles or the *Kuleana* Act empowered the Land Commission to award fee simple title to native tenants for their plots of land or *kuleana*.[20] The *kuleana* land of the people consisted primarily of irrigated taro patches located in the valleys. The awards were limited to the amount of land actually cultivated, plus small houselots distinct from the cultivated lands.[21] When the Land Commission confirmed an individual's land claim, it issued an award of that land to the claimant. Generally, upon payment of a commutation tax to the government, the minister of the interior conveyed complete title in the form of a royal patent. However, no commutation was required to secure title to *kuleana* land on the presumption that such commutation had already been paid by the *konohiki* of the *ahupuaʻa*.[22]

The act creating the Land Commission required that its decisions be based on existing law and native usages with regard to land, including among other things "water privileges."[23] Despite that language, the Land Commission did not determine or award water rights. However, the right to use water for irrigation has invariably been *implied* in an award of taro land by the Land Commission, even if the deed did not mention water rights.[24] Such rights came to be viewed as "appurtenant" to taro lands by reason of ancient custom and usage.

Section 7 of the *Kuleana* Act also contained the following water rights provision:

> The people also shall have a right to drinking and running water, and the right of way. The springs of water, and running water, and roads shall be free to all, should they need them, on all lands granted in fee simple: provided, that this shall not be applicable to wells and water courses which individuals have made for their own use.[25]

Over 100 years later, the Hawaiʻi Supreme Court held that this provision codified the common law doctrine of riparian water rights in Hawaiʻi.[26]

After the *Mahele*, the sugar companies began playing a prominent role in the life of the islands. Much of the land that had been transferred to the chiefs in the *Mahele* soon moved into the hands of Western sugar interests. The acquisition of lands allowed the sugar companies to assert water rights associated with those lands. Advancements in engineering made it possible to irrigate lands which had never before been irrigated. The first large irrigation canal, 11 miles long, was built at the Lihuʻe Plantation on Kauaʻi in 1856. A decade later, there were three sugar plantations in the Iao Valley on Maui, each of them diverting irrigation water from the Wailuku River. Disputes over water rights in the Wailuku River resulted in several early water rights cases decided by the Hawaiʻi Supreme Court.[27] In 1878, a group of cane planters, led by Alexander & Baldwin, constructed a 17-mile ditch from the high rainfall areas of eastern Maui to the plains of central Maui. The construction of several other great ditches followed, turning central Maui into one of the most productive sugar producing areas in the islands. In 1892, the Hawaiian Sugar Company completed a 13-mile system of tunnels, ditches, and flumes on Kauaʻi to divert water from the Hanapēpē River to the sugar lands of Makaweli. As the century drew to a close, the sugar industry's need for water continued to increase.[28]

As land titles became established pursuant to the *Mahele* and Land Commission Awards, controversies arose over water rights connected with those lands. In 1860, the legislature created the Commission of Private Ways and Water Rights to settle these controversies. Originally, the commission consisted of three persons appointed in each election district; however, by subsequent amendments the number of commissioners was reduced to one per district, and a right of appeal was allowed to the Hawaiʻi Supreme Court. In 1907, the office of commissioner was abolished and those duties were transferred to circuit court judges.[29]

The early proceedings before the commission were apparently informal in nature. The disputes related to small amounts of water used for domestic purposes and for irrigation of taro patches. The commissioners decided these cases based upon ancient custom and usage as reflected in the water rights of the parties just prior to the Land Commission Awards. In other words, they tried to determine the amount of water which each party was entitled to by customary usage. On this issue, the oral testimony of *kama'aina* or old timers from the district was often decisive. The proceedings generally resulted in a decree permitting each party to divert and use water for a specified period of time.[30]

The resolution of water disputes became more complicated with the rise of the sugar industry. As the companies acquired taro lands and extended their operations far beyond those lands, it became apparent that they needed much more water than the amount allowed by ancient taro rights. The law began to develop principles relating to the use of "surplus waters," meaning the amount of water flowing in a stream in excess of that required to satisfy ancient irrigation rights.[31] By purchasing an *ahupua'a*, a sugar company could claim ownership of all surplus waters originating in or flowing through the *ahupua'a*. Ownership of the surplus water was supposedly derived from the ancient right of the *konohiki* to control all the waters of the *ahupua'a* and to use them for whatever purpose desired, subject only to the tenants' taro rights. Thus, the sugar companies claimed the right to use much more water than their appurtenant rights would permit; and they also claimed the right to divert these waters to lands which historically were without water rights.[32] However, the assertion of ownership of surplus waters appears to be a misinterpretation of the traditional powers and duties of the *konohiki*. It has already been noted that the ancient Hawaiians had no concept of ownership of waters; nor did they have the capacity to use surplus waters to any appreciable extent.

To some extent, the Hawaiian government assisted the sugar companies in their acquisition of land and private water rights. In 1876, King Kalākaua signed legislation creating a commission to report on lands suitable for growing sugar cane and the cost to develop such lands. The minister of finance was authorized to issue bonds to finance improvements and to make government water and land available for new enterprises without compensation to the government. The minister of the interior was also authorized to apportion government water to various landowners. Another law passed in 1876 allowed persons to acquire rights-of-way over other lands in order to develop their own lands. The government thus made the waters of Hawai'i freely available to the sugar industry.[33]

4. HAWAI'I SUPREME COURT CASES

Hawai'i case law has recognized several kinds of water rights: some arising out of ancient custom and usage; some having their origin in the English common law; and some reflecting the needs of agriculture and business. These various influences have created a unique system of water rights.

a. *Ancient Appurtenant Rights*

Appurtenant water rights arise from the ancient Hawaiian agricultural system. The taro farmers, who cultivated taro on lands adjacent to a stream or *'auwai* were entitled to use a certain amount of water for domestic purposes and irrigation. The *konohiki* of the *ahupua'a* or *'ili kūpono* controlled the distribution of water privileges among tenants.

Through ancient custom and usage, the right to use water for irrigation became attached or "appurtenant" to taro lands. This customary right evolved into a legal right when land titles were awarded by the Land Commission.[34] The quantity of water covered by the appurtenant right was the amount customarily used at and immediately prior to the Land Commission Award.[35] The earliest Hawai'i water rights case established the appurtenant rights of the parties. In *Peck v. Bailey* (1867),[36] a dispute arose between two landowners within the *ahupua'a* of Wailuku on Maui. The plaintiff, a sugar plantation and mill, filed suit against the defendant, a taro and cane planter, alleging that the defendant had illegally diverted excessive waters of the Wailuku River from the sugar company's property. The company claimed a "right of Lord paramount"[37] over the waters of the Wailuku, based upon title derived from the *konohiki* of the *ahupua'a*. The company further alleged that the defendant had no right to use the waters of the Wailuku except in the limited amount customarily allowed by the *konohiki* to water defendant's taro patches.

The court rejected the sugar company's claim to paramount rights in the Wailuku River. Both the sugar company and the defendant derived title to their lands from the *konohiki* of the *ahupua'a*. Pursuant to the *Mahele* and Land Commission Awards, these lands were conveyed to both parties, along with certain rights associated with those lands. "If any of the lands were entitled to water by immemorial usage," said the court, "this right was included in the conveyance as an appurtenance."[38] Therefore, both sides were limited to their ancient appurtenant rights to use water for their lands, neither party having any exceptional rights.

Also at issue in *Peck* was whether appurtenant waters could be transferred to *kula* lands -- arid lands with no traditional water right. The defendant had dried up some of his taro patches, extended the *'auwai* which watered those patches, and was using the taro water to cultivate sugar cane. The court held that the defendant had the right to use taro water on other lands provided no injury was done to the water rights of others. However, the court limited the quantity of water that could be transferred to *kula* lands to the amount which the defendant was entitled to use on his taro lands by immemorial usage.[39]

Since the *Peck* decision, the Hawai'i Supreme Court has consistently reaffirmed the doctrine of appurtenant water rights. It has become a fundamental principle of Hawai'i's water law.[40]

b. *Prescriptive Water Rights*

A prescriptive water right is one that is acquired by adverse use. It is similar to the acquisition of land ownership through adverse possession. In general, a person who uses water "belonging" to another person, may acquire a right to use such water provided certain legal requirements are met. The requirements are that the use of water be actual, open, notorious, hostile to the rightful holder of the water right, and continuous for a statutory length of time, for example, 20 years.[41] If all of these elements are proved, the person has acquired a prescriptive right to use the water. The quantity of water covered by the prescriptive right is the amount actually used during the period of adverse use.[42] Prescriptive water rights cannot be acquired against the government.[43]

In some early cases, the court loosely applied the term "prescriptive" to ancient appurtenant rights.[44] Later cases made a clear distinction between prescriptive rights which are acquired by adverse use, and appurtenant rights which arise out of ancient permissive use.[45] As a practical matter, however, the acquisition of either right permits landowners to use a certain quantity of water to irrigate their land.

Prescriptive water rights were adjudicated in *Lonoaea v. Wailuku Sugar Co.* (1895).[46] In that case, several taro growers complained that the sugar company had taken more than its share of water from the Wailuku River and from two ancient *'auwai* leading from the river. This illegal diversion was allegedly accomplished by construction of dams and a flume, and by enlargement of the *'auwai*. The flume carried water to *kula* lands owned by the sugar company.

By ancient usage, it had become settled that the stream and the two *'auwai* would each take one-third of the water in times of normal flow. The owners of lands along these water courses would then divide the water according to their ancient appurtenant rights. Historically, the taro farmers had irrigated their fields by day and night. With the introduction of cane culture in the district, however, the cane planters began to irrigate their fields only during the day, leaving the taro growers to take the water at night. This day and night division of usage continued for over 30 years.

The court held that the sugar company had established a prescriptive right to use the day water, despite the fact that the customary day usage appears not to have been adverse. Acknowledging that the cane planters had taken the day water with the acquiescence of the taro growers, the court nevertheless found the company's claim sufficiently hostile to the taro growers' rights. On that issue, the court merely stated: "Its use was adverse. This is proved by the fact that it was taken and enforced."[47] The taro growers were entitled to the amounts of water which they had acquired by prescription pursuant to their night usage.

Citing the *Peck* case, the court also held that the transfer of water to *kula* lands was permissible provided it caused no injury to others.[48] The sugar company had purchased 20 to 30 acres of taro land which was entitled to water by ancient usage. The company ceased cultivation of those taro lands, transferring the taro water by flume to 120 acres of sugar cane fields. The court apparently limited the transfer to the amount customarily used on the taro lands during the period of adverse use. However, it does not appear that the court actually placed any clear restriction on the amount of day water which the company could transfer to its sugar lands. The court simply stated that the sugar company's use of the water by day could not diminish the taro grower's supply, since the latter had use of the water at night.[49]

In *Hawaiian Commercial & Sugar Co. v. Wailuku Sugar Co.* (1902),[50] a later case involving the Wailuku Sugar Company, the court clarified the extent of the prescriptive right which the company had acquired. The company had not acquired the right to use *all* the day water, but only that amount which had been used "for its present estate" during the period of adverse use. If the company later acquired additional *kula* lands, it still could not take more water than its original lands were entitled to by prescription.[51]

In *Davis v. Afong* (1884),[52] the court held that a prescriptive right could be acquired to spring waters which came to the surface from an underground source. In that case, the springs or ponds originated on the defendant's property, but flowed through an ancient *'auwai* to farm lands owned by several plaintiffs. The plaintiffs complained that the defendant had wrongfully diminished the flow of water which normally flowed from the springs into the *'auwai*. The court noted the general principle that landowners are entitled to use water originating on their land subject to the rights others may acquire by prescription. Since the plaintiffs had taken water from the *'auwai* for well over 20 years, however, the court held that they had acquired a prescriptive right to use those waters.[53]

155

c. Surplus Water Rights

Although the concept has been defined in several ways, surplus water is generally the amount of water not covered by other water rights. It is the amount of water theoretically remaining in the stream after all users have taken their appurtenant, prescriptive, or riparian share. (Riparian rights are discussed below.) The courts have divided surplus waters into at least three categories. Normal surplus refers to the ordinary flow of a stream. Freshet surplus is the occasional overflow caused by normal rainfall. Storm surplus is a large freshet or flood caused by a storm.[54]

Surplus water rights supposedly arise out of the ancient power of the *konohiki* to control all of the waters within the *ahupua'a*, subject only to the tenants' taro rights.[55] The right to use surplus water was crucial to the development of the sugar industry, which needed far more water than the amount covered by ancient appurtenant rights.

The *Lonoaea* decision touched briefly on the issue of surplus water rights. In an introductory paragraph, the court commented that storm waters were free to anyone who desired to appropriate them, provided that no one took all the storm waters and deprived others of the opportunity to make use of them.[56] However, in *Hawaiian Commercial*, the court held that it had not intended in *Lonoaea* to decide the surplus or storm water rights of the participants.[57] The question of surplus water rights was "one of great difficulty, and the court has carefully avoided passing upon it until compelled to do so and has always regarded it as an unsettled question."[58]

The court confronted the issue two years later in *Hawaiian Commercial & Sugar Co. v. Wailuku Sugar Co.* (1904)[59] [hereinafter *Hawaiian Commercial II*]. The two sugar companies owned almost all of the *ahupua'a* of Wailuku on Maui. The Wailuku River originated on lands owned by Hawaiian Commercial and flowed its entire length within the *ahupua'a*. The Wailuku Sugar Company had constructed a dam and flume which diverted water from the Wailuku to *kula* lands located more than a mile from the river. Hawaiian Commercial sued to restrain the diversion. The court divided surface waters into two classes: (1) surplus water, meaning the water, whether storm water or not, that is not covered by prescriptive rights and excluding also riparian rights, if there are any; and (2) water which is covered by prescriptive rights.[60] In this instance, the term "prescriptive" included ancient appurtenant rights. The court held that surplus waters were the property of the *konohiki*, to do with as the *konohiki* pleased, and were not appurtenant to any particular portion of the *ahupua'a*.[61] The *konohiki* in this instance was the Hawaiian Commercial & Sugar Company.

The court, in effect, permitted the private ownership of surplus waters, its decision in this regard purportedly based on ancient Hawaiian custom. According to the court, the king had been the sole owner of both the land and the water, and he could do with both as he pleased. The court admitted that the king's powers had been limited somewhat by tenants' taro rights. However, there had never been any limitation on the king's power to use surplus waters. The court also noted that in recent years, *konohiki* landowners had in many instances diverted surplus water from the *ahupua'a* either wholly or in large part.[62] This last statement may have been a reference to sugar company practices in the years preceding the case rather than to truly ancient Hawaiian practices. In any event, the *Hawaiian Commercial II* case held that the surplus waters of a stream which flowed through a single *ahupua'a* belonged to the *konohiki* of the *ahupua'a*.

Subsequently, in *Carter v. Territory* (1917),[63] the court dealt with the issue of surplus water rights in a stream which flowed from one *ahupua'a* to another. The stream in that

156

case originated in an *ahupua'a* owned by the territory and flowed into an *ahupua'a* owned by a sugar company.[64] The territory had dammed the stream and constructed a pipeline system to provide domestic water for local homesteaders, thereby diverting some of the sugar company's irrigation supply. After disposing of several issues, the court turned to the sugar company's claim to "storm or freshet waters" of the stream where a stream flowed from one *ahupua'a* to another. The court held that such waters were to be shared, subject to "reasonable use," by both *ahupua'a* according to riparian principles.[65]

The *Carter* decision created some confusion as to the nature of surplus waters. While the sugar company's claim was to "storm or freshet waters," the court framed the issue with reference to "the rights in the *surplus* waters of a stream which flows from one *ahupua'a* to another."[66] The court's syllabus of the case states the holding on this issue as follows:

> Where a stream flows through one ahupua'a into another each ahupua'a is entitled to a reasonable use of the *surplus* water of the stream according to the principles applicable to riparian rights at common law.[67] (Emphasis added.)

Moreover, the court held that the territory was the owner of the stream to the extent of the "ordinary or normal flow."[68] It then held that the sugar company was entitled to the "surplus normal flow" for irrigation purposes to the extent of its ancient appurtenant rights, but only after all domestic requirements had been satisfied.[69] Finally, the court held that the "surplus flood and freshet waters" were subject to the reasonable use of both *ahupua'a* according to riparian principles.[70] Despite this imprecise language, later courts have interpreted the *Carter* riparian rule as applying only to storm or freshet surplus water flowing from one *ahupua'a* to another.[71]

The next case to deal with surplus water rights was *Territory v. Gay* (1930).[72] In that case, the territory owned the *ahupua'a* of Hanapēpē on Kaua'i. The partnership of Gay and Robinson, a sugar company, owned two *'ili kūpono* within the upper portion of the *ahupua'a*. Several streams originated in these *'ili* and flowed through the *ahupua'a* to the sea. By means of dams, ditches, and pipelines, Gay and Robinson had diverted water to sugar lands outside the Hanapēpē watershed. The territory sued to prevent the sugar company from depriving downstream *kuleana* owners and others of their water rights.

The sole issue before the court in *Gay* was the question of title to the "normal, daily surplus water" of the Hanapēpē Stream.[73] The court first ruled that an *'ili kūpono* was a land unit independent of an *ahupua'a*, and was therefore entitled to equal rights with an *ahupua'a* on the question of surplus water use.[74] As *konohiki* of the *'ili* on which the Hanapēpē Stream originated, the court held that Gay and Robinson owned the normal surplus waters of the stream and could do with those waters whatever it wished.[75] Thus, the court gave the sugar company the unlimited right to divert the normal surplus to sugar lands outside the *ahupua'a*, even though the diversion decreased the available supply to downstream landowners within the *ahupua'a*. In so doing, the court reaffirmed the position it took in *Hawaiian Commercial II*.

However, the court contradicted its previous holding in *Carter* with regard to storm or freshet surplus. Chief Justice Perry stated that there was "no distinction in history, in principle, or in law between surplus waters of the normal flow and surplus waters which come in freshets as a result of storms."[76] He advocated overturning *Carter* and applying the private ownership rule to both categories of surplus. In a separate opinion, Judge Banks agreed that one rule should apply; however, he urged that the *Carter* riparian rule be applied to both classes of surplus.[77] Judge Parsons sided with Judge Perry on the question of normal surplus water rights, but refused to join him in overturning the *Carter* rule on storm or freshet surplus.[78]

In summary, surplus water law is based primarily on the three cases discussed above -- *Hawaiian Commercial II*, *Carter* and *Gay*. It does not appear that any clear principles emerged from these cases.[79] Each case treats the subject of surplus waters differently. In *Hawaiian Commercial II*, the court, citing *Hawaiian Commercial*, defined surplus water as "water, whether storm water or not, that is not covered by prescriptive rights and excluding also riparian rights, if there are any."[80] (Citation omitted.) That court held that such waters belonged to the *konohiki* of the *ahupua'a* of origin. The *Carter* court apparently ignored the previous definition, and made a distinction between normal surplus and storm or freshet surplus. In *Carter*, storm or freshet waters did *not* belong to the *ahupua'a* of origin, but were to be shared with an adjoining *ahupua'a* according to riparian principles. In the *Gay* case, the Chief Justice attacked the distinction between normal surplus and storm or freshet surplus, but could not convince a majority of the court to abandon the *Carter* rule. Surplus waters were defined in *Gay* as "all water not required for the satisfaction of . . . prescriptive or . . . appurtenant rights."[81] This definition differs from the one stated in *Hawaiian Commercial II* in that it makes no mention of riparian rights. In *Gay*, the court held that the normal surplus water belonged to the *konohiki* of an *'ili kūpono* of origin. In none of these cases did the court determine the quantity of surplus that a particular party was entitled to use. The law of surplus waters appeared to be unsettled.

d.   *Riparian Rights*

The doctrine of riparian rights is part of the common law of England. The word "riparian" comes from the Latin word "*ripa*" meaning bank. Therefore, a riparian landowner is one whose land is situated on the banks of the stream; and riparian rights are those which the landowner has to use of waters from the stream.

Riparianism is a doctrine of mutual and correlative rights.[82] The owner of riparian land does not own the water. The owner merely has a right of use or a "usufruct"[83] while the water flows past the owner's property. The riparian landowner is entitled to make reasonable use of the water, keeping in mind that all other riparian owners have a similar right. Stated another way, each riparian owner is entitled to the natural flow of the stream, diminished only by the reasonable use of others. If water is diverted from the stream, the unused amount must be returned to the stream. The riparian owner cannot transfer water to nonriparian lands or to lands outside the watershed, since such a transfer would necessarily deprive others of the natural flow. The latter rule has been modified, however, to allow reasonable diversions unless they result in actual damage to another riparian owner.

Riparian law makes a distinction between domestic and artificial uses. Domestic uses include drinking, washing, cooking, and watering domestic animals. These uses have priority over artificial uses, which include irrigation, mining, and other commercial enterprises.[84]

The riparian doctrine is incompatible with the concept of ownership of surplus waters.[85] Riparianism focuses on maintaining the integrity of the stream, subject to the reasonable and correlative use of all riparian landowners. On the other hand, the "owner" of surplus waters can use or divert all the surplus without regard to the wholeness of the stream or the needs of downstream owners. The tension between these competing principles can be seen in the separate opinions written in *Territory v. Gay*.

158

In 1892, the Hawaiian legislature declared that the common law of England was the common law of Hawaiʻi, subject to Hawaiian statutes, Hawaiian judicial precedent, or Hawaiian custom and usage.[86] Prior to this time, several cases referred to riparian rights, but none of them specifically decided water rights on riparian principle.[87] In *Peck v. Bailey*, for example, the court said: "A riparian proprietor has the right to enjoy the benefits of a flow of water, as an incident to his estate, and he can use the water for irrigation, watering his cattle, and other domestic purposes, provided he does not materially diminish the supply of water or render useless its application by others."[88]

As stated previously, however, only appurtenant rights were adjudicated in *Peck*. It was not necessary to decide riparian rights because neither party was entitled to more than its appurtenant share of water. In other words, neither party was entitled to any surplus in excess of appurtenant waters. If surplus waters had been at issue in *Peck*, it is possible to infer that the court might have discussed riparian principles in the apportionment of such waters.[89] Moreover, the court in *Peck* noted that the king's conveyance of land bordering on the river would include rights in the river which had not been granted before.[90] At the very least, it is clear that the *Peck* case recognized the riparian rule.

In *Hawaiian Commercial II*, the court defined surplus water with reference to water both (1) not covered by prescriptive rights, and (2) not subject to "riparian rights, if there are any."[91] This language implies that there are certain riparian rights which limit the use of surplus waters, just as appurtenant and prescriptive rights limit surplus use. By this language, it appeared that the court intended to reserve a discussion of riparian rights for a future case.[92]

In any event, *Carter v. Territory*, discussed above, was the first case to explicitly decide water rights according to the riparian doctrine. The dispute in that case was essentially between public and private water usage. The territory was diverting approximately 570,000 gallons of water per day for the domestic use of local homesteaders. The court termed this diversion a new and highly beneficial use.[93] However, it diminished the flow of water to the neighboring *ahupuaʻa* owned by a sugar company. The company had extensive appurtenant rights.[94] Moreover, the supply of water in the stream had steadily diminished over the years.

The court held that "[p]rivate water rights in this Territory are governed by the principles of the common law of England except so far as they have been modified by or are inconsistent with Hawaiian statutes, custom or judicial precedent."[95] Moreover, the right to use water for domestic purposes was superior to the right to use it for artificial or irrigation purposes.[96] Furthermore, the court noted that the *Kuleana* Act of 1850 gave homesteaders "a right to 'drinking water . . . and running water'" even if their *kuleana* had no appurtenant water rights. Therefore, each homesteader enjoyed a personal right to use the stream for domestic purposes.[97] Applying these riparian principles and the 1850 statute, the court gave priority to the domestic use of all parties over the ancient appurtenant rights of the sugar company.[98] The fact that the company could not establish the extent or amount of its appurtenant rights was significant to the court.

As noted earlier, *Carter* also held that each *ahupuaʻa* had riparian rights in the surplus storm or freshet waters of a stream flowing from one *ahupuaʻa* to another. In the *Gay* case, Chief Justice Perry criticized the riparian principles adopted in *Carter*, particularly the holding with regard to storm and freshet surplus.

> Our system of water rights is based upon and is the outgrowth of ancient Hawaiian customs and the methods of Hawaiians in dealing with the subject of water. No modifications of that system have been engrafted upon it by the application of any principles of the common law of England. To apply the principle of riparian rights to the matter of surplus freshet waters as was done in the *Carter* case is entirely at variance with preceding history and judicial precedents.[99]

Judge Perry pointed out that no other case except *Carter* had ever made an award of water rights based upon riparian principles. Riparianism was inconsistent with the ancient Hawaiian system of water usage, which according to Perry favored the use of water on both riparian and nonriparian land. His essential criticism was that riparianism did not serve the needs of Hawaiian agriculture, since it limited the right to transfer waters to nonriparian lands and allowed surplus waters to go unused. Consequently, he believed that riparianism posed a danger to the economic and political system of the territory.[100]

In a dissenting opinion, Judge Banks urged that the riparian rule in *Carter* be extended to normal surplus waters as well as to storm or freshet surplus.

> This rule is so inherently just in its regulation of the use of an element that is vital to the well being of mankind and is so consonant with natural rights and human necessities that I think it should be finally adopted as the law of this Territory.[101]

A system of correlative rights based on reasonable use was preferable to one based on absolute and exclusive ownership of surplus waters. The economic reasons for applying the absolute ownership rule, said Judge Banks, were legally insufficient. Riparianism was the sounder principle because it protected individual rights.[102]

Moreover, Banks argued, riparian doctrine was not inconsistent with prior law. Banks found recognition of riparian principles in *Peck*, *Hawaiian Commercial II*, and *Carter*. He also made reference to *City Mill Co. v. Honolulu Sewer and Water Commission* (1929), a case decided one year earlier.[103] In *City Mill*, the court had applied the doctrine of correlative rights to artesian well waters. All owners of land above the artesian basin were entitled to make reasonable use of the waters with due regard for the rights of other owners. Banks felt that the same rule should logically be applied to surface waters.[104] In *Territory v. Gay*, the court was clearly in conflict over the application of the riparian doctrine versus the concept of private ownership of surplus waters. The divided court held that the doctrine of riparian rights was not in effect with regard to the normal surplus waters of a stream. These waters were the property of the *konohiki*. However, the court let stand the *Carter* riparian rule affecting storm or freshet surplus water flowing from one *ahupua'a* to another.

e. Sovereign Water Rights

Forty-three years after the *Gay* decision, the Hawai'i Supreme Court issued its opinion in the controversial case of *McBryde Sugar Co. v. Robinson* (1973).[105] The case once again involved the apportionment of water rights in the Hanapēpē Valley. Gay and Robinson continued to own two *'ili kūpono* in the upper portion of the *ahupua'a*. McBryde Sugar Company owned two *'ili kūpono* in the lower part of the *ahupua'a*, downstream from the Gay and Robinson property. The State of Hawai'i, as successor to the territory, was now the owner of the *ahupua'a* of Hanapēpē. In 1949, Gay and Robinson improved its irrigation system and began transporting even greater quantities of surplus waters outside the Hanapēpē watershed. (The *Gay* case had awarded Gay and Robinson ownership of the normal surplus waters of the Hanapēpē river.) This diversion decreased the amount of flow

160

available to McBryde Sugar. McBryde Sugar sued to secure rights to the water it had been using before Gay and Robinson's improvements. The trial court then quantified the appurtenant and prescriptive rights of the parties.[106]

The Hawai'i Supreme Court took the occasion in *McBryde* to re-examine the entire issue of Hawaiian water rights, and in so doing the court rejected the concept of private ownership of water. The court looked to the *Mahele* of 1848 and the laws that implemented the *Mahele* to examine what the king intended to convey pursuant to his division of lands. The Land Commission Act created the Board of Land Commissioners, which adopted certain principles to be followed in settling land title claims. The court noted that the Land Commission was authorized to convey the king's private or feudal rights in the land, but not his "sovereign prerogatives" as head of the nation. One of these enumerated prerogatives was "to encourage and even to enforce the usufruct of lands for the common good." The principles further provided that the king could not surrender his sovereign prerogatives and that all conveyances were subject to them.[107]

With these principles as a foundation, the court reasoned that the right to use water was one of the most important "usufructs" of land. The principles mentioned above showed the king's intent to reserve the right to use water to himself in trust for the common good. In other words, no right to private ownership of water had ever passed with any grant of land title by the Land Commission. The court held that the state, as successor to the king, was the owner of all waters flowing in natural water courses. Gay and Robinson, among others, could no longer claim surplus water rights.[108] The court further attacked the concept of private ownership by holding that the *Kuleana* Act of 1850 had codified the riparian doctrine in Hawai'i. As already noted, one portion of the statute guaranteed the right to "drinking water and running water." The *Carter* case had already used this statute to legitimize the domestic water rights of nonriparian homesteaders. In *McBryde*, the court said that the term "running water" must have meant water flowing in natural water courses, since artificial water courses were excepted from the statute. The court found the origin of this statute in the English common law, which was brought to Hawai'i by missionaries from Massachusetts. The cases cited by the court indicated that natural water courses were *publici juris;* meaning that such waters were public and common to the extent that all who had a right of access could make reasonable use of them.[109]

Accordingly, the court held that an owner of land adjoining a natural water course had riparian water rights. As defined by the court, those rights included the right to use water flowing on land adjoining the water course without prejudicing the riparian rights of others, or the rights of others to the natural flow of the water course without substantial diminution and in the shape and size given it by nature.[110]

The court upheld the appurtenant rights of all parties. However, it overruled previous case law on the issue of transfer of water to *kula* lands. The right to the use of water acquired as appurtenant rights could only be used in connection with the particular parcel of land to which the right was appurtenant.[111] Thus, neither McBryde nor Gay and Robinson could transfer their appurtenant (or riparian) share of water to *kula* lands.

Finally, the court abandoned the concepts of normal surplus waters and storm or freshet surplus. With the adoption of riparian principles, the concept of normal surplus had no meaning. And, since all waters now belonged to the state, the court overruled the *Carter* holding with regard to storm or freshet surplus.[112]

To summarize the *McBryde* decision:[113] All of the waters flowing in natural water courses belonged to the state in trusteeship for the people. Owners of land adjacent to a

161

water course had appurtenant or riparian rights to *use* the water, but no property interest in the water itself. Appurtenant and riparian water rights had to be exercised on the lands to which they appertained; they could not be "severed" from those lands and transferred to other lands. There was no "right" to divert waters outside the watershed. Since all waters belonged to the state, no one could claim prescriptive water rights through adverse use.

In response to a request for a rehearing of the case, the court reaffirmed its initial *McBryde* decision in all respects.[114] However, Judge Levinson took the occasion to write a lengthy dissenting opinion, in which he urged the court to overrule *McBryde* and return to pre-*McBryde* principles. Judge Levinson also raised certain constitutional issues. Both the federal and state constitutions prohibited the state from taking private property without just compensation. The *McBryde* decision deprived Gay and Robinson of its "ownership" of normal surplus waters, and its right to transfer such waters to lands beyond the watershed. According to Judge Levinson, these rulings effected an unconstitutional "taking" of Gay and Robinson's property rights without compensation.[115]

Gay and Robinson appealed *McBryde* to the U.S. Supreme Court, which declined to review the case.[116] The company then sued in U.S. District Court to prevent the state from enforcing the *McBryde* decision. In *Robinson v. Ariyoshi* (1977)[117] [hereinafter *Robinson I*], Senior Judge Martin Pence issued a lengthy and critical opinion of *McBryde*. The court found the case completely revolutionary, a public policy decision which overturned established water rights without legal justification.[118] Moreover, Pence believed the decision was unconstitutional in that it deprived the landowners of valuable property rights without just compensation. The *McBryde* holdings, which gave ownership of surplus waters to the state, and prohibited the diversion of waters to *kula* lands, were "untenable and void." The court granted Gay and Robinson's request for an injunction against enforcement of these rulings.[119]

The State of Hawai'i then appealed to the Ninth Circuit Court of Appeals. Before deciding the case, the Ninth Circuit certified six water rights questions to the Hawai'i Supreme Court. In 1982, the Hawai'i Supreme Court responded in *Robinson v. Ariyoshi*[120] [hereinafter *Robinson II*]. The decision by Chief Justice Richardson strongly reaffirmed the principles set out in *McBryde*. The court explained that the question of surplus water rights had not been settled prior to *McBryde*. Therefore, the *McBryde* decision represented a clarification of ambiguous law, rather than a departure from settled principles. Under these circumstances, it was proper for the court to review the entire history of Hawaiian water usage, and to settle on the public trust doctrine as the one appropriate to modern usage.[121]

With regard to the transfer of water to nonriparian lands, the court noted that *McBryde* had not actually prohibited any party from transferring water outside the watershed. Rather, *McBryde* merely held, in a reversal of that part of the trial court's decision on surplus and prescriptive water rights, that there was no vested and enforceable right to transfer water to *kula* lands.[122] *McBryde* had affirmed the trial court's determination of the quantity of water covered by the appurtenant rights of the parties. However, it had not instructed the trial court to do anything on remand given its partial reversal of the trial court's decision. In addition, it did not exercise its power to render a final judgment on those issues. It had simply voided the trial court's decision as to surplus and prescriptive water rights. Furthermore, the parties had not sought to return to the trial court for a final disposition on all the issues. Thus, the Hawai'i Supreme Court maintained that *McBryde* was not a final determination of the sugar companies' rights, except for the court's affirmation of the trial court's conclusion on appurtenant rights.[123]

The Hawai'i Supreme Court later reaffirmed and extended the *McBryde* decision in *Reppun v. Board of Water Supply* (1982).[124] In that case, the Honolulu Water Board maintained a natural reservoir and dike system at the source of the Waihe'e Stream. The Water Board drilled a tunnel into the dike system and began pumping water to its domestic users. This reduced the stream flow to downstream taro growers, who sued to stop the diversion. Pursuant to *McBryde*, the taro growers claimed riparian rights to the natural flow of the stream substantially undiminished in quantity, as well as ancient appurtenant rights. The Water Board countered that it had previously purchased these water rights from the taro growers by deed; and that, therefore, the riparian and appurtenant rights had been severed from the taro lands.

The court found that the board's purchase of riparian rights was void, because riparian rights could not be severed from the land. In accordance with *McBryde*, the court noted that riparian rights were statutory in origin. The purpose of that statute was to assure landowners of a right to water to make their lands productive, not to provide an independent source of profit for possessors of water rights. To permit severance of water rights from the land would defeat the purpose of the statute. The court concluded that riparian rights could not be separated from riparian lands.[125]

Likewise, the court held that appurtenant water rights could not be severed or transferred to other lands. Since appurtenant rights were not statutory in origin, however, they could be extinguished by conveyance. It appeared that the taro growers had purchased their lands subject to the grantor's reservation of water rights in those lands. This attempt to separate the appurtenant water rights from the land effectively extinguished those appurtenant rights.[126] *Reppun* thus extended the *McBryde* principles to prohibit the purchase and sale of water rights apart from the lands to which they appertained.

The court in *Reppun* also restated its commitment to riparianism:

> First, the doctrine is consistent with the needs of native commoners at the time of the law's passage. Taro, the predominant agricultural crop, grew best where a steady flow of running water, most of which could be subsequently utilized by lower riparian users, occurred; the cultivation of taro took place principally upon riparian lands; and grants to commoners were restricted to lands they had in fact cultivated. Second, the principles underlying the doctrine are consistent with those that appear to pervade the native system of water allocation and preexisting civil law inasmuch as: "title" to the water was not equated with the right to use; each person's right to use was a "correlative" nature; and rights to use were predicated upon beneficial application of the water to the land. And third, the presence of the riparian doctrine in this jurisdiction had, prior to 1930, been repeatedly adverted to in our caselaw.[127] (Citations omitted.)

However, the court recognized that the doctrine's requirement of undiminished stream flow might lead courts to prohibit certain reasonable and beneficial uses. The court therefore held that a riparian owner could not sue to prohibit the reasonable use of another, unless he demonstrated actual harm to his own reasonable use. Thus, the emphasis shifted slightly from maintaining the natural flow to permitting reasonable uses.[128]

In 1985, the Ninth Circuit Court of Appeals issued its opinion in *Robinson v. Ariyoshi*[129] [hereinafter *Robinson III*]. The court held that the Supreme Court of Hawai'i had the authority to overrule earlier cases and declare that common law riparianism was the law of Hawai'i. However, the change in law could not deprive the parties of vested property rights which they enjoyed prior to *McBryde*. The court found that Gay and Robinson had acquired a vested property interest in the surplus waters of the Hanapēpē Stream. The state could not interfere with this property right unless it instituted condemnation proceedings and compensated the company for "taking" the property. The court affirmed the district court's decision insofar as it declared the rights of the parties. However, it lifted the injunction against the state on grounds that the state had not actually attempted to enforce the *McBryde* decision against Gay and Robinson.

In 1986, the case went to the United States Supreme Court as *Ariyoshi v. Robinson*.[130] The court vacated the decision of the Ninth Circuit Court of Appeals and remanded the case to that court for further consideration in light of *Williamson County Regional Planning Commission v. Hamilton Bank* (1985).[131] The Ninth Circuit in turn, remanded the case to the U.S. District Court with the same instruction. The case once again came before District Judge Martin Pence, who ten years earlier had written the opinion in *Robinson I*.

In the *Williamson County* case, a developer obtained approval from a county planning commission to develop a tract of land. Several years later, the commission disapproved further development, after deciding that more recent ordinances and regulations should be applied to the project. The developer claimed that the commission's refusal to approve further development constituted a "taking" of his property without just compensation. The U.S. Supreme Court held that the developer's "taking" claim was premature, since he had not obtained a final decision regarding the application of the new regulations to his property, and had not used the state procedures for obtaining just compensation. The court was concerned that an adjudication of a "taking" claim would require the court to evaluate

> the economic impact of the challenged action and the extent to which it interferes with reasonable investment-backed expectations. Those factors simply cannot be evaluated until the administrative agency has arrived at a final, definitive position regarding how it will apply the regulations at issue to the particular land in question.[132] (Citations omitted.)

Since no final adjudication of rights had occurred, the case was not ripe for a decision. The U.S. Supreme Court intimated that Gay and Robinson's claim for injunctive relief was similarly premature, since the state had not actually tried to enforce *McBryde* against the company. The supreme court remanded the case so the lower court could re-examine the case in light of these procedural issues.

In *Robinson v. Ariyoshi* (1987)[133] [hereinafter *Robinson IV*], Judge Pence once again attacked the *McBryde* decision as well as the opinions expressed by Chief Justice Richardson in *Robinson II*. The court rejected the idea that surplus water law was unsettled prior to *McBryde*. Pence asserted that the law with regard to normal daily surplus waters was "settled" prior to *McBryde*. Only in the area of storm and freshet surplus waters was the law "not completely" settled.[134] Therefore, Gay and Robinson had vested property rights at least with regard to the normal surplus of the stream. Moreover, it had been firmly established prior to *McBryde* that the owners of land with appurtenant or prescriptive water rights could transfer that water to any other land, so long as the water rights of others were not affected.[135]

As to the finality of *McBryde*, the court said:

McBryde II left nothing unripe or nonfinal. [Gay and Robinson], McBryde, Olokele, the small owners -- each and all had lost all of their vested property rights to take water from the Hanapepe River, had lost the right to sell and exchange the same, and had lost the right to divert water out of the Hanapepe water shed into adjoining arid lands.[136]

According to Judge Pence, the *Williamson* case shed absolutely no light on the issues raised in *McBryde* and the subsequent appeals. The court held that the *McBryde* decision was a final judgment which took away property in violation of constitutional rights. As of November 1987, the district court stood ready to issue an injunction against any state official who attempted to enforce the *McBryde* decision against Gay and Robinson or others.[137]

In the latest chapter to the 16-year court battle over the waters of the Hanapēpē Stream, the Ninth Circuit held in *Robinson v. Ariyoshi* (1989)[138] [hereinafter *Robinson V*], that Judge Pence was wrong. Applying *Williamson*, the Ninth Circuit concluded that the federal challenge to *McBryde* was not ripe for adjudication because *McBryde* was not a final adjudication of the case, as the Hawai'i Supreme Court had conclusively determined in *Robinson II*.[139] It noted that the sugar companies could not say they "retained [no] reasonable beneficial use" of the water they claimed or that their "expectation interests had been [completely] destroyed" by *McBryde*.[140] The court dismissed the argument that *McBryde* had placed a legal cloud on the title of various property owners which constituted a taking. The state had not interfered in any way with the actual diversions and use of water from the Hanapēpē Stream by the sugar companies. Even if *McBryde* placed a cloud on title, "this inchoate and speculative cloud is insufficient to make this controversy ripe for review."[141] Therefore, the Ninth Circuit Court reversed Judge Pence's decision and ordered that the complaint be dismissed.[142]

5.   THE STATE WATER CODE

In 1978, the Hawai'i State Constitution was amended to provide for the creation of a water resources agency which would, among other things, "establish criteria for water use priorities while assuring appurtenant rights and existing correlative and riparian uses and establish procedures for regulating all uses of Hawaii's water resources."[143] The creation of the water resources agency and adoption of a water code was stalled in the legislature for many years.

Finally, in May 1987, the Hawai'i State Legislature passed the State Water Code,[144] and created a six-member commission on water resource management to handle the general administration of the code.[145] The commission was to devise and adopt a set of administrative rules not later than two years after the effective date of the code -- July 1, 1987.[146] In fact, the commission adopted rules on May 27, 1988. Within one year from the effective date of these rules, "[a]ny person making a use of water in any area of the State shall file a declaration of the person's use with the commission."[147] The commission set May 30, 1989 as the deadline for filing declarations. If the commission determines that the declared use is reasonable and beneficial, it must issue a certificate describing the use. In any dispute over water rights, the commission will recognize the certificate as signifying a "confirmed usage."[148]

Currently, the commission is processing approximately 7,000 declarations involving 2,600 declarants, in order to verify the declared uses before issuing any certificates. Because of the volume of declarations and the complexity of verifying uses, the commission has not issued any certificates. One of its major problems is to determine what uses are "reasonable and beneficial" even if the actual use is verified.

The code establishes a Hawai'i Water Plan consisting of four parts: (1) a water resource protection plan prepared by the commission; (2) water use and development plans prepared by each county; (3) a state water project plan prepared by state agencies; and (4) a water quality plan prepared by the Department of Health.[149] The plan and its constituent parts were to be adopted by the commission not later than three years (July 1, 1990) from the effective date of the code.[150]

The code regulates water use by means of a permit system. That system applies *only* to those lands designated by the commission as water management areas:

> When it can be reasonably determined, after conducting scientific investigation and research, that the water resources in an area may be threatened by existing or proposed withdrawals or diversions of water, the commission shall designate the area for the purpose of establishing administrative control over the withdrawals and diversions of ground and surface waters in the area to ensure reasonable-beneficial use of the water resources in the public interest.[151]

Such designation may be initiated by written petition or by recommendation of the chair of the commission.[152] If the chair recommends designation, the commission must hold public hearings at a location in the vicinity of the area proposed for designation, and must publish a notice of hearing in the newspaper.[153] The commission may also conduct investigations with regard to the proposed designation.[154] If the commission decides to designate a water management area, it assumes administrative control over both ground and surface waters in the designated area.[155]

Once an area is designated as a water management area, the code provides that "[n]o person shall make any withdrawal, diversion, impoundment, or consumptive use of water in any designated water management area without first obtaining a permit from the commission."[156] However, no permit is required for domestic consumption by individual users or for the use of a catchment system to gather water.[157] To obtain a permit, the applicant must establish that the proposed use of water:

(1) Can be accommodated with the available water source;
(2) Is a reasonable-beneficial use;
(3) Will not interfere with any existing legal use;
(4) Is consistent with the public interest;
(5) Is consistent with state and county general plans and land use designations; and
(6) Is consistent with county land use plans and policies.[158]

These conditions show the influence of riparian principles, and concern for the public interest as reflected in comprehensive governmental planning.

Application and issuance procedures are set forth in the code. If a permittee desires to change the use of water subject to the permit, application for a modification of the terms of the permit must be made.[159] A permit may be revoked on several grounds, including non-use of the water for a period of four years.[160] The code allows a permittee to transfer a permit to another party.[161]

Those persons who were using water prior to the passage of the code must apply for a permit within one year from the effective date of designation. Except for appurtenant rights, failure to apply within this period creates a presumption of abandonment of the use.[162] If the existing use is reasonable and beneficial, and conforms to the criteria stated above, the commission will issue a permit for the continued use.[163]

Appurtenant rights are preserved by the code. "Nothing in this part shall be construed to deny the exercise of an appurtenant right by the holder thereof at any time. A permit for water use based on an existing appurtenant right shall be issued upon application."[164]

The code provides that all existing wells be registered with the commission.[165] A permit is required for all well construction and for the installation of pumps and pumping equipment.[166] The permit requirement applies to all areas of the state, including water management areas.[167] The code likewise requires the registration of all "stream diversion works" -- meaning any artificial or natural structure emplaced within a stream for the purpose of diverting stream water.[168] A permit is needed to construct a stream diversion works, or to alter an existing one.[169]

With regard to Native Hawaiian water rights, the code contains the following provisions:

> Section 174C-101 **Native Hawaiian water rights**. (a) Provisions of this chapter shall not be construed to amend or modify rights or entitlements to water as provided for by the Hawaiian Homes Commission Act, 1920, as amended, and by chapter 175, relating to the Molokai irrigation system.
>
> (b)   No provision of this chapter shall diminish or extinguish trust revenues derived from existing water licenses unless compensation is made.
>
> (c)   Traditional and customary rights of ahupua'a tenants who are descendants of native Hawaiians who inhabited the Hawaiian Islands prior to 1778 shall not be abridged or denied by this chapter. Such traditional and customary rights shall include, but not be limited to, the cultivation or propagation of taro on one's own kuleana and the gathering of hihiwai, opae, 'o'opu, limu, thatch, ti leaf, aho cord, and medicinal plants for subsistence, cultural, and religious purposes.
>
> (d)   The appurtenant water rights of kuleana and taro lands, along with those traditional and customary rights assured in this section, shall not be diminished or extinguished by a failure to apply for or to receive a permit under this chapter.[170]

How does the State Water Code affect the various water rights which have been recognized by Hawai'i courts? In accord with *McBryde*, the code acknowledges the state's role as trustee:

> It is recognized that the waters of the State are held for the benefit of the citizens of the State. It is declared that the people of the State are beneficiaries and have a right to have the waters protected for their use.[171]

Also in line with *McBryde* is the code's abandonment of prescriptive water rights: "No right, title, or interest in the use of any water resources of the State can be acquired by prescription."[172]

As noted above, the code specifically preserves ancient appurtenant rights, and prevents their abandonment by non-use.[173] Appurtenant water rights cannot be lost by failure to comply with permit procedures.[174] However, the code reverses *McBryde* with respect to the transfer of waters:

The common law of the State to the contrary notwithstanding, the commission shall allow the holder of a use permit to transport and use surface or ground water beyond overlying land or outside the watershed from which it is taken if the commission determines that such transport and use are consistent with the public interest and the general plans and land use policies of the state and counties.[175]

The code's permit system incorporates several important riparian principles, namely protection of the water source, reasonable and beneficial use, and noninterference with the rights of others.[176] In order to obtain a permit, the applicant must convince the commission that the proposed water use adheres to these principles.

6. CONCLUSION

The Hawai'i State Water Code does not address the constitutional questions raised in the appeals from the *McBryde* decision, but it may have made many of those issues irrelevant. The code does not protect the "vested" water rights which any party may have enjoyed prior to the *McBryde* decision -- particularly the right to a fixed quantity of "surplus" water. Whether such water rights "vested" prior to *McBryde*, and whether *McBryde* resulted in an unconstitutional "taking" of these rights remain unresolved. *Robinson V* left these questions for another day, if and when the state decides to enforce the principles enumerated in *McBryde*.

Given the comprehensive regulatory mechanism established by the new water code, however, those issues may never ripen for ultimate resolution. The code was designed to place most of the fundamental questions regarding water use and allocation in the hands of land use planners where there is no designated water management area in place. It is still premature to assess whether this system will work as intended. The various agencies charged with formulating the Hawai'i Water Plan are still drafting those components at this writing. These plans will guide water allocation decisions unless the Commission on Water Resource Management has designated an area as a water management area.

Currently only the Honolulu, Wahiawā, and Pearl Harbor water districts have been designated as water management areas. The commission thus regulates water use by permits only in these areas. As more areas are designated, this agency will grow in importance and influence -- possibly more so than any other regulatory body. After all, as the ancient Hawaiians realized, the power to regulate the *wai* (water), has a profound impact on the well-being of the entire society.

NOTES

1. E.S. Handy and E.G. Handy, *Native Planters in Old Hawaii* 63 (1972).
2. A. Perry, "Hawaiian Water Rights," *Thrum's Annual, 1913,* 95 (1912).
3. R. Nakuiwa, "Ancient Hawaiian Water Rights," *Thrum's Annual, 1894,* 79 (1893).
4. H.A. Wadsworth, *A Historical Summary of Irrigation in Hawaii* 37 (Hawaiian Planters Record 134, 1933).
5. Handy and Handy, *supra* note 1, at 92-93; *id.* at 134; Perry, *supra* note 2, at 92.
6. Perry, *supra* note 2, at 94-95; Wadsworth, *supra* note 4, at 131.
7. Nakuiwa, *supra* note 3, at 79-80; Perry, *supra* note 2, at 94; Wadsworth, *supra* note 4, at 130.
8. Perry, *supra* note 2, at 93.

9.   Nakuiwa, *supra* note 3, at 83.

10.   Wadsworth, *supra* note 4, at 132.

11.   Nakuiwa, *supra* note 3, at 80; Perry, *supra* note 2, at 92; Handy and Handy, *supra* note 1, at 58.

12.   Nakuiwa, *supra* note 3, at 79.

13.   Wadsworth, *supra* note 4, at 131; Handy and Handy, *supra* note 1, at 59.

14.   Hawai'i State Dept. of Budget and Finance (Hawai'i Institute for Management and Analysis in Government), *Land and Water Resource Management* 152-153 (1979) [hereinafter *Land and Water Resource Management*]; Perry, *supra* note 2, at 95; Handy and Handy, *supra* note 1, at 76.

15.   *See* Chapter 1, *supra*, text accompanying notes 17-53.

16.   Levy, *Native Hawaiian Land Rights*, 63 Cal. L. Rev. 848, 850-852 (1975).

17.   W.A. Hutchins, *The Hawaiian System of Water Rights* 23 (1946).

18.   L. Thurston, *The Fundamental Law of Hawaii* 29-30 (1904).

19.   *See Reppun v. Board of Water Supply*, 65 Haw. 531, 543, 656 P.2d 57, 65-66 (1982).

20.   Hutchins, *supra* note 17, at 30.

21.   *Id.* at 30-31.

22.   *Id.* at 25, 30.

23.   2 *Revised Laws of Hawaii, 1925*, § 7, at 2123.

24.   *Peck v. Bailey*, 8 Haw. 658 (1867); Hutchins, *supra* note 17, at 45-46.

25.   2 *Revised Laws of Hawaii, 1925*, at 2142.

26.   *McBryde Sugar Co. v. Robinson*, 54 Haw. 174, 504 P.2d 1330 (1973).

27.   *Peck v. Bailey*, 8 Haw. 658 (1867); *Lonoaea v. Wailuku Sugar Co.*, 9 Haw. 651 (1895); *Hawaiian Commercial & Sugar Co. v. Wailuku Sugar Co.*, 14 Haw. 50 (1902); *Hawaiian Commercial & Sugar Co. v. Wailuku Sugar Co.*, 15 Haw. 675 (1904).

28.   *See generally* Wadsworth, *supra* note 4, at 136-157.

29.   Wadsworth, *supra* note 4, at 139; Hutchins, *supra* note 17, at 50.

30.   Hutchins, *supra* note 17, at 50-64.

31.   *Id.* at 58.

32.   Wadsworth, *supra* note 4, at 140.

33.   *Land and Water Resource Management, supra* note 14, at 165-166.

34.   *Peck v. Bailey*, 8 Haw. 658, 661 (1867).

35.   *Carter v. Territory*, 24 Haw. 47, 66 (1917); *Territory v. Gay*, 31 Haw. 376, 383 (1930).

36.   8 Haw. 658 (1867).

37.   *Id.* at 659.

38.   *Id.* at 661.

39.   *Id.* at 666.

40.   Hutchins, *supra* note 17, at 103.

41.   *Territory v. Gay*, 31 Haw. 376, 383 (1930).

42.   *Hawaiian Commercial & Sugar Co. v. Wailuku Sugar Co.*, 14 Haw. 50, 61-62 (1902).

43.   Hutchins, *supra* note 17, at 117.

44.   *See Hawaiian Commercial & Sugar Co. v. Wailuku Sugar Co.*, 16 Haw. 113 (1904) (Motion for Rehearing).

45.   *Territory v. Gay*, 31 Haw. 376, 383-384 (1930).

46.   9 Haw. 651 (1895).

47.   *Id.* at 662.

48.   *Id.* at 665.

49.   *Id.*

50.   14 Haw. 50 (1902).

51.   *Id.* at 61-62.

52.   5 Haw. 216 (1884).

53.   *Id.* at 224.

54.   *Hawaiian Commercial & Sugar Co. v. Wailuku Sugar Co.*, 15 Haw. 675, 680 (1904).

55.   *Id.*

56.   *Lonoaea v. Wailuku Sugar Co.*, 9 Haw. 651, 659 (1895).

57.   *Hawaiian Commercial & Sugar Co. v. Wailuku Sugar Co.*, 14 Haw. 50, 66 (1902).

58.   *Id.* at 63.

59.   15 Haw. 675 (1904).

60.   *Id.* at 680.
61.   *Id.*
62.   *Id.*
63.   24 Haw. 47 (1917).
64.   *Id.* at 48-49.
65.   *Id.* at 70.
66.   *Id.*
67.   *Id.* at 48.
68.   *Id.* at 70.
69.   *Id.* at 71.
70.   *Id.*
71.   *Territory v. Gay*, 31 Haw. 376, 394-395 (1930); *McBryde Sugar Co. v. Robinson*, 54 Haw. 174, 199-200, 504 P.2d 1330, 1344-1345 (1973).
72.   31 Haw. 376 (1930).
73.   *Id.* at 382.
74.   *Id.* at 378-382.
75.   *Id.* at 388.
76.   *Id.* at 393.
77.   *Id.* at 409.
78.   *Id.* at 404, 409.
79.   *But see* Hutchins, *supra* note 17, at 77.
80.   *Hawaiian Commercial & Sugar Co. v. Wailuku Sugar Co.*, 15 Haw. 675, 680 (1904).
81.   *Territory v. Gay*, 31 Haw. 376, 384 (1930).
82.   *See generally* 78 Am. Jur. 2d *Waters* §§ 260-280, 281-296 (1975).
83.   Black's Law Dictionary defines "usufruct" as follows: "In the civil law, the right of enjoying a thing, the property of which is vested in another, and to draw from the same all the profit, utility and advantage which it may produce, providing it be without altering the substance of the thing." (5th ed. 1979.)
84.   *Carter v. Territory*, 24 Haw. 47, 66 (1917).
85.   *Territory v. Gay*, 31 Haw. 376, 415 (1930).
86.   Haw. Rev. Stat. § 1-1 (1985).
87.   Hutchins, *supra* note 17, at 87-89.
88.   8 Haw. 658, 662 (1867).
89.   *But see id.* at 671 in which the court states, in *dicta*: "[w]hile the King owned [the] ahupua'a, he had a right to apply the water to what land he pleased . . . ."
90.   *Id.*
91.   *Hawaiian Commercial & Sugar Co. v. Wailuku Sugar Co.*, 15 Haw. 675, 680 (1904).
92.   *Territory v. Gay*, 31 Haw. 376, 413-414 (1930).
93.   *Carter v. Territory*, 24 Haw. 47, 67 (1917).
94.   *Id.* at 49-50.
95.   *Id.* at 57.
96.   *Id.* at 66-67, quoting *Revised Laws of Hawaii*, § 471 (1850).
97.   *Id.* at 67.
98.   *Id.* at 70-71.
99.   *Territory v. Gay*, 31 Haw. 376, 395 (1930).
100. *Id.* at 397-403.
101. *Id.* at 409.
102. *Id.* at 410, 415.
103. *Id.* at 413-416.
104. *City Mill Co. v. Honolulu Sewer and Water Commission*, 30 Haw. 912 (1929).
105. 54 Haw. 174, 488 P.2d 1406 (1973).
106. *McBryde Sugar Co. v. Robinson*, SP No. 108 (5th Cir. Ct. of Hawai'i, Dec. 10, 1968).
107. *McBryde Sugar Co. v. Robinson*, 54 Haw. 174, 186, 504 P.2d 1330, 1338 (1973), quoting from 2 *Revised Laws of Hawaii, 1925*, at 2124 (appendix).
108. *Id.* at 185-186, 504 P.2d at 1337-1339.
109. *Id.* at 186-187, 504 P.2d at 1339; *Land and Water Resource Management, supra* note 14, at 195-196.

110. 54 Haw. 174, 191-197, 504 P.2d 1330, 1341-1344 (1973); *Land and Water Resource Management, supra* note 14, at 197.

111. *Id.* at 198, 504 P.2d at 1345.

112. *Id.* at 191, 199-200, 504 P.2d at 1344-1345.

113. *Id.* at 200, 504 P.2d at 1345-1346.

114. *McBryde Sugar Co. v. Robinson*, 55 Haw. 260, 261, 517 P.2d 26, 27 (1973).

115. *Id.* at 298-303, 517 P.2d at 47-50 (Levinson, J., dissenting).

116. *Robinson v. Hawaii*, 417 U.S. 976 (1974). No. 73-1440 6/17/74.

117. 441 F.Supp. 559 (1977).

118. *Id.* at 566-567.

119. *Id.* at 585-586.

120. 65 Haw. 641, 658 P.2d 287 (1982).

121. *Id.* at 667-677, 658 P.2d at 305-312.

122. *Id.* at 647-650, 658 P.2d at 294-295.

123. *Id.* at 651-653, 658 P.2d at 296-297.

124. 65 Haw. 531, 656 P.2d 57 (1982), *cert. denied*, 471 U.S. 1014 (1984).

125. *Id.* at 549-551, 656 P.2d at 69-70.

126. *Id.* at 551-552, 656 P.2d at 70-71.

127. *Id.* at 545, 656 P.2d at 67.

128. *Id.* at 552-553, 656 P.2d at 71-72.

129. 753 F.2d 1468 (1985).

130. *Ariyoshi v. Robinson*, 477 U.S. 902 (1986).

131. 473 U.S. 172 (1985).

132. *Williamson County Regional Planning Commission v. Hamilton Bank*, 473 U.S. 172, 191 (1985).

133. 676 F.Supp. 1002 (D.Haw. 1987).

134. *Id.* at 1012.

135. *Id.* at 1006.

136. *Id.* at 1008.

137. *Id.* at 1020.

138. 887 F.2d 215 (9th Cir. 1989).

139. *Id.* at 219, n.3; *see also supra* note 120.

140. *Robinson v. Ariyoshi*, 887 F.2d 215, 219 (1989), citing from *Williamson County Regional Planning Commission v. Hamilton Bank*, 473 U.S. 172, 190, n.11 (1985).

141. *Id.*

142. *Id.* The period for petitioning for *certiorari* to the U.S. Supreme Court has lapsed.

143. Haw. Const. art. XII, § 7.

144. Haw. Rev. Stat. ch. 174C (1989 Supp.).

145. Haw. Rev. Stat. § 174C-7 (1989 Supp.).

146. *Id.* at § 174C-8.

147. *Id.* at § 174C-26(a).

148. *Id.* at § 174C-27(a).

149. *Id.* at § 174C-31(a).

150. *Id.* at § 174C-32(c).

151. *Id.* at § 174C-41(a).

152. *Id.* at § 174C-41(b).

153. *Id.* at § 174C-42.

154. *Id.* at § 174C-43.

155. *Id.* at §§ 174C-41(a), 44, 45.

156. *Id.* at § 174C-48(a).

157. *Id.*

158. *Id.* at § 174C-49(a).

159. *Id.* at § 174C-57.

160. *Id.* at § 174C-58.

161. *Id.* at § 174C-59.

162. *Id.* at § 174C-50(c).

163.   *Id.* at § 174C-59(b).
164.   *Id.* at § 174C-63; subject to §§ 174C-26, 27, 58-62.
165.   *Id.* at § 174C-83.
166.   *Id.* at § 174C-84(a).
167.   *Id.*
168.   *Id.* at §§ 174C-91, 92.
169.   *Id.* at § 174C-93.
170.   *Id.* at § 174C-101.
171.   *Id.* at § 174C-2(a).
172.   *Id.* at § 174C-4(d).
173.   *Id.* at §§ 174C-63, 50(c).
174.   *Id.* at § 174C-101(d).
175.   *Id.* at § 174C-49(c).
176.   *Id.* at § 174C-49(a).

CHAPTER 8

KONOHIKI FISHING RIGHTS AND MARINE RESOURCES

1.   INTRODUCTION

The term *"konohiki* fishing rights"[1] encompasses a set of nearshore fishing rights unique in the United States. Prior to annexation, the Kingdom of Hawai'i codified this ancient system of fishing rights, recognizing the interests of both the *konohiki* and *ahupua'a* tenants. This system allowed the *konohiki* to regulate the taking of fish and other marine life from the reefs and fishing grounds abutting the *ahupua'a*. Tenants of the *ahupua'a* also had a right to take fish, subject to the right of the *konohiki* to manage and conserve the fisheries. Shortly after annexation in 1898, congress sought to terminate "exclusive" fishing rights and open the fisheries to all, subject to "vested rights." In the 1900 Hawai'i Organic Act, congress recognized the "vested rights" of those who registered and established their fishing rights within a two-year period.

Even today, experts continue their attempts to determine what rights survived as a result of this registration process. Existing cases reveal a split between the federal and local courts on the applicable law. As a result, the current status of these fishing rights is clouded, inviting further exploration into their viability and the effect they will have on modern activities involving nearshore fisheries. Furthermore, current federal efforts to define rights in the Fisheries Conservation Zone and the Exclusive Economic Zone beyond the territorial seas will have to consider traditional Native Hawaiian open sea fishing rights.

2.   ANCIENT RIGHTS AND CUSTOMS

Prior to Western contact, Hawaiians had no concept similar to private property ownership. Traditionally, the ancient Hawaiians operated under a system of land tenure that allowed use of the land, fisheries, and other natural resources, subject only to religious or political restrictions.

From the most ancient times, the *ali'i nui* or high chief held -- personally and as sovereign of the people -- all of the land and the adjacent fishing areas. In this system, the *ali'i nui* favored the chiefs by allowing them to exercise political control over a large division of an island -- a *moku* -- in return for, and in expectation of, martial allegiance and tribute in the form of a share of the land's bounty.

The ruling chiefs who controlled the land were "supreme executives" bound by trust to see to the welfare of the people and the land. Along with the power and authority to distribute the assets of the kingdom, the chiefs had the duties of trustees, obligated to insure the beneficial use of the land for all of the people. Implicit in ancient Hawaiian regulations regarding water and land is the concept of mutual benefit and sharing.[2]

Each *moku* was divided into subdivisions of land, *ahupua'a*, which stretched from the mountains to the sea. The *'ili kūpono* was smaller, a tract lying within an *ahupua'a* but outside, and independent of, the distribution and tribute practices of the *ahupua'a*. At times, these *'ili* were associated with separate mountain and ocean areas called *'ili lele* which provided the occupants with resources for basic sustenance.[3] These *ahupua'a* and *'ili*, which were distributed to lesser chiefs or land agents called *"konohiki"*[4] in return for the same fealty, became the basic units of land. Each unit was self-sustaining, possessing a section of high forest, mid-level cultivated land, and sea-level coastal area. These areas provided the firewood, timber, crops and seafood that for centuries sustained the ancient Hawaiians in their traditional lifestyle.

Within the *ahupua'a*, the people tilled small tracts of land for the chief's tax on certain days, for the king's on other days, and for their own sustenance on the rest.[5] These tenants or occupants, the *"hoa'aina,"*[6] were free to roam and gather the resources within the *ahupua'a* which sustained them, subject to the regulation of the *konohiki*.

Under the ancient system of land tenure, *ahupua'a* occupants shared fishing areas appurtenant to the *ahupua'a*, which were exclusively used by them. However, all were free to fish in the open ocean,[7] except as might be directed by the *ali'i*, or restricted by the king or by religious or other practices.[8]

Kamehameha III officially acknowledged the ancient fishing practices and uses of the ocean by Hawaiians in the Law of Kamehameha III, June 7, 1839.[9] Under that proclamation, the king formally distributed the fishing grounds among the different classes of people, foreshadowing[10] the land distribution to come in the *Mahele* almost a decade later. The subsequent statute, section 8, chapter III of the Laws of 1842, stated, in part:

> His Majesty the King hereby takes the fishing grounds from those who now possess them, from Hawaii to Kauai, and gives one portion of them to the common people, another portion to the landlords, and a portion he reserves to himself.
>
> These are the fishing grounds which His Majesty the King takes and gives to the people; the fishing grounds without the coral reef, viz. the Kilohee grounds, the Luhee ground, the Malolo ground, together with the ocean beyond.
>
> *But the fishing grounds from the coral reef to the sea beach are for the landlords, and for the tenants of their several lands, but not for others.*[11] (Emphasis added.)

While the law specifically recognized the people's rights in the fisheries, it went on to sanction the practice of the *konohiki* of placing a *kapu* on certain fish and fishing seasons. If the *konohiki* exceeded this limitation by unduly seizing or taxing the people for his catch, the law provided a penalty.[12] It also reserved for the king certain species from the fishing grounds seaward of the *konohiki* fisheries.[13]

This revolutionary 1839 law was the first formal recognition of the people's fishing rights. Significantly, it was also the first time that the ability of the *konohiki* to regulate these fishing rights was limited.

a. *The Statutory Changes*

In later statutes, the kingdom amended and redrafted the 1839 law with only minor changes.[14] With the passage of the organic acts establishing the kingdom's governmental structure in 1845-46, fishing rights within the *ahupua'a* remained basically the same.[15] Difficulties with enforcement and conflicts with the *konohiki* led to subsequent legislative amendments that, in effect, opened the ocean fisheries seaward of the *konohiki* fisheries "to everyone with respect to all fish."[16] In 1851, a major revision granted all fishing grounds adjacent to any government land or otherwise belonging to the government to the people for free and equal use of all persons.[17]

The kingdom codified *konohiki* fishing rights into sections 384 to 396 of the Civil Code of 1859. These statutes were carried forward without material change and incorporated into section 358 of the Civil Code of 1892[18] and chapter 84 of the Penal Laws of 1897. Despite errors and ambiguity in the English translation of the 1839 law,[19] few material changes were made to the original statute. Hence, *konohiki* fishing rights, as expressed in the kingdom's statutes, can be summarized as follows:

(1) The private fisheries of the *konohiki* extended from the beach at low watermark to the edge of the reefs and, where there was no reef, to one geographical mile seaward of the beach.

(2) Within these private fisheries, fishing was restricted to the exclusive but joint use of the *konohiki* and the tenants of the *ahupua'a* to which the fisheries were assigned.

(3) The *konohiki* could regulate fishing within these private fisheries:

   (a) By reserving aside or placing a *kapu* on one specific type of fish for exclusive use; or

   (b) After consultation with the tenants, by prohibiting fishing during certain months of the year and, during the fishing season, taking from each tenant one-third of the fish caught in the fishery.

b. *Hawai'i Supreme Court Cases 1850-1900*

During the years following the *Mahele*, the Hawai'i Supreme Court defined the scope of fishing rights in the context of the newly created private property system.

(1) *The Shared Right to the Fishery* The *konohiki* held the fishery as a nonexclusive form of private property. Accordingly, a *konohiki* could freely transfer this nonexclusive ownership of the fishing ground. On the other hand, the tenant merely held a restricted fishing right, by virtue of the tenancy, to the same fishery. A tenant could transfer a nonexclusive right to fish, but only as an appurtenance to a tenancy or fee interest in property within an *ahupua'a*.

In *Haalelea v. Montgomery* (1858),[20] Haalelea, the owner of the *ahupua'a* of Honouliuli, sued Montgomery, who owned a portion of the same *ahupua'a* known as Pu'uloa. Montgomery sought to prevent Haalelea and the *ahupua'a* tenants from fishing in the *konohiki* fishing grounds of Honouliuli. Kekauonohi, once the owner of the entire *ahupua'a*, had sold Pu'uloa to Montgomery's brother, who had subsequently conveyed it to Montgomery. When Kekauonohi died, her will left Haalelea, her second husband, the remaining lands of Honouliuli. Montgomery claimed that he had obtained an exclusive right to fish in the area adjacent to his land by express grant in the deed. Haalelea also claimed an exclusive right.

The Hawai'i Supreme Court reasoned that neither Montgomery nor Haalelea had an exclusive right to the disputed fishery. Kamehameha III had redistributed much of the fishing grounds, expressly reserving the areas from the coral reefs to the beaches for the exclusive, but joint, use of the landlords and their tenants.[21] The court found that the deed from Kekauonohi conveying Pu'uloa, which was only a portion of the *ahupua'a*, did not expressly convey her *konohiki* fishing rights. Moreover, the court considered it doubtful that Kekauonohi could have conveyed the portion of the fishing ground adjacent to Pu'uloa or her rights therein without infringing upon the rights of the tenants living in Honouliuli. The court stated:

> Certainly if her grantee had tabooed one kind of fish, on his part of the ground, while she tabooed another kind upon the other part, the rights of the tenants would have been violated. And if she could have divided the fishing ground into two parts, she could have divided into twenty, and so have rendered the rights of the tenants worthless.[22]

Therefore, the court held that the *konohiki* rights had passed by will to Haalelea.

However, these *konohiki* rights did not entitle Haalelea -- and had not entitled Kekauonohi either -- to exclusive fishing. The tenants had the joint right to fish in the same waters. The court found that the Act of 1845 supported this point by establishing the relationship between the *konohiki* and *hoaʻaina*:

> The landlords shall be considered in law to hold said private fisheries for the *equal use* of themselves and of the tenants on their respective lands; and the tenants shall be at liberty to use the fisheries of the landlords, subject to the restrictions in this article imposed.[23] (Emphasis added.)

Consequently, when Montgomery acquired a portion of the *ahupuaʻa* of Honouliuli, he acquired along with it a common right of piscary[24] in the adjoining fishing ground. As such, he became a tenant of Honouliuli entitled in common with other tenants and the *konohiki* to take fish in the adjoining sea. The court defined the term "tenant" in this context:

> We understand the word tenant, as used in this connection, to have lost its ancient restricted meaning, and to be almost synonymous, at the present time, with the word occupant, or occupier, and that every person occupying lawfully, any part of "Honouliuli," is a tenant within the meaning of the law.[25]

Thus, the Hawaiʻi Supreme Court made several important statements in the *Haalelea* case. The tenant, defined by the court as any person lawfully occupying any part of the *ahupuaʻa*, possesses a right to use of the fishery, subject only to the right of the *konohiki* to *kapu* or tax the catch. Neither the *konohiki* nor the tenant can exclude the other from fishing. The *konohiki* can convey fishing rights but only by express grant. Moreover, a *konohiki* cannot divide *konohiki* fishing rights with another or amongst others. A tenant can only convey a common right to fish on the fishing grounds of a *konohiki* in conjunction with a conveyance of a part of the *ahupuaʻa* to another.

(2)   *The Scope of the Right to the Fishery*   Despite having a more limited right, the tenant can apparently take fish subject only to taxation or *kapu* by the *konohiki*. In *Hatton v. Piopio* (1882),[26] the *konohiki* Hatton sued Piopio for trespass on the fishery. Piopio lived in Puʻuloa in the *ahupuaʻa* of Honouliuli as a tenant and employee of Dowsett. Piopio had caught fish in the waters adjacent to Puʻuloa and subsequently sold the fish for $34, which he gave to Dowsett. Hatton contended that Piopio, owning no *kuleana*, was not a legal tenant, and that even if he were, he did not have the right to sell his catch from these waters.

The Hawaiʻi Supreme Court rejected Hatton's arguments. Citing *Haalelea v. Montgomery*, the court held that any *bona fide* resident is a tenant of the *ahupuaʻa*. Since there was no dispute that Piopio resided in Puʻuloa, he had the legal rights of a tenant.[27] Further, the court held that a tenant had the right to sell fish, since sections of the Civil

Code regulating fisheries did not expressly prohibit the sale of fish. In so deciding, the court compared the statute relating to fisheries with another statute reserving native tenant rights:

> It is noticeable that in Section 1477 of the Civil Code, where certain specific rights of the people are secured, the people on the lands are allowed to take firewood, house timber, aho cord, thatch and ki leaf from the land on which they live, "for their own private use, but they shall not have a right to take such articles for profit." *No such restrictions are made in the statute respecting the fisheries.*[28] (Emphasis added.)

The court found that if the legislature had intended to limit or prohibit the sale of fish, it would have stated so in the statute regulating the fisheries. In addition, the court believed that the interest of the *konohiki* would not be adversely affected by the sale.[29] Therefore, the tenant was not liable for trespass.

Thus, the court reaffirmed that any *bona fide* resident of the *ahupua'a* would be considered a tenant under the fisheries statute. Moreover, a tenant could sell fish caught for profit, subject only to the superior right of the *konohiki* to taboo or tax the catch.

However, a tenant of an *'ili kupono* within an *ahupua'a* only had the right to take fish from the fisheries of that *'ili*. The tenant did not have the same right to fish from the fishing grounds adjacent to the *ahupua'a* as a tenant of that *ahupua'a*. In *Shipman v. Nawahi* (1886),[30] the Hawai'i Supreme Court held that a lessee of the *'ili* of Piopio, which was located within the *ahupua'a* of Waiākea, only held those rights associated with the "separate and independent title" of that *'ili*. Accordingly, the lessee of the *'ili* could not claim, as a tenant of Waiākea, the right to fish from the sea fishery adjacent to Waiākea. On the other hand, the court reaffirmed the right of the lessee of a *kuleana* to assert fishing rights in the Waiākea fishery.[31]

c. *The Organic Act of 1900*

In 1898, the United States "annexed" Hawai'i as a territory. Congress passed Hawai'i's Organic Act in 1900, establishing a governmental structure for the new territory. Section 95 of the act opened the oceans to all citizens by repealing exclusive fishing rights except rights which had already "vested."[32] However, section 96 provided that fishing rights would be deemed to have vested only if the owner "established" them by filing a petition within a two-year period and proving the claim in circuit court.[33] Finally, section 96 allowed fishing rights which had vested and been established to be condemned upon payment of "just compensation."

The express intent of these provisions of the Hawai'i Organic Act was "to destroy, so far as it is in its power to do so, all private rights of fishery and to throw open the fisheries to the people."[34] The act appears to have succeeded. Unfortunately, no one has definitively identified nor accurately inventoried all the *konohiki* fisheries in the islands, leaving the number of such fisheries uncertain.[35] However, of a total of 1,200 to 1,500 fisheries, there were an estimated 300 to 400 privately owned fisheries in 1900.[36] As of 1939, only 101 fisheries had been established and registered by some 35 owners.[37] Furthermore, one expert estimates that between 1900 and 1953, the federal and territorial governments condemned or acquired 37 fisheries,[38] while 248 fisheries were not registered and purportedly were lost. Another source relates that anywhere from 311 to 342 fisheries may have been forfeited.[39] Thus, anywhere from two to four private fisheries were forfeited for every one established.

After the passage of the Organic Act, legal disputes arose over the vesting and establishment of fisheries, the constitutionality of section 96, and valuation of both *konohiki* and tenant rights in the fisheries. The Hawai'i courts have supported the essential purpose of the act by upholding its requirements and procedures. However, they have protected fishing rights claimants where their rights have vested and been established pursuant to the Hawai'i Organic Act's provisions. On the other hand, federal courts have construed the law more cautiously to protect rights which may have vested *despite* the failure of the *konohiki* or *hoaʻāina* to register a fishery. Finally, where the territory or U.S. exercised the power to condemn a fishery, valuation has raised a whole new set of problems for courts adjudicating fishing rights claims.

(1)   *Vesting*   Section 95 of the Hawai'i Organic Act repealed all exclusive rights except those which had vested. Consequently, the courts had to resolve controversies over what constituted a vested right.   The territorial courts attempted to construe vesting narrowly, thereby limiting the survival of fishing rights.   In contrast, the federal courts tended to view *konohiki* rights as a legitimate form of property ownership protected by due process requirements.

In *Carter v. Territory* (1902) [hereinafter *Carter I*],[40] trustees of the Bishop Estate, pursuant to section 96 of the Organic Act, sought to establish *konohiki* fishing rights in the Wai'alae Iki and Moanalua fisheries. The Hawai'i Supreme Court first examined whether the claim could be based on ancient custom and prescription, and concluded that the 1839 Act of Kamehameha III had revoked and annulled any claim to the fisheries based on ancient custom or prescription.[41] Accordingly, the court required fishing rights claimants to base any claims on the Act of 1839 or some subsequent grant or conveyance. Moreover, the court stated:

> Under the common law the right of fishing in the open sea like that of navigation was a public right. The grant of an exclusive right to a sea fishery cannot be presumed. Every presumption is against the grant and in favor of the public. Every ambiguity or doubt in the instrument by which the right is claimed to be granted will be construed most strongly against the grantee.[42]

Plaintiffs argued that the Act of 1839 and subsequent statutes were in the nature of a grant, but the court rejected that argument, finding that these laws were not intended to be grants of property but merely grants of special privilege to the landlord.[43] Finally, the court also rejected the idea that the *konohiki* fisheries were appurtenances[44] to the *ahupuaʻa* and passed automatically to the *konohiki*. The court cited *Haalelea v. Montgomery* for the proposition that *konohiki* fishing rights are private property and can only be conveyed by specific words of grant.[45] The court also examined the original royal patent on the *ahupuaʻa* of Moanalua which had conveyed the "fishing right in the adjoining sea." and contained a specific metes and bounds description.[46]   The court determined that the royal patent only conveyed land and therefore this language merely *described* the fishery so that the landlord could exercise his privileges given under the fishing statute.

The plaintiffs appealed the Hawai'i court's ruling as it related solely to Moanalua fishery to the U.S. Supreme Court.   In *Damon v. Hawaii* (1904),[47] that court reversed the Hawai'i Supreme Court's decision. Justice Holmes, writing for the court, refused to require "technically accurate" words expressly granting fishing rights in a royal patent.[48] Conceding the unique nature of such rights, the U.S. Supreme Court nevertheless recognized *konohiki* fishing rights as vested property rights established under Hawai'i law. The court even intimated that the general laws of the kingdom had independently granted a right to private title to the fisheries "and if they imported a grant or a confirmation of an existing title, of course *the repeal of the laws would not repeal the grant.*"[49] (Emphasis added.) Nevertheless, focusing on the specific property description in the royal patent, the court held that the intent to convey the fishery was plain.

In *Carter v. Territory* (1906) [hereinafter *Carter II*],[50] the U.S. Supreme Court considered a claim to a fishery where the royal patent to the adjacent land did not explicitly describe the fishery. The court again decided in favor of the plaintiffs, upholding their claim to *konohiki* rights. Unlike the *Damon* case, which involved an explicit description in a royal patent of a fishery, the plaintiffs in *Carter II* based their claim on (1) the traditional use of the fishery since time immemorial, (2) ancient prescription, and (3) the 1839 Act of Kamehameha III and subsequent statutes granting fisheries to the *konohiki*. Justice Holmes, again delivering the opinion of the court, reaffirmed that the statutes "created vested rights."[51] Thus, in the court's view, a "vested" *konohiki* right need not have been based on an express grant or be appurtenant to the land. If the statute's intent to convey was clear, the right was created. The court declined to rule whether prescription and ancient tradition could also have been the basis for vested fishing rights.[52]

In *Smith v. Laamea* (1927),[53] the Hawai'i Supreme Court implied that one who acquired title to a portion of an *ahupua'a* by adverse possession would become entitled to tenants' fishing rights. In this quiet title action, La'amea occupied land he claimed by adverse possession, although he conceded that the trustees of the Bishop Estate held paper title. La'amea began his occupancy after 1900. On the other hand, plaintiffs contended that such occupancy by La'amea was permissive. One significant but undisputed fact was that La'amea and his predecessor-in-interest had paid plaintiffs one dollar a year for the right to fish. A jury found that the use by La'amea was permissive and concluded that he did not possess fee simple ownership of the land. La'amea appealed and the supreme court upheld the jury's decision. However, in *dicta*, the court declared that an adverse possessor acquiring title is a tenant and is entitled to a common right of fishing.[54] Strictly speaking, this holding recognized a potential right to fishing rights even if they vested after 1900, irrespective of section 95 of the Hawai'i Organic Act.

However, in *Damon v. Tsutsui* (1930),[55] the Hawai'i Supreme Court changed its position. In this case, Damon Estate, the *konohiki*, sought to restrain Tsutsui, the tenant, from catching shrimp in the fishery of Kaliawa. Tsutsui had acquired his rights from a lease with C.Q. Yee Hop Co., Ltd., which had purchased a portion of Kaliawa known as Panāhāhā from Waller. Waller had obtained the land from Beckley. Beckley, however, upon conveying Panāhāhā to Waller, purportedly had reserved and retained for herself the fishery and fishing rights of Kaliawa, which she had then conveyed to Ke'elikōlani. Damon claimed to have received these reserved rights from Ke'elikōlani along with the title to the *ahupua'a*.

The court held that even if Beckley had reserved the fishery and subsequently it had passed to Damon, the reservation was not binding against successors to Waller's interest. The court reasoned that the tenants' fishing rights derived not from a grant but rather from the statutes of the kingdom regulating the fisheries. The court stated:

> In our opinion each tenant in turn derived his fishing rights from the King or his successor, the Territory, by means of the statute.

. . . If a tenant sells or leases and moves away from the land he has nothing left (of what was granted him) to pass on to another tenant. The next tenant receives his rights through the statute, just as his immediate predecessor did . . . . The release, therefore, by Waller, if there was any, and the estoppel, if any such resulted from the deed of Emma [Beckley], did not operate to deprive C.Q. Yee Hop & Company or Tsutsui from acquiring or enjoying the fishing rights granted to tenants by the statute.[56]

Nevertheless, the court found that Tsutsui did not have a valid interest in the fishery. Waller, Tsutsui's predecessor, who owned the land at the time the Hawai'i Organic Act was passed, had not established his vested right and therefore had lost it. In fact, no tenant ever commenced a proceeding to establish a fishery right pursuant to section 95 of the Organic Act.[57] Therefore, since Waller had not established a vested interest, he could not have conveyed one to Yee Hop. If Yee Hop did not have a vested interest, then Tsutsui, as Yee Hop's tenant, could not claim one either.

The court further held that anyone who became a tenant after 1900 could not hold vested rights. Since Yee Hop had not purchased the land from Waller until well after 1900, it was impossible for his interest to have vested. Yee Hop and tenant Tsutsui acquired no interest in the fishery since they had no interest which had ripened at the time of their acquisition of their property rights.[58]

Tsutsui had also claimed that Damon's establishment of its vested interest was sufficient to establish and vest Waller's interest. However, the court rejected this argument, stating:

> Assuming, without deciding, that konohikis were by the statute created trustees for the tenants and that Mr. Damon's decree protected the rights of the tenants of Kaliawa, it could only operate at most so as to protect the *vested rights* of such tenants. Neither Tsutsui nor C.Q. Yee Hop & Company was referred to, by name, in the decree. Neither was even in existence as a tenant when the decree was rendered (in 1905). The Statute of Congress [Organic Act] itself did not protect any rights other than those which were vested and by "vested rights" could only have been intended those which were vested at the date of the Act. The decree could not add to the rights of those who might thereafter become tenants. It could operate at best to preserve the class of rights which the statute excepted from its repealing effect, to-wit, rights then vested. Therefore, even assuming that the konohikis were trustees on behalf of the tenants, that Mr. Damon's suit was filed on behalf of his tenants as well as for himself, and that the decree could be deemed to operate in favor of the tenants, that of itself would still leave unsettled the question of whether the rights of Tsutsui and of C.Q. Yee Hop & Company were vested or were prevented by the repealing law from becoming vested.[59]

The court finally concluded that Tsutsui had encroached on the rights of other tenants who had vested rights, as well as on those of the *konohiki*, Damon.[60]

Thus, contrary to *Laamea* and the U.S. Supreme Court's approach in *Damon v. Hawaii* and *Carter II*, the Hawai'i Supreme Court in *Damon v. Tsutsui* held that tenants whose tenancy began after 1900 did not have "vested rights."[61] Such tenants' rights did not vest even if their landlord's rights had vested.

The vesting issue took another turn in a subsequent federal court decision. In *United States v. Robinson* (1933),[62] the federal government condemned the Hō'ae'ae and Apoka'a fisheries at Pearl Harbor in 1930. The U.S. District Court determined that the value of the two fisheries was approximately $5,833. The Dowsett Company claimed all tenant rights in the Hōʻaeʻae fishery by virtue of its fee simple ownership of a *kuleana* within the *ahupuaʻa* of Hōʻaeʻae.

The government contended that the tenant did not have an exclusive fishing right, and that even if it did, it had no vested right. Further, the government argued, even if the tenant had a vested right, it had lost it by failing to register that right pursuant to the requirements of sections 95 and 96 of the Organic Act.

The federal district court held that the Dowsett Company did have valid fishing rights as a tenant, for it had "exclusive" fishing rights vis-a-vis the public. These rights had vested because Dowsett Company owned the land *prior* to the passage of the Hawaiʻi Organic Act. The court explicitly restricted its holding to the facts of the case, declining to decide whether fishing rights of those who become tenants after the effective date of the Organic Act vested.[63]

Despite this disclaimer, the court implied that vesting could occur subsequent to 1900, citing the Hawaiʻi court's earlier decision in *Smith v. Laamea*.[64] Furthermore, the court found that although the tenant had not complied with the provisions of the Hawaiʻi Organic Act in establishing that right,[65] the filing of the petition by the *konohiki* was sufficient. Under a joint ownership/trusteeship doctrine, the court believed that any action taken by the *konohiki* operated also on behalf of the tenant:

> [I]t is my view that the judgment establishing these fisheries in the name of Mark P. Robinson
> as konohiki of same, would, in legal contemplation, establish the vested right of Dowsett Co.,
> Ltd. as a tenant.[66] (Citation omitted.)

Finally, the court inferred that congress did not intend to require individual tenants to file petitions, given the sheer magnitude of the potential claims that could have been filed and the limited resources typically available to individual tenants.[67] Consequently, the court held that the tenant, Dowsett Company, had a valid vested *hoaʻaina* fishing right to the Hōʻaeʻae fishery and was entitled to compensation.

Thus, at least in federal court, *hoaʻaina* who own a *kuleana* in fee simple also hold a vested fishing right in the adjacent *ahupuaʻa* fishery. Furthermore, because custom and statute indicate that the landlord acts as trustee for the tenants, the establishment of a vested right by the *konohiki* also serves as establishment of the tenants' vested rights. In addition, even if fee simple title to a portion of an *ahupuaʻa* originated after 1900, the owner would be entitled, upon acquisition of title, to an appurtenant fishing right.[68] This holding leaves the federal court diametrically opposed to the Hawaiʻi Supreme Court's holding in *Damon v. Tsutsui*.[69]

(2)   *The Preclusion of Co-owner Rights*   In *State v. Hawaiian Dredging* (1964),[70] the Territory of Hawaiʻi instituted a condemnation action on August 29, 1941 as part of a project to develop a trans-Pacific seaplane harbor in Keʻehi Lagoon. The government sought to condemn the sea fishery of Mokauea, which was located in the lagoon. Defendant Hawaiian Dredging claimed *konohiki* rights in the fishery, which the government did not dispute.

Hawaiian Dredging's predecessor was the Kapiʻolani Estate, which had received its interest from King Kalākaua. The original owner was Moehonua, whose heirs had conveyed their interests to the king. The Kapiʻolani Estate had established its vested rights to the fishery by following the requirements set out in the Hawaiʻi Organic Act.

A number of persons intervened in the condemnation action, claiming an interest in the *konohiki* rights based on descent from Kema, an heir of Moehonua, and through conveyances from Keawe, another Moehonua heir.[71] The government contended that even if the intervenors had legal title at one time, it had been lost as a result of their predecessors' failure to establish their rights pursuant to the Hawai'i Organic Act. In response, the intervenors claimed that establishment by Kapi'olani Estate had preserved their rights.

The Hawai'i Supreme Court held that the prior judgment establishing *konohiki* fishing rights by one co-owner was not sufficient to preserve such rights in other co-owners; third-party establishment would be contrary to the Hawai'i Organic Act's purpose of restricting *konohiki* rights, particularly where the party claimed an adverse interest. Hawaiian Dredging's petition and subsequent judgment to establish its *konohiki* rights clearly indicated only one owner, and the intervenors claimed as co-owners of the *konohiki* rights, not as tenants.[72]

The court based its reasoning on the clearly expressed desire of congress to destroy, as much as it was in its power to do so, "all private rights of fishery and to throw open the fisheries to the people."[73]

(3) *Condemnation and Problems of Valuation*[74] The United States readily exercised the power to condemn fisheries through the authority granted under section 96 of the Hawai'i Organic Act, primarily to fulfill military needs. In contrast, the Territory of Hawai'i only sparingly exercised the same power on behalf of the general public.[75] Despite periodic attempts between 1913 and 1953 to comprehensively open up the fisheries to the public by condemnation, the territory failed for financial or other reasons.[76] The few times the territory or the United States attempted to open the fisheries to the public involved not only condemnation, but a suspension of *konohiki* fishing rights during the depression and World War II in order to expand food supplies.[77] In all, different researchers have reported that the government acquired anywhere from 16 to 60 fisheries by deed or condemnation.[78]

When a fishery was condemned, the lack of precedents and the uniqueness of *konohiki* fishing rights complicated the appraisal process. The federal district court, in attempting to establish the value for the 14 *konohiki* fisheries condemned by the U.S. Navy in the Pearl Harbor area in 1934, noted that the fisheries had no specific market value.[79] The court thus relied on expert testimony and set the condemnation price in terms of the marketable fish found in the fishery.[80]

Little is known of the territory's method of appraising *konohiki* fishing rights.[81] Often, the method of appraisal itself became the major point of litigation.[82] A particular problem related to *konohiki* rights is deciding whether value should be limited to either the value of the taboo fish or one-third of the normal catch, or whether it should include the value of the entire fishery. The federal district court has held that the *konohiki* owners were entitled to the full value of the fishery, subject only to the value of the tenants' interests.[83] In a subsequent case, the Hawai'i Supreme Court agreed.

In *Territory v. Trust Estate of Kanoa* (1956),[84] the Territory of Hawai'i condemned the Kanoa Estate's fishing rights in the fisheries of Niumalu and Nāwiliwili on the island of Kaua'i. The government did not dispute that the estate had *konohiki* rights to these fisheries since they had been vested and established by the estate's predecessor-in-interest pursuant to section 96 of the Organic Act.

Instead, the government argued that the estate did not possess fee ownership but merely had user rights. The territory contended that the Hawaiian words used in the 1846 fisheries statute had been mistranslated to mean private ownership and that the concept of fee ownership did not exist at that time. The government further argued that even if the owner possessed fee ownership, such ownership rights were limited to the power to taboo one species of fish, or to declare open and closed seasons and to take one-third of the catch made during the open season.

The court held that the owner's *konohiki* right was a private property right in fee simple, tracing its source back to the 1839 Law of Kamehameha III.[85] It cited the 1842 codification, which provided:

> fishing grounds from the coral reefs to the sea beach are for the *landlords*, and for the *tenants* of their several lands, but not for others.[86]

The court found that a long line of cases had consistently treated the fishery as the private property of the *konohiki*, subject only to the rights of the tenants.

In addition, the court found that those particular sections of the statute dealing with *konohiki* rights were repeatedly re-enacted by the kingdom and the territorial legislature up and until 1945.[87] It inferred that legislative re-enactment of a law after judicial construction of that law constituted legislative approval of that construction.[88] Moreover, an 1874 opinion of the attorney general had stated that the *konohiki* held the fishery as his private property. Finally, the court noted with regard to claims of mistranslation, section 1493 of the Civil Code of 1859 stated that in any conflict between English and Hawaiian, the English would control.[89]

The court also held that the successor of the *konohiki* was entitled to compensation for private ownership of all fish in the fishery, even if the *konohiki* had previously established a right to take only one specie of fish in registering the fishery pursuant to section 96 of the Hawai'i Organic Act.[90] The court held that the registration procedure did not limit the right of the *konohiki* to the ownership of the fishery, which was exclusive except for the right of a *hoa'aina* who resided in the *ahupua'a*. Thus the *konohiki* had the right to the *whole* fishery.[91]

This holding created an obvious advantage for the successors of the *konohiki*. As a holder of a fee title to the fishery, a *konohiki* can convey the rights of title to the fishery subject only to the rights of the *hoa'aina* to take fish. The tenant may not independently convey any right. Furthermore, under *Damon v. Tsutsui*, only those tenants alive in 1900 can claim an exclusive right to a fishery. They could have only vested their right by registering it in accordance with section 95 of the Organic Act. The *konohiki* could not register this right on the tenant's behalf. No tenant registered any rights to fish. Thus, the scope of registered title of the *konohiki* to the fishery grows as tenants die off, until the *konohiki* or his successor holds an *exclusive* interest in *all* the fishery, after the death of the last tenant of the *ahupua'a* who was alive in 1900. The ironic result of these decisions was to concentrate ever-increasing rights over the registered fisheries in the *konohiki* -- precisely what congress sought to avoid by passing section 95 of the Organic Act.[92]

Even more difficult than the problem of valuation of the interest of the *konohiki* is the question of how to value the tenants' rights in the fishery. In *United States v. Robinson* (1933), the federal district court held that the tenant was entitled to share in the award and should receive a portion which represented the value of the "Hoaaina right of piscary."[93]

However, the court was not able to compute an actual figure and left it up to the parties to resolve. In other cases, courts have generally refused to award more than nominal damages on the grounds that the tenant failed to submit sufficient evidence.[94]

(4) *Constitutionality of Section 96 of the Organic Act* In *Bishop v. Mahiko* (1940),[95] a condemnation action by the government, Bishop Estate, the *konohiki*, and Mahiko, the tenant, claimed rights to the fishery adjacent to the *ahupua'a* of Makalawena. Both *konohiki* and tenant had held their interests prior to the Hawai'i Organic Act of 1900.

The government claimed that the owners had failed to establish their rights pursuant to section 96 of the Hawai'i Organic Act because they had not filed a petition in circuit court. The owners contended that section 96 violated due process and constituted a taking without just compensation in violation of the Fifth Amendment to the U.S. Constitution.

The Hawai'i Supreme Court held that the Organic Act, while putting the burden on the owners to establish their rights, did not violate due process. The court felt that the procedure in the act would have been unconstitutional only if it was arbitrary, oppressive, and unjust. To the contrary, the court believed that the act was reasonable because the required filing in circuit court was (1) simple and not overly burdensome on the owners; (2) necessary to fix the exact boundaries of the fisheries, since there were no prior written descriptions; and (3) a necessary part of the government's effort to condemn the fisheries, since the owners were in the best position to provide the court with relevant information.

In addition, the court held that the act's provision as applied was not a taking without just compensation. The owners' failure to establish fishing rights was a waiver of their right to compensation.[96] The court mentioned, but did not resolve, whether establishment of a right of a *konohiki* was sufficient to establish rights on behalf of his tenants.[97]

Thus, at least the territorial supreme court deemed section 96 of the Organic Act of 1900 constitutional. Furthermore, no compensation was due fishery owners who failed to establish rights according to the act. However, those holdings may not be the last word on the issue. The U.S. Supreme Court had already declared in *Damon v. Hawaii* and *Carter II* that the rights to the fisheries vested as a result of the 1839 law.[98] Given that premise, the court might well have decided there was a taking without just compensation. However, that issue was never presented to the U.S. Supreme Court since Mahiko did not seek an appeal. Moreover, given the subsequent depletion in the economic value of fisheries, and apparent abandonment of most of the remaining private fisheries, the issue will probably remain open.[99] One commentator has suggested a renewed interest in the state to recognize the perpetuation of "traditionally" vested fishing rights "inherently held by Hawaiians and [which] do not run with the land" so long as they were not condemned.[100] Under this theory, the residency of a *hoa'aina* predating the Organic Act would be immaterial.[101]

3.   CURRENT STATE LAW

At statehood, Hawai'i reaffirmed the federal policy of opening the fisheries to all. On the other hand, the state continued to recognize "vested rights."[102] Thus, under Hawai'i's statutes, the state has preserved the essence of the 1839 Law of Kamehameha III by recognizing vested *konohiki* and tenant fishing rights.[103] The statute sets aside the same area, from the reefs or for a distance of one geographic mile seaward of the beach at low watermark adjacent to a respective *ahupua'a*, for "the equal use by the konohiki and tenants on their respective lands."[104] The law declares this area to be the private fishery of the konohiki, whose lands by ancient regulations, belong to the same."[105] The law recognizes these rights as "vested," if registered pursuant to section 96 of the Organic Act. Tenants may take any aquatic life "for home consumption or commercial purposes" subject only to restriction by the *konohiki* or other law or rule.[106]

As with the ancient law, a *konohiki* may either set apart for exclusive use or *kapu* a species of fish each year or exact up to one-third of the aquatic life taken by a tenant upon proper posting of notice.[107] The statute also provides for criminal penalties in cases of noncompliance.[108] Furthermore, it allows the state to condemn any private fishery.[109]

With regard to fisheries adjacent to government lands, the statute grants the free and equal use of these fisheries to all persons, subject to regulation by the state, regardless of any future disposition of the government's fee in the associated *ahupua'a*.[110] On the other hand, the federal government has reserved an exclusive right to fish or gather seafood above the highwater mark along the coastline of the Kalapana extension area of the Hawai'i Volcanoes National Park for Native Hawaiian residents of adjacent villages and their guests.[111]

In addition, under Article XII, section 7 of the Hawai'i State Constitution, "[t]he State reaffirms and shall protect all rights, customarily and traditionally exercised for subsistence, cultural, and religious purposes and possessed by ahupua'a tenants who are descendants of native Hawaiians." This provision forms a partial basis for establishing continuing rights of *hoa'aina* to exclusively fish and gather in the nearshore fisheries of Hawai'i,[112] despite the Hawai'i Supreme Court's prior contrary rulings limiting or extinguishing those rights under sections 95 and 96 of the Organic Act.

In contrast, the state has anticipated the establishment of state-licensed "mariculture operations" which will "protect the *public's* use and enjoyment of the reefs."[113] (Emphasis added.) The operation of sea farms and potential ocean leasing may pose conflicts with the exercise of traditional fishing rights.

Finally, the attitude of the federal courts toward the recognition of a continuing right to fish suggests that re-examination of *Damon v. Tsutsui* and *Bishop v. Mahiko* may be appropriate. However, in their current depleted state, the *konohiki* fisheries offer potential litigants few, if any, practical opportunities to test these propositions.[114]

4.   FEDERAL ACTIONS AND THE EXCLUSIVE ECONOMIC ZONE

Konohiki fishing rights have not been intensely contested in recent years.[115] In fact, most conflicts have not involved the *konohiki* fisheries. With recent technological developments, most fish can be detected and caught well outside the reef, thereby reducing the value of the traditional *konohiki* fishing areas. As noted earlier, Kamehameha III granted the right to fish seaward of the reefs to all the people. These traditional open sea fishing rights could become more important with the development of ocean resources, including fish, marine resources, and seabed minerals in the area beyond the *konohiki* fisheries.

In 1953, congress passed the Submerged Lands Act (SLA),[116] in which the U.S. relinquished all right, title, and interest to the states to develop the resources contained within the territorial sea, which lies within the three-mile limit. The U.S. retained control of commerce, navigation, national defense, and international affairs.[117] Simultaneously, congress passed the Outer Continental Shelf Lands Act (OCSLA),[118] establishing a regulatory system for the leasing, exploration, and exploitation of the non-living resources of the continental shelf beyond the three-mile limit. Congress made the OCSLA and SLA applicable to Hawai'i upon statehood in 1959.[119]

The state and federal governments, however, disagree over the exact boundaries of federal-state jurisdiction.[120] In 1978, the Hawai'i State Constitution was amended to include archipelagic waters, including waters between the islands, within the boundaries of the state.[121] Nevertheless, the federal courts have concluded that congress did not intend to include the channels between the islands within state boundaries.[122] As recently as 1990, the Hawai'i State Legislature considered legislation purporting to extend Hawai'i's territorial sea boundaries from three to 12 miles from the shoreline.[123] The legislature later deleted the specific number of miles and passed the bill in an amended form, providing for an extension of its dominion to the limit of the territorial sea.[124] It also requested that congress extend the territorial sea from three to 12 miles.[125]

In 1976, congress also passed the Magnuson Fishery Conservation and Management Act (MFCMA) to exclusively manage the fisheries, not including the "highly migratory fish," in "a zone contiguous to the territorial sea extending out to a line 200 nautical miles from shore."[126] In passing the MFCMA, congress intended to place the U.S. fishing industry under a management system that treated the fisheries as a "common property resource in which there is no ownership of the resource."[127] Accordingly, the United States exercises its management role over this resource as a public trustee.[128]

On March 10, 1983, President Ronald Reagan issued Proclamation 5030, claiming the United States' sole jurisdiction of the Exclusive Economic Zone (EEZ), an area extending 200 nautical miles from U.S. coastal boundaries.[129] In the proclamation, the United States asserted "sovereign rights for the purpose of exploring, exploiting, conserving and managing natural resources, both living and nonliving, of the seabed and subsoil and the superadjacent waters."[130]

The effect that these actions will have on Hawaiian fishing rights within Hawai'i's EEZ is unknown. The Hawai'i EEZ covers an immense area of 695,000 square nautical miles.[131] The Western Pacific Regional Fishery Management Council,[132] in developing its limited entry proposal for the Northwestern Hawaiian Islands bottomfish fishery, must consider whether there is a legal basis for granting preferential consideration to Native Hawaiians.[133] Under the MFCMA, the council is responsible for considering "historical fishing practices in, and dependence on the fishery" in developing any system for limited entry into that fishery.[134] Accordingly, the council is examining traditional fishing practices of Hawaiians to determine whether Hawaiians have preferential status to take from the Nothwestern Hawaiian Islands fisheries.[135]

The establishment of historic offshore fishing grounds still being used by Hawaiians opens the door to claiming preferential native fishing rights in the EEZ.[136] While those rights may or may not constitute vested rights, preferential fishing rights for Native Hawaiians can be justified under: (1) the MFMCA, (2) international law recognizing such rights based on peaceful and continuous usage, (3) the failure of either the provisional government of Hawai'i or the Republic of Hawai'i to repudiate the traditional usage and practice of the *maka'ainana* to fish beyond the three-mile limit, and (4) state law recognizing "Hawaiian usage" that does not otherwise conflict with state common law or statutes.[137]

Early Hawaiians not only fished within the *konohiki* fisheries, they also made extensive use of the deep sea fishing grounds in the open ocean beyond the nearshore reefs. These deep sea fishing grounds were called *ko'a* and were found in waters up to 300 fathoms deep.[138] Kamehameha III recognized these traditional rights in his 1839 proclamation.[139] The kingdom reaffirmed these rights in later statutes, declaring that "no restrictions whatever shall by any means be laid on the sea *without the reef even to the deepest ocean.*"[140] (Emphasis added.) In the Constitution of 1840, the kingdom further declared that "nothing whatever shall be taken from any individual except by express provision of the laws."[141] In fact, the kingdom, the Republic of Hawai'i, the United States, and the State of Hawai'i expressly protected the continuation of Hawaiian usage and custom, so long as it did not conflict with other laws.[142] Finally the language of *Carter II* and *Damon v. Hawaii* suggests that the grants under the 1839 law created vested rights which survived any later statutory repeal.[143]

The extent of Native Hawaiian fishing rights will remain unclear until congress formally resolves the claims for restitution and self-governance resulting from U.S. involvement in the illegal 1893 overthrow of the Hawaiian Kingdom. In *United States v. Washington* (1975),[144] the Ninth Circuit Court of Appeals held that treaties are "not a grant of rights to Indians, but a grant of rights from them -- a reservation of those not granted."[145] In that case, the Ninth Circuit recognized a preferential communal property right in an Indian tribe to take salmon from fisheries from which the tribe fished at the time the case was filed, as opposed to the time a treaty guaranteeing the right to fish their usual and traditional places was signed.[146] The court upheld this right as a matter of tribal sovereignty, in recognition of the status of these tribes as independent nations.[147] If the Kingdom of Hawai'i never took away the rights of the *maka'ainana* to fish beyond the reefs, and the United States never obtained a grant of those rights from the Republic of Hawai'i, then those rights still survive today. Of course, no treaty with the United States ever specifically reserved fishing rights following the 1893 overthrow. However, given the Hawaiian Kingdom's prior sovereign status and current attempts to resolve the myriad of political issues related to the 1893 overthrow, the potential rights of the *maka'ainana* to the fisheries in the EEZ cast a cloud on the scope of U.S. jurisdiction over this area.

Similarly, congress may have to determine whether Native Hawaiians are entitled to a portion of the sizeable revenues that could be derived from the harvesting of precious corals, crustaceans, fish, and other minerals in the EEZ.[148] This entitlement could be based on existing statutory law granting Native Hawaiians a portion of ceded land trust revenues.[149] It could also be based on the illegal overthrow of the Hawaiian monarchy in 1893 and the uncompensated cession in 1898 of Hawaiian Government and Crown Lands by the Republic of Hawai'i to the United States. The illegality of the overthrow and subsequent cession are at the crux of Native Hawaiian claims for restitution and self-governance.[150]

At annexation, the United States did not expressly take possession of, nor extinguish, Kamehameha III's grant of the fisheries beyond the reef to all the Hawaiian people.[151] While history appears to strongly support the theory that traditional fishing continued in the EEZ during the period of the kingdom, there is no remaining documented evidence of such usage prior to the 1920s.[152] Nevertheless, the absence of resolution of these complex legal issues clouds any definition of rights to the resources of the EEZ and the political jurisdiction over them. Hence, Native Hawaiians may still have a basis to assert rights to the revenues from, and management over, the fisheries and resources of the EEZ around the Hawaiian Islands.[153]   These issues must be resolved before the United States can clearly articulate the nature and extent of its dominion over the EEZ.

5.   CONCLUSION

Although *konohiki* and *hoaʻaina* fishing rights have been severely restricted by the Organic Act and interpretations of the Hawaiʻi Supreme Court, federal courts have continued to recognize them as a legal form of property ownership.   The federal courts have taken a much broader view in protecting fishing rights.   This disparate treatment of the vesting issue for both *konohiki* and tenant has lent ambiguity to the respective rights involved.   What rights have vested remains a particularly problematical question.   Despite the lack of practical significance of such ownership, the legacy of fishing rights, particularly in judicial decision-making, provides a legal framework to apply to other Native Hawaiian rights based on ancient customs and practices.

Finally, as the United States continues to assert progressively greater power over marine resources, particularly in the EEZ, it will have to confront the claims of Native Hawaiians to fishing rights and other marine resources based on their historic usage of this area and the application of various legal authorities governing its use.

NOTES

1.   Although in ancient times a *konohiki* was merely a manager of the *ahupuaʻa*, the term eventually came to mean landlord/chief of the *ahupuaʻa*.   Fishing rights are called "*konohiki* fishing rights," but in law, the term encompasses the fishing rights of the owner of the *ahupuaʻa* and the joint rights of the tenants to take from the same fisheries.

2.   D. Malo, *Hawaiian Antiquities* 195 (1951 ed.).

3.   N. Meller, *Indigenous Ocean Rights in Hawaii* 2 (paper presented December 1985).

4.   In later statute and common use, the word *konohiki* came to be translated as the English *landlord*, and came to apply to the chief himself, the "owner" of the *ahupuaʻa*. J. Chinen, *The Great Mahele* 24 n.19 (1958).

5.   One difference between the Hawaiian land tenure system and the European feudal system lay in the tenancy of those who dwelled upon and worked the land.   They were bound to neither chief nor land.   They could move at will.   On the other hand, they could be dispossessed, being themselves vulnerable to the will of the chief, and at greater distance, to the will of the king who favored that chief.   But since it was the responsibility of the chief to make the land productive, instances of abuse were rare.   Nevertheless, this relative "insecurity" -- in the eyes of the influential missionary, merchants, and advisers to the Hawaiian kings -- in great part inspired the land reforms and the fishing rights redistributions which marked the revolutionary changes to the system in the mid-eighteenth century.

6.   The term *makaʻainana* referred to the people in general while *hoaʻaina*, meaning friend of the land, was a more specific term meaning tenant of the *ahupuaʻa*.

7.   Meller, *supra* note 3, at 2-3 n.9.

8.   S. Kamakau, *Ruling Chiefs of Hawaii* 177 (1961).

9.   Malo, *supra* note 2, at 25-26.   There is some debate as to whether the law merely memorialized these traditional practices and uses of the fisheries, or legally acted to terminate custom as the basis for those practices.   Meller, *supra* note 3, at 3-4.

10.   Meller, *supra* note 3, at 2 n.13, citing T. Morgan, *Hawaii: A Century of Economic Change* 130 (1948).

11.   L. Thurston, *The Fundamental Law of Hawaii* 21 (1904).

12.   *Id.*

13.   *Id.*

14.   The 1839 proclamation of King Kamehameha III was subsequently enacted under the Laws of 1842, § 8, ch. III.

15.   Laws of 1845-46, ch. VI, art. V, § 8 (Kingdom of Hawaiʻi), Thurston, *supra* note 11.

16. For details as to these early amendments, *see* D.S. Jordan and B.W. Evermann, *Preliminary Report on the Investigations of the Fishes and Fisheries of the Hawaiian Islands*, H.R. Doc. No. 249, 57th Cong., 1st Sess. 11-15 (1902). This report was made pursuant to An Act to Provide for a Government for the Territory of Hawaii, ch. 339, § 94, 31 Stat. 141 (1900) [hereinafter, "Hawai'i Organic Act"].

17. Meller, *supra* note 3, at 8 n.38, citing section 2, Act of July 11, 1851.

18. One change made in 1892 expanded the right of the tenant to take fish only to the right to take "all fish, seaweed, shellfish, and other edible products . . . ." This change merely formalized the practice of gathering these resources which probably had continued since ancient times in spite of the narrower language in earlier statutes. Meller, *supra* note 3, at 6 n.28.

19. Meller notes several major discrepancies between the Hawaiian version and English translation of this law. *Id.* at 7.

20. 2 Haw. 62 (1858).

21. *Id.* at 65-66.

22. *Id.* at 70-71.

23. *Act of 1845*, ch. VI, art. V, § 3 (superseded by the Hawai'i Organic Act). *See* Jordan and Evermann, *supra* note 16, at 15-16.

24. Piscary is a legal term, often used in early cases, meaning the right to fish in certain areas.

25. *Haalelea v. Montgomery*, 2 Haw. 62, 71 (1858).

26. 6 Haw. 334 (1882).

27. *Id.* at 336. The court stated:

   > Every resident on the land, whether he be an old hoaaina, a holder of a Kuleana title, or a resident by leasehold or any other lawful tenure, has a right to fish in the sea appurtenant to the land as an incident of his tenancy.

28. *Id.* at 336-337.

29. *Id.* at 337.

30. 5 Haw. 571 (1886).

31. *Id.* at 572.

32. § 95 of the Hawai'i Organic Act of 1900 reads:

   > [A]ll laws of the Republic of Hawaii which confer exclusive fishing rights upon any person or persons are hereby repealed, and all fisheries in the sea waters of the Territory of Hawaii not included in any fish pond or artificial inclosure shall be free to all citizens of the United States, subject, however, to vested rights; but no such vested rights shall be valid after three years from the taking effect of this Act unless established as hereinafter provided.

33. § 96 of the Hawai'i Organic Act of 1900 reads:

   > [A]ny person who claims a private right to any such fishery shall, within two years after the taking effect of this Act, file his petition in a circuit court of the Territory of Hawaii, setting forth his claim to such fishing right, service of which petition shall be made upon the attorney-general, who shall conduct the case for the Territory, and such case shall be conducted as an ordinary action at law.
   >
   > . . . if such fishing right be established the attorney-general of the Territory of Hawaii may proceed, in such manner as may be provided by law for the condemnation of property for public use, to condemn such private right of fishing to the use of the citizens of the United States upon making just compensation, which compensation, when lawfully ascertained, shall be paid out of any money in the treasury of the Territory of Hawaii not otherwise appropriated. *Id.*

34. *In re Fukunaga*, 16 Haw. 306, 308 (1904).

35. Traditionally, fisheries were committed to memory. Over time, memories faded. In addition, Hawaiians may have referred to several under a single name, while at other times referred to them singly. No records existed either in ancient times or at annexation. Meller, *supra* note 3, at 9.

36. *Id.* at 10.

37. PRIVATE FISHERIES IN THE TERRITORY OF HAWAII (1939)

   I.   Registered under authority of sec. 96 of Organic Act.

Island	Number	Acquired by U.S.	Acquired by T.H.	Number of owners	Approximate value $
Hawaii	8			3	$ 800.00
Maui	27			3	2,000.00
Molokai	3			2	600.00
Lanai	2			1	200.00
Oahu	53	13 plus part of 1	3	20	19,650.00
Kauai	8	—	—	6	8,300.00
Total	101	13 plus	3	35	$ 31,550.00

II.   Unregistered fisheries.

Island	Number	Number of owners	Approximate value
Hawaii	140	62	$14,000.00
Maui	54	21	5,350.00
Molokai	25	15	2,500.00
Lanai	2	1	200.00
Oahu	11	9	1,100.00
Kauai	16	11	1,600.00
Total	248	119	$24,750.00

Table taken directly from R.H. Kosaki, *Konohiki Fishing Rights* 10 (Legislative Report No. 1, 1954).

38.   *KONOHIKI* FISHERIES ACQUIRED, 1900-1953

Fishery	Acquired by	Title	Date	Acquired from
Honouliuli, Oahu (one-half portion)	U.S.	Deeds	04/04/45	(Campbell Estate (Oahu Railway & (Land Co., Dowsett (Co., Ltd.
Waiawa, Oahu Kaluaoopu, Oahu Waiau, Oahu Kaonohi, Oahu Kalauao, Oahu Halawa, Oahu Kunana, Oahu Pipiloa, Oahu	U.S.	Deeds	04/28/45 04/19/45	(McCandless (Bishop Estate
Hanapouli, Oahu Waipio, Oahu Homaikaia, Oahu Miki, Oahu	U.S.	Civil 291 (Fed. Dist. Court, Honolulu)	1934	Ii Estate
Apokaa, Oahu Hoaeae, Oahu	U.S.	Civil 292 (Fed. Dist. Court, Honolulu)	1934	Robinson, et al.
Moanalua, Oahu Kaliawa, Oahu	T.H.	Law 16653		Damon Estate
Kaehu a ka moi, Maui Paukukalo, Maui Malehaakoa, Maui Kaihuwaa, Maui Makawela, Maui Kahului, Maui Puuiki, Maui Kaipuula, Maui Kanaha, Maui Palaeke, Maui Kalua, Maui Kaa, Maui Hopukoa nui, Maui Hopukoa iki, Maui Papaula, Maui Kapahu, Maui Palaha, Maui Kawaau, Maui Kanepaina, Maui Kahue, Maui	T.H.	Law 1538 (These collectively known as the Wailuku Fishery)	1949	(Haw'n Com'l & (Sugar Co. (Wailuku Sugar Co.

In counting *konohiki* fisheries, it is important to note that they greatly vary in size and in value, that a contiguous series is often referred to under one name, and that some are known by more than one name. *Id.* at 13.

39.   Meller, *supra* note 3, at 10, n.61, n.62.

40.   14 Haw. 465 (1902).

41.   *Id.* at 473.

42.   *Id.* at 479-480.

43.   *Id.* at 473-474.

44.   Appurtenance is a legal term meaning a right attached or belonging to a principal property.

45.   *Carter v. Territory*, 14 Haw. 474-479 (1902).

46.   *Id.* at 479.
47.   194 U.S. 154 (1904).
48.   The court stated:

> [I]t does not follow that any particular words are necessary to convey [a fishing right] when the intent is clear. When the description of the land granted says that there is incident to it a definite right of fishery, it does not matter whether the statement is technically accurate or not; it is enough that the grant is its own dictionary and explains that it means by 'land' in the habendum land and fishery as well. *Id.* at 161.

49.   *Id.* at 160.
50.   200 U.S. 255 (1906).
51.   *Id.* at 256.
52.   *Id.* at 256-257. On the other hand, the Court of Claims has expressly ruled that traditional use alone cannot be the basis of a presumed grant of an exclusive fishery. *The Tee-Hit-Ton Indians v. U.S.*, 132 F.Supp. 695, 697, 132 Ct.Cls. 624, 627 (1955).
53.   29 Haw. 750 (1927).
54.   *Id.* at 756.
55.   31 Haw. 678 (1930).
56.   *Id.* at 688-690. The court's view contrasts with *Haalelea's* finding that fishing rights are appurtenant to the land and transmitted as incident to the land.
57.   The court noted:

> In the cases of those who were konohikis at the date of the Organic Act it has been held that their rights were "vested" within the meaning of that Act and suitable to be perpetuated by judicial decree. *Damon v. Territory* and *Carter v. Territory, supra.* Many such decrees were obtained by konohikis throughout the Territory within the time prescribed. It may be assumed that those persons who were "tenants" at the date of the Organic Act also had "vested" rights, within the meaning of section 95, which would remain unaffected by the repeal contained in that section, provided only that they were judicially established as there required. *No proceedings whatever were instituted directly by any tenant subsequent to the passage of the Organic Act.* (Emphasis added.) *Id.* at 692-693.

58.   *Id.* at 693. This holding appears to directly conflict with the rationale in *Damon v. Hawaii*, 194 U.S. 154, 159-160 (1904), and holding in *Carter II*, 200 U.S. 255, 256 (1906), that fishing rights became vested by the statutes creating them.
59.   *Damon v. Tsutsui*, 31 Haw. 678, 695 (1930).
60.   *Id.* at 698.
61.   This Hawai'i Supreme Court holding might be questioned in light of Justice Holmes' decisions in *Damon* and *Carter II*. In those opinions his premise was that a repeal of the statute would not affect vested fishing rights.
62.   Civil No. 292 (D. Haw. 1933).
63.   The court stated:

> [T]his court need not now (and does not) decide whether or not tenants other than a *kuleana owner with title antedating June 14, 1900,* (when the Organic Act took effect) owned "vested" rights of piscary in the sea fishery adjacent to the ahupuaa of which they were (prior to June 14, 1900) tenants (residents). Nor have we anything to do, in the case at bar, with claims of those becoming tenants of the ahupuaa after the passage of the Organic Act, whether kuleana owners or tenants under leases or merely by sufferance. It is the claim of Dowsett Co., Ltd., which has owned, in fee simple, this kuleana of "Kaulu" since January, 1900, with which we are now concerned. *Id.* at 6-7. (Emphasis added.)

64.   *Id.* at 11-12.
65.   As reported in *Damon v. Tsutsui*, 31 Haw. 678, 693 (1930), no tenant had attempted to establish the right pursuant to the Hawai'i Organic Act.
66.   *United States v. Robinson*, Civil No. 292, at 15 (D.Haw. 1933).
67.   The court stated:

> A practical consideration bearing on this matter is the question whether Congress *intended* the many hundreds (or thousands) of tenants to validate each of their rights by proceedings in the courts. While the konohikis, with fisheries worth $5,000 to $50,000 might justly and reasonably be expected to validate their titles, it seems almost unbelievable that the humble tenant with in many cases his quarter-acre holding was intended to be compelled to sue in the courts to quiet his title to his incidental fishing right under the new law. I am loath to believe that Congress had any such drastic requirement in mind. *Id.* at 17-18.

68. The court relied on the *dicta* in *Smith v. Laamea* to reach this conclusion:

> The case of *Smith v. Laamea*, 29 Haw. 750 (1927), unequivocally states that one who acquires title "to a portion of an ahupuaa, by adverse possession for . . . ten years next preceding the commencement of the action" (begun Oct. 13, 1924 -- as the Hawaiian Circuit Court files show) becomes entitled to a right of piscary in the adjacent fishery -- the court quoting at length, and with approval, the language in the Montgomery case (2 Haw. 62, 71) declaring that, upon a conveyance of a *kuleana*, the common right of piscary would pass as an appurtenance thereto. The significant feature of the Laamea case is that it was decided by the present Hawaiian Supreme Court *as now constituted*; and it states that if a fee-simple title to a portion of the ahupuaa originated even as late as approximately 1924 (certainly long after the repeal of the fishing laws in 1900) the owner of such parcel of land would become entitled, upon acquiring title, to an appurtenant right of fishery. *Id.* at 11-12.

69. The federal court took pains to explain that the Hawai'i Supreme Court had not decided the issues presented to the federal court:

> The case of *Damon v. Tsutsui*, 31 Hawaii 678 (1930), decided by the Supreme Court of Hawaii, is the most recent decision on Hawaiian fishery rights. The subject of fishing rights under the laws of the Hawaiian Kingdom and the succeeding forms of government including the existing Territorial government is covered with careful thoroughness in so far as the facts of that case presented questions for decision. The three points now under consideration were all adverted to in that decision although only one of them was definitely decided. Whether or not this Federal Court is bound by the decision of the Hawaiian Supreme Court on these matters is a question that need not be determined in this case as all that the court herein is called upon to decide, and hereafter decides, are matters not definitely decided in the *Tsutsui* case. The decision in that case must, at all events, be accorded deference and respect, and *if this present decision is not in harmony with certain intimations of the Court in the Tsutsui case or with comment therein not necessary to that decision, it will be seen that the matters here decided are matters which the Hawaiian Supreme Court definitely refrained from formally determining. Id.* at 5-6. (Emphasis added.)

70. 48 Haw. 152, 397 P.2d 593 (1964).

71. Intervenors' claim was based on the fact that the deed from the heirs of Moehonua to Kalākaua granted 266 acres. However, in a subsequent judgment, Kalākaua's interest was held to consist of 480 acres. Intervenors claimed that the difference remained in the heirs and so subsequently passed or was conveyed to them. *Id.* at 184, 397 P.2d at 611.

72. *Id.* at 190, 397 P.2d at 614.

73. *Id.* at 187, 397 P.2d at 612, citing *In re Fukunaga*, 16 Haw. 306, 308 (1904); *Territory v. Matsubara*, 19 Haw. 641, 643-644 (1909).

74. Much of this section is based on information taken directly from R.H. Kosaki, *supra* note 37, at 21 *et seq.*

75. The territory condemned only three fisheries. *See* Kosaki, *supra* notes 37, 38.

76. Kosaki, *supra* note 37, at 19.

77. *Id.* at 19-20.

78. Meller, *supra* note 3, at 11, n.65.

79. Kosaki, *supra* note 37, at 22.

80. In the Pearl Harbor fisheries, just compensation was awarded in terms of the market value of mullet, *pua*, and *nehu*. In one judgment the court said that the fair market value of the sea fisheries owned by the John Ii Estate was $90,000 -- this being an aggregate of $10,000 as *nehu* value, $20,000 as *pua* value, and $60,000 as commercial mullet value. *United States v. John Ii Estate, Ltd.*, Civil No. 291.

    In another judgment, the court awarded to the Bishop Estate $30,800, calculated in terms of $10,400 for *nehu* and *iao*, $10,000 for *pua*, and $10,400 for commercial mullet. *U.S. v. E. Faxon Bishop*, Civil No. 296.

81. Supposedly, appraisers apply the "income capitalization" approach in determining *konohiki* appraisal values. However, appraisal figures are largely dependent upon the "income" that serves as the base. Some feel that the "income" to be capitalized is the annual rental fee; others hold that the gross income to be derived from fishing operations within the *konohiki* fishery is properly the income to be capitalized.

    Thus, in *Territory v. Bishop Trust Co.*, the territorial appraisers valued the Nawiliwili fishery at $13,500 and $17,696. The defendant's appraisers presented valuations of $50,000, $60,000, and $64,000. The jury awarded the sum of $30,000.

82. The difficulties of appraisal were highlighted in a *Honolulu Star-Bulletin* article of July 14, 1947. In a 1931 attempt by Territorial Attorney General Hewitt to condemn the most popular fisheries of O'ahu between Kahalu'u, around Makapu'u to Pearl Harbor, the government assembled an appraisal team of Samuel Wilder King, Oscar P. Cox, and Paul Beyer. The team ultimately recommended an appraised value for these 21 fisheries of $56,170. Kosaki, *supra* note 37, at 17. However, the newspaper reported

the practical difficulties encountered at the time the territorial appraisal team of Crozier, King, and Child was in action:

> A few facts and a lot of educated guesses go into the work of appraising the value of a private fishing right. First, there is nothing comparable to them in the U.S. According to one of the appraisers, Campbell Crozier, there never has been. In short, there are no precedents or comparative values as there are in other type of property construction.
>
> Next, there are no well defined boundaries in the ocean areas. Policing them is difficult. If a fisherman is thrown out of a private area, he often can move next door to a public one that reduces the value of a private area.
>
> In addition, few people have kept records of the annual catches in their fisheries. Even fewer have recorded the market value of them. *Id.*

83. Kosaki, *supra* note 37, citing *U.S. v. Shingle*, Civil No. 290 (D. Haw. 1933).

84. 41 Haw. 358 (1956).

85. *Id.* at 370.

86. Laws of 1842, ch. III, § 8.

87. *Territory v. Trust Estate of Kanoa*, 41 Haw. 358, 366, 370 (1956).

88. *Id.* at 367.

89. *Id.* at 366-367. *Compare* with *Haalelea v. Montgomery*, 2 Haw. 66 (1858) (earlier supreme court case requiring the Hawaiian version to control).

90. The former *konohiki* had technically registered only the taboo rights, but the court held that such registration had no effect on the present owner's rights, stating:

> The circuit court found that the petitioner was entitled to the fisheries but it did state, as had been pleaded, a paragraph regarding the right of the owner to taboo one species of fish to his exclusive use. This surplusage related merely to the rights as between *konohiki* and *hoaaina* and, further, did not restrict the *konohiki* from selecting another species the next year or electing to take one third of the catch as he might choose to do from year to year. There was no authority in the circuit court to modify the rights of the owner of the *ahupuaa* as defined by the statutes. All the court could do legally was to recognize and confirm the title to the fisheries; the statutes set forth the rights of the *konohiki* and *hoaaina* in great detail.

Territory v. Trust Estate of Kanoa, 41 Haw. 597, 598 (1957). (Petition for rehearing denied.)

91. *Id.* at 599.

92. Meller, *supra* note 3, at 12.

93. Civil No. 292, at 19 (D. Haw. 1933).

94. Kosaki, *supra* note 37, citing *United States v. John Ii Estate*, Civil No. 291 (D. Haw. 1934), and *United States v. Bishop*, Civil No. 296 (D. Haw. 1934).

95. 35 Haw. 608 (1940).

96. *Id.* at 681.

97. *See United States v. Robinson*, Civil No. 292 (D. Haw. 1933) and *Damon v. Tsutsui*, 31 Haw. 678 (1930). As noted earlier, the federal court in *Robinson* stated that establishment by the *konohiki* was sufficient to establish on behalf of his *kuleana*-owning tenants. *Id.* at 17-18. This view has been neither adopted nor rejected by the Hawai'i Supreme Court. However, the court held in *State v. Hawaiian Dredging*, 48 Haw. 152, 190, 397 P.2d 593, 614 (1964), that establishment of *konohiki* rights by one co-owner was not sufficient to establish those rights on behalf of an adverse co-owner.

98. *See* discussion of *Damon v. Hawaii* and *Carter II, supra* text accompanying notes 47-52.

99. Meller, *supra* note 3, at 12-13.

100. *Id.* at 15, citing the Hawai'i Constitutional Convention Committee on Hawaiian Affairs, Standing Committee Report No. 57, at 6 (August 25, 1978).

101. *Id.* Meller cites art. XII, § 7 of the Hawai'i State Constitution to suggest that traditional rights to the fisheries may still be valid. That 1978 amendment to the constitution provides:

> The State reaffirms and shall protect all rights, customarily and traditionally exercised for subsistence, cultural and religious purposes and possessed by ahupua'a tenants who are descendants of native Hawaiians who inhabited the Hawaiian Islands prior to 1778, subject to the right of the State to regulate such rights.

102. Haw. Const. art. XI, § 6 declares in part:

> All fisheries in the sea waters of the State not included in any fish pond, artificial enclosure or state-licensed mariculture operation shall be free to the public, *subject to vested rights* and the right of the State to regulate the same; provided that the mariculture operations *shall* be established under guidelines enacted by the legislature, which shall protect the public's use and enjoyment of the reefs. The State may condemn such vested rights for public use. (Emphasis added.)

103. Haw. Rev. Stat. § 187A-23 (1985).

104. *Id.* § 187A-23(b).

105. *Id.* § 187A-23(a).

106. *Id.* § 187A-23(b).

107. *Id.* § 187A-23(c), (d).

108. *Id.* § 187A-23(h).

109. *Id.* § 187A-23(g).

110. *Id.* §§ 187A-21, -22.

111. 16 U.S.C. § 391(b). This reservation is limited to those of not less than half Hawaiian blood. 16 U.S.C. § 396(a).

112. Meller, *supra* note 3, at 14-15.

113. Haw. Const. art. XI, § 6, *supra* note 102.

114. Meller, *supra* note 3, at 4.

115. As of 1954 there were approximately 80 registered and therefore legally recognized *konohiki* fisheries still in existence. However, many of the owners seemed to exercise no *konohiki* rights over their fisheries. *Id.* at 12, citing J. Shon, *Hawai'i Constitutional Convention Studies, 1978, Article X, Article XI,* at 117 (Honolulu: Legislative Reference Bureau, 1978).

116. 43 U.S.C. § 1301, *et seq.*

117. *Id.* § 1314.

118. *Id.* § 1331, *et seq.*

119. § 5(i) of the Hawai'i Admission Act, Pub. L. No. 86-3, 73 Stat. 4 (1959) provides:
    > The Submerged Lands Act of 1953 (Public Law 31, Eighty third Congress, first session; 67 Stat. 29) and the Outer Continental Shelf Lands Act of 1953 (Public Law 212, Eighty third Congress, first session; 67 Stat. 462) shall be applicable to the State of Hawaii, and the said state shall have the same rights as do existing states thereunder.

120. *Note, State-Federal Jurisdictional Conflict Over the Internal Waters and Submerged Lands of the Northwestern Hawaiian Islands,* 4 U. Haw. L. Rev. 139 (1982).

121. Haw. Const., art. XV, § 1. There may be precedents for the state's position, since it once was an independent kingdom. For example, in 1951, the International Court of Justice [hereinafter "ICJ"] recognized Norway's claim to waters within a baseline that connected a line of outer islands based on long, continued and peaceful use coupled with its economic dependence on the fisheries of those waters that had not been challenged by other nations. In 1974, the ICJ also recognized Iceland's preferential right to fish the high seas off its coast on a similar basis but also allowed the United Kingdom access to the same area. R.T.B. Iverson, T. Dye, and L. Paul, Draft Report, *Rights of Native Hawaiian Fishermen with Specific Regard to Harvesting of Bottomfish in the Northwest Hawaiian Islands and With Regard to Harvesting of Bottomfish, Crustaceans, Precious Corals, and Open-Ocean Fish in Offshore Areas Surrounding the Entire Hawaiian Island Chain,* Phase 1 33-34 (November 20, 1989) (unpublished report to the Western Pacific Regional Fishery Management Council) [hereinafter *WPRFMC Report*]. If the state can demonstrate similar uses, it could establish a basis for an archipelagic claim.

122. *Island Airlines v. Civil Aeronautics Board,* 352 F.2d 735 (9th Cir. 1965).

123. H.R. 2233, HD1, 15th Leg., Reg. Sess. (Haw. 1990).

124. H.R. 2233, HD1, SD1, CD1, 15th Leg., Reg. Sess. (Haw. 1990).

125. H. Con. Res. 10, H.D. 1, 15th Leg., Reg. Sess. (Haw. 1990).

126. 16 U.S.C. §§ 1801-1882 (1982).

127. *WPRFMC Report, supra* note 121, at 35, citing H.R. Rep. No. 445, 94th Cong., 2nd Sess. (1976).

128. *WPRFMC Report, supra* note 121, at 35, citing Jarman, *The Public Trust Doctrine in the Exclusive Economic Zone,* 65 Or. L. Rev. 1 (1986).

129. Proclamation No. 5030, Exclusive Economic Zone of the United States, 48 Fed. Reg. 10,605 (1984) (codified at 3 C.F.R. 5030). The international community legitimized the concept of the EEZ in the 1982 United Nations Convention on the Law of the Sea (UNCLOS III). The U.S. chose not to sign the UNCLOS III because of its provisions relating to seabed mining. However, U.S. officials have informally agreed with its other provisions and are following it in all other respects. J.M. Van Dyke, J.C. Clark, T.N. Pettit, A.L. Clark, *An Analysis of Existing and Future Policy Options for Development of Marine Mineral Resources in the U.S. Affiliated Territories -- the Johnston Island Exclusive Economic Zone* 34 (1986) [hereinafter *Johnston Island Analysis*] (unpublished paper).

130. Proclamation No. 5030, Exclusive Economic Zone of the United States, 48 Fed. Reg. 10,605 (1984) (codified at 3 C.F.R. 5030).

131. This EEZ includes the 200-mile limit extending out around the Northwest Hawaiian Islands as well as the main islands. *WPRFMC Report, supra* note 121, at 8.

132. The council is a quasi-government agency established under the MFCMA to assist in the development of fishery management plans for fishery areas within the jurisdiction of the United States and located around the State of Hawai'i. It is now focusing on implementing its fishery management plan for the northwest Hawaiian islands (NWHI). *Id.* at 1.

133. G. Anders, *Native Hawaiian Rights in a Regulated Fishery: An Exploratory Analysis* 1 (1987) (unpublished research paper, Pacific Islands Development Program, East-West Center).

134. 16 U.S.C. § 1853(b)(6)(B) (1988).

135. *WPRFMC Report, supra* note 121, at 11, 3.

136. *Id.* at 45.

137. *Id.*

138. The location and identification of deep sea fishing grounds or *koʻa* by master fishermen was extensive. E.M. Beckley, *Hawaiian Fisheries and Methods of Fishing* 10 (1883). One master fisherman could name 100 deep sea fishing grounds or *koʻa* located five miles from shore. One was 15 to 20 fathoms deep, another was 1,200 fathoms deep. Meller, *supra* note 3, n.9; citing A.D. Kahaulelio, "Fishing Lore," translated by Mary Kawena Pukui from *Ka Nupepa Kuokoa*, February 28-July 4, 1902 [on file in library of Hawaiʻi Institute of Marine Biology] at 22, 24.

139. Thurston, *supra* note 11, at 21-22.

140. *Id.* at 23.

141. First Constitution of the Kingdom of Hawaiʻi, *id.* at 1.

142. Haw. Rev. Stat. § 1-1 (1985), which was originally enacted in 1892, and continues in effect, provides:

> Common Law of the State, exceptions. The common law of England, as ascertained by English and American decisions, is declared to be the common law of the State of Hawaii in all cases, except as otherwise expressly provided by the Constitution or laws of the United States, or by the laws of the State, or fixed by Hawaiian judicial precedent, or *established by Hawaiian usage*; provided that no person shall be subject to criminal proceedings except as provided by the written laws of the United States or of the State. (Emphasis added.)

See also § 6 of the Hawaiʻi Organic Act which provided:

> That the laws of Hawaii not inconsistent with the Constitution or laws of the United States . . . shall continue in force, subject to repeal or amendment by the legislature of Hawaii or the Congress of the United States.

143. Compare, *WPRFMC Report, supra* note 121, at 45.

144. 520 F.2d 676 (9th Cir. 1975), *cert. den.*, 423 U.S. 1086, *reh'g denied*, 424 U.S. 978 (1976).

145. *Id.* at 684, citing *United States v. Winans*, 198 U.S. 371, 381 (1905).

146. *United States v. State of Washington*, 520 F.2d 676, 685 (9th Cir. 1975).

147. *Puget Sound Gillnetters Assn. v. U.S. District Court*, 573 F.2d 1123 (9th Cir. 1978), *vacated, Washington v. Fishing Vessel Assn.*, 443 U.S. 658 (1979). The U.S. Supreme Court upheld the Ninth Circuit approach, recognizing that:

> [T]he peculiar semisovereign and constitutionally recognized status of Indians justifies special treatment on their behalf when rationally related to the Government's "unique obligation toward the Indians." *Id.* at 673 n.20 (citations omitted).

148. The U.S. presently depends on imports to satisfy its need for strategic metals. The cobalt-rich ferromanganese crusts of the Hawaiian Islands are a potential alternative to a continued dependence on land-based strategic minerals. The estimated resource potential of the Hawaiian Islands crust deposits is 2.6 million tonnes of cobalt, 1.4 million tonnes of nickel, 78 million tonnes of manganese, and 63 million tonnes of iron. *See* C.J. Johnson, A.L. Clark, J.M. Otto, D.K. Pak, K.T.M. Johnson and C. Morgan, *Resource Assessment of Cobalt-rich Ferromanganese Crusts in the Hawaiian Archipelago* (1985) (unpublished paper, East-West Center).

149. Scholars have questioned whether a share of the proceeds must be designated under § 5(f) of the Hawaiʻi Admission Act for Native Hawaiians. *Johnston Island Analysis, supra* note 129, at 5, 33-34.

150. A. Murakami and R. Freitas, *Native Hawaiian Claims Concerning Ocean Resources* (August 7, 1987) (unpublished paper presented to Hawaiʻi Ocean Affairs Conference, East-West Center); *WPRFMC Report, supra* note 120, at 33. This section does not attempt to fully explore the basis for any claim to the resources and fisheries in the EEZ, except to suggest the possible theory supporting such an assertion.

151. *See generally* Murakami and Freitas, *supra* note 150, and *Johnston Island Analysis, supra* note 129.

152. *WPRFMC Report, supra* note 121, at 41-42.

153. Scholars may find a comparative study of the fishing rights of Hawaiians as opposed to Maoris useful to an understanding of this question. Maoris have relied on the Treaty of Waitangi of 1840 to reassert their dominion over their fishing rights. R. Talon, *A Comparison of Maori Fishing Rights Under the Treaty of Waitangi and the Fishing Rights of Native Hawaiians Under the Statutory and Common Law of Hawaiʻi* (May 11, 1989) (unpublished paper).

CHAPTER 9

SHORELINE BOUNDARIES

1. INTRODUCTION

Access along the shoreline and use of shoreline areas for cultural and subsistence purposes was a vital aspect of ancient Hawaiian life. Today, Native Hawaiians continue to access and use the shoreline area for many purposes, including fishing, gathering *limu*, *'opihi*, and other ocean resources, and for recreation. Consequently, the correct location of shoreline boundaries is of great importance to Hawaiians in order to prevent private encroachment onto public areas so that traditional usages may continue. This chapter will discuss Hawai'i cases which have established principles for the location of shoreline boundaries as well as principles for determining the ownership of submerged lands and newly created ocean front lands.

2. LOCATION OF SHORELINE BOUNDARIES

a. *Validity of Grants to Low Water Mark*

In *Territory v. Liliuokalani* (1902),[1] one of the earliest cases to discuss shoreline boundaries, the Hawai'i Supreme Court held that seaward boundaries to private lands granted by the monarchy could extend to the low water mark if such terms were expressly contained in the original award. The case involved a dispute between plaintiff, the Territory of Hawai'i, and defendants, Lili'uokalani and her lessee, Wilson, as to the ownership of lands at Waikīkī between the high and low water mark of the seashore. The royal patent issued by King Kamehameha V described the shoreline boundary as "running to the sea; thence along the sea at low water mark to commencement."[2] Accordingly, defendants argued that they owned the area between the high and low water marks and had the right to mine sand and gravel from that area for commercial purposes. The Territory of Hawai'i sought to prevent Wilson from removing the sand and gravel by asserting that the area between the high and low water marks belonged to the territorial government.

The territory argued that the provisions of the royal patent conveying lands between the high and low water marks were null and void because: (1) the king had no lawful power or authority to convey such lands; and (2) the words "*koe nae ke kuleana o na kanaka*" ("reserving however the people's *kuleana* therein") contained in the royal patent reserved all rights below the high water mark to the public. The territory cited a privy council resolution to support its first argument. The resolution stated:

> Resolved, that the rights of the king as sovereign extend from high water mark a marine league to sea, and to all navigable straits and passages among the Islands, and no private right can be sustained, except private rights of fishing and of cutting stone from the rocks, as provided and reserved by law.[3]

The court rejected both arguments. First, it found that Kamehameha V, as sovereign, had the power to grant lands between the high and low water marks to private parties because under common law other sovereign bodies, such as counties and states, had the power to make such grants with an express declaration of an intent to convey below the high water mark.[4] Second, the court opined that the privy council was only an advisory body to the king, so that its resolution did not have the force of law.[5] Finally, the court determined that the phrase "*koe nae ke kuleana o na kanaka*" referred only to *kuleana* house lots and taro patches occupied and farmed by tenants and had no reference to any public rights to the shoreline.[6] Consequently, the court held that the king had the power and authority to convey lands to the low water mark, and that the seaward boundary of this particular parcel extended to low water mark.

The case of *Brown v. Spreckels* (1902)[7] contains important language which suggests that while the monarchy had the power to alienate lands between the high and low water marks, conveyances of public lands between the high and low water marks could not be made *after* annexation.

Brown involved a title dispute between plaintiff, Charles Brown, and defendants, John and Adolph Spreckels, over two parcels of land located on the Hilo seashore.[8] Most of this land was accreted land, land that had accumulated on the shore due to the movement of the sea and Wailuku River. The deed for one parcel conveyed title from Kamehameha III to plaintiff's predecessor by specifically describing the property as extending to a street "[a]nd also the sea beach in front of the same down to low water mark."[9] The deed for the second parcel described the seaward boundary as being "along the edge of the sea . . . ."[10]

The plaintiff claimed that his two parcels contained all of the beach front area down to the low water mark. The defendants argued that the word "beach" in the deed to the first parcel and in the survey notes to the second parcel conveyed title only to the shore area between the high and low water mark and excluded the lands between the street and the high water mark. Hence, the defendants argued, the strip of land between the street and the high water mark did not belong to the plaintiff.

While the court interpreted both deeds as describing the shore lands from the road to at least the high water mark,[11] the court also implied that grants of public land below the high water mark could no longer be made after annexation. In reversing the lower court's judgment for the defendants, the court stated:

> This order was based by the trial Judge on the ground that the King or Government could not under the old regime alienate the shore between high and low water marks, and perhaps on the ground also that even if the power to alienate did exist then, the federal law now controls and forbids such alienation . . . .
>
> There can be no doubt that the power *formerly* existed here to alienate land between high and low water marks. There can also be no doubt that if such alienation was made in these cases, the fact that these islands have since become annexed to the United States would not affect the private rights previously granted, even if the law as held by the federal courts differed from the law that previously obtained in these islands in this respect.[12] (Citations omitted; emphasis added.)

b.   Grants Along the "Shoreline," "Seacoast" or "High Water Mark"

Many original grants, however, described shoreline boundaries in general terms, using phrases such as "*ma ke kai*," "along the shoreline" or "along the seacoast." The exact meaning of such phrases was not established until the Hawai'i Supreme Court decided the case of *In re Ashford* (1968).[13] In *Ashford*, a private landowner petitioned the land court to register title to land on Moloka'i. The original royal patents issued in 1866 described the seaward boundary of this property as *"ma ke kai"* (along the sea).[14] The private landowner asserted that *"ma ke kai"* described the boundaries at mean high tide, which could be calculated by the intersection of the shore and horizontal plane of mean high water based on U.S. Coast and Geodetic Survey publications.[15] The state contended that according to tradition, custom, and usage in old Hawai'i, *"ma ke kai"* is the high water mark along the edge of vegetation or the line of debris left by the wash of waves during ordinary high tide.[16]

At trial, the state presented *kama'aina* (native-born, one born in a particular place and familiar with its customs) witnesses to support its contention. Although objections to such testimony were sustained, the court allowed the *kama'aina* witnesses to testify in order to preserve the record on appeal.[17] The trial court then found that *"ma ke kai"* was the intersection of the shore with the horizontal plane of mean high water.[18]

The Hawai'i Supreme Court reversed, holding that: (1) *kama'aina* witnesses may testify to the location of shoreline boundaries according to ancient Hawaiian tradition, custom, and usage; and (2) according to ancient Hawaiian tradition, custom, and usage, seaward boundaries described as *"ma ke kai"* are located along the upper reaches of the wash of waves, as evidenced by the edge of vegetation or line of debris left by the wash of the waves.[19]

The court reasoned that it was necessary to examine the methods used to determine seaward boundaries at the time the royal patents were issued, since property rights are determined by the law in existence at the time such rights are vested. The court then found that in 1866 when Kamehameha V issued the royal patents for the property, it was the custom of the government survey office to have *kama'aina* witnesses point out shoreline boundaries to government surveyors, who would then record such boundaries. In this case, testimony by the state's *kama'aina* witnesses established that according to ancient tradition, custom, and usage, shoreline boundaries dividing public beaches and private lands were located along the upper reaches of the waves as represented by the edge of vegetation or line of debris.[20]

In contrast, there was no evidence to indicate that shorelines in 1866 had been based on calculations involving the intersection of the shore and horizontal plane of mean high water based on U.S. Coast and Geodetic Survey publications. The court thus held that seaward boundaries described by general terms such as *"ma ke kai"* or "along the sea" would be located along the upper washes of the waves as evidenced by the debris or vegetation line.

The Hawai'i Supreme Court further developed this position in *County of Hawaii v. Sotomura* (1973)[21] [hereinafter *Sotomura I*], by holding that: (1) the *Ashford* standard applied to properties which had been registered in land court; and (2) where seaward boundaries are evidenced by both a debris line and a vegetation line lying further *mauka* (toward the mountains, inland), the boundary is presumed to be at the vegetation line.

In *Sotomura I*, the County of Hawai'i initiated eminent domain proceedings to acquire private ocean front property located at Kalapana for the development of a beach park.[22] In 1962, the property had been registered in the land court with the seaward boundaries being described in both general terms as "along the seashore in all its windings along high water mark," as well as by specific azimuths and distance course measurements.[23] However, these distance and azimuth measurements had been located at the *limu* or seaweed line, and not at the upper wash of the waves. The landowners argued that the seaward boundary of the property was located at the azimuth and distance

198

measurements as stated in the land court decree, since land court proceedings are *res judicata* and conclusive against all other persons.[24] The county argued that the seaward boundary lay more *mauka* because the property had eroded since the 1962 land court decree, and because the actual location of the upper wash of the waves, as enunciated in the *Ashford* decision was more *mauka*.[25]

The trial court found that the property had eroded, and applied the *Ashford* standard to locate the new boundary along the debris line.[26] The trial court awarded the landowners $1.00 for the property located between the debris line and the land court decree measurements as just compensation for the taking.[27] The landowners appealed.

The Hawai'i Supreme Court concluded that the trial court erred in locating the boundary along the debris line, given the existence of a more *mauka* vegetation line. The court stated:

> We hold as a matter of law that where the wash of the waves is marked by both a debris line and a vegetation line lying further mauka; the presumption is that the upper reaches of the wash of the waves over the course of a year lies along the line marking the edge of vegetation growth. The upper reaches of the wash of the waves at high tide during one season of the year may be further mauka than the upper reaches of the wash of the waves at high tide during the other seasons. Thus while the debris line may change from day to day or from season to season, the vegetation line is a more permanent monument, its growth limited by the year's highest wash of the waves.[28]

In *Sotomura v. County of Hawaii* (1978)[29] [hereinafter *Sotomura II*], the same private landowners brought an action in the U.S. District Court for the District of Hawai'i claiming that the use of the *Ashford* standard and vegetation line to locate the high water mark by the Hawai'i Supreme Court in the *Sotomura I* decision violated their constitutional due process rights.[30]

The landowners argued that the use of the *Ashford* standard and vegetation line to locate the seaward boundary on land which had been registered in the land court was a taking of property without just compensation, since such standards for determining the location of the shoreline were radical departures from prior state law.[31]

The federal district court found that the Hawai'i Supreme Court's use of the *Ashford* standard and vegetation line to locate the shoreline boundary violated the landowners' substantive due process rights.[32] After reviewing the records of the state trial and supreme court proceedings, the district court found no authority for the Hawai'i Supreme Court's use of the *Ashford* standard and vegetation line. The court found that all relevant precedents except the *Ashford* decision used the mean high water level to determine the high water mark. Such precedents included land court rulings, attorney general opinions and statements by the legislature.[33]

The district court also attacked the *Ashford* decision by stating that the Hawai'i Supreme Court's holding regarding the definition of "*ma ke kai*" was only *dictum* since it was based on *kama'āina* testimony in the record as an offer of proof not subject to cross-examination or rebuttal evidence.[34] The district court also found that *Ashford* did not involve or apply to land court registered land. In addition, the court found that there was no reputation evidence regarding customary practices for relocating shoreline boundaries at the vegetation line after erosion had occurred.[35] Finally, the district court asserted that no legal or factual basis was stated in *Sotomura I* to support the presumption that the upper reaches of the wash of waves lie at the vegetation line when there is both a debris and a vegetation line.[36]

The district court then ruled that even though registered land may be subject to erosion, the land court's identification and use of the *limu* line to fix the location of the seaward boundary was *res judicata* or binding on subsequent actions.[37] Therefore, the state courts should have: (1) determined the exact extent of erosion; and (2) used the *limu* line to determine the location of the new seaward boundary.[38]

In an apparent response to the anticipated federal district court opinion in *Sotomura II*,[39] the Hawai'i Supreme Court reconfirmed its *Sotomura I* holding in the case of *In re Sanborn* (1977).[40] *Sanborn* involved an appeal by the state surveyor from a land court determination locating a shoreline boundary which shifted due to seasonal tides. As in the *Sotomura* case, the land had been registered in the land court and the court's 1951 decree described the seaward boundary both as "along high water mark at seashore," and by specific azimuth and distance measurements.[41]

The land court determined that the vegetation and debris line represented the upper reaches of the wash of waves during the winter season when the tide was furthest *mauka*. The court found that there had been no permanent erosion of the land since 1951, but that during the course of the year the high water mark varied due to the washing out of beach sands during the winter months and the return of such sands in the summer months.[42] This winter vegetation and debris line lay *mauka* of the azimuth and distance line stated in the land court decree. However, the land court still found that the landowner's beach front title line was fixed by the 1951 land court decree azimuth and distance measurements because there was no permanent erosion of the land.

The Hawai'i Supreme Court reversed, holding that despite the lack of permanent erosion of the land, the seaward boundary lay at the vegetation and debris line.[43] Citing the earlier case of *McCandless v. Du Roi* (1915),[44] the court reiterated the rule that in construing land court decrees, natural monuments such as "along the high water mark" are controlling over azimuth and distance measurements. Since the land court decree described the seaward boundary both by reference to a natural monument ("along high water mark at seashore") and by azimuth and distance measurements, the natural monument description was controlling. Therefore, the specific azimuth and distance measurements in the 1951 decree were inconclusive evidence of the high water mark, carrying only a presumption of accuracy which could be rebutted. The court then reaffirmed its *Ashford* definition of the high water mark as being along the upper reaches of the wash of waves. Because the land court found that the upper wash of waves during the winter season was the vegetation and debris line, the supreme court held that the seaward boundary lay along this line.

The landowners also argued that failure to adhere to the measurements in the 1951 land court decree and the relocation of the shoreline at the vegetation and debris line violated constitutional due process and constituted a taking of private property without compensation.[45] The court, however, found that there was no taking or violation of due process since the landowners had no reasonable expectation that the shoreline boundaries of their property would be conclusively fixed by the 1951 land court decree azimuth and distance measurements. This was because: (1) as of 1951, neither the Hawai'i Supreme Court, Hawai'i State Legislature, nor U.S. Congress had defined the location of "high water mark" in Hawai'i; and (2) during a subsequent 1951 reapplication to register the land, the landowners acknowledged that the high water mark varied from season to season.[46] Citing Justice Stewart's concurring opinion in the U.S. Supreme Court case of *Hughes v.*

Washington (1967),[47] the court found that determination of the shoreline boundary at the vegetation or debris line conformed to the reasonable expectations of the landowner and did not constitute a sudden change in state law.

c. *Alteration of Seaward Boundaries by Erosion, Accretion, or Avulsion*

Shorelines may be altered by erosion, accretion, or avulsion. Erosion has been defined as the gradual and imperceptible wearing away or covering of the land by natural water action.[48] Accretion is the process by which new lands are created by the gradual deposit of soil brought in by the wave action of tide waters, rivers, streams, lakes or ponds.[49] Avulsion is a sudden, violent, rapid loss or addition to lands caused by storms, floods or channel breakthroughs.[50]

The legal seaward boundaries of both regular and land court registered land may be changed due to erosion or accretion. In *Sotomura I*, the Hawai'i Supreme Court held that land court registered ocean front property is subject to the same burdens and incidents as unregistered land, including erosion.[51] This was based on its reading of Land Court Rule 26, allowing a landowner to register title to additional lands formed by accretion to previously registered land, as well as its holding in *In re Castle* (1973).[52] In *Castle*, the court had allowed the state to challenge the location of a seaward boundary on a map accompanying a land court certificate where a later survey showed that a portion of the property had become submerged due to erosion. Therefore, although a land court decree which describes a seaward boundary at the high water mark is conclusive, the court held that the *precise location* of the high water mark on the ground is subject to change and may always be altered by erosion or accretion.[53]

In *Sotomura II*, the private landowners did not dispute the Hawai'i Supreme Court's ruling that the location of a shoreline, even with regard to land court registered lands, could be altered by erosion.[54] The U.S. District Court impliedly agreed that shoreline boundaries on registered as well as non-registered land could be altered by erosion.[55]

In terms of shorelines altered by avulsion, the Hawai'i Supreme Court has adopted common law principles which hold that pre-existing boundaries are retained:

> Likewise, in cases where there have been rapid, easily perceived and sometimes violent shifts of land (avulsion) incident to floods, storms or channel breakthroughs, preexisting legal boundaries are retained notwithstanding the fact that former riparian owners may have lost their access to the water.[56] (Citations omitted.)

3. OWNERSHIP OF SUBMERGED LANDS

In *King v. Oahu Railway and Land Company* (1899),[57] the Hawai'i Supreme Court adopted the public trust doctrine, holding that all lands under navigable waters are public lands held in trust by the government for public uses.

In this case, the Hawaiian Kingdom had leased shoreline property around Honolulu harbor to defendant Oahu Railway and Land Company to develop and manage railroad and wharf facilities.[58] Pursuant to the lease and the Railroad Act of 1878, the railway company became an agent of the government and had the authority to exercise eminent domain powers.[59] However, the lease also allowed the government to reclaim the land and any improvements after giving the railway company 90 days notice. The government wanted to reclaim the land to make extensive wharf improvements. The railway company wanted to condemn the land for railroad and wharf purposes and a perpetual right-of-way to sail and anchor its vessels. The issue before the court was whether the government had released its control over lands under the navigable waters of Honolulu harbor when it issued the lease so that the railroad company could condemn such submerged lands over the objections of the government.

The court held that the railway company could not condemn these submerged lands over the objections and plans of the Hawaiian government because of the special nature of such lands.[60] Quoting from the U.S. Supreme Court case of *Illinois Central R.R. v. Illinois* (1892),[61] the court found that title to submerged lands is "different in character" from title held in lands by the states or federal government which are subject to preemption and sale. Title in lands under navigable waters is instead held in trust for the people so that they may "enjoy the navigation of the waters, carry on commerce over them and have liberty of fishing therein freed from the obstruction or interference of private parties."[62] Furthermore, the court found that the "control of the state for the purposes of the trust can never be lost, except to such parcels as are used in promoting the interests of the public therein, or can be disposed of without any substantial impairment of the public interest in the lands and waters remaining."[63]

The court then declared that:

> The people of Hawaii hold the absolute rights to all its navigable waters and the soils under them for their own common use. The lands under the navigable waters in and around the territory of the Hawaiian Government are held in trust for the public uses of navigation.
>
> It will be noticed that in the opinion of the *R. R. v. Illinois* above quoted . . . an exception is mentioned to the inalienable character of the state's right to submerged lands. The court concedes that the state can grant parcels of land under navigable waters that may be used for foundations of piers, wharves, &c., in order to subserve the public interest, and which do not substantially impair the public interest in the lands and water remaining.[64] (Citations omitted.)

The case of *Bishop v. Mahiko* (1940),[65] although dealing with the issue of *konohiki* fishing rights, contains an important discussion regarding ownership of submerged lands. In *Bishop*, the Hawai'i Supreme Court traced the ownership of submerged lands by the Kingdom of Hawai'i, to ownership by the republic, to the subsequent ceding and transfer of such lands to the United States pursuant to annexation.[66] The case, however, is inconclusive as to the exact boundaries of the submerged lands formerly owned by the kingdom and republic. Some authorities cited state that the kingdom's jurisdiction extended from low water mark to one marine league seaward,[67] while another authority cited states that the kingdom's jurisdiction extends from high water mark to one marine league seaward.[68] The case, however, reaffirms the public trust doctrine by stating that such submerged lands were not owned by the government in a proprietary sense, but in trust for the benefit of the people.[69]

In the *Sotomura I* and *Sanborn* cases, the Hawai'i Supreme Court held that submerged lands created by erosion or by the seasonal change of the tides are owned by the state in trust for the people.

In *Sotomura I*, the Hawai'i Supreme Court held that title to lands lying *makai* (toward the ocean, seaward) of the *Ashford* seaward boundary, including land lost by erosion, belongs to the state.[70] This holding was based on common law principles of erosion and the public trust doctrine, since there was no *kama'aina* testimony or other evidence of Hawaiian custom on this question.[71] The court pointed to an earlier Hawai'i case in which it had adopted the common law principle of accretion whereby title to additional lands formed by accretion passed to the private ocean front landowner.[72] It then reasoned that it should follow the common law of erosion where land lost by erosion generally returns to the ownership of the state. The court also reasoned that based on its adoption of the public trust doctrine in 1899, land beneath the high water mark had thenceforth been considered public lands held in trust for the people by the state.[73]

In *Sotomura II*, the landowners argued that the Hawai'i Supreme Court's holding that all property seaward of the vegetation line belonged to the state violated their procedural due process rights because no hearing on the issue of ownership of property located seaward of the vegetation line had been held.[74] In reviewing the record of the state trial and appellate proceedings, the federal district court found that the Hawai'i Supreme Court, without holding a hearing on the issue, determined on its own that the land was owned by the state. The county had argued that the land below the debris line was only worth $1.00, but never asserted that the land was owned by the state, while the landowners in turn argued that the value of the land was much higher.[75] After the Hawai'i Supreme Court's decision, the landowners petitioned for a rehearing on the issue of land ownership, claiming that because the issues had not been argued before the court, their right to a hearing and presentation of evidence on the matter had been violated. The Hawai'i Supreme Court subsequently denied the petition for rehearing. The U.S. District Court found that the state supreme court's decision not to hold a hearing on the issue of ownership of land below the debris line constituted a taking of property without a hearing, and violated the landowners' procedural due process rights.[76]

Because the district court found that the land court's use of the *limu* line to fix the location of the seaward boundary was binding, it held that lands between the vegetation line and *limu* line were owned by the private landowners.[77] Because no compensation was given by the state for its taking of this land area, the federal district court found that the *Sotomura I* decision violated the landowners' substantive due process rights.[78]

In contrast, the Hawai'i Supreme Court found in the *Sanborn* case that the public trust doctrine[79] created an exception to the land court statute and served to invalidate any registration of land below the high water mark. Since the public trust doctrine had been adopted in Hawai'i several years prior to the land court statute, the land court statute was subject to the doctrine. The court then confirmed its holding in *Sotomura I* that submerged lands previously registered in land court as below the high water mark are owned by the state in trust for the public.[80]

In terms of submerged lands created by sudden violent losses of beach front lands due to storms or floods (avulsion), the Hawai'i Supreme Court's agreement with common law principles which hold that pre-existing shoreline boundaries are retained[81] implies that submerged lands created by avulsion remain as private lands and that lost lands may be restored.

4.   OWNERSHIP OF NEWLY CREATED BEACH FRONT LANDS

New beach front lands may be added to existing beach front lands by accretion,[82] reliction, avulsion or lava extensions. Reliction is the gradual and imperceptible recession of water causing lands submerged under water to become fast or dry lands.[83] Lava extensions are created by lava flows which flow over seaward boundaries into the ocean onto formerly submerged lands.

Hawai'i case law holds that lands created by accretion or reliction are owned by the owners of the contiguous land to which the addition is made. In *Halstead v. Gay* (1889),[84] the Hawai'i Supreme Court upheld a finding of trespass, stating that title to the accreted area upon which defendant had entered was held by the plaintiff, as owner of the contiguous land. In citing common law, Justice Preston, sitting as an Intermediary Court, stated:

> Land formed by alluvion, or the gradual and imperceptible accretion from the water, and land gained by reliction, or the gradual and imperceptible recession of the water, belong to the owner of the contiguous land to which the addition is made.[85] (Citations omitted.)

The defendant did not challenge this principle on appeal, but argued that the description given in the patent for the land did not permit the landowner to claim the accreted land. The supreme court rejected this argument, holding that the phrase *"kahakai"* as used in the patent description, meant high water mark on the sea beach and that the intention to grant to the sea was clear in the patent.[86]

However, in 1985, the Hawai'i State Legislature enacted Hawai'i Revised Statutes (Haw. Rev. Stat.) sections 669-1(e) and 501-33[87], which require persons seeking to quiet title or register accreted land to show that the accretion is natural and has been in existence for at least 20 years. This is the same period required for proof of an adverse possession claim.[88] These, however, raise questions as to who holds title to the accreted land during the 20-year period. A legislative committee report[89] states that the statutes are not intended to affect pre-existing law on ownership of accreted land, and it appears that the comon law principles enunciated in *Halstead* continue despite this limitation on actions. The statutes also classify accreted lands to which title has been obtained as conservation district lands on which the construction of structures, retaining walls, or dredging, grading or other activities which may interfere with the future course of the beach, are prohibited.[90]

In *State v. Zimring* (1977),[91] the Hawai'i Supreme Court appeared to agree with common law principles regarding ownership of lands created by avulsion. By stating that pre-existing boundaries are retained where a sudden violent shift of lands due to floods or storms creates new lands,[92] the court implied that lands created by avulsion are owned by the state.

The Hawai'i Supreme Court held in *Zimring* that lands created by lava extensions are owned by the State of Hawai'i. In *Zimring*, a 1955 volcanic eruption on the island of Hawai'i resulted in the creation of 7.9 acres of new coastal lands.[93] In 1960, the Zimrings purchased two parcels of land which were contiguous to the lava extension, and began making improvements on the lava extension area. In 1968, the state demanded that the Zimrings vacate the lava extension area, and thereafter filed a complaint to establish title to the area.

Based on equity principles, the Hawai'i Supreme Court held that lava extensions are public lands owned by the state. The court found that there was no established Hawaiian custom or usage regarding ownership of lava extensions.[94] Between 1846[95] and 1892[96] there had only been two lava flows which created lava extensions. The court found that an 1868 lava extension had been awarded by the Boundary Commission in 1876 to a private individual, while there had been no government action on an 1887 lava extension. The court therefore held that these two pre-1892 governmental actions did not establish any traditional Hawaiian custom and usage with regard to ownership of lava extensions.

The court also found no prior common law cases that dealt with the ownership of lava extensions.[97] The court then based its decision on equitable principles by balancing the interests of contiguous landowners against the interests of the public at large. The court stated:

> Rather than allowing only a few of the many lava victims the windfall of lava extensions, this court believes that equity and sound public policy demand that such land inure to the benefit of all the people of Hawaii, in whose behalf the government acts as trustee. Given the paucity of land in our island state and the concentration of private ownership in relatively few citizens, a policy enriching only a few would be unwise. Thus we hold that lava extensions vest when created in the people of Hawaii, held in public trust by the government for the benefit, use and enjoyment of all the people.
>
> Under public trust principles, the State as trustee has the duty to protect and maintain the trust property and regulate its use. Presumptively, this duty is to be implemented by devoting the land to actual public uses, *e. g.*, recreation. Sale of the property would be permissible only where the sale promotes a valid public purpose.[98]

Alternatively, the Zimrings asserted that the federal government, and not the state, held title to the 1955 lava extension.[99] They argued that the state could not claim title to the lava extension since it was not part of the lands ceded by the republic to the federal government in 1898 and returned to the state pursuant to the Admission Act and was not land created after statehood in 1959.

The Hawai'i Supreme Court rejected this argument. It found that according to the Joint Resolution of Annexation, the Republic of Hawai'i had ceded all of its property interests, including future interest to any lands added to the territory through conquest, discovery, or volcanic activity, to the United States.[100] Thus, since the right to future lava extensions was conveyed to the United States at the time of annexation, any lava extension created thereafter would be considered ceded lands which were returned to the state in 1959. The court also reasoned that retention of title to the lava extension by the federal government would be inconsistent with the intent of the Admission Act, which was to convey all lands not set aside for federal use to the state.[101] Since the lava extension had not been set aside for federal use, it was clearly owned by the state.

5.   CONCLUSION

In recent years, the Hawai'i Supreme Court has shown greater concern for preserving the shoreline area for public, rather than private, use. Fortunately, early Hawai'i law adopting the public trust doctrine and recognizing Hawaiian tradition, custom, and usage has provided a basis for the court's decisions. While the U.S. District Court believed that the *Ashford* and *Sotomura I* standard for locating the shoreline constituted a radical departure from prior law, this standard has been codified[102] and recognized as the law of Hawai'i.

In terms of the alteration of seaward boundaries and the ownership of newly created submerged or fast lands by erosion, accretion, reliction and avulsion, the court has generally adopted common law principles. In addition, the court has held lava extensions to be public lands owned by the state in trust for the public.

NOTES

1. 14 Haw. 88 (1902).
2. *Id.* at 89.
3. Resolution of the Privy Council of August 29, 1850, 3 Privy Council Record 425 (1850).
4. *Territory v. Liliuokalani*, 14 Haw. 88, 89-90 (1902).
5. *Id.* at 91-92.
6. *Id.* at 95.
7. 14 Haw. 399 (1902).
8. *Id.* at 401-402.
9. *Id.* at 402.
10. *Id.* at 405-406.
11. *Id.* at 409-411.
12. *Id.* at 404.
13. 50 Haw. 314, 440 P.2d 76 (1968).
14. *Id.*
15. *Id.*
16. *Id.* at 315, 440 P.2d at 77.
17. *Id.*
18. *Id.*
19. *Id.*
20. *Id.* at 316, 440 P.2d at 78.
21. 55 Haw. 176, 517 P.2d 57 (1973).
22. *Id.* at 177, 517 P.2d at 59.
23. *Id.* at 177-178, 517 P.2d at 59.
24. *Id.* at 178, 517 P.2d at 60.
25. *Id.* at 179, 517 P.2d at 60.
26. *Id.* at 180, 517 P.2d at 60.
27. *Id.* at 182-183, 517 P.2d at 62.
28. *Id.* at 182, 517 P.2d at 62. The Hawai'i Supreme Court again affirmed this definition in a *per curiam* decision. *See In re Hanahuli Ass'n., Ltd.*, 56 Haw. 160, 532 P.2d 397 (1975).
29. 460 F.Supp. 473 (D. Haw. 1978).
30. The landowners had appealed the *Sotomura I* decision to the U.S. Supreme Court, but *certiorari* was denied. *Id.* at 477.
31. *Id.* at 476.
32. *Id.* at 478.
33. *Id.*
34. *Id.* at 479.
35. *Id.*
36. *Id.* at 480.
37. *Id.* at 482.
38. *Id.* at 483.
39. A preview of the district court's formal opinion was published in 1975 when the court denied the state's motion to dismiss. *See Sotomura v. County of Hawaii*, 402 F.Supp. 95 (D. Haw. 1975).
40. 57 Haw. 585, 562 P.2d 771 (1977).
41. *Id.* at 589, 562 P.2d 774.
42. *Id.* at 588-590, 562 P.2d 774.
43. *Id.* at 598, 562 P.2d 779.
44. 23 Haw. 51 (1915).
45. *In re Sanborn*, 57 Haw. 585, 596, 562 P.2d 771, 777-778 (1977).
46. *Id.* at 597-598, 562 P.2d at 778.
47. 389 U.S. 290 (1967).
48. R.R. Powell, 5 *Powell on Real Property*, para. 717[2] (1989).
49. *Id.*
50. *State v. Zimring*, 58 Haw. 106, 120, 566 P.2d 725, 734 (1977).

51.   55 Haw. 176, 180, 517 P.2d 57, 61 (1973).

52.   54 Haw 276, 277, 506 P.2d 1, 3 (1973).

53.   *County of Hawaii v. Sotomura*, 55 Haw. 176, 180, 517 P.2d 57, 61 (1973).

54.   460 F.Supp. 473, 476.

55.   *Id*. at 482.

56.   *State v. Zimring*, 58 Haw. 106, 120, 566 P.2d 725, 734 (1977).

57.   11 Haw. 717 (1899).

58.   *Id*. at 718.

59.   *Id*. at 721.

60.   *Id*. at 723-725.

61.   146 U.S. 387 (1892).

62.   *King v. Oahu Railway and Land Company*, 11 Haw. 717, 723, quoting from *Illinois Central R.R. v. Illinois*, 146 U.S. 387 (1892).

63.   *Id*. at 724 (still quoting from 146 U.S. 387).

64.   *Id*. at 725.

65.   35 Haw. 608 (1940).

66.   *Id*. at 641-645.

67.   *Id*. at 643-644.

68.   *Id*. at 644.

69.   *Id*. at 645.

70.   55 Haw. 176, 183, 517 P.2d 57, 62. The supreme court then vacated the lower court's award of $1.00 to the private landowners as compensation for the lands lying between the debris line and the land court survey line condemned by the county for park purposes.

71.   *Id*.

72.   *Halstead v. Gay*, 7 Haw. 587, 590 (1889).

73.   *County of Hawaii v. Sotomura*, 55 Haw. 176, 183-184, 517 P.2d 57, 63-64 (1973).

74.   460 F.Supp. 473, 477.

75.   *Id*.

76.   *Id*. at 477-478.

77.   *Id*. at 482.

78.   *Id*.

79.   Under the public trust doctrine adopted in 1899 pursuant to *King v. Oahu Railway and Land Company*, 11 Haw. 717 (1899), all land below the high water mark is owned by the state in trust for the public. Such land cannot be relinquished by the state unless for public purposes.

80.   *In re Application of Sanborn*, 57 Haw. 585, 593-594, 562 P.2d 771, 776 (1977).

81.   *State v. Zimring*, 58 Haw. 106, 120, 566 P.2d 725, 734 (1977).

82.   *Id*. at 119, 566 P.2d at 734, citing *Halstead v. Gay*, 7 Haw. 587, 588 (1889).

83.   Powell, *supra* note 48.

84.   7 Haw. 587 (1889).

85.   *Id*. at 588 (citing from lower court opinion).

86.   *Id*. at 589.

87.   1985 Haw. Sess. Laws, Act 221.

88.   *See* Chapter 6, *supra,* text accompanying notes 101-111.

89.   Water, Land Use, Development and Hawaiian Affairs and Judiciary Comm. Rep. No. 346, *1985 House Journal,* 1142-1143.

90.   *See* Haw. Rev. Stat. § 183-45 (1985).

91.   58 Haw. 106, 566 P.2d 725 (1977).

92.   *Id*. at 120, 566 P.2d at 734.

93.   *Id*. at 107, 566 P.2d at 727.

94.   *Id*. at 116-117, 566 P.2d at 732-733.

95.   In 1846, the Land Commission was created and given the power to issue individual Land Commission Awards. This generally is acknowledged as the year in which private land ownership originated in Hawai'i. *Id.* at 111-115, 566 P.2d at 730.

96.   November 25, 1892 is the date the common law of England was adopted and by which ancient Hawaiian usage must have been established in practice. *State v. Zimring*, 52 Haw. 472, 474-475, 479 P.2d 202, 203-204 (1970).

97.   *State v. Zimring*, 58 Haw. 106, 119, 566 P.2d 725, 734 (1977).

98.   *Id*. at 121, 566 P.2d at 735.
99.   *Id*. at 121-122, 566 P.2d at 735-736.
100.   *Id*. at 122-123, 566 P.2d at 736.
101.   *Id*. at 124-125, 566 P.2d at 736.
102.   *See* Haw. Rev. Stat. § 205A-1 (1985).

PART FOUR

TRADITIONAL AND
CUSTOMARY RIGHTS

CHAPTER 10

ACCESS RIGHTS

1.   INTRODUCTION

Access along the shore, between *ahupua'a* or districts, to the mountains and sea, and to small areas of land cultivated or harvested by native tenants was a necessary part of early Hawaiian life. With Western contact and the consequent changes in land tenure and lifestyle, gaining access to landlocked *kuleana* parcels, and to the mountains and sea, have become important rights which Native Hawaiians must assert if they are to retain their lands and their traditional cultural practices. The following chapter examines the unique access rights of Native Hawaiians, as well as those exercised in common with the general public.

2.   ANCIENT HAWAIIAN TRAIL SYSTEM

Although foot travel along trails was the primary means of transportation over land for early Hawaiians, little has been written by Hawaiian scholars regarding the construction or use of ancient trails. As one commentator has noted, this is probably because trails were so widespread and commonplace that their construction and use was not considered noteworthy.[1] However, given a general understanding of the land tenure system in ancient Hawai'i, several conclusions about ancient trails can be drawn.

Like the construction of an aqueduct system in Hawai'i, the *ali'i 'ai moku* or district chief, or the *ali'i 'ai ahupua'a* or resident *ahupua'a* chief, probably determined the need for a trail in a particular location.[2] After that, it was usually the task of either a *konohiki* or land agent, or a *kahuna* or professional, to plan and design the location of a trail in the most direct but least obtrusive route.[3] The planning and design of a trail probably required an intimate knowledge of the climate and geography of a particular region. For instance, during normal weather, the coastal trail built near Hōnaunau, Kona, Hawai'i was located well inland from the shoreline but was slightly above the high water mark during stormy weather, so that travelers could pass safely under all weather conditions.[4]

The final step of actually constructing the trail was carried out by hand by the *maka'āinana*, people of the land, under the direct supervision of the *konohiki*.[5] The size and type of trail constructed varied from one island to the next, depending largely on the surrounding terrain and the materials available at the time. For instance, practically all of the shoreline trails along the Ka'ū and Kona coast on the island of Hawai'i were constructed across lava flows.[6] Trails in these areas were only wide enough to accommodate single-file pedestrian traffic and, in areas where the trail crossed *a'ā* or clinker type lava, medium sized, smooth waterworn stones from the shore were placed approximately every two and one-half feet apart so that traveling by foot would be less painful.[7] On the other hand, the Alaloa (Long Road) on the island of Maui, built by the famous chief Kihaapi'ilani during the 16th Century, was so wide it could have accommodated modern single-lane vehicular traffic.[8] Although many sections of the Alaloa have since been destroyed, it originally ran completely around the island, primarily near the shoreline, and was inlaid with stones, giving it the appearance of cobblestones.[9]

Trails ran primarily in two directions. Vertical trails within an *ahupua'a* running from the sea to the mountains provided *ahupua'a* residents with access inland to tend to their taro terraces or their cultivated crops as well as for hunting, gathering, and religious purposes. Horizontal trails running through more than one *ahupua'a*, primarily along the shoreline, served as thoroughfares for people traveling from one *ahupua'a* to another, or one district to another. Use of Hawai'i's trails was open to all classes of people. However, the *ali'i* appear to have preferred, where possible, travel by canoe rather than by foot.[10]

There are no detailed rules and regulations governing the use of trails in Hawai'i's written history. The lack of a highly stratified system of rules regulating use may indicate that access by foot, unlike the consumption and use of Hawai'i's water, was not considered a valuable commodity by Hawaiians. Thus, any restrictions placed on use of trails were an extension of general restrictions defined by the Hawaiian culture (*e.g.*, prohibition of outdoor night activity during certain moon phases or the *kapu noho* requiring prostration in the presence of chiefs). The lack of rules and regulations may also be attributed to a declaration by the early O'ahu ruler Kūali'i during the 16th Century allowing old men, women, and children to sleep in safety along the highway.[11] This law was later adopted by Kamehameha I and came to be known as *Māmalahoe.*

3.   WESTERN INFLUENCE

Following Captain James Cook's arrival to Hawai'i, Hawaiian trails were not extensively developed or exploited by Western interests, probably because establishing sea ports and transporting goods by boat was a less expensive, and more efficient, means of transportation for the merchant class.[12] That is not to say, however, that some trails were not significantly altered. Prior to the *Mahele* of 1848, many trails were altered due to the introduction of horses in Hawai'i. Originally brought as gifts for King Kamehameha I by Captain Richard J. Cleveland aboard the Lelia Byrd in 1803, horses flourished in the islands. In 1851, there were recorded 11,700 horses in the islands.[13] To accommodate travel by horse, many trails, such as the shoreline trails along the Kona and Ka'ū coast, were enlarged and even rerouted into areas which previously had been almost inaccessible.

In addition, certain new laws provided the Hawaiian government with a continuous source of labor, so that roads could be constructed through areas which had been inaccessible due to the huge amount of labor required. In 1841, the Hawaiian monarchy officially passed a law allowing citizens to pay out their road tax by labor on government roads.[14] In addition, prisoners were also required to work on construction and maintenance of all roads.[15] As a result, many ancient trails were altered or rerouted to accommodate horses, and later, vehicular traffic.[16]

Although there was a network of trails on all the major Hawaiian islands, the Board of Land Commissioners, in awarding individual land titles in the mid-19th Century, considered trails as incidental to the determination of boundaries in making land awards.[17] Thus, most trails were never recorded, a process which could have established their origin and use. As large tracts of land were developed for sugar or pineapple cultivation, or ranching operations, many *mauka-makai* (mountain to sea) trails were destroyed. Still other trails within the *ahupua'a* fell into disuse and became overgrown as settlement patterns shifted, or the Native Hawaiian population within the *ahupuaʻa* decreased due to disease or the necessity of seeking employment in the cities.

4.   PRESENT-DAY ACCESS RIGHTS

In modern times, rights of access can be divided into two major categories: (1) access rights to a *kuleana* parcel, and (2) access rights between two or more *ahupuaʻa* or districts. Access rights to *kuleana* parcels may involve access along ancient trails, or expanded access not limited to any particular route. Access rights between two or more *ahupuaʻa* or districts generally involve access along ancient or well-established trails.

a.   Kuleana *Access*

(1)   *Common Law Theories*   Early Hawaiʻi Supreme Court cases held that *kuleana* owners are entitled to access to their property under the English common law concept known as an easement. An easement is simply a right to use the land of another; it does not give the user title or possession to the property.[18] The width and length of an easement depends upon the intent of the parties as evidenced by several factors, including the type of use, the continuity of use, and the circumstances surrounding the transaction.[19] Land subject to an easement is called the servient tenement while the land that is benefitted by the easement is known as the dominant tenement.[20] While an easement can be created at common law using different legal theories, the Hawaiʻi courts have held that an easement to a *kuleana* parcel is created either expressly or impliedly.

(a)   *Express Grant of an Easement*   During the *Mahele*, all Government and Crown Lands were awarded subject to the rights of native tenants. Deeds executed to the *konohiki* conveying private interests in land usually contained the Hawaiian phrase "*ua koe ke kuleana o na kanaka*," which has been interpreted by Hawaiʻi courts to mean "reserving the rights of native tenants."[21] In *Rogers v. Pedro* (1982),[22] plaintiffs sought to quiet title to certain parcels of land located *makai* of a government road at Kaluaʻaha, Molokaʻi. Defendants counterclaimed and, among other things, demanded access to the highway as owners of a landlocked *kuleana* parcel.[23] The Hawaiʻi Intermediate Court of Appeals held that the phrase "*ua koe ke kuleana o na kanaka*," contained in the plaintiffs' original grant operated as an express reservation of certain rights to *kuleana* owners, including an unrestricted right of access to their property.[24]

(b)   *Implied Grant; Easement by Necessity*   In *Kalaukoa v. Keawe* (1893),[25] the Hawaiʻi Supreme Court adopted the common law doctrine of implied easement by necessity. In *Kalaukoa*, a common grantor had sold adjoining parcels to the predecessors-in-interest of Kalaukoa and Keawe. Keawe's parcel was landlocked. Although there was no mention of a grant of an easement across Kalaukoa's land in favor of Keawe's land, a trail was plainly visible and had been used for nearly 20 years by Keawe's predecessors-in-interest as a carriage road.[26] The court held that an easement by implication may be created either because of "strict" necessity, *e.g.*, because one of the parties is landlocked, or by reasonable necessity, *e.g.*, where a way has been actually and continuously used and, while an alternate route is possible, it is very difficult or expensive.[27]

The actual dispute in the *Kalaukoa* case, however, involved the width and purpose for which the easement would be put to use. Kalaukoa claimed that the easement should be strictly limited to horse or even foot traffic.[28] Keawe, on the other hand, contended that travel by carriage was acceptable.[29] The court found that since Keawe's predecessors-in-interest had actually used the path for carriage travel for an uninterrupted and considerable length of time, continued carriage use would not unreasonably burden Kalaukoa's land.[30]

One year later, the supreme court extended the implied easement by necessity doctrine to include owners of landlocked *kuleana* parcels. In *Henry v. Ahlo* (1894),[31] Henry, a *kuleana* owner, filed suit to obtain access to his property which was surrounded by Crown Lands leased to Ahlo. Basing its decision largely on *Kalaukoa*, the court found that a right-of-way must be determined by evidence such as the lands' condition and character, and uses made of the lands, including any acts or acquiescence by the parties.[32] Consequently, the court established a ten-foot-wide roadway to Henry's *kuleana*.[33]

(2) *Statutory Basis* On August 6, 1850 the legislature of Hawai'i enacted a statute, now popularly known as the *Kuleana* Act, which was designed to insure and provide the tenant farmers residing within an *ahupua'a* the opportunity to obtain fee simple title to the lands upon which they resided and cultivated their crops.[34] Over the years, every section of the *Kuleana* Act was repealed with the exception of section 7, which survives today in the form of Hawai'i Revised Statutes (Haw. Rev. Stat.) section 7-1:

> Where the landlords have obtained, or may hereafter obtain, allodial titles to their lands, the people on each of their lands shall not be deprived of the right to take firewood, house-timber, aho cord, thatch, or ki leaf, from the land on which they live, for their own private use, but they shall not have a right to take such articles to sell for profit. The people shall also have a right to drinking water, and running water, and the right of way. The springs of water, running water, and roads shall be free to all, on all lands granted in fee simple; provided that this shall not be applicable to wells and watercourses, which individuals have made for their own use.[35]

The legislative history of the *Kuleana* Act indicates that this particular section was included at the insistence of King Kamehameha III. The privy council minutes reflect the king's concern that a "little bit of land even with allodial title, if they [the people] be cut off from all other privileges would be of very little value."[36] The privy council thus adopted the king's suggestion:

> [The] proposition of the King, which he inserted as the seventh clause of the law, as a rule for the claims of common people to go to the mountains, and the seas attached to their own particular lands exclusively, is agreed . . . .[37]

The *Kuleana* Act was expansive in scope because it not only provided the native tenants a statutory right of access to their *kuleana*, but also gave them unobstructed access within the *ahupua'a* to obtain items necessary to make the *kuleana* productive.

The first Hawai'i Supreme Court case to discuss the scope of Haw. Rev. Stat. section 7-1 was *Oni v. Meek* (1858).[38] In this case, Oni, a tenant of the *ahupua'a* of Honouliuli, O'ahu, filed suit against John Meek, an entrepreneur who had leased the entire *ahupua'a* of Honouliuli from its *konohiki* through several lease agreements. Oni filed suit when some of his horses, which had been pastured on Meek's land, were impounded by Meek and sold as strays. Oni claimed that he had an unqualified right to pasture his horses. This right stemmed from, among other things, the Act of 1846, predecessor to the *Kuleana* Act, which allowed a tenant the right of pasturage with the consent of the resident *konohiki* and minister of interior.[39] Since Oni had obtained the consent of the *konohiki* prior to Meek's lease agreement, Oni contended that the consent controlled.[40]

The Hawai'i Supreme Court rejected Oni's argument, concluding that while the Act of 1846 was not expressly repealed by subsequent legislation, it was implicitly repealed by the passage of the *Kuleana* Act of 1850.[41] Any right of pasturage was repealed since no right of pasturage was included in section 7 of the *Kuleana* Act.[42] The court noted that several attempts made in subsequent legislatures to include a right of pasturage were unsuccessful.[43] Moreover, the *Kuleana* Act had been amended several times thereafter, but no right of pasturage was included.[44] The court held that only those rights expressly included within section 7 would prevail over any fee simple title claim of a *konohiki* or the lessee of a *konohiki*.[45]

While *Oni* dealt generally with the scope of section 7-1, the first Hawai'i Supreme Court case to specifically address access under section 7-1 was *Palama v. Sheehan* (1968).[46] In *Palama*, plaintiff Palama filed an action to quiet title to land as well as a fishpond located in Kalāheo, Kaua'i. Defendants owned several *kuleana* parcels located *makai* of Palama's property and one *kuleana* located within Palama's land.[47] Defendants claimed that they were entitled to access to their *kuleana* parcels under Haw. Rev. Stat. section 7-1.[48] The court held that defendants had established access rights under section 7-1 since their predecessors-in-interest had used a trail since historic times to gain access between other taro lands located *mauka* of Palama's property and the *makai kuleana* parcels.[49] The court also held that defendants were entitled to a right-of-way across plaintiff's land by reason of necessity.[50] Palama claimed that even if a right of access was found, such right should be limited to pedestrian use which existed at the time the original grant was made in 1850.[51] The court did not reach Palama's second claim, holding that Palama's predecessor-in-interest had enlarged the path in 1910 for vehicular access so that the present width of the easement did not unreasonably burden Palama's land.[52]

Twelve years after *Palama*, the Hawai'i Intermediate Court of Appeals was faced with the issue of whether the right of access to a *kuleana* under section 7-1 included the right to park vehicles next to the *kuleana* property. In *Haiku Plantations Association v. Lono* (1980),[53] residential leasehold owners of the upper portion of Ha'ikū filed an action for declaratory relief against the owner of a *kuleana* parcel within 'Ioleka'a, an *'ili* that is landlocked *mauka* of Ha'ikū, to determine the access rights of each of the parties.[54] The court held that while an easement for access to the *kuleana* existed, it did not include a right to park vehicles along the easement.[55]

Subsequently, the Intermediate Court of Appeals in *Rodgers v. Pedro* (1982), as previously discussed, held that a landowner could establish a right of access under section 7-1 if the parcel is (1) landlocked and (2) a *kuleana* or other ancient tenancy whose origin is traceable to the *Mahele*.[56] Since neither party in *Pedro* disputed the *kuleana* owner's chain of title, the court entered judgment in favor of the *kuleana* owner.[57]

A second statutory basis for securing access to *kuleana* parcels can be found in Haw. Rev. Stat. section 1-1, which provides that:

> The common law of England, as ascertained by English and American decisions, is declared to be the common law of the State of Hawaii in all cases, except as otherwise expressly provided by the Constitution or laws of the United States, or by the laws of the State, *or fixed by Hawaiian judicial precedent, or established by Hawaiian usage* . . . .[58] (Emphasis added.)

215

However, this section has never been used by the Hawai'i courts in a *kuleana* access case. It has been interpreted in other decisions as supporting certain native tenant rights.[59] Consequently, it remains a viable basis for asserting *kuleana* access rights.

(3)   *Constitutional Basis*   In November 1978, Hawai'i's State Constitution was amended by Hawai'i's voters. Among the sections approved was Article XII, section 7:

> The State reaffirms and shall protect all rights, customarily and traditionally exercised for subsistence, cultural and religious purposes and possessed by ahupua'a tenants who are descendants of native Hawaiians who inhabited the Hawaiian Islands prior to 1778, subject to the right of the State to regulate such rights.[60]

Although this section could be interpreted to include *kuleana* access rights, no Hawai'i cases have applied this section specifically for this purpose.[61] The plain language of Article XII, section 7, however, indicates that such rights would be limited to those tenants who are of Hawaiian ancestry, unlike the rights under Haw. Rev. Stat. section 7-1, which have been interpreted to apply to any person who lawfully occupies a *kuleana* parcel or is a lawful tenant of the *ahupua'a*.[62]

b.   *Access Between* Ahupua'a *or Districts*

There appears to be statutory protection for access to and along trails running across government property.[63] With regard to private land, however, there are several theories that Native Hawaiians can utilize to assert their rights to access along existing trails.[64]

(1)   *Common Law Theories*
(a)   *Custom*   The doctrine of custom, which recognizes uses or rights that have been exercised for long periods of time and have been commonly consented to, developed in feudal England. One justification for the doctrine was the theory that a centuries-old usage must have been founded on a legal right and conferred in the distant past.[65] In determining whether a specific right or use is based on custom, the use must be (1) ancient; (2) exercised without interruption; (3) peaceable and free from dispute; (4) reasonable; (5) certain; (6) applied uniformly to all lands similarly situated; and (7) not repugnant to other customs or other laws.[66] The custom doctrine has been applied in other jurisdictions to provide public rights-of-way to beaches.[67]

In Hawai'i, the supreme court has not applied the common law custom doctrine to public access along Hawaiian trails. In *Oni v. Meek* (1858), one basis upon which tenant Oni claimed a right of pasturage was custom.[68] While such a right may have been accepted in England,[69] the Hawai'i Supreme Court rejected the argument in *Oni*, finding it repugnant to existing Hawai'i property laws.[70] The Intermediate Court of Appeals, in *Haiku Plantations Association v. Lono* (1980), did not reach the issue of whether the right to park vehicles on lands next to a *kuleana* parcel was customary, finding no evidence that vehicles were actually parked in historic times on the right-of-way.[71]

One Hawai'i case, however, has held that a right established by custom does exist for use of Hawaiian trails. In *Barba v. Okuna* (1980),[72] fishermen and certain residents of Ka'ū filed suit against a private landowner to establish access to Hawaiian shoreline trails as well as along a government road running through the landowner's property. The trial court found, among other things, that such trails were used by Hawaiians in prehistoric times to move from place to place and that such use continued through to the present and was not inconsistent with Hawai'i's existing property laws.[73] The trial court concluded that the fishermen and residents had shown that a right-of-way over the Hawaiian trail was established by custom.[74] On appeal, the supreme court affirmed the trial court's holding without publishing an opinion.[75] Although the supreme court has not officially recognized the doctrine as it relates to access, *Barba* does indicate that customary use is a viable doctrine in Hawai'i.

(b) *Implied Dedication of Public Right-of-Way* A second theory used to establish access along Hawaiian trails is implied dedication of a public right-of-way across private land. In *King v. Cornwell* (1869),[76] the Hawaiian government prosecuted defendant Cornwell for erecting a fence over a public highway. Cornwell claimed, among other things, that the highway was not "public."[77] The court found that two elements are required to establish an implied dedication: (1) an intention and act of dedication by the property owner; and (2) an acceptance by the public.[78] The court further stated that if public use is the *only* evidence of a dedication, then such use must be for 20 years,[79] the statutory period required to show a prescriptive use at the time.

Courts in other jurisdictions have held that an intent to dedicate by the owner may be express, implied-in-fact, or implied-in-law.[80] Intent is express if it is manifested by a deed, or by any other oral or written manifestation that is consistent with statute.[81] Intent may be implied-in-fact if the public has used the trail for a period less than the prescriptive period but the owner has consented to its use.[82] A court may find an implied-in-law dedication where the owner has merely acquiesced to use, but the public has used the property for longer than the statutory prescriptive period and has enjoyed substantial benefit from the use of the land.[83] Implied-in-fact dedication focuses on the owner's intent while the public's actual use of the trail is the focus of implied-in-law dedication.

In addition to the elements stated in *Cornwell*, other jurisdictions have considered the following factors in finding implied dedication: (1) use by more than one public group or individual members; (2) continuous use; (3) knowledge of use, either actual or constructive, on the part of the owner; (4) use sufficient to satisfy the statutory period required for adverse possession; (5) acceptance by the public, either by actual use or by maintenance of the trail; (6) failure of the owner to affirmatively assert that the public has no property right to the land; and (7) acquiescence by the owner during the statutory period required for adverse possession.[84]

(c) *Public Trust Doctrine* A third possible legal theory for securing access along Hawaiian trails is the public trust doctrine. The doctrine stems from the ancient English principle that all submerged and tidal lands are owned in fee by the king, but are held in trust for the common use of the people.[85] Under this doctrine, all public lands and interests in land are held in trust by a state or municipality for the benefit of the people and must be preserved and maintained for public purposes.[86]

The public trust doctrine is well recognized in Hawai'i law, and has been used to: (1) lay public claim to navigable waters;[87] (2) insure the public's right to take fish;[88] (3) claim lava extensions as public land;[89] (4) claim lands below the high reaches of the waves as a natural resource owned by the state in trust for the enjoyment of the public;[90] and (5) declare that water is a resource which the state must manage for the common good.[91]

The public trust doctrine may also be applicable to establish public ownership and the public's right to access along ancient Hawaiian trails.[92] Prior to the creation of private property rights, trails, like all lands of the Hawaiian kingdom, were held by the king in trust for the people in common.[93] In adopting a private property system the king, in his sovereign capacity, retained his interests in all ancient trails and held such interests in trust for the benefit of the public. Pursuant to the Principles Adopted by the Board of Land Commissioners,[94] certain sovereign prerogatives could not be conveyed away by the board:

> What is the nature and extent of that power which the King has bestowed upon this board? It can be no other than his private or feudatory right as an individual participant in the ownership, *not* his sovereign prerogatives as head of the nation. Among those prerogatives which affect lands, are the following:
>
> . . . .
>
> 3rd. To encourage and even to enforce the usufruct of lands for the common good.
> 4th. To provide public thoroughfares and easements, by means of roads, bridges, streets, etc., for the common good.
>
> . . . .
>
> These prerogatives, powers and duties, His Majesty ought not, and ergo, he cannot surrender. Hence the following confirmations of the board, and *the titles consequent upon them must be understood subject to these conditions.*[95] (Emphasis added.)

Under these principles, public trails and rights-of-way are specifically reserved, and can also be deemed as important usufructs of land. This public trust status attached to public trails, highways, and rights-of-way continued through the territorial period to the present. While the Hawai'i Supreme Court has never specifically applied the public trust doctrine to trails, it would be a logical extension of existing public trust law to do so.

(2) *Statutory Basis* Haw. Rev. Stat. chapter 264, section 1, formerly known as the Highways Act of 1892, was amended in 1988 to specifically define public trails within the state. Section 264-1(b) provides:

> All trails, and other nonvehicular rights-of-way in the State declared to be public rights-of-ways, by the highways act of 1892, or opened, laid out, or built by the government or otherwise created or vested as nonvehicular public rights-of-way at any time thereafter, or in the future, are declared to be public trails. A public trail is under the jurisdiction of the state board of land and natural resources unless it was created by or dedicated to a particular county, in which case it shall be under the jurisdiction of that county.[96]

Although no cases have interpreted subsection (b), the plain language suggests that an ancient trail becomes public if: (1) it was a public right-of-way at the time the Highways Act of 1892 passed; or (2) it was built by the government; or (3) it became a public right-of-way subsequent to passage of either the 1892 Act or subsection (b).

A trail became a public right-of-way under the Highways Act of 1892 if it was either dedicated, surrendered, or abandoned to the government.[97] Usually dedication was by deed from a private landowner to the government.[98] Surrender or abandonment of a privately owned trail occurred when the owner exercised no act of ownership over the trail for a period of five years after the passage of the Highways Act in 1892.[99] If there has been a dedication, surrender, or abandonment by the private owner, fee ownership of the trail vests in the government. Two Hawai'i Supreme Court cases have discussed what constitutes sufficient proof to show surrender of a roadway to the government.

In the case of *In re Hawaiian Trust Co.* (1906),[100] the Territory of Hawai'i appealed from a decree of the land court granting the territory an easement over a certain roadway. The territory claimed that since the easement had been used for more than five years following the passage of the 1892 Highways Act, fee simple title to the roadway vested automatically in the territory.[101] The only evidence presented at trial, however, was that the road was used by the public as early as 1853.[102] The Hawai'i Supreme Court held that a mere legislative enactment could not vest title in the territory and that the fee could only be acquired by the territory through condemnation, or by the owner's consent, express or implied.[103] While there was evidence to establish that the territory had acquired an easement in the roadway, the court held that in the absence of further affirmative acts of surrender, the territory did not acquire the fee simple title to the road.[104]

In the case of *In re Kelley* (1968),[105] Kelley, an owner of fee simple beach front property near Ka'alāwai, O'ahu, petitioned the land court to register lands fronting his property, which he claimed extended to the shoreline. The evidence showed that the original owner had sold the subject property in 1885 to Kelley's predecessor-in-interest, but had delineated the *makai* boundaries of the property as going to "*the mauka side of the road near the sea*[.]"[106] Other evidence showed that a deed executed in 1884 to a parcel adjoining Kelley's had expressly reserved to the government a 50-foot-wide right-of-way running *mauka* of the shoreline alongside Kelley's property.[107] The court held, among other things, that if an owner had surrendered, by affirmative act, a highway to the government five years *prior* to the passage of the 1892 Highways Act, the highway automatically became government property upon passage of the act; formal acceptance by the government was not necessary.[108] Since the evidence showed that the owner adjoining Kelley's property dedicated the roadway to the government in his 1884 deed and that, by the 1885 deed, Kelley's predecessor-in-interest acquired property situated *mauka* of the road, the court held that title to the roadway vested with the government.[109]

Another possible means of protecting access along Hawaiian trails is through the Hawaiian usage exception under Haw. Rev. Stat. section 1-1, as previously discussed. However, no cases have yet interpreted section 1-1 with regard to public access along Hawaiian trails.

In 1988, Haw. Rev. Stat. chapter 198D was adopted to establish a state-wide trail and access system known as *Na Ala Hele*.[110] To establish and maintain this system, the state's Department of Land and Natural Resources (DLNR) has been directed to: (1) inventory all the existing trails located in the state;[111] (2) adopt rules to regulate the use of trails and accesses;[112] (3) identify areas which have inadequate access;[113] and (4) acquire additional trails and accesses in areas with inadequate access to enhance the state-wide trail and access system.[114] To date, an inventory has not been completed. However, it is anticipated that once inventoried under this system, trails and access along such trails will be protected and enforced by the DLNR.

5.   CONCLUSION

Access rights in Hawai'i are based on a mixture of Hawaiian custom and usage, English common law, and statutory and constitutional provisions. For the most part, Native Hawaiians hold access rights in common with members of the general public. However,

Native Hawaiians also have unique access rights arising under the state constitution relating to the exercise of traditional and customary rights as *ahupua'a* tenants.

The law regarding access to *kuleana* parcels is well established in Hawai'i statutory and case law. While it is clear that owners of *kuleana* parcels enjoy an unrestricted right of access to their property as either an express grant, an implied easement by necessity, or by statute, there are still many landlocked *kuleana*. Access to a *kuleana* will usually be by way of a trail that has existed since the *Mahele*, or earlier, and which subsequently may have been modified for vehicular traffic. Implicit in cases decided by Hawai'i courts is that usage may be enlarged to include any reasonably foreseeable changes in the use of the dominant parcel. This is a general principle in the law of easements and has been adopted by other jurisdictions.

However, even if there is no evidence of a trail or roadway either on old maps or on the ground, *ahupua'a* tenants still have access rights to their *kuleana* under Haw. Rev. Stat. section 7-1 and the doctrine of easement by necessity. In such cases, a court can designate the location and width of the access or right-of-way. Unfortunately, this is a time consuming and expensive process. Moreover, many *kuleana* owners do not have the finances to pursue this type of court action.

The law regarding access to the mountains and sea, and between *ahupua'a* or districts, is less well-defined. Although there are no Hawai'i Supreme Court cases which deal directly with the issue of access and protection of trails which run between two or more *ahupua'a* or districts, such rights can be established under the theories of common law custom, implied dedication, the public trust doctrine, and under Haw. Rev. Stat. sections 264-1 and 1-1. In addition, cases which discuss the preservation of highways under Haw. Rev. Stat. section 264-1 could extend to ancient trails. An issue that remains unresolved is the proof required to establish a surrender or abandonment of ownership to the public.

The recent enactment of statutes to establish a statewide trail system is a positive sign for the future preservation of traditional trails and access routes. With increased development, however, it will be more difficult for Native Hawaiians, as well as the general public, to assert and maintain their access rights.

NOTES

1. R.A. Apple, *Trails: From Steppingstones to Kerbstones* 1 (1965).
2. E.S.C. Handy and M.K. Pukui, *The Polynesian Family System in Ka'u, Hawaii* 5 (1958).
3. E.S.C. Handy and E.G. Handy, *Native Planters in Old Hawaii* 321-24, 325-26 (1972).
4. *See* Apple, *supra* note 1, at 28.
5. *See* Handy and Handy, *supra* note 3.
6. *See* Apple, *supra* note 1.
7. *Id.* at 9-17.
8. *See* Handy and Handy, *supra* note 3, at 489-491.
9. *Id.*
10. *See* Apple, *supra* note 1, at 1, 2, 17.
11. S.M. Kamakau, *Ka Po'e Kahiko: The People of Old* 14-17 (1964).
12. R. Kuykendall, *The Hawaiian Kingdom, 1854-1874*, at 3-11 (1938).
13. *See* Apple, *supra* note 1, at 33, 43.
14. *Id.* at 45.
15. *Id.*

16. *Id*. at 33-35, 60.

17. *See, e.g., Jones v. Meek*, 2 Haw. 9, 12 (1857).

18. R.R. Powell, 3 *Powell on Real Property* Para. 404 (1987).

19. *Id*. at Para. 415, 416.

20. *Id*. at Para. 404.

21. *Rogers v. Pedro*, 3 Haw. App. 136, 138 n.3, 652 P.2d 549, 551 n.3 (1982); *Palama v. Sheehan*, 50 Haw. 298, 300, 440 P.2d 95, 97 (1968). *But see Liliuokalani v. Territory*, 14 Haw. 88, 95 (1902), interpreting the phrase "*koe nae ke kuleana o na kanaka*" to refer only to *kuleana* house lots and taro patches occupied and farmed by tenants.

22. 3 Haw. App. 136, 642 P.2d 549 (1982).

23. *Id*. at 138, 642 P.2d at 551.

24. *Id*. at 139, 642 P.2d at 552.

25. 9 Haw. 191 (1893).

26. *Id*. at 194.

27. *Id*. at 193.

28. *Id*. at 192.

29. *Id.*

30. *Id*. at 194.

31. 9 Haw. 490 (1894).

32. *Id*. at 491.

33. *Id*. at 492.

34. 2 *Revised Laws of Hawaii, 1925*, at 2141.

35. Haw. Rev. Stat. § 7-1 (1985).

36. 3 Privy Council Record 713 (1850).

37. 3 Privy Council Record 763 (1850).

38. 2 Haw. 87 (1858).

39. *Id*. at 91-95.

40. *Id.*

41. *Id*. at 94.

42. *Id.*

43. *Id*. at 95.

44. *Id.*

45. *Id.*

46. 50 Haw. 298, 440 P.2d 95 (1968).

47. *Id*. at 298, 440 P.2d at 96.

48. *Id.*

49. *Id*. at 301, 440 P.2d at 97-98.

50. *Id.*

51. *Id*. at 303, 440 P.2d at 99.

52. *Id.*

53. 1 Haw. App. 263, 618 P.2d 312 (1980).

54. *Id*. at 265, 618 P.2d at 312-313.

55. *Id*. at 266, 618 P.2d at 314.

56. 3 Haw. App. 136, 139, 642 P.2d 549, 551-552 (1982).

57. *Id*. at 140, 642 P.2d at 552.

58. Haw. Rev. Stat. § 1-1 (1985).

59. *See Kalipi v. Hawaiian Trust Co.*, 66 Haw. 1, 9-10, 656 P.2d 745, 750-751 (1982).

60. Haw. Const. art. XII, § 7.

61. *But see Kalipi v. Hawaiian Trust Co.*, 66 Haw. 1, 5-9, 656 P.2d 745, 748-750 (1982).

62. *Oni v. Meek*, 2 Haw. 87, 95-96 (1858).

63. *See* Haw. Rev. Stat. § 171-26 (1985); Haw. Rev. Stat. § 198D (1989 Supp.).

64. Other legal theories such as public prescriptive easements, or implied reservation of an easement in the public are plausible. However, since Hawai'i has not, as of this writing, adopted either theory, they will not be discussed in this chapter.

65. McKeon, *Public Access to Beaches*, 22 Stan. L. Rev. 564, 583 (1970).

66. W. Blackstone, 1 *Commentaries on the Laws of England* 75-78 (1979 ed.).

67.   *See State Ex. Rel. Thornton v. Hay*, 254 Or. 584, 462 P.2d 671 (1969).

68.   2 Haw. 87, 89-91 (1858).

69.   Gray, *The Rule Against Perpetuities* 577 n.2 (4th ed. 1942); McKeon, *Public Access to Beaches, supra* note 65, at 582.

70.   2 Haw. 87, 90 (1858).

71.   1 Haw. App. 263, 267, 618 P.2d 312, 314 (1980).

72.   No. 4590 (3rd Cir., Oct. 14, 1980).

73.   *Id*. at 10-19.

74.   *Id*. at 24-25.

75.   *Barba v. Okuna*, No. 8160, mem. (Dec. 3, 1982).

76.   3 Haw. 154 (1869).

77.   *Id*. at 158.

78.   *Id*. at 161.

79.   *Id*. at 162.

80.   *See, e.g., Gion v. City of Santa Cruz*, 2 Cal. 3d 29, 84 Cal. Rptr. 162, 465 P.2d 50 (1970); *Seaway Co. v. Attorney General*, 375 S.W.2d 923 (Tex. Civ. App. 1964).

81.   R.R. Powell, 6 *Powell on Real Property* Para. 935 (1987).

82.   *Gion v. City of Santa Cruz*, 2 Cal. 3d 29, 38, 84 Cal. Rptr. 162, 167, 465 P.2d 50, 55 (1970).

83.   *Id*. at 29, 38-39.

84.   *See King v. Cornwell*, 3 Haw. 154, 162 (1869); Note, *The Acquisition of Easements by the Public through Use*, 16 S.D. L. Rev. 150, 153 (1971).

85.   *See Bishop v. Mahiko*, 35 Haw. 608, 645-46 (1940).

86.   *See* McQuillan, *Municipal Corporations*, §§ 10.31, 28.38 (1981); Sax, *The Public Trust Doctrine in Natural Resource Law: Effective Judicial Intervention*, 68 Mich. L. Rev. 471 (1970).

87.   *King v. Oahu Railway and Land Co.*, 11 Haw. 717 (1899).

88.   *Bishop v. Mahiko*, 35 Haw. 608 (1940).

89.   *State v. Zimring*, 58 Haw. 106, 121, 566 P.2d 725, 737 (1977).

90.   *Bishop v. Mahiko*, 35 Haw. 608, 647 (1940); *County of Hawaii v. Sotomura*, 55 Haw. 176, 183-184, 517 P.2d 57, 62-63 (1973).

91.   *McBryde Sugar Co. v. Robinson*, 54 Haw. 174, 186-87, 504 P.2d 1330, 1338-1339 (1973); *Reppun v. Board of Water Supply*, 65 Haw. 531, 544, 656 P.2d 57, 66 (1982).

92.   *See generally* Town and Yuen, *Public Access to Beaches in Hawaii: "A Social Necessity,"* 10 Hawaii Bar Journal 3, 25-28 (1973).

93.   *State v. Zimring*, 58 Haw. 106, 111, 566 P.2d 725, 729 (1977).

94.   Act of October 26, 1846, 2 *Revised Laws of Hawaii, 1925*, at 2124-2137.

95.   2 *Revised Laws of Hawaii, 1925*, at 2128.

96.   Haw. Rev. Stat. § 264-1(b) (1989 Supp.).

97.   *See id.* § 264-1(c)1-2.

98.   *Id.*

99.   *Id.*

100.   17 Haw. 523 (1906).

101.   *Id*. at 524.

102.   *Id*. at 523. *See In re Kelley*, 50 Haw. 567, 580 n.4, 445 P.2d 538, 546 n.4 (1968).

103.   17 Haw 523 (1906).

104.   *Id*. at 524-525.

105.   50 Haw. 567, 445 P.2d 538 (1968).

106.   *Id*. at 570, 445 P.2d at 541.

107.   *Id.*

108.   *Id*. at 579-80, 445 P.2d 546-547.

109.   *Id*. at 581, 445 P.2d 547.

110.   Act 236, L. 1988.

111.   Haw. Rev. Stat. § 198D-3, 198D-4 (1989 Supp.).

112.   *Id*. at § 198D-6.

113.   *Id*. at § 198D-5.

114.   *Id*. at § 198D-8.

CHAPTER 11

GATHERING RIGHTS

1.   INTRODUCTION

In early Native Hawaiian life, gathering activities served to supplement the everyday food and medicinal supplies of the people. Hawaiians often cultivated various crops in the mountain areas and gathered both cultivated and non-cultivated items. Other food supplies and resources were gathered at the seashore. The laws at the time of the *Mahele* and immediately thereafter recognized the importance of such gathering rights to the native people. However, early case law restricted native tenants' rights[1] and over the years, the tension between Western private property concepts and the exercise of native gathering rights has resulted in increasing limitations on those rights.

2.   ANCIENT HAWAIIAN GATHERING SYSTEM

Gathering activities, primarily dependent upon access rights, appear to have served at least three important purposes in early Hawai'i. First, gathering allowed the tenant farmer to supplement a subsistence lifestyle with plants and animals that either could not grow or could not be supported on or near the tenant's houselot or cultivated plot of land.[2] In this instance, gathering included items for both medicinal as well as religious purposes. Second, gathering allowed the tenants within an *ahupua'a*, when called upon by the resident chief, to retrieve large products from the land for communal purposes, such as a tree for a canoe or rafters for a *hālau*.[3] Third, during times of famine, gathering helped the people to survive. When crops or sea life had diminished significantly due to drought or other adverse climate conditions, gathering or foraging for food became the primary means of survival for Hawaiians.[4]

Early Hawaiians gathered both cultivated and non-cultivated items and the type of items gathered varied from one *ahupua'a* to the next depending upon the availability of the item. In the uplands above the plains and in the lower forests, Hawaiians usually cultivated plants such as taro and yam, *pi'a, 'ōlena, 'ohe, olonā* and *'awa*.[5] These items served to supplement the tenants' lifestyle at home. Other plants, such as the *'ōhi'a lehua, māmaki,* and *'awapuhi* were gathered growing in the wild. These items had medicinal, ornamental, practical, and aesthetic as well as ceremonial uses.[6] In Hawai'i's streams, Hawaiians would gather *'o'opu, 'ōpae,* and *hihiwai* for food.[7] Hunting was also considered a form of gathering as Hawaiians went hunting for feral pigs.[8]

Gathering, however, was not limited to the uplands. Along the sea coast and in the ocean, Hawaiians would gather items such as *limu, 'opihi, wana,* and other marine products to supplement their daily diet.[9] Fish, the primary source of protein for Hawaiians, was also gathered in areas ranging from coral reef beds to deep water.[10] As one early Westerner commented:

Hawaiian life vibrated from uka, mountain, whence came wood, kapa, for clothing, olona, for fishline, ti-leaf for wrapping paper, ie for ratan lashing, wild birds for food, to the kai, sea, whence came ia, fish, and all connected therewith.[11]

While early Hawaiians may have cultivated only small areas compared to the total acreage on each major island, they were able to utilize much greater land areas through gathering.

As with access along trails, little has been written by Hawaiian scholars regarding the *kapu*, or rules and regulations, surrounding gathering practices. Several conclusions, however, can be reached about such *kapu*. Apart from their religious significance, the *kapu* served as an efficient means of conserving resources. For instance, with regard to sea gathering practices, there was a *kapu* placed on deep water fishes such as the *aku* and the *ʻōpelu* during spawning season.[12] Such fish were susceptible to overfishing since they bore their young in the open ocean and not in protected tidal pool areas as did the *manini, uhu, palani* or *kala*.[13] Since many *kapu* were imposed by the chiefs, the size, type and number of items gathered, as well as the manner in which they were gathered, were probably established by the resident chief. A higher ranking chief, however, could overrule a lower chief's *kapu*. One Hawaiian scholar noted that Queen Kaʻahumanu, a high chiefess and wife of Kamehameha I, sometimes allowed the people on Oʻahu to gather fish that were usually reserved for the chiefs.[14]

The earliest attempt to establish uniform gathering practices on all islands emerged with the codification of laws in 1839.[15] Many of these laws were, no doubt, a carry-over from the *kapu* system. In the laws of 1839, gathering practices were established for both the uplands as well as the sea. The laws of 1839 allowed a tenant use of the *ahupuaʻa* to gather items subject, however, to several reservations.[16] First, the *konohiki* or resident chief, was allowed to reserve one kind of tree for exclusive use.[17] This kind of tree must be non-cultivated, and growing in the wild.[18] If a tree reserved by the *konohiki* was taken, the law of 1839 required that the tenant split the haul equally with the *konohiki*.[19] A second reservation was imposed by King Kamehameha III and prohibited the taking of sandalwood until the king lifted the decree.[20] A third reservation prohibited the taking of any tree by the tenant, and presumably by the *konohiki*, that was so large a man could not place his arms completely around it, unless the tree was taken to make a canoe or paddles.[21] Finally, the native *ʻōʻō* and *mamo* birds were reserved exclusively for the king.[22]

The laws of 1839 also imposed restrictions with regard to sea life. The tenants and common people were allowed unrestricted fishing in the ocean waters beyond the fringing reef.[23] The area between the shoreline and the fringing reef, however, was subject to regulation by the *konohiki* and only tenants could fish therein. The *konohiki* was allowed to reserve one kind of sea life that lived in this area, usually either fish or squid.[24] If a tenant took a restricted sea life, the tenant could not fish in the area for a period of two years.[25] If the *konohiki* restricted fishing rights or collected a portion of the fish caught by tenants, then the *kapu* fish of the *konohiki* could be fished by the tenants unrestricted for one year.[26] In addition to the restriction placed by the *konohiki*, the king imposed a restriction by either exclusively reserving entire fishing districts or by placing a restriction on certain kinds of fish within selected districts on each major island.[27] Unlike the "shore-to-reef" regulation, however, the king's restriction applied regardless of the area that the fish frequented.

3. WESTERN INFLUENCE

Several factors appear to have contributed to the decline in gathering practices by Hawaiians. With the arrival of Westerners, the islands' subsistence economy dramatically changed. The first major change probably occurred in the early 1800s when Hawai'i's sandalwood was discovered as an exportable crop to the Orient. Resident chiefs, attracted by Western products offered in exchange for sandalwood, immediately began to summon tenants into the uplands to harvest and transport the sandalwood to the trading ships.[28] While the sandalwood trade probably did not have an immediate impact on the tenants' ability to gather other products upland, the continual demand by resident chiefs for Western products greatly increased over a period of time, resulting in many tenants neglecting their own fields as well as their health.[29] The once prized sandalwood eventually became a curse, as both men and women tenants worked from dawn till dusk cutting sandalwood. To end this "curse," women would pull up young sandalwood seedlings so that their children would not be required to continue the arduous task of harvesting sandalwood.[30] At the height of trading, sandalwood produced enough income for Kamehameha I to buy six foreign ships.[31] The laws of 1839 restricted sandalwood to the exclusive use of the king. Any person cutting sandalwood or breaking young seedlings without permission of the king would be fined 100 house rafters, each rafter being five yards long.[32]

A second major change occurred when sugar, and then pineapple, became Hawai'i's major cultivated export crops. Since large tracts of land were required for these crops, many *ahupua'a* had to be cleared for this purpose. Early Hawaiians raised plants in small areas in the mountains. These small fields, as well as uncultivated areas rich in plants and herbs used by Hawaiians, were destroyed in the clearing process. The total acreage used in this manner has not been recorded, but given the number and size of plantations on each major island during the late 19th and early 20th Centuries, there was undoubtedly a significant effect on the ability of tenants to exercise gathering rights.[33] Moreover, the introduction of cattle and goats into the islands, together with the clearing of large tracts of land for ranching operations, also played an important role in the decrease of traditional gathering practices.[34] Finally, as Hawai'i changed from a subsistence to a mercantile economy, tenants abandoned their subsistence lifestyle and traveled to the cities to take up other jobs, contributing to the decline of traditional gathering practices.

4. PRESENT-DAY GATHERING RIGHTS

a. *Gathering Rights of Native Tenants*

Although there are no cases that directly address gathering rights of early Hawaiians, the Hawai'i Supreme Court has generally recognized the existence of such rights in its early decisions. For instance, in the case of *In re Boundaries of Pulehunui* (1879),[35] the court stated:

> A principle very largely obtaining in these divisions of territory [*ahupua'a*] was that a land should run from the sea to the mountains, thus affording to the chief and his people a fishery residence at the warm seaside, together with the products of the high lands, such as fuel, canoe timber, mountain birds, and the right of way to the same, and all the varied products of the intermediate land as might be suitable to the soil and climate of the different altitudes from sea soil to mountainside or top.[36]

More than a century after the *Mahele*, the supreme court finally addressed the gathering rights of native tenants in *Kalipi v. Hawaiian Trust Co.* (1982).[37] In that case, Kalipi, who owned a taro field in Manawai and an adjoining houselot in 'Ohi'a, Moloka'i, filed suit against owners of the *ahupua'a* of Manawai and 'Ohi'a when he was denied unrestricted gathering rights in both *ahupua'a*. Kalipi sought to gather certain items for subsistence and medicinal purposes.[38]

(1)   *Statutory Basis* One basis Kalipi asserted for his rights to gather was the Hawaiian usage exception set forth in Hawai'i Revised Statutes (Haw. Rev. Stat.), section 1-1.[39] This section declares the common law of England to be the law of Hawai'i "except as otherwise expressly provided by the Constitution or laws of the United States, *or by the laws of the State,* or *fixed by Hawaiian judicial precedent, or established by Hawaiian usage* . . . ."[40] (Emphasis added.) The court interpreted the Hawaiian usage exception as allowing for "native understandings and practices which did not unreasonably interfere with the spirit of the common law."[41] The court stated that to determine whether such Hawaiian practices would interfere with recognized property interests involved "balancing the respective interests and harm once it is established that the application of the custom has continued in a particular area" on a case-by-case basis.[42] However, because there was an insufficient basis to find that gathering rights customarily extended to persons who did not reside within the *ahupua'a* in which the rights are claimed, and because Kalipi was not a resident of the *ahupua'a* at the time the case was heard, the court held that he could not assert gathering rights under section 1-1.[43]

Kalipi's second claim stemmed from section 7 of the *Kuleana* Act (now Haw. Rev. Stat. section 7-1).[44] Section 7-1 specifically enumerates certain items which can be gathered within an *ahupua'a* by a native tenant: firewood, house-timber, *aho* cord, thatch, or *ki*-leaf.[45] The court held that in order to assert a right to gather under section 7-1, three conditions must be satisfied: (1) the tenant must physically reside within the *ahupua'a* from which the item is being gathered; (2) the right to gather can only be exercised upon undeveloped lands within an *ahupua'a*; and (3) the right must be exercised for the purpose of practicing Native Hawaiian customs and traditions.[46] Although the second condition was not stated in the statute, the court reasoned that it must be deemed a condition precedent to the exercise of such rights since gathering on developed lands would conflict with Western concepts of property law as well as the traditional "Hawaiian way of life" in which the "cooperation and non-interference with the well-being of other residents were integral parts of the culture."[47] Under the court's view, only if all conditions were satisfied would a tenant be allowed to gather and even then such gathering would be restricted solely to those items expressly enumerated in the statute.[48] The court held, however, that Kalipi did not meet the first condition because he did not physically reside within the *ahupua'a* of Manawai or 'Ohi'a, and thus could not assert rights under section 7-1.[49]

In summary, *Kalipi* reaffirmed the traditional gathering rights of *ahupua'a* tenants. While the items listed in Haw. Rev. Stat. section 7-1 are limited to materials primarily used for constructing a house or starting a fire, Haw. Rev. Stat. section 1-1 as interpreted by *Kalipi,* has the potential of expanding tenants' gathering rights. This could include gathering materials which are essential to the tenants' lifestyle, such as medicinal plants, and could even lead to limited upland subsistence farming as practiced by early Hawaiians. In addition, section 1-1 could be interpreted to include the right to gather plants and animals which were introduced after 1778 (*e.g., kiawe* or *koa haole* wood, hunting for feral goat, sheep, cattle or deer), but which have been gradually incorporated over time into the tenants' lifestyle.

(2) *Constitutional Basis*   Article XII, section 7 of the Hawai'i State Constitution, discussed in the previous chapter on access rights, could provide an additional basis for asserting traditional gathering practices. The plain language of the constitutional provision, however, limits claims to those tenants who are of Hawaiian ancestry. This language is narrower in focus than Hawai'i Supreme Court cases, which have held that the rights of a tenant would attach to any person who lawfully occupies a *kuleana* parcel or lawfully resides in the *ahupua'a*.[50]

b.   *Rights of Non-residents*

It is clear from *Kalipi* that Haw. Rev. Stat. section 7-1 rights only apply to tenants who reside within an *ahupua'a*. It is possible that gathering rights of non-residents could be asserted under other legal theories such as the customary rights doctrine of Haw. Rev. Stat. section 1-1 if it could be shown that Hawaiian custom allowed gathering by non-residents under limited conditions.

5.   CONCLUSION

The *Kalipi* decision left many questions unanswered and indicated that the Hawai'i Supreme Court would examine the unique factual situation of each case in order to determine whether native gathering rights conflict with Western concepts of private property. The court appeared to believe that in situations where private property interests would be affected, gathering rights must be limited. As rural areas of the islands become increasingly more populated and developed, native gatherers may not be able to obtain the necessary resources within their own *ahupua'a* and will be forced to gather in *ahupua'a* in which they do not reside. The 1978 constitutional amendment protecting *ahupua'a* tenant rights and Haw. Rev. Stat. section 1-1 may provide a basis for such expanded gathering practices if it can be shown that these practices were customary in early Hawaiian society. Nevertheless, it is clear that in spite of the 1978 constitutional amendment, in the coming decade Native Hawaiian gathering rights could be restricted to an even greater extent by the imposition of Western private property concepts.

NOTES

1.   *See Oni v. Meek*, 2 Haw. 87 (1858).
2.   *See generally* E.S.C. Handy and E.G. Handy, *Native Planters in Old Hawaii* (1972).
3.   E.S.C. Handy and M.K. Pukui, *The Polynesian Family System in Ka'u, Hawaii* 216-19 (1958).
4.   *Id.* at 224; *see also* Handy and Handy, *supra* note 2, at 234-35.
5.   Handy and Pukui, *supra* note 3, at 223.
6.   *See* Handy and Handy, *supra* note 2, at 236-42.
7.   Titcomb, *Native Use of Fish in Hawaii* 4 (1983).
8.   *See* Handy and Handy, *supra* note 2, at 253.
9.   *Id.* at 304.

10. Titcomb, *supra* note 7, at 1.

11. C.J. Lyons, *Land Matters in Hawaii No. 1*, 1 The Islander 103 (1875).

12. *See* Titcomb, *supra* note 7, at 13-14.

13. *Id*. at 14.

14. *See id.* at 16.

15. *The Declaration of Rights and the Laws Regulating Property in Hawaiian for these Hawaiian Islands*, promulgated by King Kamehameha III (1840). *See also* L. Thurston, *The Fundamental Law of Hawaii* 21-23 (1904).

16. *See generally, id*. at 6.

17. *Id*. at 22.

18. *Id.*

19. *Id.*

20. *Id*. at 22-23.

21. *Id.*

22. *Id.*

23. *Id*. at 6.

24. *Id.*

25. *Id.*

26. *Id*. at 6-7.

27. *Id*. at 7. These areas were as follows: (1) O'ahu: the districts of Kalia, Ke'ehi, Kapapa, Malaeakuli and Pahihi. (2) Moloka'i: the districts of Punalau, O'oia, Kawai, Koholanui, Kaonini, Aiko'olua. (3) Lana'i: the districts of Kaunolu (*aku* only), Kaohai (*uhu* only). (4) Maui: the districts of Honua'ula (*akule* only) and other districts having *akule*. (5) Hawai'i: all districts that have *ahi*. (6) Kaua'i: all districts that have transient fish where fishermen have caught two or more canoe loads. (This *kapu* would equally apply to all transient schools of fish belonging to the kingdom.)

28. *See* Handy and Pukui, *supra* note 3, at 234-35.

29. *Id.*; R. Kuykendall, *The Hawaiian Kingdom, 1778-1854*, 89-90 (1938).

30. *Id*. 89-90.

31. *Id*. at 87.

32. *See* Titcomb, *supra* note 7, at 23.

33. R.C. Schmitt, *Historical Statistics of Hawaii* 293 (1977).

34. *See generally* Kuykendall *supra* note 29.

35. 4 Haw. 239 (1879).

36. *Id*. at 241.

37. 66 Haw. 1, 656 P.2d 745 (1982).

38. *Id*. at 3-4, 656 P.2d at 747.

39. *Id*. at 9, 656 P.2d at 750.

40. Haw. Rev. Stat. § 1-1 (1985).

41. 66 Haw. at 10, 656 P.2d at 750-751.

42. *Id.* This test as applied to gathering rights would probably include access rights as well.

43. *Id*. at 12, 656 P.2d at 752.

44. *Id*. at 5, 656 P.2d at 748.

45. *See* Haw. Rev. Stat. § 7-1 (1985).

46. 66 Haw. at 7-8, 656 P.2d at 745-750; for a discussion of who is a lawful resident within an *ahupua'a, see* *Dowsett v. Maukeala*, 10 Haw. 166 (1895).

47. 66 Haw. at 8-9, 656 P.2d at 750.

48. *Id.*

49. *Id*. at 9, 656 P.2d at 750.

50. *See, e.g., Haalelea v. Montgomery*, 2 Haw. 62, 71-72 (1858).

CHAPTER 12

RELIGIOUS FREEDOM

1.   INTRODUCTION

The Free Exercise Clause of the First Amendment to the United States Constitution guarantees to citizens the freedom to practice their religion. The United States Supreme Court, however, in recent decisions has narrowed the scope of Free Exercise Clause protection, rendering Native Hawaiian religious freedom in serious jeopardy. Even the American Indian Religious Freedom Act, passed by congress in 1978 in recognition of the inherent right of Native Americans to the free exercise of religion, appears devoid of meaningful protection.

The Hawai'i State Constitution guarantees freedom of religion in language almost identical to the federal constitutional provision. Moreover, Article XII, section 7 of the state constitution specifically protects the rights of Native Hawaiian *ahupua'a* tenants to practice their religion. However, neither of these provisions has provided any greater protection to Native Hawaiians than the Free Exercise Clause.

After a brief review of Native Hawaiian religion, this chapter will discuss the Free Exercise Clause, the American Indian Religious Freedom Act, and the state constitutional provisions, and trace their impact on the exercise of Native Hawaiian religion.

2.   NATIVE HAWAIIAN RELIGION

To attempt a detailed description or definition of Hawaiian religious concepts and practices is beyond the scope of this work and certainly beyond the knowledge of the authors. However, based on the works of those with greater knowledge, the following is offered as a brief synopsis of major Hawaiian religious concepts.

In Hawaiian thought, life was not confined to physical existence or to the concrete world felt and seen by the physical body. Life continued after death, in the spiritual realm, and physical life was viewed as a place of preparation for the after life. All human beings had "spiritual origin, material birth, and spiritual eternity of complete unceasing existence."[1] Thus, besides the *kino* or physical body, an individual also had a second separable spirit[2] which could move during sleep, and the *'uhane* or eternal spirit which survived death.[3]

Native Hawaiian religion rested upon a basic belief in spirits and the realm of the spirit. Spirits, in the form of the *akua* or gods, and spirits in the form of the *'aumākua* or family guardians, were involved in every aspect of life. In farming, fishing, tapa making, dancing, sports, or any activity of Hawaiian life, Hawaiians were able to ask for the guidance and support of the appropriate *akua* or *'aumakua*.[4] To Hawaiians, religion was a way of life.[5]

According to *The Kumulipo*, a genealogical prayer chant linking the last ruling monarchs of Hawai'i to the primary deities, *Papa* and *Wākea* were the identified progenitors of all Hawaiians.[6] Each of the four major *akua* of the Hawaiian religious system, *Kū, Kāne, Lono*, and *Kanaloa*, governed an aspect of Hawaiian life.[7] These four *akua* personified the natural forces and were generally referred to with an epithet signifying the particular force being invoked.[8] Since many of the same attributes characterized each *akua*, the particular human activity involved determined to which deity an appeal would be made.[9]

Kū, the male generating power and god of medicine and war, had the most elaborate *heiau* or temples.[10] As the god of war, *Kū* required human sacrifice for the most important rituals.[11] Amongst the best known manifestations of *Kū* are *Kūkā'ilimoku* (*Kū* the snatcher of land), the war god of the 'Umi-Kamehameha line of chiefs; *Kūkeoloewa* (*Kū* the supporter), the god of the Maui chiefs; and *Kū'ulakai* (*Kū* of the abundant red things of the sea), the god of fishermen.[12]

Kāne, the procreator, the god of life, fresh water, sunlight, and all natural phenomena occurring in the sky,[13] had more than 70 forms. These include *Kānenuiākea* (*Kāne* of the broad expanse), the maker of heaven, earth, and the things that filled them; *Kānehoalani* (*Kāne* of the heavens); and *Kānehekili* (*Kāne* of thunder), the god of thunder.[14] Unlike *Kū*, *Kāne* allowed no human sacrifices during his worship.[15]

Lono, the god of peace, agriculture, fertility, and medicine, is most well known as the patron of the *Makahiki* and god of the first fruits of the season.[16] The *Makahiki* occurred during the rainy season of the year.[17] It was the time when the *ali'i* collected their share of the produce and, since war was prohibited during the *Makahiki* season, there was leisure for sports and games. *Heiau* called *māpele* were dedicated to *Lono* and were used to pray for rain, fertility, and abundant crops.[18] Pigs and products of the land were offered on the *māpele*, but never human sacrifices.

Kanaloa, the god of the ocean and ocean winds, is most closely associated with *Kāne*.[19] They often traveled together in their human forms opening up springs of fresh water.

Hawaiians had numerous other *akua*, most representing some aspect of nature.[20] These *akua* include *Pele*, goddess of fire and the volcano.[21] *Pele*, who had come from lands to the south seeking a home in Hawai'i, traveled down the island chain from Kaua'i to the Big Island, testing each volcano until she and her family finally settled at Kīlauea on the island of Hawai'i. *Pele* was also a feared sorceress, able to assume contrasting forms.[22] She displaced the older god *'Aila'au*, the wood eater, as the god of fire.[23]

Pele had many brothers and sisters who were deities in their own right, but the most famous were her brother, *Kamohoali'i*, the shark god, and *Hi'iaka-i-ka-poli-o-Pele*, *Pele*'s youngest sister.[24] *Hi'iaka* undertook a long and arduous journey to Kaua'i to bring *Pele*'s lover, *Lohi'au*, to her side at Kīlauea.[25] The chants and *hula* telling of *Hi'iaka*'s journey form an epic story as intricate and moving as any of the great sagas of the world.

In Hawai'i, as in much of Polynesia, an ancient line of *mo'o* or lizard deities was worshipped. While the female *mo'o* most often were guardians and protectors, the male *mo'o* were usually fierce and to be feared. The guardian *mo'o* include *Mo'oinanea*, the matriarch of all *mo'o* gods and goddesses; *Kihawahine*, a Maui chiefess who, after death, became a lizard goddess; and *Hauwahine*, the guardian of Kawainui Fishpond at Kailua, O'ahu.[26]

There were also numerous deities of the arts and crafts including *Kapo* and *Laka*, the patron deities of the *hula*; *Lea*, goddess of canoe makers; *Ha'inakolo*, goddess of *kapa* makers and bird catchers; *Maikohā*, the god of *kapa* makers; and *Ma'iola*, a god of healing.[27]

In addition to the *akua*, Hawaiians also worshipped *ʻaumākua* or personal gods transferred through ancestral history and unique to a particular family or *ʻohana*.[28] Hawaiians not only worshipped the *ʻaumākua*, but considered themselves related to their *ʻaumākua*.[29] Most *ʻaumākua* had been respected and wise humans who, after death, were able to offer advice and guidance. As one author states:

> The bond between humans and their personal, ancestral gods was very real. By the age of seven a child was expected to say his own prayers to his *ʻaumākua*. His family and his *ʻaumākua* expected him to refrain from breaking the laws of the many gods, to observe and obey the *kapu* pronounced by the chiefs and *kāhuna* and to be a helpful person and refrain from hurting his fellow men in any way.[30]

Akua and *ʻaumākua* manifested themselves in *kinolau*, or numerous earthly forms, as animals, plants, or forces of nature.[31] The *ʻaumākua* especially could be called upon for aid in difficult times. Many stories are told of the shark, owl, or lizard *ʻaumākua* rescuing families from peril.[32] To Hawaiians, the soul existed separate from the body.[33] *ʻAumākua* worship, therefore, embodied the concept of spirit worship in which each family carried its own accounts concerning the association between the spirit and particular animals, plants, or natural forces.[34]

Hawaiian religion also encompassed ceremonies and rites, and a prescribed code of behavior. Basic to these was the concept of *mana*, the animating force of all life forms.[35] *Mana* was strongest in the *akua*, the high chiefs, and the *kāhuna* or priests. However, all persons, places and things had *mana* either as active or dormant energy.[36] *Mana* could increase or decrease and was transferable. Thus, many actions were performed in order to preserve or increase *mana*. *Mana* could be used for either good or evil and the mere strength of one's *mana* did not guarantee the bounty of eternal life.[37] "No spirit (*ʻuhane*) of man or woman ascends into the spiritual life guaranteed into eternity except by *pono*, which means duty, responsibility, justice, and righteousness. Without *pono* no good life for mankind either on earth or beyond earth develops."[38] Professor Rubellite Johnson has defined *mana* as the three-fold manifestation of power:

(1) The *mana* or supernatural power of sacred spiritual beings;

(2) The *mana* of human beings which could be inherited by descent from the gods and *aliʻi* or acquired by intelligence and goodness (*pono*); and

(3) The residual *mana* resting in sacred objects.[39]

One way of imparting *mana* was through performance of ceremonies and rites.[40] Through chanting, prayer, or human sacrifice, the *mana* of the gods could exist in persons or objects.[41] *Kāhuna* directed *mana* by using a ritual.[42] Ritual preserved and protected the concept of *mana* to such a large extent that even after the overthrow of the early Hawaiian religious system, belief in the power of certain rituals remained.[43] To the Native Hawaiian, ritual was a vital link to *mana* and thus to the entire religious system.[44]

The *kapu* system, a complex structure of rules and laws, protected the *mana* of individuals and places, and prevented *mana* from harming others.[45] It manifested in many ways. A major impact was in the relationship between humans and the gods, where the various *kinolau* of the gods were *kapu* to followers and the *kinolau* of a family's *ʻaumākua* were *kapu* to family members.[46] Another example of the *kapu* system involved the relationship between men and women, where members of the opposite sex were not allowed to eat together.[47] It has been argued that the *kapu* system imposed severe hardships on

Hawaiians, eventually leading to its abolishment.[48] However, *kapu* also regulated the conservation of natural resources and undoubtedly served a vital function in preserving the Hawaiian social structure.[49]

In 1819, the *kapu* system was abolished by the breaking of the *'ai kapu*, the eating law which forbade men and women to eat together.[50] The young King Liholiho (Kamehameha II) and his brother Kauikeauoli (later Kamehameha III) publicly ate with the chiefesses Ka'ahumanu and Keōpūolani, who were the surviving wives of Kamehameha I. Subsequently Liholiho ordered the destruction of the temple images. However, the *kapu* system could not have been abolished without the support of the priesthood, and indeed, the high priest Hewahewa has been identified as the moving force behind abolishment of the *kapu* system.[51] While there was a strong opposition movement led by the *kahuna* Kekuaokalani, a nephew of Kamehameha I, against abolishing the *kapu*, the movement was defeated in late 1819.[52] The Christian missionaries arrived a few months later.

While the *kapu* system itself vanished, certain basic Hawaiian religious concepts have remained. These include the concept of *mana* or sacredness attached to places, persons, or things, *aloha 'āina* or respect and love for the *'āina* and its natural resources, and the reverence and honor due the ancient gods of Hawai'i and the *'aumākua* of each family. Today, these religious beliefs and the practices which actualize them continue to permeate Native Hawaiian life.

3. THE FREE EXERCISE CLAUSE

a. *History*

Since religion is a way of life for Native Hawaiians, its protection in modern times is of paramount concern. The freedom of Hawaiians to practice their native religion is secured by the Free Exercise Clause of the First Amendment to the U.S. Constitution, which states that "Congress shall make no law respecting an establishment of religion, or prohibiting the free exercise thereof . . . ."[53] Despite its apparently clear language, courts have given the Free Exercise Clause various interpretations. The original meaning of the clause, as evidenced by the intention of its drafters, is uncertain.[54] History, however, provides some clues regarding the purpose of the Free Exercise Clause. The drafters were well aware of the longstanding European conflict between government and religion.[55] The drafters also saw the decline in the establishment of state churches and a rise in toleration for other religious sects.[56] Given this historical context, it is likely that the Free Exercise Clause was intended to prohibit restrictions being placed on less popular religious groups in order to bolster a particular religion or belief.[57] It is also clear that the clause was designed to forbid federal interference in the religious exercise of any denomination.[58]

b. *Early Judicial Interpretation*

The free exercise of religion guaranteed by the First Amendment is not unlimited. In *Reynolds v. United States* (1878),[59] the first case to examine the Free Exercise Clause, the United States Supreme Court made a distinction between religious belief and religious practice.

In *Reynolds*, members of the Mormon Church challenged a federal law prohibiting polygamy, a practice required under Mormon doctrine. Reynolds was married to two women simultaneously in violation of the statute.[60] The court rejected the argument that the Free Exercise Clause protected Reynolds from punishment and held that the clause protected religious belief and opinion but not necessarily religious practice.[61] By its decision, the court adopted Thomas Jefferson's narrow view of religious freedom, which allowed belief but did not protect action even if religiously motivated.[62] The court further reasoned that congress had the power to forbid subversive religious practices and concluded that criminalizing polygamy was a legitimate expression of congressional power.[63]

In *Cantwell v. Connecticut* (1940),[64] the supreme court modified the strict action-belief dichotomy advanced in *Reynolds*. The court acknowledged that freedom to believe was absolute.[65] However, the court also stated that restraints on the freedom to act could not be unduly restrictive.[66] Thus, in subsequent cases, courts focused on whether government restraints were reasonable or unduly restrictive.

In *Braunfeld v. Brown* (1961),[67] the supreme court applied the *Cantwell* approach to decide a challenge to Pennsylvania's Sunday closing law by Orthodox Jewish merchants. The merchants claimed that the closing law seriously infringed on free exercise of their religion and imposed financial hardships on their businesses.[68] The state law coupled with the Jewish religious requirement of a Saturday Sabbath resulted in a weekend closing for the merchants. The court held that while religious action was protected, the state law requiring Sunday closing only incidentally burdened the free exercise of religion.[69] Furthermore, in *Braunfeld*, the court made its own determination that state legislative action was reasonable, resulting in only very limited free exercise protection.[70]

In *Reynolds, Cantwell,* and *Braunfeld,* the supreme court established that religious belief was absolutely protected, but religious action was subject to some restriction. However, free exercise restrictions by the government had to be "reasonable."

c. *Compelling Interest Test*

This course took an abrupt turn in *Sherbert v. Verner* (1963).[71] In *Sherbert*, a Seventh Day Adventist member was denied unemployment benefits after she lost her job for refusing to work on the Saturday Sabbath.[72] The U.S. Supreme Court held that the state's denial of unemployment compensation was a serious burden on the free exercise of religion and required the state to show a compelling interest for its action.[73] This standard contrasted greatly with the reasonableness standard used in prior cases. *Sherbert* also established that if the effect of a statute hinders religious observance, then it is unconstitutional.[74]

State courts followed *Sherbert*'s lead. In *People v. Woody* (1964),[75] a group of Navajo Indians challenged a California statute proscribing the possession of peyote.[76] The California Supreme Court found that the statute imposed a burden on Navajo religion since peyote "constitutes in itself an object of worship[.]"[77] The court further held that no compelling state interest existed to justify the ban on religious use of peyote.[78] Fifteen years later, the Alaska Supreme Court would also rely on *Sherbert* in allowing Athabascan Indians to transport illegally obtained game for use in religious ceremonies.[79]

Nine years after *Sherbert*, in *Wisconsin v. Yoder* (1972),[80] the U.S. Supreme Court again relied upon the compelling interest test. In *Yoder*, members of the Amish sect refused to permit their children to continue formal education beyond the eighth grade.[81] The Amish valued and practiced agricultural work and feared higher education would endanger their children's salvation.[82] Their refusal to allow their children to attend school, however, violated Wisconsin's compulsory school attendance laws.[83]

The court first reviewed the burden imposed by the school attendance law on Amish religion. In so doing, it determined that the law placed a very serious burden on Amish religion.[84] The court then held that the state's interest in education was not sufficiently compelling to overcome the Free Exercise Clause protection of Amish religious practices.[85] The court's detail of Amish life and reliance on expert testimony, however, suggested that Free Exercise Clause protection might prevail only on the unique facts found in *Yoder*.[86] Nonetheless, the decision was a major advance over the action-belief dichotomy of *Reynolds* and reasonableness test advanced in *Braunfeld*.

d. *Modern Interpretation*

The contradictory aspects of *Yoder*, its holding and strong language protecting religious conduct combined with its pronounced reliance on unusual facts, presented a problem for post-*Yoder* courts.[87] Consequently, federal courts often adopted inconsistent interpretations of the Free Exercise Clause and the compelling state interest test.

In *Palmer v. Board of Education of City of Chicago* (1979),[88] the compelling state interest requirement was significantly diminished. *Palmer* involved a teacher whose religious beliefs prevented her from engaging in certain classroom activities.[89] The board of education terminated Palmer's employment based on her conduct.[90] The Seventh Circuit Court of Appeals affirmed the lower court's grant of summary judgment for the board of education.[91] Both courts virtually dispensed with any analysis of the state interest involved. In fact, the lower court's language indicated an outright assumption that a compelling state interest existed.[92]

The Sixth Circuit Court of Appeals, relying on *Yoder*, also took a restrictive view of Free Exercise Clause protection. In *Sequoyah v. Tennessee Valley Authority* (1980),[93] the Cherokee Indian Nation sought an injunction against the proposed impoundment of a reservoir. The Cherokee claimed the impoundment would flood and destroy sacred sites.[94] In considering this claim, the Sixth Circuit required the Indians to show that religious practice in the area was central or vital to Cherokee religion.[95] Following the implication in *Yoder* that religion must be both organized and founded on external authority, the Sixth Circuit also considered whether the Indian religious conviction was held by an organized group.[96] The Sixth Circuit found the evidence insufficient to meet the two tests it had formulated.[97] By imposing these requirements, the court placed the rights of native religious practitioners, and other religious sects outside of the Judeo-Christian tradition, in jeopardy.

In another situation, the United States Supreme Court seemingly broadened the basis for establishing religiously motivated conduct. In *Thomas v. Review Board of the Indiana Employment Security Division* (1981),[98] a Jehovah's Witness was deemed ineligible for state unemployment benefits because he had quit his position at a military manufacturing plant due to his religious beliefs against the production of war materials.[99] Another Jehovah's Witness had not objected to the activity.[100] The court held that free exercise protection applied even though the particular religious belief involved was not shared by all Jehovah's Witnesses.[101] Based on *Thomas*, it appeared that religious beliefs, even though not uniformly held by all members of a religious group, were a protectible interest under the Free Exercise Clause.

These three cases showed a lack of clear guidance in the post-*Yoder* era. The compelling state interest determination established in *Sherbert* and *Yoder* appeared to provide little protection to free religious exercise after the decision in *Palmer*. *Thomas* and

Sequoyah seemed to be inconsistent. Under *Sequoyah*, religious practice had to be central to religion, but *Thomas* held that religious belief need not be consistent among religious group members. These cases provided little instruction on the scope of free exercise protection. They also foreshadowed the current direction of free exercise analysis.

e. *The American Indian Religious Freedom Act*

The free exercise of Native American religions gained significant recognition in 1978 when congress passed the American Indian Religious Freedom Act (AIRFA).[102] The act states that:

> [I]t shall be the policy of the United States to protect and preserve for American Indians their inherent right of freedom to believe, express, and exercise the traditional religions of the American Indian, Eskimo, Aleut and Native Hawaiians, including but not limited to access to sites, use and possession of sacred objects, and the freedom to worship through ceremonials and traditional rites.[103]

The express purpose of AIRFA was to require that federal policies comply with the constitutional mandate of free exercise of religion.[104] Section 2 of AIRFA illustrates this purpose by instructing federal agencies to consult with native religious leaders concerning the changes in policies or practices necessary to preserve traditional religions.

Despite its congressional directive to safeguard traditional religious practices, AIRFA has afforded little protection. In *Badoni v. Higginson* (1980),[105] Navajo Indians raised free exercise and AIRFA violations in the government's management of the Rainbow Bridge National Monument and the Glen Canyon Dam and Reservoir.[106] The Navajo claimed the government infringed on religious practices by impounding water in Lake Powell and drowning certain Navajo gods, and by permitting tourists to frequent a sacred area.[107] The Tenth Circuit Court of Appeals held that with regard to the flooding of Lake Powell, the government was sufficiently justified in its actions since the water supply of four states was affected. As to the second claim, the court found no legal basis for excluding the public from the sacred area.[108] It dispensed with the Indians' AIRFA claim with little discussion.[109]

Wilson v. Block (1983)[110] provided a better opportunity to determine the effectiveness of AIRFA. In *Wilson*, the Navajo and Hopi Indian tribes resisted the expansion of a skiing area known as the Snow Bowl located in the San Francisco Peaks. The Peaks, visible from both the Hopi and Navajo Reservations, are sacred to the tribes. The Hopi believe the Kachinas, spiritual emissaries from the Creator, live on the Peaks and create the rain which sustains the Hopi villages. The Navajos also believe the Peaks are one of four sacred mountains and the home of certain deities. Both tribes collect herbs and plants from the area, and the Navajo perform religious ceremonies in the mountains. After finding no burden on religious beliefs or practices, the D.C. Circuit Court of Appeals stated that AIRFA did not require "native traditional religious considerations always to prevail to the exclusion of all else."[111] According to the court, the American Indian Religious Freedom Act clearly did not require deference to Indian religious concerns.

AIRFA also received minor attention in *Crow v. Gullet* (1983).[112] Leaders of the Lakota and Tsistsistas Nations sought injunctive relief against state construction and development at Bear Butte, an important religious site used for various religious ceremonies including the Lakota's vision quest.[113] The Eighth Circuit Court of Appeals concluded that the state's actions did not infringe upon Indian religious practices.[114] Furthermore, the court found that AIRFA's provisions created no legal rights or cause of action independent of the First Amendment.[115] AIRFA appeared a hollow shield for traditional native religions.

These early cases invoking the American Indian Religious Freedom Act demonstrate the act's shortcomings in furnishing substantial free exercise protection.[116] Only in situations involving failure by a federal agency to investigate charges of misconduct associated with free exercise claims has AIRFA served its intended function.[117]

4.   FREE EXERCISE PROTECTION TODAY

a.   *Recent U.S. Supreme Court Decisions*

Given the seemingly inconsistent treatment of free exercise claims in post-*Yoder* cases and the judicially confining interpretation of AIRFA, recent cases have offered an opportunity to dispel past ambiguities in both areas. Unfortunately, recent cases have increasingly limited free exercise protection.

In a 1986 case, *Bowen v. Roy*,[118] the U.S. Supreme Court considered whether the Free Exercise Clause compelled the government to exempt an Indian welfare recipient from having to obtain a statutorily required social security number.[119] An Indian couple had refused to acquire a social security number for their daughter based on religious grounds.[120] The court held that the Free Exercise Clause did not require an exemption under the circumstances.[121] In reaching its decision, the court distinguished the statutory conditions in *Sherbert* and *Thomas*, cases involving unemployment compensation benefits, from the "facially neutral" and uniformly applied provisions requiring a social security number.[122] Furthermore, the court believed the social security number prerequisite furthered a valid public interest.[123]

However, in a subsequent unemployment compensation case, *Hobbie v. Unemployment Appeals Commission of Florida* (1987),[124] the supreme court surprisingly reverted to its earlier decisions, finding *Sherbert* and *Thomas* controlling. In *Hobbie*, a member of the Seventh Day Adventist Church was discharged for refusing to work on the Saturday Sabbath.[125] The employee was later denied unemployment benefits because her refusal to work constituted misconduct.[126] Based on *Sherbert* and *Thomas*, the court failed to find any compelling state interest sufficient to justify the burden on religious freedom.[127] As a result, the court held that denial of unemployment benefits violated the Free Exercise Clause.[128] One portion of the decision also extended free exercise protection to those religious beliefs adopted *after* employment is obtained.[129]

Free exercise protection was dealt a severe blow by the court's decision in *Lyng v. Northwest Indian Cemetery Protective Association* (1988).[130] In *Lyng*, members of three Northwestern California Indian tribes sought to halt construction and development of a road by the United States Forest Service in a sacred area.[131] A study commissioned by the Forest Service documented the importance of the area to Indian religious practice and recommended no further construction of the planned Gasquet to Orleans roadway.[132] The Forest Service ignored this recommendation, prompting a series of legal disputes.[133]

The U.S. Supreme Court reversed the Ninth Circuit's decision, which had permanently halted construction.[134] The court relied on *Bowen v. Roy* in holding that the Free Exercise Clause did not preclude the Forest Service from conducting activities affecting

Indian religion.[135] According to the court, no distinction existed between the social security number requirement in *Roy* and the construction of a railroad or harvest of timber on lands having religious significance.[136] It believed that neither instance of government action violated religious belief or penalized religious activity.[137]

Another significant consequence of *Lyng* was the court's disregard of the "effects" test established in *Sherbert* and followed in *Yoder, Thomas,* and *Hobbie.* These precedents require that the effect of government action on free exercise of religious rights be assessed. If there is a burden on free exercise, then the government must show a compelling state interest. Instead of applying this accepted analysis, the court confined free exercise protection only to situations where government conduct *coerces* violations of religious beliefs or *penalizes* individuals for their religious beliefs.[138] However, applying a standard of coercion or penalty undoubtedly restricts the application of free exercise protection to a narrow range of cases.

Lyng also departed from *Thomas* and *Hobbie* by seeming to require unanimity of religious belief, where those cases appeared to dispel any need for such unanimity among members of religious sects. In *Lyng,* however, the court suggested that the lack of unanimous Indian opposition to the construction illustrated only a minimal impact on Indian religion.[139] Contrary to earlier precedent, the court subjected the Indians to a higher level of factual proof by imposing the unanimity of belief requirement.

The *Lyng* court also resolved any ambiguity concerning the American Indian Religious Freedom Act. In response to the argument that AIRFA authorized the injunction entered by the lower court, the court stated that AIRFA was not a source of legal rights or a cause of action.[140] Such a glaring expression of AIRFA's ineffectiveness stands in stark contrast to congress' intent in adopting it.

The most recent and profound limitation on free exercise protection was announced by the U.S. Supreme Court in *Oregon Employment Division v. Smith* (1990).[141] Two members of the Native American Church, one a Klamath Indian and the other a non-Indian, were fired from their jobs as drug counselors because each ingested a small amount of peyote at church ceremonies. One of the job requirements was that counselors be drug-free. Moreover, under Oregon law, those fired for "misconduct connected with work" are not entitled to receive unemployment compensation. The two church members were denied unemployment compensation on that basis. The state appeals court, in a decision upheld by the Oregon Supreme Court, held that denying unemployment compensation substantially burdened the employees' rights to exercise their religion.

On review in the U.S. Supreme Court in 1988,[142] the case was remanded to the Oregon Supreme Court to determine whether the use of peyote for religious purposes was a crime under Oregon law. The court reasoned that this information was necessary to determine the federal question since, if the state could jail the employees for use of peyote, it could impose lesser penalties including the denial of unemployment compensation.[143]

On remand,[144] the Oregon Supreme Court determined that sacramental use of peyote violated, and was not exempted from, the state's criminal law prohibition.[145] The court refused to decide whether the state criminal law violated the state constitution, but did find the state law prohibition was invalid under the federal constitution's Free Exercise Clause.

In a six-to-three decision issued in April of 1990, the U.S. Supreme Court held that the Free Exercise Clause allows the state to prohibit religious use of peyote and Oregon could deny unemployment benefits to persons discharged for peyote use, even if the use was of a sacramental nature. The court determined that while banning the performance of physical acts (such as ingesting peyote) *solely* because of their religious motivation would be a violation of the Free Exercise Clause, the clause does not relieve individuals of the obligation to comply with a law that only incidentally forbids the performance of the act if the law is not specifically directed to religious practice and is otherwise constitutional.[146] Moreover, the court rejected the balancing test set forth in *Sherbert* and subsequent cases since that test was developed in a context -- unemployment compensation eligibility rules -- which lent itself to individualized assessment.[147] The balancing test would be inapplicable, the court reasoned, to an across-the-board prohibition of a particular form of conduct. Finally, the court concluded that while it is constitutionally permissible for a state to exempt religious peyote use from the operation of drug laws, it is not constitutionally required.[148]

b. *The Free Exercise of Religion in Hawai'i*

In Hawai'i, Native Hawaiian religious freedom claims initially have arisen in the context of access to sacred lands. In *United States v. Mowat* (1978),[149] several members of the Protect Kaho'olawe 'Ohana were charged with trespassing upon Kaho'olawe Island, contrary to federal statutes and regulations. Based on regulations, entry onto Kaho'olawe was banned without advance consent by the Commandant of the Fourteenth Naval District. Defendants claimed access based upon free exercise of religion. However, the Ninth Circuit Court of Appeals concluded that requiring advance approval before entry was not unreasonable as Kaho'olawe was used as a bombing target area and might contain live unexploded ordnance which could put trespassers at risk. This risk outweighed any burden on free exercise of religion. The case did not specify exactly what religious ceremonial activities were to be practiced on the island by the defendants, but the religious, cultural, and historical significance of Kaho'olawe to Native Hawaiians is similar to the claims made by Indians in *Badoni* and *Sequoyah* regarding Indian sacred lands. Citing *Sherbert*, the court in *Mowat* found that the proper standard would be to balance the burden placed on defendants' free exercise of religion against the government's interests. The court concluded that "the compelling Government interest . . . in keeping outsiders off dangerous land . . . outweighs any burden on defendants' free exercise of religion."[150]

In *Aluli v. Brown* (1977),[151] Kaho'olawe was also at issue. In this case, plaintiffs sought to stop military bombing of the island and to prevent further destruction of archeological sites of religious and historical significance to Native Hawaiians. Although the federal district court denied an injunction, it required the military to file annual environmental impact statements pursuant to the National Environmental Policy Act (NEPA), 42 U.S.C. section 4321. The court stated:

> An action that significantly affects the quality of the human environment is one that either directly affects human beings or indirectly affects human beings through adverse effects on the environment . . . .
>
> . . . [A]n EIS must consider the possible effects of major federal actions upon historic and cultural resources . . . . 89 archeological sites [have been discovered so far] on Kahoolawe which . . . [are of] possible importance to Hawaiian history and culture . . . . [A]n adverse effect upon the archeological sites *may* have a direct effect upon human beings; for example the plaintiffs. Regardless, the court believes that an adverse effect upon the sites would be an adverse effect upon the environment which would have an indirect effect on human beings . . . .

[D]efendants' . . . bombardment of Kahoolawe is a major federal action significantly affecting the quality of the human environment.[152]

While the court did not support the plaintiffs on their religious exercise claim, the court reminded the government that even archeological sites are important to the welfare of human beings and every effort must be made to follow the mandate of NEPA. Subsequently, however, the U.S. District Court's ruling, requiring the filing of an environmental impact statement every year, was reversed.[153]

Hawai'i state courts have had limited opportunity to invoke Free Exercise Clause analysis. Moreover, they have never interpreted the requirements of the state constitutional provision on free exercise of religion to extend greater protection than the federal provision.[154] For the most part, Hawai'i courts have applied the *Yoder* test by examining the legitimacy of the religious belief involved, the burden on the religious belief, the impact on religious practices and the existence of a compelling state interest.[155]

In *State v. Lono* (1985),[156] members of the Temple of Lono were arrested and charged with camping without a permit at Kualoa Regional Park. Kualoa is a sacred site and the location of an ancient *heiau* dedicated to *Lono*. Park regulations did not allow extended camping periods and temple members had entered and remained in the park for periods from three weeks to four months in order to perform various ceremonies. One of the religious practices involved sitting in a meditative state until experiencing *hō'ike a ka pō* or night visions, which provide inspiration and guidance. In their defense, temple members challenged the park regulation as an infringement upon religious freedom. The trial court determined that defendants' "religious interest in participating in dreams at Kualoa Regional Park are not indispensable to the Hawaiian religious practices, and further the Defendants' practices in exercising their religious beliefs . . . are philosophical and personal and therefore not entitled to First Amendment protection."[157] The Hawai'i Supreme Court also gave short shrift to the religious freedom argument, affirming the trial court in a memorandum opinion.

In the most recent case dealing with the exercise of Native Hawaiian religion, *Dedman v. Board of Land and Natural Resources* (1987),[158] the Hawai'i Supreme Court applied the *Yoder* test. In *Dedman*, Native Hawaiians challenged a Board of Land and Natural Resources' (BLNR) decision permitting geothermal development in an area significant to native religious practitioners who honor the deity *Pele*.[159] The *Pele* practitioners claimed that the proposed development would impinge on their right to free religious exercise, since geothermal development requires drilling into the body of *Pele* and taking her energy and lifeblood.[160]

The Hawai'i Supreme Court first acknowledged the sincerity of the religious claims at issue.[161] It then considered whether the BLNR's approval of the proposed geothermal development would unconstitutionally infringe upon Native Hawaiian religious practice.[162] On this question, the court found controlling the absence of proof that religious ceremonies were held in the area proposed for development. Without evidence of a burden on the free exercise of native religion, the court did not reach the compelling state interest question. Accordingly, the court concluded that no Free Exercise Clause violation had occurred.[163]

The *Dedman* court's application of a narrow analysis of free exercise infringement accounted for its failure to find any burden on Native Hawaiian religious practices. Under the court's view, a burden on the free exercise of religion exists when government action regulates or directly impinges on Native Hawaiian religious practices. Furthermore, only government conduct which compelled irreverence of religious beliefs or penalized individuals for their religious actions would warrant free exercise protection. Certainly, few practitioners of native religion could meet this standard. Such a constricted approach consigns free exercise protection to the far end of a rapidly diminishing spectrum of native rights.

Any doubt concerning the *Dedman* court's constitutional analysis of free exercise protection dissolved with the U.S. Supreme Court's decision in *Lyng* and its subsequent refusal to review the Hawai'i Supreme Court's decision in *Dedman*.[164] *Lyng* reinforces the limited interpretation of the Free Exercise Clause advanced in *Dedman* and thereby places the unfettered practice of Native Hawaiian religion at serious risk. Moreover, the distinctiveness of Native Hawaiian religion, so different from traditional Judeo-Christian doctrines, makes it especially vulnerable and renders its continued protection under the Free Exercise Clause elusive.

In the *Dedman* case, the state constitutional amendment protecting traditional and customary rights of Native Hawaiian *ahupua'a* tenants was not specifically implicated. This may have been because those challenging the BLNR action did not claim to live within the *ahupua'a* where the land was located nor to have such rights. Thus, the Hawai'i courts have never interpreted this constitutional amendment in the context of a religious freedom claim.[165] Nevertheless, it is clear from the committee reports and floor debates on this amendment, that delegates to the 1978 Constitutional Convention were aware of and concerned about limitations placed by large landowners and government on access to traditional religious sites.[166] However, since the amendment's adoption in 1978, neither the state legislature nor individual state departments have enacted legislation or rules protecting traditional religious practices or access to sacred sites.

5.   CONCLUSION

The Free Exercise Clause of the First Amendment guarantees to Native Hawaiians the freedom to practice their religion. To Native Hawaiians, this includes the freedom to practice a way of life which acknowledges the sacredness of certain places, animals, and natural forces. The scope of free exercise protection, however, depends on how the courts have interpreted the Free Exercise Clause. Such interpretation has a long and varied history. Originally, the Free Exercise Clause, as interpreted in *Reynolds*, only shielded religious belief from government interference. *Sherbert* and *Yoder* combined to incorporate religiously motivated conduct within the ambit of free exercise protection. Those cases also established that government action which burdens religious freedom implicates free exercise protection. Both cases required the government to justify its conduct by demonstrating a compelling interest. In the *Lyng* case, however, the U.S. Supreme Court severely limited these established precedents. Free Exercise Clause protection now requires infringement born of coercion or penalty on religious freedom. *Lyng* also rendered the American Indian Religious Freedom Act, originally designed to protect and preserve traditional native religions, less effective than congress intended. The U.S. Supreme Court's most recent pronouncement in the *Smith* case casts an unsettling specter of doubt upon the survival and continued practice of native religions. In Hawai'i, the state constitution has not provided any greater protection for Native Hawaiian religion than the federal constitution. Strengthening the American Indian Religious Freedom Act and enforcing the 1978 state constitutional amendment protecting rights customarily and traditionally exercised by *ahupua'a* tenants for religious purposes appear to offer Native Hawaiians the greatest promise in attempts to safeguard their unique native religion.

NOTES

1. R.K. Johnson, *Native Hawaiian Religion*, in Native Hawaiians Study Commission, *Report on the Culture, Needs and Concerns of Native Hawaiians (Majority Report)* 226 (1983).

2. Some have termed this soul or spirit the *kino wailua*, but that term also has been applied to the spirit of a deceased person.

3. Johnson, *supra* note 1, at 226.

4. M. Pukui, *Hawaiian Religion* 1 (1963).

5. J. Mulholland, *Hawaii's Religions* 17 (1970).

6. M.W. Beckwith, *The Kumulipo* 118 (1951). There are several interpretations of *The Kumulipo*. One interpretation considers it an account of evolutionary development. Another suggests an analogy to conception and birth. W.H. Davenport, *The Religion of Pre-European Hawaii*, in 16 Social Process in Hawaii 20 (1952).

7. *Id.*

8. *Id.*

9. V. Valeri, *Kingship and Sacrifice* 14 (1985).

10. D. Mitchell, *Resource Units in Hawaiian Culture* 72 (1982).

11. *Id.*

12. *See* Johnson, *supra* note 1, at 235-237, for a listing of the numerous forms of *Kū*.

13. Mitchell, *supra* note 10, at 72.

14. *Id. See also* Johnson, *supra* note 1, at 239-241.

15. Davenport, *supra* note 6, at 26.

16. Mitchell, *supra* note 10, at 72.

17. Davenport, *supra* note 6, at 27.

18. Mitchell, *supra* note 10, at 73.

19. *Id.* at 73-74.

20. Mulholland, *supra* note 5, at 14.

21. N.B. Emerson, *Pele and Hiiaka -- A Myth* xxv-xxxii (Tuttle ed. 1978).

22. *See* Valeri, *supra* note 9, at 19.

23. Mitchell, *supra* note 10, at 75.

24. Emerson, *supra* note 21, at xxv-xxxii.

25. *See generally* Emerson, *supra* note 21, for the chants recounting this epic journey.

26. Mitchell, *supra* note 10, at 75.

27. *Id.*

28. *See* Mulholland, *supra* note 5, at 15 and Valeri, *supra* note 9, at 20.

29. *Id.*

30. Mitchell, *supra* note 10, at 77.

31. *See* Johnson, *supra* note 1, at 234-235 for a discussion of the *kinolau* concept.

32. *Id.*

33. *See* Davenport, *supra* note 6, at 22.

34. *Id.* at 23.

35. Johnson, *supra* note 1, at 228.

36. *Id.*

37. *Id.* at 229.

38. *Id.*

39. *Id.*

40. *See* Valeri, *supra* note 9, at 99. *Mana* was also imparted by descent or by both descent and ritual simultaneously.

41. *See* Mulholland, *supra* note 5, at 16-17.

42. *Id.*
43. *Id.*
44. *See* Davenport, *supra* note 6, at 22.
45. Mulholland, *supra* note 5, at 16.
46. Valeri, *supra* note 9, at 21.
47. *Id.* at 114.
48. Mulholland, *supra* note 5, at 16.
49. Mitchell, *supra* note 10, at 81.
50. *See however* Johnson, *supra* note 1, at 234, noting that there had been at least one prior breach by the *ali'i* of the *kapu* system.
51. *Id.*
52. A.I. Kroeber, *Cultural Patterns and Processes* 211-212 (1963).
53. U.S. Const. amend. I.
54. Pepper, *Reynolds, Yoder and Beyond: Alternatives for the Free Exercise Clause*, Utah L. Rev. 309, 311 (1981) [hereinafter *Alternatives*].
55. *Id.* at 312.
56. *Id.*
57. *Id.* at 313-314.
58. *Id.* at 313.
59. 98 U.S. 145 (1878).
60. *Id.* at 146.
61. *Id.* at 164.
62. *See Alternatives, supra* note 54, at 320-321.
63. *Reynolds v. U.S.*, 98 U.S. 145, 165-166 (1878).
64. 310 U.S. 296 (1940). The case involved members of the Jehovah's Witness sect who were convicted of solicitation under a state statute. The court reversed the conviction based on the Free Exercise Clause. *Id.* at 311.
65. *Id.* at 303-304.
66. *Id.* The court, however, failed to explain what constituted undue restrictions. *See Alternatives, supra* note 54, at 329.
67. 366 U.S. 599 (1961).
68. *Id.* at 601-602.
69. *Id.* at 605-607.
70. *See Alternatives, supra* note 54, at 331.
71. 374 U.S. 398 (1963).
72. *Id.* at 399-401.
73. *Id.* at 403.
74. *Id.* at 404, citing *Braunfeld v. Brown*, 366 U.S. 599, 607 (1961).
75. 61 Cal. 2d 716, 394 P.2d 813, 40 Cal. Rptr. 69 (1964).
76. 394 P.2d 813, 814-815.
77. *Id.* at 817.
78. *Id.* at 820.
79. *Frank v. State*, 604 P.2d 1068, 1074-1075 (Alaska 1979).
80. 406 U.S. 205 (1972).
81. *Id.* at 207-209.
82. *Id.*
83. *Id.*
84. *Id.* at 218-219. The court emphasized that the law burdened not only religious practice, but religion itself.
85. *Id.* at 228-229. In articulating the compelling interest test, the court stated: "The essence of all that has been said and written on the subject is that only those interests of the highest order and those not otherwise served can overbalance legitimate claims to the free exercise of religion." *Id.* at 215.
86. *See Alternatives, supra* note 54, at 333. The court itself recognized that only a handful of other religious groups could meet the requirements of Free Exercise Clause protection. 406 U.S. 205, 235-236 (1972).
87. Pepper, *The Conundrum of the Free Exercise Clause--Some Reflections on Recent Cases*, 9 N. Ky. L. Rev. 265, 267-268 (1982).
88. 466 F.Supp. 600 (1979), *aff'd*, 603 F.2d 1271 (7th Cir. 1979).

89. 466 F.Supp. 600, 601 (1979). Specifically, plaintiff Palmer refused to recite the pledge of allegiance, teach patriotic songs or organize activities celebrating common holidays.

90. *Id.* at 602.

91. 603 F.2d 1271, 1274 (1979).

92. *Palmer v. Board of Education of City of Chicago*, 466 F.Supp. 600, 603 (1979). To the district court, it was "self-evident" that the state had a compelling interest at stake.

93. 480 F.Supp. 608 (1979), *aff'd*, 620 F.2d 1159 (6th Cir. 1980), *cert. denied*, 449 U.S. 953 (1980).

94. 480 F.Supp. 608, 610 (1979).

95. 620 F.2d 1159, 1164 (6th Cir. 1980).

96. *Id.*

97. *Id.*

98. 450 U.S. 707 (1981).

99. *Id.* at 710-711.

100. *Id.* at 711.

101. *Id.* at 715-716.

102. 42 U.S.C. § 1996 (1982).

103. *Id.*

104. H.R. Rep. No. 1308, 95th Cong., 2d Sess. 2-3, *reprinted in* 1978 U.S. Code Cong. & Admin. News 1262.

105. 638 F.2d 172 (10th Cir. 1980).

106. *Id.* at 175.

107. *Id.* at 176.

108. *Id.* at 178-179.

109. *Id.* at 180.

110. 708 F.2d 735 (D.C. Cir. 1983), *cert. denied*, 464 U.S. 456 (1983).

111. 708 F.2d 735, 747 (1983).

112. 706 F.2d 856 (8th Cir. 1983) (per curiam).

113. *Id.* at 858.

114. *Id.*

115. *Id.*

116. The questionable effectiveness of the act has led to recent attempts to amend it. The proposed amendment protects the management of lands "historically indispensable" to Indian religion from interference.

117. *New Mexico Navajo Ranchers Association v. Interstate Commerce Commission*, 702 F.2d 227 (D.C. Cir. 1983) (per curiam).

118. 476 U.S. 693 (1986).

119. *Id.* at 695.

120. *Id.* The couple believed a social security number would "rob" their daughter's spirit.

121. *Id.* at 712.

122. *Id.* at 708.

123. *Id.* at 710-711.

124. 480 U.S. 136 (1987).

125. *Id.* at 138.

126. *Id.* at 139.

127. *Id.* at 140.

128. *Id.* at 141-142.

129. *Id.* at 143-144.

130. 485 U.S. 439 (1988).

131. *Id.* at 442-43

132. *Id.* at 441-443.

133. *Id.* at 443-445. *See Northwest Indian Cemetery Protective Association v. Petersen*, 565 F.Supp. 586, 595, 606 (N.D. Cal. 1983) (the court held that the Forest Service's development activities constituted a violation of the Free Exercise Clause and permanently enjoined construction of the road); *see Northwest Indian Cemetery Protective Association v. Petersen*, 795 F.2d 688, 698 (9th Cir. 1986) (the Ninth Circuit upheld the district court's grant of a permanent injunction).

134. *Lyng v. Northwest Indian Cemetery Protective Association*, 485 U.S. 439, 458 (1988).

135. *Id.* at 447-453.

136. *Id.* at 449-453.

137. *Id.*
138. *Id.*
139. *Id.* at 451-452.
140. *Id.* at 454-455.
141. 1990 WL 42783 (U.S. April 17, 1990).
142. *Oregon Employment Div. v. Smith*, 485 U.S. 660 (1988).
143. *Id.* at 673-674.
144. *Oregon Employment Div. v. Smith*, 307 Ore. 68, 763 P.2d 146 (1988).
145. *Id.* at 72-73, 763 P.2d at 148.
146. 1990 WL 42713, at 11 (U.S. April 17, 1990).
147. *Id.* at 17.
148. *Id.* at 21-22.
149. 582 F.2d 1194 (9th Cir. 1978).
150. *Id.* at 1206.
151. 437 F.Supp. 602 (D. Haw. 1977).
152. *Id.* at 608.
153. 602 F.2d 876 (9th Cir. 1979).
154. *See, e.g., Medeiros v. Kiyoski*, 52 Haw. 436, 441-444, 478 P.2d 314, 318-319 (1970).
155. *See State v. Andrews*, 65 Haw. 289, 291, 651 P.2d 473, 474 (1982); *State v. Blake*, 5 Haw. App. 411, 413, 695 P.2d 336, 337-338 (1985).
156. S.Ct. No. 9571 (4/03/85).
157. *State v. Lono*, Case Nos. CTR 1-21 of 9/2/82; CTR 1-26 of 9/9/82; CTR 22 of 9/10/82; and CTR 5-8 of 10/1/82. Order Denying Motion to Dismiss at 4.
158. 69 Haw. 255, 740 P.2d 28 (1987), *cert. denied*, 108 S.Ct. 1573 (1988).
159. *Id.* at 256, 740 P.2d at 31.
160. *Id.* at 259-260, 740 P.2d at 32. According to Native Hawaiian religious belief, the area proposed for geothermal development is considered the home of *Pele*, the volcano goddess.
161. *Id.* at 260, 740 P.2d at 32.
162. *Id.*
163. *Id.* at 261-262, 740 P.2d at 32-33.
164. *Cert. denied*, 108 S.Ct. 1573 (1988).
165. *But see Kalipi v. Hawaiian Trust Co.*, 66 Haw. 1, 11-12, 656 P.2d 745, 751-752 (1982).
166. Hawaiian Affairs Comm. Rep. No. 57, 1 *Proceedings of the Constitutional Convention of Hawaii of 1978*, 639.

CHAPTER 13

NATIVE HAWAIIAN BURIAL RIGHTS

1.   INTRODUCTION

Since the beginning of time, people have faced the inevitable reality that one day the physical functions of the human body would cease. Caring for the repose of the dead, as well as the sensibilities of the living, are largely universal values. Consequently, in each society, the dead and their remains have been cared for pursuant to cultural beliefs and customs. For Native Hawaiians, beliefs and customs associated with death are deeply ingrained in Hawaiian culture, calling for utmost respect and reverence.

The first written accounts by Native Hawaiians of traditional burial practices were unmistakably influenced by Western thought and Christian belief. Nevertheless, early Native Hawaiian scholars also reported traditional beliefs and customs. These writings clearly reveal that the care and protection of Hawaiian human remains are firmly in the hands of living Native Hawaiian descendants.

There is no case law with respect to Hawaiian burial rights. Historically, Native Hawaiians did not avail themselves of judicial forums for the protection of family grave sites or community burial grounds. Specific reasons for this failure are unclear. However, legal impediments, including procedural standing requirements and the lack of statutory protection, may have been significant factors. In addition, the courts or other public forums may not have been considered appropriate places to raise matters of private family concern. Moreover, fundamental and radical changes in the traditional land tenure as a result of the *Mahele* left Native Hawaiians disenfranchised from *ʻāina* (land) traditionally occupied for generations. This resulted in the loss of lands in which the remains of ancestors rested, and consequently the loss of the ability to care for and protect such remains.

Recently, opposition to the exhumation of approximately 1,100 Hawaiians at Honokahua, Maui resulted in deeper awareness of the burial issue. Native Hawaiians have since become more keenly conscious of the cultural responsibility to protect and care for *nā iwi o nā kūpuna* (the bones of the ancestors). One result of this awakening, was the call for protection of unmarked prehistoric and historic Hawaiian burial sites.

In the Hawaiʻi State Legislature, a two-year struggle to amend existing statutory law in order to protect unmarked prehistoric and historic Hawaiian burial sites culminated in 1990 with the passing of H.B. 3296. Similarly, in states across the nation, legislation recognizing the need to protect prehistoric unmarked Native American burial sites has been enacted.

The State of Hawaiʻi's largest repository of Hawaiian and other Polynesian human remains is the Bernice Pauahi Bishop Museum. There, approximately 3,600 remains have been collected or donated over the years. To its credit, the museum recently passed a release policy providing for the repatriation of *nā iwi o nā kūpuna*. However, 1,504 *kūpuna* exhumed from Mōkapu, Oʻahu, present site of the Kāneʻohe Marine Corps Air Station, are viewed as "federal property" and consequently not subject to the release policy. Additional authority may be required for their *hoʻihoʻi* (return).

245

In 1989, congress passed an unprecedented law requiring the Smithsonian Institution to inventory, identify, and repatriate the remains and funerary objects of Native Hawaiians, American Indians and Alaskan Natives. In addition, pending measures in both congressional houses may extend the inventory, identification, and repatriation process to Native American remains, funerary objects, sacred objects, and inalienable communal property in the present possession and control of any federal agencies and private institutions receiving federal funding.*

Laws often reflect important societal values. Society in a very real sense believes that all human remains, regardless of race, gender, creed, or religious orientation should be treated with care and respect. In fact, the common law of England, as adopted in many states including Hawai'i, reflects this societal value.

Until recently, modern statutory law limited protection to marked burial sites and cemeteries. By enacting laws protecting unmarked Native American burial sites and calling for the repatriation and reinterment of Native Hawaiian, American Indian and Alaskan Native remains, lawmakers across the country are finally affording America's first people the same protection as other citizens.

2. TRADITIONAL HAWAIIAN BURIAL BELIEFS AND CUSTOMS

For Hawaiians, the death[1] of a loved one was a powerful emotional and spiritual event. Even today, beliefs and customs centuries old permeate modern Native Hawaiian life:

> Grandfather was dying, and the entire 'ohana [family clan] was gathered around his sleeping mat. Soon the old man's spirit would leave his body to join the family 'aumākua [ancestor gods] in the eternity called Pō. But before this final moment, the patriarch, with almost his last breath, would impart his specific mana, his canoe-building talent, to a chosen descendant.
>
> But now, Kulikuli! Noho mālie. [Hush! Be silent.] The moment has come. Grandfather motions his grandson, Kelala, to come closer. Summoning his last strength, the dying man chants briefly. Then come the solemn words:
>
> "To you my dear and beloved mo'opuna [grandson], I give my mana. May this mana, the gift of the aumākua passed down through me, guide your hand so that your canoes may be fleet as the makani [wind], as strong as nalu nui [high surf], and as bold in ocean waves as the manō [shark]."
>
> Bending down, Kelala places his mouth close to his grandfather's. The old man draws a deep breath, and exhales directly into Kelala's mouth.
>
> "Through this hā, you have received my mana," he says, and in peace and serenity meets death.[2]

a.   Make (Death)

Hawaiians believed that following make (death), the 'uhane (spirit) remained near nā iwi (the bones). Thereafter, the 'uhane could leave and enter Pō (eternity) to join the 'aumākua.[3] A transfiguration ritual called kākū'ai helped to speed the spirit on its way.[4] On the other hand, the 'uhane might stay in the burial area, then depart for Milu (the

---

*   As this book went to press, congress passed H.R. 5237, providing for the repatriation of remains in the possession and control of federal agencies, including the Department of Defense.

246

underworld). The time frame for this process is difficult to predict.[5] The ritual of *'unihipili* (deification) kept the *'uhane* alive in *nā iwi* for future service to its *kahu* (keeper). In such instances, the *'uhane* did not go on to *Pō*, but instead remained in the present world.[6]

b.   Nā Iwi *(The Bones)*

For Hawaiians, *nā iwi*[7] are the essential physical material of a person and the *'uhane* is the psychic. The two are necessary for the makeup of a complete person.[8] Moreover, the manifestation of immortality was in *nā iwi*. Only *nā iwi* survived and remained the lasting embodiment of an individual.[9] As a result, the link between *kūpuna* (ancestors) and the eventual immortality of living Native Hawaiians is symbolized by *nā iwi*.[10]

Nā iwi are placed in the ground to eventually become part of *Haumea* (Earth), thereby insuring a place for the bones forever. Most importantly, *nā iwi* impart the *mana* of the deceased to that ground, to that *ahupua'a* and eventually to the island. The entire area therefore becomes sacred with *mana*.[11]

Nā iwi[12] were highly respected by loved ones. Accordingly, certain *nā iwi* were guarded and treasured. The epitome of veneration resulted in *'unihipili*[13] of bones in which the spirit of the deceased was kept alive in *nā iwi*. Just short of *'unihipili* was the practice of secretly exhuming the body of a beloved, cleaning the bones, and keeping them in the home, even near bedside when sleeping. However, *nā iwi* could also be despoiled by enemies. Consequently, spiritual beliefs associated with bones led to practices designed to protect them from coming into the possession of foes.[14]

c.   *Forms of Bone Desecration*

Hawaiians believed that following death, the *'uhane* stayed near *nā iwi* and that desecration of *nā iwi* insulted the *'uhane*. Desecration resulted in injury and spiritual trauma to the living descendants of the deceased.[15] For this reason, Hawaiians considered certain treatment of bones as desecration.

First, leaving bones uncovered and exposed to sunlight was highly disrespectful if not outright profane.[16] In addition, turning bones into fish hooks was considered insulting. Much worse was the misuse of a skull as a spittoon or an item in which to carry discarded food.[17] The ultimate desecration was complete destruction of *nā iwi*, because then the *'uhane* was prevented from joining the *'aumākua* in eternity. Thus, burning bones was considered the ultimate act of desecration.[18] In modern times, however, the wishes of the decedent must be honored, even superseding the *kapu* associated with cremation.

d.   Kia'i Kupapa'u *(The Wake)*

Kia'i kupapa'u was traditionally the time to both mourn the passing of the beloved and to celebrate the sanctity of the family. Family members sat around the body, whose feet faced the door of the *hale*. As mourners arrived, a close relative would whisper their names to the deceased.[19] As *uwe* (wailing) commenced, memories of the deceased were recalled. At times, the favorite *mele* (songs) and *hula* (dances) of the deceased were performed. These traditional funerary practices amounted to farewell communications to the still-lingering *'uhane*.[20] Following burial and purification came the *'aha 'aina make*[21] (feast of death) when the entire *'ohana* came together to comfort one another, share food, and strengthen family bonds.

e. Kaumaha *(Grief)*

Hawaiians had various mourning practices which were largely dependent upon the status of the decedent. The intensity of *uwe* (wailing) was much more prominent upon the death of an *ali'i* (royalty). For certain royal members, *na'au'auwā* (deepest grief) was expressed by loyal followers through violent manifestations called *mānewanewa*, which could include knocking out front teeth, gashing the head, and scarring the body.[22] Moreover, *oli* (chants) were composed and expressed to reflect deep sorrow and love for the departed *ali'i*.[23]

For the *maka'āinana*, mourning by family members was openly expressive, but usually did not amount to the mass emotion expressed with the passing of an *ali'i*.[24] Traditionally, the length of the grief period was about one year. After one year, the same persons held a second feast, *'aha 'aina waimaka* (feast of tears), which was "a joyful reunion of all who had previously shed tears together."[25]

f. Kanu 'Ana *(Burial Sites)*

Hawaiians chose burial sites for symbolic purposes. The western side of each island, symbolizing the sunset of life (death), was most desirable. Therefore, places like Honokahua on Maui, Mo'omomi on Molokai,* and Ka'ena on O'ahu were significant burial sites.[26]

Burial sites were chosen as places of safekeeping for *nā iwi*. Some bones were hidden in caves, cliffs, sand dunes, or deposited in the ocean. *'Ohana* members were often buried near the home, to be near the family so proper care and participation in family affairs could continue. Burials were often *hūnākele* or secret to keep *nā iwi* from being abused or disturbed.[27]

g. Kanu *(Burial)*

There were many ways of disposing of *nā iwi*[28] following preparation for burial.[29] Often an appointed person or group, related to the deceased, did the actual interment, usually at night in a designated burial area. However, the exact spot would not be made known. Many times sand, cave and rock burials were selected over dirt interment because no evidence of ground disturbance was left.[30]

A *kahu* was sometimes chosen to care for the bones and funerary objects placed with the deceased. This task was kept within the family for generations until the last *kahu* died, sometimes without naming a successor.[31]

As Western influence on Hawaiian culture grew, Hawaiians gradually discontinued two traditional funerary practices. The first, *pūholoholo*, was the removal of flesh from the corpse by steaming. Thereafter, the flesh was usually disposed of in the deepest part of the ocean. The second, *kākū'ai*, called for the transfiguration of the bones into a form of *'aumākua*.[32]

At about the same time, two Western funerary practices became readily acceptable to Hawaiians. The first was the use of wooden coffins. In earlier times, *ali'i* were buried in canoes made of *koa* and *kukui*, so it is not surprising that Hawaiians accepted this practice. The second was use of morticians to prepare the corpse for sepulture.

---

* The author was taught by his *tūtū wahine*, Harriet Ahiona Ne, that there is no *'okina* or glottal stop in Molokai. That teaching is followed throughout this chapter.

Traditionally Hawaiians had been very strict as to which individuals could handle a corpse. With an *ali'i*, only highly trusted blood-related retainers were permitted and for *maka'ainana*, only close family members.[33] Following interment, family members purified themselves through rituals called *pī kai* (sprinkling of sea or salted water for purification) or *kapu kai* (ceremonial bath in the sea).[34]

h.   Ho'omoe Pū *(Funerary Objects)*

Hawaiians also believed that funerary objects interred with the dead body were taken by the *'uhane* to *Pō*.[35] This belief was expressed by saying "*ho'omoe pū*" ("put to sleep together"). These funerary objects accompanied the body both as comfort and sustenance for the journey to the spirit world. In earlier times such items usually included food and ornaments.[36]

i.   Kō Ka'uhane *(Spiritual Matters)*

Hawaiians also believed that the *'uhane* took intangible matters with it beyond the grave.[37] Regarding promises, requests, reconciliations, or other emotional or spiritual matters, the belief that such were taken with the *'uhane* was expressed by saying "*lawe i ka wā make*" ("take in time of death"). In addition, the *'uhane* could take family grudges, curses, or a name that carried harmful connotations. Moreover, unless the decedent's *mana* was passed on, the *'uhane* could take its special talent back to *nā 'aumākua*.[38]

Nā iwi o nā kūpuna are the surviving receptacles of the *'uhane* of deceased Hawaiians. The cultural responsibility to protect *nā iwi* from desecration is firmly in the hands of living Native Hawaiians. Due to the absence of traditional Hawaiian beliefs and practices of *kanu hou* (reburial), present day Native Hawaiians are left to establish such funerary practices based on traditional Hawaiian values, in order to reinter disturbed ancestral remains.[39]

3.   THE LAW OF DEAD BODIES[40]

To date, the treatment of Hawaiian remains has primarily been handled in political forums. Native Hawaiians simply have not utilized the courts to implement the responsibility of caring for *nā iwi*. Many Native Hawaiians believe proper treatment should not be determined by the courts, but must be found in cultural beliefs and practices that call for spiritual preparation and appeasement.[41] However, in a modern context, Native Hawaiians may be forced to resort to the courts in order to protect Hawaiian remains. In doing so, there are procedural and substantive barriers which must be faced.

a.   *Standing*

In order to initiate a legal action, the asserting party must have the requisite standing. This means that the party must have sustained or been threatened with harm or injury as a result of the action complained of, or must assert an interest within the "zone of interests" intended to be protected by the particular law being asserted.[42] An "attenuated line of causation to the eventual injury" complained of is sufficient to maintain standing.[43] If the asserting party lacks the required interest in the action, a court will normally dismiss the case without reaching its merits. The standing requirement must be satisfied in order to initiate any judicial proceeding.

Next-of-kin traditionally have been recognized as having standing to sue regarding the disposition of their relative's remains.[44] The issue becomes more complex, however, in cases involving reburial when no direct descendants can be identified.

In *Beatty v. Kurtz* (1829),[45] the U.S. Supreme Court held that an unincorporated church congregation did have standing to sue other congregation members who wished to take church property, including the graveyard, for private purposes. The court stated:

> [C]ertain persons, belonging to a voluntary society, and having a common interest may sue in behalf of themselves and others having the like interest, as part of the same society, for purposes common to all and beneficial to all.[46]

Recently, courts have demonstrated a willingness to stretch the ancestral tie connection far enough to grant standing even where no specific descendants can be identified. For example, in *Charrier v. Bell* (1986),[47] a Louisiana Appeals Court reasoned that at least some members of the present day Indian tribe were descendants of the exhumed Indian remains at issue in the case. Hence the tribe, which necessarily included the "direct descendants" had standing to sue to recover the remains.[48] In other cases where no direct descendants could be identified, more distant relatives, those most interested in the proper disposition of the body, have been granted the authority to represent the interests of the deceased.[49]

Based on the fact that living Native Hawaiians are descended from the original people to occupy the Hawaiian Islands, courts may be inclined to grant standing to Native Hawaiians to speak for the interests of otherwise undefended ancestral remains. Thus, judicial standing for Native Hawaiians could be established to protect ancestral Hawaiian burials.

The difficulty in asserting claims to Hawaiian remains extends beyond the procedural standing requirement, however, raising questions as to the nature of the legal interest in human remains.

b. *Development of the Common Law*

English common law did not recognize an ownership interest in human skeletal remains. American courts have followed that rule and do not recognize property rights to a dead body.[50] Instead, American jurisprudence recognizes the right of the nearest next-of-kin to determine proper disposition of the deceased.[51]

This common-law rule originated in Roman law. Under Roman law, certain categories of things were "beyond human proprietary interest" (*in nullius bonis*) and were exclusively of "divine understanding" (*in divini iuris*). Human burials were included in the category of inherently "sacred things" (*res religiosae*).[52] This view continued into English common law, with the exclusion of human burials from the general law of property.[53]

The Roman rule that burial sites were sacred was significant because it recognized that burial of a human body consecrated the area, dedicating the site in perpetuity to the decedent and the gods who dwelled below. The site became hallow ground, beyond the scope of proprietary concern and instead within the realm of Roman criminal law.[54]

With the recognition that burials were matters of divine understanding, ecclesiastical figures gained authority and exclusive jurisdiction over the repose of the dead. Thereafter, under early English common law, disinterment and relocation of human remains was lawful only with the consent of appropriate church officials. No one else had enforceable rights.[55]

While the rule against any proprietary interest in human remains was firmly embedded in the common law, English real property law did recognize that one could hold a proprietary interest in the *land* in which human remains were interred.

An early Hawai'i case illustrates this point. In *Mott Smith v. Wilder* (1879),[56] the Estate of Lunalilo filed suit in equity against the Minister of Interior over possession of the Lunalilo Mausoleum. Earlier, Kamehameha III and his wife Kekāuluohi deeded what is now Kawaiaha'o Church to church members. Following Lunalilo's death, in accordance with his will and with the concurrence of Kawaiaha'o Church, a site on church grounds was set aside for the establishment and dedication of a mausoleum for the deceased king. Thereafter, following a grant of $400 by the legislature for the mausoleum's upkeep, the government took possession, prompting the suit. The Hawai'i court acknowledged the common law principle, stating that:

> According to common law in cases of ordinary interments in the ground, *the heir has no property in the bodies or ashes of his ancestors*, and he cannot sustain an action against such as disturb the remains, but as the body after burial becomes a part of the ground where it was committed, "earth to earth, ashes to ashes, dust to dust," the person who has the freehold of the soil can bring an action of trespass *quare clausum fregit*, against those who disturb or disinter it; and any person who has the actual possession of the land may sustain this action against a wrong doer.[57] (Emphasis added.)

The common law seems clear that remains of a deceased individual cannot be "owned" the same way other objects may.[58] For example, a dead body is not considered an asset to an estate nor is it considered larceny to steal a corpse.[59] Instead, dead bodies are considered "quasi-property" in that one can possess certain rights in the deceased, such as control over proper disposition, but does not have the entire "bundle of rights" granted to an owner of other property.[60]

The Legislature of the Kingdom of Hawai'i formally adopted the English common law in 1892. At statehood, Hawai'i codified the same common law principles "as ascertained by English and American decision."[61] Since there exists no contrary state statute or law, the common law rule that human remains are not private property is the law of Hawai'i and applicable to thousands of exhumed Hawaiian remains.[62] This view is consistent with recent case law in other jurisdictions.

For instance, in *Charrier v. Bell* (1986),[63] remains and grave goods of Tunica-Biloxi Indians were removed by plaintiff Charrier and offered for sale to Harvard University's Peabody Museum. After leasing the remains, Harvard declined to purchase, doubting Charrier's title to the remains and grave goods. As a result, Charrier filed for declaratory relief confirming his ownership in both the remains and grave goods.

Following a trial on the merits, the court held the Tunica-Biloxi Tribe to be the lawful owner of the remains and grave goods. The court of appeals affirmed, ruling that the remains and grave goods were not "abandoned" such that a subsequent landowner could claim title to them:

> *[T]he fact that descendants of fellow tribesmen of the deceased Tunica Indians resolved, for some customary, religious or spiritual belief, to bury certain items along with the bodies of the deceased, does not result in a conclusion that the goods were abandoned.* While the relinquishment of immediate possession may have been proved, an objective viewing of the relinquishment does not result in a finding of abandonment. Objects may be buried with a decedent for any number

251

of reasons. The relinquishment of possession normally serves some spiritual, moral, or religious purpose of the descendant/owner, but is not intended as a means of relinquishing ownership to a stranger. Plaintiff's argument carried to its logical conclusion would render a grave subject to despoliation either immediately after interment or definitely after removal of the descendants of the deceased from the neighborhood of the cemetery . . . . *The intent in interring objects with the deceased is that they will remain there perpetually, and not that they are available for someone to recover and possess as owner.*[64] (Emphasis added.)

c. *Causes of Action*

Under the theory that human remains are quasi-property, descendants retain certain rights in the body. Noted commentator W. Echo-Hawk believes no apparent reason exists why American common law protections for the sanctity of the grave and the sensibilities of the living[65] should not apply to protect Native American burials regardless of their age,[66] whether the native decedent can be identified,[67] or who owns the land containing the burials.[68]

With respect to human remains and funerary objects, there is a presumption against the propriety of removal of a dead body.[69] Thus, wrongful exhumation of a body or interference with a burial[70] may give rise not only to a trespass action by the owner of the land in which the body is interred,[71] but also to an equitable action in tort by the descendants.[72] Moreover, any subsequent purchaser of the property in which a burial is located is not free to disturb the remains.[73] Descendants have a right similar to an easement and permission of either the descendants or a court of equity is necessary in order to disturb the repose of the dead.[74] Further, a lineal descendant may exhume a body for reburial elsewhere.[75] Significantly, some courts have recognized that the religious beliefs of the deceased are a factor in determining whether disinterment is appropriate.[76]

Common law also has developed regarding disposition of grave sites and cemeteries. Like dead bodies, graves do not fall under normal principles of property law.[77] For example, the land surrounding burials in a cemetery is considered sacrosanct and protected along with the burials.[78] Even though cemeteries are protected under the law, they can be deemed "abandoned" if they have not been used in a long period of time or if they are not properly maintained. If a cemetery is deemed to have been abandoned, the bodies must still be exhumed and reburied elsewhere before the land may be used for another purpose.[79] However, there is a strong legal presumption against finding that a cemetery has been abandoned.[80]

In addition to the common law, Hawai'i has statutes regarding the management and protection of cemeteries.[81] Most statutory provisions define cemeteries in Judeo-Christian terms[82] and thus are less likely to afford much protection to Native American burials. Nevertheless, the definition of "cemetery" in Hawai'i may be broad enough to implicitly include unmarked Hawaiian burial grounds.[83] However, Hawai'i statutory law also provides for the removal or redesignation of cemeteries.[84]

In spite of the existence of substantial case law, the "quasi-rights" of descendants primarily have been applied to recently dead bodies, not ancient skeletal remains. In fact, Hawai'i statutory law defines dead body to include bones, "from the state of which it reasonably may be concluded that death recently occurred."[85] "Skeletons" or bodies which have been dead for an extended period of time, often are not considered "dead bodies."[86] Nevertheless, "if respect for the dead and their descendants is the basis of these quasi-rights, there should be no distinction between skeletons and recently dead bodies."[87] Thus, these common law concepts could be applied in suits brought by living Native Hawaiians seeking to protect ancestral Hawaiian remains.

4. HAWAI'I'S HISTORIC PRESERVATION LAW

a. *Hawai'i Revised Statutes Chapter 6E*

Recognizing the public interest in preserving historic and cultural property in the state, the 1976 Hawai'i legislature enacted an historic preservation law, codified at Hawai'i Revised Statutes, chapter 6E.[88] The law, structured after the National Historic Preservation Act of 1966, is administered by the Department of Land and Natural Resources (DLNR), and requires a comprehensive historic preservation program.[89] Historic property was defined as "any building, structure, object, district, area and site, including heiau and underwater site, that is significant in the history, architecture, archaeology, or culture of this State, or its communities, or the nation."[90]

Ancestral Hawaiian burial sites, however, were not specifically addressed by the historic preservation law. In 1988, Act 265 amended chapter 6E,[91] establishing provisions regarding discovery of prehistoric and historic burial sites.[92] Act 265 required that the Office of Hawaiian Affairs (OHA) and lineal descendants, where known, be notified of discovery. Native Hawaiians, however, were not included in the decision-making process to determine appropriate treatment of ancestral remains.

The exhumation activities at Honokahua, Maui and the efforts of concerned Native Hawaiians to respond to the crisis, sparked a demand for legislative protection for Hawaiian burial sites and the sensibilities of living Native Hawaiian descendants. The events at Honokahua made one thing clear: Native Hawaiians must be involved in the decision-making process regarding proper treatment of the bones of their ancestors.

b. *House Bill 3296*

On the last night of the 1989 Hawai'i legislative session, a joint house and senate committee failed to pass out of conference a bill relating to burials. The bill was an attempt to protect unmarked prehistoric and historic Hawaiian burial sites. The bill failed due to opposition by pro-development and large landowner interests, but concerned Native Hawaiians vowed to continue their efforts to seek a burials protection law.

On October 28, 1989, Hui Mālama I Nā Kūpuna o Hawai'i Nei organized the Native Hawaiian Burials Seminar.[93] One purpose of the seminar was to educate the public regarding Native Hawaiian spiritual beliefs and customs associated with burials and provide a forum for the scientific view.[94] Another purpose was to discuss issues relating to unmarked prehistoric and historic Hawaiian burials, and by so doing, raise the level of community awareness. The seminar leaders hoped to address concerns raised about pending legislation. Proceeding through congress at the time was a bill mandating the return of more than 18,500 Native American human remains in possession of the Smithsonian Institution.[95] Moreover, pending in the Hawai'i legislature was the burials legislation.

A clear theme emerged from the seminar -- living Native Hawaiians must be involved in the decision to protect or relocate the remains and funerary objects of ancestral Hawaiians. Native Hawaiians from each island expressed the unequivocal desire to care for *nā iwi* located or exhumed from their respective islands.

In November of 1989, the DLNR, of its own accord, administratively established island burial councils[96] and initiated a series of meetings between the councils, Hui Mālama I Nā Kūpuna o Hawai'i Nei, Bishop Estate, Hawai'i Resort Developers, the Land Use Research Foundation, and OHA, to clarify issues and attempt to overcome opposition. Due to the magnitude of revisions, new bills were introduced in both houses in the 1990 legislative session.[97] Months of good faith efforts by concerned Native Hawaiians culminated in both houses voting in unanimous support of H.B. 3296. On July 3, 1990, Governor John Waihe'e signed the historic legislation into law as Act 306.[98]

c. *Act 306 (Session Laws 1990)*

Act 306 provides a process by which the universal need to protect the repose of the dead is addressed, at the same time recognizing legitimate interests of private landowners. Important provisions of the new law are discussed below.

(1) *Island Burial Councils* The DLNR, through its State Historic Preservation Division (SHPD), will establish burial councils for Hawai'i, Maui and Lana'i, Molokai, Kaua'i and Ni'ihau, and O'ahu to implement the new burials law.[99]

Members of each council must reside in various regions of the respective islands and represent both Native Hawaiian and large landowner interests. Regional representatives from the Native Hawaiian community must demonstrate an understanding of Hawaiian cultural beliefs regarding burials. Council members will be appointed by the governor from a list developed by the DLNR, following consultation with appropriate Native Hawaiian organizations.[100] OHA will submit a list of nine candidates to the governor from which 20 percent of the regional representatives will be chosen. Membership ratio on the councils must always favor regional representatives.[101]

Councils will assist SHPD with the inventory and identification of unmarked prehistoric and historic Hawaiian burial sites and make recommendations regarding appropriate treatment and protection. Most importantly, the councils will "determine the preservation or relocation of previously identified native Hawaiian burial sites."[102]

(2) *Criteria Defining "Significance" Will Be Promulgated Through Administrative Rule-Making* The new law states, "[a]ll burial sites are significant and shall be preserved in place until compliance with this section is met, except as provided . . . ."[103] Act 306 does not define the criteria that will guide council decisions. Instead, the criteria will be developed through administrative rule-making by DLNR.[104]

An important issue during the 1990 legislative session was clarification of the term "significant" when referring to burial sites. Act 306 addresses this concern by stating:

> The appropriate island burial council shall determine whether preservation in place or relocation of previously identified native Hawaiian burial sites is warranted, *following criteria which should include recognition that burial sites of high preservation value, such as areas with a concentration of skeletal remains, or prehistoric or historic burials associated with important individuals and events, or areas that are within a context of historic properties, or have known lineal descendants, shall receive greater consideration for preservation in place.*[105] (Emphasis added.)

Due to the varying and complex instances in which Hawaiian remains may be found, flexibility in responding to each situation is important. Thus, a process which encourages broad public participation, lengthier comment period, and a reasoned pace may help establish the needed flexibility.

(3) *Notification to Councils of Projects That May Affect Unmarked Burial Sites; Determination Whether Such Sites Will Be Preserved in Place or Relocated* Before a proposed state project which may affect unmarked prehistoric or historic Hawaiian burials commences, the DLNR must be notified, allowed to review, comment and concur. If an archaeological assessment reveals evidence of burials on the proposed development property, the DLNR shall refer the matter to the appropriate island burial council. Thereafter, the council shall have 30 days to make a determination whether to preserve or relocate the remains. The council's decision will be based on criteria to be developed by the DLNR and the councils in administrative rule-making.[106]

With regard to projects located on private property, before any agency of the state or its political subdivisions approves any project involving a permit, license, land use change or other entitlement for use which may affect burials, the agency must advise the DLNR who will in turn notify the appropriate council.[107] Act 306 authorizes the councils to decide whether Hawaiian burials are to be protected *in situ* or relocated.

(4) *Appeal of Island Burial Council Decisions* Council determinations regarding whether to protect *in situ* or relocate remains may be administratively appealed to a panel composed of three members of the Board of Land and Natural Resources and three island burial council chairpersons, with the DLNR chair voting only in case of a deadlock.[108]

The appeals panel will hold contested case proceedings pursuant to applicable law. Within 90 days following a final determination of the matter, a preservation or mitigation plan will be approved by the DLNR in consultation with any known lineal descendants, the respective council, other Native Hawaiian organizations and the affected property owner.[109] Should the burials prove not to be Hawaiian, the DLNR will decide proper treatment in consultation with appropriate ethnic organizations and the affected property owner.[110]

(5) *Inadvertent Discovery of Hawaiian Burials* Where Hawaiian remains are inadvertently discovered, the DLNR, using the same criteria as the councils, will decide proper treatment,[111] *i.e.*, whether to preserve *in situ* or relocate due to the prospect of imminent harm.[112] In either instance, a mitigation plan will be developed by the DLNR or with its concurrence. If construction activities do not pose a threat to the remains, preservation in place will be the mitigation plan.[113] In land alteration projects, the landowner or developer is responsible for executing the mitigation plan, but in non-project situations, the DLNR is responsible.[114]

If removal is warranted due to imminent harm, council members will be notified and allowed to oversee the process. The DLNR will determine the place of relocation after consulting with the property owner, any lineal descendants, and the council. Relocation may be accompanied by traditional ceremonies determined by lineal descendants.[115]

(6) *"Burial Site" Defined* Act 306 defines "burial site" to address the concern raised by Native Hawaiians that, consistent with the common law, human remains are not to be considered property in the ordinary commercial sense. In addition, the area surrounding a burial is sacrosanct and should be distinguished from other types of historic

property. Thus, burial sites are "unique class[es] of historic property."[116] Act 306 amends chapter 6E to emphasize the special treatment needs of burial sites by adding the phrase "or burial site" each time the term "historic property" appears.

(7) *State Title to Hawaiian Burial Sites* The State of Hawai'i will hold title[117] to known Hawaiian burial sites in trust for preservation or proper disposition by Native Hawaiian descendants.[118] In addition, the state cannot transfer any burial site without first consulting the appropriate island burial council.[119] Thus, Act 306 creates a state trust responsibility regarding Hawaiian burial sites.

(8) *Penalties for Violation* Act 306 makes it unlawful for any person to knowingly take, appropriate, excavate, injure, destroy or alter any burial site[120] or its contents located on private or public lands, except as permitted by the provisions of the new law.[121] A civil penalty of $10,000 is set for each separate offense. If other loss occurs, the violator shall be fined the value equal to the damage caused. In addition, equipment used by a violator may be seized and sold by the state without compensation to the owner.[122] Finally, any person violating the section will be prohibited from participating in the construction of any state- or county-funded project for ten years.[123]

(9) *Reproductions, Forgeries, and Illegal Sales* It is unlawful to offer for sale or exchange any exhumed prehistoric or historic human remains or burial goods, or remove such from the jurisdiction without a permit from the DLNR. The penalty for violating this section was set at $10,000 in order to deter black marketing and interstate transportation of Hawaiian burial remains and grave goods.[124]

(10) *Enforcement* The state attorney general has the power to bring an action for restraining orders and injunctive relief to enjoin violations or threatened violations. In addition, any person may maintain an action for restraining orders or injunctive relief against the state, its political subdivisions, or any individual, in order to protect a burial site from unauthorized disturbance.[125]

(11) *Implementation* Following passage of Act 306, a burials program was established within SHPD. Primary responsibilities of the burials program include coordinating burial council matters, and drafting rules and regulations as charged by the new law. The success of Act 306 depends on how well SHPD staff interacts with, and is able to get the cooperation of, the councils, the Native Hawaiian community, developers, and landowners. Indeed, due to the large number of development activities taking place throughout the islands, implementation can only be successful if developers and landowners are aware of and sensitive to the cultural and spiritual issues involved, as well as the new legal procedures.

5.   REPOSITORIES OF EXHUMED HAWAIIAN REMAINS

a.   *Bernice Pauahi Bishop Museum*
The largest repository of Hawaiian remains and funerary objects in Hawai'i is the Bernice Pauahi Bishop Museum. As of 1982, an estimated 3,662 Polynesian skeletal remains

have been identified as being in the possession of the museum. Of that total, approximately 3,124 are Hawaiian.[126]

To its credit, the Bishop Museum has adopted a formal policy of repatriation, which states:

> When a request is made for the reburial of specific groups of remains, Bishop Museum will make remains available in response to a reinterment plan meeting all legal and regulatory requirements. Such a plan will be developed in cooperation with all applicable parties and agencies, including but not limited to lineal descendants, the landowner, Office of Hawaiian Affairs, Department of Health, and the Department of Land and Natural Resources State Historic Preservation Officer.
>
> It is and has been the policy of Bishop Museum that skeletal remains will be released to lineal descendants who identify the remains of specific individuals.
>
> Note: Objects directly associated with a burial are an integral part of that burial and would accompany the remains.[127]

The policy seems to involve two classifications of reburial requests. The first is "specific groups of remains." These groups are identified by origin or provenance. Hence, one assumption is that the museum will only release remains to members of the particular Polynesian group, *e.g.*, Hawaiian remains to Native Hawaiians. More importantly, a request for repatriation of remains identified to a particular island should be honored only if the requesting party can establish that they are "from" that particular island.[128] Once again standing is important. However, due to the nature of informal negotiation, the burden of proof is considerably easier to overcome than with judicial standing.[129]

The second classification involves instances where the remains of an individual can be identified by name. Following proper establishment of the nexus to the deceased individual, lineal descendants would be allowed to take possession for proper disposition, consistent with the common law. Interestingly, according to the museum, "[t]he only Native Hawaiian remains at Bishop Museum identified by names are those in the two sennit caskets, or ka'ai. The names Liloa, Lonoikamakahiki, Hakau, and Umi are recorded in the documentation accompanying the ka'ai. No other Native Hawaiian remains presently at Bishop Museum are identified by name."[130] Thus, it would appear that the remains of the identified individuals may be released to lineal descendants. However, there is some controversy over the acquisition of both *kā'ai* by the Bishop Museum. The *kā'ai* were originally housed at the royal mausoleum at Mauna 'Ala, and should be returned with their remains to Mauna 'Ala and the exclusive company of *ali'i*.[131]

On its face, the museum's release policy envisions a cooperative effort between parties. More importantly, the language in the policy requiring a reinterment plan that comports with all "legal requirements" seems to place primary responsibility for reinterment efforts in the hands of SHPD.[132] Thus, an interested party would initiate the process by requesting an inventory for a specific provenance. Upon completion, a repatriation request would then be made and details of a reinterment plan developed between the requesting party, the Bishop Museum, and the landowner where reinterment is expected to take place. Consultation with OHA and the Department of Health[133] could then occur. However, the "legal requirements" preface in the policy indicates that SHPD must approve the final plan.[134]

The Bishop Museum's release policy implicitly recognizes living Native Hawaiian descendants as having an important interest in proper disposition of the Hawaiian remains in the museum. By adopting the policy, the museum has made a firm commitment to address a longstanding concern within the Native Hawaiian community over the mistreatment of Hawaiian remains.[135] In that respect, the Bishop Museum stands as an excellent example, evidencing respect for the beliefs and customs of the native people, especially regarding proper treatment of their dead. Moreover, the museum's action demonstrates that, in some instances, Hawaiian cultural and spiritual needs outweigh scientific demands for analysis.[136]

b. *The University of Hawai'i -- Mānoa*

Until recently, the remains of approximately 100 humans had been stored at the University of Hawai'i's Department of Anthropology.[137] The collection included remains collected by the DLNR and the University of Hawai'i, as well as remains exhumed from federal lands.[138]

The DLNR series was acquired both through inadvertent discoveries and development projects. By mutual agreement, the University of Hawai'i was used as a storage facility until final disposition of remains could be determined. Until recently, SHPD did not have a laboratory in which state archaeologists could conduct identification analysis or store remains pending final disposition.

The University series came by way of a field laboratory established at Lapakahi, Kohala, on the Island of Hawai'i. The project was conducted in conjunction with the State Parks Division in the early 1970s. There are about 27 remains in this series, which were procured for research purposes.[139]

The federal series includes three remains exhumed from the Kāne'ohe Marine Corps Air Station, and Bellows and Hickam Air Force Bases. Such remains were procured through inadvertent discovery and removal due to erosion or pending development. Arrangements are being made to transfer the three to the Bishop Museum for storage.

The SHPD recently transferred the University collection to its office and will proceed with reinterment of all remains following analysis to determine ethnicity.[140] Due to strong reservations expressed by the Native Hawaiian community,[141] osteological analysis will be limited principally to determination of ethnicity, sex, age and number of individuals.[142] This information can be derived through examination, rather than physical injury to the bones.[143] Once ethnicity is determined, appropriate ethnic community organizations will be notified as to final disposition. In addition, a determination of which remains were inadvertently discovered and removed as a result of development will be made in order to identify which parties will be included in reinterment agreements and bear costs.[144]

c. *Smithsonian Museum of Natural History*

Until recently, the Smithsonian Museum had in its possession approximately 212 Hawaiian skulls and various infracranial remains.[145] In July of 1990, 80 remains identified to the islands of Hawai'i, Maui, Lana'i and O'ahu were repatriated. This historic endeavor was conducted by Hui Mālama I Nā Kūpuna o Hawai'i Nei, pursuant to the National Museum of the American Indian Act, discussed below.

The skulls of 132 Hawaiians from the island of Kaua'i await repatriation. Living descendants requested that the skulls not be included in initial repatriation efforts. Repatriation and reinterment for the Kaua'i *kūpuna* is being scheduled for the near future.

Remains of Hawaiians and other Polynesians are located in other institutions or collections throughout the world.[146] Strong concern and support of living Native

Hawaiians will one day result in the repatriation and reinterment of all known Hawaiian remains. However, since many Hawaiian remains were simply thrown away, incinerated, or destroyed, it may never be possible to repatriate and reinter all of the *kūpuna*.

6.   FEDERAL PRESERVATION LAW

Through archaeological excavation, the remains of 1,593 Hawaiians have been removed from federal lands at Mōkapu and placed in the Bernice Pauahi Bishop Museum. The Bishop Museum has taken the position that the remains are the rightful property of the federal government. Since then, Hawaiian remains continue to be found and removed from Mōkapu. In addition, Hawaiian remains have been exhumed from Bellows Air Force Base, Hickam Air Force Base, and the island of Kahoʻolawe.

Moreover, approximately 212 Hawaiian remains were exhumed for scientific purposes and sent to the U.S. Army Medical Museum.[147] Thereafter, the same Hawaiian remains, along with thousands of American Indian and Alaskan Native remains, were transferred to the Smithsonian Museum of Natural History. The exhumation of Hawaiian remains from federal lands in Hawaiʻi and the storage of these remains in institutions under the guise of federal ownership warrant a brief review of applicable federal law and pending legislation.

a.   *Antiquities Act of 1906*

In 1906, congress passed the Antiquities Act.[148] The act's purposes include curtailment of destruction of cultural sites (including burial sites) located on federal lands, prevention of international black marketing of cultural objects, and establishment of a federal policy to preserve historic places, structures, and objects of scientific importance. The act outlawed the excavation, injury or destruction of "any historic or prehistoric ruin or monument or *any object of antiquity,* situated on lands owned or controlled by the Government of the United States"[149] except with government permission. Under the act, however, certain educational and scientific institutions were allowed to examine and excavate archaeological sites and gather "objects of antiquity," "with a view to increasing the knowledge of such objects, and [provided] that the gatherings shall be made for permanent preservation in public museums."[150]

The act showed less concern for the cultural and spiritual value[151] of the sites and objects found on federal lands, and more concern for their educational and scientific value.[152] Native American human remains on federal lands were viewed as objects of antiquity or property, contrary to well-established common law principles.[153] In addition, the act assumed that Native American remains were owned by the federal government.[154] Although still law, the act's provisions regulating management of archaeological resources have been replaced by the Archaeological Resource Protection Act.

b.   *Reservoir Salvage Act of 1960*

The presumption that the federal government owned cultural resources, including Native American burials, continued with the Reservoir Salvage Act.[155] The Salvage Act amended the 1935 Historic Sites Act, which had established the preservation of historic buildings and objects of national significance as a national policy.[156] By the Salvage Act, congress recognized that construction of large-scale water control projects posed a threat to "the preservation of historical and archaeological data (including relics and [human] specimens) . . . ."[157] As a result, salvage archaeologists were given unrestricted access to American Indian cultural and burial sites that would have been destroyed by construction. Consequently, thousands of American Indian remains, funerary objects, and cultural objects were removed to the nation's museums.[158]

As with the 1906 Antiquities Act, the federal government sought to preserve Native American remains, funerary objects and cultural objects for scientific and educational research and data. The cultural and spiritual concerns of Native Americans were not considered in the expropriation of these remains.

c. *National Historic Preservation Act of 1966*

The 1966 Historic Preservation Act[159] established a national preservation[160] program and regulatory scheme. Congress declared it a national policy to encourage identification and preservation of the nation's historic and cultural resources.[161] This policy was to be implemented in three ways: the National Register of Historic Places,[162] the Advisory Council on Historic Preservation,[163] and Section 106 Review.[164]

As with its predecessors, the 1966 Preservation Act did not provide substantive protection to Native American cultural and burial sites and funerary objects. Largely procedural in nature, the Section 106 review process merely requires federal agency heads prior to licensing to "take into account the effects of the undertaking on any [area] . . . that is included in or eligible for inclusion"[165] in the National Register of Historic Places. Prior to approval, the federal agency head is required to afford the Advisory Council on Historic Preservation reasonable opportunity to comment on the proposed undertaking.[166] Federal agency heads, however, are not bound to follow the advice of the Advisory Council and may choose to ignore its comments and proceed with the undertaking. At best, the Section 106 procedure may result in burial site avoidance. More often than not, the outcome is preservation by mitigation resulting in exhumation and removal of the burial remains and goods, rather than protection of the burial remains in their original site.[167]

d. *Archaeological Resources Protection Act of 1979*

Motivated in part by the inability of federal land management agencies to enforce the 1906 Antiquities Act and the overall inadequacy of federal preservation law,[168] the Archaeological Resources Protection Act[169] (ARPA) protects archaeological resources on federal lands by narrowly defining "archaeological resources"[170] and substantially increasing the severity of civil[171] and criminal penalties[172] imposed on unqualified and unpermitted[173] looters. Within the definition of "archaeological resources," ARPA includes:

> any material remains of past human life or activities which are of archaeological interest . . . includ[ing], but not limited to . . . *graves, human skeletal materials or any portion or piece of any of the foregoing items*.[174] (Emphasis added.)

Contrary to common law principles, American Indian and Alaskan Native remains found on federal public land[175] or Indian land are deemed the property of the federal government. Thus, ARPA retains the presumption of federal ownership and control of Native American remains.

Under ARPA, however, permits for removal of graves and human remains cannot be issued without the consent of Native Americans. Moreover, ARPA requires that American Indian tribes be notified[176] prior to any negative impact on cultural and spiritual sites located on federal lands. Although ARPA specifically applies to federal lands, including national parks and wildlife refuges in all 50 states, Native Hawaiians were not included in the act's provisions.[177] This failure may be construed as allowing excavation and removal of Hawaiian remains from federal lands and national parks[178] without the consent of, or even notice to, living Native Hawaiians.

Since its passage, various federal departments and agencies have adopted policies and guidelines implementing ARPA. In 1982, the Department of Interior (DOI), National Park Service (NPS), established "Guidelines for the Disposition of Archaeological and Historical Human Remains," which recognize that:

> proper treatment [of Native American human remains] . . . involves . . . sensitive issues in which scientific, cultural, and religious values must be considered and reconciled through consultation with affected Indian tribes or "ethnic groups."

To accomplish proper consideration of competing values, early consultation is encouraged. However, noted commentator S. Moore argues both ARPA's "notice" requirement and NPS Guidelines' "consultation" requirement amount to little, if any, reprieve for American Indians, primarily because most DOI bureaus have interpreted the 1982 guidelines to elevate the scientific value of cultural sites over the cultural value.[179] Moreover, the common interpretation of ARPA is that it precludes reinterment since Indian remains are considered property of the United States to be curated in qualified institutions.[180]

As a result of pending federal legislation and the growing concern of Native Americans for proper treatment of ancestral remains, DOI Secretary Manuel Lujan has ordered a reassessment of DOI policies governing the protection and treatment of human remains and sacred objects in federal lands, including the possibility of repatriation.[181]

While ARPA provides limited protection for Native American remains on federal lands, it fails to specifically include Native Hawaiians. This failure withholds even ARPA's limited protection for the repose of the Hawaiian dead.

e.   *American Indian Religious Freedom Act of 1978*[182]

Humanity has always acted to protect the sanctity of the dead and these actions have been regarded as religious in nature.[183] Thus, in 1978, when the American Indian Religious Freedom Act (AIRFA)[184] was enacted to protect the religious rights of Native American people to access sacred sites,[185] burial sites were included.[186] Native Hawaiians were specifically included in AIRFA's provisions.[187]

However, neither AIRFA nor the United States Constitution[188] have prohibited the federal government from taking action that infringes upon the religious practices[189] of Native Americans, including spiritual practices associated with honoring the dead.[190] Thus, AIRFA amounts to no more than a recognition that Native American religious practices warrant consideration prior to federal administrative actions.[191]

AIRFA cannot be relied upon to prevent the disturbance of Hawaiian remains located on federal land. Instead, AIRFA merely insures that the federal agency involved must consider the impact of the proposed action on Hawaiian religious beliefs and customs. Due to the obvious limitations of AIRFA, proposed amendments await further action by congress.

f. *The National Museum of the American Indian Act*[192]

On November 28, 1989, President Bush signed into law S. 978,[193] which established "a living memorial to Native Americans and their traditions which shall be known as the 'National Museum of the American Indian.'"[194] In addition, the act requires that the Secretary of the Smithsonian Institution inventory and identify all Native American human remains and funerary objects in its possession. If by a preponderance of the evidence, Indian remains are identified to specific tribal origin, the secretary must notify the affected tribe. If by the same standard, remains are identified as being Native Hawaiian, the secretary shall:

> enter into an agreement with appropriate Native Hawaiian organizations with expertise in Native Hawaiian affairs (which may include the Office of Hawaiian Affairs and the Malama I Na Kupuna o Hawai'i Nei) to provide for the return of such human remains and funerary objects.[195]

On May 14, 1990, Hui Mālama I Nā Kūpuna o Hawai'i Nei discovered that a partial inventory of the Hawaiian remains had been completed on December 1, 1989.[196] Thereafter, Hui Mālama completed the inventory and arranged for the *ho'iho'i* (return). On July 18, 1990, 13 members of Hui Mālama entered the Smithsonian Museum of Natural History and prepared the remains of 80 *kūpuna* for repatriation and reinterment, leaving behind the skulls of 132 *kūpuna* from Kaua'i which await repatriation by identified descendants. Native Hawaiians were the first to implement the provisions of the Museum Act.

The Museum Act acknowledges a long overdue obligation to repatriate Hawaiian and other Native American human remains and funerary objects to their rightful caretakers, living native descendants. Despite the promise that the Museum Act holds, however, its provisions apply only to the Smithsonian. Many federal agencies and private institutions across the United States have in their possession the remains and funerary objects of thousands of Native Americans including Hawaiians. Hence, for living Native Hawaiians and other Native Americans who wish to repatriate such remains for proper reburial, there must be a process to inventory, identify, and repatriate these human remains and funerary objects from the possession of institutions across the country.

g. *Pending Federal Legislation**

At the time of publication, the United States Congress had before it two bills designed to address the difficult problems created by the exhumation of thousands of Native Americans.[197] S. 1980 and H.R. 5237 provide for the repatriation and reinterment of Native American human remains, funerary objects, sacred objects, and items of cultural patrimony from federal agencies and instrumentalities and private institutions across the United States. Congress may extend federal authority to regulate private institutions because these institutions receive federal funding.

These bills address a problem perpetuated throughout federal law and policy, the presumption that the federal government owns Native American remains. The "federal property" problem of Native American remains created by antiquity laws would be resolved

---

* As this book went to press, congress passed H.R. 5237, providing for the repatriation of remains in possession and control of federal agencies. On November 16, 1990, President Bush signed H.R. 5237 into law.

by providing for repatriation of native remains or objects excavated under a federal permit by the federal agency that issued such permit. Native American human remains and objects would no longer be considered "archaeological resources" and future disturbance of remains and objects will not be allowed without prior consent of native heirs or governments.

Like the Museum Act, S. 1980 and H.R. 5237 identify the two Native Hawaiian organizations to receive notice and make repatriation requests as Mālama I Nā Kūpuna o Hawai'i Nei and the Office of Hawaiian Affairs. The language includes other Native Hawaiian organizations as well.

Congress is now in a position to make significant changes in the future treatment of Native American remains and funerary objects by no longer classifying them as federal property. This action would be a major step in recognizing the cultural and spiritual values of Native Americans.[198]

7.   CONCLUSION

The unforgettable events at Honokahua were the single most important turning point in the development of contemporary Hawaiian burials rights. Those events released energy so positive that Native Hawaiians have since become keenly aware, through *nā iwi*, of their spiritual and cultural responsibilities to their *kūpuna*.

Due in large part to this *mana*, the Hawai'i Historic Preservation Act was amended to become one of the most protective state laws in the nation. Unmarked prehistoric and historic graveyards are now protected under the auspices of state law. Moreover, Native Hawaiians were integral in obtaining passage of the new legal protections. Under the new law, Native Hawaiians are directly involved in the determination of proper treatment of their ancestors, helping the entire community to understand and respect traditional Hawaiian burial beliefs and customs. These advancements in legislative protection on the state level are mirrored on a national level by the Museum Act and pending legislation before congress. With respect to known skeletal collections, the Bishop Museum has agreed to provide for the return of *nā iwi* in its possession, and the DLNR will repatriate the Hawaiian remains once held by the University of Hawai'i at Mānoa. Moreover, the Kaua'i ancestors in the Smithsonian Institution should be home by the time of publication.

Na wai e ho'ōla i nā iwi? (Who will save the bones?)

The responsibility to care for the graves and remains of the Hawaiian *kūpuna*, whether based on cultural or legal foundations, is clearly in the hands of living Native Hawaiians.[199] For Native Hawaiians, proper treatment of *nā iwi o nā kūpuna* is a human rights issue inextricably tied to the question of sovereignty. One fundamental expression of sovereignty is the right to live in a way which is culturally and spiritually fulfilling to a people. Native Hawaiian customs and beliefs call for careful and respectful treatment of *nā iwi* and for their return to the *'āina* of Hawai'i. Only in this manner can the continuity of life between those who have gone before and those who live today be maintained; and only by maintaining this continuity can the *'āina* and spirit be restored to the people.

263

NOTES

1. S.M. Kamakau, *Ka Po'e Kahiko: The People of Old* 33-35, 43-44 (1987 ed.).
2. M.K. Pukui, E.W. Haertig, C. Lee, *Nānā I Ke Kumu (Look to the Source)* Vol. I, 43-44 (1972) [hereinafter *Nānā I Ke Kumu*].
3. Kamakau, *supra* note 1, at 28-32.
4. *Nānā I Ke Kumu, supra* note 2, at 115-118; *see also* Kamakau, *supra* note 1, at 63-91.
5. Affidavit of Pualani Kanaka'ole Kanahele regarding the cultural significance of Honokahua, Maui at 4 [hereinafter Kanaka'ole Kanahele].
6. *Nānā I Ke Kumu, supra* note 2, at 195-196.
7. For Hawaiians, the bones of the dead were cherished and were hidden to be protected. See Mary Kawena Pukui, *Hawaiian Dictionary* 104 (1986 ed.).
8. *See* Kanaka'ole Kanahele, *supra* note 5, at 4.
9. *Koko* (blood) was *haumia* (defiled) and *pela* (flesh) following death was *kapu* (taboo). *Nānā I Ke Kumu, supra* note 2, at 107.
10. *Id.* at 111-112.
11. Kanaka'ole Kanahele, *supra* note 5, at 4-5.
12. For a discussion of the Hawaiian names for the bones of the human body and the origin of such names, *see* K. Blaisdell, M.D., *Na Iwi o ke Kino (The Bones): Na Inoa (The Names) Mokuna 'elua (Part II)*, 6 Ka Wai Ola O Oha, No. 7, at 22 (July 1989).
13. *Nānā I Ke Kumu, supra* note 2, at 148; 195-196.
14. *Id.* at 108-109.
15. *Id.* at 109, 136.
16. This raises issues regarding proper cultural treatment of Hawaiian remains exposed to the sun for long periods due to erosion and/or other ground-disturbing activities.
17. *Nānā I Ke Kumu, supra* note 2, at 109.
18. *Id.* at 109-110.
19. *Id.* at 135.
20. *Id.*
21. *Id.* at 139.
22. *Id.* at 133.
23. *Id.* at 135.
24. *Id.*
25. *Id.* at 139.
26. Kanaka'ole Kanahele, *supra* note 5, at 3.
27. *Id.* Today, Native Hawaiians view unnecessary analysis as disturbance and abuse of *nā iwi*.
28. Kamakau, *supra* note 1, at 38-43.
29. D. Malo, *Hawaiian Antiquities (Mo'olelo Hawai'i)* 96-99 (1987 ed.).
30. Kanaka'ole Kanahele, *supra* note 5, at 3.
31. *Id.* at 4.
32. *Nānā I Ke Kumu, supra* note 2, at 134, 115.
33. *Id.* at 134.
34. *Id.* at 122-123, 180.
35. *Id.* at 137.
36. *Id.*
37. *Id.* at 136-137.
38. *Id.* at 137-138.
39. Members of Hui Mālama I Nā Kūpuna o Hawai'i Nei were taught six ceremonial *pule* (prayers) in order to conduct the repatriation of 80 *kūpuna* from the Smithsonian Museum of Natural History. Some prayers were borrowed, while others were created by Kumu Pualani Kanaka'ole Kanahele.
40. Hawai'i State Public Health Statistics Act, Haw. Rev. Stat. § 338-1 (1985) defines "dead body" as "lifeless human body, or such parts of the human body, or the bones thereof, *from the state of which it reasonably may be concluded that death recently occurred.*" (Emphasis added.)
41. E. Kanahele, *Native Hawaiian Burials: A Native's Point of View*, Pleiades -- the Journal of the University of Hawai'i Community Colleges 73-75 (1990 ed.).
42. *Sierra Club v. Morton*, 405 U.S. 727 (1970); *see Life of the Land v. Land Use Commission*, 63 Haw. 166, 623 P.2d 431 (1981).

43. *United States v. SCRAP*, 412 U.S. 669, 688-90 (1973).

44. *See, e.g., Pao v. Diamond Head Memorial Park Assoc.*, 38 Haw. 270, 271 (1948); *Lum v. Fullaway*, 42 Haw. 500, 516 (1958) ("[t]he duty of burial rests upon the persons who have the right of sepulture. In the absence of a spouse, the right of sepulture belongs to next of kin."); *citing also*, 15 Am. Jur., *Dead Bodies*, § 10; 25 C.J.S., *Dead Bodies*, §§ 3, 5; *see also Codell Constr. Co. v. Miller*, 304 Ky. 708, 713-14, 202 S.W.2d 394, 397 (1947); *Brownlee v. Pratt*, 77 Ohio App. 533, 68 N.E.2d 798 (1946); *see also* T. Stueve, *Mortuary Law* 70-71 (6th ed. 1980).

45. 27 U.S. (2 Pet.) 566 (1829).

46. *Id.* at 585; *see also* Rosen, *The Excavation of American Indian Burial Sites: A Problem in Law and Professional Responsibility*, 82 Am. Anthropologist 5, 9 (1980).

47. 496 So.2d 601 (La. Ct. App. 1986), *cert. denied*, 498 So.2d. 753 (La. 1986).

48. *Id.* at 604 ("Despite the fact that the Tunicas have not produced a perfect 'chain of title' back to those buried at Trudeau Plantation, the tribe is an accumulation of the descendants of former Tunica Indians.").

49. *See, e.g., Pettigrew v. Pettigrew*, 207 Pa. 313, 318-19, 56 A. 878, 880 (1904) (distant relatives or even a friend); *Sullivan v. Catholic Cemeteries, Inc.*, 113 R.I. 65, 69, 317 A.2d 430, 432 (1974) (most interested individuals); *Larson v. Chase*, 47 Minn. 307, 309, 50 N.W. 238, 239 (1891) (those most intimately and closely connected with the deceased by domestic ties).

50. *See Dead Bodies*, 22 Am. Jur. 2d, § 4; *Dead Bodies*, 25A C.J.S., § 2; Martin, *Annotation: Corpse-Removal and Reinterment*, 21 A.L.R. 2d. 472, 480, 486; P. Jackson, *The Law of Cadavers and of Burial and Burial Places* 129-31, 133-34 (1950, 2d ed.).

51. *See note* 44, *supra*. American common law parted company with English antecedents by recognizing the right of next-of-kin to the respectful treatment and disposition of the remains of loved ones. In the absence of ecclesiastical courts, next-of-kin did not have a legal forum in which to raise concerns regarding deceased ancestors. Hence, American courts of equity in effect succeeded to the jurisdiction of ecclesiastical courts in interment matters and standing was recognized in the next-of-kin and friends to safeguard the burial of their beloved. *See Ruggles' Report* (N.Y. Surr. 1857) 4 Bradf. Rept. 503; *see also Beatty v. Kutz* (1829) 27 U.S. (2 Pet.) 566, 584-585.

    Despite being characterized as a "quasi-property" right, the interest of next-of-kin is nonetheless not predicated upon a property in remains but rather derived from acknowledged concerns of family and friends to dignified treatment. *See Pierce v. Proprietors of Swan Point Cemetery* (R.I. 1872) 14 Am. Rep. 667, 676-677, 681; *see also, Keyes v. Konkel* (Mich. 1899) 78 N.W. 649; Harper, James & Gray, *The Law of Torts*, § 9.4, 654 (2d ed. 1986); *Prosser & Keaton on Torts* 63 (5th ed. 1984).

52. *See Tomkins & Lemon, Gaius*, §§ 4, 6, 9 (1869); Abdy & Walker, *Gaius and Ulpian*, 412 quoting "The Rules of Ulpian," Tit. XXIV, §§ 4-6 (1874); Cooper, *Justinian's Institutes*, Lib. II, Tit. I. §§ VII, IX, X, 69 (3d ed. 1852).

53. *See, e.g.*, Throne (trans.), 2 *Bracton on the Laws and Customs of England* 40-41 (1968); Guterbock, *Bracton and His Relation to the Roman Law* 24 (1866); Britton, *Of Purchase*, § 84b(2), 176 (1901); Nichols (trans.) *Britton* 214 (1865).

54. The inviolable character of the burial place under Roman law rendered the Catacombs a safe meeting place for early Christians.

55. *See Martin, supra* note 50, at 472, 478; *see also* Mathews, *Whose Body? People as Property*, Curr. Legal Probs. 193, 197-198 (1983).

56. 6 Haw. 228 (1879).

57. *Id.* at 229-30.

58. *See* S. Moore, *Federal Indian Burial Policy -- Historical Anachronism or Contemporary Reality?*, 12 NARF L. Rev. No. 2, 5 (Spring 1987); Jackson, *supra* note 50, at 129; *Pettigrew v. Pettigrew, supra* note 49, at 315-16.

59. Jackson, *supra* note 50, at 129.

60. *See* Stueve, *supra* note 44, at 12-13; H. Bernard, *The Law of Death and Disposal of the Dead* 17 (2d ed. 1979); Kuzenski, *Property in Dead Bodies*, 9 Marq. L. Rev. 17, 22 (1924); *Sullivan v. Catholic Cemeteries, Inc.*, 113 R.I. 65, 68, 317 A.2d 430, 432 (1974).

61. Haw. Rev. Stat. § 1-1 (1985); *see supra* note 51.

62. Walter R. Echo-Hawk, Senior Attorney with the Native American Rights Fund in Boulder, Colorado, argues forcefully that American common law "which so strongly protects the legitimate interests of the living in the dead also include[s] Native people within its equitable protections." *See*, Echo-Hawk, *Tribal Efforts to Protect Against Mistreatment of Indian Dead: The Quest for Equal Protection of the Laws*, 14 NARF L. Rev. No. 1 (Winter 1988). *See also infra* note 126.

63. *See supra* note 47.

64. *Id.* at 604-605.

65. For an excellent discussion of the moral view, *see* V. Deloria, Jr., *A Simple Question of Humanity -- The Moral Dimensions of the Reburial Issue*, 14 NARF L. Rev. No. 4 (Fall 1989).

66. The older the burial site, the broader the legal standing to protect the same from desecration. *See generally* 25A C.J.S. at 520 n.51; *see also Female Union Band Assoc. v. Unknown Heirs*, 403 F. Supp. 540 (D.D.C. 1975), *aff'd*, 564 F.2d 600 (D.C. Cir. 1976); *St. Peter's Evangelical Lutheran Church v. Kleinfelter*, 8 Pa. Dist. & Co. 612, 29 Daugh Co. 240 (Pa. 1926); *Wormley v. Wormley*, 64 N.E. 864 (Ill. 1904); *Matter of Indian Cemetery, Queens County, N.Y.*, 169 Misc. 584 (N.Y.Sup.Ct. 1938) (Indian remains in abandoned burial ground safeguarded by the court upon condemnation).

67. *Hamilton v. Individual Mausoleum Co.*, 80 P.2d 501 (Kan. 1939); *see also* 25A C.J.S. at 516, 21 A.L.R. 2d. at 487.

68. *See Female Union Band, supra* note 66; *Charrier v. Bell, supra* note 47, at 601, 607 (the court ruled that the grave goods belonged to the tribe, stating "[we] cannot agree that ownership of such objects may be acquired by reducing them to possession and over the objections of the descendants of the persons with whom the objects were buried. Reason dictates that these objects, when and if removed, rightfully belong to the descendants if they be known and such disposition as the descendants may deem proper.").

69. *See Martin, supra* note 50, at 472, 480, 486; *see also* Bieder, "A Brief Historical Survey of the Expropriation of American Indian Remains" (April 1990) (copyright NARF/Bieder) (NILL No. 006376); *State v. Johnson*, 50 P. 907 (1897) (the unexplained possession of a dead body illegally removed is *prima facie* evidence of wrongful possession); *State v. Schaffer*, 95 Iowa 379, 64 N.W. 276 (1895) (the burden is on a defendant to show he had lawful authority to disinter a dead body).

70. Desecration of a place of burial is prohibited, amounting to a criminal misdemeanor under Haw. Rev. Stat. § 711-1107 (1985). Desecration is defined as "defacing, damaging, polluting, or otherwise physically mistreating in a way that the defendant knows will outrage the sensibilities of persons likely to observe or discover his action."

71. *See Mott Smith v. Wilder, supra* note 56, at 230; *see also, e.g., Meagher v. Driscoll*, 99 Mass 281, 284 (1868) (landowner has action in trespass); *Jacobus v. Congregation of Children of Israel*, 107 Ga. 518, 520-21, 33 S.E. 853, 854-55 (1899) (same).

72. *See, e.g., Pao v. Diamond Head Mem. Park Assn., supra* note 44, at 274 (defendant cemetery owner wrongfully "dug and disinterred the body of the plaintiff's father" after due interment in the plaintiff's burial plot within the cemetery belonging to the defendant); *Larson v. Chase*, 47 Minn. 307, 312, 50 N.W. 238, 240 (1891) (wife has action for mutilation of dead body); *see also Goldman v. Mollen*, 168 Va. 345, 355, 191 S.E. 627, 632 (1937) (trustees of cemetery have right to object to dead being disturbed); *Moore, supra* note 58, at 5; P. Jackson, *supra* note 50, at 41, 104, 176. However, *c.f.* Haw. Rev. Stat. § 338-25.5 (1985) which provides:

> No corpse, nor the remains of any dead human body, exclusive of ashes, shall be exposed, disturbed, or removed from its place of burial, nor shall the receptacle, container, or coffin holding the remains or corpse be opened, removed, or disturbed after due interment, *except upon written application made to the director [of the Department of Health] for a permit therefor and upon the issuance and according to the terms of a permit granted therefor by the director. After any removal or disturbance the grave shall be filled at once and restored to its former condition.* (Emphasis added.)

Act 306 (Sess. 1990) amended Haw. Rev. Stat. § 338-25.5 to exempt historic and prehistoric remains from the permit requirement.

73. *Anderson v. Acheson*, 132 Iowa 744, 758, 110 N.W. 335, 340 (1907); *see also* Rosen, *supra* note 46, at 8.

74. *Heiligman v. Chambers*, 338 P.2d 144, 150 (Okla. 1959); *United States v. Unknown Heirs*, 152 F.Supp. 452 (W.D. Okla. 1957) (when a burial ground was condemned, it was a federal court of equity's duty to see that a Comanche Indian chief was properly reinterred in an appropriate cemetery); *Matter of Indian Cemetery, Queens County, N.Y., supra* note 66 (Indian remains in a long-abandoned burial ground were carefully safeguarded by a court of equity when the area was condemned for highway purposes).

75. *See* P. Jackson, *supra* note 50, at 107.

76. *See, e.g., Goldman, supra* note 72, at 358 (child cannot disinter orthodox Jewish father because religion forbids disinterment); *Yome v. Gorman*, 242 N.Y. 395, 403, 152 N.E. 126, 128 (1926) (wife cannot disinter husband due to Catholic beliefs); *see also* Rosen, *supra* note 46, at 8.

77. The court in *Anderson, supra* note 73, at 758 stated: "The peculiar use to which such property is dedicated, and the sentiment of sanctity with which mankind regard the burial place of the dead, furnish ample reason for declining to apply to it the ordinary rules of ownership and devolution."

78. Jackson, *supra* note 50, at 186.

79. *See The Reburial of Native American Skeletal Remains: Approaches to the Resolution of Conflict*, 13 Harvard Env'tal L. Rev. 147, 168 (1989).

80. *See Anderson, supra* note 73, at 757; *Heiligman, supra* note 74, at 148; Jackson, *supra* note 50, at 395-96; Rosen, *supra* note 46, at 7.

81. Haw. Rev. Stat. § 441-11 (1967).

82. *See, e.g.,* Cal. Health & Safety Code §§ 8100, 8101 (West 1970 & 1988 Supp.).

83. Haw. Rev. Stat. § 441-1 (1985) states:

> "cemetery" means any property, or part interest therein, dedicated to and used or intended to be used for the permanent interment of human remains. It may be a burial park with one or more plots, for earth interment; a mausoleum with one or more vaults or crypt interments; a structure or place with one or more niches, recesses,

or other receptacles for the interment of cremated remains, or any combination of one or more thereof.

84. Haw. Rev. Stat. § 6E-41 (1989 Supp.).

85. Haw. Rev. Stat. § 338-1 (1985).

86. *See* Stueve, *supra* note 44, at 9.

87. *See* Bowman, *supra* note 79, at 169.

88. Haw. Rev. Stat. § 6E-1 (1985) states in part that:

> The Constitution of the State of Hawai'i recognizes the value of conserving and developing the historic and cultural property within the State for the public good. The legislature declares that the historic and cultural heritage of the State is among its most important assets and that the rapid social and economic developments of contemporary society threaten to destroy the remaining vestiges of this heritage . . . . *The legislature further declares that it shall be the public policy of this State to provide leadership in preserving, restoring, and maintaining historic and cultural property, to ensure the administration of such historic and cultural property in a spirit of stewardship and trusteeship for future generations* . . . . (Emphasis added.)

89. *Id.* § 6E-3 (1985).

90. *Id.* § 6E-2 (1985).

91. *Id.* § 6E-43 (1989 Supp.).

92. Hawaiian remains would be found in prehistoric burials, whereas historic burials could be of any of a number of ethnic groups including Hawaiians.

93. Hui Mālama's efforts were supported both by the Native Hawaiian Legal Corporation and the Office of Hawaiian Affairs.

94. University of Hawai'i Prof. Dr. Terry Hunt was the featured speaker on the scientific interests in exhumed human remains. At the time, Dr. Hunt was the president of the Society for Hawaiian Archaeology.

95. The bill sought to establish a National Museum for American Indians to be administered by the Smithsonian Institution. In return the Smithsonian would agree to inventory, identify and repatriate the more than 18,500 Native American remains (including 212 Hawaiians) in its collection. The bill was sponsored by Hawai'i Senator Daniel K. Inouye and was signed into law by President Bush on November 28, 1989; *see* National Museum of the American Indian Act, 20 U.S.C. § 80q (1989).

96. The principal role of the councils was to advise the DLNR of matters regarding unmarked Hawaiian burial sites. The administrative action was taken as an interim means to address the concerns of the Native Hawaiian community until legislation protecting burial sites could be passed.

97. Senator Eloise Tungpalan introduced S.B. 2981, while Representative Peter Apo introduced H.B. 3296.

98. H.B. 3296 became Act 306 (Session Laws 1990).

99. Haw. Rev. Stat. § 6E-43.5(a) (1990 Supp.).

100. As with the National Museum of the American Indian Act, Hui Mālama I Nā Kūpuna o Hawai'i Nei was identified as an appropriate Native Hawaiian organization with cultural expertise in reburial matters.

101. Haw. Rev. Stat. § 6E-43.5(b) (1990 Supp.).

102. *Id.* § 6E-43.5(f).

103. *Id.* § 6E-43(b).

104. *Id.* § 6E-43.5(c).

105. *Id.* § 6E-43(b).

106. *Id.* § 6E-8. At the time of writing, the rules and regulations defining the criteria had not been promulgated. *See supra* note 104.

107. Haw. Rev. Stat. § 6E-42 (1990 Supp.).

108. *Id.* § 6E-43(c).

109. *Id.* § 6E-43(d).

110. *Id.* § 6E-43(e).

111. *Id.* § 6E-43.6(c)(2).

112. *Id.* § 6E-43.6(c)(3).

113. *See* letter from Don Hibbard, Director SHPD, to Kazu Hayashida, Manager of the Board of Water Supply of the City and County of Honolulu (August 7, 1990) ("If the remains can be left in the ground, then preservation is the mitigation plan. . . . If the remains cannot be left in the ground because they would be severely damaged, disinterment/reinterment becomes the plan.").

114. Haw. Rev. Stat. § 6E-43.6(e) (1990 Supp.).

115. *Id.* § 6E-43.6(f).

116. *Id.* § 6E-2.

117. Testimony from Native Hawaiians indicated that state title should be temporary, and that subsection (c) should be amended to state:

> [W]hereupon formal recognition of a Native Hawaiian sovereign entity is restored by the United States, the State of Hawaii shall transfer trust title to Hawaiian burial sites to the Hawaiian sovereign.

See Testimony of Edward Halealoha Ayau and Terri-Lee Keko'olani Raymond Before the Senate Committee on Culture, Arts, and Preservation, February 7, 1990. However, the proposed language was not included in the final draft.

118. Haw. Rev. Stat. § 6E-7(c) (1990 Supp.).

119. *Id.* § 6E-7(d).

120. *See also* Haw. Rev. Stat. § 711-1107(1)(b) (1985).

121. Haw. Rev. Stat. § 6E-11(b) (1990 Supp.).

122. *Id.* § 6E-11(c).

123. *Id.* § 6E-11(d).

124. *Id.* § 6E-12(b)(c).

125. *Id.* § 6E-13(b).

126. At present, the collection of human remains in the Bernice Pauahi Bishop Museum is summarized as follows:

Hawaiians	
O'ahu (Mōkapu)	1,593
O'ahu	838
Lana'i	226
Hawai'i	205
Kaua'i	80
Maui	60
Molokai	47
Nihoa	11
Necker	1
Locality Unknown	63
Subtotal	3,124
Eastern, Western & Southern Polynesians	
Guam	311
Marquesas	64
Society Islands	42
Tinian	29
Fiji	28
Tonga	17
Tuamotu	10
Gambier	8
Saipan	9
New Zealand	3
New Guinea	3
Australia	2
Line	2
New Hebrides	2
Samoa	5
Epao	2
Palau	1
Subtotal	538
TOTAL	3,662

127. On May 23, 1989, the Board of Directors of the Bishop Museum approved the "Policy on Release of Human Remains."

128. There is still the problem of defining who is "from" an island or area and, therefore, may speak on behalf of that island or area. For living Native Hawaiians, genealogical connections can be found on many islands. Pualani Kanaka'ole Kanahele, a respected Native Hawaiian, suggests that a good guideline to follow is whether or not that person has at least three generations of *'ohana* buried in that island; the principle being that one may speak for a place if in fact there exists a foundation of ancestors upon which one's words may stand.

129. *See* Ubelaker and Grant, *Human Skeletal Remains: Preservation or Reburial?*, Yearbook of Physical Anthropology Vol. 32 at 263 (1989).

130. *See* Letter of W. Donald Duckworth, President and Director of the Bishop Museum, August 10, 1990, to Mr. Edward Halealoha Ayau, Esq., of the Native Hawaiian Legal Corporation, in response to the query "whether any of the more than 3,000 Native Hawaiian remains in the present possession of the Bishop Museum are identified by name."

131. *See* Letter to Governor Lucius Pinkham from Prince Jonah Kūhio Kalaniana'ole, January 15, 1918, formally requesting the *kā'ai* be removed from Mauna 'Ala to the Bishop Museum; *see* Gov. Pinkham's response, January 17, 1918, agreeing to the removal in order to exhibit the *kā'ai; see* Kalaniana'ole's rebuttal to Pinkham, January 22, 1918, to arrange an inspection of the remains; *see,* Pinkham's response, January 29, 1918, recognizing Kūhio's ownership interest in the "relics"; *see also* "Inventory of Specimens Taken Into Custody by the Bishop Museum," March 15, 1918; *finally, see* letter from the Bishop Museum Curator to Gov. Pinkham stating the museum's assumption of custody over the *kā'ai.*

132. The division is part of the Department of Land and Natural Resources. The Hawai'i historic preservation law, amended in 1990 by Act 306, does not specifically address repatriation of skeletal collections. Nevertheless, Haw. Rev. Stat. ch. 6E, § 43.6 does place responsibility for treatment of historic and prehistoric burials under the authority of the division. Moreover, the amendment includes a procedure for treatment of inadvertent discoveries of historic and prehistoric burials:

> In the event human skeletal remains are inadvertently discovered . . . *[t]he department [DLNR] shall* gather sufficient information including oral tradition, to document the nature of the burial context and *determine appropriate treatment of remains.*
>
> . . . .
>
> In cases where remains are archaeologically removed, *the department shall determine the place of relocation,* after consultation with the appropriate council, affected property owners, representatives of the relevant ethnic group, and any identified lineal descendants, as appropriate. (Emphasis added.)

Since there exists no specific grant of authority to any other entity, including the Department of Health and the Office of Hawaiian Affairs, legal responsibility for reinterment from the Bishop Museum seems to rest with the State Historic Preservation Division.

133. State law treats "dead bodies" and "skeletons" differently. The State Department of Health has jurisdiction over "dead bodies" defined as "lifeless human body . . . from the state of which it reasonably may be concluded that death recently occurred." Haw. Rev. Stat. § 338-1 (1985). "Skeletons" are considered ancient dead bodies and come under the authority of the Department of Land and Natural Resources. Haw. Rev. Stat. §§ 6E-43, 43.5, 43.6. Moreover, although state law requires permits from the Department of Health for disinterment, a recent amendment to Haw. Rev. Stat. § 338-25.5, exempts the SHPD from this requirement when prehistoric or historic remains are discovered.

134. At present, preparation for the return of 47 remains exhumed and removed from the island of Molokai is underway. The process was initiated in January, 1990 with a request for an inventory of all remains from the island in the present possession and control of the museum. On August 20, 1990 a physical inventory of the remains was conducted to verify the listed inventory with the physical collection. Repatriation and reinterment will proceed following development of a reinterment plan approved by SHPD.

135. *See Forms of Bone Desecration* discussed in part 2 *supra; see also* transcript of Native Hawaiian Burials Seminar, *infra* note 141.

136. For perspectives on both sides of the longstanding struggle of spirituality versus science, *see* Pietvsewsky, *The Reburial Issue: Justification for Studying Human Remains* (Feb. 1989); Ubelaker and Grant, *Human Skeletal Remains: Preservation or Reburial?,* Yearbook of Physical Anthropology Vol. 32, 249-287 (1989) (forceful argument in favor of scientific research); *see also* J. Johnson Cleghorn, "Hawaiian Burial Reconsideration: An Archaeological Analysis," A Thesis (August 1987) ("Human burials are one of the most frequently encountered classes of archaeological data. As a result, mortuary practices have long been a central concern for archaeologists"); *see* K. Blaisdell, M.D., *Na Iwi o ke Kino (the Bones) Mokuna 'Ekolu (Part III) Na ma'i iwi (bone disease),* 6 Ka Wai Ola O 'Oha, No. 8, at 19 (August 1989); *see also* K. Blaisdell, M.D., letter of Sept. 12, 1990 to Edward J. Morgan, M.D. (in favor of DNA analysis on a 300-year-old bone of a Hawaiian *wahine*); Deloria, *A Simple Question of Humanity -- The Moral Dimensions of the Reburial Issue,* 14 NARF L. Rev. No. 4 (Fall 1989) (statement of respect for Native American dead as defined by Native Americans themselves).

Moreover in response to concerns that the repatriation of Native American human remains will result in loss of an important research resource necessary for advancing human health, Emery A. Johnson, M.D., Assistant Surgeon General, Retired, United States Public Health Service, in a letter, May 8, 1990, to Gary Kimble, Executive Director of the Association of American Indian Affairs, stated:

> In discussing this issue with the other physicians who now hold or have held senior positions in the Indian Health Service, we can all identify contributions made in the past to the understanding of the natural history of disease and can speculate on possible value, such as in establishing baselines for environmental pollution, but did not identify any current research activity that promises to assist in elevating the health status of American Indian and Alaskan Native people.
>
> A search this past week of the medical literature collected by the National Library of Medicine, which contains essentially all of the significant scientific medical journals, did not reveal any significant publication relating to the utilization of Native American skeletal remains to prevention, diagnosis or treatment of disease. While there are theoretical potentials, the evidence does not suggest that there has been any significant research in recent years that will impact on the health of humans. If there had been such research, it would be found in the collected literature in the National Library of Medicine.
>
> . . . .

As a final comment, I cannot believe that the theoretical potential of medical research on Native American human remains in museum collections can outweigh the current negative impact on Indian mental health that the present condition of disrespect for human rights has on today's Native American people . . . .

Note: Although Dr. Johnson did not specifically refer to Native Hawaiians in his letter, at a congressional hearing before the Senate Select Committee on Indian Affairs, May 14, 1990, on S. 1980, Johnson made it clear that no such research currently exists on any Native American human remains, *including Native Hawaiians.*

137. Approximately 50 remains from Kualoa, O'ahu were returned to an on-site storage facility at the direction of University of Hawai'i President Al Simone following a request by Ed L. Kanahele, president of Hui Mālama I Nā Kūpuna o Hawai'i Nei.

138. *See* "Human Skeletal Remains in U.H. Archaeological Facilities as of 10/05/90," compiled by Jo Lynn Gunness.

139. *See* Letter from Don Hibbard, Director Historic Preservation Program, July 2, 1990, to Dr. P. Bion Griffin, Department of Anthropology, University of Hawai'i at Mānoa at 1.

140. *Id.* at 2.

141. *See* transcript of Native Hawaiian Burials Seminar, October 27, 1989.

142. Hibbard makes it clear that "none of these [DLNR] remains will be used in classrooms or for study. Rather they will be in storage awaiting any needed analysis and reinterment." *See,* note 139, *supra.*

143. University of Hawai'i-Mānoa researchers have conducted a study of mitochondrial DNA (mt DNA) from the *iwi* of a pre-contact Hawaiian *wahine.* The process involves "destructive analysis," in that fragments of the bone must be obtained. *See* letter from Dr. K. Blaisdell, Sept. 12, 1990, to Edward J. Morgan, III, M.D.

144. *See supra* note 139.

145. *See* letter from L.E. St. Hoyne, Associate Currator, Department of Anthropology, National Museum of Natural History, Feb. 26, 1979, to Dr. Michael Pietvsewsky.

146. For instance, the American Museum of Natural History confirmed a collection of 31 Hawaiian skulls predominantly from Lana'i (22), Molokai (4), Kaua'i (3), and O'ahu. There are two Melanesians. *See* letter and inventory from J.L. Brauer, Oct. 22, 1990, to William Paty. Unconfirmed reports indicate that the British Museum in London and Harvard's Peabody Museum possess Hawaiian remains. Moreover, the Maoris temporarily postponed the sale of a preserved, tatooed head of a Maori warrior by an auction house in London, England. It is estimated that 150 Maori heads have been removed from New Zealand. *See* K. De Young, *Controversy Comes to a Head,* Washington Post (May 20, 1988).

147. The taking of American Indian bones was official federal policy under an 1868 U.S. Surgeon General Order to Army personnel to procure Indian crania for the Army Medical Museum (AMM). The official reason given by the AMM was for comparative racial study. An estimated 18,500 American Indians were removed from their graves or beheaded on the battlefields. Following examination of "osteological peculiarities," Dr. George A. Otis of the AMM announced in 1870 that the data indicated that American Indians "must be assigned a lower position on the human scale than has been believed heretofore." *See* Bieder note 69, *supra,* at 39-40. In addition, Hawaiian crania were also removed from ancestral graves or collected for analysis. For one such account, *see* letter from Dr. C.H. Mastin to Army Medical Museum, National Anthropological Archives, April 19, 1874:

When I parted with you a month ago, I told you I would send you "a skull" and I now comply -- for I send by express to you *a present,* the skull of a "Sandwich Islander." It is genuine for "*I knew him well,*" attended him in his last illness, and made his head responsible for his medical bill -- It has served my purpose, and I turn it over to you. . . . I procured his head . . . I now place it, a native offering, on the Alter [sic] of Science . . . .

See also supra note 145.

148. 16 U.S.C. § 431 *et seq.,* 34 Stat. 225 (1906).

149. *Id.* § 433. However, application of the criminal sanction did not withstand judicial scrutiny; the terms *ruin* and *object* were found to be vague and to fail constitutional requirements of due process. *United States v. Diaz,* 499 F.2d 113 (9th Cir. 1974).

150. 16 U.S.C. § 432, 34 Stat. 225 (1906).

151. The congressional record is simply devoid of evidence of any Native American cultural or religious perspectives. *See* Moore, *supra* note 58, at 2.

152. Proponents included national archaeological societies and prominent educational institutions.

153. *See* part 3, *supra.*

154. *See* Moore, *supra* note 58.

155. 16 U.S.C. § 469 *et seq.,* Pub. L. No. 86-523 (1960); Pub. L. No. 93-291 (1974).

156. 16 U.S.C. § 461 *et seq.* (1935).

157. *See* note 155, *supra.*

158. *See* Moore, *supra* note 58, at 3 ("As in the 1906 Antiquities Act, the 1960 Reservoir Salvage Act in effect opened the door to widespread 'looting' and unrestrained expropriation of sites by the professional archaeological community, and made qualified public and private museums and other institutions the repository for 'relics and [human] specimens' removed from sites.").

159. 16 U.S.C. § 470, Pub. L. No. 89-665 (1966); as amended by Pub. L. No. 91-243 (1970); Pub. L. No. 93-54 (1973); Pub. L. No. 94-422 (1976); Pub. L. No. 94-458 (1976); Pub. L. No. 96-189 (1980); Pub. L. No. 96-244 (1980); Pub. L. No. 96-515 (1980).

160. Preservation *in situ* calls for protection in place whereas preservation by mitigation calls for storage in the confines of museums and universities after removal and documentation.

161. 16 U.S.C. § 470(b)(6), Pub. L. No. 89-665 (1966); as amended by Pub. L. No. 96-515 (1980).

162. 16 U.S.C. § 470a, Pub. L. No. 89-665 (1966); as amended by Pub. L. No. 91-383 (1970); Pub. L. No. 93-54 (1973); as added Pub. L. No. 94-458 (1976); as amended by Pub. L. No. 96-205 (1980); Pub. L. No. 96-515 (1980).

163. 16 U.S.C. § 470i, Pub. L. No. 89-665 (1966); as amended by Pub. L. No. 91-243 (1970); Pub. L. No. 93-54 (1973); Pub. L. No. 94-422 (1976); as amended by 1977 Reorg. Plan No. 2; Pub. L. No. 96-515 (1980).

164. 16 U.S.C. § 470f, Pub. L. No. 89-665 (1966); as amended by Pub. L. No. 94-422 (1976); for a summary review of federal preservation legislation including the National Historic Preservation Act, *see* Thalia Lani Ma'a, *Kanawai Mau Mo'olelo -- Laws of Historic Preservation in Hawai'i.*

165. *Id.*

166. Procedures governing the Section 106 process are set forth at 36 C.F.R. Part 800 (1986). *See Working with Section 106, 36 C.F.R. Part 800: Protection of Historic Properties -- Regulations of Advisory Council on Historic Preservation Governing the Section 106 Review Process,* Advisory Council on Historic Preservation (1986).

167. Unlike the Western notion of preservation of human remains, traditional Hawaiian culture provided that such remains must be allowed to deteriorate and decompose and become part of *Haumea* once again. Such action completes the circle for the Hawaiian of coming from *ka 'aina*, feeding off *ka 'aina* and then in time, returning to become part of *ka 'aina* once again.

168. 16 U.S.C. § 470aa(a)(3), Pub. L. No. 96-95 (1979).

169. 16 U.S.C. § 470aa *et seq.*, Pub. L. No. 96-95 (1979).

170. 16 U.S.C. § 470bb(1), Pub. L. No. 96-95 (1979); as amended by Pub. L. No. 100-588 (1988).

171. 16 U.S.C. § 470ff, Pub. L. No. 96-95 (1979).

172. 16 U.S.C. § 470ee, Pub. L. No. 96-95 (1979); as amended by Pub. L. No. 100-588 (1988) (extended prohibition against defacement of archaeological resources to include any attempt to excavate, remove, damage, or otherwise alter or deface any such resources); Pub. L. No. 100-588, § 1(c) decreased requirement relating to value of archaeological resources and cost of restoration and repair of such resources to $500 from $5,000.

173. 16 U.S.C. § 470cc, Pub. L. No. 96-95 (1979).

174. 16 U.S.C. § 470bb(1), Pub. L. No. 96-95 (1979); as amended by Pub. L. No. 100-588 (1988).

175. The term "public lands" includes lands owned and administered as part of the national park system and national wildlife refuge system and "all other lands the fee title to which is held by the United States." 16 U.S.C. § 470bb(3), Pub. L. No. 96-95 (1979); as amended by Pub. L. No. 100-588 (1988).

176. 16 U.S.C. § 470cc(c)(2); Pub. L. No. 96-95 (1979).

177. 16 U.S.C. § 470bb(5), Pub. L. No. 96-95 (1979); as amended by Pub. L. No. 100-588 (1988).

178. Pu'u Honua o Hōnaunau National Historic Park has 150 human remains, presumably Hawaiians, from Pu'u Honua o Hōnaunau, Hawai'i Volcanoes National Park and Kaloko-Honokōhau National Historic Park, "located in a lava tube that has been blessed by all of the major religious groups including Native Hawaiians." *See*, "Native American Human Remains in the National Park Service -- A Preliminary Survey" (August 1988; updated February 1990).

179. *See* Moore, *supra* note 58, at 4.

180. A National Park Service representative testified before the Nebraska legislature in opposition to the passage of a state burial law which called for repatriation of remains in the Nebraska State Historic Society stating:

> [T]he National Park Service is concerned that the bill, as now written, will jeopardize the integrity of federally-owned collections now curated in Nebraska institutions. Uniform rules and regulations of the Antiquities Act of 1906 require that archaeological collections acquired under the authority of that Act and prior to the enactment of this Archaeological Resource Protection Act of 1979 be preserved in a public museum.

See Testimony of Douglas Scott, before the Committee on Government, Military, and Veterans Affairs on L.B. 340, January 25, 1989, at 1.

181. The Department of Interior presented testimony to the U.S. Senate Select Committee on Indian Affairs on May 14, 1990 that department policy regarding the appropriate treatment of Native American remains which could include repatriation, was in the process of being revised based on input of Native Americans across the country including Native Hawaiians. *See* Testimony of Jerry L. Rogers, Associate Director, Cultural Resources, National Park Service on S. 1980.

182. 42 U.S.C. § 1996, Pub. L. No. 95-341 (1978).

183. One legal commentator has stated:

> The sepulture of the dead has, in all ages of the world been regarded as a religious rite. The place where the dead are deposited all civilized nations, and many barbarous ones, regard in some measure at least, as consecrated ground. In the old Saxon tongue the burial ground of the dead was "god's acre."
> [American cases] all agree in principle: The normal treatment of a corpse, once it is decently buried, is to let it lie. This idea is so deeply woven into our legal and cultural fabric that it is commonplace to hear it spoken of as a "right" of the dead and a charge on the quick. [No] system of jurisprudence permits exhumation for less than what are considered weighty, and sometimes compelling reasons. (Citations omitted.)

> *Annotation: Removal and Reinterment of Remains*, 21 A.L.R. 2d 472, 475-76.

184. *See* discussion of the American Indian Religious Freedom Act in Chapter 12, *supra*.

185. 42 U.S.C. § 1996, Pub. L. No. 95-341 (1978) states:

> On and after August 11, 1978, it shall be the policy of the United States to protect and preserve for American Indians their inherent right of freedom to believe, express, and exercise the traditional religions of the American Indian, Eskimo, Aleut, and Native Hawaiians, including but not limited to access to sites, use and possession of sacred objects, and the freedom to worship through ceremonial and traditional rights.

186. Native American religions, along with most religions, provide standards for the care and treatment of cemeteries and human remains. Tribal customary laws generally include standards of conduct for the care and treatment of all cemeteries encountered and human remains uncovered, as well as for the burial sites and bodies of their own ancestors. Grounded in Native American religious beliefs, these laws may, for example, require the performance of certain types of rituals at the burial site, specify who may visit the site, or prescribe the proper disposition of burial offerings.

    The prevalent view in the society of applicable disciplines is that Native American remains are public property and artifacts for study, display, and cultural investment. It is understandable that this view is in conflict with and repugnant to native people.

    Most Native American religious beliefs dictate that burial sites once completed are not to be disturbed or displaced except by natural circumstances. *American Indian Religious Freedom Act Report* 64 (August 1979).

187. *See* note 185, *supra*.

188. Where state action is involved, the first amendment may be violated. *Fuller v. Marx*, 724 F.2d 717 (8th Cir. 1984); where the action is racially motivated, the equal protection clause is implicated. *Rice v. Sioux City Cemetery*, 349 U.S. 70, 80 (1955) (Black, J., dissenting).

189. Certain traditional Native Hawaiian practitioners stated strong opposition to use of the term "religion" or the reference to themselves as "religious leaders." They believe that due to the high degree of respect Hawaiians held for all things, the more accurate term was "Hawaiian spiritual beliefs." *See* Transcript of Native Hawaiian Burials Seminar (Oct. 27, 1989).

190. The language of AIRFA delineates why First Amendment freedom of religion protections apply to Native Americans, resolves that congress will protect such Native American religious freedoms, and thereby orders the president of the United States to "direct the various Federal departments, agencies, and other instrumentalities responsible for administering relevant laws to evaluate their policies and procedures in consultation with native traditional religious leaders in order to determine appropriate changes necessary to protect and preserve Native American religious cultural rights and practices." 42 U.S.C. § 1996. However, the courts have been uniform in finding that AIRFA merely requires federal agencies to consider Native American religious issues. *See, e.g., Wilson v. Block*, 708 F.2d 735 (D.C. Cir. 1983), *cert. denied sub nom Navajo Medicinemen's Ass'n v. Block*, 464 U.S. 1056 (1984); *see also Lyng v. Northwest Indian Cemetery Protective Ass'n*, 108 S.Ct. 1319 (1988).

191. Note, *Indian Religious Freedom and Governmental Development of Public Lands*, 94 Yale Law Journal 1447, 1458 (1985), states:

> Yet, if nothing else, the Act [AIRFA] is a formal congressional acknowledgement that government action on public lands does infringe Native American beliefs and practices to some extent, and that Indian religions must be accorded meaningful protection in ways not generally necessary for protection of Euro-American religious interests.

192. 20 U.S.C. § 80q, Pub. L. No. 101-185 (1989).

193. S. 978 was introduced by Senator Daniel K. Inouye, Chairman of the Senate Select Committee on Indian Affairs.

194. 20 U.S.C. § 80q-1, Pub. L. 101-185 (1989).

195. 20 U.S.C. § 80q-11(a)(2).

196. *See* Letter from Dr. Donald J. Ortner, Chairman, Department of Anthropology, Museum of Natural History, to State Office of Hawaiian Affairs Chairman Thomas Kaulukukui, notifying OHA of the completion of an inventory pursuant to the provisions of the Museum Act and requesting further direction as to the disposition of the Hawaiian remains. However, Ortner did not notify Hui Mālama I Nā Kūpuna o Hawai'i Nei, nor was a formal response made by OHA.

197. *See Report of the National Dialogue on Museum-Native American Relations* (1990). The dialogue was sponsored by the Heard Museum in Phoenix, Arizona after calls for increasing channels of communication between Native American Indians and the science community on the sensitive burials issue. The majority opined in favor of repatriation. Native Hawaiians were not included in the panel discussions. A strong minority report was published by Dr. Diane Goldstein of the University of Wisconsin.

198. The adverse impact of federal preservation statutes on native burials, and hence on the spiritual sensibilities of Native Americans, was described in 1979 by the *AIRFA Report, supra* note 186.

199. In keeping with Hawaiian burial custom after activities involving the dead, a prayer of purification is offered here:

Kahuna:	*He mu oia!*	(Protect us!)
Hui:	*He mu!*	(Protect!)
Kahuna:	*He mu na moe inoino,*	(Protect us from nightmares
	na moemoe a, na	bad dreams, evil and
	punohunohu, na haumia,	defilement,
	he mu oia!	protect us!)
Hui:	*He mu!*	(Protect!)
Kahuna:	*Elieli!*	(Free of the *kapu*!)
Hui:	*Noa!*	(Free!)
Kahuna:	*Ia e!*	(Praise to Ia!)
Hui:	*Noa honua!*	(Free!)

CHAPTER 14

CUSTOMARY ADOPTION

1.   INTRODUCTION

Adoption comprised an integral part of ancient Hawaiian life. Today, customary adoption practices continue to exist,[1] though in modified form compared with their traditional counterparts.[2] Despite the many distortions in Hawaiian adoption patterns imposed by time, their present legal ramifications bear on the inheritance rights of Native Hawaiians. The following chapter discusses the cultural history and legal consequences of Hawaiian customary adoption.

2.   CULTURAL HISTORY OF ADOPTION

Traditional and modern adoption practices have assumed three basic forms: *ho'okama*, *hānai* and fosterage.[3] Literally translated, *ho'okama* means "to make a child," son or daughter.[4] It refers to a non-related child adopted in friendship.[5] Love, companionship and loyalty characterize the ensuing relationship.[6] However, in the traditional system, responsibility for the child did not include economic support.[7] Today, in contrast to its traditional aspects, *ho'okama* is commonly used to refer to *legal* adoption.[8]

Perhaps the more generally known form of adoption is *hānai*. Meaning "to feed," *hānai* refers to a child who is reared, educated, and loved by someone other than the natural parents.[9] The *hānai* relationship most often occurs within the family, so a child is rarely raised by strangers.[10] Moreover, natural parents maintain a relationship with their child, although they can only reclaim their child in the event of death or incapacity of the *hānai* parents.[11]

Traditionally, the permanent quality of the *hānai* relationship made it a near equivalent of legal adoption.[12] In modern times, however, the meaning of *hānai* varies.[13] It can encompass the temporary care of a child or a permanent relationship in which *hānai* parents assume complete responsibility for the child.[14]

Luhi, meaning "tiredness," represents a foster care relationship.[15] The notable feature of this relationship is its temporariness. Normally, parents who are ill or away from home place their child with relatives until they are able to resume care of the child.[16] Underlying the *luhi* relationship is the understanding that the child will return to the natural parents upon request.[17] Modern-day variations of *luhi* include a child placed in a foster home or child care facility.[18]

3.   LEGAL CONSEQUENCES OF CUSTOMARY ADOPTION

Three phases in Hawai'i court decisions summarize the legal effect given Hawaiian adoption practices. A pre-written law period, in which courts differentiated between a *ho'okama* or legal adoptive relationship and a *hānai* relationship, constituted the first phase.[19] During this period, the courts recognized adoptions implemented according to Hawaiian customs[20] and supported by evidence clearly showing a right of inheritance.[21] In *In re Estate of Nakuapa* (1873),[22] the Hawai'i Supreme Court held that a child adopted as an heir by ancient custom inherited to the exclusion of collateral kindred, but the relationship must be established by clear and unambiguous evidence. In *Nakuapa*, a jury had rendered the decision that one Kaaoaopa was the *keiki hānai* of the deceased Nakuapa. The supreme court set aside the verdict and ordered a new trial because it was unclear whether Kaaoaopa's status as *keiki hānai* also carried with it the right to inherit. The court stated:

> It is contended that numerous instances can be cited where children of high chiefs were adopted, and they did not inherit property by virtue of this relationship. It is not made apparent to the Court why they did not inherit, but doubtless for the reason that they were not adopted as children with the rights of heirship. In this country, the adoptions were of such a various relationship, some as temporary, and others as permanent, that a Court and Jury must be satisfied that the adoption caused the relationship of a child of the blood, so far as kind treatment, support, and right of inheritance were concerned.
>
> . . . .
>
> The majority of the Court are of the opinion that there was, prior to the written law, a custom and usage which recognized an adoption, if clearly defined in the contract, by which the child adopted might be an heir to the property of the adopter.[23]

Similarly, in *Mellish v. Bal* (1869),[24] the question presented to the Hawai'i Supreme Court was whether a child adopted as a *keiki hānai* was the heir at law of the deceased. The supreme court found that no evidence had been presented at trial on the ancient customs of Hawai'i from which it could be inferred that the child had been adopted as an heir. The court recognized that not every relation of *keiki hānai* carried the right of inheritance and the one claiming the *hānai* relationship had the burden to establish that right.

In 1841, the Hawai'i legislature promulgated the first written law of adoption, stating:

> If parents wish to commit their child to the care of another, it is well for them to go before an officer, and make their agreement in writing, and he being a witness to the correctness of the transaction, and signing his name as such, the writing shall be legal. If there be no writing or no officer sign his name, the child can not be transferred. The true parents still have the direction of the child.[25]

Various statutes after 1841 also provided procedures for adoption.

After the passage of these statutes regulating adoption, the courts continued to recognize Hawaiian oral customary adoptions only if they were made *prior* to enactment of such statutes. Thus, in *Kiaiaina v. Kahanu (1871)*,[26] the Hawai'i Supreme Court held that an adoption of a child as heir, according to Hawaiian custom and usage, *made prior to the written law*, was valid under existing law. In *Abenela v. Kailikole* (1863),[27] the court refused to recognize an adoption which had not been made in strict compliance with an 1846 statute governing adoptions. Although the facts in *Abenela* do not state whether the child had been adopted as a *keiki hānai* or in customary manner, the natural and adopting parents did sign an agreement of adoption in 1847. However, the document was not produced at trial and the court found that the agreement had not been executed before a notary and then sent to the principal notary public in Honolulu for registration as required by the 1846 statute. The court stated:

The Legislature having made it necessary, and we think wisely so, that all agreements of adoption which are of great importance, as affecting rights in property, should be made in writing, and duly recorded; and as no compliance with this requirement has been shown in the present case, the plaintiff cannot prevail in this action, in the absence of the necessary legal evidence of his having been adopted . . . .[28]

Later in 1915, the last stage in adoption law, the Hawai'i legislature enacted a comprehensive statute detailing the legal consequences of adoptions.[29] This statute indicated that more than Hawaiian custom and usage was necessary to effect a legal adoption.[30]

Today, Hawai'i's courts continue to distinguish between legal adoption and *hānai* relationships. In *Maui Land and Pineapple Co. v. Naiapaakai Heirs of John Keola Makeelani* (1988),[31] the *hānai* children of John Keola claimed an interest in his property based on customary adoption. The Hawai'i Supreme Court stated:

[W]hile adoption by custom was recognized in early times beginning in 1841 and continuing until the present time (and thus in effect during the period when appellants were hanaied by John Keola), there were written statutes of adoption which had to be followed in order to constitute the adoptee's legal heirs of the adopters. Even prior to the enactment of any statutes on the subject of adoption, the mere fact that one was a "keiki hanai" did not, by Hawaiian custom, carry with it a right of inheritance.[32]

Moreover, the court refused to apply the doctrine of equitable adoption in which an adoption is implied by law based upon the actions of the parties, even though no formal adoption exists.[33] This doctrine had been used in Alaska to uphold Alaskan Native cultural adoptions with attendant inheritance rights.[34]

4. CONCLUSION

Since the enactment of specific statutes governing adoption, Hawai'i courts, while recognizing traditional adoptive practices, have not given formal legal effect to such practices. The *Naiapaakai* case reaffirms that while Native Hawaiians may continue to practice *hānai* and customary adoption, there is no right of inheritance within customary adoption relationships unless formal adoption requirements are satisfied.

NOTES

1.   *Adoption in Eastern Oceania* 21 (V. Carroll ed. 1970).
2.   *Id.* at 29.
3.   *Id.* at 21.
4.   *Id.*
5.   M. Pukui, E.W. Haertig, C. Lee, *Nānā I Ke Kumu (Look to the Source)* 167 (1972) [hereinafter *Nānā I Ke Kumu*].
6.   *Id.*
7.   *Id.*
8.   *Adoption in Eastern Oceania, supra* note 1, at 30.
9.   *Nānā I Ke Kumu, supra* note 5, at 49.

10. *Id.*

11. *Id.* at 50.

12. *Id.*

13. *Adoption in Eastern Oceania, supra* note 1, at 31.

14. *Id.*

15. *Nānā I Ke Kumu, supra* note 5, at 50.

16. *Adoption in Eastern Oceania, supra* note 1, at 29.

17. *Id.*

18. *Nānā I Ke Kumu, supra* note 5, at 50.

19. *O'Brien v. Walker*, 35 Haw. 104, 118-119 (1939).

20. *Estate of Nakuapa*, 3 Haw. 410, 411 (1873).

21. *O'Brien v. Walker*, 35 Haw. 104, 118-119 (1939).

22. 3 Haw. 342 (1872).

23. *Id.* at 346-47.

24. 3 Haw. 123 (1869).

25. L. Thurston, *The Fundamental Law of Hawaii* 73 (1904).

26. 3 Haw. 368 (1871).

27. 2 Haw. 660 (1863).

28. *Id.* at 662.

29. Act 47, 1915 Haw. Sess. Laws 50.

30. *Id.* Though children adopted in the customary manner cannot inherit by intestate succession, some Hawai'i cases have recognized the customary relationship in other contexts. In *O'Brien v. Walker*, 35 Haw. 104 (1939), the court, in construing the term "lawful issue" in a trust instrument, extensively discussed the ancient custom and tradition of adoption. The court drew the distinction between *ho'okama*, the type of customary adoption in which inheritance rights attached, and *keiki hānai*, a foster child relationship in which no inheritance rights attached. (*See* 35 Haw. 128-29.) In *O'Brien*, the court examined the background and heritage of the trustor (a part-Hawaiian born around 1841 to an *ali'i* family who married into another Hawaiian family and who would have been familiar with the practice of adopting children with inheritance rights) to conclude that he intended the words "lawful issue" to include an adopted child of one of his natural children. Of course, in *O'Brien* the adopted child had been adopted in conformance with applicable statutory requirements. Customary adoption was also discussed in *Leong v. Takasaki*, 55 Haw. 398, 410-11, 520 P.2d 758, 766 (1974), in order to show that a blood relationship may not be necessary in order to recover for emotional distress caused by seeing a stepgrandmother struck and hit by a car.

31. 69 Haw. 565, 751 P.2d 1020 (1988).

32. *Id.* at 568, 751 P.2d 1021-1022.

33. *Id.*

34. *See Calista Corporation v. Mann*, 564 P.2d 53 (Alaska 1977), in which the Alaska Supreme Court applied the equitable adoption doctrine to allow two Native Alaskan women who had been adopted in the culturally accepted manner of their tribes to receive shares of stock in their parents' native corporations organized under the Alaska Native Claims Settlement Act.

PART FIVE

RESOURCES BENEFITING

NATIVE HAWAIIANS

CHAPTER 15

NATIVE HAWAIIAN CHARITABLE TRUSTS

1.   INTRODUCTION

Native Hawaiians have beneficiary status under certain private charitable trusts. These trusts include: the Bernice Pauahi Bishop Trust, the Queen Lili'uokalani Trust, the Lunalilo Trust, and the former Queen Emma Trust. As beneficiaries, Native Hawaiians not only enjoy trust benefits but, in some instances, possess rights to legally enforce the trusts. The following chapter briefly discusses each trust, the provisions establishing the trust, and how each trust affects Native Hawaiian beneficiaries today.

2.   THE KAMEHAMEHA SCHOOLS/BISHOP ESTATE

In 1883, Bernice Pauahi Bishop, the great-granddaughter of Kamehameha I and the last descendant of his royal line, established a charitable trust for the educational benefit of Hawaiian children. Devoted to the welfare of her people and cognizant of the rapid social changes occurring at the time, Mrs. Bishop considered education the means toward future advancement of Hawaiian children. Named the Kamehameha Schools/Bishop Estate, Mrs. Bishop's legacy to her people has become the wealthiest and most influential charitable trust in Hawai'i.

a.   *Trust Provisions*

In three provisions of her will, dated October 31, 1883, Mrs. Bishop implemented her concern for the education of Hawaiian children. In paragraph 13, Mrs. Bishop directed five trustees to hold the remainder of her personal and real estate in trust for the purpose of building and maintaining two educational institutions.[1] The institutions, one for girls and one for boys, were to be called the Kamehameha Schools. Mrs. Bishop authorized the trustees to expend the amounts required to purchase land and construct and furnish the schools' facilities.[2] While the trustees had complete discretion in spending the necessary monies, they could not spend more than half the monies then accumulated.[3] Mrs. Bishop also permitted the trustees to use the annual income from the trust for the maintenance of the schools and for the support and education of orphans and other indigents, giving preference to Hawaiians of pure and part aboriginal blood.[4]

In addition to the construction and maintenance of the schools, paragraph 13 also gave the trustees power to lease or sell the real estate and make any subsequent investment decisions.[5] The trustees, however, were required to submit an annual inventory of all receipts, expenditures and property to the supreme court.[6] Mrs. Bishop also directed that such information be published in a Honolulu newspaper.[7]

Paragraph 13 also detailed Mrs. Bishop's wishes regarding the administration of the schools. She instructed the trustees to provide good education and moral guidance to foster the students' mature development.[8] All teaching positions were restricted to persons of the Protestant faith.[9]

Paragraph 14 designated Charles Bishop, Samuel Damon, Charles Hyde, Charles Cook, and William Smith as the first five trustees.[10] Any action by the trustees required the concurrence of at least three trustees.[11] Vacancies were to be filled by the choice of a majority of the supreme court justices.[12] Mrs. Bishop also restricted the selection of her trustees to persons of the Protestant religion.[13]

Paragraph 17 of the first codicil or amendment to the will, executed on October 14, 1884, gave the trustees full discretion to sell, exchange, purchase, or lease any lands necessary for the establishment or maintenance of the schools or for the best interests of the estate.[14]

In her second codicil executed on October 9, 1884, Mrs. Bishop expressed her priority in establishing the boys school and allowed the trustees to defer construction plans for the girls school.[15] The trustees were also given the power to decide curriculum and tuition matters.[16]

Mrs. Bishop died on October 16, 1884. At her death, she owned approximately one-tenth of the entire land area of Hawai'i, or about 400,000 acres of land, all of which she devised to the Kamehameha Schools.[17] This included the 353,000 acres she inherited from her cousin, Princess Ruth Ke'elikōlani.[18] Three years later and pursuant to the will provisions, the Kamehameha School for Boys was opened with 37 students and four teachers.[19]

b. *Cases Interpreting Trust Provisions*

(1) *Powers and Duties of the Trustees* Soon after the trust provisions became effective, the trustees sought to clarify their various responsibilities. The issue of trustee resignations provided the court with its first opportunity to interpret the trust provisions. When trustee Samuel Damon wished to resign, the supreme court held in *Damon v. Hyde* (1897),[20] that an accounting, official appointment of a new trustee, and a decree conveying the estate to the new trustee were necessary prerequisites to any resignation.

Court interpretations of paragraph 13 of the will comprise much of the case law defining trustee duties and powers. The court has affirmed the language of paragraph 13 by requiring the filing and publication of an estate inventory.[21] The court restricted all trustee expenditures to the support of education at the Kamehameha Schools only,[22] and concluded that the trustees possessed the power to sell estate lands or use estate *corpus* to construct the school facilities.[23]

However, in *Bishop v. Pittman* (1935),[24] the supreme court held that the trustees had no authority to compensate tenants for the loss of their leased lands by eminent domain. The court later found that paragraph 13 limits trustee charges related to construction costs to the *corpus* account.[25]

The Hawai'i Supreme Court has also interpreted the provisions of paragraph 17 of the first codicil. In *Hyde v. Smith* (1898),[26] the court held that paragraph 17 empowered the trustees to sell and convey the trust lands at their discretion and without prior court approval. This holding supported later court decisions concerning the trustees' power to convey lands or expend trust monies.[27]

The Hawai'i Supreme Court has also addressed the provision on vacancies in the fourteenth paragraph of Mrs. Bishop's will. In *Estate of Bishop* (1917),[28] the court held that the power of appointing a trustee rested with the majority of the supreme court justices, acting as individuals. Furthermore, such appointments could not be reviewed by any court. The case overturned a decision by the circuit court, which had disapproved the appointment of a new trustee and had named its own choice. The court was again faced with the issue of trustee appointment in *Kekoa v. Supreme Court* (1973).[29] In that case, the appointment process withstood a challenge based on federal and state constitutional grounds.

Other cases pertaining to trustee duties and powers reflect general tenets of trust law. In *Richards v. Midkiff* (1964),[30] the court reiterated the general rule that a minority trustee has standing to question the judgment of the majority trustees in situations involving a breach of trust. However, a matter within the discretion of the trustees is only reviewable by a court when the trustees have abused their discretion.[31]

Similarly, the court in *Midkiff v. Kobayashi* (1973)[32] held that a minority trustee had standing to challenge the actions of the majority trustees. Furthermore, the court established that trustees must obtain court approval of actions which deviate from the provisions of the trust document.[33]

Attendant to their managerial responsibilities, the trustees also receive compensation, at a rate determined by statute.[34] In two instances, the attorney general has challenged the amount of compensation given to the trustees. In *Estate of Bernice P. Bishop* (1945),[35] the attorney general objected to the trustees' commissions on income derived from the wartime rental of the schools and to the amount of those commissions. The court held that the lease rents were legitimate bases for commissions but agreed with the attorney general on the appropriate percentage rate.[36]

In a later case, the court similarly held that sums collected from lessees of the estate constituted income, even though those sums were paid to the state for real property taxes.[37] Considered as income, the trustees could appropriately base their compensation on the rental amounts.

(2) *Trust Corpus* While the trustees enjoy complete discretion under the trust provisions, the Hawai'i Land Reform Act of 1978[38] seriously limited the exercise of those powers as they pertained to the trust *corpus*. Essentially, the act allows the state to condemn leasehold land and sell it to lessees in fee simple.[39] In a lengthy series of cases, the trustees challenged the act as an unconstitutional taking without a public purpose, a requirement under eminent domain proceedings.[40] The United States Supreme Court held that when the use of eminent domain power is rationally related to a conceivable public purpose as determined by the legislature, a court will not question such legislative enactments.[41] At present, the trustees have embarked on a formal policy to sell residential-zoned land in bulk rather than develop and lease subdivided house lots.[42] Currently, it has less than 4,000 leases.[43]

c. *Current Trust Status*

The trust's landholdings now represent about eight percent of the state's total land area. The land is distributed over the five larger islands; 95 percent of the trust lands are located on O'ahu and Hawai'i.[44] Approximately one-half of the lands are classified as conservation areas.[45] Of the remaining lands, 48 percent are classified as agricultural areas and two percent are used for commercial and residential purposes.[46] The latter landholdings account for the trust's primary source of income.[47]

In accordance with the trust provisions, all revenues obtained primarily through land rentals fund the maintenance of the Kamehameha Schools. Presently, the Kamehameha Schools is the richest private school in the country with an endowment of approximately $1.57 billion.[48] It has an operating budget estimated at $31 million yearly.[49]

The Kamehameha Schools is comprised of more than 75 buildings,[50] situated on a 600-acre campus.[51] In 1965, the boys and girls schools, established separately pursuant to the trust provisions, were combined.[52] The institution offers classes from kindergarten through high school. In 1971, the trust established the Kamehameha Elementary Education Program to conduct research to help academically "at-risk" Hawaiian children.[53] The schools also provides a variety of extension programs, a decision which received court approval in the 1970s.[54] These programs include summer school, adult education, and the Hawaiian Studies Institute.[55]

3.   LILIʻUOKALANI TRUST

Queen Liliʻuokalani, Hawaiʻi's last reigning monarch, also established a charitable trust for the benefit of Hawaiian children. Although the Crown Lands were confiscated when Liliʻuokalani was deposed in 1893, her private landholdings comprised the *corpus* of the trust.

a.   *Deed of Trust*

Section VII of the Queen's Deed of Trust, dated December 2, 1909, states in pertinent part:

> From and after the death of the Grantor, all of the property of the trust estate, both principal and income . . . shall be used by the Trustees for the benefit of orphan children in the Hawaiian Islands, the preference to be given to Hawaiian children of pure or part aboriginal blood.[56]

The trust instrument also directed the trustees to establish and maintain an institution, bearing Liliʻuokalani's name, for Hawaiian orphans.[57] The three original trustees, A.S. Cleghorn, Colonel Curtis P. Iaukea, and William O. Smith, and all trustees thereafter, were expressly authorized to exercise complete discretion in fulfilling the terms of the trust.[58]

Section VIII of the trust provided for the appointment of trustees when a vacancy occurred.[59] Under this provision, the remaining trustee or trustees are required to nominate a replacement, who is to be confirmed and appointed by a judge. If the remaining trustees fail to submit a written nomination to the court, the court can appoint a new trustee upon the application of any trustee or beneficiary.

The trust provision absolved the trustees of personal liability and limited trustee liability to situations of willful misconduct or gross negligence.[60] These provisions have never been legally challenged, although the queen's will survived an unsuccessful contest.[61]

On October 11, 1911, Queen Liliʻuokalani amended the Deed of Trust to substitute Samuel Damon as trustee for the deceased A.S. Cleghorn.[62] More importantly, Queen Liliʻuokalani also extended the trust beneficiaries to include "other destitute children."[63] A second amendment on September 2, 1915 resulted in the transfer of some of the queen's Waikīkī property to her nephew, Prince Jonah Kūhiō Kalanianaʻole.[64]

b.   *The Queen Lili'uokalani Children's Center*

The Queen Lili'uokalani Children's Center (QLCC), is the culmination of the trustees' efforts to establish an institution for the benefit of Hawaiian children. The earliest years of the center reveal its association with the Hawaiian Humane Society, an organization formed in 1883 to protect the island's animal population.[65] In 1920, the society focussed its efforts on providing temporary or permanent homes for children.[66] The organization continued its work in this area and by 1933, 55 percent of the caseload included children of Hawaiian ancestry.[67]

During this time, child welfare practices moved away from the concept of orphanages as a means of assisting orphaned or destitute children. The trustees responded to this movement by seeking court approval of a postponement in the establishment of an institution for the trust beneficiaries.[68] The court responded in 1934 by permitting the trustees to act within their discretion in placing the beneficiaries in suitable foster homes or boarding schools.[69]

In 1935, the Lili'uokalani Trust launched its child welfare program.[70] Upon the recommendation of the Child Welfare League of America, the Lili'uokalani Trust collaborated with other social agencies in serving the needs of children.[71] In so doing, however, the Lili'uokalani Trust adhered to the mandates of the trust provisions by maintaining an independent staff who worked specifically with Hawaiian children.[72]

In 1941, two social service organizations, the Children's Service Association and the Family Consultation Service, merged to form the Child and Family Service. For the next five years, the Lili'uokalani Trust continued its singular work under the auspices of the Child and Family Service. By this time, the trust's financial condition had improved, a circumstance which encouraged the trustees to consider establishing an autonomous child welfare agency. In 1946, the Child Welfare Department, Lili'uokalani Trust was created.[73]

As part of its plan to build an independent child welfare agency, the trustees sought legal clarification concerning the trust beneficiaries. Specifically, the trustees requested legal definitions of the terms "orphan" and "destitute" used in the trust instrument. A 1941 legal opinion from its attorneys deemed orphans to include children having only one legal parent.[74] A legal definition of "destitute," rendered by the trust's attorneys in 1951, concluded that the trustees were empowered with full discretion in selecting the beneficiaries of the trust.[75] Furthermore, this discretion included the decisions concerning termination of benefits. Both opinions served to reinforce the wide latitude possessed by the trustees under the trust provisions.

The 1950s witnessed the growth of the Child Welfare Department, Lili'uokalani Trust. In 1952, the Department of Public Welfare licensed the agency as a child-placing organization.[76] The agency also functioned as a field placement site for graduate students studying social work. By 1958, a staff of six professionals provided casework services and financial assistance to approximately 350 children.[77]

The agency proceeded to expand and diversify its services. In 1963, the agency created a Social Work Trainee Program to interest Hawaiian students in social work careers.[78] The agency also opened a Nānākuli office in 1965 to meet the need for services in that area.[79] It constructed its present headquarters and formally dispensed its services as the Queen Lili'uokalani Children's Center in 1966.[80]

Throughout the 1960s and early 1970s, the QLCC established units on Moloka'i and in Hilo.[81] It also began the first phase in the development of its Kona lands.[82] Simultaneously, the QLCC matched its geographical growth with an enhanced commitment to serve not only the needs of its beneficiaries but also the related needs of the Hawaiian community.[83] This perspective resulted in active community development and group service efforts by QLCC staff to complement the direct casework services offered to individual beneficiaries.

The QLCC maintained its concentration on its beneficiaries and in 1972 sought a legal response from the state attorney general as to age limitations of beneficiaries.[84] The attorney general opined that the trust could furnish services to beneficiaries beyond the legal age of majority.[85] Based on this determination, beneficiaries may retain educational assistance and counselling services even after they attain 18 years of age.

Throughout the 1970s, the QLCC offered distinct services in three areas, Individual, Group, and Community Development.[86] These services comprised the core of the center's work with beneficiaries. Individual services involved helping children and their families cope with the loss of parents or single parenthood. Group services facilitated the social, educational, and cultural development of beneficiaries through peer group experiences. Community development services assisted parents in self-help activities aimed at creating improved services and opportunities for their families.

In 1986, the trustees adopted a permanency planning policy, which essentially channelled all trust resources towards assuring a stable home and family for each beneficiary.[87] Staff and beneficiary work as partners in planning for a permanent and stable home environment.

Presently, the QLCC has extended its services to the islands of Maui and Kaua'i. In addition to its Honolulu, Hilo and Moloka'i offices, units are also located in Kona and Windward O'ahu. The center now services approximately 2,000 Hawaiian children statewide yearly.[88]

4. LUNALILO TRUST

King William Charles Lunalilo was among the first *ali'i* landowners to establish a charitable trust to benefit Hawaiians. His intent was to create a home for the care of poor Native Hawaiians.

a. *Will Provisions*

In his will, dated June 7, 1871, Lunalilo directed his trustees to dispose of his property and invest the proceeds until the sum of $25,000 had been accumulated.[89] Once this amount was raised, Lunalilo ordered the trustees to "expend the whole amount in the purchase of land and in the erection of a building or buildings on the Island of O'ahu, of iron, stone, brick or other fire-proof material, for the use and accommodation of poor, destitute and infirm people of Hawaiian (aboriginal) blood or extraction, giving preference to old people."[90]

Lunalilo instructed a majority of the supreme court justices to nominate and appoint three trustees to administer the trust.[91] Any two of the trustees could decide all matters pertaining to the trust.[92] Furthermore, the trustees were required to submit an accounting to the court and could be removed by a majority of the court.[93]

b. *Case Law*

Over a 27-year period, the trustees of the Lunalilo Trust sought legal clarification in administering the trust. Soon after Lunalilo's death in 1874, his will was contested based on his status as a spendthrift at the time the will was made.[94] The court held that although Lunalilo was under guardianship as a spendthrift, he was not incapacitated so as to void the will.[95]

In 1879, the trustees first petitioned the court for direction concerning the investment of the proceeds, which had exceeded $25,000, from the sale of Lunalilo's property.[96] Since the amount of money mentioned in the will had been aggregated, the court ordered the trustees to purchase land and begin construction of a building according to the will's directives.[97]

Two years later, the trustees again sought court assistance in determining their authority to execute leases of the trust estate.[98] Applying a strict interpretation of the will, the court concluded that the trustees could not lease the property, but must sell the trust property even though the realized amounts had already exceeded $25,000.[99] The sales compelled by this decision account for the investment portfolio of securities possessed by the trust today.

The trustees also submitted the question of their compensation to the court.[100] The trustees had purchased and sold stock resulting in a $29,000 gain. Under a state statute, the court determined that the monies constituted receipts realized from securities which should be viewed as principal rather than income.[101] As a result, the court ordered that the trustees should be given a commission based on the 2.5 percent rate applied to receipt of principal rather than a higher rate applied to receipt of income.[102]

c. *Lunalilo Home*

Pursuant to the mandate of Lunalilo's will, the first Lunalilo Home was constructed of volcanic stone on 21 acres located in an underpopulated Makiki area.[103] The home was completed in 1883 and had a capacity to house 50 residents. Forty-four years later, however, the expanding residential area posed a threat to the care of the home's occupants. The trustees sought and found a more secluded area of 20 acres near Koko Head. In 1927, the trustees sold the original Makiki site and purchased the Koko Head land. The Brown family gifted the trust with the purchase price for 11 acres; the trustees bought the remaining nine acres with the proceeds from the sale of the Makiki site.[104] The new Lunalilo Home, once the Radio Corporation of America building, accommodated 56 residents.

In 1969, the trustees developed 15 of the 20 acres into a residential tract of 80 leasehold lots due to the residential and business growth in the Hawai'i Kai area.[105] The home retained the remaining five acres for its operations. In 1983, the trustees sold 73 lots in accordance with a state law concerning leasehold-to-fee conversions.[106]

The Lunalilo Home is a state-licensed adult residential care home, subject to Department of Health regulations.[107] Residents must be ambulatory and continent to qualify for admittance, requirements which are mandated by the licensing criteria, but difficult to satisfy. The trustees are working toward acquiring a license as an intermediate care facility, which would allow a greater eligibility among Hawaiian elderly. Still, the home reflects Lunalilo's concern for his people and offers an important service to those Hawaiian elders who qualify for its benefits.

5.   QUEEN EMMA TRUST

As a young queen, Emma, wife of King Kamehameha IV, had great compassion for the sick and indigent people of her time. She envisioned a medical facility where those who were ill and without financial means could receive hospital care.[108] Queen Emma enlisted her husband's assistance and both personally solicited monies from among Hawai'i's residents to raise funds for a hospital.[109] Their efforts resulted in the founding of the Queen's Hospital in 1859.[110]

The hospital's charter of incorporation empowered the incorporators to establish a permanent medical facility in Honolulu for the treatment of sick and disabled Hawaiians.[111] The charter also authorized the treatment and accommodation of "foreigners and others who may choose to avail themselves."[112] Any surplus money would be used to establish other hospitals.[113] In 1860, the first building was completed. By 1931, through private monetary contributions and legislative appropriations, the Queen's Hospital offered comprehensive medical services.[114]

Queen Emma's lifetime efforts to provide medical care continued beyond her death in 1885. In her will, dated October 21, 1884, Queen Emma assured the Queen's Hospital of ongoing financial support to maintain and expand its medical services by devising several parcels of land and income from other lands to the hospital.

a.   Trust Provisions

Queen Emma's will contains 16 paragraphs, six of which comprise the pertinent trust provisions. Aside from provisions for the hospital, the first ten paragraphs provide for usual expenses, bequeath monies to servants, devise small tracts of land, and permit residence on two of the queen's premises.[115] Paragraph 11 bequeaths life annuities in the amount of $2,100 to four persons. Paragraph 12 establishes four yearly scholarships totalling $600 at St. Andrew's Priory.[116]

Paragraph 13 creates the trust estate. It devises seven pieces of real estate to Alexander Cartwright in trust, with the subsequent rents, income and profits earmarked to satisfy the previously mentioned annuities and scholarships.[117] Paragraph 13 also directs that one-half of the surplus rents, income or profit from the real estate, after payment of the annuities and scholarships, goes to the Queen's Hospital.[118] The queen's cousin, Albert Kūnuiākea, receives the other half under the same conditions as above.[119] The trustee is authorized to sell the tracts upon the death of the annuitants, provided the remaining real estate produced income sufficient to fund the four scholarships.[120] Proceeds from any sale were to be divided one-half to the Queen's Hospital and one-half to trustee Cartwright, in trust, to pay to Albert Kūnuiākea.[121]

Paragraph 14 devised eight other tracts of Honolulu real estate and the remainder of the queen's Maui lands to the Queen's Hospital.[122] In paragraph 15, trustee Cartwright also received five pieces of Hawai'i and Maui lands in trust for Albert Kūnuiākea.[123] Paragraph 16 allots the residue of the queen's estate in equal portions to the Queen's Hospital and Albert Kūnuiākea.[124] In the event of Kūnuiākea's demise without issue, the hospital would receive the entire residue.[125]

The trust provisions indicate that the annuities and scholarships were of prime importance to Queen Emma.[126] Secondarily, the queen intended to benefit the Queen's Hospital and her cousin Albert.[127] These purposes would bear on future judicial interpretations of the trust provisions.[128]

b. Case Law

The few cases addressing the trust provisions cover a range of issues. In *Rooke v. Queen's Hospital* (1900),[129] the court held that the lands devised to the Queen's Hospital in paragraph 14 were not legally Queen Emma's property. Title belonged to C.C.K. Rooke, not to Queen Emma. Therefore, the hospital had no claim to the lands. In a 1904 case, *In re The Queen's Hospital*,[130] the territorial auditor challenged a legislative appropriation for the Queen's Hospital. Based on the hospital's charitable functions, the court held that legislative appropriations were lawful.

In a case more directly related to the trust, Queen's Hospital sought to obtain the monies and property in excess of the payment of annuities and scholarships.[131] Interpreting paragraph 13 as empowering the trustee to modify the land investments only after or upon the death of the annuitants, the court refused to terminate the trust prior to that time.[132]

The court faced a contrary situation in *Hite v. Queen's Hospital* (1942)[133] when the successor trustee questioned the lack of preference in treating Hawaiian patients, which he felt conflicted with Queen Emma's intent in establishing the hospital.[134] After reviewing the hospital's charter as well as the queen's will, the court held that the hospital was for the use of the general public and Hawaiians alike.[135]

Five years later, the Queen's Hospital again attempted to terminate the trust.[136] The court dismissed the suit, indicating that the discontinuance of the $600 scholarship to St. Andrew's Priory would violate the express provisions contained in Queen Emma's will.[137]

The Queen's Hospital finally succeeded in its attempt to effect a partial distribution of the trust estate. In *Queen's Hospital v. Hite* (1950),[138] the court ordered the successor trustee to determine the real estate needed to fund the scholarships to the Priory and to transfer the excess land to the Queen's Hospital.[139] A factor in the court's decision was the costly administrative charges incurred in generating funds for a mere $600 scholarship.[140]

In 1967, citing the economic infeasibility of maintaining the trust to provide $600 in scholarships, Judge Allan Hawkins terminated the Queen Emma Trust.[141] The court, however, retained a separate trust account of $25,000 to fund the Priory scholarships.[142] Pursuant to the will provisions, the Queen's Hospital obtained the two remaining lots, worth approximately $1 million.[143]

At the present time, the Queen's Health Systems manages the Queen's Medical Center, formerly the Queen's Hospital. It is the twentieth largest corporation in the state, with revenues of $192.3 million.[144] A portion of revenues is allocated to fund cancer research.[145] Although the Queen Emma Trust no longer exists, the success of the Queen's Health Systems signifies the far-reaching benefits of the trust and symbolizes the timelessness of Queen Emma's gift to her people.

6. CONCLUSION

The Hawaiian *ali'i* demonstrated their concern for the Native Hawaiian people by establishing trusts to provide education, health care, and social welfare benefits for Hawaiians. The trusts, particularly the Kamehameha Schools/Bishop Estate, represent a vast resource for Hawaiians. While the trusts undoubtedly have aided many Hawaiians, they are faced with difficult challenges as the needs of the Native Hawaiian community become more complex. Whether the trustees and courts will interpret specific trust provisions broadly enough to meet these changing needs is unknown. Surely, in interpreting the trust provisions, the intent of the *ali'i* to benefit their people must be the guiding principle.

NOTES

1. *Wills and Deeds of Trust: Bernice P. Bishop Estate, Bernice P. Bishop Museum, Charles R. Bishop Estate* 17-18 (3rd ed. 1957).
2. *Id.* at 18.
3. *Id.*
4. *Id.*
5. *Id.*
6. *Id.*
7. *Id.* at 18-19.
8. *Id.* at 18.
9. *Id.* at 19.
10. *Id.*
11. *Id.*
12. *Id.*
13. *Id.*
14. *Id.* at 24.
15. *Id.* at 27.
16. *Id.*
17. Kamehameha Schools/Bernice Pauahi Bishop Estate, The Land of KS/BE (1983).
18. *Id.*
19. Honolulu Star-Bulletin, Aug. 31, 1987, at A6, col. 1.
20. 11 Haw. 153 (1897).
21. *In re Bishop Estate*, 16 Haw. 804 (1905).
22. *Smith v. Lindsay*, 20 Haw. 330 (1910).
23. *Smith v. Lymer*, 29 Haw. 169 (1926) in which the court also approved the hiring of a real estate broker to sell estate lands and allowed trustee commissions based on the construction costs of the new buildings. In *In re Estate of Bishop*, 36 Haw. 403 (1943), the court applied general trust law in concluding that the trustees could employ others necessary in assisting the trustees in the discharge of their duties.
24. 33 Haw. 647 (1935).
25. *Collins v. Hodgson*, 36 Haw. 334 (1943).
26. 11 Haw. 535 (1898).
27. *Smith v. Lymer*, 29 Haw. 169, 176 (1926); *Bishop v. Pittman*, 33 Haw. 647 (1935).
28. 23 Haw. 575 (1917). On appeal, the Ninth Circuit agreed with the Hawai'i court that an appointment by a majority of the justices was final. 250 F. 145 (9th Cir. 1918).
29. 55 Haw. 104, 516 P.2d 1239 (1973). (A beneficiary challenged the appointment of Matsuo Takabuki as violative of procedural due process, the state constitution and the Canons of Judicial Ethics.)
30. 48 Haw. 32, 396 P.2d 49 (1964). (Trustee Atherton Richards sued the majority trustees for breach of trust relating to the lease of estate lands by the trustees which had previously been leased to Richards.)
31. *Id.* at 56, 396 P.2d at 62.
32. 54 Haw. 299, 507 P.2d 724 (1973). (Minority trustee sued majority trustees over proposed development plans for Keauhou, which had been approved by the attorney general but never submitted to the circuit court. The court held that trustees need court authorization of any deviation from the trust instrument.)
33. *Id.* at 336, 507 P.2d at 745.
34. Haw. Rev. Stat. § 607-20 (1985) states as follows:

    Charitable trusts, special provisions. Notwithstanding any other provisions, in the case of an estate of a charitable trust, the commissions of the trustees shall be limited to the following schedule of percentages on all moneys received in the nature of revenue or income of the estate, such as rents, interests, and general profits: ten per cent on the first $1,000; seven per cent on the next $4,000; five per cent on the next $100,000; three per cent on the next $100,000; and two per cent on all over $205,000. This schedule of percentages shall be applied not oftener than once a year.

The trustees shall also be entitled to just and reasonable allowances for bookkeeping, clerical, and special services and expenses incidental thereto.

This section shall apply as well to future accounting in existing estates as to new estates.

In 1989, the trustees each received $659,558 in compensation. Honolulu Advertiser, June 1, 1990 at A-4.

35. 37 Haw. 111 (1945).

36. *Id.* at 149.

37. *In re Estate of Bishop*, 53 Haw. 604, 499 P.2d 670 (1972).

38. Haw. Rev. Stat. § 516-23 (1985).

39. *Id.* The section states:

> **Exercise of power of eminent domain.** Within twelve months after the designation of all or part of the development tract for acquisition, the Hawaii housing authority shall acquire through voluntary action of the parties, or institute eminent domain proceedings to acquire the leased fee interest in the tract or portion so designated; provided that negotiations for acquisition by voluntary transaction shall not be required before the institution of eminent domain proceedings. Except as otherwise provided in this part, the authority shall exercise its power of eminent domain in the same manner as provided in chapter 101. If the development tract or applicable portion thereof, as the case may be, is not acquired or eminent domain proceedings are not instituted within the twelve-month period, the authority shall reimburse the fee owner, the lessor and the legal and equitable owners of the land so designated for actual out-of-pocket expenses of appraisal, survey, and attorney fees as the owner, the lessor, and the legal and equitable owners may have incurred as a result of the designation.

40. *Midkiff v. Tom*, 471 F. Supp. 871 (D. Haw. 1979); *Midkiff v. Tom*, 483 F. Supp. 62 (D. Haw. 1979); *Midkiff v. Tom*, 702 F.2d 788 (9th Cir. 1983); *Hawaii Housing Authority v. Midkiff*, 463 U.S. 1323 (1983); *Midkiff v. Tom*, 725 F.2d 502 (9th Cir. 1984); *Hawaii Housing Authority v. Midkiff*, 467 U.S. 229 (1984); *Midkiff v. Tom*, 740 F.2d 15 (9th Cir. 1984).

41. *Hawaii Housing Authority v. Midkiff*, 467 U.S. 229, 241-244 (1984).

42. *Id.*

43. *Id.* The trustees initiated a formal, voluntary lease conversion program in 1978. However, after initial success with the program, many lessees opted to initiate condemnation proceedings.

44. Kamehameha Schools/Bernice Pauahi Bishop Estate, The Land of KS/BE (1983).

45. *Id.*

46. *Id.*

47. *Id.*

48. Honolulu Star-Bulletin, Aug. 31, 1987, at A1, col. 1.

49. *Id.*

50. Honolulu Star-Bulletin, Sept. 1, 1987, at A6, col. 1.

51. Honolulu Star-Bulletin, Sept. 2, 1987, at A1, col. 2.

52. Honolulu Star-Bulletin, Aug. 31, 1987, at A6, col. 4.

53. Honolulu Star-Bulletin, Sept. 1, 1987, at A6, col. 3.

54. Honolulu Star-Bulletin, Aug. 31, 1987, at A6, col. 4.

55. Honolulu Star-Bulletin, Sept. 1, 1987, at A6, col. 3.

56. *In re Estate of Lydia K. Dominis, a.k.a. Liliuokalani*, Probate No. 5342, First Circuit Court (1923).

57. *Id.*

58. *Id.*

59. *Id.*

60. *Id.*

61. *In re Estate of Liliuokalani*, 25 Haw. 127 (1919). (The court dismissed claim of inheritance brought by Mrs. Theresa Belliveau on the grounds that she could not establish her genealogical relationship to the queen.)

62. *In re Estate of Lydia K. Dominis, a.k.a. Liliuokalani*, Probate No. 5342, First Circuit Court (1923).

63. *Id.*

64. *Id.*

65. Queen Liliuokalani Children's Center, 1987 Manual 7 (1987) (Section 1: History, Philosophy, Agency Mission, Goals, Programs, Eligibility and Priorities, Organization and Administration).

66. *Id.*

67. *Id.*
68. *Id.*
69. *Id.*
70. *Id.* at 8.
71. *Id.*
72. *Id.*
73. *Id.*
74. *Id.* at 9.
75. *Id.* at 9-10.
76. *Id.* at 10.
77. *Id.* at 11.
78. *Id.* at 12.
79. *Id.*
80. *Id.* at 12.
81. *Id.* at 14.
82. *Id.*
83. *Id.* at 15.
84. *Id.* at 14.
85. *Id.* at 14-15.
86. Queen Liliuokalani Children's Center, 1982 Annual Report 8.
87. Queen Liliuokalani Children's Center, 1987 Annual Report 5.
88. *Id.*
89. *In re Estate of William Charles Lunalilo*, Probate No. 2414, First Circuit Court (1874).
90. *Id.*
91. *Id.*
92. *Id.*
93. *Id.*
94. *In re Estate of Lunalilo*, 3 Haw. 519 (1874).
95. *Id.* at 520, 522.
96. *In re Estate of Lunalilo*, 4 Haw. 162 (1879).
97. *Id.* at 165.
98. *In re Estate of Lunalilo*, 4 Haw 381 (1881).
99. *Id.* at 383.
100. *In re Estate of Lunalilo*, 13 Haw. 317 (1901).
101. *Id.* at 318.
102. *Id.*
103. Lunalilo Home (pamphlet published by Lunalilo Home, 1982).
104. *Id.*
105. *Id.*
106. *Id.*
107. *Id.*
108. Honolulu Advertiser, July 2, 1931, at Sec. 3-17, col. 1.
109. *Id.*
110. *Id.*
111. *In re Queen's Hospital*, 15 Haw. 663, 665 (1904).
112. *Id.*
113. *Id.*
114. *Id.* In 1931, the Queen's Hospital provided emergency, maternity, surgical, x-ray, laboratory, clinic, dietary, training, social and physiotherapy services. As a private charitable organization, the hospital qualified for legislative appropriations. *In re Queen's Hospital*, 15 Haw. 663 (1904).
115. *Queen's Hospital v. Hite, Trustee, et al.*, 38 Haw. 494, 496 (1950).
116. *Id.*
117. *Id.*
118. *Id.* at 497.
119. *Id.*

120. *Id.* at 496.
121. *Id.* at 496-497.
122. *Id.*
123. *Id.* at 497-498.
124. *Id.* at 498.
125. *Id.*
126. *Id.* at 499.
127. *Id.*
128. The courts would rely on the priority of the annuities and scholarships in decisions regarding termination of the trust. In addition, the queen's subordinate purpose of benefitting her cousin proved short-lived. Albert Kūnuiākea died without issue in 1903, thereby entitling the Queen's Hospital to the entire residue of the estate.
129. 12 Haw. 375 (1900).
130. 15 Haw. 663 (1904).
131. *Queen's Hospital v. Cartwright*, 19 Haw. 52 (1908).
132. *Id.* at 62.
133. 36 Haw. 250 (1942).
134. *Id.* at 258-259.
135. *Id.* at 268.
136. Honolulu Advertiser, Nov. 25, 1947, at 4, col. 7.
137. *Id.*
138. 38 Haw. 494 (1950).
139. *Id.* at 520-521.
140. *Id.* at 518.
141. Honolulu Star-Bulletin, Mar. 8, 1967, at A10, col. 1.
142. *Id.*
143. Honolulu Advertiser, Mar. 8, 1967, at A1, col. 6.
144. Chang and Yoneyama, *The Fifth Annual Ranking of the Largest Public and Private Corporations in Hawaii*, Hawaii Business 51, 76 (August 1988).
145. Honolulu Star-Bulletin, May 4, 1988, at B1, col. 1.

CHAPTER 16

FEDERAL PROGRAMS AND BENEFITS FOR NATIVE HAWAIIANS

1. INTRODUCTION

In limited instances, the federal government has recognized a responsibility to the Native Hawaiian people by enacting specific provisions for their benefit. Most often these provisions, acknowledging the social, health, and educational problems of Native Hawaiians, are based on need and social policy rather than the unique status of Native Hawaiians as native people. Nevertheless, the increasing number of federal programs and benefits for Native Hawaiians is a positive step.

The following chapter briefly outlines the relevant acts and provisions specifically directed to Native Hawaiians. In almost all of these acts, congress has defined a Native Hawaiian as one with any quantity of Hawaiian blood. The few acts that do set a blood quantum requirement are specifically tied to the Hawaiian Homes Commission Act.

2. EDUCATION PROVISIONS

a. *Hawkins-Stafford Elementary and Secondary Education Improvement Act*[1]
In 1988, congress passed legislation releasing federal money for educating Native Hawaiians.

(1) *Title I, Basic Requirements, Subtitle V, Drug Education*[2] Under this program, the Secretary of Education is authorized to make grants to organizations that primarily serve or represent Native Hawaiians. To qualify, the organization must be recognized by the governor of Hawai'i, and monies received under the grant must be used to plan, conduct, and administer drug education programs for the benefit of Native Hawaiians.

(2) *Title IV, Education for Native Hawaiians*[3] As the result of a study showing that Native Hawaiians performed poorly in schools, congress determined that federal assistance in education was necessary. Title IV was enacted to develop supplemental educational programs to benefit Native Hawaiians.[4] These programs include:
  (a) *Native Hawaiian Model Curriculum*[5] The Kamehameha Elementary Education Program (KEEP) receives partial federal funding. The KEEP program primarily involves the Kamehameha Schools and the Department of Education acting together to provide a Reading Comprehension Program. The elementary schools that have been targeted by KEEP are (1) Pāhoa, (2) Waimea, (3) Hau'ula, (4) Keaukaha, (5) Kekaha, (6) Nānā I Ka Pono, (7) Wai'anae, and (8) Mākaha.
  (b) *Native Hawaiian Family-Based Education*[6] Grants may be made to Native Hawaiian organizations for parent-infant programs, preschool programs, research and development, and assessment programs. The purpose is to develop a minimum of 11 statewide family-based education centers to carry out the programs. Kamehameha Schools receives funding for its Pre-educational Kindergarten Program (PREP). PREP is comprised

of a traveling preschool program, a home visiting program, and three learning centers with additional centers to be established.

(c)   *Native Hawaiian Higher Education Demonstration Program*[7]   The Kamehameha Schools receives a grant to administer this program to aid Native Hawaiian students in their pursuit of post-high school education. Accordingly, the funds can be used for the following purposes:

(1)   Full or partial fellowships for students enrolled in any accredited two- or four-year college, business, or vocational training institution. Applicants for these grants must be residents of Hawai'i of Hawaiian ancestry. Awards are based on academic potential and financial need;

(2)   Counseling and support services for the college students;

(3)   College preparation and guidance for secondary students;

(4)   Research and evaluation related to college preparation and guidance; and

(5)   Faculty development programs to aid Native Hawaiian students.[8]

Also authorized are similar programs for post-bachelor degree education for Native Hawaiians. Post-bachelor degree grantees must provide professional services to the Native Hawaiian community upon completion of their degree.

(d)   *Native Hawaiian Gifted and Talented Demonstration Program*[9]   A federal grant was awarded to the University of Hawai'i at Hilo to establish a Native Hawaiian Gifted and Talented Center on its campus. The purpose of the center is to address the emotional, psychological, and educational needs of gifted and talented Hawaiian students enrolled in elementary and secondary schools. To meet the special needs of these students, the use of the Hawaiian language, culture and tradition is encouraged. The center also provides support services for the parents of these students.

The initial grant was made to the University of Hawai'i at Hilo for a three-year period. At the end of this period, the four-year accredited college in Hawai'i that has made the greatest contribution to Native Hawaiian students will be eligible for this grant.

(e)   *Native Hawaiian Special Education Program*[10]   Grants were made to the State of Hawai'i Department of Education to meet the special education needs of Hawaiian children. These grants may be used for the identification of special needs children, to conduct educational activities, and for research and evaluation activities.

b.   *Library Service and Construction Act*[11]

This act is designed to assist states in the growth and improvement of public library services. As part of this effort, the Secretary of Education is authorized to make grants to organizations that primarily serve or represent Hawaiians. Alu Like, Inc. is the sole recipient of money under this act.

Funds may be used for training and salaries of Native Hawaiian library personnel; library materials; conducting special library programs for Native Hawaiians; constructing, renovating, purchasing, or remodeling library facilities; transportation allowing Native Hawaiians access to library services; disseminating information about library services; and assessing Native Hawaiian library needs.[12]

3. TRAINING, ECONOMIC DEVELOPMENT AND EMPLOYMENT PROVISIONS

a. *Vocational Training*

Congress has established various programs to improve vocational skills and education. Native Americans have been particularly targeted for assistance.

(1) *Vocational Education*[13] The purposes of this measure include assisting the states to improve vocational education programs in order to meet the needs of the nation's work force, insuring access to vocational education programs for inadequately served or disadvantaged individuals, and assisting the economically depressed areas of a state.[14]

The Secretary of Education is directed to enter into contracts with organizations primarily serving and representing Native Hawaiians which are recognized by the governor of Hawai'i. Alu Like, Inc. is the primary recipient of these funds.

(2) *Job Training Partnership Act*[15] The purpose of this act is to establish programs to prepare youth and unskilled adults for entry into the job market and to provide similar assistance for those facing serious barriers in obtaining employment.[16]

Congress found that serious unemployment and economic disadvantages exist among members of Indian, Alaskan Native, and Native Hawaiian communities. Further, congress believed that there was a compelling need to provide training to these groups and that such programs are essential to the reduction of the disadvantages these groups suffer.[17]

Due to the special relationship which exists between the federal government and native peoples, programs should be administered on the national level. The Secretary of Labor is authorized to arrange such programs for Native Hawaiians through such organizations as the secretary determines will best meet their needs.[18] Preference is to be given to groups which are directly controlled by Native Hawaiians.[19]

The act authorizes job search assistance; job development; training in skills in which demand exceeds supply; supportive services, including community assistance and financial and personal counseling; pre-layoff assistance; relocation assistance; and programs conducted in cooperation with employers and labor organizations to provide early intervention in the event of plant closing.[20]

Relocation assistance may be provided if the individual cannot obtain employment within the commuting area and if the individual has obtained a *bona fide* long-term employment offer.[21] Services must be provided to eligible Native Hawaiian populations on an equitable basis.[22]

Summer Youth Employment and Training Programs for Native Americans are also authorized by the act.[23]

b. *Economic Opportunity Program, Native American Program Act*[24]

The purpose of this act, as amended in 1987, is to promote the goal of economic self-sufficiency for American Indians, Native Hawaiians, other Native American Pacific Islanders (including American Samoan Natives), and Native Alaskans.[25]

The Secretary of Health and Human Services is authorized to provide financial assistance, on a single- or multi-year basis, to public and nonprofit private agencies serving Native Hawaiians.[26]

The secretary awards grants to one agency of the State of Hawai'i, or to a community-based organization whose purpose is the economic and social self-sufficiency of

Native Hawaiians. This grant shall be used to carry out a five-year demonstration project which shall establish a loan fund. This loan fund will be used to make loans to Native Hawaiian organizations or individuals for the purpose of promoting economic development in Hawai'i. The Office of Hawaiian Affairs was awarded the grant and has established a Native Hawaiian loan fund.

In order to qualify for a loan, a prospective borrower must show that financing from other sources is not available on reasonable terms and that there is a reasonable chance of paying back the loan. The loan terms cannot exceed five years and the interest is to be two percent below the current yield on Treasury bills. Borrowers may be required to provide collateral. A written copy of any collection procedure should be given to the borrower at the time the loan is made. No loans may be made after November 29, 1992.[27]

The secretary may provide grants to help public or private organizations test or develop new approaches that will help Native Americans overcome problems which prevent them from becoming economically self-sufficient.[28]

c. *Employment Preferences*

(1) *Kaloko-Honokōhau National Historic Park*[29] In 1978, congress passed the National Parks and Recreation Act, which established the Kaloko-Honokōhau National Historical Park. The park encompasses 1,300 acres on the Big Island.[30] Congress created the park to provide a center for the preservation, interpretation, and perpetuation of traditional Native Hawaiian activities and culture.[31] It intended that the park reflect historic land use patterns and offer a needed resource for the education, enjoyment, and appreciation of traditional Native Hawaiian activities and culture by local residents and visitors.[32]

The Secretary of Interior manages the park in accordance both with the laws regulating the national park system and with a study report entitled "Kaloko-Honokohau" of May 1974.[33] The secretary is authorized to acquire lands for the park by donation, exchange or purchase.[34] Surplus federal lands may also be acquired for the exchange of park lands. Any exchange, however, must involve lands of equal value or include equalizing cash payments.[35]

The act also regulates the secretary's management of park activities. The secretary may furnish traditional Hawaiian accommodations.[36] The submerged lands located within the park must be managed in compliance with state marine policies.[37] Fishing and shoreline food gathering as well as access to the small boat harbor are permitted, subject to regulation.[38] The air and water quality of the park and the scenic and aesthetic values of surrounding areas are preserved in ways compatible with traditional Native Hawaiian land and water management concepts.[39] Furthermore, the act directs the secretary to employ Native Hawaiians within the park.[40]

The secretary appoints a nine-member Advisory Committee to advise the National Park Service on matters relating to park management. Native Hawaiian organizations nominate five prospective appointees. All members are residents of Hawai'i; at least six members must be Native Hawaiian. Committee members do not receive compensation, although they may be reimbursed for expenses reasonably incurred in official duties. Ex-officio, non-voting members of the committee include the park superintendent, the National Park Service State Director, a gubernatorial appointee, and a Hawai'i County mayoral appointee.[41]

(2) *Kalaupapa National Historical Park*[42] Congress established the Kalaupapa National Historical Park in 1980. Located on Moloka'i's north shore, the park consists of the entire Kalaupapa peninsula, which was used to isolate leprosy victims in 1865. The leprosy settlement was created as a result of an 1865 law authorizing the Minister of the Interior to allocate government-owned lands for the isolation of any persons with Hansen's disease. Beginning in 1866, the settlement served as an exile for more than 7,000 persons suffering from the disease. The settlement's best-known resident was Father Damien who gained worldwide attention by caring for patients for 14 years until he succumbed to the disease.[43]

Given the history of the settlement, congress sought to preserve its internationally unique cultural, historical, educational and scenic resources.[44] In 1980, it established the Kalaupapa National Historical Park to preserve these resources and to pay tribute to the inspirational work of Father Damien. In creating a national park, congress guaranteed that Kalaupapa patients would be able to maintain their community and provided for the maintenance of historic sites and cultural values.[45] However, when there is no longer a resident patient community, the Secretary of Interior is authorized to re-evaluate the park's policies.[46] Congress also intended that patients and Native Hawaiians manage the settlement and accordingly provided for training opportunities.[47]

The Secretary of Interior is authorized to acquire lands within the boundaries of the park from the state or its political subdivisions by donation or exchange. Some of the lands within the park are held by the Department of Hawaiian Home Lands and thus any lands conveyed to the state in exchange for DHHL lands will be held in trust for the benefit of Native Hawaiians as defined in the Hawaiian Homes Commission Act. The secretary can also acquire privately owned lands for the park by donation, purchase or exchange.[48]

The secretary is empowered to form agreements with other park property owners for the preservation and improvement of resources having historic, architectural and cultural significance.[49] Kalaupapa patients decide many of the settlement's visitor policies, such as the restriction permitting only 100 visitors daily. Patients are also allowed to hunt and fish within the park without regard to federal fish and game laws.[50] Patients and Native Hawaiians receive preference in appointments to positions established for the administration of the park. They are also provided with training opportunities to develop the skills necessary to qualify for such positions.[51] Under this provision, Native Hawaiians must meet the 50 percent blood quantum requirement.

The park has an advisory commission to advise the secretary on matters of park development and operation. The commission consists of 11 members, seven of whom are former or present patients elected from the community. The remaining four members are recommended by the governor. At least one of these four must be Native Hawaiian.[52]

4. HOUSING PROVISIONS

a. *National Housing Act*[53]

The National Housing Act creates a General Insurance Fund which the Secretary of Housing and Urban Development may use to insure qualifying single-family mortgages on Hawaiian Home Lands.[54] This provision holds particular relevance for Native Hawaiians. A section of the act extends the insurance program to one- to four-family residences on

Hawaiian Home Lands.[55] The limitations of the act with respect to marketability of title are waived if:

(1) The mortgagor is Native Hawaiian and the property is within Hawaiian Home Lands and is under a homestead lease;

(2) The property will be the principal residence of the mortgagor; and

(3) The Department of Hawaiian Home Lands of the state is a co-mortgagor and guarantees to reimburse any claims paid or offers other acceptable security.[56]

Applicants must meet the 50 percent blood quantum requirements of the Hawaiian Homes Act or be a spouse or child successor as provided under the act.[57]

5. CULTURE AND ARTS

a. *Program for Native Hawaiian Culture and Arts Development*[58]

Native Hawaiian culture and arts receive congressional support through grants authorized by the Secretary of the Interior for Native Hawaiian culture and arts development. Any private, nonprofit organization which primarily serves Native Hawaiians and is recognized by the governor of Hawai'i qualifies for congressional aid.[59] The grants provide support for scholarly study and instruction in Native Hawaiian art and culture, create degree-awarding programs in Native Hawaiian culture and arts, and establish Native Hawaiian culture and arts centers.[60]

Organizations receiving grants must have a managerial board consisting of Native Hawaiians or individuals widely recognized in the field of Hawaiian culture and art. Representation on the board by the Office of Hawaiian Affairs, the president of the University of Hawai'i, and the president of Bishop Museum is required.[61] Presently, the Bishop Museum is the primary recipient of the grant.

6. HEALTH PROVISIONS

a. *Native Hawaiian Health Care Act of 1988*[62]

Congress determined that a policy of the United States is to raise the health status of Native Hawaiians to the highest possible level and to encourage the maximum participation of Native Hawaiians in order to achieve this objective. In keeping with this, the Secretary of Health and Human Services has been authorized to grant federal monies to Papa Ola Lōkahi, the Native Hawaiian Health Board, which is comprised of (1) the Office of Hawaiian Affairs; (2) E Ola Mau; (3) Alu Like; (4) the University of Hawai'i John A. Burns School of Medicine; and (5) the newly established State Health Planning and Development Agency.

Papa Ola Lōkahi will develop a Native Hawaiian comprehensive master health care plan, and with the secretary, may make grants to qualified entities for the purpose of providing comprehensive health promotion, disease prevention services as well as primary health services. Qualified entities would be a Native Hawaiian health center or a Native Hawaiian organization.

b. *Grants for Supporting and Nutritional Services to Older Hawaiians*[63]

This program was established to meet the unique needs and circumstances of older Native Hawaiians, as provided by the Older Americans Act. Eligible entities are public and nonprofit private organizations providing supportive and nutritional services to at least 50 Native Hawaiians over the age of 60.

c. *Research and Demonstration Hearing Screening and Follow-Up Program for Native Hawaiian Children*

Due to the high hearing loss statistics affecting Native Hawaiian children, monies were appropriated in 1988 under the authority of the Rehabilitation Act of 1973, as amended. Kamehameha Schools received the grant award in March of 1989.

7. SUBSTANCE ABUSE PROVISIONS

a. *Drug Abuse Prevention, Treatment, and Rehabilitation*[64]

The growing extent of drug abuse led congress to consider a coordinated program and effort on the international, national, state, and community levels to combat both supply and demand for illicit drugs. Accordingly, congress implemented a drug abuse prevention, treatment and rehabilitation program using federal government resources to reduce the incidence of costs of drug abuse.

Congress authorized the National Institute on Drug Abuse to provide funds to individuals and entities for training seminars, educational programs and developing drug abuse prevention, treatment, and rehabilitation programs. Funds are also available to identify new drug abuse programs and conduct early intervention services. Programs addressing alcohol abuse and alcoholism also qualify for grants from the National Institute on Drug Abuse.[65]

State substance abuse agencies receive and review all funding applications. Applications submitted by public or state agencies have priority over those received from the private or local sector. Grantees must substantially supervise the activity, provide efficient program administration and account for the disbursement of funds. Applicants must also offer a program evaluation scheme.[66] Applications aimed at underserved populations such as racial and ethnic minorities, including Native Hawaiians and Native American Pacific Islanders, are given special consideration.[67] The state governor must approve all grants.[68]

Grantees must offer services that are community based, responsive to the needs of clients, especially handicapped persons, and integrated with other agencies and programs. Grantees must utilize the services of persons fluent in a language other than English if a substantial number of the target population is of limited English-speaking ability. In addition, grantees should rely on existing community resources where appropriate.[69]

b. *Drug-Free Schools and Communities*[70]

Congress has appropriated federal funds to establish programs for drug abuse education and prevention.[71] Of the total funds appropriated, 0.2 percent are earmarked for Native Hawaiian programs.[72] The Secretary of Education is directed to enter into contracts with organizations which primarily serve Native Hawaiians and which are recognized by the governor to plan, conduct, and administer programs for drug abuse education. These programs target school-age Native Hawaiians for drug abuse prevention services. Kamehameha Schools/Bishop Estate has received the grant to administer the program. One such targeted community is Nānākuli.

c. *Comprehensive Alcohol Abuse and Alcoholism Prevention, Treatment, and Rehabilitation Program*[73]

Congress established a comprehensive community care program to address national alcohol-related needs. The program incorporates federal, state, and local planning of federal assistance and concentrates on developing ways to lower the incidence of substance abuse. It also implements methods for diverting problem drinkers from the criminal justice system into training programs. In addition, the program seeks to develop effective occupational prevention and treatment services and increase federal research on causation and prevention of alcohol abuse.[74]

Congress also established the National Commission on Alcohol and Other Alcohol Related Problems to conduct a needs assessment of special and underserved population groups. The needs of Native Hawaiians are expressly identified as requiring study, as is the adequacy of existing services to fulfill such needs.[75]

d. *Grants and Contracts for the Demonstration of New and More Effective Alcohol Abuse and Alcoholism Prevention, Treatment, and Rehabilitation Programs*[76]

The National Institute on Alcohol Abuse and Alcoholism awards grants to and may contract with public and nonprofit private entities to conduct projects specializing in prevention and early intervention of alcohol abuse. The institute may also fund coordinating efforts of all alcohol abuse programs and offer education and training to treatment personnel.[77] Grantees must adhere to the service guidelines listed under the Drug Abuse Prevention, Treatment and Rehabilitation Program.[78] Applications are handled in the same manner as those for drug abuse funding, except that the National Advisory Council on Alcohol Abuse and Alcoholism reviews all applications for alcohol abuse appropriations.[79]

Congress expressly considered Native Hawaiians in enacting these funding provisions. Based on data indicating that although Native Hawaiians comprise 22.6 percent of the state's population in need of alcohol treatment services, only seven percent of this group receive treatment services, congress determined that Native Hawaiian demonstration projects deserve special consideration.[80] As a result, Native Hawaiians are designated recipients of substance abuse funding.

8. CONCLUSION

Congress has not included Native Hawaiians in all programs or acts benefiting other Native Americans. This appears to be an appropriate and rational decision given the different historical and political relationships developed with the federal government by Native Hawaiians and other native groups. A blanket classification as Native Americans would contain as many disadvantages for Native Hawaiians as advantages. Thus, while Native Hawaiians continue to seek federal recognition of their self-governing rights, they also acknowledge that their situation and claims are unique and different from those of other Native Americans.

NOTES

1. Pub. L. No. 100-297, 102 Stat. 130 (1988).
2. *Id.* at § 1001, § 5134.
3. *Id.* at §§ 4001-08, 102 Stat. 358-63.
4. *Id.* at § 4004.
5. *Id.* at § 4003.
6. *Id.* at § 4004.
7. *Id.* at § 4005.
8. *Id.* at § 4005(a).
9. *Id.* at § 4006.
10. *Id.* at § 4007.
11. 20 U.S.C. § 351 (1988).
12. *Id.* at § 351c(d)(2); *see* 34 C.F.R. § 771 *et seq.* (1988) (implementing regulations).
13. 20 U.S.C. § 2301 *et seq.* (1982).
14. *Id.*; 34 C.F.R. § 400 *et seq.* (1988).
15. 29 U.S.C. § 1501 *et seq.* (1987). *See* 20 C.F.R. § 632 (1988) (implementing regulations).
16. 29 U.S.C. § 1501 (1987).
17. *Id.* at § 1671(a).
18. *Id.* at § 1671(c)(1)(B); implemented at 20 C.F.R. §§ 626-32, 36 and 684 (1988).
19. 20 C.F.R. § 632.10(f) (1988).
20. 29 U.S.C. § 1653(a) (1987).
21. *Id.* at § 1653(b). For a more detailed list of activities allowed *see* 20 C.F.R. §§ 632.78-632.81 (1988).
22. 20 C.F.R. § 632.87 (1982).
23. *Id.* at § 632.250 *et seq.*
24. 42 U.S.C. § 2701 *et seq.* (1986); 42 U.S.C. 2991 *et seq.* (1986).
25. 42 U.S.C. § 2991 as amended Nov. 29, 1987, Pub. L. No. 100-175, §§ 504(b)(1), 506(c)(1), 100 Stat. 975-78; implementing regulations at 45 C.F.R. § 1336 *et seq.* (1988).
26. 42 U.S.C. § 2991b.
27. *Id.*
28. *Id.* at § 2291d.
29. Kaloko-Honokōhau National Historical Park, Pub. L. No. 95-625, § 505, 92 Stat. 3499 (1978), amended Pub. L. No. 96-87, § 401(i), 93 Stat. 666 (codified at 16 U.S.C. § 396d).
30. 92 Stat. 3499 § 505(a).
31. *Id.*
32. *Id.*
33. *Id.* at § 505(c).
34. *Id.* at § 505(b).
35. *Id.* at § 505(e).
36. *Id.* at § 505(d)(1).
37. *Id.* at § 505(d)(2).
38. *Id.* at § 505(d)(3).
39. *Id.* at § 505(d)(4),
40. *Id.* at § 505(e).
41. *Id.* at § 505(f).
42. Act of Dec. 22, 1980 to establish the Kalaupapa National Park. Pub. L. No. 96-565, § 101, 94 Stat. 3321. (Codified at 16 U.S.C. § 410jj.) [Hereinafter *Act of Dec. 22, 1980.*]
43. S. Rep. No. 1027, 96th Cong., 2d Sess. (1980).
44. *Act of Dec. 22, 1980, supra* note 42, at § 102-103.
45. *Id.*
46. *Id.* at § 109.
47. *Id.* at § 102-103.
48. *Id.* at §104.
49. *Id.* at § 105.
50. *Id.* at § 107.

51. *Id.* at § 102-103.
52. *Id.* at § 108.
53. 12 U.S.C. § 1701 *et seq.* (1986).
54. 12 U.S.C. § 1715z-12 (1986).
55. *Id.* at § 1715z-12(a).
56. *Id.*
57. *Id.* at § 1715z-12(d).
58. 20 U.S.C. § 4441 (1986).
59. *Id.* at § 4441(a).
60. *Id.* at § 4441(b).
61. *Id.* at § 4441(c).
62. 42 U.S.C. § 11701, P.L. 100-690, 102 Stat. 4223 (1988).
63. Older Americans Act of 1965, Public Law 89-73, as amended; Public Law 100-175, Title VI, Part A -- Native Hawaiian Program, *et seq.*
64. 21 U.S.C. § 1101 *et seq.* (1982).
65. *Id.* at § 1177(a).
66. *Id.* at § 1177(c).
67. *Id.* at § 1177(d).
68. *Id.* at § 1177(g); *see* 42 C.F.R. § 52 (implementing regulations).
69. 20 U.S.C. § 1177(f).
70. 20 U.S.C. § 4601 *et seq.* (1986).
71. *Id.* at § 4602.
72. *Id.* at § 4612.
73. 42 U.S.C. § 4541 *et seq.* (1982).
74. *Id.* at § 4541.
75. *Id.* at § 4541(b)(10).
76. 42 U.S.C. § 4577 (1982).
77. *Id.* at § 4577(a)(1)-(3).
78. *Id.* at § 4577(b).
79. *Id.* at § 4577(c)(2)(b).
80. *Id.* at § 4577(c)(4).

GLOSSARY OF TERMS

aʻā   Clinker-type lava.

accretion   Process by which new lands are created by the gradual deposit of soil brought in by the wave action of tide waters, rivers, streams, lakes or ponds.

ʻaha ʻaina make   Funeral feast, intended to comfort the mourners; feast of death.

ʻaha ʻaina waimaka   Feast of tears, held on the first anniversary of a death, a happy occasion, as the death by this time has been accepted by the family; joyful reunion of all who had previously shed tears together.

ʻaho   Thatch; cord.

ahupuaʻa   Land division usually extending from the uplands to the sea, so called because the boundary was marked by a heap *(ahu)* of stones surmounted by an image of a pig *(puaʻa)*, or because a pig or other tribute was laid on the altar as tax to the chief; the land unit most closely related to the everyday life of the people.

ʻai kapu   To eat under taboo; to observe eating taboos; eating law which forbade men and women to eat together.

ʻāina   Land, earth.

aku   Bonito, skipjack.

akua   God, goddess, spirit; divine, supernatural, godly.

aliʻi ʻai ahupuaʻa   Chief who rules an *ahupuaʻa.*

aliʻi ʻai moku   High chief, controlling an island or district; the one who receives the produce of the district.

aliʻi nui   High chief.

allodial   Free; not holden to any lord or superior; the opposite of feudal; fee simple title.

aloha ʻāina   Respect and love for the *ʻāina,* land.

ʻaumakua, ʻaumākua (pl.)   Family or personal gods, deified ancestors who might assume the shape of animals, plants or natural forces. Humans did not harm or eat *ʻaumākua. ʻAumākua* guided and warned mortals in dreams and visions.

ʻauwai   Ditch or canal for irrigation purposes.

avulsion   A sudden, violent, rapid addition or loss to lands caused by storms, floods or channel breakthroughs.

ʻawa   Kava shrub, native to Pacific islands, the root being the source of a narcotic drink used in ceremonies.

ʻawapuhi   Wild ginger.

collateral estoppel   Doctrine that a judgment on an issue or controverted point bars raising same issue again in subsequent litigation on a different cause of action between the same parties.

corpus   The main body or principal of a trust.

dicta, dictum   Statements and comments in an opinion concerning some rule of law or legal proposition not necessarily involved nor essential to a determination of the case at hand and therefore not binding in subsequent cases.

erosion   To wear away by the action of water, wind, currents, tides or other elements.

hālau   Long house, as for canoes or hula instruction; meeting house.

hale   House, building, hall.

hānai   Refers to a child who is reared, educated and loved by someone other than the natural parents; often occurs within the family; can encompass either temporary care of a child or a permanent relationship.

heiau   Hawaiian place of worship, temple; some *heiau* were elaborately constructed stone platforms, others simple earth terraces.

hīhīwai   Endemic grainy snail, found in fresh or brackish water, eaten both cooked and raw.

hoaʻāina   Tenant, caretaker, occupant, as on a *kuleana.*

hoʻihoʻi   To return, send back, restore.

hōʻike a ka pō   Night visions providing inspiration and guidance.

hoʻokama   "To make a child," a non-related child adopted in friendship; in modern times, commonly refers to legal adoption.

ho'omoe pū   "Put to sleep together," funerary object interred with the dead.

hui   Club, association, society, corporation, company.

hula   Hawaiian dance, dancer; to dance the *hula*.

hūnākele   To hide in secret, as the body of a loved one in a secret cave.

'ili   Land section, next in importance to *ahupua'a* and usually an administrative subdivision of an *ahupua'a*.

'ili kūpono   A nearly independent *'ili* land division within an *ahupua'a*, paying tribute to the ruling chief and not to the chief of the *ahupua'a*.

'ili lele   Portion of an *'ili* land division separated from the main part of the *'ili* but considered a part of it.

in personam   A legal term used to designate jurisdiction or power that a court may acquire over an individual in contrast to jurisdiction over property.

in rem   A legal term used to designate proceedings or actions instituted *against the thing*, in contradistinction to personal actions, which are said to be *in personam*.

in situ   In place; in natural or original condition.

kā'ai   Sennit caskets; sometimes container for bones.

kahakai   Beach, seashore, seacoast, seaside.

kahu   Honored attendant, guardian, keeper of *'unihipili* bones.

kahuna, kāhuna (pl.)   Priest, expert in any profession (whether male or female).

kahuna nui   High priest and councilor to a high chief.

kākū'ai   To dedicate the dead to become *'aumākua*; to transfigure, transfiguration.

kala   Surgeonfish, unicorn fish.

kama'āina   Native-born, one born in a place, familiar, "old timer."

kanu   To plant, bury; planting, burial.

kanu 'ana   Burial site.

kanu hou   Reburial.

kapa   Tapa, as made from *wauke* or *māmaki* bark.

kapu   Taboo, prohibition; sacred.

kapu kai   Ceremonial sea bath for purification, purification by sea water, as after contact with a corpse.

kapu noho   Taboo requiring prostration in the presence of chiefs.

***kapu* system**   A complex structure of rules and laws; protected the *mana* of individuals and places, and prevented *mana* from harming others.

keiki hānai   Foster child, or sometimes adopted child. Child reared, educated and loved by someone other than natural parents.

kī   Ti, a woody plant in the lily family. The leaves were used for house thatch, food wrappers and sandals.

kia'āina   Governor.

kia'i kupapa'u   The wake; the time to both mourn the passing of the beloved and to celebrate the sanctity of the family.

kiawe   Algaroba tree, originally brought from Peru to Hawai'i in 1828, where it has become very common.

kino   Body, person, individual, self.

kinolau   Earthly forms, such as animals, plants or forces of nature, taken by a supernatural being or spirit.

kō ka'uhane   Spiritual matters.

koa   The largest of native forest trees, a valuable lumber tree, used for canoes, surfboards, calabashes.

ko'a   Fishing grounds; deep-sea fishing grounds found in waters up to 300 fathoms deep.

koe nae ke kuleana o na kanaka   "Reserving however the people's *kuleana* therein," words contained in royal patents reserving the rights of native tenants.

konohiki   Land agent of an *ahupua'a* land division under the chief. In modern times, landlord or chief of *ahupua'a*.

***konohiki* fishing rights**   Fishing rights under control of the *konohiki*; in law, term encompasses the fishing rights of the owner of the *ahupua'a* and joint rights of tenants to take from the same fishery.

kuhina nui   Powerful office in the days of the monarchy. Usually translated as "prime minister" or "premier," but said to have carried greater power. The office was abolished in 1864.

kukui   Candlenut tree, with white, oily kernels which were used for lights; the tree is a symbol of enlightenment.

kula   Plain, field, open country, pasture.

kuleana   Right, privilege, responsibility, title, property; as a result of the 1850 *Kuleana* Act, a tenant's plot of land, which could only include land which the tenant had actually cultivated plus a houselot of not more than a quarter acre.

Kuleana Act   August 6, 1850 act authorizing the award of fee simple title to native tenants for their cultivated plots of land and house lots.

kupuna, kūpuna (pl.)   Grandparent, ancestor, relative or close friend of the grandparent's generation.

lawe i ka wā make   Promises, requests, reconciliations or other emotional or spiritual matters taken with *'uhane* at time of death. Phrase meaning "take in time of death."

limu   A general name for all kinds of plants living under water; seaweed.

limu line   Seaweed line on the beach or shore.

luhi   A foster care relationship; in the *luhi* relationship the child returns to the natural parents upon request.

luna wai   Water master, one in charge of water distribution, appointed by the *konohiki* or land agent.

ma ke kai   Along the seashore, along the sea coast.

Mahele   1848 division of Hawai'i's lands between king and chiefs.

Mahele Book   Recordation of all of the lands of Hawai'i divided between the king and chiefs.

maka'āinana   Commoner, people in general; citizen, subject. Literally: people of the land; supported the chiefs and priests by their labor and its products.

Makahiki   Annual festival beginning in October and lasting about four months, with sports and religious festivities, and a *kapu* on war. During this period, the *ali'i* collected their share of the produce of the land from the people.

makai   On the seaside, toward the sea, in the direction of the sea.

makani   Wind, breeze; windy; to blow.

make   To die, perish; dead, killed; death.

māmaki   Small native trees with broad white-backed leaves and white mulberry-like fruit; the bark yielded a fiber valued for a kind of tapa, similar to that made from *wauke* but coarser.

mamo   Black Hawaiian honey creeper; its yellow feathers above and below the tail were used in choice featherwork. Formerly found only on Hawai'i, not seen since the 1880s.

mana   Supernatural or divine power, miraculous power; authority; miraculous, divinely powerful, spiritual.

mānewanewa   Grief, sorrow, mourning; exaggerated expression of grief, as by knocking out teeth.

manini   Very common reef surgeonfish, also called convict tang in the adult stage.

manō   Shark (general name).

māpele   *Heiau* for the worship of *Lono* and the increase of food; the offerings were of pigs, not humans.

mauka   Inland, upland, towards the mountain.

mele   Song or chant of any kind.

Milu   Underworld, ruler of underworld.

mō'ī   High chief, king, sovereign, monarch, ruler, queen.

moku   District, island, section.

mo'o   Lizard, reptile of any kind, dragon, serpent; water spirit.

mo'opuna   Grandchild; relatives two generations later, whether blood or adopted; descendent; posterity.

Na Ala Hele   Statewide trail and access system.

nā iwi   The bones.

nā iwi o nā kūpuna   The bones of the ancestors.

na'au'auwā, na'au'auā   Intense grief; anguish so great that it may lead to suicide; to mourn, grieve.

307

nalu nui   High surf.

'ohana   Family, relative, kin group; related.

'ohe   All kinds of bamboo; reed; flute; bamboo tube for preserving fish.

'ōhi'a lehua   Flowering tree having many forms, from tall trees to low shrubs.

'ōlena   Turmeric, a kind of ginger distributed from India into Polynesia.

oli   Chant that was not danced to, especially with prolonged phrases chanted in one breath.

olonā   A native shrub related to the *māmaki*.

'ō'ō   A black honey eater with yellow feathers, endemic to island of Hawai'i, now extinct.

'o'opu   General name for fishes included in the families Eleotridae, Gobiidae, and Blennidae. Some live in salt water near the shore, others in fresh water, and some said to be found in either fresh or salt water.

'ōpae   General name for shrimp; *'aumākua* for some people.

'ōpelu   Mackerel scad; *'aumākua* for some people.

'opihi   Limpets. Hawaiians recognize three kinds: *kō'ele* (the largest), *'ālinalina, makaiauli*. For some persons, *'ophi* are *'aumākua*.

palani   A surgeonfish famous for a strong odor.

pī kai death.   To sprinkle with sea water or salted fresh water to purify or remove taboo, as formerly done after a death.

pi'a   A kind of yam, a climber with lobed leaves known throughout Pacific islands and in tropical Asia.

piscary   The right of fishing; the right of fishing in waters belonging to another person.

Pō   Night; the realm of the gods, pertaining to or of the gods.

pono   Goodness, uprightness, moral qualities, correct or proper procedure, excellence, well-being, prosperity.

pūholoholo   To steam; to steam a corpse so that the flesh *(pela)* will separate from the bones.

reliction   The gradual recession of water which causes submerged lands to become fast or dry lands.

res   Subject matter of a trust or will.

res judicata   Rule that a final judgment rendered by a court of competent jurisdiction on the merits is conclusive as to the rights of the parties and their privies, and, as to them, constitutes an absolute bar to a subsequent action involving the same claim, demand or cause of action.

ua koe ke kuleana o na kanaka   "Reserving the rights of native tenants."

'uhane   Soul, spirit; spirit which survived death.

uhu   The parrot fishes.

uka   Inland, upland, towards the mountain.

'unihipili   Spirit of a dead person, present in bones or hair of the deceased and kept lovingly; deification.

usufruct   In civil law, the right of enjoying and using the property of another, and to draw from the same all the profit, utility, and advantage which it may produce.

uwē, uē   Wail, cry, lament, mourn.

wai   Water, liquid or liquor of any kind other than sea water; fluid.

wana   A sea urchin considered an *'aumakua* by some.

TABLE OF CASES

INDEX

INDIANS
See NATIVE AMERICANS

INDIGENOUS PEOPLES, 95-98
Blue water thesis, 96
Definition of peoples, 97
Self-determination and, 95-98

INSTITUTE FOR THE ADVANCEMENT
OF HAWAIIAN RIGHTS, 94-95

JOB TRAINING
See FEDERAL PROGRAMS AND
BENEFITS

KA LĀHUI HAWAI'I, 92-94, 98

KA PĀKAUKAU, 79, 90

KAHO'OLAWE, 30, 93, 238-239

KALĀKAUA, KING DAVID, 11, 44, 78, 153

KALANIANA'OLE, PRINCE JONAH
KŪHIO, 13, 46, 48, 284

KALAUPAPA NATIONAL HISTORIC
PARK, 298-299

KALOKO-HONOKŌHAU NATIONAL
HISTORIC PARK, 297-298

KAMA'ĀINA TESTIMONY, 153, 198, 199,
203

KAMEHAMEHA I, 5, 212, 225

KAMEHAMEHA II, 5, 232

KAMEHAMEHA III, 5, 7, 10, 174, 187, 214,
224, 232, 251

KAMEHAMEHA IV, 10, 11, 288

KAMEHAMEHA V, 11, 196-197

KAMEHAMEHA SCHOOLS/BISHOP
ESTATE
See TRUSTS, NATIVE HAWAIIAN
CHARITABLE

KE'ELIKŌLANI, PRINCESS RUTH, 126,
282

KING'S LANDS, 7, 10, 151

KINOLAU
See RELIGIOUS FREEDOM

KONOHIKI
See FISHING RIGHTS
LAND TENURE

KUALOA, 239

KULEANA
See ACCESS RIGHTS
LAND TENURE

KULEANA ACT OF 1850, 8, 151-152, 159,
161, 214-215, 226

KŪNUIĀKEA, ALBERT, 288

LAND COMMISSION, 6-9, 128, 151-152,
161, 218

LAND COURT SYSTEM, 112-113
Adverse possession, 112, 113
Background, 112-113
Decree of registration, 113
Prescription, 112, 113
Procedures, 113
Title examiner, 113

LAND TENURE, 3-10, 150-152, 173-174
Ahupua'a, 3-4, 9, 173-174
'Ali'i 'ai ahupua'a, 3
'Ali'i 'ai moku, 3
Board of Land Commissioners, 6-9
Boundary Commission, 8
Constitution of 1840, 5-6
Crown Lands, 10
Government Lands, 7, 9, 10
'Ili, 4
'Ili kūpono, 4, 8, 173
'Ili lele, 173-174
King's Lands, 7, 10
Konohiki, 3, 7-8, 9, 174
Konohiki lands, 7-8, 9
Kuleana Act of 1850, 8, 151-152
Kuleana lands, 8, 9
Land Commission Awards, 7-9, 151-152
Law of 1825, 5
Law of 1839, Declaration of Rights, 5,
150-151
Mahele of 1848, 6-8
Maka'āinana, 4, 8
Mō'ī, 3
Traditional, description of, 3-5

ABOUT THE EDITOR
Melody Kapilialoha MacKenzie

Ms. MacKenzie was born and raised in Kailua, Oʻahu. She is a graduate of Kailua High School, and also earned a Bachelor of Arts degree in Religious Studies/Anthropology from Beloit College in Beloit, Wisconsin. Prior to beginning her law studies, she was the law librarian for the National Indian Law Library of the Native American Rights Fund in Boulder, Colorado. She attended Antioch Law School in Washington, D.C. before returning to complete her law degree at the University of Hawaiʻi in 1976.

After graduation, she clerked for then Chief Justice William S. Richardson of the Hawaii Supreme Court for four years. She joined the staff of the Native Hawaiian Legal Corporation in 1980, and served as its executive director from 1982-86. She currently serves as senior staff attorney for NHLC. In 1988, she was appointed a per diem judge of the District Court of the First Circuit, State of Hawaiʻi.

Ms. MacKenzie also has taught the Native Hawaiian Rights course at the William S. Richardson School of Law, and has been an advisor to the Board of Trustees of the Office of Hawaiian Affairs regarding land claims and Native Hawaiian self-determination and self-governance.

A *kumu hula*, Ms. MacKenzie has danced *hula* for more than 15 years and was graduated by Māpuana de Silva in 1989. She currently teaches *hula* for Hālau Mōhala ʻIlima.